Sin[...]a's best-selling bargain shopping guidebooks, including *The Underground Shopper* and her most recent books, *Great Buys for People Over 50* and *Great Buys for Kids* (both in Penguin). Value and getting your money's worth is her bargain "buy-line." Called America's diva of discounts, she was born to shop at half-price out of necessity. Now she shops at half-price because she's smart. Since launching her publishing career, she has appeared on hundreds of talk shows—"Donahue," "Oprah," "Hour Magazine," "Good Morning America," "Real People," and "CBS News"—and has had countless newspaper and magazine articles written about her, which have appeared in everything from *Money* to *Newsweek*. She lives in a lakefront house outside Dallas with her two dogs and five cats. Her son, Josh, is a college student/photographer/TV grip and waiter in his spare time and is decorating his own apartment with the help of *Great Buys*.

GREAT BUYS BY MAIL

(and Phone!)

How to Save Money on Everything

Sue Goldstein

PENGUIN BOOKS

PENGUIN BOOKS
Published by the Penguin Group
Penguin Books USA Inc., 375 Hudson Street,
New York, New York 10014, U.S.A.
Penguin Books Ltd, 27 Wrights Lane,
London W8 5TZ, England
Penguin Books Australia Ltd, Ringwood,
Victoria, Australia
Penguin Books Canada Ltd, 10 Alcorn Avenue,
Toronto, Ontario, Canada M4V 3B2
Penguin Books (N.Z.) Ltd, 182–190 Wairau Road,
Auckland 10, New Zealand

Penguin Books Ltd, Registered Offices:
Harmondsworth, Middlesex, England

First published in Penguin Books 1993

1 3 5 7 9 10 8 6 4 2

LIBRARY OF CONGRESS CATALOGING IN PUBLICATION DATA
Goldstein, Sue, 1941–
Great buys by mail (and phone!): how to save money on everything/
Sue Goldstein.
p. cm.
Rev. ed. of: The 3rd underground shopper. 1986.
Includes index.
ISBN 0 14 01.4782 9
1. Mail-order business—United States—Directories. 2. Discount houses (Retail trade)—United States—Directories. I. Goldstein, Sue, 1941– 3rd underground shopper. II. Title.
HF5466.G6 1993
381'.142'029473—dc20 92–42284

Printed in the United States of America
Set in New Baskerville
Designed by Kathryn Parise

To Josh,
whose passage into adulthood
was one giant step for mankind.
And to my dad, Bill Elkin,
who is one giant in
all of mankind.

Acknowledgments

'Tis nobler in the pocketbook to look for value in every aspect of your life, from friends to FRANCISCAN CHINA, colleagues to CARTER's, associates to AVIA, and employees to ESPRIT.

When it comes to the latter, there's no better group than those who work on my books and "buylines": GREAT BUYS, THE UNDERGROUND SHOPPER, THE UNDERGROUND SHOPPER TV SHOW, DIAL-A-DEAL and other money-saving related projects.

Thanks are due to the line-up of stars in this stable of workhorses: Steve Walker, a multi-talented native Texan whose standards of excellence would make any winning racehorse pale by comparison; Debra Rodia, the leader of the pack, who took the files and ran with them—head of the research team, her nose was always to the grindstone and she came away smelling like a rose; Timothy Pope, her back-up, who picked up when she rounded the bend; and Tammy Pennington, who trailed with all the last-minute details when all else failed.

And special thanks to Julie Norman, who is my right-hand when I leave my left somewhere and cannot find it; and whose calm and collectedness convened 24 hours a day when one of my hare-brained ideas hit. Everyone needs and deserves at least one Julie in his life to survive.

To Dave Tanner, who went from radio co-host to TV co-host—

to help me get my ratings up. And to Norman Payson, who saw me as the walking-talking "diva of discounts" and decided to join me as my partner in Dial-a-Deal, in the free Underground Shopper and occasionally for lunch.

To Steve Goodrick, and the entire Visual Dynamics cast and crew, who keep my lips in sync and my hips—well, they continue to promise a different angle shot every time.

To my agent, Jane Dystel, the only top New York agent who can pull off having a baby boy, Zack, in secret (guess her husband and her daughter knew about it), and still return calls within an hour all nine months long. And to my editor, Lori Lipsky, who continues to provide superb guidance and direction when I'm all over the place.

To the merchants themselves, who provide the material from which we derive such pleasure as well as savings. And to the phone company and post office, who deliver the message usually without fail, through rain, sleet, and sometimes hail. (Remember, we had almost continual hail storms this year in Texas.)

To my friends and family, who resist telling me to turn off the computer and take a day off once in a while, I am eternally grateful. Without this opportunity to shop and tell, I might not be able to shop 'til I drop.

And that is every woman's dream. Mine, too! Thank you readers and shoppers everywhere.

Contents

Introduction

Remember the fun you had reading *Through the Looking Glass* when you were a kid? It's probably been a long time since you imagined yourself walking through a wonderland—unless you're a mail-order shopper!

Today's mail-order catalogs, with their glossy pages, stunning photography, and alluring copy, are contemporary looking glasses into a wonderland of modern living. You'll find thousands of things to add sparkle and zest to your life. Thumbing through a modern-day wish-book brings out the child in all of us; it's our boarding pass to a flight of fancy. A well-designed catalog is like a springboard that lets you dive into a pool of possibilities and splash into a new, brighter world of imagination.

Speaking of another world, price-quote firms, while not as glamorous or well-known as catalog companies, have some out-of-this-world discounts. Cost-conscious consumers with the shopping smarts to check out *all* the alternatives, including price-quote firms, can find savings of several hundred dollars (sometimes thousands) on a major purchase. Savings like that are no idle chatter; they're real and really fantastic! Price-quote firms often offer unsurpassed savings on large, functional items like appliances, furniture, and stereos, among other things. These companies don't provide you with a glossy catalog—at best you'll get a flier listing the lines they carry. It's up to you to decide what you want—learn the manufacturer, model number, and other descriptive details—and write or call to get a price quote. If you like the price quoted, go ahead and order. It's that simple.

Direct marketing makes a lot of sense for today's consumers. It's cost-efficient and *convenient*. There are savings in time and gas, no wear and tear on your car, and best of all no wear and tear on your nerves from battling crowds or locking horns with pushy salespeople. Some of the larger direct marketing companies even have 24-hour toll-free lines so you can order anytime, day or night. And don't forget, you often don't pay sales tax when you buy out-of-state, though that may soon change.

Many mail-order firms have excellent prices. Direct marketing companies avoid the overhead expense of maintaining retail storefronts and they usually don't have a large number of employees, so payroll expenses are kept down. The bottom line is that it usually costs less to sell by mail, so even by charging lower prices they still make a profit. That's good for consumers, who come out ahead.

When you stop to think that the corresponding disadvantages are only a small shipping charge, a delay of one to a few weeks (except in the case of some larger items like furniture, where you may experience much longer delays), and occasionally the price of a phone call (if you phone in your order rather than write), shopping direct offers big benefits. You get more than just convenience, you get savings. It's no wonder the popularity of shopping by phone is at an all-time high and that direct marketing is being hailed as one of the tidal waves of retailing in the future.

If there was ever any doubt about the popularity of mail-order shopping, it was dispelled by the first edition of this book, which was published in 1983 under the title *The Underground Shopper's Guide to Discount Mail Order Shopping*. Today's value consumer wants it all—quality, service AND price. So in the '90s, we call our book *Great Buys by Mail (and Phone).*

Shoppers today are clearly pressed for time and money, so it's only natural to want to pick up the phone and get the best buys. But who to call and what they sell takes research. Hopefully, our efforts will pay off in great dividends—not only in the savings afforded the consumer, but to the companies we listed, who deserve both recognition and increased sales. In short, everybody wins.

You might wonder how we went about deciding which companies to include and which to exclude. What criteria did we use and how did we research our book? Because this was the fourth edition things were a little easier for us. We wrote and called all the companies listed in our previous editions as well as the companies we had been collecting information about since our last edition. Then we added those companies we knew about from our local bargain shopping guides that would ship their merchandise nationwide.

We collected new catalogs, new fliers, and new brochures, and checked prices. We carefully reviewed our Reader Response files, and companies that were the object of complaints were red-flagged; some new companies recommended to us by our readers or that we uncovered on our own were also added.

For all of you who are skeptical about mail-order shopping, out of the almost 1000 companies listed in the past, we have received only a handful of serious complaints. Even better news is that any problems were quickly resolved when we intervened. The most common complaint was a delay in getting a catalog.

When we finished our data gathering, we added this new research to the information we already had on file (such as questionnaires filled out by company personnel, newspaper and magazine articles, and catalogs, brochures, and fliers). We then revised our earlier write-ups to include all the new information we thought would be useful to our readers.

Overall, we've expanded and revised our earlier editions, and made a number of changes suggested by readers, from reorganizing the CONTENTS to noting the different types of payment accepted by each company. We've dropped some; added many. The vast majority of our listings were dropped not because they went out of business, but because they asked not to be listed; or they could not or would not respond to requests for information; or because we simply uncovered other, *better* companies with lower prices. Very, very few of the companies listed in our previous editions, by the way, went out of business, a tribute both to the viability of mail-order shopping and to our own strict standards for evaluating companies.

To sum it all up, we're back. We've tried to make meaningful rather than cosmetic changes and to incorporate as many reader suggestions as possible. We've tried not just to put out another book, but a *better* book. This is it—we hope you like it.

Twelve Questions about Mail-Order

1. When ordering apparel, how can I be sure I get the right size?

You may be a perfect "10" in most clothing, but each manufacturer cuts its garments differently. There's always the chance the clothes you order might not fit. That's why it is smart to send your measurements. Then, if there is any variation in clothing size due to fabric, style, or cut, whoever is filling your order can double-check your measurements with their clothing sizes. It's a way of reducing the chance you'll get something that doesn't fit.

Here are some tips about taking your own measurements that we found in the Land's End catalog:

- Shirts—Neck: Pick a shirt with a collar that fits well. Lay the collar flat and measure from the center of the button to the far end of the button hole. The number of inches is your neck size. Sleeve: Bend elbow, measure from center of neck to elbow and down to wrist. The number of inches is your sleeve length.

- Chest or bust—Measure around the fullest part of chest, keeping tape up under arms and around (not below) your shoulder blades. Size equals the number of inches.

- Waist—Measure around waist and over shirt, but not over slacks or skirt. Measure at the height you normally wear your slacks or skirt. Keep one finger between your body and the tape. The number of inches equals your size.

- Seat and hips—Stand with your heels together and measure yourself around the area of greatest circumference.

- Inseam—Chose a pair of pants that fits you well. Measure from the crotch seam to the bottom of the pants. The number of inches (to the nearest half-inch) gives you the inseam length.

2. I've never shopped by mail. How do I get started?

A good place to start is with this book. Read through the sections that interest you and mark the companies that sound good to you. You'll be able to tell from the write-up how the company is set up to do business. For example, we've coded the listings in this book so you'll know if a company has a catalog (C), a brochure (B), a flier (F), or whether they just give price quotes (PQ). When you write or call a company for the first time, either to ask a question or to request a catalog, be sure to mention that you read about it in *Great Buys by Mail*.

The next step is to read the literature you receive very carefully. Make sure everything is clear to you. Read product descriptions like size, weight, color, and contents very carefully; check the order form closely. Understanding the return policy is particularly important, since you'll want to know what your rights are if a problem develops. Type or print (legibly) all the relevant information like code numbers, etc., on the order form, and (optional) specify substitutions or second choices (you must be flexible at times). Observe minimum order requirements—a few companies can only offer a discount on quantity purchases.

In filling out the order form and adding up the total, don't forget to include the shipping or other charges indicated on the order blank. Always request insurance if it's not already provided. Include sales tax when applicable.

When ordering, it's preferable to use a credit card number, but checks and money orders are acceptable. Many companies won't ship your order until after your personal check has cleared the bank (meaning a delay of two to three weeks), so credit card orders are faster. Money orders and cashier's checks are readily accepted and will speed the processing of your order. *Never send cash!* If you send cash and your money "disappears" and you don't receive your order, you have no proof that you paid.

Whether you order by phone or by mail, be sure to keep complete, accurate records. Note the date the order was placed and the name of the order-taker, keep your receipts, etc. When you ask for a price quote, send a business-size SASE (self-addressed, stamped #10 envelope), and you'll get your price quote faster.

3. What's a price quote, and how do I get one?

Many of the companies listed in our book have access to thousands of products from SONY to SAMSONITE. If one of these discount retailers created a catalog, it would be twice the size of the Los Angeles Yellow Pages. Rather than try to publish a series of massive volumes and then continually update them, these companies have chosen a less expensive way to operate: quoting prices to people who call or write.

The price quote system is an extremely cost-efficient way to let you know: a) that the item is available and b) what the current (discounted) price is. Don't be afraid of price quotes—the system is simple. Just write or call and give the specifics of the item you're interested in (model number, style number, etc.), and wait to see if they have what you want, and how much they're selling it for.

Here's an example of how the price quote system works. Suppose you want to buy some Christian Dior panties that normally cost $7 a pair in a department store. After finding the stores in our book that sell lingerie, you'd write each one a letter. The letter might sound something like this:

> "Dear Sir,
> Do you have CHRISTIAN DIOR (manufacturer) INTIMATES (model) #82500 (style) size 6 (size) panties (item) in beige (color)? If so, what's the cost per pair, per six, and per dozen?" (Because clerks in these businesses are usually pressed for time, we suggest you ask about no more than three items.) Also ask: "How much is the shipping cost and how fast will they be shipped?"

Remember to include a large, self-addressed, stamped envelope with your letter. You'll get an answer sooner and you'll know the letter they send back to you is properly addressed.

4. My porcelain heart is broken. Can I return it?

Maybe. The first thing to remember is *never* send anything back without first writing the company and okaying a return with them. Wait for their answer before you do anything. It's all right to telephone, but if you do, write down the name of the person who authorized your return and record his instructions to you. Some companies will pay the return postage; most won't.

It's always wise to ask for the return policies if they aren't spelled out in the catalog. (They should be.) Save the original packaging if you think there's a chance you'll return something.

5. Can you tell me what a restocking charge is? I've seen this mentioned in some catalogs I have.

Glad you asked. Restocking charges are definitely worth knowing about: they can be as much as 25 percent of an order in some cases. A restocking charge is a labor fee charged by a company when it has to take back an item. Restocking fees aren't charged in the case of items that have been damaged in transit, but if you decide to send back something you've ordered because you've changed your mind or your purchase wasn't just right after all, you may have to pay a penalty. That does increase your risk, but if you don't like the merchandise, well, that's why we suggest doing your homework before you shop by phone. If, for instance, you buy a $1,000 sofa from a furniture company that has a 25 percent restocking charge and then you decide to send the sofa back, you'll be out $250. That's why, when it comes to companies with restocking charges, you'd better be sure what you buy is what you want. Mistakes can be expensive.

Restocking fees are usually charged only by companies selling larger and more expensive items such as furniture and stereos.

6. I want to get a price quote. Where do I find the manufacturer, model, and style number of the item I want?

Catalogs usually include this information in their write-ups, but you may not have a catalog with the item you want. If you can find the item in a store, check the price tag. Price tags often have the model number (although sometimes it's coded). Some people just ask the salesperson for this information, but if you're going to turn around and order the item somewhere else, that's a pretty shabby way to treat a salesman who works only on commission. Another alternative is to send an ad or photograph from a magazine and hope someone can figure out what you want.

7. Can you explain the 30-day mail-order rule to me? I've heard about it but I don't know what it is.

Six to eight weeks is as long as you should have to wait to receive your order under normal conditions, and many companies deliver your order much faster than that. According to the FTC 30-day mail-order rule, companies are required by law to either a) ship your goods within 30 days after receipt of your order or b) advise you there will be a delay. They must do this unless their catalog specifically notes shipment will take longer. In the event that the company can't ship your order within 30 days, they must offer to refund your money and give you a cost-free way of canceling (either with an 800 number or a collect call).

8. My order never arrived, the company's phone is disconnected, and my check's been cashed. Help!

One trade organization that will intervene on your behalf or put you in touch with the proper agencies is the Direct Marketing Association (DMA). Write to them at DMA, P.O. Box 9008, Farmingdale, NY 11735. Calling the Better Business Bureau or the Postmaster General to alert them is also a good idea, and you can alert the FTC and your state attorney general's office if you think you've been ripped off. We at *Great Buys* will intervene and do what we can if you have a problem with a company listed in our book. We'll keep your written complaint on file and eliminate a listing if it proves necessary. (See the Reader Response page.)

9. After I pay shipping charges, am I really saving money?

If the item you want is available at a local discount store or will go on sale soon, it might be better to buy it locally, but not always. Some companies have charts in their catalogs to figure shipping charges according to weight and distance; other companies charge depending on the dollar amount of your order. Figure the shipping costs, calculate the savings in sales tax if you're ordering out-of-state, and *then* compare prices. That way you'll be comparing final cost to final cost.

There are three ways an order can be shipped. Parcel Post (PP) is one way. The United States Postal Service charges from 50 cents to $4.40 to insure parcels valued up to $500. Packages valued over $500 must be registered and sent First Class. These can also be insured. *The only way goods can be sent to a post office box is by Parcel Post.* To use this method, mark both your order and check "Deliver by Parcel Post Only" if you want delivery to your post office box. COD orders are more expensive since the carrier collects a money order fee of $1.50 or more, depending upon the value of the package.

United Parcel Service (UPS) automatically insures each package for $100 in value and charges 25 cents for each additional $100 in value on the same package. UPS charges should not include insurance unless the cost is greater than $100. The cost of using UPS is determined by the package's weight and measurement, the package's point of origin, and its destination. The price is usually worth it. Most people agree that UPS is the most efficient and reliable carrier.

A third means of shipping an item is by truck. Truckers are used for non-mailable orders (goods over 50 pounds in weight). The weight of the goods and the distance they will be shipped determine the amount of the charges. The shipper specifies on the bill of lading the amount due (if any) and the form of payment the trucker should collect when he delivers the merchandise. On **COD** orders, for example, the shipper must specify that a personal check is acceptable. This may not include the freight company's charges, in which case an additional check may be required. You'll often see the abbreviation **FOB**, meaning "freight on board." "FOB factory" means you pay the shipping charges from the factory to you.

10. Will the trucker's charges on a large purchase like furniture be so big that they eat up all the money I saved?

It's highly unlikely. If they did, no one would mail-order furniture! Often the price of having a piece of furniture shipped offsets the savings in sales, but doesn't significantly reduce the amount you saved off the retail purchase price. This depends, though, on the distance a piece of furniture must be shipped (whether it must cross the Mississippi River or the Rockies), the sales tax charged in your state (and the amount of your sales tax savings), and the price charged by the carrier used.

Deregulation of the trucking industry has caused freight companies to lower their rates for both long and short hauls. The price of shipping a single item has dropped a lot, too.

On the topic of savings, you'll save about 50 percent on freight charges on items like bookcases if you ship them "knocked down" or disassembled. The reason disassembled merchandise costs less is that it takes up less room on the truck.

Another money-saving tip is that residents of the east and southeast who are buying from the North Carolina furniture district should look for companies with their own trucks and crew. Their rates are generally lower than those of common carriers.

11. The idea of ordering from a foreign country scares me. What if I order a kaftan but get back an afghan?

Getting catalogs with exotic stamps, quaint idiomatic letters, and unusual products is like taking a small trip to a foreign country. It's fun! Just like taking a trip, though, there are some precautions.

Read the catalogs closely and look for such things as insurance, duty (each item is taxed at a different rate), the return policy, and delivery information. You'll pay a premium for air mail delivery, but the alternative is delivery via surface mail on a "slow boat."

The method of payment should be explained in the catalog. If not, write to the company before sending any money. Because of fluctuating currency markets, Deak International, a currency broker with offices in most major cities, suggests that a foreign company bill you in their own currency and you then pay in that currency. Currency brokers and most banks will issue a check based on the current rate of exchange. You can obtain a currency conversion table for approximate values from Deak International, 29 Broadway, New York, NY 10006. Paying by credit card when possible is another way to avoid exchange rate hassles.

Another tip you should follow in the U.S., but *especially* when you do business with a foreign company, is that if you must return your purchase for any reason because of damage, write for instructions first. If you don't take this step and get clearance *first*, you may end up paying duty *twice*.

12. Please explain customs duties. How much extra will I have to pay?

Any purchase made outside the U.S. is subject to customs examination. That's the law. The U.S. Postal Service sends all incoming packages to customs to be examined, and each dutiable item is charged a percentage of its appraised value. The different percentages for individual items are obtained from the exhaustive *Tariff Schedules of the United States*. The duty on a silk blouse might be 18 percent while that on a cotton blouse may be 25 percent. It's hard to estimate what the duties will be beforehand: Duties on different products are often based on political, rather than economic, considerations. It's a complicated process. Call your local customs office for details.

After customs has written the duty bill, the parcel is returned to the Post Office. The Post Office handles the delivery and the collection of the duty, along with a $1.75 postal handling fee.

In Canada, the procedure for paying duty is roughly the same, except you will be notified by Canadian customs that your package is ready for pickup. Canadians pay slightly higher duties than U.S. citizens, plus a 9 percent federal sales tax.

While everything you buy out of the country must be inspected, not everything is subject to duty charges. Items classified as "duty free" under the Generalized System of Preferences (GSP) come from over 140 under-developed nations, and include about 2,800 items that range from cameras to wood carvings. In order to take advantage of the GSP, you must buy an eligible article in the same beneficiary country as it was grown, manufactured, or produced. Bona fide "unsolicited" gifts aren't exempted under the laws for returning travelers.

Symbols Key

I. Types of Payment Accepted

CK Personal checks. A few firms don't accept personal checks. They think that the inconvenience of waiting until the checks clear, and the resulting impatience of customers due to the delay in receiving their order, make checks more trouble than they're worth. Firms that *do* take personal checks have a "CK" symbol in the line beneath the address where types of payment are listed. When you pay by check, expect a delay in receiving your order of two to three weeks since most firms will wait until your check clears the bank before processing your order. Certified checks, cashier's checks, and money orders are all commonly accepted as payment by mail-order companies and won't mean a delay in processing your order.

MC MasterCard. Using a credit card is advisable for orders you want to get quickly, since there isn't the delay there is with a check that first must clear the bank. Using credit cards for orders that don't total large sums of money also makes some sense because you'll get your order faster and the credit charges won't be large in absolute terms. Credit card orders aren't always advisable, however, when purchasing large or expensive items since delivery of large merchandise usually takes a long time and because credit charges (in absolute terms) on expensive items will be high. It almost goes without saying that credit orders are mandatory when you order by phone. As a final word of warning, when you use credit, it's still a good idea to write down the model and style number, etc., of the merchandise you ordered, as well as the name of the person you spoke with if you ordered by phone. If a problem arises, this information may prove useful.

V Visa

AE American Express

O Optima

DC Diner's Club

CB Carte Blanche

D Discover

CH Choice

COD Cash on Delivery. Firms that accept COD payments usually qualify that with some type of restriction, such as a 25 percent deposit, which serves to protect them in case you change your mind and decide not to accept the order. When you order COD, know that COD means *cash* on delivery. If you expect to receive your order and pay by check, you'll probably be disappointed. You'll have to pay by cash or by some other form of payment that's "safe" for the seller.

MO Money Order

IMO International Money Order

II. Information about the Supplier

C Catalog. When it costs something to get a catalog, we've noted the amount immediately after the entry, as in "C/$2." The charge for a catalog is generally small (if anything), only enough to cover postage and handling, and to discourage catalog requests from people who wouldn't actually order. We have indicated when the catalog price is refundable with a first order.

B Brochure. A brochure is smaller than a catalog and often folds out. For our purposes, a brochure is eight pages or less in length.

F Flier, or price sheet. Usually one or two pages.

PQ Price quote. Companies with a "PQ" following their heading will answer telephone queries or letters requesting information about specific merchandise. To get a price quote, you must know the manufacturer's name, the item's stock number, etc.

SASE Send a self-addressed stamped envelope #10 size. Sometimes it is requested that you send two first-class stamps. Follow the instructions, please.

FAX The fascimile machine facilitates your order by placing it or a photo of what you're looking for within seconds, and that means almost instant gratification.

FOB When getting price quotes long-distance, often companies will quote you the price from their factory to you. FOB means "freight on board."

III. 800 Numbers

Note: We did not put a number 1 before dialing for bargains long-distance or before the toll-free 800 number. However, you must dial a 1. We were disappointed to learn that many of the best money-saving furniture resources in North Carolina have been pressured into eliminating their toll-free numbers because they were discounting and threatening to take business away from full retail accounts. Well, we didn't say it was going to be easy. Still, even with the price of a phone call, you will be saving hundreds, if not thousands.

IV. Prices

Remember, prices are quoted to give you a feel for the listing's pricing structure, reflecting the percentage, if applicable, off retail. Do not expect to see that exact item and dollar amount when you order the latest catalog or receive the most current price.

V. Address Information

Dept. GBBM: You'll notice that some listings contain Dept. GBBM in their addresses. That stands for **Great Buys by Mail**. We've included this as a convenience to the companies listed, since many companies like to know where their new customers heard of them. It also helps us if our book becomes more important to the companies listed; they have a greater incentive to provide us with the information we ask for as we try to update our files and ask them to reward readers with a special offer. It gives us more clout. Ultimately, our power helps you because if there is ever a problem and you contact us, there's a greater chance the company will listen to us when we intervene on your behalf.

VI. Apologies for Goofs

We admit it ahead of time. We know, in spite of meticulous research and many hands and eyes on the manuscript, there are probably a few mistakes. We hope, only a few. Expect a few OOBs (out-of-businesses) and "This number has been disconnected" since there is some lag time between the shopping and publishing of this information. Though we may have goofed and inadvertently transposed a phone number or address, for any of these snaffus, please know we didn't mean it.

Turn to the Reader Response page if you want to tell us if and where we've failed, or which merchant has failed you. And if you know of a place we've omitted, please let us know that, too. The more the merrier.

Tips for Ordering by Mail

- Never send cash; order by check, money order, or credit card.

- Find out the company's policy on warranties, exchanges, and refunds.

- Keep a record of your order: name, address, telephone number, date of order, copy of advertisement.

- Know shipping charges.

• Orders (unless othewise stated) must be shipped within 30 days of receipt of your order. If there is going to be delay, the company must notify you.

• You are not required to pay for anything you did not order. Write "REFUSED" on the package and send it back (no postage needed).

• Complaints or questions regarding warranty policy, misrepresentation, or fraud, contact:
Postmaster or Chief Postal Inspector
U.S. Postal Service
Room 3517
Washington, DC 20260
(202) 245-5445

• Questions or complaints about unordered merchandise or delay of your order, contact:
Consumer Inquiries
Federal Trade Commission
Washington, DC 20580
(202) 523-3598

Complaints

So you've got a problem. After attempts at resolution with the merchant in question and after you've correctly followed the procedures for complaints covered in the catalog, brochure, or by phone, you can seek outside counsel. If you've written or spoken to the company first and still aren't satisfied, you can turn to the following agencies. (It is a good idea to include all of your correspondence and photocopies of the documentation when seeking help.)

BETTER BUSINESS BUREAU (BBB): Always check with the local BBB *before* ordering from a mail-order company. This local BBB is in the area where the company resides, not *your* hometown. If you send a SASE to the Council of Better Business Bureaus, Inc., 1515 Wilson Boulevard, Arlington, VA 21209, you will receive a directory of BBB offices. Though the BBBs are funded by the participating businesses, they do maintain files on firms, help resolve consumer complaints, and provide an overview on the firm's selling history. That way, if a firm has 100 unresolved complaints on file, chances are they're not a good bet.

CONSUMER ACTION PANELS (CAPs): These are third-party dispute resolution programs established by the industries they represent. For example, for a problem with a major appliance, you can write MACAP (Major Appliance Consumer Action Panel), 10 North Wacker Drive, Chicago, IL 60606 or call 800-621-0477. For help with other industries, consult a standard reference source in the public library called *Encyclopedia of Associations*.

DIRECT MARKETING ASSOCIATION (DMA): This is the trade association for mail-order merchants and direct-marketing companies. Its Mail Order Action Line (MOAL) helps resolve nondelivery problems with a mail or direct marketer. To get help, send a copy of your complaint letter and documentation to:

Mail Order Action Line
DMA
P.O. Box 9008
Farmingdale, NY 11735

You may also get your name added to or removed from mailing lists through the DMA's Mail Preference Service. Write to the DMA at the address above to receive the "MPS" form.

FEDERAL TRADE COMMISSION (FTC): Though this law-enforcement agency does not act on individual complaints, every letter helps build a case. The Fair Credit Billing Act (FCBA) of 1975 offers mail-order shoppers who use credit cards some leverage if there's a problem of nondelivery. Disputes regarding the quality of goods or services are also covered, but this coverage varies from state to state. It's best to contact your local consumer protection agency for clarification before proceeding to the federal level.

UNITED STATES POSTAL SERVICE (USPS): Probably the most effective of all the agencies; their track record of resolution is almost 85 percent. Send a copy of your final complaint letter and documentation to:

Chief Postal Inspector
U.S. Postal Service
Washington, DC 20260

Contacting the local postmaster nearest the firm in question is often quicker.

Reader Feedback

We'd like to hear from you! Comments, both good and bad, help shape our next edition and other books in the *Great Buys* series. Of course, we'd like to hear from you, our readers, and from merchants who would like to be listed.

If you've had a problem, and have failed to resolve it with the merchant directly, don't hesitate to state your case to us, %

GREAT BUYS
P.O. Box 294042
Lewisville, TX 75029

Be sure to include all the pertinent information and *copies* of any documentation relating to the transaction and what you would like done. Don't forget, too, to give your name, address, and your daytime phone number.

GREAT BUYS BY MAIL

(and Phone!)

Apparel: Baby's and Children's

Baby your baby by buying diapers at wholesale prices. Rack up the savings on suits for your little prince, pinafores for your princess, and hand-knit clothing for toddlers and tykes at way below retail prices. Natural fibers imported from Europe are an alternative. If you're planning on more than one child, choose better quality clothing—it will last longer. Also, consider stocking up on items like sleepers and diapers. You'll have them when you need them, and you'll save money, too. And now for the rites of offspring, here are some ways to shop 'n coo.

After the Stork
1501 12th Street NW — (800) 333-5437
Albuquerque, NM 87104 — CK, MC, V, AE, D, MO, C

Here's lookin' at you, kid, in 100-percent natural cotton clothing. After the Stork has been in business since 1980, selling children's clothing that's safe for little ones' delicate skin. From birth through size 14, this apparel is a natural for the apple of your eye without taking a bite out of your budget. Though retail, they're reasonable. They guarantee customer satisfacton; and the catalog's free before, during, or after the stork.

The B2 Products
P.O. Box 1108 (800) 695-7073
Haymarket, VA 22069 MC, V, AE, F

Cheaper by the dozen? You betcha! B2 Products sells infants' undershirts (expanding to crawlers' and older children's soon) by the dozen to save you TIME and MONEY! Imagine never having to wait for a sale or driving to the store only to find they're sold out of the size you need. As a B2 customer, you'll receive: superior quality products, delivery within 15 days, special savings on personal care items, bonus coupons, packing list specials, updates on new product lines, gift wrapping on request, and a special monthly health newsletter. Sizes 3–36 months. Don't "B2" slow, or you'll miss out on a *Great Buy*! Call for a free price list.

Baby Bunz & Co.
P.O. Box 1717 (707) 829-5347
Sebastopol, CA 95473 CK, MC, V, MO, B

The environmentally conscious movement is on, and disposable diapers are out. But that's no problem, baby; your diapering needs are covered. Baby Bunz sells NIKKY diaper covers in waterproof cotton, vinyl-lined cotton, and lambswool, in sizes newborn to three years (or 34 pounds, whichever comes first), all up to 30 percent off. The Baby Bunz diaper line is also available and features flat, prefolded, and contour diapers at up to 20 percent off. To "wet" your appetite further, they carry biodegradable "Dovetails" diapers, nylon diaper and pants covers, training pants, WEEWEAR and FIX OF SWEDEN layettewear, Merino wool and pima cotton blankets, a lambskin blanket for the crib, soft booties, a cuddly "First Doll," bath products by WELEDA, a flowered diaper bag, and more. If you're not happy with your order, you've got thirty days to return the unused item(s) for a refund, credit, or exchange. A $10 minimum is required when you charge it, and only U.S. funds are accepted. Tricks of the diapering trade are revealed in their brochure.

Baby Clothes Wholesale
70 Ethel Road West (908) 572-9520
Piscataway, NJ 08854 C/$2.95 (refundable), B

Baby Clothes Wholesale makes a believer out of "I can't believe I bought the whole sale"! What a selection of boys' and girls' clothing, size newborn to 7 years, at prices that are 50 percent off retail. The cost of their 52-page, full-color catalog ($2.95) will be recouped after your first purchase, and it is loaded with year-round values. If you choose not to spring for the catalog, send a SASE (business-size #10-envelope) and they'll send you the latest full-color brochure free, with information on the merchandise and the catalog.

Esprit
499 Illinois Street (415) 648-6900
San Francisco, CA 94107 MC, V, AE, C (Spring 1993)

Join the corps of dedicated outlet shoppers and save up to 40 percent on this popular California manufacturer's trendy kids' and moms' sportswear and accessories. Visit Esprit in person, or shop by phone from their catalog (available Spring 1993) or outlet stores located in Boulder, CO; Palm Springs and San Francisco, CA; Dallas, TX; and New Orleans, LA.

Hanna Andersson
1010 Northwest Flanders (800) 222-0544
Portland, OR 97209 (800) 346-6040 (customer service)
MC, V, AE, D, C

Your kids will go bananas over Hanna's brightly colored, 100-percent cotton sweaters, knit pants, jackets, caps, gloves, socks, and more all waiting to be worn. And worn. And worn again. Then, it's off to the "Hannadowns" program, where you can trade in those in "good used condition" and receive a 20-percent credit towards a new purchase. The Hannadowns are then donated to a worthy charity. This Swedish import sure makes good on her promises. Quality clothing is within earshot even if you can't make it to their outlet stores in Portland.

Jolene Company
1050 W. 350 South
P.O. Box 1446 (801) 373-3206
Provo, UT 84603 PQ

If you haven't seen Jolene, you haven't dressed a little girl or boy in a while. This is a major supplier to department and chain stores nationwide offering the labels JOLENE, HAPPY KIDS, and TOM

SAWYER at discounts of 20 percent to 70 percent off retail on first-quality closeouts and overruns and some seconds. Shop by phone without leaving home.

Kids at Large
Building 32, Endicott Street
Dept. 900 (617) 769-8575
Norwood, MA 02062 CK, MC, V, C

Having fits over finding clothes for hard-to-fit kids? Chubby children have finally found a home. This catalog offers fun and fashionable clothing for the overweight and larger child, at last, for less. They are the only company in the United States that makes clothes exclusively for overweight children and offers them by mail only. Chock-full of trendy and stylish clothes, from acid-washed jeans to funky neon shorts. Shipping via UPS within 48 hours of placing order.

Natan Borlam Co., Inc.
157 Havemeyer (718) 387-2983; (718) 782-0108
Brooklyn, NY 11211 CK, PQ

Since 1951, Natan Borlam has been featuring the clothes you grew up with. Kids and moms can shop both the domestic as well as the imported front of boys' clothing in sizes infants to 20; girls' clothing, infants to juniors, preteen sizes 4 to 14; and women's clothing. Slim and husky, too. From casual to dressy, everything sports tags and fabrics from the finest domestic and European manufacturers and is made expressly for Borlam. Savings run 25 percent to 50 percent. Borlam's offers a 14-day refund policy and tacks on $2 for shipping. So what's a $2 shipping charge between friends? They're open Sunday through Thursday from 10 a.m. to 6 p.m. and Friday from 10 a.m. to 2 p.m.

Natural Baby Co., Inc.
114 W. Franklin Avenue (800) 388-BABY; (609) 737-2895
Pennington, NJ 08534 CK, MC, V, AE, MO, COD, C

The Natural Baby Co. has been around since 1983, but don't expect them to be just another diaper company. They *do* have diapers, of course; their own, called "Rainbow," are pinless, foldless, and made of cloth. Then there are diaper covers called NIKKYS, diaper pads, unfolded cloth diapers, a cushioned changing pad to use in creating a changing table out of furniture you already have (suggestions included), a baby sling, crib blankets, STORKENWORKS shoes, plus apparel for older kids, like mittens, scarves, sweaters, and heavyweight pants by NIKKYS for kids up to 110 pounds. As if all that wasn't enough, they also offer "The Incredible Toypack" program. Send them a $30 deposit check and they in turn send you a variety of other manufacturers' catalogs. Such things as puppet theaters, dolls, books, tapes, wagons, building sets, art supplies, and many other toys and games to pass down to the next generation, all discounted by 25 percent. When you return the catalogs to Natural Baby, along with an order ($60 minimum), they'll return your deposit check. But choose carefully; no returns unless goods are defective. Expect delivery to take up to two months.

Oshkosh B'Gosh

P.O. Box 300 (800) 537-4979
Oshkosh, WI 54902 CK, MC, V, AE, D, C

The great American coverup is none other than OSHKOSH B'GOSH. Golly, gee, Miss Molly, from baby to school age, your kid can't leave home without a pair from here. Call for their overall(s) free quarterly catalog so you'll have it in front of you when you call (414) 231-8800 to find out the outlet store nearest you.

Rubens & Marble, Inc.

P.O. Box 14900 (312) 348-6200
Chicago, IL 60614-0900 F (SASE)

This company's over a hundred years old and is still kicking. They may be old-timers, but they never lose their touch. Since 1890, they have been outfitting babies while they're still in the hospital, but you can get in on the act, too, and save up to 60 percent. Undershirts are mostly seconds with small flaws, with short or long sleeves in plain, double-breasted, snap, and tie styles for sizes newborn to 36 months, plus first-quality cotton/wool blends and preemie sizes. Waterproof pants, kimonos, training pants, baby gowns with drawstring bottoms, terry bibs, and fitted crib and bassinet sheets round out the baby boom. There's a one-package minimum order; the number of items in a package varies. Send a SASE for a price list.

Small Fry
330 Sunset (817) 387-9915
Denton, TX 76201 CK, MC, V, MO, PQ

Save big with Small Fry—30 percent to 50 percent off on designer wardrobes for kids, sizes infants to 20 for boys and infants to juniors for girls. Preemie sizes, too. And the names are stellar: GUESS?, GENERRA, KNITWAVES, OSHKOSH B'GOSH, MALLEY, CHOOZIE, BUGLE BOY, IMP . . . the list goes on. Call if you're looking for a specific item, and they'll ship it. This is one small fry you won't want to throw back.

Starbaby
Warehouse Row
1110 Market Street (615) 265-7552
Chattanooga, TN 37401 PQ

This California manufacturer is spreading its outlet stores faster than a speeding bullet. Permission in writing is requested before they will allow a credit card order to be fulfilled by phone. Just write to the outlet above to authorize a purchase in advance. Save up to 50 percent on darling children's clothing.

Sultra (Camp Beverly Hills)
Corporate Office: Sultra Corporation
472 Seventh Avenue, 17th Floor (212) 967-5980
New York, NY 10018 PQ

Can't afford to send your kids to camp, much less Beverly Hills? Well, outfit them instead in Camp Beverly Hills clothes. It's certainly cheaper than a ride down Rodeo Drive. Detour to their outlet stores in Saratoga or Central Valley, New York or order by phone direct to their outlet store at (914) 928-2507 (not the corporate number above) and save up to 50 percent. All first-quality and all fashionably in-season.

The Wabby Company
3331 Gold Run Road
Boulder, CO 80302
(303) 449-2120
CK, MC, V, MO, B

Every baby loves a Wabby, this diaper cover with a difference. Instead of nylon or rubber, the Wabby is made of Gore-Tex®, a breathable fabric that keeps wetness in and lets vapors escape, so babies stay cooler. Wabbies are machine washable (and dryable, too), and available in sizes newborn to XL, or 29–34 pounds, in yellow, white, or a print, at $12.25 each (four or five are necessary for one baby). Hats, long underwear, booties, and diaper-sack hampers are also part of the booty. The Wabby Company offers discounts with quantity orders.

Apparel: Family

What's your pleasure? Chances are you'll find it here. From fashion to function, professional to playful, we'll bet you'll find the look you like. Be a sport and dive into the discounts at the All-American T-Shirt Company. Or dress to excess in a gown from Hollywood. In this section, you'll find a variety of bargains ranging from custom apparel for men and women to designer "standbuys"—Manhattan, Damon, Anne Klein, Henry Grethel —to warm winter woolens to the preppy, durable clothing that never falls by the wayside. It's all here for you, and it's fit to be tried.

American T-Shirt
1228 Scyene Road Whse. 209 (800) 782-0214; (214) 289-8262
Mesquite, TX 75149 CK

Since 1988, American T-Shirt has been offering patriotic deals on activewear by HANES, ONEITA, FRUIT OF THE LOOM, and SCREEN STARS. They offer long and short-sleeved T-shirts, leggings, and skorts in 28 colors, in 50/50 blends and 100-percent cotton, at prices as low as $2.65 a piece. This wholesale distributor has no minimum orders, but you'll save even more when you buy by the dozen, and you can mix and match colors and sizes, from small through XXX-large. Their toll-free number accepts orders Monday through Friday from 8:30 a.m. to 8 p.m. Call or write for a free brochure.

A Star Is Worn
7303 Melrose Avenue (213) 939-4922
Los Angeles, CA 90046 CK, MC, V, AE, C/$5

You can wear it again, Samantha, at this specialty store, but trust me, this is no ordinary thrift shop. All the clothes here have the cachet that comes with having once belonged to a star. You might cheer up in a T-shirt of Cher's for $20, or shimmy out in a red strapless gown made especially for Farrah Fawcett at $600. Some stars specify that their favorite charity receive a percentage of sales, and many of the items are even autographed by their donors. Besides clothing, there are accessories including jewelry and miscellaneous odds and ends that are also recycled to star-struck shoppers.

Babouris Handicrafts
56 Adrianou Street
105 55 Athens 01-32-47-561
Greece CK, MO, B/$3

For those interested in weaving a fantastic yarn for entertaining after-dinner guests, why not tell the story of Babouris. Since 1958, they've been home-spinning woolen yarns and fancy cotton yarns in a variety of natural and fast-dyed colors, hand-knit sweaters, and knitted wear made from the above yarns at prices 70 percent off comparable U.S. products. Minimum order is five kilos of yarn or one sweater, and your order is processed immediately.

Bemidji Woolen Mills
P.O. Box 277 (218) 751-5166
Bemidji, MN 56601 MC, V, D, COD, B

Play ragtime with a ragg knit cap or grab some woolens for your next ski trip to the wild and wooly, wintry West. Founded in 1920, this family-owned business specializes in men's, women's, and children's outerwear; yarns; LADY SLIPPER design products (decorative stuffed animals); plus they manufacture 100-percent wool and polyester batting. They'll also go to bat for you by reprocessing your old wool batting. Most famous for their jackets and coats, they've even made jackets for 15 northern governors. Yarns are another good buy: 100-percent pure wool yarn was $2.75 per skein. Department store brands (WOOLRICH and PENDELTON), for example, are found at prices about 30 percent lower. There's a 100-percent satisfaction guarantee, with exchanges or refunds made on request. Goods that must be back-ordered take two to three weeks; normal orders are shipped the same day.

Cahall's Department Store/Cahall's Brown Duck Catalog

P.O. Box 450 (513) 444-2094
Mount Orab, OH 45154 CK, MC, V, D, MO, C/$1

Here's your chance to duck retail on jeans, jackets, overalls, and more. Cahall's Brown Duck Catalog offers all these, from names like LEVI'S, JERZEES, OSHKOSH B'GOSH, WRANGLER, HANES, and others at up to 40 percent below retail. Their work shoes are something to quack about, too, for men and women, featuring sizes that are hard to find. T-shirts, hats, sturdy socks, bandanas, and more won't ruffle your feathers with high prices. They ship worldwide, and your satisfaction is guaranteed.

Cambridge Wools, Ltd.

(See **Arts and Crafts**, p. **54**.)

Clothkits

(See **Kits and Kaboodle**, p. **348**.)

Custom Coat Company, Inc.

P.O. Box 230 (414) 361-5050
Berlin, WI 54923 MC, V, C

Custom Coat can transform raw hides into jackets, coats, vests, gloves, purses, hats, moccasins, and many other leather accessories. They tan deer, elk, and moose hides (yours or theirs). All garments (ladies' and men's) can be made with rayon, satin fleece, or pile lining. Their free 21-page catalog provides excellent information concerning care and shipping of your raw hides at 25 percent below retail costs for similar products. If you bag a small one and need some extra leather to complete your order, they can supply it at $3.50 a square foot.

D. MacGillivray & Coy
Muir of Aird 011-44-0870-2525
Balivanich Benbecula CK, Bank Check, V, AE, Access, MO, IMO,
Western Isles, Scotland Postal Orders, C/$4
PA88 5LA

Here's the Harris tweed and Shetland knitwear specialist "patronized by royalty and nobility." Even Her Majesty the Queen and Princess Margaret own their hand-knit Shetland shawls. For the materialistic, hand-woven Harris tweed was a good buy, as well as Harris wool sweaters, knitted by hand, for less than $50. They have Scotch tweeds and Donegals, Scottish clan tartans, Shetland tweeds, mohair and camel's hair, sweaters, socks, bedspreads, caps, ties, rugs, kilts, and even hand-blended Hebridean perfume! We were intrigued by their "real grouse claw brooches." There's no minimum order, no restocking charge, and a 15-day exchange or refund policy if not satisfied.

Damon/Enro Shirt Company
7601 River Road (201) 861-1115
North Bergen, NJ 07047 CK, MC, V, AE, PQ

For out-of pocket savings that are completely out-of sight, try this outlet for men's and women's apparel. No more will you be roamin' the stores looking for clothing by DAMON or ENRO, or paying prices only royalty can afford. You can leave your chariot at home and get first-quality sportswear at close to wholesale. This store is owned by DAMON and (predictably) carries their own brands: DAMON and ENRO. Prices are a whopping 30 percent to 60 percent off retail on shirts, ties, sportswear, and knitwear. They even have retail outlet locations in Indiana, Kansas, Kentucky, New Jersey (Secaucus), New York, South Carolina, and Tennessee. They have a five-day refund and a 30-day exchange policy. Shipping's a flat $3 rate.

Deerskin Place
283 Akron Road (717) 733-7624
Ephrata, PA 17522 CK, MC, V, COD, C/$1, PQ

"Deer-ly beloved, we are gathered here . . ." Those who don't run with the herd can let their fingers do the stalking through this catalog. You can fawn over sheepskin coats and jackets, handbags, shoes, moccasins, gloves, and wallets for men and women at 30 percent to 50 percent off retail. (Talk about saving some bucks! Bargains like that belong on our trophy rack—where the interest is mounting!) A woman's belted leather jacket was $395; men's slip-on deerskin shoes were $69.95. We set our sights on a pair of women's unlined deerskin gloves for $29.99, and bagged a coonskin cap ($9.95) for the bambi-no. Baby moccasin boots in sizes 1 to 6 were $13.95, while suede knee-high moccasins in sizes 4 to 10 with hard or soft soles were $45. Men's sizes typically run 6 to 13. There's no minimum order and no restocking charge on returns, although there is an exchange-only policy (no refunds). If you haven't gotten your order in two to four weeks, start hunting. Now that you don't have stiff leather prices to dis-suede you from buying, you won't have to lock horns with these guys. Satisfaction guaranteed.

Deva Cottage Industry
303 E. Main Street (301) 663-4900
Burkittsville, MD 21718 CK, MC, V, D, MO, C/$1

According to their catalog, "Deva is an attempt to humanize work and integrate it with home life." That's a worthy goal, and manufacturing natural fiber clothing for men and women is the means they've selected. Though "gentlemen often prefer blends," Deva's au natural drawstring pants at $21 postpaid are close kin to the surgical team look, and very comfortable. The pants come in many colors and are perfect for running, lounging, or meditating. They also make drawstring shorts ($14 postpaid), wrap skirts ($24 postpaid), a wonderful "Spring Moon" kimono for $39, and many other products. They sell direct, so you can expect to save around 20 percent. Clothing comes in sizes small, medium, large, extra large, and extra-extra large. Everything carries an unconditional guarantee, entitling you to exchange or claim a refund. They also sell books for devotees of Eastern philosophy and culture. Fabric samples are enclosed with their catalog.

Dharma Trading Co.
(See **Arts and Crafts**, p. **60**.)

Down Generation/Sylvia & Sons
725 Columbus Avenue (212) 663-3112
New York, NY 10025 CK, MC, V, AE, DC, COD, PQ

Get down, get down! More than 35,000 down-filled garments including jackets, vests, and full-length coats are discounted 15 percent off retail. We found enough skiwear to outfit Jean-Claude Killy and his whole family for at least ten seasons, and that's no snow job. Some of their most popular brands include WOOLRICH, CB, HEAD, OBERMEYER, TRAILWISE, and THE NORTH FACE. No shipping charges unless order is over ten pounds (and that would take a lot of down). Exchanges or refunds offered for a 60-day period.

Edinburgh Woolen Mill, Ltd.
Langholm, Dumfriesshire Dept. 58 (05418) 0092
Scotland DG 130BR MC, V, AE, C

Are you on a kilt trip about spending too much money? Don't skirt the issue, address it—and send it off to Scotland! (You'll be coming back for moor.) Tweed and tartan skirts and suits for men and women are priced well below those found in comparable stores in the United States. Sweaters by PRINGLE and their own brand cost from $20 to $75 ($35 to $125 retail). There's a 100-percent satisfaction guarantee, and they'll gladly accept exchanges on items purchased through the mail or at one of their 80 retail shops in Britain. Since all prices are in pounds, it's easier to use your credit cards. They will honor prices for the duration marked in the catalog. A 6-pound (surface) or 12-pound (air mail) postage fee is required on any size order.

Eisner Bros.
76 Orchard Street (212) 475-6868
New York, NY 10002 Certified Check, COD, C

Eisner Bros. is one of the world's largest headquarters for all active wear and printables. They carry T-shirts in white and over 20 colors.

They also carry sweatshirts, sweatpants, minidress sweatshirts, oversized T-shirts and sweatshirts, night shirts, tank tops, golf shirts, jackets, and baseball caps. They stock sizes from infant (six months) through adult 4XL in a full variety of colors. Eisner Bros. is a distributor for FRUIT OF THE LOOM, HANES PRINTABLES, HANES UNDERWEAR, JERZEES, RUSSELL, and SCREEN STARS. Orders are shipped the same day they are placed.

The Finals
(See **Sporting Goods and Apparel**, p. **455**.)

Gohn Bros.
105 S. Main
P.O. Box 111 (219) 825-2400
Middlebury, IN 46540 CK, B, PQ

Going, going, Gohn to the Brothers from Middlebury! This 85-year-old company sells Amish men's and women's clothing, plain clothing, underwear, hosiery, yard goods for quilting, and supplies and notions. (Their Amish Country Cookbook is $7.50 and features 600 old-fashioned Amish farm cooking recipes. That's one notion that really whetted our appetites.) Their line of 100-percent cotton underwear, socks, and bedding is their most popular offering. Clothing brands include HANES, HEALTH KNIT, GERBER, CHATHAM, RED WING (shoes), CANNON (towels), and V.I.P. SPRINGMILLS (fabrics). Prices were about 30 percent off retail. Gohn carries a line of sewing supplies, too, in their eight-page brochure. Exchanges and refunds upon request.

HTC, Inc.
P.O. Box 217
2191 S. Main (517) 523-2167
Pittsford, MI 49271 CK, COD, C

Park your car in the Harvard yard because they carry that classic from the fifties, the car coat. HTC is the manufacturer of top-quality insulated, washable nylon outerwear. Ladies' jackets, car coats, and long coats are all lightweight in a fantastic selection of colors. They also carry men's jackets, hunting jackets, work clothes, and snowmobile suits. Women's sizes ranged from 8 to 34 and men's sizes ranged from small to XXX-large. All American-made at the HTC factory and sold at factory prices—40 percent to 70 percent off. This company's been around since 1926—the time of the model A Ford. No wonder their prices are so affordable!

As a special for *Great Buys* readers, when you buy one coat at the catalog price, you'll get the second for 15 percent off.

Howron Sportswear
295 Grand Street (212) 226-4307
New York, NY 10002 CK, MC, V, AE, D, COD, PQ

How, Ron! We spent heap big pile of wampum at this place. (And we didn't need a reservation!) Chief labels were STANLEY BLACKER, DAMON, and OSCAR DE LA RENTA really Siouxted our tribe. (Squaw won't squawk when she can Chippewa-y for OSCAR DE LA RENTA, STANLEY BLACKER, DAMON, MEMBERS ONLY, SANSABELT, GIVENCHY, and many others!) Ladies' dressy and sportswear styles (sizes 4 to 18 or 38 to 48) by ACT III, VILLAGERS, BRECKENRIDGE, PRESTIGE, STUART LANG, and LEE would catch any brave's eye. (Give 'em the old pow-wow!) Ladies' HANES panty hose and underwear were discounted 25 percent; men's JOCKEY shorts carried the same discount. Most merchandise was 25 to 50 percent off retail. Orders take about a week. Indian givers get store credit only on returns.

Jos. A. Bank Clothiers
25 Crossroad Drive (800) 284-3225; (301) 837-8838
Owings Mills, MD 21117-5499 CK, MC, V, AE, C

For investment dressing, this is a manufacturer you can Bank on. Savings of 25 to 30 percent on fine-quality traditionally styled men's, women's, and preppie clothing and accessories were tastefully tailored to fit our fiscal budget. Bank's holdings included good buys on silk ties (at $12.50 each, these are the ties that *won't* bind); men's Oxford cloth shirts (for just $18.50, they put us in high cotton, but left a little "lettuce" in our pockets); men's 100-percent wool worsted suits (for $210 they blasted their competition in worsted suits); women's khaki slacks ($26.50); and ragg wool sweaters (for $20.50 they wouldn't leave even the Pillsbury doughboy looking like a rag-a-muffin). Other Bank assets included shoes, belts, rain gear, handbags, hats, and caps. Returns are accepted within 30 days for exchange or refund (if the garment hasn't been worn or altered). If you write a personal check, your order will be held until your check clears. If you would like to put a finger on the supple fabrics they use, ask for a sample.

Land's End
1 Land's End Lane (800) 356-4444 X 4947
Dodgeville, WI 53595 CK, MC, V, AE, D, C

Land's End is a landmark with their line of clothing; just trekking through their catalog makes you want to take a Tibetan hike or go white water rafting in Wisconsin. Their clothing is sturdy, comfortable, classic, and fun. We saw beautiful lambswool and ragg sweaters for men and women, colorful polo and rugby shirts, twill pants, women's skirts, and shorts and shoes along with belts, shoulder bags, and nautical gifts fit for even land-locked sailors. Even boomerangs were available for those one-step-above-the-average Frisbee freaks. While not technically an "off-price" merchant, they do offer particularly high-quality clothing at factory direct prices. Satisfaction guaranteed or complete refund; shipping charges at a flat rate of $3; free full-color 48-page catalog (a trip by itself). Specialty kids catalog also available.

Lee-McClain Co., Inc.
1857 Midland Trail (502) 633-3823
Shelbyville, KY 40065 CK, MC, V, PQ

Tired of jockeying for clothing at retail? (You bet!) Well, you can't get a Kentucky derby here, just suits, sport coats, and slacks at 40 to 60 percent off. This 50-years-plus-old company manufactures its own line of STRATHMORE suits—other suits are given private labels and sold in retail stores under that store's name. Summer-blend suits were 55-percent dacron and 45-percent wool, while winter suits were 100-percent wool. Only one suit style is available—every suit has a two-button front with a center vent in the back. Prices on STRATHMORE suits ranged from $175 to $185 (suits comparable in quality run $295 and up). Navy blazers and navy suits with pinstripes are their most popular offerings, although a 100-percent camel's hair sports jacket for $175 is also a good seller. Suits are stocked in sizes 36 to 50 in extra-long, long, regular, and short. About 90 percent of their inventory is for men, but they do have some tailored suits and blazers for women, too. If you send them your suit size, they'll send you fabric samples (since not all fabrics are available in all sizes). Make your decision, and you'll be off to the races (looking like a thoroughbred) with their finished lines.

Manhattan
New Braunfels Mills Store Plaza
651 Highway 81 East (512) 620-7528
New Braunfels, TX 78130 CK, MC, V, AE, D, MO, COD, PQ

You can order by mail from these Manhattan aisles and save 20 percent to 70 percent on men's and women's clothing without climbing to the top of the Empire State Building. I'll take MANHATTAN, ANNE KLEIN, LADY MANHATTAN, HENRY GRETHEL, JOHN HENRY, YVES ST. LAURENT, and PETERS & ASHLEY.

Natan Borlam Co., Inc.
(See **Apparel: Baby's and Children's**, p. **4**.)

O'Connor's Yankee Peddler Warehouse Sale
116 Newman Street (517) 362-3437
East Tawas, MI 48730 CK, MC, V, AE, D, PQ

Wanna be the tog of the town? The answer's just around the O'Connor. These Yankees peddle last season's stock along with first-quality closeouts from over 100 manufacturers including PENDLETON, WHITE STAG, JANTZEN, COLLEGE TOWN, CALVIN KLEIN, LEVI'S, HAGGAR, ARROW, GANT, MISTY HARBOR, and others at 30- to 70-percent discounts. They also have men's clothing, gifts, and furniture. There's an exchange policy on returns less a 10-percent restocking charge—they'll honor justifiable returns only. Call for a price quote.

Prince Fashions Ltd.
GPO Box 2868 5-742938; 5-744106
Hong Kong CK, IMO, C/$2 (refundable)

You don't have to kiss a frog to find a prince among the high cost of clothing. Just look to the east—the Far East. Prince Fashions

Ltd. offers high-quality clothing at royal savings. They are one of the biggest mail-order companies in Hong Kong and have been in business for 25 years. Princess-pleasing prices abound in their full-color catalog. We discovered a kingdom of royal bargains. A hand-knit cardigan was $22.20; a men's lambswool sweater, just $14.50; and a jade bangle bracelet was only $27.80. We couldn't possibly list all the items this Prince of fashion carried, but we can name a few: jewelry, watches, sport suits, dresses, jackets, and fans.

Great Buys readers receive an additional 10 percent off, as well as a souvenir gift. If not pleased, you won't lose your crown. The Prince takes returns without a frown.

Pueblo to People
2105 Silber Road, Suite 101
Houston, TX 77055
(800) 843-5257;
(713) 523-1197 (Houston);
(713) 956-1172 MC, V, AE, D, C

This nonprofit organization provides products exclusively from South American cooperatives with its central goal to aid native artisans in selling and distributing their handicrafts. The catalog is filled with a bounty of ecologically sound and economically appealing items to wear yourself, or for gift giving. Appliqued skirts and vests, mohair sweaters, hand puppets, Guatemalan sisel baskets, gourmet gift nuts, and more grace this colorful catalog with a cause.

Rammagerdin of Reykjavik
Hafnarstraeti 19
P.O. Box 751-121
Reykjavik, Iceland
011-354-1-627270
C, B (with samples)/$1

Question: What's the favorite comic strip of an Icelandic sheep shearer? Answer: Mutton Jeff! This company sells wool and fur clothing for the whole family, plus ceramics, souvenir gifts, and knitting products. Prices on their woolen sweaters, ponchos, coats, caps, mittens, shawls, and vests are about 50 percent less than U.S. retail for comparable quality (around $35 to $40 usually, versus $70 to $80). If you've been hankering to weave your own bargain, they also sell Icelandic yarn made from the mountain sheep fleece. It is well known for being warm, yet very light and soft. There's a minimum yarn order of eight skeins.

Royal Silk
6117 Harrison Place, Dept. 1557 (800) 962-6262; (201) 854-6611
West New York, NJ 07093 CK, MC, V, AE, DC, CB, C/$2

Although Royal Silk isn't a bona fide discount company (they sell their own wares rather than discounting those made by others), you can still find excellent values on silk blouses, dresses, and menswear. Prices are usually 30 percent to 60 percent lower than those on retail lines of comparable quality. The *Royal Man* collection exhibited a shantung silk tuxedo shirt, silk shorts for $18, and several styles of silk and cotton shirts. Batiste shirts for men and women (60-percent silk, 40-percent cotton) ranged from $22 to $27. The women's *Royal Silk* catalog featured their most popular item, a stylish silk T-shirt, for $19. The silk crepe de chine tank top came in a close second, also $19. Royal Silk has a 100-percent guarantee, so if you're unhappy for any reason, they'll refund, exchange, or offer credit. Their basic, 40-page, full-color catalog displays over 70 items.

St. Laurie Ltd.
897 Broadway @ 20th Street (212) 473-0100
New York, NY 10003 CK, MC, V, AE, DC

Halo out there! This Sainted discounter can save you pennies from heaven on classic business suits. Sharp-looking men's and women's suits are discounted, as can be seen in their semi-annual combination swatch brochure. At St. Laurie, men's suits cost from $295 to $350; women's suits from $295 to $350. Dressing for corporate America doesn't come cheap, but for custom clothing, these can't be beat. Fabric swatches of tweed, silks, mid-weight wools, linens, cashmeres, worsted wool, and camel's hair give you a feel for what you're buying. There's a two-week refund or exchange period; orders normally are delivered in about a week, although back-ordered items can take two to three weeks to arrive. If you're in the neighborhood, take a factory tour from 9 a.m. to 4 p.m., Monday through Friday. We don't want to make a suitcase out of this, but here is where the worst-ed can be the best. Swatch Club Membership: $10/year, two seasons, Fall and Spring.

Sara Glove Company, Inc.
P.O. Box 1940 (800) 243-3570; (203) 574-4090
117 Benedict Street (203) 574-3500
Waterbury, CT 06722-1940 MC, V, C

It's not tough to find clothes that work as hard as you do; just look into the Sara Glove catalog and you'll find the industrial-strength duds they've sold since 1974. Shoes by CAROLINA, DICKIES uniforms, custom-printed T-shirts, personalized satin jackets, smocks and work shirts, boots, all kinds of gloves, and more. Sizes range from small to very large. Satisfaction's guaranteed and orders are often shipped immediately.

Spiegel, The Ultimate Outlet
(See **Buying Clubs and One-Stop Shopping**, p. **118**.)

Waco Thrift Stores Inc.
P.O. Box 143
201 Atlantic Avenue (404) 537-2702
Waco, GA 30182 MC, V, COD, B

I dream of jeanies with the light brown wrappers. For men's and women's first-quality jeans (including LEE) for just $18.95, you're wacko if you pass up Waco. Goosedown jackets for kids cost just $49.95 and are ideal for school or play in colder climates. They've got family clothing gently worn by gentle people. Men's clothing, including slacks and suits, are their best buys. They'll exchange on new merchandise; you can expect your order in about a week. Write for their brochure and price list with labels and styles for a prompt reply.

WinterSilks
2700 Oaura Lane
P.O. Box 130 (800) 621-3229
Middleton, WI 53562 CK, MC, V, AE, C

When the weather outside is frightful, cozy up to this color catalog for "silk clothing at factory direct prices." Cotton/silk-blend sweaters, silk nightshirts, robes, tanks, long johns, men's boxer shorts and briefs, bras, turtlenecks, scarves, blouses, pants, and more add style at a savings. Prices in the sale section were especially pleasing, like silk cardigans for $29.95, a handknit silk/cotton scarf for $11.95, or a pair of silk/wool bootie slippers for $8.95. Returns are accepted; UPS and Federal Express delivery are available.

W.S. Robertson (Outfitters) Ltd.

40/41 Bank Street 0896-2152
Galashiels Scotland CK, MC, V, IMO, C/$5

If you're a chip off the ole block, you'll really love these PRINGLES—probably the finest name in knitwear for men and women since 1815. We won't pull the wool over your eyes—you'll save about one-third off the specialty store prices in the U.S. Choose from cardigans and pullovers in cashmere, lambswool, shetland, camel's hair—all natural fibers. Other names noted are BALLANTYNE, BRAEMAT, and LYLE & SCOTT LTD. knitwear. All prices are quoted in pounds; be sure to deduct the value added tax not charged on exported goods (15 percent), after you've figured the conversion to dollars. Minimum order—one garment.

Apparel: Maternity

The nine months of waiting should pay off with the birth of a baby, not a nation of debt. The savings here will keep those instincts maternal rather than just having you spill your guts for the material, girl. Stretch out those stretch or stirrup pants with an elastic stomach insert rather than always panting for a new pair of pants if you're expecting. Then invest in a top or two for several mix 'n match looks for less. Complete the wardrobe with ensembles from these select sources.

Mother's Place
P.O. Box 94512 (800) 829-0080
Cleveland, OH 44101-4512 CK, MC, V, D, MO, C

Save on maternity clothes with flair. With your ever-expanding waistline, it is no longer necessary to waste money dressing to the nines (months.) Save up to 60 percent on a full maternity wardrobe: dresses, separates, activewear, and more to take you from work to play with no hassles. These fashions are generously cut but will still please the tightwadded budget-conscious; some activewear is less than $20, and career separates are around $30. Check out this little catalog with big potential; satisfaction's guaranteed with this delivery. Minimum credit card order, $10.

Mothers Work
1309 Noble Street (215) 625-9259
Philadelphia, PA 19123 MC, V, AE, C/$3 (refundable)

Are you one of the many working mothers of the '90s? Then let Mothers Work work for you. Exclusive pre- and post-maternity business suits help you look stunning before, during, and after. We discovered jackets, dresses, and skirts, made of 100-percent worsted wool. You won't find this quality under just any cabbage leaf. Many of the dresses and blouses coordinate with the suits for a complete look. Their full-color 32-page catalog arrives with a wardrobe design aid and a swatch card to help you mix and match so you can put together the perfect working wardrobe. You won't have to work hard at looking professional. Mothers Work will deliver a 100-percent refund or exchange within 10 days of receipt, and they offer next-day shipping so your precious bundles won't be overdue.

Reborn Maternity
1449 Third Avenue (212) 737-8817
New York, NY 10028 CK, MC, V, AE, C/$2

For a pregnant pause that refreshes, flip through Reborn Maternity's catalog. Revive your maternity wardrobe with moderate to better sportswear and evening wear: You'll find born-again bargains in sizes 4 to 20. It won't be long before you'll be singing praises, either, when you see the 10-percent to 40-percent savings on name brands like SASSON, DENNIS GOLDSMITH, BELLE FRANCE, and FINE SPORT. The minimum order's just $20 and you won't have to wait nine months, either—most are delivered in two and a half weeks, or well before the stork makes *his/her* delivery.

Apparel: Men's

For investment dressing without cashing in your cache of blue chips, you've come to the right spot. Check out the stock marketed here and get everything from ADOLFO to ZEROS at bargain margins. Classic clothing is never out of fashion. Natural fabrics feel better, wear better, and last longer, so indulge yourself—your clothing is an investment, remember? When you dress for success, good taste pays big dividends. If you're conscious of the bottom line, the least you can do is not sacrifice the designer names. Here's looking at them for less: GIORGIO ARMANI, STANLEY BLACKER, CHRISTIAN DIOR, LONDON FOG, RALPH LAUREN, PERRY ELLIS, YVES ST. LAURENT . . . we've got you covered at over-the-counter prices.

A. Rubinstein and Son
63 E. Broadway — (212) 226-9696
New York, NY 10002 — CK, MC, V, AE, DC, CB, COD, B, PQ

Unlike the great musician, this A. Rubinstein's no pianist, although his prices on men's clothing definitely struck a responsive chord. This family's been playing our song for 64 years; three generations of Rubensteins work in the store! Everything is first quality. Suit sizes range from 34 short to 52 long. There are dozens of brands, including ADOLFO, PIERRE CARDIN, CHARLES JOURDAN,

STANLEY BLACKER, YVES ST. LAURENT, GUESS?, GIORGIO ARMANI, and OLEG CASSINI—not to mention SAN REMO, MARZOTTA, DAMON, and LONDON FOG. Shirts, ties, sportswear, rainwear, and outerwear were also available at 20-percent to 30-percent discounts. There's a $25 minimum order; no restocking charge. They'll make refunds or exchanges up to two weeks after delivery. Alterations are free for New York City residents. No wonder note-able New Yorkers have kept in tune with the times by making this store their fashion forte.

Dallas Menswear
1704 Commerce (214) 741-6738
Dallas, TX 75201 MC, V, AE, DC, PQ

Since 1976, Dallas Menswear has been selling quality menswear, and putting the stress on *quality*, not your wallet. Savings of 25 to 60 percent can turn any Tom, Dick, or Billy Bob into a sharp-dressed man. They carry private labels, as well as BARTOLINI and BAGIR men's apparel, in sizes 36 to 46 regular, 40 to 50 long, and 38 to 42 short. Call to check their stock for something suitable for you; they don't have a catalog. But their normal delivery time is seven days, and merchandise that hasn't been altered may be returned within four weeks.

Eisenberg & Eisenberg
Fifth Ave @ 16th Street (212) 627-1290
New York, NY 10003 CK, MC, V, AE, MO, COD, PQ

Dress to kill without wounding your budget. Eisenberg & Eisenberg has been in business since 1898, selling men's clothing and specializing in elegant tuxedos. Dapper Dans can save enough to buy roses and still put gas in the Jaguar. Have your eye out for brands such as RALPH LAUREN, PERRY ELLIS, TALLIA, LORD WEST, DIMITRI, PIERRE CARDIN, and CHRISTIAN DIOR. If you buy from the store, alterations are available on the premises. For mail-order customers, they ship UPS insured to all locations. Call for a price quote on a terrific tux and take the walk for less. Returns are accepted within 30 days for full refund. No restocking fee.

Factory Wholesalers
United Ramex Division
P.O. Box 938 (612) 693-3413
Litchfield, MN 55355 Money Orders only, B, PQ

Their name tells you what you need to know. This is no place for cads and dandies, but if you're a working man, their duds are no duds. Used men's work clothes including pants, shirts, coveralls, jackets, socks, white shirts, and pants. Ladies' smocks made from washable linen are also available. A bundle of five pants and five shirts was $19.50 plus $4.50 handling. You can't beat that no matter how many times you strike! Shop coats were four for $8 plus shipping, another nicely coated bargain. They tell us their clothes are made in America for American-sized bodies. This company says they'll save working men a minimum of 90 percent over a year. A 100-percent satisfaction or your money refunded.

Great Buys readers get a free bonus work shirt with their order.

G & G Projections
62 Orchard Street (212) 431-4531
New York, NY 10002 CK, MC, V, AE, DC, CB, COD, PQ

Gosh, golly, and gee whiz! They'll take the shirt right off their racks and mail it to you! For another option, order your name brand and designer shirts and sweaters in names such as HATHAWAY and CHRISTIAN DIOR from their affiliated stores, called Penn Garden and Liberty Menswear, phone (212) 966-5600. Shirts range in size from 14½ to 18; suits and jackets bearing labels by GEOFFREY BEENE, STANLEY BLACKER, YVES ST. LAURENT, ADOLFO, PIERRE CARDIN, and CALVIN KLEIN. Virtually everything they carry is a name brand. You'll save 20 percent to 35 percent, and they pay the shipping (with no G-strings attached!). Alterations are free on suits, jackets, and raincoats. Orders are delivered in about two weeks; a full refund or exchange policy should also put you at ease. Order by phone Sunday through Friday with credit cards.

Gelber's Menswear
1001 Washington Avenue (314) 421-6698
St. Louis, MO 63101 MC, V, AE, D, COD, PQ

The St. Louis Cardinals may make us see red, but Gelber's is far from our Arch enemy. The inventory of discounted men's clothing changes weekly at this 100-year-old, St. Louis–based company. Everything's first quality and discounted 30 percent to 70 percent off regular prices. Current styles are available in names such as SAN LORENZO, OLEG CASSINI, BOSA, RAFFINATTI, and JOHN ALEXANDER. High on the best-selling list are 100-percent wool single- or double-breasted gabardine suits in solid colors with silk-lined pants, made in the U.S.A. by FIORAVANTE, for $249; retail $499. Tie one on with silk FRATELLI tie sets at $19. They do alterations at little or no charge. Customers usually receive their orders in about ten days.

Send them a style description for prices and tell 'em you're a *Great Buys* reader—you'll get an additional $30 to $50 off on their everyday low prices posted on the sleeves of their garments.

Harry Rothman
200 Park Ave South — (212) 777-7400
New York, NY 10003 — CK, MC, V, COD, PQ

Rothman is to the discount men's clothing business what Loehmann's is to women's. Suits, jackets, shirts, ties, rainwear, and haberdashery in a wide variety of styles hang out on the racks here. Sizes run from 36 to 56; there are extra-longs and extra-shorts, too. Many top men's manufacturers are represented, always in season, and always in large quantities; prices are from 25 percent to 50 percent off. (Though they wouldn't reveal labels to us over the phone, we know that many a Hick has become a Free Man after leaving his shop.) Write to their mail-order department describing your size, weight, height, waist measurements, and preference of patterns and fabric. They'll provide you with top-of-the-line menswear. Returns are accepted (if not worn or altered).

Huntington Clothiers
1285 Alum Creek Drive — (800) 848-6203
Columbus, OH 43209 — (614) 252-4422 (OH residents)
CK, MC, V, AE, DC, CB, C

The Huntington Clothiers' catalog proves once and for all that "good things come in small packages." The 82-page booklet is a *must* for devotees of the classic cultured look. However, their super-soft, spun-cotton afghan-comforter-warmer-throw-big boy's wubbie is still a security blanket to some big boys I know. Shirts come in striped and solid Oxfords, straight collar, button-downs, long and short sleeves, pinpoint Oxfords, "graph check," broadcloth, tartan plaids, and gingham. Pure silk ties with tropical fish, florals, medallions, sailboats, from $19.50 to $26. Suitable savings were found on camel's hair, worsted wool, alpaca, lambswool, corduroy, and flannel suits and sport coats. Dress trousers, jackets, trenchcoats, shoes, briefcases, cotton boxers, terry robes, fountain pens, watches, and Swiss army knives complete this ground-floor opportunity to dress for success for less.

The King Size Company
P. O. 9115
Hingham, MA 02043
(800) 343-9678; (617) 877-4100
(MA residents)
MC, V, AE, D, C

The kingpin of King Size, James Kelley, stands tall when he professes his motto, "A 6′ 8″ man should not have to pay a penalty for being tall." They try to position their prices within 10 percent of what a 5′ 8″ man would pay for the same clothing. They also have clothing to outfit large men (pants sizes 44 to 60; shirts from 17 to 22). They have their own label as well as JOCKEY, HAGGAR, BOTANY 500, PALM BEACH, HUSH PUPPIES, and LONDON FOG. Shipping via UPS costs 10 percent of the order; there's an unconditional guarantee. Their free catalog comes out ten to twelve times a year; January and June are sale issues.

Lee-McClain Co., Inc.
(See **Apparel: Family**, p. **16**.)

Master Fashions
P.O. Box 37559
5318 Normandy Boulevard
Jacksonville, FL 32205
(904) 786-8121
CK, MC, V, AE, D, B

Hee-ey, men! Master Fashions been the savior for many a man of the cloth; they're called to serve preachers, pastors, and Christian groups. Bless their hearts, they have basic black, brown, and navy suits in two basic styles. Many brands are carried, and savings of 40 percent to 60 percent will leave you a lot of bread to be thankful for. Sizes run all the way from 36 to 70. At the risk of sounding judgmental, we noted their offerings also included a simply styled two-button blazer in electric blue, orange, red, green, or gold. They tithe one free suit for every ten religiously ordered. Shipping charges are $3 or five percent of the total order, whichever is greater; most orders are received in two to three weeks; satisfaction guaranteed.

Paul Frederick Shirt Company

140 W. Main (800) 247-1417; (215) 944-0909
Fleetwood, PA 19522 CK, MC, V, AE, D, DC, MO, C

Collar great deals on shirts and ties and look the part for 35 percent less than retail. Paul Frederick makes it easy. They've been manufacturing shirts since 1954, and selling directly to the public since 1986. We saw Paul Frederick's own pinpoint Oxford buttondowns at $33 or two for $64; pique bib evening shirts for $47.50; cummerbunds and bow ties, $44 a set; plus silk ties, cufflinks, and other shirts galore in sizes 14½ to 18½ collar and 32 to 37 in sleeve lengths, all for the businessman who knows how to work as hard as he plays. And speaking of playing, the color catalog also features a sports crossword puzzle. Satisfaction is guaranteed, and most orders take seven to ten days.

Quinn's Shirt Shop

Route 12, P.O. Box 131 (508) 943-7183
North Grosvenordale, CT 06255 COD only, B/$2 (with SASE; refundable)

Fly straight to the mighty Quinn's for shirts by ARROW at up to 60 percent off. No tricks up these sleeves; the shirts are all slightly irregular, which accounts for the super-low prices. Regular, big, and tall sizes for 14½" to 20" necks and 31" to 38" sleeves are available. Specify if you want long or short sleeves. If you have a shirt in mind, get the style number or code and call them for a price quote. There's a four-shirt ordering minimum; if the shirts you receive are too flawed for your taste, they may be exchanged. Send a SASE along with your $2 check when ordering a price list.

Sussex Clothes Ltd.

302 Fifth Avenue (212) 279-4610
New York, NY 10001 CK, MC, V, AE, C/$5

Dress for Sussex means "power dressing" for the man who's upwardly mobile. This prestigious manufacturer "sells retail to the public at wholesale prices." They carry suits, from $205 to $260, and sport jackets, starting from $175. We saw a blue wool blazer for just $159 and a 100-percent camel's hair sport jacket for just $200. All fall and winter suits are 100-percent wool. Regularly stocked imported fabrics include: camel's hair, herringbone, flannel, pinstripe, plaid, tweed, and solid wool. You'll also find 100-percent silk sport jackets; trousers in sizes 30 to 40; two- and three-piece suits; tuxedos for $250. All bear the SUSSEX label; they're about 50 percent less than comparable retail price. Shipping costs $5 for the first suit and $1 for each additional garment. Return policies are very flexible: they'll swap sizes, or refund on anything within 10 days as long as the garment hasn't been altered or the tags removed.

Apparel: Women's

Sport an international look without taking a bumpy ride. At the right prices, you can snag souvenirs from around the world and dress the part of the cosmopolitan lady. Go international with Danish or Irish hand-knit sweaters, or fine woolen clothing from the famous looms of Iceland. And here's a tip: If you're on the smallish side, save $$ on your IZODS by shopping in the boys' department. The conversions are: boys' 20 equals women's size large (38-40); boys' size 18 equals women's medium (34 to 36); boys' sizes 14 to 16 equals women's small (30 to 32). No matter what you're looking for, use your ingenuity. With a little shopping savvy, you can get an upstairs wardrobe at a bargain-basement price.

Anthony Richards
P.O. Box 94503 (216) 826-3008
Cleveland, OH 44101-4503 CK, MC, V, MO, PQ

The Anthony Richards label means clothing for the mature working woman that doesn't overwork your budget. Save up to 60 percent on their classy ensembles and separates that keep you looking as smart as you are. If you have a particular piece of clothing in mind, and know the size and color you need, call for a price quote. Skirt the issue of full price and hit the boardroom in savvy chic.

Arthur M. Rein

32 New York Avenue (516) 379-6421
Freeport, NY 11520-2017 Certified or Cashier's Check, MO, PQ

Arthur has put a Rein on high prices. His prices of 10 percent to 50 percent below retail should win an Academy Award. Leading ladies are always in top fur fashions with BLACKGLAMA, EMBA, BLACK WILLOW, SAGA, and more. If it's a brand, it's on hand, as well as unbranded generics that were also available at a lesser price. Arthur produces fur garments and any item capable of being made of fur. For example, review these box office hits: 99-percent custom-made fur coats, jackets, capes, boas, wraps, earrings, teddy bears—the list continues for several scenes. Custom-made garments are guaranteed to fit properly. If you would like an autograph from Arthur and a tour of his factory and showroom, you only have to make an appointment. Want a price quote? Send a SASE with your height, weight, bust or chest size, sleeve length, color, kind of fur, and estimated budget. About 90 percent of his inquiries are answered the same day. Additionally, sometimes older styles in used fur garments are available in excellent condition at about one-third the cost of a new one, especially if you are in the market for a hide but don't want to lose yours paying for one!

Great Buys readers will receive a free Rein mink fur teddy bear on a purchase of $3,000 or more (bears retail for $195).

Avon Fashions

Avon Lane (800) 322-1119
Hampton, VA 23630 CK, MC, V, AE, D, MO, C

Avon calling, this time with a selection that's dressy, sporty, and everything in between. Their prices are right, and they get even better with sales. How about a coatdress in red, white, or lime for $24.99, or a floral print cotton/polyester skirt for $19.99? Swimsuits start as low as $14.99. Jumpsuits, career separates, casualwear, lingerie, evening wear, belts . . . even shoes, all packed into their 83-page color catalog. They even offer petite and tall sizes on many items. Orders are usually shipped right away; satisfaction guaranteed.

Chadwick's of Boston
35 United Drive (508) 583-8110
W. Bridgewater, MA 02379 CK, MC, V, AE, D, MO, C

We were impressed with the mail-order division of Hit or Miss, a Boston-based off-price chain, featuring brand names direct to your doorstep. You'll recognize the models in the Chadwick's catalog from the pages of your popular fashion magazines, but the prices won't sound the same. They are 20 percent to 50 percent below retail. We found a variety of fashion formats from casual khakis and polo shirts to elegant evening wear. Gabaradine suits, silk blouses, shirtwaist dresses, and many other garments are featured. For a discounter, Chadwick's spares no expense in presenting a well-organized layout of merchandise. Much of the selection is classic, but trendy themes pop out occasionally. We highly recommend this catalog, but watch out: Reading May Be Hazardous to Your Wealth.

The Chelsea Collection
340 Poplar Street, Building #20 (800) 722-7888
Hanover, PA 17333-0018 (800) 435-8330 (customer service)
CK, MC, V, AE, D, CB, DC, MO, C

Save on stylish separates and suits from The Chelsea Collection. You can dress for success without losing your shirt with reasonable prices on polished and distinctive dresses, blouses, skirts, accessories, and more. Their return policy allows for exchanges or refunds at any time if a customer is dissatisfied.

Dion-Jones Ltd.
Dept. GBBM
3226 S. Aberdeen (312) 927-1113
Chicago, IL 60608 CK, MC, V, AE, C

Outwit the cost of fuller figure fashions by buying them direct (at wholesale or close to wholesale) prices. Former large-size model, Laura Dion-Jones, has created a dynamic and dramatic fashion collection with a multitude of expandable possibilities. This is the ultimate fashion solution to, "I have nothing that fits!" tale of woes. Separates and dresses are easy to care for, sophisticated, and sensible. Cold water wash, hang to dry, roll to pack. You can actually arrive, wrinkle-free! Dresses, tops, skirts, pants, jackets, dusters, coats, baseball/bomber jackets, vests, and big-shirts styled in luscious colors and textures—all interchangeable offering a myriad of wardrobe possibilities. No matter what your figure type, height, or size, from formal affairs, to wedding gowns, office functions, to a stroll down Park Avenue, this is the only ample size designer that provides a smashing "in" look without cashing out. Whether petite, average or tall, a size 12 or a super-size 70, Dion-Jones has it made . . . for less. Custom orders also welcome.

Reader special: Take an additional 20 percent off their already factory-direct prices.

Essence By Mail

P.O. Box 62
Hanover, PA 17333-0062
(800) 882-8055
(800) 553-4578 (customer service)
CK, MC, V, AE, D, CB, DC, MO, C

From understated elegance to bold fashion statements, Essence distills distinctive looks for women. Apparel, hats, accessories, home accents, and more are available in the color catalog. Prices are reasonable, and their seasonal sales catalogs feature discounts up to 55 percent. There is a $20 minimum on credit card orders, and nonpersonalized items may be returned at any time for a full refund or exchange.

Great Lines, Inc.

389 Fifth Avenue
New York, NY 10016
(212) 213-8890; (212) 725-3697
CK, MO, COD, B

Wanna hear a Great Line? We know, you've heard them all. Well, this one's got a leg up on the competition. Women are already forming lines to save on these fashion accessories including jazzy ladies' hosiery and tights, hair accents, jewelry, belts and sunglasses. Whoa! What a way to walk out in style even if your name is not Legs Diamond. In business for 12 years, they provided the extra oomph for hoisery and accessories that pack a high fashion punch without the high-fallutin' price tags. No wait to get their free brochure; just call. No returns unless merchandise is defective. Allow three to six weeks for delivery.

Irish Cottage Industries
44 Dawson Street
Dublin 2, Ireland C/$1

You can't earn a living churning cottage cheese, so the crafty Irish turned to making fine-quality sweaters. It o'curd to them that the cottage industry could churn out homemade wool-you-be-mine's faster that granny could say, "I feel a draft." Best of all, their prices on hand-knit Aran sweaters, scarves, and mittens won't get your Ire up (not with savings of about 25 percent.) With luck and a buck, you can get a charming catalog by air mail (free by surface mail).

Lane Bryant
2300 Southeastern Avenue (800) 477-7070; (317) 266-3311
Indianapolis, IN 46201 CK, MC, V, D, C

This isn't Anita's company, but orange you glad you discovered them? We won't tell any tall tales: they carry "taller misses" sizes 16 to 24. If you're 5′ 7″ or over, they have you covered in sizes 10 to 24. Big deal, you're a little larger now—sizes 36 to 60 and half sizes 12½ to 34½ are also carried. Brands include HUNTER'S RUN, EXQUISITE FORM, VANITY FAIR, GLORIA VANDERBILT, and more. Prices are reasonable on everything from lingerie to shoes in sizes 6 and up. Satisfaction is guaranteed and orders take eight to ten business days.

The Loft Designer Sportswear
491 Seventh Avenue (212) 736-3358
New York, NY 10018 CK, PQ

When we saw the loft's less-than-lofty prices on designer sportswear, we didn't hit the roof. With 30-percent to 60-percent discounts, we found prices much less steep-le than we expected; and even though we had a ceiling on our budget, here we could put a designer on our back. Nothing comes between us and our CALVINS (Kleins, that is), except high price tags. We found the latest PERRY ELLIS, and even ANNE KLEIN-ing the walls here. No price quotes by phone. Write in describing item requested. Include a $20 deposit per garment, refundable if they cannot locate requested item. Then, a balance-due invoice will be mailed. After your check clears, item will be shipped. Pretty complicated, eh?

Mixables
2636 Walnut Hill Lane #206 (800) 541-7057
Dallas, TX 75229 CK, MC, V, C

Mix 'n match is a woman's way to versatility. Shop-from-home direct to one of the largest manufacturers of ladies' and girls' interlock knit 50/50 poly-cotton sportswear and dresses at wholesale prices. (That's half price, ladies.) A full size range, from petites, regulars, and plusses, at prices around $20 or less. If you join their Fashion Club for $10 a year, you can save even more. Call Monday–Saturday, 9 a.m.–5:30 p.m. CST.

Ms., Miss and Mrs.
Third Floor (800) 223-6101
462 Seventh Avenue at 35th Street (212) 736-0557
New York, NY 10018 CK, MO, PQ

Whether you're a Ms., Miss, or Mrs., you'll find what you're looking for here. TV anchorwomen, governor's wives, society mavens, and Sue Goldstein are big fans of this New York floor of fame. They carry over 500 designer labels in sportswear, dresses, coats, and suits. There's a style to fit your way of life and budget. Everything is at least one-third off retail, with some items marked 50 percent off and more, in sizes 4 through 20. Call to tell them what you're interested in, and if they don't have it in stock (with 25,000 items in stock, this is rare), they'll order it for you. This unique combination of quality, personal service, great selection, and the right price keeps their customers satisfied. Take care choosing your purchase: all sales are final.

Philip Reiner Furs
345 Seventh Avenue (212) 675-2900
New York, NY 10001 CK, V, AE, MC, PQ

If you're into furs, get into Philip Reiner for furs with or without a history. Unclaimed, estate, and new designer furs by ANNE KLEIN, OSCAR DE LA RENTA, LANVIN, HARVÉ BERNARD, and others from designer and department stores around the country in every price range are bound to please. Here's a taste of the prices: minks in assorted colors that would cost nearly $6,000 new were going for $395. Included in their selection are sable, lynx, and stone marten furs. Don't get skinned when you put on the ritz.

Phillippe Marcel
P.O. Box 94610
6800 Engle Road
Cleveland, OH 44101-4610
(800) 869-9901
CK, MC, V, MO, C

Petite to full-figure sizes all fit in at Philippe Marcel. Ooh, la la. Vive la fashionable designs, in vibrant colors, tailored or loose-fitting styles, sold by the manufacturer to save you money. Coordinating accessories, such as bracelets, earrings, and necklaces, were also shown to help pull together a perfect look. Smell rich in designer perfumes like OSCAR DE LA RENTA and POISON at up to 80 percent off. They guarantee satisfaction, and offer a no-questions-asked return policy.

Premier Editions
340 Poplar Street, Bldg. 20
Hanover, PA 17333
(800) 447-3164; (201) 863-7300
CK, MC, V, AE, D, CB, DC, MO, C

Hanover packs another popularly priced catalog into the mailboxes of American women. And all sizes are covered. Career separates, casual wear, lingerie, sleepwear, or something for a night on the town can be found, sometimes with coordinating jewelry to match. Accent your wardrobe with these positives and don't settle for something inbetween.

Roaman's
Dept. 46206-8368
2300 Southeastern Avenue
Indianapolis, IN 46206-8368
(800) 274-7130 (orders)
(800) 274-7240 (customer service)
CK, MC, V, AE, D, Lane Bryant, Lerners, Roaman's, C

Roaman's has the fit and the fashion to keep you casual and comfortable even if you're an ample sample. Their color catalog of mature and full-size fashions features women's, misses, and half sizes 14 through 52. Separates, lingerie and shoes from GLORIA VANDERBILT, BONJOUR, LE CHUTE, and SUE BRETT will keep you looking smart for less. When last we checked, popular buys included trapeze tops prices from $19.99 to $34.99, Lycra® stretch pants from $21.99 to $31.99, and big, comfy shirts from $17.99 to $36.99. "No sale is ever final"; returns are accepted for credit, refund, or exchange. Most orders are delivered in seven days or less.

The Swiss Konnection

(see **Jewelry**, p. **342**.)

Willow Ridge

421 Landmark Drive (919) 763-6500
Wilmington, NC 28410 MC, V, AE, C

A store that never closes gets high marks in my book. Misses' and petites' clothing to size 20 is covered in versatile and inexpensive fashions from the golf course to the club. And what about price? Well, everything's on sale from the first page to the last. Choose from tops, bottoms, sportswear, dresses, and cover-ups, and your budget will not go bust. Everything's under $50.

Appliances (Large and Small)

What do you do if your mail-order appliance starts humming and hooing? If your video game is on the blink or your vacuum cleaner is upchucking more that it's sucking in, don't despair. First, write the manufacturer and/or retailer and give them the opportunity to respond. If your problems aren't ironed out that way and you're still dissatisfied, write the Major Appliance Consumer Action Panel (MACAP), 20 N. Wacker Drive, Chicago, IL 60606 or call their toll-free recording (800) 621-0477 or their office (312) 984-5858 during working hours. The recording gives you a step-by-step plan of action when your major appliance problem isn't resolved by the dealer. Supply them with the manufacturer's name, the type of appliance, and the model number, the date the appliance was purchased, a description of the problem, copies of correspondence, and all receipts. They'll take it from there.

Bernie's Discount Center, Inc.
(See **Housewares**, p. **323**.)

Bondy Export Corp.
(See **Buying Clubs and One-Stop Shopping**, p. **112**.)

Cole's Appliance & Furniture Co.
4026 Lincoln Avenue (312) 525-1797
Chicago, IL 60618 CK, MC, V, D, MO, PQ

Apply yourself to Cole's for furniture and more—for less. Up to 40 percent (and sales tax, outside of IL) is a pretty penny to save on appliances, TVs, VCRs, and furniture. A call or letter won't get you a glossy brochure, but it will get you a price quote that's surprisingly low on brand-name appliances and furniture. Try Cole before you fiddle around with retail.

Discount Appliance Centers
2908 Hamilton Street (301) 559-6802
Hyattsville, MD 20782 CK, MC, V, AE, MO, O, DC, C, PQ (send SASE)

Clean up the deals on vacuum cleaners and sewing machines, plus all the accessories, attachments, and supplies that go with 'em. Savings of up to 60 percent are nothing to sneeze at; neither are names like ELECTROLUX, HOOVER, KIRBY, PFAFF, SINGER, NECCHI, CONSEW, and others. Write and send a SASE for a price quote on the latest in vacuums and sewing machines. Minimum order is $25.

EBA Wholesale
2361 Nostrand Avenue (718) 252-3400
Brooklyn, NY 11210 CK, MC, V, PQ

At last, at last! There'll be no more suffering by savings suffragettes! This company voted to pass this EBA (Equal Bargains Amendment) and give up to 60-percent discounts on all major and small appliances, TVs, and video equipment. Become un-fettered and liberate yourself from the economic heat of high-priced air conditioners. (In other words, stay cool, fool!) It's a g-ratifying experience to find dozens of products from over 50 top-name manufacturers like ADMIRAL, PANASONIC, LITTON, KITCHENAID, WESTINGHOUSE, GENERAL ELECTRIC, and many others. Send a description of the item to EBA (including the model number) and they'll quote a price. If you decide you want to exchange for another model, they'll be glad to make amends, but there's a 20-percent restocking charge on returned merchandise. Expect your order to arrive in about two weeks.

Focus Electronics
(See **Electronics: Audio/Video/Stereo/TVs**, p. **186**.)

Harry's Discounts & Appliances Corp.
8701-18th Avenue (718) 236-3507
Brooklyn, NY 11214 CK, MC, V, MO, PQ

The truth about Harry's is that they've been in business for 40 years and they'll save you 30 percent on electronic equipment and appliances. We're just wild about Harry. No kidding, these aren't bush-league names: TOSHIBA, BLACK & DECKER, SONY TVs, EMERSON, GE, HITACHI, OSTER, SUNBEAM, and more. No gray-market goods here. And cross my heart, they'll give you a price quote by phone. Outsized goods are shipped only in the five boroughs of New York City, Long Island, and parts of New Jersey (by truck).

Kaplan Bros. Blue Flame Corp.
523 W. 125th Street (212) 662-6990
New York, NY 10027-3498 CK, Certified Check, MO
B (SASE), PQ (SASE)

Serious cooks who want serious equipment are attracted to this flame for up to 50 percent off list prices on commercial fryers, stoves, storage units, and more. These restaurant-sized products are not for everyone, but for those with catering aspirations, big families, or just a love of cooking. You will find industrial and commercial equipment by VULCAN, BLODGETT, GARLAND, and others at great prices. They ship to 48 states and offer price quotes by phone or by letter with SASE. Brochures are available from individual manufacturers only.

MidAmerica Vacuum Cleaner Supply Co.
(See **Vacuums**, p. **514**.)

Oreck Corporation
(See **Vacuums**, p. **515**.)

Percy's Inc.
19 Glennie Street (508) 755-5269
Worcester, MA 01605 MC, V, D, MO, PQ

No small appliances or catalog here, just savings of up to 40 percent on washers and dryers, ranges, freezers, all kinds of TV and video equipment, radar detectors, office equipment like fax machines and copiers, stereo components, and more by WESTINGHOUSE, LITTON, MAGIC CHEF, MITSUBISHI, MAYTAG, WHIRLPOOL, RCA, SHARP, FISHER, ZENITH, and others. Call or write for a price quote on the brand or model of your choice.

Art and Collectibles

Are you basically a pack rat—but one with good taste? Maybe you're someone who just loves collecting. You live for the thrill of discovery and the pleasure of creating a nest for yourself with interesting "found" objects. On the other hand, maybe you're someone who knows exactly what you want, and you're motivated by the excitement of the chase. You've been on the trail of a particular ivory Netsuke statue ever since you brought one back from Japan last year. Finally, maybe you just have a taste for the unusual. You're struggling with that room in your house that needs some pizazz, and a hand-loomed rug from Tibet would be just perfect. Whatever you want, your search is over. You'll find it (whatever "it" is) here.

A. Goto
Shibuya, P.O. Box 261
Tokyo, Japan 150 — Bank Draft, MO, F

Goto this dealer if you want a deal in Japanese antiques! A. Goto specializes in Netsuke (pronounced NUTSKE—and you'll go nutsky over their prices), Inro, snuff bottles, wood block prints, and cloisonne. You'll find these antiques up to snuff for they are all in good to excellent condition, dating from the 1850s to the 1900s. Prices average 40 percent to 80 percent less than retail. Prices vary for several reasons: quality, age, the artist, etc. Many of these items are rare collectibles not available in retail stores. We must bow to the variety of Netsuke: ivory, black coral, amber, stag horn, hornbill, ivory nut, porcelain, and Manju. Stock is subject to change, so alternates must be indicated on the order. Be warned: Items may not be returned. We found the price list and photos that were sent somewhat incomplete, so be sure to ask for complete shipping information. Orders will be processed within five days. Items are shipped by sea mail; there is a surcharge of 15 percent for air mail. Insurance is not automatic, so be sure to request it. (There is also an extra charge for it.) No sales tax or duty on items over 100 years old.

Antique Imports Unlimited
P.O. Box 2978, Dept. GBBM (504) 892-0014
Covington, LA 70434 CK, MC, V, MO, C (rates vary)

This company's made some intercontinental moves in their day, beginning in Ireland and crossing the Atlantic ultimately to land in Louisiana. What you lose by forgoing browsing through the antique shops is about 60 percent to 70 percent off the retail prices. If you know your stuff, period, you'll love to order from their ample lists in a variety of categories. From their antiquities (ancient items of Egypt, Greece, Rome, Persia, etc.), with a minimum order of $30, you could choose from the fifth century A.D., a semi-circular stamp seal of mottle quartz in orange, red, and white, the face (intaglio) engraved with the figure of a stag's head, and pierced for suspension. Listed in good condition. That's just one detailed listing from one of the categories available. Others include: Antique & Collectible Jewelry; Antiques & Collectibles; Antique Maps, Prints, and Paintings.

Central Carpet
(See **Carpets and Rugs**, p. **131**.)

Cinema City
P.O. Box 1012-0301 (616) 722-7760
Muskegon, MI 49443 CK, MC, V, MO, C/$3 (refundable)

Since 1975, Cinema City has been thrilling film buffs and collectors of movie memorabilia with hard-to-find and unique items. Picture this: movie posters from the hottest new films to classic oldies, scripts, autographed material, foreign items, press kits, and more, wrapped-to-show in one catalog, all at up to 50 percent off. Cinema City's black & white catalog is a concise listing of the one-sheets, stills, and scripts available, and their collection is impressive. The price of one-sheets is $15 to $20 on average; an internationally released poster from *Casablanca* was $25. It's wise to call to ensure that your selection is still available. Most orders are shipped within 48 hours; returns are accepted within seven days. Checks take two to four weeks to clear.

Great Buys readers will receive a coupon good on their first order when they order a catalog.

Dewynters Licensing & Distributing

116 W. 29th Street, 12A (212) 268-6660
New York, NY 10001 CK, MO, COD, C, PQ

The show must go on, and sometimes we never want it to end. If Broadway's your bag, Dewynters is your bounty; mugs, T-shirts, sweatshirts, posters, and other Broadway memorabilia are featured in their catalog and usually cost less than in theater gift shops: T-shirts average $13; posters, around $6. The selection is constantly updated, so if what you're after isn't included, write or call to see if they have it. They also give price quotes by phone or mail. There's no business like the mail-order business!

The Friar's House

Bene't Street 0223-264110
Cambridge, England CB2 3QA CK, MC, V, AE, DC, C

The elegance of merry old England can be yours at a very low cost. From traditional to modern, this company carries a selection of china, crystal, and enamel collectibles to start or complete your collection. Values include modern glass paperweights in British and European styling, enamel decorator boxes in true BILSTON and BATTESEA style, DAVID WINTER COTTAGES, and all the crystal and china available for collecting. Names include almost all British companies, with special added discounts offered at certain times throughout the year. Money refunded if not completely satisfied with purchase, and immediate delivery is provided by air mail. From The Friar's House to your house, this worldwide service is sure to please.

Gallery Graphics, Inc.
P.O. Box 502
227 Main Street (417) 475-6116
Noel, MO 64854 CK, COD, C/$5 (refundable)

Stop waiting for your Prints Charming! Gallery Graphics carries over 250 art prints and reproductions of antique classics at a savings of up to 50 percent. Everything is in stock, including Christmas cards, note and greeting cards reproduced from antique prints, and framed and matted prints. Orders normally go out the same day; none take longer than 72 hours. Customer satisfaction is guaranteed, and in all their years of business, there's never been a single request for a refund. Their price list is wholesale prices. Shipping charges are 5 percent of the invoice price of the merchandise. Smile with the *Mona Lisa*, turn green with envy at *Blue Boy*, or kick up your heels with a Degas for as little as $2. This place has the largest selection of antique reproductions in the world! Minimum first order is $100.

Gifts and More, Inc.
802 Kings Highway (718) 998-0192
Brooklyn, NY 11223 CK, MC, V, MO, C/$3
(deductible from your first order)

Remember that rock promoter, Murray the Clay? (He had to go underground after the mass kiln.) Well, this Murray offers a 170-page catalog filled with sculptured replicas of famous as well as contemporary works, from ancient Chinese pieces to cowboys and horses at very reasonable prices. In addition to the familiar (Rodin, Michelangelo, etc.), he carries many lesser-known works by even lesser-known artists. Glassware, barware, crystal, and coffee mugs are also available, but only for walk-in customers (they are not shippable). Murray's glassware and crystal are "misprints" from famous-name manufacturers (whom Murray prefers to keep quiet about). Decorated barware retailing for $18 for four pieces is priced as low as $3.95 in some cases. Catalog prices are about 20 percent to 25 percent less than retail, but if you visit, you'll find even bigger discounts: up to 80 percent in some cases. Shipping is done by UPS, and refunds are made at your request.

Good Shepherd's Store
P.O. Box 96
Manger Street
Bethlehem, Israel C/$2

Holy mother of pearl! While Good Shepherd's Store watches its stock by night, wise men won't have to travel to get good buys on religious icons. You won't have to dip into your cache of cash to get a creche you like. We'd have walked a mile for one of their camels, starting at $6, or a Bible, $14 ($21 at U.S. flea markets) both in olive wood. Chess sets, candlesticks, religious figures, and jewelry boxes are all available. An inlaid mother-of-pearl cross was $4. Minimum order is $30.

Miscellaneous Man
P.O. Box 1776 (717) 235-4766
New Freedom, PA 17349 CK, MC, V, C/$3

Who is the Miscellaneous Man and why does he collect miscellany? Well, George Theofiles, ephemerologist (probably a fancy name for pack rat) travels the globe searching for items some would consider trash: old stamps, handbills, labels, guides, and other memorabilia. One man's trash is another man's treasure should be his calling card. All items are original and some even classified as antiques. Among his huge collection you'll find circus posters, cigar labels, war posters, and more. Post this: Prices are 30 percent to 50 percent below retail. He claims every one of his items represents a piece of history. This diversified man looks twice at things the rest of us ignore. He has accumulated enough miscellaneous items to fill the Taj Mahal. If you are adding to your collection or just adding a focal point to your wall, give this man a call. Twelve hundred posters, books, etc., are offered in his semi-annual catalog. Every item is shipped in gorilla-proof tubes and is insured. No monkeying around. The next time you clean your attic, think twice about what you throw away.

Museum of Fine Arts, Boston
P.O. Box 1044 (617) 427-7791
Boston, MA 02120 (800) 225-5592 (credit card orders only)
CK, MC, V, AE, MO, C

Are you ready to get artsy? From a bronze statue of the three Graces to black onyx earrings, you'll find a treasure trove of goodies to give or receive from this museum. Jewelry, notecards, prints and posters, and more are all inspired by various artists and historical periods. A 14K Graeco-Roman ring was $348; a silk scarf, $45. Not exactly cheap, but when you consider that your money goes, in part, toward preserving culture for future generations, who can complain? Their selection for kids is both educational and just plain fun—a variety of books and puzzles for $12.95; wooden toys for $20; plus stuffed toys, videos, games, and more. Look into items that are unusual, beautiful, useful, and add a little class to your life. All in-stock items are shipped within two business days and delivered in seven to ten days.

Nepal Craft Emporium
(See **Arts and Crafts**, p. **68**.)

Passport Furniture Classics
(See **Furniture and Accessories**, p. **260**.)

Prints of Peace Gallery
P.O. Box 534
13813 State Street (219) 627-2905 (credit card orders only)
Grabill, IN 46741 CK, MC, V, MO, C

We bow to these fellow punsters for offering a fine selection of Victorian and art nouveau prints fit to grace any wall. Even if you're not Victorian principled, you'll love this charming assortment of Amish country prints, antique reproduction lithographs, and animal and fine art prints priced as low as $15, including shipping and handling. Mats and frames are available for most prints, too. Once on their mailing list, you'll receive supplementary pages as new prints and gift items are added to their repertoire. Only preauthorized returns are accepted. When in the neighborhood, visit their showroom, 15 minutes outside Fort Wayne, Indiana.

Quilts Unlimited
P.O. Box 1479 (804) 253-8700
440-A Duke of Gloucester Street CK, MC, V, C/$5
Williamsburg, VA 23185 (refundable to readers)
$20 for annual monthly subscription

This company believes that where there's a quilt, there's a way to buy it for less. So if you appreciate the fine crafting and fascinating colors found in American antique quilts, send for their 16-page catalog. In addition to describing each quilt's colors, fabric, and design elements, the catalog lists prices, sizes, and any flaws the quilt might have. A packet of 12 to 20 photographs, each showing eight quilts, is sent with every catalog. Quilts Unlimited is "America's largest antique quilt shop," selling to over 1,000 mail-order customers each year. Bette Midler, Lauren Bacall, and many overseas customers each year have bought from this shop. Avid collectors themselves, owners Joan and Albie Fenton issue a new catalog "once per month, generally" as new quilts are acquired. Prices are about 20 percent to 30 percent less than antique dealers would charge for the quilts; stuffed animals made from quilts and crib quilts are discounted 10 percent and 30 percent, respectively. The Fentons guarantee authenticity and if you're not satisfied, return the purchase within three days and your $5 will be applied to your next order.

Rick's Movie Graphics, Inc.
P.O. Box 23709 (904) 373-7202
Gainesville, FL 32602-3709 CK, MC, V, MO, C/$3, PQ (SASE)

Take your pick from Rick's posters for flicks and save from 10 percent to 65 percent. The selection of movie posters in their 95-page catalog includes everything from domestic oldies to foreign posters of current releases, and that's just scratching the surface; they carry more than they could fit into a catalog! If you don't see what you want, send an inquiry along with a SASE for information.

Sturbridge Yankee Workshop
90 Blueberry Road (800) 343-1144
Portland, ME 04102 CK, MC, V, AE, D, MO, C

Any damn Yankee would appreciate the sturdy, practical furniture found at this classic workshop. Since 1953, Sturbridge has been selling Early American and traditional home furnishings, Cape Cod weather glass, and Shaker style and Victorian pieces to all-American bargain hunters. Tambour clocks, Persian rugs, brass quilt racks, tapestry pillows, and much more are affordable by mail. Don't worry, the reproduction soda fountain and gas station signs, from $12.99 to $17.99, would not have to be stuffed in the mailbox. Customer satisfaction is guaranteed. In-stock items are shipped within three days; custom or special orders take six to eight weeks. Federal Express delivery is available.

W. M. Wauters' Original Paper Collectibles

700 Clipper Gap Road — CK, MO
Auburn, CA 95603 — F (Send a *long* SASE for a free flier)

Label it an original if it's from W. M. Wauters. Bill's been collecting labels from California fruit crates, soda pop, and others for years and began his crateful dead hobby selling to the public in 1972. A fantastic selection and the lowest prices around on these charming and nostalgia-inspiring labels give even Mrs. Peel a second chance. Many are just 14 cents a piece. Orange, apple, lemon, asparagus, and pear labels; used stock certificates; broom, cigar box and bottle labels, and others make this a collector's or decorator's dream. Send for his list of label descriptions and prices and get a piece of history at the same time. C.O.D. orders add $7.50; no phone orders accepted.

Works of Max Levine

19-18 Saddle River Road — (201) 797-7216
Fair Lawn, NJ 07410 — MC, V, B/$1

Max Levine's three-dimensional, original wall sculptures are made from heavy-gauge steel finished with a patina of gold leaf and solid brass accents. Many of these "limited edition" contemporary works are specially designed to blend artistically in homes or offices. Prices range from $65 to $325. Since this is the only outlet for Max Levine's work, it's impossible to compare prices. There's a ten-day full-refund policy; orders are typically delivered in four to six weeks.

Wurtsboro Wholesale Antiques

P.O. Box 386 — (914) 888-4411
Wurtsboro, NY 12790 — CK, MC, V, COD, C/$2 Antique

These folks aren't afraid to peddle their wares (accessories and smaller items only) through the mail, Wurts and all. (Do you suppose Wurtsboro got its name when somebody toad the county line?) This company sells European primitive antiques that are at least 100 years old. (However, American primitive pieces are sold in the store only.) Their hottest-selling items are spinning wheels, carousel horses, butter churns, and wooden hay forks. Although they are mainly wholesalers (Bloomingdale's buys from them for resale), if you buy, you can buy-pass the middle man. Orders are usually shipped by UPS; there are five-day return privileges.

Arts and Crafts

Art for art's sake, without the art ache? Free expression often isn't, at least not when you're the artist. Art supplies are expensive. But now starving artists can put food on the table, by buying their art supplies at a discount. It's as easy as setting up your easel. Just draft a letter from your drafting table, and quality products like LIQUITEX acrylics, WINSOR & NEWTON Designer's Gouache, GRUMBACHER oils, and REMBRANDT pastels will come to you—by mail. Discounts can be up to 50 percent off the prices in an art supply store. And if you're a member of an artist's guild or a student in a class, you can buy in larger quantities and save even more. Van Gogh for it! Do-it-yourself or buy from the artist's hand that provides a touch of class.

A. I. Friedman
44 W. 18th Street — (212) 243-9000
New York, NY 10011 — CK, MC, V, AE, O, C/$5, PQ

Supplying the fashion industry with markers, paints, and drafting supplies contributes to this man's Fried-dom. Their other clients include publishers, Fortune 500 companies, and even the Muppets. This 63-year-old company features a complete, state-of-the-art inventory from airbrushes to zipatone in their thick 324-page catalog, $5. Over 10,000 brands are carried and many items are discounted 20 percent or more. A special list of items including LIQUITEX acrylics and oils, WINSOR & NEWTON watercolors, REMBRANDT and BOCOUR BELLINI oils, and a large selection of brushes discounted up to 40 percent (provided you place an order of $50 or more). Canvas panels, watercolor papers, stretchers, canvas, and turpentine are also discounted. You'll have to add 10 percent to your purchase for shipping, handling, and insurance. Exchanges or refunds are made up to seven days after purchase.

Allen's Shell-a-Rama
(See **Hard-to-Find and Unique Items**, p. **277**.)

American Frame Corporation
1340 Tomahawk Drive (800) 537-0944
Maumee, OH 43537-3553 CK, MC, V, AE, O, MO, C

We've been framed! Get into the picture at American Frame and find great deals on sectional frames in cherry, mahogany, oak, and other woods, as well as metal frames in a variety of colors, mats, and other picture-framing aids. Hang the expense; their frames were as much as 50 percent less than those found elsewhere. Nail one of their 10-page catalogs and you'll be able to picture your posters, photos, and prints hanging out for less.

Art Express
P.O. Box 21662 (800) 535-5908
Columbia, SC 29221 CK, MC, V, AE, D, MO, C/$3.50

This Express, which started out in 1969 as a retail store before hitching its wagon to the mail in 1989, is an artist's one-way ticket to saving up to 60 percent on art supplies, furniture, books, videos, and accessories. Their catalog is an easy-to-read, 72-page joyride; prices vary from low to average. Paper, paints, brushes, pastels, canvas, easels, lights, and much more by GRUMBACHER, REMBRANDT, ART BIN, KOHINOOR, WEBER, ANCO, HOLBEIN, and others will help your budget stay within the lines. A ten-tube starter set of WINSOR & NEWTON gouache colors was $36.40/list was $45.50; a set of twelve 30 ml bottles of ROTRING ink was $35.99. They ship items already in stock within 48 hours; returns only when previously authorized.

Art Supply Warehouse, Inc.
360 Main Avenue (203) 846-2279
Norwalk, CT 06851 CK, MC, V, MO, C

Saving 40 percent and more on art supplies is a stroke of genius. Get smart and throw your creativity into high gear with this gear, including paints, brushes, furniture, inks, canvas, paper, books, and much more. Their free 76-page catalog features CREATIVE MARK, LIQUITEX, and GRUMBACHER, among others. Check out these prices: WINSOR & NEWTON artists' oils (seven series) run from $5.75 to $53.45 retail; A.S.W.'s prices were from $2.85 to $29.90. Orders arrive within seven to ten working days, and returns are accepted, provided they're in resaleable condition and in their original package(s).

Berman Leathercraft
25 Melcher Street
Dept. GBBM (617) 426-0870
Boston, MA 02210-1599 CK, MC, V, C/$3 (refundable)

Berman has a complete line of leathers and suedes, hardware, accessories, dyes, and books on leathercraft. Prices are competitive and better than you'll find many other places, with the best buys coming on quantity orders. Sorry; no buffalo, Bill, just belt strips, brass buckles, clothing leathers, scraps, and more from BERMAN, BARGE, and FIEBINGS. Unaltered leathers may be returned within 30 days; delivery takes about seven.

Cambridge Wools, Ltd.
Box 2572 011-64-9-390-769
Auckland 1, New Zealand IMO, B

What will you find here? Cheerful, bright knitting yarns, or knitting yarns in earthy, toasty tones sold by the ounce or by the pound. These yarns are hard to find in the U.S. and when they're available, are often very expensive. Cambridge also sells Aran sweaters and sheepskins, plus knitting, spinning, and weaving supplies. Satisfaction is guaranteed and shipping (via sea mail) is included in the price. If you return the merchandise, they'll refund your money; minimum order is $30.

The Caning Shop
929 Gilman Street, Dept. GBBM (415) 527-5010
Berkeley, CA 94710 CK, MC, V, MO, C/$1

Have a seat—or a basket, for that matter—at The Caning Shop and you'll find able and cane materials at reasonable prices. Their catalog warned us to beware of "hairy flat reeds, brittle round reeds, and cane that splits," and added that they are the only repair shop that actually uses the materials they sell. They offer a wide selection of supplies for basketry and caning, plus a wide assortment of how-to books. Their chair cane, cane webbing, round and flat reeds, rattan, seagrass, raffia, Danish cord, rawhide, and 24 colors of waxed linen were their best sellers; braided wheat straw, Japanese basket nippers, and many more tools and supplies were also offered. In business since 1969, they offer friendliness and know-how, along with a "no problem" return policy. Orders are shipped within 24 hours of receipt; minimum order with charge cards is $10.

Identify yourself as a reader of *Great Buys by Mail* and they'll send you their $1 catalog *free*.

Ceramic Supply of New York & New Jersey, Inc.
10 Dell Glen Avenue (201) 340-3005
Lodi, NJ 07644 CK, MC, V, MO, C/$4

Spin into this catalog and you'll come out a ceramic whiz! Roll your bowls on their potters' wheels, or try colorful glazes, tiles, raku kilns, underglazes, brushes, airbrushing supplies . . . even an electric kiln. If you need it for a ceramic project, they probably have it, and you'll save as much as 40 percent. All kinds of extras, too, for making ceramic music boxes, clocks, and jewelry, plus books and much more. It's packed into Ceramic Supply's 150-page catalog. Residents of New York and New Jersey will be pleased to note they'll receive free delivery on orders of $100 or more. They'll give you a price quote by letter or phone; there's a ten-day return policy, although there are sometimes restocking fees.

Cheap Joe's Art Stuff
300A Industrial Park Road (800) 227-2788
Boone, NC 28607 CK, MC, V, D, MO, C, PQ

You can reap the benefits by shopping cheap in more ways than one. This outfit may be small, but the savings aren't. Joe's been discounting paper, paint, canvas, brushes, mat cutters, books, videos on art, and more, by WINSOR & NEWTON, WILTON, ROBERT SIMMONS, WHITNEY, and other big names in the art biz, by an average of 30 percent since 1986. The company's goal is to stay in touch with its customers, which it does by encouraging suggestions on inventory and questions about materials. Customer satisfaction is guaranteed and quantity discounts are available.

Circle Craft Supply
P.O. Box 3000 — (813) 659-0992
Dover, FL 33527-3000 — CK, MO, COD, C/$1 (refundable), PQ

Round and round and round we go; where we stop . . . is Circle Craft Supply, a company that's not much more than ten years old, but what a wheeler and dealer. Painting, jewelry, doll making, and crocheting are only a few of the pastimes they cater to, with clay, paints, brushes, books, and loads of supplies to keep you in one place for hours. Let your imagination soar with their great selection (the catalog's 152 pages) and sear off about 20 percent less than you would have to pay elsewhere. No matter what your hobby, art, or craft choice, Circle probably will hit the bulls-eye. Returns are accepted within ten days when authorized.

Columbus Clay Company
1049 W. Fifth Avenue — (614) 294-1114; (614) 294-7040
Columbus, OH 43212 — CK, MO, C

At the Columbus Clay Company, they take discounting for granite. In business since 1939, this company is well known as one of the best sources for ceramic supplies. Owned and operated by George Rigrish, a graduate of ceramic engineering at Ohio State, the business manufactures a wide variety of clays and glazes, which are sold direct to the public or to schools and studios. They also carry kilns and other instruments for the potter.

Country Handcrafts Magazine
P.O. Box 643 — (800) 558-1013
Milwaukee, WI 53201 — (800) 242-6065 (WI residents)
(414) 423-0100
CK, MC, V, AE, MO

If you were into country when country wasn't in, you may want to pick up this publication. It continues the tradition of catering to crafters who want country projects by giving patterns and project instructions in every bimonthly issue. Every pattern is full size and shown in full color. All are down home and money-saving buys.

Great Buys readers can subscribe for $12.98 to the magazine (regularly $16.98).

Craft King, Inc.
P.O. Box 90637 (813) 686-9600
Lakeland, FL 33804 CK, MC, V, MO, C/$2, PQ

What makes royalty? Divine Right prices, of course. Pay homage to the up to 60-percent-off savings that rule the kingdom here. Craft King has won the crown with crafts for kids and adults, like painting, embroidery and cross-stitch, quilting, and more. Beads, felt, wood carving tools, and other supplies are included in the 128-page catalog in which they hold creative court. Pay tribute to their instructional book selection, as well as their craft kits. We had to bow to their policy of guaranteeing satisfaction; authorized returns are accepted.

Craft Resources, Inc.
P.O. Box 828 (203) 254-7702
Fairfield, CT 06880-0828 CK, MC, V, MO, C/$1

Embroidery aficionados will appreciate the selection here, as will anyone learning crewel, needlepoint, wood crafting, basket-making, and any number of crafty projects. Craft Resources offers kits for making them all, including rugs and afghans, for up to 50 percent less. All the tools of the trade are offered: floss, crochet hooks, picture-framing supplies, canvas, yarn, and other supplies, too, in case you're ready to head in your own creative direction. Returns on unused merchandise are accepted within 60 days. There is a minimum of $10 when ordering with credit cards. Head for this resource to do-your-own-thing, baby, ah eh!

Craftsman Wood Service Co.
1735 W. Cortland Court (708) 629-3100
Addison, IL 60101 CK, MC, V, MO,
C/$2 (for postage and handling)

Wood you like to pay 15 percent less for woodcrafting tools like chisels, shaves, drill presses, coping saws, plus brass finishes for cabinets and doors? We thought so. Here are some more options: Craftsmen drawings for a gun cabinet cost $11.95; build-your-own veneer backgammon board from scratch for $40.95. One exceptional bargain was ten pounds of small pieces of imported wood for $18.95. They've got over 50 brands, including BOSCH, DREMEL, AMERICAN MACHINE TOOL, FOREDOM, ROCKWALL, and STANLEY, so you're not sacrificing quality. Discounts vary, but they give an additional 10-percent discount for quantity purchases. Minimum order is $10 for cash; $15 for charge cards; and $25 for an open account. There is a 60-day return-for-refund (with approval) period. Merchandise orders should arrive in three to five days. Check out their 130-page catalog for the full story.

Craftways Corporation/Cross Creek

4118 Lakeside Drive
Richmond, CA 94806
(800) 421-9948 (CA residents)
(510) 223-3144
CK, MC, V (for orders over $15),
C/$1 (published twice a year)

Charted designs and iron-on transfers from Sesame Street, Walt Disney, Norman Rockwell, and the National Football League were among the many patterns in this catalog. Cheer up any child's room with favorite characters from Mickey Mouse to the Dallas Cowboys. Cross your fingers to remind you to order this 32-page catalog stuffed full of crafts from award-winning designers and craftspersons. At the top of the list are such items as cross-stitch charts and books, folk art dolls, wooden dolls and soft sculpture patterns, band boxes, and scherenschnitte (a traditional paper cutting art). A stitch in time saves more than a dime with accessories for stitchers: platinum needles, towels, and potholders with AIDA inserts, tote bags, and many "country" decorating items that include frames and precut mats, wooden cupboards, and towel racks. All have been selected for their high quality and reasonable prices. Look for their bimonthly magazine called *Cross Stitch and Country Crafts* at your local newsstand; subscription price $14.97 a year.

Crown Art Products Co., Inc.

90 Dayton Avenue
Passaic, NJ 07055
(201) 777-6010
CK, MC, V, D, MO, C

Silk-screening's a snap when you go with a pro. Since 1974, Crown has sold reasonably priced silk-screening kits, AIROTEX puff paints, fabric dyes, and all kinds of ink: their own ink for textiles, POSTERELLE paper inks, AIROTEX airbrush inks, and more. They also carry everything you need to learn to silk screen with the best of them, including chemicals and equipment. (They have classes, too, if you happen to live near Passaic.) Special discounts are available to professionals, including art teachers; call for more information. They'll give price quotes on large orders. With credit cards, the minimum order is $25. Make a smooth move and get on their mailing list for a free 15-page catalog.

Daniel Smith
4130 First Avenue South
Seattle, WA 98134-2302
(800) 426-6740; (206) 223-9599
CK, MC, V, AE, MO, C/$5, PQ

Daniel Smith lays it on thick when it comes to style and selection. If painting whets your palette, try mixing with WINSOR & NEWTON, HOLBEIN, SENNELIER, and MAIMERI, to name a few; or try Daniel Smith's own brand. They've also got paper galore, for drawing, painting, sketching, prints, and more by ARCHES, STRATHMORE, and CANSON. Ornate and extraordinary specialty papers, too, including papers made from exotic barks and leaves. Canvases, paint brushes, pencils, pens, airbrush equipment and supplies, drafting and graphic arts tools, furniture . . . there's nary an end in sight. While it's possible to save up to 30 percent, it's the extensive selection that makes this company's catalog a work of art. Minimum order is $25 (for paper); satisfaction's guaranteed.

Deepak's Rokjemperl Products
61, 10th Khetwadi
Bombay 400004, India
91-22-3888031 (dial 01 for operator assistance with the call)
Bank Check, Certified Check, Bank and Postal Order, B

Besides owning Deepak's, personable Vijay Shah also owns Shah's Rock Shop, Vijay World Traders, and Gemcraft India International. (He's into everything, and everything seems to be in his brochure.) So many hundreds of items are packed into the pages, it's almost impossible for shoppers to wade through the bargains. (It's the mail-order equivalent of the "can't see the trees through the forest" phenomenon.) If you're persistent, you can draw upon beads that you can string yourself and give as a handmade gesture of good will. The cost is next to nothing: about 50 percent to 80 percent less than retail. Amethysts (faceted) were 50 cents a carat (retail $1 per carat); moonstones were ten cents per carat (retail 25 cents per carat); rubies were 64 cents (retail $1.50 and more). There were also tourmalines, opals, garnets, sapphires, emeralds, and other sparkling stones. Digging through their catalog, we also excavated pendants and earrings at inexpensive prices. Quantity purchases equal maximum savings. Orders are filled in a week or two.

Dharma Trading Co.

P.O. Box 150916 (800) 542-5227; (415) 456-7657
San Rafael, CA 94915 CK, MC, V, D, C

You won't find any bums at Dharma Trading Co., just friendly folks and discounted craft supplies and clothing. Find yourself in their 100-percent cotton and silk clothing in adult and children's sizes for dyeing and painting. Discover tie-dying supplies, or get the goods on marbling, printing, painting, and more. Their color-fast dyes and fabric paints will have you expressing yourself at savings of up to 50 percent. Artists, crafty types, and schools alike have been "into" Dharma since 1969; drop by the store at 1604 4th Street when in San Rafael. Otherwise, call or write for their free (and very groovy) 95-page newsprint catalog.

Reader special: Any size FREE T-shirt with first order.

Dick Blick Company

P.O. Box 1267 (800) 447-8192; (800) 322-8183
Galesburg, IL 61501 (309) 343-6181
CK, MC, V, AE, D, COD, C

Use your Bic to write Dick Blick and get their 480-page, full-color catalog of creative materials. Whether you're into calligraphy, painting, jewelry-making, ceramics, drafting, airbrushing, printing, weaving—even making crafts—this leading supplier of high-school and university art departments is your best bet for savings and selection. In their sale supplement, LIBERTE'S watercolor sketchbook, (30) 80-pound sheets, was 15 percent off at $20.40. A STAR SAPPHIRE artist's portfolio, 14″ × 18″, was 40 percent off at $29.40. Most discounts are between 10 and 20 percent (although sale discounts average 40 percent); temperas and acrylics are the most popular purchases. Most orders arrive at their destination in about two weeks.

Reader special: $5 gift certificate to readers with first order, plus a special sale flier for preferred customers.

Eloxite Corporation
806 Tenth Street (307) 322-3050
Wheatland, WY 82201 CK, MC, V, MO, COD, C/25 cents

Jewelry-making geniuses (and the rest of us!) will be pleased to discover a source for parts that only costs part of what you'd expect. Slash 75 percent off on wires for earrings, stones for settings, buckles for belting, rings, tie tacks; even clock-building components; plus jewelry-making tools and equipment on a par with those used by professionals. So don't lose your mind; find these findings and save! Eloxite offers a 15-day return policy with a small restocking fee in some cases; the minimum order is $15.

Enterprise Art
P.O. Box 2918 (813) 536-1492
Largo, FL 34649 CK, MC, V, MO, COD, C

Enterprising jewelry and craft nuts can put on the glitz for peanuts. Enterprise Art specializes in supplies for making jewelry, T-shirts, hair accessories, and more—glass and crystal beads, TULIP slick and glitter paints, covered buttons, bead caps, bar pins, filigrees, barrettes and barrette bases, doll-making kits, friendly plastic, glue guns, cord, and much, much more. Supplies are available individually, but the savings are bigger when you buy in bulk. Ethnic pony beads, for example, were $1.19 for a seven-piece set; $13.49 for 144 pieces. Nine jingle bells were 69 cents; a dozen packages were just $6.90. Outfox them, and get crafty by never paying full price again!

The Fiber Studio
P.O. Box 637 (603) 428-7830
Henniker, NH 03242 CK, MC, V, D, MO, COD, C/$1, B/$4, PQ

The Fiber Studio can tie you in to great bargains on knitting and weaving supplies, equipment, and more. They're spinning out discounts of up to 40 percent on a wide selection of yarns, including cotton, wool, linen, and silk. They also offer looms and spinning accessories, natural dyes, and books on knitting, weaving, and spinning. A sample card of their yarns or spinning fibers (be sure your request is clear) was $4. Once you've ordered the yarn sample, $1 and four self-addressed #10 envelopes, with two stamps a piece, you will get their sale catalogs, which feature more yarn in a wide range of colors at sew low prices. There's a minimum order of $15 when you order with a credit card. Price quotes, by phone or mail, are available.

Flax Artist's Materials
240 Dolly Drive (415) 468-7530
Brisbane, CA 94005 CK, MC, V, AE, MO, C/$5, PQ

Don't take any flak from full-price retailers when it comes to art supplies. Flax creates an alternative with savings of up to 30 percent in their supplemental sale catalogs. Advertising artists, painters, airbrush artists, and graphic designers will find a large and diverse selection of equipment, supplies, portfolios, furniture and more in the large catalog at full retail prices. Sale catalogs are smaller, but the savings are clearly visible. The minimum order is $25; once you pay for the big catalog, sale catalogs are free.

Frank Mittermeier, Inc.
3577 E. Tremont Avenue (212) 828-3843
Bronx, NY 10465 CK, COD, C

Whenever Mister Chips goes to the Bronx, he always calls on Frank. Frank's no chiseler, but his collection of tools will steel your heart away. He carries over 40,000 tools for wood-carvers, sculptors, engravers, ceramists, and potters, plus many how-to books for the know-so inclined. Discounts of 10 percent and a "no charge for shipping" policy when you buy six or more tools will whittle down your bill. DASTRA woodcarving tools, finely crafted by DAVID STRASSMANN & COMPANY of Germany, were 10 percent lower than retail including shipping. Send for the free illustrated catalog—"every whittle bit helps."

Gettinger Feather Corp.
16 W. 36th Street (212) 695-9470
New York, NY 10018 CK, MO, B/$2 (with samples)

Boa, oh boa, we feathered our nest for chicken feed! Not only that, we got ostrich, marabou, turkey, and peacock feathers that tickled our fancy and can be used in all sorts of crafts. The price on pheasant tails brought pleasant dreams. Your hats will welcome the many styles of feathers available from this company. Our sample packet included a bright green "fashion" feather, as well as some beautiful black speckled plumage. Send $2 for your own samples without feather delay.

Identify yourself as a *Great Buys* reader and get a special deal on your first order.

Ginger Schlote
P.O. Box 19523DD (303) 936-7763
Denver, CO 80219 CK, MO, Certified Check, C/$2.50

Jewelry buffs with a penchant for doing it their way will love this mounting parts catalog. Gingerly flip through these 36 pages for the hobbyist with the creative drive and a desire to save 40 percent to 60 percent. Jewelry boxes, rings, pendant mountings, chains, and accessories all delivered in one week to ten days. Policy of fast, friendly service with a quibble-free guarantee is a nice clincher to the deals.

The Goodfellow Catalog of Wonderful Things
P.O. Box 4520 (510) 845-2062
Berkeley, CA 94704 CK, MC, V, MO, C/$13.95 plus $2.50 shipping

Here's a source book for handmade items you can mail-order direct from the artisan. This 720-page compendium features 680 selected artisans' jewelry, sculpture, canoes, kayaks, kimonos, teepees, stained glass, roller skates, walking sticks, quilts, rocking horses, photographs, and a myriad of other good and wonderful things. By shopping by the book and ordering direct from the particular craftsperson, you can save at least 20 percent off the prices charged by fancy specialty stores and boutiques. Other books from these same goodfellows (each at $14.95 plus $2.25 shipping): *The Goodfellow Catalog of Wonderful Things for Kids of All Ages; The Goodfellow Catalog of Gifts under $50; The Goodfellow Catalog of Wonderful Things to Wear and Wear and Wear; The Goodfellow Christmas Catalog*; and *The Goodfellow Catalog of Things for the Home and Office*. Each book has approximately 150 to 170 artisans and comes complete with ordering information and pictures.

Great Northern Weaving
P.O. Box 361-D (616) 731-4487
Augusta, MI 49012 CK, MO, COD, C/$1

If you can't stay on the straight and narrow with your budget, try weaving into this catalog for a little help. Create woven and braided rugs with reed hooks, shuttles, and rug filler in a number of colors, rags and more at savings of up to 50 percent. If your skills are rusty, they offer books to smooth you over the rough spots. You won't stagger at the price of their catalog, either, especially when you know it comes with samples!

Great Tracers
3 N. Schoenbeck Road-1771 (708) 255-0436
Prospect Heights, IL 60070-1435 CK, MO, B/$1 (refundable)

This family of Great Tracers will trace a trail to your hearts but not your wallets. They offer *great* savings of up to 50 percent. You won't be tracing these low prices to other firms, and that's nothing to shake a pencil at! They provide made-to-order letter stencils in a variety of sizes. The most popular is a three-line stencil cut in ⅝″ letters on oil board, with a maximum of 20 letters per line, with a company or organization's name, address, slogan, or other message, for $5. Satisfaction is guaranteed. They're "concerned and dedicated" to making sure "customers are happy with their purchases."

When you mention you're a *Great Buys* reader, you'll get free shipping and handling, which usually amounts to saving another 20 percent.

Grieger's Inc.
P.O. Box 93070
900 South Arroyo Parkway (800) 423-4181; (818) 795-9775
Pasadena, CA 91109 CK, MC, V, AE, C

These folks have been in the mail-order business for more than 50 years, so they definitely know what works. A glance through their color catalog will tell you they mean business. It's a fact that once you've found them, you won't need a Grieger-counter to locate precious price-saving craft projects. They've got jewelry mounts for earrings, pendants, rings, chains, bead-stringing kits, wax supplies, tumble-polished gemstones, belt buckles, lariat tie slides, clock parts, stained-glass kits, music boxes, wood burning supplies, soldering supplies, adhesives, kilns, tools, and more. Jewelry mounts and supplies are their most popular items. Top brands included FORDOM and DREMAL. They also sell cubic zirconia. There is a $5 minimum order; customers usually receive their order in about a week.

Holcraft's Catalog
P.O. Box 792, Dept. US92
211 El Cajon Avenue (916) 756-3023
Davis, CA 95616 CK, MC, V, C/$2

It just wouldn't be the holiday season without tradition. And where do traditional figurines, ornaments, chocolate molds, cookie cutters, mugs, pillows, gift tags, and other festive accoutrements come from? Holcraft, of course. They know if you've been sleeping or awake, because you'd have to be out like a light to miss these very reasonable prices on items you couldn't even find elsewhere. Their 32-page catalog was full of charming drawings of items like their Victorian Santa chocolate mold for $29, or the Old World Christmas ornaments from $10 to $14. Their excellent customer service department will refund your money with no questions asked within 30 days; orders are normally delivered within a week.

Great Buys readers who identify themselves as such will receive a 10-percent discount on orders over $25, along with free craft instructions with all molds.

The H.O.M.E. Craft Catalog
P.O. Box 10 (207) 469-7961
Orland, ME 04472 CK, MC, V, AE, D, MO, COD, B/$1

Homeowners Organized for More Employment not only is a delightful community group, it's a handicrafters' haven. If you fancy appliqued pot holders, pottery, Christmas wreaths, or patchwork quilts like Granny used to make, you'll like what you find in this 8-page brochure. Other items include handwoven towels, mats, and coverlets; hand-knit sweaters, socks, and hats; and stuffed toys and dolls. Pot holders, quilts, and toys are their most popular products because of their craftsmanship and discount prices. These are the genuine articles; everything is handmade. For those of you cynics who wonder just who gets your money, 70 percent of the item's selling price goes to the Maine craftspeople. Most orders are received in about three weeks, but allow four to six weeks' delivery on larger items. Full refunds or exchanges are made, but aren't often needed—everything is inspected by Sister Lucy Polin, president and designated fault-finder.

Hong Kong Co.
2801 University Drive (305) 755-8777
Coral Springs, FL 33065 CK, MC, V, C/$3 (refundable)

If you have some good cents, you can sparkle with all sorts of stones. Hong Kong is oriented to saving you money on all sizes and types of semi-precious stones for use in jewelry-making. They've been in business offering semi-precious stones, beads, and jewelry since 1979 offering same-day delivery and a 12-day return policy (postage is not refundable). The minimum order is $25; order less and add a $5 surcharge.

Hudson Glass Co. Inc.
219 N. Division Street (800) 431-2964; (914) 737-2124
Peekskill, NY 10566 CK, MC, V, D, MO, C/$3 (refundable)

If you can't have breakfast at Tiffany's, have breakfast under one. "The Source" catalog from Hudson Glass Co. featured three pages of patterns for Tiffany-style lamps you make yourself. If you don't think that's impressive, the rest of the thick catalog had patterns for stained-glass windows, mirrors, boxtops, hangings, and lamp bases. Besides books and patterns, we found 15 types of glass plus tools, hardware, and forms for projects of any level of proficiency. No longer is buying your stained-glass-making supplies going to be a pane in the pocketbook.

Idea Art
P.O. Box 291505 (800) 433-2278; (615) 889-4989
Nashville, TN 37229-1505 CK, MC, V, AE, MO, C/$2

If your letters are lackadaisical or your memos morose, take a look at these paper tigers. Idea Art's illustrated letter paper may be just the punch your communication needs. They've got designs for holidays, office use, invitations, computer paper, announcements and celebrations, plus presentation folders and certificates that may be personalized with gilt imprinting. If the environment's high on your list of things to protect, check out their recycled products from KIMBERLY-CLARK. Minimum order is $25; satisfaction is guaranteed.

Jerry's Artrama, Inc.

P.O. Box 1105
Dept. GBBM — (800) 221-2323 (orders)
117 S. Second Street — (516) 328-6633
New Hyde Park, NY 11040 — CK, MC, V, D, C/$2

A trial by Jerry probably means you'll get hung in some art gallery. Brands like WINSOR & NEWTON, ROTRING, D'ARCHES, GRUMBACHER, and STRATHMORE are witnesses for the state (of the art, that is) in paints, frames, mats, brushes, storage furniture, and all kinds of other supplies. Character witnesses give testimonials to Jerry's discount of "20 percent to 70 percent off" (a charge to which he pleads "guilty"). They usually deliver the goods within ten working days; refunds and exchanges are accepted up to 30 days.

JewelryMaker's Source Book

P.O. Box 2918 — (813) 536-1492
Largo, FL 34639 — CK, MC, V, MO, C

Makers of jewelry make out like bandits at this store on a range of supplies: filigrees, acrylic rhinestones, earring clips and hoops, brass studs, barrettes and bases, bar pins, and watch parts, among others. Then, JewelryMaker's Source Book plies the tools of the trade, like elastic waxed linen and glue guns. All prices are reasonable; the greatest savings, though, are on bulk orders. They prefer mail orders to phone orders; there's a $10 minimum on credit card purchases. Quantity discounts are available; they ship orders within 24 to 48 hours.

McKilligan Industrial and Supply Corp.

(See **Hardware, Tools, and Home Improvement**, p. **292**.)

Meisel Hardware Specialties

P.O. Box 70
2313 Commerce Boulevard (800) 441-9870; (612) 472-5544
Mound, MN 55364 CK, MC, V, D, MO, C/$1

Near the shores of Lake Minnetonka, Meisel Hardware Specialties await your requests for the latest in woodwork specialty hardware. Wood wheels with rubber tires, metal spoke wheels, doll stroller wheels, brass jewelry box hardware, 24K-gold–plated cabinet hardware, plans and parts for classic wood toys, and many country and Folk Art projects are available through their 48-page, beautifully crafted and discounted catalog. They will sell wholesale to anyone who can meet their $15 minimum order—and expect generally about 40 percent below craft store prices. This is probably one of the largest single sources of woodworking hardware in the country.

Nepal Craft Emporium

G.P.O. Box 1443 12500-21220
Katmandu, Nepal C/$3

Nepal Craft Emporium's handsome handicrafts should be featured in "House Buddha-ful." Thirty Buddha gods and goddesses ranging in price from $2 (for children of a lesser god) to $99 are cast by the ancient "lost wax process," which apparently has been found again. As a result, these pieces are sought-after collector's items. Turquoise-and-coral-studded filigree boxes, birds, animals, and jewelry make unique and inexpensive gifts priced from $1 to $8. The minimum order is $300 (FOB Katmandu).

Newburgh Yarn Mills

P.O. Box G (914) 562-2698
Newburgh, NY 12551 CK, MC, V, D, MO, B/$2.80 (w/samples), PQ

Batten down the hatches on your budget! Their own cotton and wool yarns weave a pretty picture at up to 35 percent off. They hold down the prices at this Fort on a variety of yarn weights and colors that were meant for weaving. Yarn is sold in eight-ounce cones, and quantity discounts are available. Call or write for a price quote, or get their brochure and samples for $2.80.

New England Basket Co.

P.O. Box 1335 (508) 759-2000
N. Falmouth, MA 02556 CK, MC, V, MO, B, PQ

Skip to Grandma's house in style with baskets fit for filling with food or something a little more crafty. Dried or silk flowers, Easter eggs, a handmade gift for a friend; baskets have loads of uses, and New England sells loads of them. My, what big discounts they have: up to 50 percent less than in your average store, in rattan, willow, and others. Ask about their quantity discounts (the better to save you money, my dear). Call or write (with SASE) for a price quote.

New York Central Art Supply Co.

62 Third Avenue (800) 950-6111; (212) 473-7705
New York, NY 10003 CK, MC, V, AE, D, DC, O,
MO, C (cost varies), PQ

"We cater to our mail-order customers," says Steven Steinberg, third-generation owner of one of New York's oldest fine art supply stores. Discounts of up to 40 percent do nothing to discount his claim. They have "the most complete artists' supply inventory in the world," so even hard-to-find items pose no problem. Every major brand in every type of artists' supplies is available. Their paper department covers the entire second floor of their three-story building: It includes over 2,000 papers from 17 countries. New York Central really showed their true colors with 250 lines of paints by WINSOR & NEWTON, LIQUITEX, REMBRANDT, GRUMBACHER, and BELLINI. Besides their free catalog of paints and painting supplies, there are special catalogs for drawing, batik, calligraphy, and more, $2, and for paper, $3. Ask about quantity discounts; minimum order is $25.

Passport Furniture Classics

(See **Furniture and Accessories** , p. **260**.)

Pearl Paint
308 Canal Street (800) 221-6845 (outside NY)
New York, NY 10013-2572 (212) 431-7932 (NY residents)
CK, Certified Check, MC, V, MO, C, PQ

Now there's a string of Pearls (Paramus, Woodbridge, and Cherry Hill, New Jersey; Fort Lauderdale, Tampa, Miami, and Altamonte Springs, Florida; Atlanta, Georgia; Alexandria, Virginia; Cambridge, Masachusetts; Rockville, Maryland; East Meadow, New York; and two in New York City) to help you paint the town red, white, or cobalt blue (but only one by mail order!). Pearl is a huge supplier of arts and crafts materials with "more artist's paints than anybody else in the world," with brands such as BEROL, DESIGN, ROTRING, KOH-I-NOOR, BADGER, WINSOR & NEWTON, and MORILLA. Discounts are from 20 percent to 70 percent off everyday, with four yearly sales. If you send them a product description, they can usually fill it (as they've done for folks like Peter Max, the late Andy Warhol, and Helen Frankenthaler). Orders are shipped UPS, Federal Express, or by truck; minimum order's $50.

The Potter's Shop
31 Thorpe Road (617) 449-7687
Needham, MA 02194 CK, MO, C

Has your reading been going to pot lately? If so, let it go to pottery, instead. Specializing in books and videos on ceramics and pottery, Steve Branfman's mail-order business will keep you fired up about the subject with 15-percent to 70-percent discounts and more on a wide range of titles. All books are discounted at least 15 percent off list. Discontinued and out-of-print books get discounted even further. They have hundreds of different titles in stock and on display. Their catalog keeps you abreast of special promotions. When you're in the area, visit The Potter's Shop studio and retail store and find the work of local and resident potters for sale. Special orders are welcome.

Print's Graphic Design Book Store
3200 Tower Oaks Boulevard
Rockville, MD 20852
(800) 222-2654 (credit card orders only); (301) 770-2900
CK, MC, V, AE, O, C

Those with artistic inclinations are inclined to love this one. PrintBooks has been offering great prices on great design books since 1940. Their free color catalog makes its mark with an excellent selection of books on graphic art, type, computer design—even good old-fashioned figure drawing. Many of the books are used as standard reference material in professional advertising departments. One graphic artist was delighted to find a book on ADOBE ILLUSTRATOR 3.0 for $19.95; *Illustrators Reference Manual: Nudes* was $19.50. Your satisfaction is guaranteed and returns are accepted within 15 days for credit, refund, or exchange.

Pueblo-to-People
(See **Apparel: Family**, p. **18**.)

Pyramid Products
P.O. HOC1 Box 21, Dept. GBBM
Niland, CA 92257
(619) 354-4265
C/$1

With a Pyramid foundry set, mechanics, hobbyists, artists, inventors, jewelers, and sculptors can make metal castings for model parts, figurines, plaques, and jewelry. Precious metal miners can use the Pyramid Furnace for smelting ore. Their furnaces provide the Pyramid power of temperatures up to 2,400°F for melting iron, bronze, aluminum, copper, gold, white metal, and silver. Casting supplies are also available, as you'll see if you check out their 12-page catalog.

Readers of *Great Buys by Mail* get the $1 catalog *free*.

Rammagerdin of Reykjavik
(See **Apparel: Family**, p. **18**.)

Sax Arts & Crafts
2405 S. Calhoun Road
New Berlin, WI 53151
(800) 558-6696; (414) 784-6880
CK, MC, V, AE, MO, C/$4 (refundable), PQ

If $4 sounds a bit steep, keep in mind that this color catalog is over 450 pages deep, and contains an encyclopedic inventory of materials and supplies. Up to 50 percent off isn't too shabby, either, on supplies for painting, weaving, making ceramics, framing pictures, dyeing clothing, stringing beads, making paper, creating jewelry, marbling, making baskets, lithography . . . the possibilities are mind-boggling. There are loads of kids' supplies (they can practically eat them and still live to tell about it), as well as products for serious artists, plus helpful books. STRATHMORE, WINSOR & NEWTON, and LIQUITEX are a few of the trusted names available. They have a minimum order of $10; quantity discounts are yours for the asking if you meet their quantity standards. Customer satisfaction always a priority.

Smiley's Yarns
92-06 Jamaica Avenue
Woodhaven, NY 11421
(718) 847-2185 (mail orders)
(718) 849-9873 (store),
CK, B

You'd be smiling, too, if you knew everybody was going to love your discounts. Smiley's, the "largest yarn store in New York City," is grinning about discounts of 30 to 70 percent off on PINGOUIN, BERNAT, PHILDAR, SCHAFFHAUSER, and many other brands of yarn and knitting accessories. Afghan hooks, cable stitch needles, marker rings, circular needles, crochet hooks, and various weights and colors of yarn make for a great selection as well as low prices. They sell PHILDAR Superwash Lenox Bulky, a 100-percent wool yarn, for $2.50 (retail is $6.95). RIVIERA Antibes, an acrylic/viscose/nylon blend, was just 50 cents a ball (ten balls are necessary for a medium-sized, long-sleeved woman's cardigan). Fact sheets, with yarn samples, are free with a SASE; new fact sheets are mailed every six weeks.

Sonshine Crafts
437 Clinton Avenue
RD 1
Salt Point, NY 12578
(914) 266-5955
CK, COD (plus $1.90), C/50 cents

If you're pressed for a special something, calligrapher Pat Smith can custom letter and decorate just what would bring that personal touch to gift giving. Allow three to four weeks for delivery of matted and framed verses, and quotes written in calligraphy and accented with pressed flowers. Many quotes (yours or hers) are available in a choice of six frames. Price list and quotes available, along with a color catalog. The shopper in me loved "Life is not a dress rehearsal," but the old favorite "Footprints in the Sand" was still appealing.

Stavros Kouyoumoutzakis Workshop Spun Wools
166 Kalokerinou Avenue 011-30-81-284-466
712-02 Iraklion, Crete, Greece CK, B/$1 (w/samples)

You'll ab-Zorba the Greek bargains here. Don't go up and down the Isles—just flip through the Greek pages. We'll be dis-Crete in revealing their beautiful, unusual weaving and knitting yarns from Crete and Australia, in various weights and undyed colors, would cost twice as much in the States. So, feta your paper and pen and write away.

Straw into Gold, Inc.
3006 San Pablo Avenue (510) 548-5247
Berkeley, CA 94702 CK, MC, V, MO, F

Since 1971, Straw into Gold has been spinning out the savings on craft supplies. Purses can be made from these sows' ears, including yarns and special fibers for weaving and spinning, looms, knitting needles, crochet hooks, and more. Yarns come in silks, wools, cottons, and other blends from names like VILLAWOOL and ROWAN. They have sample cards so you can examine the weights and textures yourself, as well as offering a good selection of instructional books. To receive their flyers and other mailers, send two double-stamped SASEs. Discounts are available when you buy in quantity.

Stu-Art Supplies, Inc.
2045 Grand Avenue (800) 645-2855; (516) 546-5151
Baldwin, NY 11510-2999 CK, MC, V, MO, C, PQ

Artichoke you up. Get your framing and presentation supplies cheaper (approximately 50 percent) and wind up on the Dick Cabbage show. We'll be art-iculate about their discounted NIELSON metal frame sections, wood and tenite sectionals, five varieties of mats, shrink wrap, D'ARCHES watercolor, paper, and all-media art boards. Minimum orders of $15 on frame sections and $25 on mats, but if you combine the two, there's just a $25 minimum. Orders over $300 are shipped free in UPS delivery areas only. Authorized refunds are given to dissatisfied customers.

Suncoast Discount Arts & Crafts
9015 U.S. Route 19 North (813) 577-6331
Pinellas Park, FL 34666 C/$2

From coast to coast, you can save up to 40 percent on arts and crafts supplies by shopping Suncoast. Over 300 pages of crafty and floral ideas can be mustered up with a little help from these friends. Think of the endless hours of boredom and stimulate those hazy, lazy days of summer with creative craft projects. The list is endless: dolls, toys, rugs, jewelry, wreaths, handcrafted calligraphed note cards, floral arrangements, cross-stitchery, quilted frames, macramé wall hangings, baskets, beadery, handpainted T-shirts and more. Page after page of possibilities, with closeout specials soaring to 90 percent off retail.

Squadron Mail Order
(See **Kits and Kaboodle**, p. **356**.)

Taylor's Cutaways and Stuff
2802 E. Washington, Dept. GBBM
Urbana, IL 61801-4699 CK, MC, V, B/$1

Get a "good idea by mail" and cutaway retail craft supplies. Snip into Taylor's for scraps of felt, fake fur, satin, velvet, flannel, velour, and cotton, plus craft packs, buttons, elastic, lace, bows, needles, doll patterns, toy patterns, puppet-making kits, and more. They can save you up to 70 percent on your crafty needs, but sorry—there's no store location, only mail order. Refunds are given when necessary; normal delivery time is one to two weeks. Write for a brochure.

Texas Art Supply Co.
2001 Montrose Boulevard, Dept. GBBM (800) 888-9278;
Houston, TX 77006 (713) 526-5221 (Houston)
CK, MC, V, AE, D, C/$7

You know the old cliché about the size of things in Texas, and the savings (from 10 percent to 80 percent) at Texas Art Supply is no exception. Since 1948, they've been roping big names like GRUMBACHER, WINSOR & NEWTON, LIQUITEX, LETRASET, SPEEDBALL, MONT BLANC, and CHART PAK. Altogether, they offer over 600 brands of art, drafting, engineering, craft, hobby, sign, and display supplies to corral any inspiration. And as long as they're in resaleable condition, they won't steer you wrong in the returns department either. Visit their two stores in Houston when in the Lone Star State.

Reader special: Free catalog ($7 value).

United Supply Co., Inc.

P.O. Box 9219 — (800) 322-3247
Fort Wayne, IN 46899-9219 — CK, MC, V, MO, C

Let's get together and refuse to pay list price on arts and crafts supplies. We can start by shopping United Supply, where 25 percent is knocked off the list price on average, and savings are visible on paint, airbrushes, print and craft supplies galore, plus books, videos, and more. Join up with discounted REMBRANDT, SHIVA, STRATHMORE, LIQUITEX, KOHINOOR, and D'ARCHES products and ask about saving even more when you buy in quantity. Educational slides and filmstrips dealing with art history and art appreciation are also available. Shipping is often included in the price of their supplies; customer satisfaction is guaranteed.

Utrecht Art and Drafting Supply

33 35th Street — (718) 768-2525
Brooklyn, NY 11232 — CK, MC, V, MO, C

To etch his own. With over 100 brands here, there's a big enough selection for everyone to draw from with a stroke of a phone call. Their extensive inventory is discounted up to 70 percent off and is available on art and drafting supplies ranging from acrylics, brushes, canvas, and drafting machines to frames, watercolors, and zipper cases. We found a complete line of D'ARCHES, K&E, BIENFANG, and DESIGN ART MARKER. Quantity discounts on UTRECHT products rounded out their portfolio. There's a $40 minimum order and a two-week delivery time. Returns are accepted only with prior authorization. Before u trek all over town, try Utrecht.

Vanguard Crafts, Inc.
P.O. Box 340170 (718) 377-5188
Brooklyn, NY 11234-9007 C/$1 (refundable)

If you meet the minimum requirements of buying $25 worth of rainy-day craft supplies, then you can maximize the savings up to 40 percent. Their 68-page catalog is a vanguard of ingenuity. Choose kits and supplies for hundreds of hours of creative pleasure. Foil pictures, shrink art, mosaic tiling, decoupaging, copper enameling, stenciling, calligraphy, woodworking . . . and the tools of the trade. Basic art supplies also included, such as the three Ps: paint, paper, and pastels.

Veteran Leather Company, Inc.
204 25th Street (800) 221-7565
Brooklyn, NY 11232 (718) 768-0300 (NY residents)
CK, MC, V, MO, C/$2 (refundable), PQ

Veteran Leather Company has a variety of leathers including suede and chamois, and they carry a large assortment of leather-working accessories and tools. You'll be able to hide behind stock brands like CRAFTOOL, MIDAS, BASIC, FIEBING, OSBORNE, ORIGINAL MINK OIL, and LEXOL. Most prices are lower than retail with discounts up to 50 percent on quantity purchases. There is a $25 minimum order (for mail order) and a 10-percent restocking charge on returns unless the material is defective. Leather you swing for their catalog (48 pages) or call for a price quote, you will still be a veteran from the war on high prices.

Warner-Crivellaro Stained Glass, Inc.
1855 Weaversville Road (800) 523-4242
Allentown, PA 18103 CK, MC, V, AE, MO, COD ($5 charge), C

Warner-Crivellaro wastes no time in letting you know that all types of glass are not created equal, and they make sure you know why. Their catalog gave us an education in "seedy," "wormy," "moss," and other types of machine-made glass textures, as well as instructions on cutting stained glass. The rest of the catalog is devoted to various types and colors of stained glass, in addition to stained-glass tools and supplies. There's soldering paste, cutting oil, decorative glass nuggets, permanent glass-marking pens, lamp bases and chains, stencils, and books on designing jewelry, making holiday ornaments, and more. Just about anything you could want for etching your name on a piece of stained glass. Minimum order is $25; Canadian, Alaskan, and overseas orders must be paid in advance by credit card.

Webs
P.O. Box 147
Dept. 1090
Service Center Road (413) 584-2225
Northampton, MA 01060 CK, MC, V, C

The Webs you weave won't be tangled if you follow a simple rule of thumb: Demand discounts of up to 80 percent on yarn. For toilers and spinners, hand and machine knitters, and weavers, this web is hard to leave. Save on name-brand and private-label yarns in a great assortment of colors. Customers that step into their parlor especially like the mohair, rayon chenille, coned cottons, and shetlands, included in their sample collection. Their "packs" were a good buy; they consist of at least ten pounds of a specific type of yarn, such as cotton flake or rug wool. Returns on correctly filled orders require a 15-percent restocking charge; delivery takes from ten days to two weeks.

Wondercraft
125 Thanes Street (401) 253-2030
Bristol, RI 02809 CK, B

Have no fear, Wonder Craft is here! A division of Robin Rug, Inc., this company offers an assortment of cottons, wool, and cotton/rayon blends, synthetics, and 2/24 acrylic yarns at very reasonable prices. The yarns are sold by the pound: for example, a pound of wool suitable for making a child's sweater was $6. Samples are sent attached to a flier with prices. If you spend over $150, an additional 35 percent is subtracted. It's no Wonder they do such a large mail-order business.

Yankee Ingenuity
P.O. Box 113 (405) 477-2191
Altus, OK 73522 CK, MC, V, COD, B/$1

It takes one Yankee to appreciate another Yankee's ingenuity. Primarily set up to wholesale clock parts to craft shops, ceramic studios, and manufacturers of handcrafted clocks for resale, by ordering through the mail, you, too, can save up to 70 percent off the retail price. The clock will only register 48 hours for a response to your order with all parts guaranteed for life against factory defects. So, if you're ready to defect, write for their eight-page illustrated brochure today.

Yarn Barn
P.O. Box 1191 (404) 479-5083
Canton, GA 30114 C/$2 (puts you on a mailing list for continuous samples), CK

Latch onto this barn for discounted yarn because the selection is incredible. Boucle, chenille, flaked cotton, cable cotton . . . to name a few samples we received. Knitters won't knit pick the selection or prices. Most yarns are mill ends, so be sure to order enough to finish the job. Fibers are natural, synthetic, and blends in various weights from thread to rug yarn. The minimum order is $15.

Yazoo Mills, Inc.
P.O. Box 369 (717) 624-8993
New Oxford, PA 17350 CK, MC, V, MO, COD, PQ

How can you trust that beautiful graphic illustration to the postal system? Professional artists don't; at least, not without the proper mailing tube. That's where Yazoo Mills comes in. They can save you more than 50 percent on tubes for storing or shipping. We're talking all sizes and *low* prices—as low as $1.18 each. They can even sharpen your professional image with your choice of colors. And they're all made of environmentally correct recycled material. Send for a free list of prices and descriptions.

Zimmerman's
2884 34th Street North (813) 526-4880
St. Petersburg, FL 33713 CK, MC, V, MO, C/$2 (refundable)

A home crafter's haven for "Have they got a deal for you!" This is the Ben Franklin of thrift when the project calls for a craft-supply source. Beads, ribbons, yarns, macramé, dolls, books, crocheting and knitting supplies, and anything else to get the job done. Free UPS shipping anywhere in the U.S.A.

Beauty and Cosmetics

If you've always wanted to shop for perfume on the Rue de la Paix, now's your chance. Buy fragrances direct from Paris, the perfume capital of the world, and do it without using all your frequent-flyer miles! Savings are up to 50 percent, so you can really parlay the "parlez-vous Français?" route into a trip to the banque. Even with the small handling fee and duty, by avoiding the thorny U.S. markups, you'll still come out smelling like a rose. Remember that most (but not all) perfumes are "restricted brands" by U.S. customs. That means there's a per-person limit of one or two bottles of each scent allowed for import. Closer to home, if you've never tried one of the various beauty sources we list, you should. Discounts of 50 percent are possible on famous-name cosmetics, and that's nothing to sneeze at.

Beauty Boutique
P.O. Box 94520 (216) 826-3008
Cleveland, OH 44101-4520 CK, MC, V, D, C

You've seen these products in your drugstore or discount chain, but never at these wholesale prices. Direct from the manufacturer, this company's cache of cosmetics includes lipsticks, nail care products, shampoo, skin care products, and fragrances discounted up to 90 percent! REVLON, MAYBELLINE, ALMAY, and ESTÉE LAUDER are just a few of the brand names you'll recognize. AZIZA eyeshadows were $1.88 a piece or three for $5 (valued individually at $4.25). Polish off .25-ounce ELIZABETH ARDEN nail polishes for only 99 cents each. So make it your strategy to send for their color catalog—start saving face and saving money at the same time.

Beauty by Spector, Inc.
Dept. GB-BM-93 (412) 673-3259
McKeesport, PA 15134-0502 CK, MC, V, B

In-spector Clousseau might say, "Hmmm, vot have ve hair?" Wigs, wiglets, cascades, falls, toupees for at least 50 percent below comparable retail are this 34-year-old company's crowning glory. Prices in the sales brochures and descriptive fliers didn't distress us: a two-ounce human-hair wiglet was $29.95 (retail $60); a ponytail switch was $49.95 (retail $90); and a man's toupee was $199 (retail $400). At these prices, you can wear someone else's hair (or a synthetic) without worrying about getting scalped.

Identify yourself as a *Great Buys* reader when ordering to get a special deal.

Beautiful Visions
P.O. Box 4002 (516) 349-7180
Hicksville, NY 11801 CK, MC, V, MO, C

Beauty is in the eyes of the beholder. Behold a vision of dazzling discounts. Beautiful Visions offers an eyeful of famous brand-name cosmetics that are truly a sight for sore eyes. A nail-polish-corrector pen was on special for 49 cents (a $4 value). REVLON eyeshadow powder pencils were 88 cents (valued at $4.25). These low prices should have you seeing double. It was love at first bite when we discovered luscious lipsticks in a mouthful of brands. For instance, L'OREAL Creme Rich lipsticks were priced right at $1.99 each. We also took time to smell the roses and a variety of other sensual scents. For example, 1.7 ounces of CHRISTIAN DIOR's POISON Eau de Toilette was smelling fine for $30. That is a savings of $15. OSCAR DE LA RENTA was a sweet flower, available for the special price of $25. There was also a selection of bath and skin care products to care for the body without removing an arm and a leg. No minimum order, just beautiful, affordable visions.

Beauty Supplies, Etc.
718 Lingco Drive (800) 783-8898; (214) 231-8848
Richardson, TX 75081 CK, MC, V, PQ

Discounts on over 3,000 nail-care products are right at your fingertips, and have been since this company began serving nail professionals six years ago. Beauty Supplies, Etc., offers 10-percent to 20-percent off on big names for your big ten: ORLY, DEVELOP 10, ALPHA 9, and JESSICA, among others. Who says you have to go to a professional manicurist to nail down great polishes and nail-care accessories? Their hottest sellers are nail tips, CALVERT nail dryers, and polishes. No catalog; call or write for a price quote.

Be sure to mention *Great Buys* with any order over $15 and you'll receive a free "blow-dry" brush.

Cosmetique
P.O. Box 94100 (800) 621-8822; (708) 913-9099
Palacine, IL 60094 CK, B

Me and m-eye shadow searched for blemishes in this cosmetics offer to no avail. In fact, we were tickled firefrost pink to find such flawless fashions. Cosmetique will send you a special introductory coupon if you ask for it. Then, for just $1, you'll receive $100 worth of cosmetics, all by top-name manufacturers like DIANE VON FURSTENBERG, ADRIAN ARPEL, and REVLON. If you decide to remain a member, you pay $15.90 (includes shipping) for each future kit. That adds up to 80-percent savings off retail—a pretty slick offer—leaving us at a g-loss for words. Even better, if you change your mind and don't want to keep your kit, it's returnable with no penalty charges. Orders come in about 30 days. Cosmetique is open Monday through Thursday, 7:30 a.m. to 5:15 p.m.

Cosmetics Plus
501 Seventh Avenue (212) 924-3493; (212) 727-0705
New York, NY 10018 CK, MC, V, AE, C, PQ

Cosmetics Plus is your ticket to big beauty at small prices. They carry brands such as LANÇOME, STENDAHL, CHRISTIAN DIOR, ELIZABETH ARDEN, CHARLES OF THE RITZ, ULTIMA II, and NEW ESSENTIALS, for less than you'd find in department and specialty stores. Even hard to find items are available, and even when you add the shipping charges, you'll still come out ahead. For a look at their own line, PIAJABE, call for a catalog; for a specific product from one of the other lines they offer, call for a price quote.

DFM Products
471 Beverly Road (800) 227-2238
Teaneck, NJ 07666 MC, V, C

Forget the copies, these are the real scents and nothing but non-scents lovers could be fooled. They are not samples, either, as when catalogs often use the name of a designer fragrance at what appears to be a ridiculously low price; the buyer quickly discovers the bottle it comes in is about as big as your thumbnail. Not these. These are the real things and the real sizes: GIORGIO, FENDI, SHALIMAR, CAROLINA HERRERA, POISON, whatever your PASSION at 20 percent to 30 percent off, including FREE shipping.

Essential Products Co., Inc.
90 Water Street (212) 344-4288
New York, NY 10005-3587 CK, B, PQ

A scent-sational fragrance find! Now you can exude the aromas of affluence and get a snootful of savings to boot. Essential Products has been copying the most successful fragrances of name designers (just about any top-seller you could want) since 1985. Since their products don't carry the burden of massive "image advertising" costs and the resultant astronomical markups, they sell the smell, not the mystique, leaving you with the sweet smell of 75 percent less for colognes and up to 90 percent less for perfumes. A one-ounce bottle of a leading women's fragrance costs $19, regardless of the brand copied; a half-ounce bottle costs $11. Men's fragrances come only in the four-ounce size and cost $10. Shipping's by UPS, and orders go out the same day. Merchandise returned within 30 days of purchase will receive an exchange or refund (your choice). Send a self-addressed stamped envelope for free sample scent cards, fragrance list, and order form without any obligation. For fragrances at prices you won't get incensed over, this place is Essential.

Great Buys readers will receive a 10-percent discount on orders over $100.

Freddy
10 rue Auber (331) 47426341
75009 Paris, France PQ

We're ready, Freddy! Freddy was the least expensive Paris-based mail-order cosmetics supplier the last time we (price) checked. Perfume extracts and toilet water matching the perfumes are about 40 percent less than you'd find in the U.S. They carry women's and men's perfumes, lotions, scarves, cosmetics, creams, and gifts. Names include PACO RABANNE, YVES ST. LAURENT, NINO CERUTTI, STENDAHL, ORLANE, HERMES, LANÇOME, OSCAR DE LA RENTA, UNGARO, GIVENCHY, BENETTON, and many others. By air mail, orders take a maximum of eight days; sent halfway by air and halfway by surface mail, the maximum time is four weeks. (With other companies, air mail can take six to eight weeks.) Freddy doesn't have a catalog (the fluctuating price of the dollar makes it impractical), but they do send customers a pro forma invoice with the prices quoted net in U.S. dollars and available for two weeks. You have to write and ask the price of everything (definitely an inconvenience), and sometimes they're a little slow in answering, but the savings can be heaven scent.

Holbrook Wholesalers, Inc.
1205 Broadway, Room 204 (800) 347-3738; (212) 880-8681
New York, NY 10001 C

"NYC's largest importer," the ad for Holbrook proclaims, and, with more than 500 designer perfumes available at up to 33 percent off, sounds like they mean business. But before you turn up your nose at mere perfume, consider this added bonus: LANÇOME's line of products to keep everything from your face to your feet looking great is up to 20 percent off. All you need to get up and glow is in the Holbrook Wholesalers' *free* catalog.

Holzman & Stephanie Perfumes Inc.
P.O. Box 921-1927 (708) 234-7667
Lake Forest, IL 60045 CK, MC, V, MO, C/$2

Welcome to the House of Holzman & Stephanie. Entering their fabulous home, you will discover a mansion of world-famous designer fragrances. In the kitchen you'll find Madame Holzman, who was educated in organic chemistry, and the French master perfumer, with his sophisticated smeller. They are cooking up their own versions of 35 sensuous perfumes, including OPIUM, COCO, CHANEL NO. 5, and CHLOE. No scrimping on their ingredients; they use only top-quality oils and alcohols aged to perfection. "Excellence is a way of life with us" is their motto. Next, off to the right, you will come to the den that is filled with colognes for him: ARAMIS, DRAKKAR NOIR, and ROYAL COPENHAGEN, to name a few. Down the hall is LAUREN, baring WHITE SHOULDERS (*pardon moi*). Finally, you will pass to the library, with its PRIVATE COLLECTION of OSCAR DE LA RENTA and HALSTON. On your way out, smell the garden of florals and spice perfumes: TEA-ROSE, and don't overlook the JASMINE. Oh, in the side court, don't miss LAGERFELD and HALSTON playing POLO in GREY FLANNEL. Original perfumes run as high as $325 per ounce; their versions average $22 per ounce (*tres bien*). Visit again and again, but at these prices, their house may become an OBSESSION. Their catalog comes with four sample vials.

Tell them you're a *Great Buys* reader and you'll receive a free ½-ounce perfume from their collection when you purchase the four perfumes in the Holzman & Stephanie line.

M. Geoffrey's Designer Fragrances

144 No. 7th Street, Dept. GBBM (800) 284-2426; (215) 434-2288
Allentown, PA 18101 CK, V, MC, AE, D, C/$1 (w/$2 coupon)

Those with designs on the original designer fragrances will be able to fulfill their passion with PASSION . . . or POLO, GIORGIO, PACO RABANNE, ESTÉE LAUDER, KARL LAGERFELD, NINA RICCI, and over 200 different designer fragrances for up to 70 percent off retail! OBSESSION cologne spray, retailing for $35, was just $19.98; two ounces of ETERNITY cologne spray were $12.98 ($25 retail). Returns are accepted if items are returned in their original condition within 30 days. Most deliveries are made in seven to ten working days, and all orders are shipped free.

Great Buys readers will receive a free gift with their first order, so be sure to tell 'em where you smelled this offer.

House of International Fragrances
4711 Blanco Road (512) 341-2283
San Antonio, TX 78212 CK, MC, V, PQ

For scents that mean savings (and savings that make sense!), order copies of the most popular fragrances under the TOUCH & GO label. Women can save over 80 percent on reproductions of OPIUM, OSCAR DE LA RENTA, CHLOE, HALSTON, ANAIS ANAIS, GIORGIO, WHITE LINEN, COCO, OBSESSION, POISON, SHALIMAR, CHANEL NO. 5, and ESTÉE LAUDER. Their men's perfumes are as poignant as the women's, with savings of 50 percent on reproductions of PACO RABANNE, POLO, GREY FLANNEL, LAGERFELD, POUT LUI, VAN CLEEF & ARPELS, and ARAMIS. Over 100 different fragrances are available: They reproduce almost every brand known to olfactory consumers who only want to smell rich. These fragrances in essence last longer than the originals: One drop of 100-percent essence lasts eight hours; one bottle at $5.99 will last three months when used daily. In-stock items are shipped within 48 hours.

J-R Tobacco Co.
(See **Tobacco**, p. **477**.)

KSA Jojoba
19025 Parthenia Street, Dept. GBBM (818) 701-1534
Northridge, CA 91324 CK, COD, F (with SASE and two stamps)

Here at the office, we like to watch the soaps. It's good, clean fun and, from time to time, we find an interesting item—such as KSA's jojoba soap. Browsing through their literature, we learned that jojoba is a plant that produces beans that contain an oil similar to sperm whale oil. The oil is used in shampoos, lubricants, cosmetics, machine and automotive oil, and even lotions. If enough jojoba plants were grown, there'd be no need to kill any whales, we also learned. The effects of this oil on healing and protecting skin are remarkable, says KSA, which sells jojoba products (including plants) wholesale to the public. A half-ounce glass gift bottle of pure jojoba oil cost $3.95; a bar of jojoba glycerin soap was $1.50. Teddy bear, whale, and rabbit soaps-on-a-rope were $2.50; they also had a glycerin snowman. Liquid soaps, creams, lotions, and lip balms were among their offerings. Eight ounces of their jojoba-and-aloe-vera shampoo was $3. A "Save Our Whales" rubber stamp will make a big impression on your ecology-minded friends at $5.50 each. "We stand behind our products and will replace and/or refund any product found to be defective."

Great Buys readers can grow their own jojoba plants with this special offer: two seed packets for the price of one, *or*, get a free oil sample with product order.

Michel Swiss

16 rue de la Paix (331) 2616884 or (331) 2616944
Paris, France CK, C

Ooh-la-la! You'll save enough at Michel Swiss to open your own Swiss bank account. OK, maybe we exaggerated a little bit on that one. Prices were terrific on palpably pungent Parisian perfumes. Franc-ly speaking, you don't knead to pay in French bread either, since prices are quoted in American dollars. Lagerfeld's CHLOE in a quarter-ounce size was $31.15; and Nina Ricci's L'AIR DU TEMPS was $27.75 for the quarter-ounce size. They have many new fragrances, such as PALOMA, GUCCI III, MISSONI, RALPH LAUREN FOR MEN, DIVA (my namesake is the Diva of Discounts) by UNGARO, and many more. Skin-tillating soaps, crystal limoges, bath oils, body creams, bubble baths, men's colognes, and after-shaves were also available at reasonable prices. Michel Swiss's prices include full insurance, and you get a gift with each order. You may go in-Seine, though, waiting two to three months for delivery via normal mail, or two to three weeks via air mail.

New Mexicraft Company, Inc./Perfumes of the Desert

P.O. Box 7036 (505) 243-0859
Old Albuquerque, NM 87194 CK, MC, V, AE, D, DC, F

Don't let good scents desert you when you're buying perfume. New Mexicraft, in business for over 40 years, can sweeten your surroundings with a variety of scents fresh from the desert of New Mexico, including perfumes, colognes, and after-shaves. From refreshing Pinon (from pine needles) to floral Purple Sage, there are ten fragrances to suit all kinds of tastes at great, low prices. One ounce of Cactus Flower perfume was $18.50; an eighth of an ounce of Desert Mistletoe was just $6. Or give your home its just desserts with fragrant incense or slow-burning perfumed candle pots. All in all, an unusual and captivating array, to bring a Southwest flavor (and scent) to your neck . . . of the woods. They even have gift-wrapping (to which you can add your own card), and "do not open 'til Christmas" stickers. Call or write for a flier.

Professional Hair Care

P.O. Box 199056 (317) 351-2002
Indianapolis, IN 46219 CK, MC, V, D, MO, C

Are your locks locked out of beauty? Never fear; your crowning glory can be achieved in the hair department, with a little help from these mail-order hair-i-tecs. Professional Hair Care has products galore to unsnarl your hair net and set you up in style. These prices will curl you: REDKEN shampoos starting at $10.50 for a half-liter, SEBASTIAN styling aids for around $11; even PAUL MITCHELL products for less than in salons. They're not giving it away here, but the time and gas saved by not having to motor or walk to your salon for these exclusive products can be worth it. There are also REDKEN and NEXXUS skin-care products, KENDRA, MATRIX, OPTIMUM and GENTILLE shampoos and conditioners, TRUCCO makeup, HAWAIIAN TROPIC tanning lotions, and more. Licensed stylists will help you solve hairy questions if you need professional guidance in your selection. Orders are shipped the same day; shipping and handling is $2, no matter what you order. Exchanges are accepted for five days after you receive your order.

Sole Food Foot Cream

3205 Bandolino Lane, Dept. 5920 (214) 867-5313
Plano, TX 75075 CK, B

If your feet can't take the heat of a full day's feast, try a little food for your feet. Sole Food, developed by a drug and cosmetic chemist, can be used on feet or hands, to soften the skin, protect against the elements, and help heal minor cuts and irritations. A small amount is all it takes to massage tired toes, even right through panythose. This nonirritating, nonprescription cream also contains anti-fungal and deodorant agents. Free brochure details the ingredients and its purposes.

Great Buys by Mail readers are eligible for an *exclusive* 20-percent discount on Sole Food. Readers get 4.25 ounces, regularly $20, for

$16; the ⅔-ounce size, regularly $6, is $4.80. You must tell them you're a reader and request the discount when ordering.

Topsy Tail Company
3529 Townsend Drive (214) 353-0884
Dallas, Texas 75229-3804 CK, MC, V

This revolutionary tool makes a plain pony tail into a sophisticated "do" in seconds. Just a few simple moves can turn shoulder-length or longer hair into twists, braids, and beautiful upswept styles. The tool ($9.95 plus $1.50 shipping), comes with a complete instruction manual. It's time to start wagging your tail behind you with a Topsy Tail.™

Valray International, Inc.
739 N.E. 40th Court (305) 563-8411
Ft. Lauderdale, FL 33334 CK, MC, V, MO, B

Let's face it—it's all in the name. Since 1974, Valray has been saving you about 50 percent off comparable skin-care products (scrubs, cleansers, masks, toners, eye and throat creams, wrinkle smoothers, bleaching creams, etc.) and makeup lines (foundations, powders, blush, eyebrow pencils, cover sticks, lipsticks, and mascara). Marketing similar products, without the zillion-dollar ad campaigns, under the house name MAXIMILIAN'S REJUVENATION® and SCENTIQUE perfumes and colognes, you'll get the benefits and the "look" without the hefty price tags. Returns accepted within 30 days for complete refund if not entirely satisfied.

Vickie-Bee Perfumes
1285 Morrow Road (412) 221-6174
Pittsburgh, PA 15241 CK, B

At Vickie-Bee, the buzz word is copy. And these folks aren't bumbling idiots when it comes to making first-rate copy perfumes of OPIUM, SHALIMAR, CHANEL NO. 5, WHITE SHOULDERS, JOY, OSCAR DE LA RENTA, and PHEROMONE ("One of the most expensive perfumes in the world"). They take the sting out of pricing, too—only $12 per ounce. Order a few bottles today and smell for yourself just how close a copy can come to "bee-ing" the real thing.

Bed and Bath

Bed and bath bargains abound between the sheets of this section. Take comfort in outfitting your bed and bathrooms at half the price. You'll salute the four-star savings on brass beds, and march to the beat of decorated deals on MARTEX towels, NETTLE CREEK bedspreads, or SPRINGMAID sheets. With the great savings you'll be getting on sheets, pillowcases, towels, etc., you may even be too excited to sleep!

Alden Comfort Mills
P.O. Box 55
1708 E. 14th Street — (800) 822-5336; (214) 423-4000
Plano, TX 75086-0055 — CK, MC, V, AE, D, C

Go to the source to discover the cover-up. And while you're keeping warm, you'll save 30 percent to 60 percent in the process. Quilt by association provides for down quilts and comforters from this manufacturer. They will even revamp your old down items. Add new life to your old comforters, shams, lap robes, crib-sized comforters, and dust ruffles. From plain to printed, flowered to striped, they've got comfort, style, and selection. Their custom recovering service for down and feather comforters can even make your old comforter bigger by adding more fill. In business since 1947, it is still family owned and operated. Choose your fabric or theirs and voilà, you're on your way to sleeping underneath a cloud. Brass beds, bed frames, bean bags, and all your bedding needs are covered. Satisfaction is guaranteed.

Clearbrook Woolen Shop
(See **Fabrics and Upholstery**, p. **193**.)

The Company Store
500 Company Store Road
La Crosse, WI 54601
(800) 323-8000
(608) 785-1400 (WI residents)
CK, MC, V, AE, D, MO, C

Get down, get down . . . and save up to 30 percent at the same time. A simple but elegant selection of pure down products is available from this factory division of Gillette Industries. We warmed up to high-quality crafted and styled down pillows, comforters, crib comforters, and booties available in classic colors (beige or blue), plus outerwear and accessories. Rest assured, you're in good company.

Cuddledown of Maine
312 Canco Road
Portland, ME 04103
(800) 323-6793
CK, MC, V, AE, D, MO, C/$3

Cuddle up to Cuddledown and never be cold again! How cozy can you go? You might be surprised. The Cuddledown-manufactured collection includes super-soft cotton sheets both treated and untreated; beautiful striped, flowered, and solid blankets and comforters; pillows, fabric shower curtains, booties, robes, and sleepwear that keep you tastefully toasty. Prices are primo, too; a gorgeous Italian-striped cream or white twin-sized comforter cover was $179; high-quality, striped English flannel sheets were $39. They have been in business since 1973, and they warmed our hearts with their slogan, "Save a gallon, shop by mail!"

D. MacGillivray & Coy.
(See **Apparel: Family**, p. **11**.)

The Decorette
(See **Windows and Walls**, p. **519**.)

Designer Secrets Catalog

P.O. Box 529 (800) 955-2559
Fremont, NE 68025 CK, MC, V, AE, D, MO, C/$2 (refundable)

Ever wonder how professional decorators can make a room look so good? Well, the secret's out. Designer Secrets, that is, where bedroom ensembles, wallpaper, fabrics, sheets, pillow cases, pillows, shower curtains, and bath accessories are up to 50 percent below retail. Queen-size comforter sets were selling for $209.90, including dust ruffle, comforter, and pillow shams. A matching sheet set was $69.90. There is no restocking fee, but there is a 30-day time limit on returns.

Domestications

P.O. Box 40 (800) 782-7722; (717) 633-3313
Hanover, PA 17333 CK, MC, V, AE, CB, D, DC, MO, C

Domestications is right at home with low domestic prices. A lovely twin cutwork comforter cover was just $39; a hand-held steamer iron was $9.99. You can afford to put your faith in these down-home savings on big-city looks for your home. Bedding, towels, robes, chairs, tablecloths, and more fill the colorful 95-page catalog. There is a $20 minimum on credit-card orders. You can return anything but personalized items, and shipment on most merchandise is guaranteed within 60 days from Hanover House to yours.

Dreams of Comfort

7606 Girard Avenue (800) 423-2725; (619) 454-2280
La Jolla, CA 92037 CK, MC, V, AE, CB, DC, C

Open your own chir-o-practice by ordering direct from this manufacturer. For over 20 years, this company has been selling "American's best-built electric adjustable bed." According to their literature, there's a five-year guarantee on lift motors (which can be replaced easily, even by an all-thumbs teenager), and a one-year guarantee on the heater. A 39″ × 74″ twin regular bed was $899 (comparable retail price: $1,498), while a twin long was $800 (typically $949 in a store). Sleep right. Shipping's not outrageously expensive either; about $75. Other products include an at-home massage unit that kneads out the competition. Usually, orders are received in seven to ten days. We'd say more, but we don't want to rub it in. (We have a hands-off policy here.)

Eldridge Textile Co.
277 Grand Street (212) 925-1523
New York, NY 10002 CK, MC, V, C/$3 (refundable)

If you're looking for a big selection for the bed, bath, or boudoir, at discounts of up to 40 percent, stop here! Their inventory of first-quality merchandise is enough to floor you. But the buck doesn't stop there, not in *this* 52-year-old business. You'll find ground-floor opportunities for name-brand and designer towels, sheets, area rugs, blankets, pillows, and closet accessories. Move on to the main attraction: custom-made headboards, comforters, bedspreads, draperies, hand-painted bedding, and valances. Their hundreds of brand names read like a "Who's Who" in home decorating: MARTEX, WAMSUTTA, DAKOTAH, FIELDCREST, SPRINGMAID, and CAMEO are just a sampling. Almost half of the orders go out the same day. Returns are accepted within 30 days if the item is unused and still salable.

Ezra Cohen Corp.
307 Grand Street (212) 925-7800
New York, NY 10002 CK, MC, V, AE, PQ

It's E-Z to save with Ezra Cohen of New York. A veritable institution for bargains in towels and bed linens, this famous discounter's been around since 1910. Name-brand, top-of-the-line linens we encountered included WAMSUTTA, UTICA BY J.P. STEVENS, BILL BLASS, SPRINGMAID, MARTEX, MARIMEKKO BY DAN RIVER, VERA, CANNON, LAURA ASHLEY, and many others. Ezra Cohen features a wide variety of products, from neck rolls and pillow shams to duvets and down comforters and bedspreads by DAKOTAH, NETTLE CREEK, CROSCILL, and BATES. Coordinated linens are presented in bedroom settings right out of the pages of *Architectural Digest*. Sheets for waterbeds, throws, quilts, draperies—the list is virtually endless. Ezra Cohen specializes in custom designs. A team of professionals will design "almost anything" using material from regular sheets. Orders on in-stock items generally take three weeks for delivery.

The Factory Store
585 Baltimore Street (717) 632-8691
Hanover, PA 17331 CK, MC, V, B

Since July of '63, the Acme Quilting Co. has been turning out the textiles (over 5,000 bedspreads alone are available for the great American cover-up). Inventory also includes bedspreads, towels, draperies, pillows, sheets, comforters, quilts, and blankets from NETTLE CREEK, BEAU IDEAL, BATES, ACME, CANNON, DAKOTAH, SPRINGMAID, and others. About 20 to 25 brands are carried. The Factory Store is probably best known for its NETTLE CREEK bedspreads, but mattress pads may be their *best* buy. Save 30 percent to 50 percent on first-quality merchandise and 50 percent to 60 percent on irregulars. (Who cares if your bottom sheet's a little faded at the corner!) There's a liberal exchange and refund policy, with shipment by UPS. (Tack on an additional 50 cents for the carton and handling.) Tightwads like us sleep cheap on bed linens without the (retail) bedbug bite.

Harris Levy, Inc.
278 Grand Street (212) 226-3102
New York, NY 10002 CK, MC, V, AE, O, MO, C, PQ

We'll Levy this Grand Street granddaddy (in the business for 98 years) our highest honors. Harris Levy throws in the towel, as well as the sheets, comforters, and other bed and bath items at 25 percent to 50 percent off. They carry every major brand, including WAMSUTTA, J.P. STEVENS, MARTEX, SPRINGMAID, FIELDCREST, DAN RIVER, and CANNON. There are over 60 different styles of sheets with an especially big selection of country-style sheets and towels. Their custom-order department can fill special requests for table linens, draperies, and shower curtains including monogramming. Returns are handled on an individual basis within 30 days as long as the item is returned in its original condition; store credit is usually given. Minimum order is $25 with a credit card.

Inter-TRADE
301 W. 16th (616) 393-8089
Holland, MI 49423 CK, COD, PQ

When we first gazed at this company, it was called Cameo. Boy, were our faces etched with relief when we found out only their name changed. Now called Inter-TRADE, they pillow-ries high-retail prices with 25-percent to 30-percent savings on piles of bed pillows, decorative pillows, down comforters, and rocker and chair pads. They even carry their own brand, called LUXURY DOWN. Orders usually come in about two weeks. There's a $15 minimum on custom orders, a 10-percent restocking charge, and a guarantee against defective workmanship. After you sleep on this decision, you'll know you've made the right choice.

J. Schachter Corp.
85 Ludlow Street (800) INTO-BED
New York, NY 10002 CK, MC, V, D, PQ

Is there a Schachter in the house? You're darn right! Since way back in 1919, they've been hiding out in the bedroom buried beneath the largest fabric selection of comforters in the country. There are over 200 to choose from, as well as other accessories to complete the ensemble: shams, ruffles, table covers, and draperies. They also carry both custom and stock comforters, and pillows and linens by PALAIS ROYAL, SPRINGMAID, CANNON, WAMSUTTA, FARIBO, and MARTEX. Favorites include a goosedown pillow retailing for $50 that Schachter sells for $30, and a down comforter ($129 retail) for just $69. Savings run 30 percent to 40 percent usually, but up to 60 percent on closeouts. Recovering old down comforters and pillows is a store specialty. Odd-sized sheets for boats and water beds are another store novelty. No returns are accepted on custom or special orders, but full credit is issued on unopened, stock merchandise. Orders generally come in two to six weeks.

The Mattress Factory
912 East Vickery Boulevard (817) 334-0361
Ft. Worth, TX 76104 CK, MC, V, AE, D, PQ

The original Mattress Factory has been bedding down for over 100 years and it's still a family tradition to bed down for less. Stop fiddling around and sleep where probably even Washington slept. All mattresses and box springs are comparable to SEALY; a queen set, regularly $349, was $299. Choose from two manufacturers of springs and seven firmnesses. Add a 20-year warranty, kids' beds, and it spells savings up to 75 percent. Manufacturing is in the back of the original warehouse, but you don't have to travel to the Stockyards to stock up. Delivery nationwide.

Mother Hart's Natural Products, Inc.
P.O. Box 4229
3330 S. Congress Avenue #21 (407) 738-5866
Boynton Beach, FL 33424-4229 CK, MC, V, MO, C, PQ

You can take savings of 50 to 70 percent to heart and take home bed and bath items, underwear, activewear, and more from Mother Hart's. Their catalog features duvet covers, pillows, comforters, and sheets (both treated and untreated) made of natural fabrics at great low prices. Great buys are also available on first-quality and irregular extras, like legwear, sweaters, camisoles, and sleepwear. They cotton to your love of comfort and savings at the same time. Call or write for a price quote. Returns are accepted in 30 days on unused goods; satisfaction is guaranteed.

Quilts Unlimited
(See **Arts and Collectibles**, p. **48**.)

Rafael
291 Grand Street (212) 966-1928
New York, NY 10002 CK, MC, V, AE, PQ

Put your money worries to bed! Rafael means pleasant dreams. They offer seductive savings of 40 percent to 50 percent off the nightmarish cost of deparment-store prices. Take comfort in comforters, or softly sink into sheets, pillowcases, towels, table linens, and more from the houses of BILL BLASS, WAMSUTTA, SPRINGMAID, CANNON, and MARTEX. They also get down and cushy, too, plus fabrics, draperies, and blinds—mini, vertical, and pleated. Most orders arrive in about two to three weeks; there are no refunds, but exchanges are allowed.

Rubin & Green Interior Design Studio
(See **Windows and Walls**, p. **524**.)

Shama Imports, Inc.
(See **Fabics and Upholstery**, p. **200**.)

Springmaid/Wamsutta Mill Store
36 Groce Road (803) 433-4645
Lyman, SC 29365 CK, MC, V, MO, PQ

You've got it made at Springmaid/Wamsutta. They sell their first-quality bath towels, sheets, window treatments, comforters, bedspreads, and other discontinued items for up to half off. With six outlets and more in the works, this is a hot spot to find linens and domestics in your area or by phone. If you know the size, pattern, style, and color of the item you want, you can call for a price quote and to find out if it's in stock. Make sure you let them know whether you want first quality or irregular; otherwise, you may decide your judgment was flawed despite the discount!

Village Linen Co.
6131 Kirby (713) 524-1040
Houston, TX 77005 CK, MC, V, AE, D, C

Looking for towels that won't hang you out to dry? Village Linen's catalog offers a load of luxurious linens at great discounts. Drift off to dreamland on authentic "paper white" linens, or spread your bed with a white night comforter. Blanket yourself in bargains from their selection of sheets, towels, table linens, bathroom accessories, and more.

Boating Supplies

Are you the seafaring type? When the sails of your boat are billowing, the wind's at your back, and you're slicing through the spume and waves with a thin, cool mist spraying your face, do you feel truly alive? If you're a boat owner, or soon will be, this section is for you. Whether you're getting ready for the America's Cup race, preparing for a weekend of waterskiing, or just planning a strategic assault on the local black bass population at an area lake, these companies can regale you with regalia. From a tiny rubber raft to equipment for the biggest yacht, when it comes to mail-order marine supplies, selection, and watered-down savings, then heads up. It's sink or swim, but it's a game well worth playing.

Bass Pro Shops
P.O. Box 4046
Springfield, MO 65808
(800) 227-7776
(417) 883-4960 (in AL, HI)
CK, MC, V, AE, C/$2; $3 credit with catalog

You'll fall for this catalog hook, line, and sinker. Their bait is mighty tempting—savings up to 50 percent on an oceanic selection of boats, rods, reels, lines, hooks, clothing—everything but the catch. Holy mackerel, that's your contribution.

Defender Industries
255 Main Street
P.O. Box 820 (914) 632-3001
New Rochelle, NY 10802-0802 CK, MC, V, MO C/$3 (refundable)

Up periscope to sight the savings! Defender torpedoes the competition with sub-marine prices—in fact, the lowest prices (35 percent to 60 percent off) we've seen on a complete line of nautical gear. Discounted items ranged from mobile phones to PATAGONIA boating apparel to first-aid kits, electronic instruments, engines, sailboat hardware—all the way to camping coolers and stoves. The depth of their fiberglass inventory (the largest in the U.S.) gave us a real charge. ACHILLES inflatable rafts weren't made for heels, either; and TIMBERLAND shoes were a good buy, as was foul-weather gear. Before you Destroyer finances paying retail, bow down to their stern discounts on boat and sailing supplies. There's a $15 minimum order ($25 with credit cards) and a 20-day refund policy.

E & B Marine Supply, Inc.
201 Meadow Road (800) 533-5007; (908) 287-3900
Edison, NJ 08818 CK, MC, V, AE, D, MO, C

No nautical disasters here: Landlubbers and boaters will discover that the prices here won't rock the boat. Their catalog is swamped with thousands of boating accessory items. Savings billow upwards from 20 percent to 60 percent on marine marvels such as depth sounders, marine radios, electronic navigational aids, cushions, furniture, toilets, pumps, water skis, etc. Names like EAGLE, BOW 'T STERN, RITCHIE, and HUMMINGBIRD are no strangers to the high seas (or your local lake). Other discounted items include fair- and foul-weather clothing, boat shoes, nautical ties, inflatable boats, clocks and barometers, and much more. Fifty convenient outlet stores are stocked with all the catalog items and then some. The minimum order is $15 ($25 for phone orders); returns within 90 days.

Fish 'n' Shack
P.O. Box 1080 (314) 346-4044
Camdenton, MO 65020 CK, MC, V, MO, C

Nothing fishy about savings of up to 50 percent below retail (and more on the house brand). Lampoon a bargain on every item in this 132-page catalog with about every product imaginable for freshwater fishing and boating. This ocean-array of inventory includes reels, rods, tackle boxes, fishing lines, bait, fly tying, and more. How-to videos even teach you the art of the catch. Though the name's deceiving (half the inventory's devoted to hunting, camping, and other outdoor gear), the savings nevertheless are no fish tales.

Goldberg's Marine Distributors

P.O. Box 3040, Dept. GBBM
Edison, NJ 08818-3040
(800) BOATING
(908) 819-9222 (international)
CK, MC, V, AE, D, C

Buoy, oh buoy, this company's been afloat since 1946, and they say they were the *first* mail-order boating accessory company to offer the discounts. Goldberg's has really gone overboard on pleasure-boating equipment and nautical clothing at seaworthy savings between 20 percent and 60 percent below retail. We piered at items like life vests, boat covers, pumps, fishing equipment, marine radios, and depth finders in their catalog of cargo. SEAFIT anchor kits held fast at $62.99, which gives us anchors away the way we want 'em—at a discount. With discount stores in New York City and Philadelphia, there's a boatload of savings to be found in their prices. Most items are delivered in three to seven days; refunds and exchanges are made.

M & E Marine Supply Co.

1715 Mt. Ephraim
Camden, NJ 08104
(800) 541-6501
CK, MC, V, D, C

Think you've seen everything in the way of marine accessories? Think again, bilge breath! Everything you've ever wanted to buy for your boat (every major brand) is contained in their two-pound, over-300-page catalog—and at discount prices! As if this massive catalog weren't enough, they even offer special "sail" supplements four times a year. You'll find power and sail equipment, marine electronics, hardware, paint, sport-fishing equipment, furniture, clothing, and gifts. They even sell marine toilet paper. Everything is offered at 25 percent to 40 percent off. Orders are shipped within 24 to 48 hours. Full refunds are given within 30 days.

Overton's Marine/Overton's Water Sports
P.O. Box 8228
111 Red Banks Road (800) 334-6541
Greenville, NC 27835 CK, MC, V, AE, D, C

Here's two great divisions of a company that go great together, with two (count 'em) catalogs, to boot! Overton's was founded in 1975, selling waterskis and accessories from a grocery store. From such shallow beginnings, they are now keeping their head above water with a multimillion-dollar business. Their Marine division stocks boating equipment and accessories, "from seatcovers and electronics to hardware, lifts and cleaners." Their Water Sports division offers "the world's largest selection of waterskis, kneeboards, inflatables, wetsuits, vests, and gloves," as well as summerwear and active apparel. Savings on all Overton's merchandise runs as high as 50 percent, plus a price-protection guarantee (see catalogs). The Overton policy is "satisfaction guaranteed" across the board; most orders are shipped within 24 hours; Federal Express service is available.

Skipper Marine Electronics, Inc.
3170 Commercial Avenue (800) 621-2378
Northbrook, IL 60062 CK, MC, V, MO, COD, C, PQ

Discounts, ho! Up to 30 percent off on nautical electronics, calibrated and properly set by Skipper before shipment, is worth dropping anchor for. Their catalog has over 100 pages of EAGLE, ECHOTEC, MICRONAR, DATAMARINE, CYBERNET, KING MARINE, and more brands of radios, navigational devices, and other boating electronics. And there's more merchandise than meets the eye; if you don't see what you want, call or write with your request for information and/or a price quote. Shipping is included in the cost of electronics. What a whale of a deal!

West Marine Products
500 Westridge Drive (800) 538-0775
Watsonville, CA 95077 (408) 476-1905 (CA residents)
CK, MC, V, MO, C, PQ

Set sale! There's a breeze blowing up to 50 percent off full retail here, and the trade winds are even more fair during seasonal catalog offerings. West Marine sells marine equipment, supplies, clothing, accessories, and electronics. Some 6,000 major brands are stocked in their more than 60,000-square-foot warehouse, including lines like PATAGONIA, NAVICO, CANNON, RITCHIE, and DATA-MARINE. There are over 22,000 different items for sale, ranging from rope to paint. Customer satisfaction is guaranteed. Most orders are shipped within 24 hours. You don't have to be into new wave to appreciate their tide-y, 124-page catalog.

Yachtmail Co. Ltd.
Admiral's Court, The Quay — 011-44-590-672784
Lymington, Hampshire SO41 9HE, England — CK, MC, V, MO
Bank Cheque, C

The sea of cruiser-yacht equipment available from this company is all-encompassing. Flares and foghorns, heads and hatches, pumps and pulleys, lights and logs, move over, you're rockin' the boat! You name it, they've got it, and we're not dinghy, either. Just a little dizzy with discounts of about 25 percent off U.S. prices. That's a lifesaver in today's economy. We found seaworthy savings on AVON, MUSTO, HENRY LLOYD, AUTOHELM, and SPLASH-DOWN sextants. The only albatross not-so-ancient mariners must contend with is freight charges on the AVON life rafts.

Books and Magazines

Turn the pages to historic proportions on books from antiquities to magazines devoted to the Paris gossip scene. Dedicated to bibliophiles who prefer to take a hike from their easy chairs, as well as to read the fine print and index the savings.

Barnes & Noble Bookstores, Inc.
126 Fifth Avenue (800) 242-6657; (212) 767-7079
New York, NY 10011-5666 CK, MC, V, AE, DC, MO, C

From a slang dictionary to military history to Faulkner, Barnes & Noble is the place to find good reading, cheap. Prices were as low as $2.98, and the selection included books on religion, philosophy, science, British history, art, literature, and reference books. " 'Tis nobler to pay less for Shakespeare's sonnets than to ever pay through the Rom-e-nos." An education in itself since 1873, this barnes-storming mail-order bookseller doesn't stop the buck with just books, either. Videos featuring comedians, great performers, and more, plus international music selections on cassette and CD, rounded out the selection. Get a free catalog and start filling in the blank spaces in your life.

Bookworld Services, Inc.
1933 Whitefield Loop (800) 444-2524
Sarasota, FL 34243 CK, MC, V, AE, D, MO, C/$1

Book it to Bookworld Services for the latest and greatest read. Turn the pages to sci-fi and fantasy, or educate yourself with nonfiction books like those on computers. One of their big sellers is *Principles of Riding* for $19.95. Of course, the horse is extra. It's all available for prices that won't cost you much more than a trip to the library . . . and there's no overdue charges!

Collegetown Magazine Subscription Services
(800) 433-1357
(Monday-Friday; 8 A.M.-4 P.M. CST)

Call Krazy Kevin's Live Hotlines for the lowest prices on over 1,400 magazine subscriptions. Choose from titles that include *People*, *Newsweek*, *Time*, *Glamour*, *Field & Stream*, *Sports Illustrated*, and many more. Save off the newsstand prices. Save off the subscription prices. Sometimes you'll even save half of half. Check with them before you subscribe to the sweepstakes of possibilities elsewhere.

Cookbook Outlet
P.O. Box 872036
Dallas, TX 75287 CK, MO, B

If you think too many cookbooks spoil the cook, you're right on the money here. Every cookbook imaginable, including more than 375 Southern cookbook titles alone is the soup to nuts base at this warehouse distributor. Save 20 percent on the suggested manufacturer's list price on current titles and start the dough rising. Taste a few of these cookbooks-for-less: *30-Minute Light Gourmet*, *A Taste of New England*, *Beyond Parsley*, *Cajun Cooking*, *Dairy-Free*, *Dirty Dining* (no kin to Dancing), *Don't Eat Your Heart Out*, *Fajita Fiesta*, *Game Fish Cookbook*, *Houston Junior League Cookbook*, *Lite Switch*, *The Mansion on Turtle Creek Cookbook*, *Mrs. Field's Cookie Book*, *Pastors' Wives Cookbook*, *Puddin Hill Cookbook*, *Santa Fe-Lite and Spicy*, *The Book of Tofu*, *Vintage Vicksburg*, *White Trash Cooking*, *Wild About Munchies* . . . does that whet your appetite yet? Write for their FREE title list and start cookin' with bargain books from this outlet's menu.

Daedalus Books, Inc.
P.O. Box 9132 (800) 395-2665
Hyattsville, MD 20781-0932 CK, MC, V, AE, MO, C

Read any good books lately? If not, consider Daedalus. Their catalogs are chock full of interesting reads: from art to gardening, children's books to unknown foreign authors, fiction and nonfiction. Most books are publishers' overstocks. Seven catalogs are put out each year. Daedalus offers a 30-day return policy, and no restocking charge.

Jessica's Biscuit/The Cookbook People
P.O. Box 301 (617) 965-0530
Newtonville, MA 02160 CK, MC, V, MO, C/$2

Jessica's a hot potato in the cookbook biz. She's kosher with us (literally), with scads of specials on cookbooks for making just what the doctor ordered. Or are you a soul man? Whatever your taste, there's a cookbook full of recipes to match it, and Jessica's probably has it. You'd be amazed at how many ways corn, potatoes, beans, and other foods can be prepared; there's a cookbook for each of those, too. Get a picky kid to eat foods that are both healthy and delicious, or learn to make a mean appetizer. Their sales will save you as much as 80 percent on cookbooks you may not even be able to *find* elsewhere.

Magazine Marketplace
One Instant Win Place (800) 662-6657; (309) 691-4610
Peoria, IL 61644 CK, MC, V, AE, D, MO, COD, B

If you don't subscribe to the idea of paying full price for magazine subscriptions, look into Magazine Marketplace. They'll pay you three times the difference if you can find an offer (excluding renewals) that's lower than their subscription rates. Or you might get lucky and win their seven-million-dollar sweepstakes. Address any mailed inquiries to "Customer Service."

Publishers Central Bureau
One Champion Avenue (201) 382-7960
Avenel, NJ 07001-2301 CK, MC, V, AE, MO, C

Books, books, and more books wind up for "Last Call: at up to 90 percent off." Be it a publisher's overstock or a producer's overrun of a video or record, it lands full circle in this catalog at gigantic savings. Monthly catalogs offer the full array of reading and listening pleasure. From art books, gardening, diet and health, beauty, children's books to classics, cookbooks to computers, classical records and tapes, golden oldies, old radio shows, PCB is the just dessert in food for thought.

Publishers Clearing House
101 Winners Circle — (516) 883-5432
Port Washington, NY 11050 — CK, MO

Subscribe to your favorite magazine and save as much as half the regular rack rate. Publishers Clearing House clears the way for great deals on more than 100 magazines, including everything from *TV Guide* to *Consumer Reports*. Pay for your selections all at once, or over a four-month period. And, of course, enter the sweepstakes; you never know when lady luck will be calling.

The Scholar's Bookshelf
110 Melrich Road — (609) 395-6933
Cranbury, NJ 08512 — CK, MC, V, MO, C

A mind is a terrible thing to waste, so don't! Feed your intellect without starving your wallet with The Scholar's Bookshelf catalog, where you can save as much as 75 percent off original publishers' prices. In business for 16 years, they stock books from university presses on such subjects as literature, art, philosophy, and fine arts. Returns are accepted within 30 days; no restocking charge.

Script City
8033 Sunset Boulevard — (213) 871-0707
Suite 1500-GBBM — CK, MC, V, AE, CB, D, DC, MO, C
Hollywood, CA 90046

Discount prices are where the action is, and Script City's line is, "We will not be undersold!" They hit the mark every time with scripts and books for at least 10 percent less than their competitors. Television scripts, new movie scripts, software, videos, books on acting, writing, directing, and more fill the pages of their catalog.

First catalog is *free*; subsequent bigger catalogs cost $2. Rush orders are available; returns must be authorized within seven days of receipt.

Strand Book Store, Inc.
828 Broadway
Dept. 1003-4805
New York, NY 10003
(212) 473-1452
CK, MC, V, AE, D, MO, C

Don't get stranded without something to read. Look at these folks for a few million; in fact, you might say they're booked solid. Since 1929, Strand has been in the book biz. They stock over 2.5 million new and used remainders, rare and limited editions, and signed or inscribed books. Art, Americana, social science, fiction, literature, chess, poetry, music, and books on a myriad of other subjects are available at an average of 50 percent off retail. Some are discounted as much as 90 percent! When we checked out, we bought Umberto Eco's *Foucault's Pendulum*, at a list price of $22.95, for $7.95; *Warhol's Diaries*, which listed for $29.95, for $9.95. Returns are accepted. On request, Strand will ship door to door within four business days via the most reasonable express service. The actual cost will be applied to your credit card. Although they do their best to ship promptly, allow four to six weeks for delivery.

Subscription Services, Inc.
29 Glen Cove Avenue
Glen Cove, NY 11542
(800) SAY-MAGS
(516) 676-4300 (in NYC)
CK, MC, V, PQ

No reading between the lines here. This is one of the lowest-priced sources for ordering magazine subscriptions. Write or call for their list of magazines and a price quote for specific subscriptions. What a great gift to a distant relative; they'll even enclose a personalized card with each subscription.

Special to *Great Buys* readers: A personalized file of all your subscriptions will be kept, and you'll be notified when it is time to renew.

Tartan Book Sales

500 Arch Street (800) 233-8467, Ext. 507 (orders)
Williamsport, PA 17705 (717) 326-2905 (inquiries and PA orders)
CK, MC, V, MO, C, B

This mail-order division of the Brodart Company offers hardbound books (returned for whatever reason from libraries) at cut-rate prices. No paperbacks, reference texts, or children's books, but adult fiction, nonfiction, romance, science fiction, Westerns, and mysteries line the shelves of these pages at up to 75 percent off. Free catalog and brochure upon request.

Bridal

You are cordially invited to the wedding of Miss Jane Frick and Mr. Jack Frack. Black Tie requested. He loves me, he loves me a lot. So before you start the quest for the best in gowns and tuxes, flowers and forget-me-knots, something borrowed and something blue, add these sources to your shopping registry.

Albert S. Smyth Co., Inc.
(See **China, Crystal, Silver, and Gifts**, p. **148**.)

Barrons
(See **China, Crystal, Silver, and Gifts**, p. **149**.)

Bridal Secrets
6138 McCart — (817) 346-4848
Ft. Worth, TX 76133 — Cashier's Check, MO, PQ

You do, you do! Say *adieu* to high-price wedding ensembles now that you know that the secret's off the rack. With their over 300 wedding gowns in stock, in sizes 3 to 22, with prices from $500 to $1,600, you can take the walk for less. Prefer to rent? They have everything for the trousseau for a borrowed price of $150 to $290 (values to $1,500). Full service for all your wedding needs, including bridesmaids' dresses, a dress for Mom, veils, slips, garters, shoes, even jewelry can be rented. As seen on *The Maury Povich Show*, it's all available for a one-night stand. Call for details.

Discount Bridal Service
7162 Ambassador Road (800) 441-0102
Baltimore, MD 21207 CK, MO

If you want to dress for less, this is your one-stop shopping source for saving on your wedding dress. Call for the representative nearest you, where you'll meet your friends in the business. These new sources for discounts are called "bridal brokers." And their business is ordering almost any name-brand bridal gown or bridesmaid's dress you can find in the major bridal magazines and have it delivered to your door for 15 percent to 40 percent off retail. Because the gown comes direct from the manufacturer, they require the dress be paid in full, including shipping and handling, before an order is placed.

Eisenberg & Eisenberg
(See **Apparel: Men's**, p. **25**.)

Goldman's
(See **China, Crystal, Silver, and Gifts**, p. **155**.)

House of 1776
(See **China, Crystal, Silver, and Gifts**, p. **157**.)

Lamrite's
565 Broadway (216) 281-3744
Bedford, OH 44146 CK, MC, V, MO, C/$2 (refundable)

Daisy, Daisy, give me your answer do, I'm half crazy over the love of you. It won't be a stylish marriage, but we'll have flowers all over the carriage. Lamrite's carries a full line of wedding supplies discounted approximately 20 percent off retail. There's a large selection of straw hats that you can decorate and a *huge* selection of ribbons. Their Pretty Petals kits for making silk flowers are a particular favorite, with 15 different flowers in 25 colors. There is a

$10 minimum order; orders typically are shipped out the same day they're received. (If more people knew about discounted wedding supplies, do you think there would be fewer tears at weddings?)

Manny's Millinery Supply Co.
(See **Shoes, Boots, and Hats**, p. **445**.)

Michael C. Fina Co.
(See **China, Crystal, Silver, and Gifts**, p. **160**.)

Michele's Silver Matching Service
(See **China, Crystal, Silver, and Gifts**, p. **160**.)

Midas China & Silver
(See **China, Crystal, Silver, and Gifts**, p. **161**.)

Skyline Color Lab
(See **Cameras, Opticals, and Photographic Equipment**, p. **126**.)

Buying Clubs and One-Stop Shopping

If you're on a fast track, why traipse all over town looking for the best buy on a SONY TV? Or a CUISENART? Need a SEIKO watch for the graduate? A pair of PORSCHE CARRERA sunglasses for the track? A BLACK & DECKER tool set, a FISHER-PRICE toy, a PANASONIC microwave, a WURLITZER jukebox, a BOSCH cappuccino/espresso machine, well, why leave home to buy it? There's hardly time to make Jell-O anymore in an average day in the life of the working mom. So, if you want to shop "buy" phone and join the ranks of the armchair bandits, these one-stop shopping sources let your fingers do the talking.

47th Street Photo
455 Smith Street
Brooklyn, NY 11219

(800) 221-7774
(800) 221-3513 (video hotline)
(212) 260-4410 (AK, HI, NY residents)
(212) 398-1410; (212) 608-6934
CK, MC, V, AE, D COD (down payment on credit card; the rest cash), C/$2, B, PQ

A broad selection of top brands, with usually efficient service, a 15-day return/exchange policy, and discounts of 25 percent to 75 percent below retail on cameras, watches, audio/video equipment, computers, copy machines, microwaves, TV games, typewriters, shredders, dictation equipment, health aids, home appliances, and cordless phones make this company a must call. Their selection of electronic products is so extensive, they've got a whole catalog devoted just to video products. (They've also got a separate division to fill corporate, industrial, and institutional requests.)

Bennett Bros., Inc.
30 E. Adams Street (800) 621-2626
Chicago, IL 60603 (312) 621-1600
(inside IL and customer service)

211 Island Road (800) 631-3838 (orders)
Mahwah, NJ 07430 (201) 529-1900 (New Jersey)
CK, MC, V, C/$5 (refundable)

Bennett Brothers has been in business for very nearly 100 years, offering deals on everything from jewelry to exercise equipment. They'll treat you like family with great prices on GORHAM, REED & BARTON, and ONEIDA stainless, silver, and gold flatware; LUNT keepsake silver; SHEFFIELD serving platters; MIKASA and NORITAKE china; MIKASA crystal, and more. Their color catalog's 450 pages also contain bargains on folding chairs, typewriters, headphones, blankets, and so much more merchandise we couldn't possibly list it all. Join up with this family and send bargains worldwide.

Bondy Export Corp.
40 Canal Street (212) 925-7785
New York, NY 10002 CK, MC, V, AE, B, PQ

Small, name-brand appliances discounted 30 percent to 50 percent pay big dividends for Bondy's. The last time we shopped Bondy's, they had the best price anywhere on KRUPS coffee grinders, $17 compared to a normal $32 retail price. In fact, they've got irons, toasters, hair dryers, coffee makers, can openers . . . it looks like a Smithsonian exhibit on "Modern Savings and Loan Gift Giveaways for People Opening New Accounts." Bondy's portfolio includes stock from hundreds of companies, including GE, OSTER, HAMILTON BEACH, CLAIROL, HOOVER, SANYO, SONY, ZENITH, CORNING, FARBERWARE, SMITH-CORONA, and SAMSONITE. Whew! Then it's on to the RAY BAN and PORSCHE CARRERA sunglasses, PANASONIC answering machines and cordless phones, SEIKO and CASIO watches, and ITT telephones. Bondy's specializes in products for use overseas (220 volts). Cameras by CANON, MINOLTA, and POLAROID, plus all kinds of film, make getting a price quote first from Bondy's a wise investment. Turn on to microwave ovens by GE, SHARP, and TOSHIBA; radar detectors by FOX, BELL, and COBRA; and "Walkmans" by SONY, SANSUI, and AIWA. Orders are shipped UPS and can arrive in anywhere between two and seven days. Buy carefully: there are no returns.

C.O.M.B.
720 Anderson Avenue (800) 328-0609
St. Cloud, MN 56935 MC, V, AE, D, C

You could scour the country with a fine-tooth comb and still not uncover a better deal than here. For the past 18 years, this over-the-counter public company (division of Fingerhut) has come up with savings of 50 percent off suggested retail on all the major brands in phones, stereos, TVs, housewares, appliances, computer hardware and software, radios, exercise equipment, and automobiles. Yes, savings of $4,000 on your bigger-ticket items is commonplace. Offering both the manufacturer's warranties and C.O.M.B.'s assurance that you'll be completely satisfied will start the bargains rolling. Call toll-free and receive your order in less than two weeks. Their 48- to 64-page monthly catalog is free, including a biweekly insider's hotline.

Comp-U-Card/Shoppers Advantage
40 Oak View Drive (800) 835-7467
Trumbull, CT 06611 (800) 526-4848 (membership)
(203) 365-2000
CK, MC, V, B, PQ ($49.95 membership)

She'll be Comp-in' round the mountain when she comes! She'll be savin' time and money, she'll be shoppin' for her honey, she'll be Comp-in' round the mountain when she comes! For $49.95 a year, subscribers to this "electronic shopping service" can get all the price quotes they want on over 250,000 items of major brands of appliances, furniture, jewelry, wallpaper, electronics, computers, china, crystal, luggage, audio equipment, etc. Subscribers also get "Best Buys," Comp-U-Card's monthly publication, which lists current bargains (including specials, immediate deals like closeouts and sales). If you've been waiting for a "big brake" on buying a new car, Comp-

U-Card claims they can get it for you from their dealers or yours for $125 over dealer cost (plus destination charges from Detroit to your door). Also, check into their *Travelers Advantage* program for some of the best deals in travel, (800) 548-1116.

Damark International, Inc.

7101 Winnetka Avenue North (800) 729-9000; (612) 566-4940
Brooklyn Park, MN 55428 (612) 531-0380 (FAX)
CK, MC, V, AE, D, MO, C

The UPS man thinks we own stock in Damark because of the number of deliveries we receive from this company. Their monthly "Great Deal" catalogs, rivaling closeout heaven, regularly command our attention. For example, we bought a 386 CORDATA computer for $1,499/retail $2,999, which is the backbone of our shopping research data base. Then, our office phone is often answered by a PANASONIC answering machine that was factory-reconditioned for $29. Then, it's on to the futons, the BOSCH cappuccino/espresso machines, the cookware, the dishes, the binoculars to see the world through rosier-colored glasses, the list is limitless.

Dial-A-Brand

57 South Main (516) 378-9694
Freeport, NY 11520 CK, MC, V, COD, PQ

One ringy-dingy, two ringy-dingies . . . well, you won't get Ernestine, but you can get the low-price lowdown on TVs, air conditioners, major appliances, videotape recorders, or microwaves. Major airlines, universities, and banks all have patronized this company in an effort to save money. Recommended by national consumer groups, Dial-A-Brand's easy to do business with. Just call and give the model number of the item you want, and lo and behold, it's whisked COD to your door in its factory-sealed carton (complete with full warranty and service). They'll exchange at no cost if your purchase is damaged or is defective on delivery. No membership fee required.

Discount Buyers of America Catalog

Dept. 92-D-240, Item #4436 (800) 722-9999
P.O. Box 2020 CK, MC, V,
Brick, NJ 08723 $29.95 + $3.95 shipping and handling

Changing the way Americans shop, this is *the* catalog for value-conscious consumers. As featured in *Family Circle*, you can buy direct from the manufacturers via this catalog. Only quality name brands such as SONY to PANASONIC, SEIKO to CITIZEN, GENIE to KITCHENAID are represented, and you will save up to 50 percent, guaranteed! Or double the refund difference if you find the exact item elsewhere within 30 days. Most of your major shopping categories are covered: appliances, home furnishings, electronics, housewares, garden and lawn supplies, jewelry, luggage, sporting goods, exercise equipment, telephones, cameras, and more. Once a member, you will get the catalog *plus* the full year's membership in the Amerishop Buying Service (a $49.95 value).

Fingerhut
11 McLeland Road (612) 259-2500
St. Cloud, MN 56395 CK, MC, V, AE, D, MO, C

Bed and bath items, housewares, lingerie, power tools, exercise equipment, apparel, you name it, they can put their finger on it. One catalog presented everything but the kitchen sink and included lingerie to a lava lamp. Fingerhut offers monthly payment plans (with approved credit) for merchandise, and prices are reasonable. The color catalog includes a price chart to help you figure out how much you'll end up spending if you pay by the month. From jewelry to vacuum cleaners, you never know what you'll find.

Heartland Industries
820 South 6th Street (800) 229-2901
Hopkins, MN 55343 CK, MC, V, AE, D, MO, C

Heartland is all heart and we love them because they sell their products wholesale (or close to), for the "best values direct to you." Their color catalogs feature consumer electronics, gifts, and household appliances. Exercise equipment, watches, dog houses, radar detectors, slot machines, and even a WURLITZER jukebox, were available at rock-around-the-clock prices. Full refund if returned within 30 days. In-stock items arrive within ten to fourteen days.

Hunter Audio-Photo Ltd.
507 Fifth Avenue (212) 986-1540
New York, NY 10017 CK, MC, V, AE, DC, CB, PQ

Watch out for these a-wrist-ocrats: SEIKO, BULOVA, and CASIO watches at savings of up to 50 percent. Or take a few cheap shots at their complete line of cameras by MINOLTA, MAXXUM, CANON, PENTAX, FUJICA, and NIKON. Feeling adventurous? Take a walk on the wild side with SONY, SANYO, PANASONIC, and TOSHIBA personal stereos, all at discount prices. (SONY Walkmans were a particularly good buy.) You can write your own ticket with pens by MONT BLANC, PARKER, and CROSS, up to 50 percent off. Write for flyers that list their prices. Getting tired? Your days are numbered with adding machines by CANON, SANYO, TEXAS INSTRUMENTS, and HEWLETT-PACKARD. Run that by us one more time: They have over 2,000 movie videos in stock, along with videos for operas and ballets, all at 10 percent to 25 percent below list price. There's no minimum order, but no refunds, either. Orders usually arrive in about two weeks. Tally ho, this Hunter's a fox!

LVT Price Quote Hotline, Inc.

P.O. Box 444, Dept. GBBM — (516) 234-8884
Commack, NY 11725-0444 — CK, MO, B, PQ

No, LVT is not E.T.'s big brother, even though a lot of people do phone, and even though some prices they quote are "out of this world." Given the model number of any item carried by one of the 75 big-name manufacturers they do business with, LVT will quote a price to you, often as much as 40 percent lower than retail. Major appliances, televisions, microwave ovens, typewriters, video recorders, radar detectors, telephone answering machines, computers, calculators, scanners, office equipment, food processors, vacuum cleaners, and air conditioners are all items they regularly handle. Videocassette recorders, telephone answering machines, CUISINARTS, and vacuum cleaners remain their most popular bargains. All merchandise is covered by manufacturers' warranties, but be sure of your selection—all sales are final; there are **no** returns. Orders are processed within 24 hours of receipt of your cashier's check, certified check, or money order. LVT pays all surface UPS shipping charges nationwide. A nice personal touch: If your order is out of stock, LVT will telephone you to inform you of the delay, rather than just send you a postcard like most firms. Write for their brands' list, find out the model numbers of the items you want (cheap!), and phone home to LVT.

Mature Wisdom
P.O. Box 28
340 Popular Street (800) 638-6366
Hanover, PA 17333-0023 MC, V, AE, D, CB, DC, C

You don't need to have earned a Phi Beta Kappa key to know that "Love of wisdom is the guide of life." One person's wisdom is another's folly, so with this catalog, just turn the page. Grow comfortably and in style as this catalog exemplifies. Page after page, you'll see fashions that fit the fuller figure or that fit for comfort, products that make for healthier and easier living, products for the traveling man or his pet, products for the home front, and more. Also, there's an exercise bike with a seat that is easy on the rear end, soft-knit shoes with orthopedic arch supports, a take-your-own blood pressure kit, an anti-wrinkle facial pillow, or a four-wheel cart for groceries. If you're a smart shopper and are blessed with mature wisdom, you'll shop by phone and save both time and money.

RSP Distributing
P.O. Box 2345 (213) 542-0431
Redondo Beach, CA 90278 CK, MO, C/$6 (refundable), B and Sales Kit/$2

Talk about closeout heaven. This 200-page catalog sure offers enough items: jewelry, gifts, novelties, housewares, cutlery, survival products, auto accessories, tools, toys, office supplies and accessories, clothing, electronics . . . whew, exhaustive enough to tire even the consummate shopper. Save up to 90 percent on closeout merchandise; and save up to 60 percent off suggested retail items in this catalog. You can choose to be the ultimate consumer of these goods, or resell them for a profit. Many products covered by factory warranty; others can be returned postpaid to RSP within 30 days for credit.

Service Merchandise
P.O. Box 25130 (800) 251-1212
Nashville, TN 37202-5130 (615) 254-2700 (Nashville residents)
CK, MC, V, D, Service Merchandise Card, C

If service is the state of the art, you can make a date with Service Merchandise, if you're smart. Their catalog is not for the fainthearted, though, with page after page of 4-color discounts on name brand items expansive enough to keep you turning for hours. Every room in the house can be considered fair game. And though known as America's Leading Jeweler, there's more in store than just diamonds and 14 kt. bracelets, earrings, charms, and rings. And remember, you'll never, never, never ring up full price for anything. Visit any one of their almost 400 stores nationwide, or shop-at-home and enjoy the creature comforts for less. SEIKO watches, SONY compact disc players, CANON calculators, AT&T phones, diamonds and 14K gold bracelets, charms, earrings, tennis bracelets, CORNING cookware, ONEIDA flatware, HOOVER vacuum cleaners, BRAUN shavers, VITAMASTER exercise bicycles, NIKON cameras, VERDI luggage . . . the list is endless. Nationwide low-cost product protection plans are also available.

Spiegel, The Ultimate Outlet

P.O. Box 88251 (800) 332-6000 (orders)
1040 W. 35th (605) 348-8100 (customer service)
Chicago, IL 60667-1494 CK, MC, V, AE, Spiegel, C/$3 (refundable)

Who misses paying retail? Not us, especially when Spiegel gets into the off-price game. Kiss full price good-bye and save 30 to 70 percent on everything from dresses to men's suits to Christmas ornaments. It's all in the Ultimate Outlet catalog, featuring style and low prices under one roof. A pair of women's chambray shorts was just $9.99; a floral print cotton/polyester dress was 25 percent off at $49.99; little girls' leggings were $12.90; boys' khaki trousers were $9.99; and men's double-breasted, lined suits were $149.99. Miscellaneous items included a SOUTHWESTERN BELL telephone with built-in answering machine for $109, picture frames, bedding, bookends, lamps, and more. A bunch of bargains for every season, and clothing for all the right reasons. Delivery usually takes three to seven days; items can be returned for a full refund or credit.

Cameras, Opticals, and Photographic Equipment

Don't look to the stars for a good buy on cameras, telescopes, and binoculars. Rather, focus your attention on our tips. Before deciding to order a camera, telescope, or binoculars by mail, visit several shops to look over the selection and get some professional assistance. When you've narrowed your choices down to a few, contact some mail-order sources to see if they stock the equipment you want. Resist the impulse to order over the phone. Always send in your order and keep copies of your correspondence. That way, if anything goes wrong, you'll have records. When your equipment arrives, unpack it carefully and save all the packing materials, in case you need to return it. Don't fill in the warranty cards until you're sure everything is in working order. If you opt to follow these few rules of the trade, with the money you save, you can buy an extra lens!

AAA Camera Exchange
43 Seventh Avenue
New York, NY 10011
(800) 221-9521 (orders only)
(212) 242-5800 (NY residents)
MC, V, D, PQ

Strictly a mail-order house, AAA features triple-good discounts on optics, many from famous makers. Discounted zoom lenses were a particularly good deal. A NIKON 80mm to 200mm f/4.5 zoom retails for $540, while AAA offered a comparable range and speed CANON 70mm to 210mm f/3.8 macro for only $180 and an unnamed 75mm to 205mm f/4.5 for only $140. That's a lot of money saved—and that's only one of the many bargains to snap! Between 30 and 50 brands are carried, and 90 percent of the merchandise pertains to 35mm cameras. Discounts are about 50 percent off, so expect low, low prices. Orders are shipped in 24 to 48 hours, with minimal shipping charges of $3.75. Merchandise is fully guaranteed and can be exchanged within 14 days. However, there is a 15-percent restocking charge on returns. If you know what you LEICA, but you're not a name snob, you'll get the picture fast.

Arlington Camera
544 West Randol Mill Road — (817) 261-8131
Arlington, TX 76011 — CK, MC, V, D, B, PQ

Arlington's staff know their stuff and can lead you on the path to a perfect camera, lens, or other photographic accessory. They maintain a complete inventory of cameras and darkroom supplies at discount prices, and you can bet they have one of the best selections around, including lots of used cameras. Used but not abused is their camera forte. And having only experienced personnel is their forte! Call for a free brochure or price quote.

Astronomics/Christophers, Ltd.
2401 Tee Circle, Suite 106 — (800) 422-7876 (orders)
Norman, OK 73069 — (405) 364-0858 (customer service)
CK, MC, V, AE, D, O, MO, C, PQ

The stellar lineup of savings and selection at this celestial crossing will have you seeing stars. Scores of binoculars, telescopes, and photographic accessories are available at great prices, and if you see any identically equipped models elsewhere for less (including freight charges), they promise to meet or beat the price whenever possible. The information they provide their customers is *quite* extensive; these guys are really heavenly! If you're a serious stargazer or photographer, their knowledgeable staff helps you see the picture clearly. The garden-variety bird-watcher will also benefit with super deals on the perfect pair of binoculars. Take a closer look at Astronomics and you won't see full retail prices. Write or call for a large collection of black-and-white, illustrated information sheets.

B & H Foto Electronics
119 W. 17th Street
New York, NY 10011
(800) 221-5662 (photo orders)
(800) 932-1977 (video orders)
(212) 807-7474 (inquiries)
MC, V, D, C

B & H has seen the light on photographic specialty equipment. They've got light meters, tripods, flash systems, and more by CANON, MINOLTA, NIKON, OLYMPUS, PANASONIC, SONY, POLAROID, HASSELBLAD, LEICA, and others. Everything's discounted, and their prices are often hard to beat. There's a 14-day exchange or refund policy for photo equipment; seven days for video. Most orders are delivered in seven to ten days.

Cambridge Camera Exchange, Inc.
Seventh Avenue and 13th Street
New York, NY 10011
(212) 675-8600
CK, MC, V, COD, C

You'll find some of the sharpest students of camera equipment at Cambridge. While Cambridge isn't in England, or even in Massachusetts, discounts are in the vicinity of 30 percent to 50 percent on cameras, lenses, and lights. We found thousands and thousands of cameras with every known brand present and accounted for. NIKON, PENTAX, and CANON were priced at far below retail; less-expensive, less-well-known equipment was also on a roll. Cambridge is one of the few stores handling European cameras like HANIMEX, PRAKTICA, and EXACTA—and these brands offered the greatest savings. Some of their specials, advertised in magazines and select mailings, are available at truly mind-boggling prices. We saw the NIMSLO Three Dimensional (stereo) camera (which regularly lists for $199.50) for an unbelievable $26.95! Cambridge has a 20-day exchange or refund policy; no restocking charge on returns; and their merchandise is fully guaranteed. Shipping's at least $4.75. They don't quote prices, but they do quote Shakespeare (and sometimes Goethe, Schiller, Pushkin, and La Fontaine). To get a catalog and free mailings, you must tell them the name of the camera you own. They separate their mailings by different camera manufacturers.

Danley's
P.O. Box 4401 (518) 664-2014
Halfmoon, NY 12065 CK, MC, V, MO, C, PQ

Stargazing lately? Or maybe the cost of telescopes is up there with Venus and Mars. Danley's has brought the price of optical products back down to Earth. You'll find the products in their assortment of brochures out of this world—and at up to 50 percent off. BAUSCH & LOMB, LEICA, NIKON, and other names in scopes and accessories are available, and a galaxy of other bargains, too. Bird-watchers, hunters, and sports spectators will goggle over name-brand binoculars like BUSHNELL, CELESTRON, SWIFT, and a flock of others at prices that won't have you up a tree. You can receive price quotes by phone or by sending a SASE. Orders are handled within 24 hours. Get this rare money-saving bird in your sights.

Edmund Scientific Company
101 E. Gloucester Pike (609) 547-8880 (orders)
Barrington, NJ 08007-1380 (609) 573-6260 (customer service)
CK, MC, V, AE, D, CB, MO, C

No book would be complete without a scientific review through one of these two giant catalogs. Serving America's budding science community, they are both *free* and almost a day's reading. The 112-page hobbyist edition and their 188-page industrial/educational catalog are jam-packed with an astronomical collection that would send stargazers to the moon. Tackle any science project with aplomb. Lasers, magnets, microscopes, optical tools and accessories, photography equipment, telescopes, measuring tools, weather and wind-speed instruments, gyroscropes, potato-powered clocks, solar-power products, and lab supplies of every kind. Edmund manufactures over 200 different magnifiers alone, plus low-vision aids for the vision-impaired. Though not discount, it is *the* one-stop shopping source if the subject has a scientific bent. They offer an unconditional warranty for 45 days. Microscopes are under warranty for two years; telescopes for one.

Ewald-Clark
17 W. Church Avenue (703) 342-1829
Roanoke, VA 24011 CK, MC, V, AE, MO, PQ

Seeing eye-to-eye on prices is easier with Ewald-Clark; their photographic and video equipment and binoculars are as much as 40 percent off the list prices. It's easy to see why brands like MINOLTA, FUJI, VIVITAR, HASSELBLAD, KODAK, POLAROID, BRONICA, and CANON are getting snapped up. They carry darkroom supplies, too, and picture-perfect accessories, plus finishing services. Give them a call or send a letter (with SASE) for price quotes, or visit their stores in Roanoke and Blacksburg, Virginia. They ship orders worldwide.

Executive Photo and Supply Corp.

120 W. 31st Street — (800) 223-7323 (orders only)
New York, NY 10001 — (212) 947-5290
MC, V, AE, D, DC, COD, PQ

We always thought executives were known more for flashing rolls of bills than rolls of film, but then again, how else can they see the Big Picture? Executive Photo's a midtown photo dealer with a less buttoned-down outlook. They sell cameras, lenses, film, paper, and photographic accessories, computers, printers, fax machines, and answering machines with names like NIKON, PANASONIC, SHARP, SONY, AT&T, CANON, and TOSHIBA. Prices are 40 to 50 percent lower than their full-retail competition (so there's no competition here!) and on a par with other NYC photo mail-order companies. (Executive sells at dealer's net.) Orders are usually delivered in seven to ten days and manufacturer's warranties apply. Whether you're the Big Cheese, or just someone who gets chewed out a lot, you'll smile anyway.

Focus Electronics

(See **Electronics: Audio/Video/Stereo/TVs**, p. **186**.)

Hirsch Photo

699 Third Avenue — (212) 557-1150
New York, NY 10017 — MC, V, AE, PQ

No "Judd-heads" need to Taxi to this Hirsch outlet. With a no-questions-asked service policy, years of reliable customer recommendations, and bargain prices, you'll cross the photo finish line without the meter running. There are no hidden surprises and over 100 leading brands of camera equipment, including NIKON, PENTAX, MINOLTA, and OLYMPUS. Audio-visual equipment such as projectors is also available. Prices are set at 10 percent above their cost, which translates to hard-to-beat savings. Orders are shipped within 48 hours, and carry a full factory warranty. Refunds are given within ten days; there's no restocking charge.

Hunter Audio-Photo Ltd.
(See **Buying Clubs and One-Stop Shopping**, p. **115**.)

KEH Camera Outlet
2720 Royal Lane, Suite 100 (214) 620-9800
Dallas, TX 75229 (214) 243-3606 (FAX)
MC, V, PQ

Shutter at the thought of shopping elsewhere for used and new equipment at picayunish prices for the professional, serious amateur, and/or collector. All major top-quality and medium-priced cameras, lenses, and accessories are available at this camera consortium of service and savings. Shipping nationwide by UPS and Federal Express. A large inventory as well as a "wish list" kept for personal customer service. Smile, even if you can't be candid, and lens us your ear.

Mardiron Optics
4 Spartan Circle (617) 938-8339
Stoneham, MA 02180 CK, MO, B, PQ

Get a closer look at Mardiron Optics for STEINER and SWIFT binoculars and telescopes at 35 percent to 40 percent off. From mini pocket-sized to long-range instruments, they've got what you need to get the big picture. Bring an 8" by 30" STEINER model, popular with bird-watchers, into focus for $218 (list price was $339). Their brochure bulges with bargain-priced binoculars, telescopes, astronomical telescopes, and night scopes to make certain you find the stars or any other faraway objects. All binoculars and scopes are factory fresh and carry the manufacturer's guarantee. Prices include shipping and handling costs. Mardiron will accept returns for a full refund, provided you contact them concerning your intent to return within 21 days. Personal checks must clear before orders are sent; otherwise, orders go out within two weeks. Immediate response to inquiries.

Olden Camera
1265 Broadway @ 32th Street (212) 725-1234
New York, NY 10001 CK, MC, V, AE, DC, PQ

Olden is one of the oldest of the mail-order camera businesses, and they've got ordering down to a science and selection down to an art. From new NIKONs to old MINOLTAs, if it's photographic in scope, they've got it. Well-known and not-so-known meters and motors, stereo cameras, and slide projectors are displayed in their 200-page catalog, and a leasing plan's available for purchases of $3,000 or more. Video equipment, electronics, computers, business machines, copying equipment, and parts for cameras made from 1900 to the present are also available. There's no set discount, but they claim their prices are "the lowest prices found." Olden's buyer protection plan lets you return equipment in 30 days (in its original condition) with no questions asked. They even take trade-ins through the mail! Olden's a top-notch organization, so you won't expose yourself to any dangers dealing with them.

Orion Telescope Center
P.O. Box 1158 (408) 464-0466
Santa Cruz, CA 95061 CK, MC, V, MO, C, PQ

Orion belts high prices on telescopes and accessories with discounts of up to 40 percent in their catalog. Set your sights well below average retail and reach for Orion's own brand, as well as EDMUND, CELESTRON, and MEADE telescopes, among others. Camera goodies are also available from PENTAX, SWIFT, BUSHNELL, OPTOLYTH, and more. And look for binoculars of all kinds; the selection won't disappoint you. Orion's catalog (over 60 pages) will have you reaching for the stars, even on a down-to-earth budget. Customer satisfaction is guaranteed; call or write for a price quote on institutional orders.

Porter's Camera Stores, Inc.
P.O. Box 628 (800) 553-2001; (319) 268-0104
Cedar Falls, IA 50613 CK, MC, V, D, MO, C

If it's stability you're after, try Porter's. A company born in 1914 isn't likely to vanish anytime soon. Old-fashioned deals fill their catalog, which resembles a Sunday newspaper supplement. Camera equipment and extras were viewed around 35 percent off, including darkroom equipment, camera cases, lens cleaner kits, filters, carrying straps, lighting accessories, lenses, chemicals, and a variety of instructional pamphlets. There's even a consulting service to answer your questions. Their catalog is free in America; $3 in Canadian funds (all orders must be paid in U.S. funds, however). Orders are shipped worldwide with a minimum of $100.

Ritz Camera
6711 Ritz Way — (301) 784-1441
Betsville, MD 20705 — CK, MC, V, AE, D, C

With the lowest prices, guaranteed for 30 days after the sale, you'll be inclined to focus on Ritz for your camera needs. INFINITI, MINOLTA, NIKON, CANON, KODAK, and OLYMPUS are some of the flashy names you'll find in their catalog. Picture new photographic equipment and accessories for less and start clicking on the Ritz. Get the picture? Retail stores nationwide but shop at home for putting on the Ritz-for-less. Plus the catalog's free.

Scope City
679 Easy Street — (805) 522-6646
Simi Valley, CA 93065 — CK, MC, V, AE, D, MO, C

Scope out Scope City and you'll see deals on telescopes, binoculars, and accessories. CELESTRON, MEADE, QUESTAR, SIMMONS, LEICA, OPTOLYTH, and other celestial names light up at up to 45 percent off. In the accessories department, look into lenses, charts, instructional manuals, and more. Satisfaction is guaranteed; returns are accepted for exchanges, refunds, or credit within 30 days. Find your way to their catalog and set your sites on some winning deals.

Skyline Color Lab
9016 Prince William Street — (703) 631-2216
Manassas, VA 22110 — CK, MC, V, AE, MO, C

Discounts of up to 30 percent are developing at Skyline (formerly ABC Photo Service); it's all part of the process of film processing. They process color or black-and-white film, duplicate slides or negatives, make enlargements, and much more, for up to 30 percent less than you'd pay elsewhere. Print packages, mounting on canvas stretchers or canvas panels, processing of underexposed film, and wedding packages are just a few of their special services. Check out their catalog and take a shot at mail-order film services. If your film is lost or damaged, alas, they'll only replace it with a new roll; there's a $25 minimum order. They'll ship anywhere in the world, but CODs are only accepted in the continental U.S.

Solar Cine Products, Inc.
4247 South Kedzie Avenue
Chicago, IL 60632
(800) 621-8796 (orders only)
(312) 254-8310 (inquiries)
CK, MC, V, DC, D, C, PQ

Get some variety in your mailbox and focus on these star performers! Solar Cine carries a full line of 35mm accessories, including screens, tripods, camera bags, and over 2,000 other items. (Photofinishing, accessories, processing, film, and video transfers are what they're best known for.) Film for movies and cameras are probably one of their best buys. Brands include KODAK, MINOLTA, CANON, PENTAX, and POLAROID, and discounts range from 40 percent to 60 percent. Most orders are shipped in 12 to 48 hours. Refunds are given only when the item proves defective.

Sugra Photo-Systems
P.O. Box 8051
Pittsburgh, PA 15206
(800) 221-9695 (orders only)
(412) 571-3770
CK, MC, V, AE, D, MO, C

Sugra is *the* camera specialty equipment store. They don't sell cameras, but they *do* sell a lot of camera accessory items. In fact, they pioneered the field of photographic accessories over 40 years ago. Their catalog displays items that will make your cameras (and you) expand your creativity to the max. They have more special filters than a Japanese tour group has cameras. Sugra does much of their own manufacturing, but they also carry SHARP, BENBO, MITSUBISHI, CLEARLIGHT, and FUJIMOTO. There's no minimum order; most orders are shipped within four to seven working days. Exchanges are accepted with prior authorization only.

T. M. Chan & Co.
(See **Jewelry**, p. **342**.)

Wall Street Camera Exchange
82 Wall Street (800) 221-4090; (212) 344-0011
New York, NY 10005 CK, MC, V, AE, D, DC, COD, C, PQ (SASE)

Go for broker at this Wall Street institution. Though they were named the largest LEICA camera dealer in the country in past years, they also carry other name brands such as NIKON, ROLLEI, HASSELBLAD, MAMIYA, OLYMPUS, and ROLEX. This wall-to-wall collection in their 100-page catalog includes photo cameras, lenses, accessories, camcorders, video cameras, video recorders, personal copiers, typewriters, keyboards, scanners, radar detectors, and more and can save you up to 75 percent off retail. Exchanges accepted within ten days of receipt of merchandise. Used photo equipment bought and sold. Repair department on the premises. Manufacturers' warranties where applicable and extended warranties available. Minimum order, $25.

Westside Camera Inc.
2400 Broadway (212) 877-8760
New York, NY 10024 CK, MC, V, AE, MO, PQ

Cool your jets and stop fighting for the lowest prices. This gang's got it, man. There's a place for us, and it's here. Westside's story is selling all photographic equipment and supplies at 25 percent to 30 percent lower than retail. Brands include camera gang leaders like NIKON, CANON, MINOLTA, and OLYMPUS. Discounted darkroom supplies like chemicals and equipment will enlighten you to the savings possibilities and, for once, keep you in the dark. (Now you won't have to be out cruising the streets.) Oriental paper, SPRINT chemicals, and a full line of KODAK products all are discounted, too. A $25 minimum order will initiate you into the Westside brotherhood. (Are you man enough to handle it?) Be tough; write to Barry Glick and ask for a price quote. That love affair with a NIKON doesn't have to be just a dream.

Carpets and Rugs

Does the price of wall-to-wall carpeting drive you up *the wall? Going barefoot on the carpet is fun (unless it's because after buying a carpet, you can't afford shoes!). Oriental, dhurrie, custom area-rug prices can be a knotty problem, but not if you shop by mail. Beautiful, high-quality rugs can be shipped to you (by truck—there's no such thing as a flying carpet). Why not try it? Instead of just being bugged, you'll be snug as a bug in a rug.*

Access Carpets
P.O. Box 1007 (404) 277-7785
Dalton, GA 30722 CK, MC, V, B

When you have Access to these guys, 30 percent to 70 percent savings on floor coverings are no big deal. Access Carpets has been rolling out the deals since 1981. They won't walk all over your budget, with an average of 40 percent off on carpet, hardwood floor coverings, padding, and vinyl, with major names including BRUCE, MANNINGTON, and CHICKASAW HARDWOOD. All carpets are first quality, and they carry the full manufacturers' warranties. Free samples and a brochure are available; most orders arrive in a week to ten days.

Bearden Bros. Carpet Corp.

3200-A Dug Gap Road
Dalton, GA 30720

(800) 433-0074
(404) 277-3265 (in GA)
(404) 277-1745 (FAX)
CK, MC, V, AE, D, O, MO, B, PQ

Let Bearden help you sweep full-price carpeting under the rug. They can save you as much as 80 percent on names like MOHAWK, ARMSTRONG, BURLINGTON, CABIN CRAFTS, MONTICELLO, J.P. STEVENS, and others. If you already know the manufacturer, style and color codes, and square yardage needed including padding, they can give you a price quote over the phone (make sure they also send you a written confirmation of it); otherwise, send for their free brochure. They ship anywhere in the U.S. (including Alaska and Hawaii) and customer satisfaction is guaranteed.

Braided Rugmaker

369 Roosevelt Avenue
Pawtucket, RI 02860

(401) 723-6734
CK, MC, V, MO

The Braided Rugmaker does just that—custom-braided rugs in many different configurations. Savings on comparable rugs anywhere from 50 percent to 70 percent. Send color swatch and size information when ordering, along with a $10 deposit (deductible from order). They'll send back a price quote including braid sample and diagram. A 50-percent deposit is then required with order; balance upon delivery. Save the COD fee by paying in full in advance. No returns on custom orders unless defective or damaged in shipment. Allow eight weeks for delivery.

Great Buys readers: Receive FREE 2 × 3-foot rug when purchasing any room-size rug measuring 5 × 8 feet or larger.

Carpet Club

11431 LBJ Freeway @ Jupiter
Garland, TX 75041

(800) 98-CARPET
(214) 840-3200
CK, MC, V, AE, D, PQ
(add 5 percent for credit card purchases)

This Carpet Club is the one to flat-out join if you are tired of being floored by the high cost of carpeting and other floor coverings. No membership fee. No long wait at the check-out counter. No more driving all over town to compare prices. This is the place that stands head and shoulders over the competition. Shop by phone for name brand carpets, vinyls, wallcoverings, hardwood floors, and marble and ceramic tiles at wholesale prices. Choose names like CABIN CRAFTS, L.D. BRINKMAN, SALEM, STEVENS, GALAXY, HORIZON, WORLD, EVANS & BLACK and more. Names that have stood the test of time. Nationwide shipping. And remember, no sales tax outside Texas (another possible 8 percent savings.)

Great Buys readers: Receive an additional 10 percent off with all orders.

Central Carpet
424-426 Columbus Avenue @ 81st Street (212) 787-8813
New York, NY 10024 MC, V, PQ

Across from the Planetarium in NYC, you'll find deals that are out of this world on rugs. These aren't just any rugs; they're all rare antiques and semi-antiques, and they're discounted 30 percent to 60 percent off the appraised values. Their motto, "8,000 rugs; 8,000 discounts." Call for a price quote and start putting your foot down on full prices. Some of these even look . . . price-less!

Cherry Hill Furniture, Carpet & Interiors
(See **Furniture and Accessories**, p. **250**.)

Elkes Carpet Outlet, Inc.
1585 Bethel Drive (919) 887-5054
High Point, NC 27260 CK, B, PQ

You've heard of having an uncle in the business? Well, now you have an ant-ler in the business! These Elkes can rack up 30-percent to 50-percent savings on first-quality carpeting and other floor coverings, and even more on top-choice irregulars, close-outs, discontinued colors, and promotional styles of name-brand contract carpet. They access most major lines (including commercial, industrial, and institutional lines) with names like CORONET, DOWNS/CARPET, PHILADELPHIA, WORLD, or ARMSTRONG. The selection is excellent; restocking charges vary between mills if after delivery you decide to return. Ordinarily, orders are delivered in two or three weeks. If you've been hunting and hunting, trying to track down a good buy on carpet (and you carribou-t savings on major brands), this just might be the place where you can bag your limit. And if you don't see what you want, call or write for a price quote.

Factory-Direct-Carpet-Outlet
P.O. Box 417 (800) 225-4351
Miles City, MT 59301 (800) 233-0208 (in MT)
CK (certified) and MO preferred
CK, MC, V (5% added to purchase), B/PQ

If you walk Miles and Miles in your sleep, be sure to buy your carpet cheap. This carpet company cushions the blow of steep carpet prices with over 40 years in the business. They promise all carpeting is first quality with full manufacturer's warranty and costs just $1 a square yard over dealer's cost. They special order from every major mill and have the carpet directly shipped to you. All you need is to take down the information off the back of the carpet sample you see in a retail store and provide the following: manufacturer's name; style name and numbers; color name and numbers; and also, if possible, the RN number (which is a 5-digit number). Their price quote is for delivered carpet direct to you. They even provide bank references at the First Security Bank (406) 232-2620 (ask for Alan Holom) and the Montana Department of Consumer Affairs (406-444-4312). Personal checks must clear before orders are sent.

Floorcrafters Wholesale
P.O. Box 644 (707) 468-0615
Ukiah, CA 95482 CK, D, MC, V, MO, C/$1 (refundable), PQ

Floorcrafters Wholesale is blind to regular retail. All they see are window treatments, carpeting, and vinyl and hardwood flooring for as much as—no, we're not kidding—75 percent off. Six years in the business has given them time to meet big names, like GALAXY, HORIZON, CONGOLEUM, BALI, QUEEN, and CALADIUM (among others), and to introduce them to you at unbelievable prices. They catalog their achievements, and request a $100 minimum order. Write or call for a price quote if you know the lowdown (manufacturer's name, style, and color) of what you want.

Guaranteed Floorcovering
3434 Doug Drive (800) 828-5610; (214) 638-7847 (RUGS)
Dallas, TX 75247 CK, MC, V, AE, D, Financing, PQ

For over twenty years, this company has been laying out the red carpet in homes from coast to coast. With names you can stand on, MOHAWK, ARMSTRONG, CORONET, SALEM, L.D. BRINKMAN, GALAXY, QUEEN, CABIN CRAFTS, in blues, grays, greens, patterns, sculptures, berbers, you name it, they can ship it. Also wood flooring by BRUCE, HARTCO, and ANDERSON, and vinyl by ARMSTRONG, CONGOLEUM, and MANNINGTON. Though you'll need to secure installation locally, Guaranteed guarantees you'll be standing on the best-for-less.

Johnson's Carpets, Inc.
3239 S. Dixie Highway (800) 235-1079; (404) 277-2775
Dalton, GA 30720 CK, MC, V, AE, D, MO, B, PQ

Why is Dalton such a carpet hot spot? Only Georgians know for sure, but here's another biggie in the savings department. Yep, y'all, up to 80 percent off retail on carpeting, custom-made rugs, padding, and installation necessities. They can give you a price quote if you know the style and color codes, manufacturer, and square yardage you'll need. Call for a brochure before you get floored by department-store prices.

K & D Supply Co.
1440A Industrial Drive (800) 477-1400; (704) 846-4345
Mathews, NC 28105 CK, MC, V, MO, C/$4

Rug rats everywhere will appreciate these genuine Oriental and flat braid rugs. K & D will supply you with a 72-page color catalog featuring a large selection of rug styles, sizes, and colors only when you fork over $4. However, since our deadline was upon us, we couldn't wait for the catalog and just requested information. Lots of luck! Questioning got us nowhere even though we passed the Dale Carnegie course in winning friends and influencing retailers.

Loftin-Black Furniture Co.
(See **Furniture and Accessories**, p. **257**.)

National Carpet
1384 Coney Island Avenue (718) 253-5700
Brooklyn, NY 11230 MC, V, MO, C/$3

Go National and save on rugs, rugs, and more rugs. Rug rats, bug out on retail; up to 40 percent off is more like it, and KARASTAN rugs are just the ticket. Satisfaction is guaranteed on these gorgeous designs; $3 will get you a catalog. It's no cover-up! Check out a KARASTAN for less.

National Furniture Gallery
(See **Furniture and Accessories**, p. **258**.)

Priba Furniture
(See **Furniture and Accessories**, p. **261**.)

S & S Mills
P.O. Box 1568 (800) 241-4013; (404) 277-3677
Dalton, GA 30722 CK, MC, V, D, MO, C (w/samples)

Be snug as a bug with a rug from this carpet manufacturer. Deep in the heart of the carpet capital of the world, S & S Mills stands on its own square yards. Comparable to ARMSTRONG and other better brands, S & S manufactures wall-to-wall savings of at least 50 percent. Call toll-free for your free carpet swatches and delivery within seven to ten days. Experienced service representatives can answer all your questions, and you can expect every style of carpet, whether it's DUPONT, ANTRON, STAINMASTER, or OLEFIN. Average homeowners can save $3,000 to $6,000, but even a small roomful can net you big bucks.

Sutton-Council Furniture
(See **Furniture and Accessories**, p. **265**.)

Tibetan Refugee Self-Help Centre
Havelock Villa 65 Gandhi Road (91)3542346 DE: Office
Darjeeling-734101 India CK, C/$2.50

Learn about "the courageous plight of the Tibetan people driven from their homeland by invaders in 1959." What price knowledge? Just $2.50, and for your money you can also learn about the many wonderful crafts made at this Centre. The Centre was created to help the Tibetan refugees not only earn a living, but also to preserve their craftmanship and cultural heritage. Using vegetable dyes and wools imported from Nepal, the refugees make a beautiful assortment of rugs. Complicated designs sell for about $10.70 per square foot. Add 10 percent for carpets larger that 50 square feet, and 5 percent if it's a custom-made carpet. Either bank transfers to the Grindlays Bank P.L.C., Darjeeling, or checks are acceptable payment.

Turner Tolson, Inc.
(See **Furniture and Accessories**, p. **266**.)

Village Carpet
1114 Conover Boulevard West (704) 465-6818
Conover, NC 28613 CK, MO, B

People are flocking to this village for up to 50 percent off and more. First-quality brands of carpet include ALADDIN, CABIN CRAFTS, DIAMOND, GALAXY, PHILADELPHIA, QUEEN, BIGELOW, MOHAWK, SALEM, WORLD, WONDAWEAVE, SUTTON and HORIZON. We found same-style, same-manufacturer carpet that retailed for $14.99 a yard for just $8.99 a yard at Village. Carpet is returnable if manufacturing defects are visible. There are minimum charges in some cases; they'll gladly estimate the cost of shipping your order (the savings in sales tax usually offsets shipping charges).

Warehouse Carpets, Inc.
P.O. Box 3233 (800) 526-2229 (outside GA)
Dalton, GA 30721 (404) 226-2229 (GA residents)
CK, C, PQ

Roll out quality carpet at 30 to 40 percent off. Every carpet this company sells is first quality, no off-brands or seconds. They roll with such major lines as QUEEN, SALEM, MOHAWK, HORIZON, EVANS & BLACK, GALAXY, LEES, CABIN CRAFTS, and PHILADELPHIA. Vinyl, too, by ARMSTRONG, MANNINGTON, TARKETT, and CONGOLEUM. These generous discounts are made possible in part by their convenient location in Dalton, Georgia, where many large carpet manufacturers are established. The shipping charge is often offset by the tax break incurred from out-of-state purchases. Simply specify the manufacturer's name and the carpet's style name, and Warehouse Carpets will almost invariably secure the same carpet at a substantial savings. There is no minimum order. Refunds are accepted only on defective merchandise; delivery usually takes between two and three weeks.

Weissrugs/ The Area Rug Store
2621 Murray Avenue (800) 422-7848
Pittsburgh, PA 15217 CK, MC, V, PQ

Don't let them pull the rug from under you. Selected carpet mills and area rugs are up to 50 percent off retail and sport such stellar names as KARASTAN, CABIN CRAFTS, MASLAND, COURISTAN, HELIOS, and CAPEL. All prices quoted include freight. And they stand behind every carpet they sell.

Young's Furniture and Rug Co.
(See **Furniture and Accessories**, p. **268**.)

Zarbin and Associates, Inc.
(See **Furniture and Accessories**, p. **268**.)

Cars and Auto Supplies

Everybody has heard horror stories about auto mechanics. And often it's true: Some mechanics couldn't fix a martini, let alone a Mercury. So what can you do to protect yourself—short of enrolling in a series of do-it-yourself auto repair courses at the local community college? One alternative is to decrease your chances of getting an incompetent mechanic. For three minutes of your time and the price of a postage stamp, you can get a listing of local service mechanics who've been certified in specialized areas of training. Write to the National Institute of Automotive Service Excellence, 1825 K Street N. W., Washington, DC 20006, or call (202) 833-9646 for more information. The name of the company they work for, address, and telephone number are given.

American Auto Brokers
24001 Southfield Road, Suite 110 — (313) 569-5900
Southfield, MI 48075 — CK, Cashier's Check
MO, PQ (SASE)

As a veteran in the business of managing car dealerships for more than 35 years, Mel Palmer decided to open his own company, American Auto Brokers. Knowing the industry inside and out, Palmer made his move and was, in fact, instrumental in lifting the ban on auto brokering. Mel and his brokering crew negotiate deals nationwide. You can save anywhere from $150 to $4,000, depending, of course, on how much margin there is to play with and whether or not the car is in great demand. A firm quotation can be issued in writing for a small fee. American Auto Brokers deal in all makes, domestic and foreign autos, and in all styles as well—cars, trucks, and vans. If you have not arranged your own financing, GMAC, Ford Motor Credit, or AMC Credit is available on domestic automobiles. The order is placed upon receipt of deposit, which is refundable if the order is canceled within 72 hours. Delivery, which is made to any dealership in the country and includes manufacturer's warranty, takes approximately six weeks. When you ask for your price quote, be sure to have specific information on model and options desired.

AutoVantage
P.O. Box 540227 — (800) 999-4CAR
Houston, TX 77254-0227 — MC, V, DC

The advantage is yours when you know a fair price from a raw deal on a used car you're buying, selling, or trading. AutoVantage is an automotive service plan whose members enjoy services like a free Used Car Summary, plus discounts on car maintenance services—10 percent off on services from GOODYEAR and FIRESTONE, car painting at Maaco, Aamco transmission maintenance, and Meineke muffler service. Specials include deals on tires, car rentals, and more. The only catch is that you must use MasterCard, Visa, or Diners Club to take advantage of most of their discounts. Call for details on becoming a member.

Belle Tire Distributors, Inc.
Performance Dept.
3500 Enterprise Drive — (313) 271-9400
Allen Park, MI 48101 — CK, MO, PQ

These belles are properly at-tired by such companies as MICHELIN, BF GOODRICH, GOODYEAR, FIRESTONE, UNIROYAL, PIRELLI, and KELLY SPRINGFIELD, priced up to 35 percent lower than most full-priced stores. (Check local sources, however, before purchasing long distance to ensure maximum savings.) This company's been in business for 70 years and rotated performance tires long before other companies jumped on the cycle. They're experts when it gets down to where the rubber meets the road. Shipping's by UPS and costs $20 per tire. Tires are shipped within 24 hours.

Capital Cycle Corporation
P.O. Box 528 (703) 444-2500
Sterling, VA 22170-0528 CK, MC, V, AE, MO, C

Too pooped to pop a wheelie? Here's a spokes-person for your mechanical cause! Capital Cycle got us charged up with the largest inventory of genuine and original BMW parts in the U.S.—and at up to 65 percent off the regular BMW list price. (They're the only BMW parts dealership in the U.S. with discounted prices.) Frankly, we aren't too exhausted to give a muffled roar of approval: Easy Riders like us don't need any price shocks to get us all choked up. You can rev up your classy chassis here with everything from a vacuum screw gasket to telescopic fork parts. They carry over 4,000 parts in stock and promise clutch performances on mail telephone orders. The catalog we got was (what else?) en-cycle-opedic. There's a $20 minimum order. Orders are shipped the same day.

Cellular World
(See **Electronics, Audio/Video/Stereo/TVs**, p. **185**.)

Cherry Auto Parts
5650 N. Detroit Avenue (800) 537-8677
Toledo, OH 43612 (800) 472-8639 (in Ohio)
(419) 476-7222
CK, MC, V, D, MO, PQ

Say "cherry-o" to high-priced auto parts! Cherry has been in business for more than 45 years, both as a store and as a mail-order (price quote) business, so they're well worth a pit stop. Cherry offers sweet deals on a large selection of quality used parts for foreign cars and trucks—there are no lemons here! Small electric parts are in particularly abundant supply. Discounts on most items are in the 50 percent to 80 percent range, since the parts are used. Most parts have been surgically removed from hapless autos that have met untimely deaths on the roadway; they are then transplanted into other autos. They also carry a full line of rebuilt foreign starters and alternators. Used engines and transmissions are perhaps the best bets: They're certainly the biggest. There's a $15 minimum order; orders are shipped the next day. Parts are guaranteed to be in good working order.

Clark's Corvair Parts, Inc.

Route 2 (413) 625-9776
Shelburne Falls, MA 01370 CK, MC, V, D, MO, COD, C/$4

Have you been racing all over the country to find parts for your Corvair? We have some great news for all of you die-hard Corvair owners. Take a u-turn and gas up on some great savings with the Clarks. Their Corvair parts company will keep you on the track and running smoothly. They stock enough parts to fill Indianapolis. Over 4,500 different items: mechanical, trim, interior, suspension, emblems, and over 1,000 items that are not available anywhere else in the world. With a pit crew like the Clarks, you'll stay in the lead. Brands like DELCO, TRW, GENERAL MOTORS, CHEVROLET, and MOOG will keep you in tune. The Clarks make hundreds of their parts themselves, including the upholstery. They've got you covered as well as making the collectible Corvair affordable. Their 400-page catalog with over 1,000 photos and sketches is worth its weight in parts. You can find anything you need at a savings of up to 40 percent. However, you may find a knock or two in their return policy. All returned parts must be in perfect condition, and a 15-percent restocking fee is charged. No returns on electrical items or incorrectly ordered parts. Speed off to savings and the checkered flag.

Clinton Cycle & Salvage, Inc.

9405-A Livingston Road (301) 248-0900
Fort Washington, MD 20744 CK, MC, V, AE, D, COD, B, PQ

Here's something that'll make you want to crack up! Clinton's a mail-order used motorcycle part business that specializes in Japanese 250cc and larger street motorcycles. (KAWASAKI, SUZUKI, YAMAHA, and HONDA are the makes.) They offer 40 percent to 60 percent off retail parts; the prices vary with the condition of the particular part. Satisfaction's guaranteed or your money back when you return the item within two weeks of purchase: There's a restocking charge when a customer changes his mind. Most orders are received within seven to ten days; there's no minimum order. If new (and very expensive) parts aren't needed for your bike's image, you might drop a note to Clinton about the state of the economy.

Consumer Reports Used Car Price Service

(900) 446-0500

Consumer Reports offers via a 900 number (it'll cost you $1.50 per minute, and the typical call lasts about five minutes) the current market value for that used car you've been thinking about. Whether you're buying from a dealer or an individual, the price you'll hear is updated frequently and takes into account mileage, major options, and general condition of the vehicle. Too, this information could be available FREE from your loan officer at a bank. Either way, though, you can use the information to your "savings advantage" and at least not pay *too* much. You will also hear information about the frequency of repair records as compiled by the editors of *Consumer Reports*.

Crutchfield Corporation

1 Crutchfield Park
Dept. EA
Charlottesville, VA 22906

(800) 336-5566 (catalog requests)
CK, MC, V, AE, D, O, DC, CB, MO, C

Use this crutch to play the field and save big on an extensive line of car stereo and home audio equipment. Highly trained technical advisers run the company and answer questions about Crutchfield's products. Even with this attention to service, prices are still very reasonable. Crutchfield's catalog looks and reads like *Stereo Review* magazine. Helpful buying tips are interspersed throughout. They're authorized dealers for all their products. Brands we found in audio components included: SONY, PIONEER, and KENWOOD, among others. In-dash car stereos are a big seller; Crutchfield carries an astounding selection from KENWOOD, CLARION, JVC, JENSEN, PIONEER, SANYO, and SONY. Crutchfield also offers a free installation guide, making it easy to install your own car stereo system and save over buying it from a new-car dealership. In addition, Crutchfield carries video products from JVC, SHARP, and PIONEER, and telephones and answering machines by SONY, PANASONIC, KENWOOD, and AT&T. If you are buying a stereo for home or car, send for this catalog first. Everyone needs a crutch when it comes to saving money, and they ship in 24 hours.

Edgewood National, Inc.
623 Meridian East (206) 927-3388
Puyallup, WA 98371 CK, MC, V, AE, D, MO, PQ

Some may say parts is parts, but Edgewood is edging out the competition with up to 40 percent off on auto parts for four-wheel-drive vehicles. Considering their merchandise is all brand-spanking new, that's quite a revolution. They even sell engines! Nearly 30 years in the business and a staff that knows their stuff make this a primo candidate for parts at prima facie discounts. Call or write for a price quote. Returns are accepted, provided they're authorized in advance.

European Parts Specialist
P.O. Box 6783 (800) 334-2749
Santa Barbara, CA 93160 MC, V, AE, COD (cash), C/$3

Ach tune-up? Is your Gesund t-heit enough? *Nein? Days ist nicht gut!* This mail-order company carries BMW parts exclusively. They have 'em all, ranging from engine to muffler to wheels to roof. Discounts of 10 percent to 30 percent will set your engine to purring like a kitten. There's a 15-percent restocking charge if you change your mind about an order after shipping; most orders are shipped within 48 hours. Their 60-page catalog costs just $3, so mail for it, *macht schnell!*

Explosafe Gasoline Cans
44 County Line Road (516) 454-0880
Farmingdale, NY 11735 CK, F, PQ

We'd like to say business is booming here, but when you're selling explosion-proof gasoline cans, the fewer booms the better. "Most ordinary gas cans emit dangerous fumes and do not have anti-explosion systems," we learned from their flier. "Explosafe cans won't explode . . . the special vent prevents escape of dangerous explosive fumes." The gasoline cans are metal and have a plastic spout, and are manufactured by KIDDE. The cans have been featured on "That's Incredible!" (remember that one?), which is more than can be said about your ordinary cans. Better yet, their prices are 50 percent off retail. Five-gallon gas cans cost $22 ($44 retail), while 2.5 gallon cans cost $18 ($36 retail). Shipping is $4/can; expect delivery seven to ten days after you place your order. Now "That's Incredible!"

Freedman Seating Company
4043 N. Ravenswood (312) 929-6100
Chicago, IL 60613 CK, MC, V, C

Have a seat . . . or two! This company offers ready- and custom-made seating for all vehicles. A full range of styles makes it simple to find just the seating arrangements you're looking for. Manufactured by Freedman, color swatches are available upon request to match your decorator auto needs. Seats, sofa beds, benches, dinettes, and pedestals for vans, recreational vehicles, four-wheel-drive vehicles, and trucks are all included in the selection. Choose elegant wood-trimmed velvet seats, plush pillow-back chairs and sofa beds, tweed and vinyl combinations, or durable vinyl seats and dinette sets. Fabric and vinyl to match all seats are available by the yard, and accessories let you adapt and adjust your vehicle's seating arrangements with swivels, pedestals, and more. Designer lighting, trays, and tables add the finishing touches. Illinois residents add 8 percent tax; prices include shipping and handling. Guarantees available upon request; orders filled within one week.

Go Cart
P.O. Box 405 (402) 289-3994
Elkhorn, NE 68022 CK, MC, V, AE, MO, C/$3

Wheels of fortune? Well, probably not, but you *can* save 20 percent on a go-cart kit complete with a welded frame, three-horsepower engine, clutch, and chain. Or order a la cart without the engine. They also make fiberglass mini-cars. Orders are shipped direct from the factory and usually take two weeks to arrive.

Impco, Inc.
909 Thompson Street (800) 243-1220; (713) 868-1638
Houston, TX 77007-5630 CK, MC, V, MO, COD, C

Impco has spritely savings on parts for your Mercedes-Benz, provided it's a diesel model made between 1977 and 1985. Flipping through their color catalog, you'll see an average discount of 30 percent on everything from a kit to build your own engine, to tools and electronic parts, to upholstery cleaner. And the parts are all brand-new, not reconditioned. Be aware that there's a minimum of $20 on phone orders. Customer satisfaction is guaranteed; returns are accepted within 30 days on unused goods if authorized. They ship worldwide.

J. C. Whitney & Co.
1917-19 Archer Avenue
P.O. Box 8410 — (312) 431-6102 (orders only, 24 hours)
Chicago, IL 60680 — MC, V, AE, D, O, C

When your car budget's been totaled, and the sum is greater than the parts, call J. C. If you've got a car, RV, or motorcycle, J. C. Whitney has everything you've always wanted to put on it, but didn't know where to get it. You'll find all sorts of customizing items from hood ornaments to fuzzy dice in their 100-page catalog. Or maybe you'd like to fix up your older car with replacement parts like ball joints, convertible tops, seat covers, or new carpets—the company (established in 1915) has perhaps the largest selection of automotive parts and accessories around. And don't forget they have all the special tools necessary for these jobs. J. C. Whitney is chock full of parts for all cars, foreign and domestic, going back to the Model T; there are hundreds of brands. Prices can range up to 60 percent off, although the average is probably more like 20 percent off. Orders are shipped within 48 hours of receipt; there's a full refund if you're not satisfied. Friendly order-takers take orders 24 hours a day, seven days a week.

Ken Tompor Auto Broker
4140 S. Lapeer Road — (313) 373-8010
Orion, MI 48057 — (out of Detroit area, call collect)
Terms available

Ken Tompor, the long-established pro of wheeling and dealing, is your personalized car connection. A legitimate $50 over dealer invoice on any car can be delivered to you anywhere as quickly as 24 hours. Most custom orders take four to six weeks, however, and come equipped with all factory warranties and service guarantees. The only difference is . . . you haven't paid for the dealer's expensive overhead, advertising costs, or salesmen's commissions, but you do pay for the car, period! No hassle, no computer price quotes to pay for, be it a FORD or a FERRARI. Specialty cars are fast replacing art as the collector's choice for investment appreciation—also a specialty service at Ken Tompor Auto Broker Company.

Manufacturer's Supply
(See **Hardware, Tools, and Home Improvement**, p. **291**.)

Nationwide Auto Brokers
17517 W. 10 Mile Road (800) 521-7257
Southfield, MI 48075 (313) 559-6661 (MI residents)
MC, V, D

In business for 22 years, Nationwide is one of the largest and best-known car brokerage firms. (They're even computerized!) For $9.95 you'll receive a form showing all the available optional equipment for the car you want. Then, check off the options desired and return it. You will get a personalized price quote for a car that's equipped just the way the doctor ordered. Nationwide charges just $50 to $125 over factory invoice on American-made cars; $125 to $300 on most foreign makes. Certain cars produced in limited quantities aren't always available. Foreign and domestic cars, trucks, and vans are available, and all come with factory warranty. Domestic autos can be financed with GMAC or Ford Motor Credit. Most deposits are about $100, but sometimes are as high as $500. Prices are quoted FOB Detroit, or delivery will be made to your local dealer. A telephone staff is available to answer your questions.

Racer Wholesale
10390 Alpharetta Street, Suite 620 (404) 886-RACE
Roswell, GA 30075 CK, MC, V, D, MO, COD,
C/$2 (free to readers)

Play it safe with Racer and save on auto racing safety equipment and accessories. You can take the lead position when saving from 40 percent to 70 percent on helmets, timing devices, filters, fuel pumps, fans, suits, harnesses, seats, steering wheels, mufflers, lighting, and more. Race to the deals from FUELSAFE, FLOWMASTER, SIMPSON, BELL, and others. Racer's been crossing the finish line with lower prices since 1985, and has a lowest-price guarantee. Most items are shipped within 24 hours; no returns are accepted on electrical parts or special orders. Other returns are subject to a 15-percent restocking fee.

Great Buys readers receive their $2 catalog free.

RSP Distributing

(See **Surplus and Volume Sales**, p. **473**.)

Tele-Tire

17642 Armstrong Avenue
Irvine, CA 92714-5791
(800) 835-8473; (714) 250-9141 (CA residents)
CK, MC, V, D, MO, B, PQ

This Tele isn't Kojak, but if your tires are bald, they can probably come to the rescue and be pretty tough on the competition. Hey baby, look at these brands: BRIDGESTONE, PIRELLI, MICHELIN, CONTINENTAL, QUANTUM, and DUNLOP. Shop around and find out what tire you need, then let them throw the book at you—a free brochure of tires and prices, with savings of about 30 percent off full retail. Returns are accepted within 30 days.

Titan Rubber International

One Bryan Drive
Wheeling, WV 26003-0137
(800) 443-8473
CK, MC, V, D, AE, MO, PQ

Titan, cycling the globe since 1959, is a giant in the savings arena—up to 50 percent off on tires, as well as tubes, valves, and batteries. Big names include GOODRICH, DUNLOP, MICHELIN, PIRELLI, and GOODYEAR. They don't have a catalog, but they give price quotes by mail or phone, and are knowledgeable about the tires your car needs. Ask about their quantity discounts.

World Wide Auto Brokers, Inc.

33523 W. Eight Mile Road
Livonia, MI 48153
(800) 841-8555; (313) 478-8555
(313) 478-8577 (FAX)
CK, MO, MC, V, AE

World Wide has got the car buying business by the horn. Forget the hassle of purchasing or leasing a new car or truck ever again.

Let the experts with a worldwide reputation do the negotiating for you . . . and save you big bucks! World Wide Auto Brokers is a bonded, State licensed, independent company which acts as your agent in the purchase or lease of a new car or truck. They handle all makes and models and they buy for you through factory-franchised dealers in your hometown. Thousands of satisfied car customers refuse to buy without them. If saving money, time, and aggravation is your desire, this is the source to driving the best bargains in town. The computerized car quote identifies all of the standard equipment as well as all of the available options with their actual factory to dealer cost and suggested retail price. That means the price is negotiated from factory to dealer cost, as opposed to negotiated from sticker price down. Computerized sticker quotes detail the standard as well as the optional equipment available.

Readers of *Great Buys* can receive the computerized car quotes by mail or fax for $9.95 (retail $19.95). The price is refundable when the car is leased or purchased through World Wide. If you choose to buy your car elsewhere, use the car quote as a negotiating tool so that your local dealer will know YOU know what his cost of the car really is.

China, Crystal, Silver, and Gifts

Are your cupboards down to the bare essentials? Bone up with china! From GORHAM to WEDGWOOD, antique English to patterns that have gone by the wayside, there are matching services that will track down your long-lost china and silver patterns. Other companies offer fine servings on current patterns. Most carry name-brand silver, china, and stemware. If you're looking for something special, be specific and tell them exactly *what you want. And whenever you write with a request, it's always smart to enclose a SASE (unless you're writing someone outside the U.S.). Replies from Europe can take a while, so be patient. And if it's a gift, don't leave home without sending one by phone.*

Albert S. Smyth Co., Inc.
29 Greenmeadow Drive — (800) 638-3333; (301) 252-6666
Timonium, MD 21093 — CK, MC, V, AE, C

When it comes to plates and china, these folks can dish it out, but when it comes to money, it's another story. They can't take it (or at least they won't take much of it!). We dug through their world of catalogs and came up in china. Since 1914, Albert S. Smyth's been in china, and in crystal and gifts, too. They carry famous makers like LENOX, REED & BARTON, ROYAL DOULTON, WEDGWOOD, and others at 25 percent to 65 percent off retail. Fine jewelry discounted 25 percent to 50 percent is also a welcome part of their serving grace. Their 24-page color catalog displayed some beautiful items at excellent discounts off the suggested list price. There's a written 30-day full-refund policy; no restocking charge on returns, and no minimum order. Orders are usually shipped within 24 hours and received within ten days. Albert S. Smyth is a member of the National Bridal Service.

Atlantic Bridge Collection Corp. Ltd.
Ballybane 011-353-91-53637
Galway, Ireland CK, MC, V, AE, Access, IMO, C/$2

Prices are falling down at Atlantic Bridge on tableware and collectible figurines. Porcelain by ROYAL DOULTON, WEDGWOOD, and SPODE; AYNSLEY and MINTON silverware; WATERFORD and GALWAY crystal, and more were priced as much as 40 percent off. From fine Irish table linens to a set of crystal candlesticks, you can save a mint on goods from the Emerald Isle. They'll give price quotes by phone if you care to spend the money on a transAtlantic call; minimum order is $25. Satisfaction is guaranteed.

Barrons
P.O. Box 994 (800) 538-6340
Novi, MI 48376 CK, MC, V, D, MO, C

There are buys fit for royalty in this Barrons' 35-page catalog. Savings of up to 65 percent on china, silver, crystal, and fine giftware will leave you sitting pretty. NORITAKE, WEDGWOOD, LENOX, ROYAL DOULTON, FRANCISCAN, GORHAM, and ONEIDA are some of the names that have made Barrons a force to reckon with since 1974. Plus LLADRO figurines, silverware chests, jewelry boxes, pictures frames, vases, and more. Brides with families scattered across the world will find their bridal registry service a blessing. Exchanges or refunds within 30 days.

Bennett Bros., Inc.
(See **Buying Clubs and One-Stop Shopping**, p. **112**.)

Beverly Bremer Silver Shop
3164 Peachtree Road, N.E. (404) 261-4009
Atlanta, GA 30305 CK, MC, V, D, AE, MO, PQ

All that glitters is not full price at Beverly Bremer's. Missing family forks that have been discontinued but not forgotten, or just difficult-to-find silverware can often be found here; just let her know the missing parts. Besides flatware, there are picture frames, jewelry boxes, vases—in short, all things fine and silver. The sparkling array includes both new and old items, although, if old, it's all been splendidly cleaned and restored. Call or send a photo of your flatware for help locating more of the same, or call for a price quote on the object of your affection. They buy and appraise silver as well; no catalog is available.

Bradbury's
1627 Westgate Road (715) 834-4013
Eau Claire, WI 54703 CK, MC, V, MO, PQ

Dip into the delicious selection of tableware here, from china to tablecloths at up to 50 percent off. And it's not just everyday china we're talking about, either; table talk centered around JOHNSON BROTHERS, ROYAL DOULTON, FRANCISCAN, ROYAL ALBERT, NIKKO, and MINTON. Set yourself up in style and don't be afraid to lay it on thick; with Bradbury's, you can afford to. Price quotes available by letter or telephone.

Buschmeyer & Company
515 S. Fourth Avenue (800) 626-4555
Louisville, KY 40202 CK, MC, V, AE, D, DC, MO, PQ

Still in the bush leagues where finding discount flatware's concerned? Wise up and try Buschmeyer & Company. Dig into deals on all sterling and silverplate flatware—in other words, if they don't have it, they'll get it, discontinued patterns included. And the discounts soar to 40 percent. Alas, they have no catalog, but a phone call or letter with SASE will get you a price quote.

Casselryd Crystal
P.O. Box 0966
Radford, VA 24141 MC, V, AE, DC, C

Home, Swede, Home at this purveyor of fine crystal. They call Sweden "The Land of Crystal," and you'll soon see why. Casselryd's the source for crystal with the endangered animal motif, charming and unusual bud vases, crystal glasses, candleholders, bowls, perfume bottles, holiday ornaments, and more, plus flatware from

ORREFORS, KOSTA BODA, ROSENTHAL, GENSE, SWAROWSKI, DAUM, and VILLEROY & BOCH, at savings of up to 50 percent. Prices are in U.S. dollars and include shipping and insurance. When visiting Stockholm or Copenhagen, you can stop by in person at their showroom; they'll even send a limo to pick you up at your hotel! Who said being price-conscious wasn't an easy ride?

China Cabinet, Inc.
24 Washington Street (800) 545-5353; (201) 567-2711
Tenafly, NJ 07670 CK, MC, V, O, MO, PQ

With discounts of up to 50 percent, this China Cabinet's no heartbreaker. They serve up savings on china, flatware, crystal, and giftware by ROYAL DOULTON, WILTON, ORREFORS, ARTHUR COURT, WEDGWOOD, DANSK, GORHAM, and JACQUES JUGEAT, to name a few. There's a $25 minimum on credit-card orders; a phone call or letter with SASE will get you a price quote.

Chinacraft of London
Parke House
130 Barlby Road (01) 9602121
London W10 6BW, England C/$5, PQ

We thought a Chinacraft was like a Christ-craft, only without the motor. (Sort of a junk?) Were we wrong, wrong, wrong! Yin-terested folk will find this company yanks their prices on china down substantially. And if you know china, we're willing Tibet you'll find a lot to yak about in their catalog. Got something particular in mind? Ask for price quotes on gorgeous china and hand-cut crystal from WEDGWOOD, SPODE, ROYAL WORCESTER, ROYAL DOULTON, BACCARAT, WATERFORD, and STUART. A price list is enclosed to give approximate costs.

The China Matchers
P.O. Box 11632 No phone
Milwaukee, WI 53211 CK, PQ (SASE)

Matchmaker, matchmaker, make me a plate . . . catch me a cup . . . do me a dish. While this may never make Broadway, if you're singing the blues over a set of china missing a few supporting players, give The China Matchers a holler. They specialize in LENOX, HAVILAND, and WEDGWOOD patterns, and it's a buyer's and seller's market. For information, send the name of the pattern or a picture of a dinner plate to The China Matchers. Then on opening night, your table will get a standing ovation.

The China Warehouse
P.O. Box 21797 (800) 321-3212; (216) 831-2557
Cleveland, OH 44121 CK, MC, V, MO, C, PQ

Has the Kosta living got you Boda tears? Well, honey, there's no need to fret. You can still have fine china on your table. Just shop the warehouse where up to 40-percent savings are given on brands like KOSTA BODA, ONEIDA, MINTON, ROYAL DOULTON, DENBY, MIKASA, FITZ & FLOYD, NORITAKE, and others. Your table will have a style all its own, but you won't be paying top dollar for china, crystal, stainless and sterling flatware—that's *not* our style. Supply manufacturer's name, pattern, and number of pieces for price quote.

Classic China
1002 N. Central Expressway, #116 (800) 825-7766
Richardson, TX 75080 (214) 238-7766
CK, MC, V, D, AE, PQ

Take a peek into this classic China Closet for china if the walls of your china are tumbling down. If the price of fine dinnerware is putting you off on feed, you'll eat up bargains of 20 percent to 40 percent on VILLEROY & BOCH, SPODE, ROYAL WORCESTER, ROYAL DOULTON, LENOX, and MIKASA. Spoon up the ONEIDA and GORHAM flatware, too, or propose a toast to the crystal. Table runners, place mats, and more abound. No catalog is available, but a phone call will get you a price quote on the menu of choices.

The Company of Women
102 Main Street
P.O. Box 742 (800) 937-1193
Nyack, NY 10960 CK, MC, V, C

If you enjoy the company of women, and support a worthy cause at the same time, this is the catalog of choice. Products displayed such as message T-shirts, stationery, cards, household items and gifts, and posters are distinguished by a "W" if they were created by a woman. Throughout this 30-page color catalog are items both useful and inspirational to women, and the bulk (81 percent) of the proceeds goes to the Rockland County Family Shelter in Rockland County, New York, that serves victims of domestic violence and rape, with the remaining 19 percent going to its creator, Melinda Little.

Coinways/Antiques Ltd.
136 Cedarhurst Avenue (516) 374-1970
Cedarhurst, NY 11516 CK, MC, V, AE, D, DC, MO, F, PQ

Coinways is the way to go when you're in search of the missing link—in your china pattern, that is. Whether Grandma left it to you, or it's part of your bridal pattern, there's a good chance they can find it. Even if you don't know the name of the pattern, sending a photograph or photocopy by mail will suffice. No need to go on a dig to dig up that lost soup spoon; Coinways/Antiques Ltd. handles GORHAM, ONEIDA, REED & BARTON, TUTTLE, TOWLE, TIFFANY, LUNT, and many, many others. There's one catch, though: They won't let you pay full price. Savings run up to 75 percent off the manufacturers' suggested retail. Call or write for a price list; it's a sterling opportunity.

David Lackey Antiques & China Matching
1186 Meyerland Plaza (713) 666-1344
Houston, TX 77096 CK, MC, V, AE, D, PQ

Buying and selling discontinued and new china and crystal plus antique and pre-owned china makes this the great call of China. Besides, this guy was no Lackey when it came to delivering first-class service per place setting. Selling by the piece makes the dinner plans easier . . . especially for solo serves. Discontinued patterns included WEDGWOOD, LENOX, ROYAL DOULTON, FRANCISCAN, METLOCK; current patterns, too, at 50 percent off (though not always available).

David's Imports
1507 Misty Cove (512) 835-7202
Austin, TX 78754 CK, MO, COD, C/$1

Well, we don't mean to give Austin's best-kept secret away, but it looks like David's *is* practically giving it away. Factory seconds and discontinued imported items at 50 percent of their *wholesale* prices are something to blab about. Hand-blown imported glassware including tumblers, carafes, hurricane lamps, tabletop and decorative pieces, and more, plus handcrafted imported ceramics, had us making a trade agreement in no time. They say they don't want to be swamped with orders, but they will ship if they have what you want. Visit them at 9701, in the Brown Lane Building, #C303, when in Austin.

Emerald Mail Order
Ballingeary, Macroom County
Cork, Ireland

280 Summer Street
Boston, MA 02210

(800) 334-3750
(617) 423-7645 (phone orders)
CK, MC, V, AE, Access, MO,
Bank Cheque, C/$2 (refundable)

No sham, Sam (and no blarney, Barney), Emerald's rock-bottom prices make them a gem on the Emerald Isle. Drink in the savings—up to 35 percent on the full line of WATERFORD crystal and BELLEEK china, plus ROYAL WORCESTER, AYNSLEY, ROYAL DOULTON, COALPORT, and LIMOGES. You won't get lepre-conned by these fine folks. Now you can thank your lucky stars and eat 'em too—from a BELLEEK bowl! Not to mention the figurines and giftware from such illustrious sources as LLADRO, IRISH DRESDEN, and HUMMEL. Their Collector's Club will keep you posted on the selection; it's $15 for a newsletter, special deals, and coupons.

Fortunoff Fine Jewelry & Silverware, Inc.
1300 Old Country Road
Westbury, NY 11590

(800) 937-4376; (516) 832-9000
CK, MC, V, AE, DC, MO, C/$2

Some folks swear by 'em, others swear at 'em; when it comes to china, everybody's got an opinion about Fortunoff. Patterns from GORHAM, TOWLE, INTERNATIONAL, REED & BARTON, KIRK-STIEFF, LUNT, and ONEIDA are put out to pasture here at passionate prices. Other goodies go for full fare. (Discounts vary depending on the category of merchandise.) Catalogs fortunately arrive to herald each major shopping season. Choose from over

500 patterns of flatware in sterling, silverplate, or stainless steel; or choose a gem from their beautiful collection of fine jewelry priced at less than you'd imagine. They also carry a line of clocks in brands like SEIKO, HARRIS & MALLOW, and DERICHRON. Others will make a Fortunoff you, but when it comes to contemporary and antique silver, Fortunoff boldly proclaims, "No one sells sterling flatware for less."

The Friar's House
(See **Art and Collectibles**, p. **45**.)

Gered
173/174 Piccadilly (01) 6292614
London WIV OPD England MC, V, AE, DC, IMO, C

SPODE from Gered, ROYAL DOULTON, MINTON, and ROYAL CROWN DERBY from Gered, WEDGWOOD from Gered—all the most sought-after names in bone china straight from the pages of this catalog giftbook. Though not a discounter by acclamation, the price savings between the U.K. price and U.S. price should net 50 percent after allowing for shipping, insurance, and U.S. Duty. Strikingly beautiful examples with sumptuous detail jump out of each page. Since our old office address was on Fitzhugh in Dallas, I was understandably tempted by SPODE's Fitzhugh offerings. Several members of the English Fitzhugh family were officials in the East India Company in Canton, and it's probably from them that the name of this Chinese pattern, introduced by SPODE in circa 1800, was derived.

Goldman's
315 Grand Street (800) 221-7457
New York, NY 10002 CK, MC, V, AE, D, MO, PQ

Goldman's is a gold mine of china, silverware, and flatware. You won't have to dig very far before you strike savings of 35 to 70 percent on in-stock items by NORITAKE, FITZ & FLOYD, SPODE, LENOX, MIKASA, ROYAL DOULTON, DANSK, WEDGWOOD, VILLEROY & BOCH, and GORHAM. Goldman's will ship anywhere in the U.S., and offers the service of a bridal registry. Allow two to four weeks for delivery. Longer for the marriage.

Grand Finale/Horchow
P.O. Box 620048
Dallas, TX 75262-0049
(800) 955-9595 (U.S. and Canada)
(214) 556-6025 (Dallas, outside U.S., Puerto Rico, Virgin Islands)
CK, MC, V, AE, D,
C ($3 refundable on first purchase)

Taking its final bow through this catalog, you'll save page after page on fine home furnishings, gifts, china and crystal, fashions, and elegant accessories. We applaud their intent, being as they were one of the first companies to offer luxury merchandise at significant savings. Designers' names are sprinkled throughout. A two-piece floral dress from CAROLE LITTLE was $158, their price $99.99. One catalog featured a line-up of linens by LAURA ASHLEY, J.P. STEVENS, DAN RIVER, and FIELDCREST at up to 50 percent off. TOWLE's stainless 44-piece set (service for eight) from TOWLE showed a retail value of $425 for $99.99. Many decorative accessories from faithful reproductions to the hand-painted and original dishing up discounts anywhere from 25 to 70 percent. Expect to receive your order in about ten to fourteen days. Write for Grand Finale's catalog. You'll soon be asking for an encore!

Greater New York Trading Co.
81 Canal Street
New York, NY 10002
(212) 226-2808
CK, V, MC, COD, B

If you don't want to let some full-price retailer take a bite out of your budget, nibble on the prices at this Big Apple business. (You won't find seeds of destruction here!) What could be tastier than tableware by: GORHAM, INTERNATIONAL, LENOX, LUNT, MIKASA, MINTON, NORITAKE, ONEIDA, ORREFORS, ROYAL DOULTON, REED & BARTON, ROSENTHAL, ROYAL WORCESTER, KIRK-STIEFF, TOWLE, WATERFORD, and WEDGWOOD? Discounts of 40 percent to 60 percent off are oh-so-sweet and are always in season. A 91-piece setting of NORITAKE china in the Vienna pattern would normally be about $1,500, but it was just $730 here. A 91-piece setting of MIKASA china in the Charisma pattern (normally $600) was just $275.

House of 1776
3110 S. Jupiter (800) 989-1776; (214) 864-1776
Garland, TX 75041 CK, MC, V, MO, C

With a hearty heigh-ho silver—and china, and crystal—you'll ride away with a steal of a deal from the House of 1776. The price of NORITAKE was tasty, as well as SPODE, ROYAL WORCESTER, ROYAL DOULTON, TOWLE, GORHAM, WEDGWOOD, and LENOX. Up to 60 percent off is nothing to horse around about. Their dog and pony show even includes a bridal registry. Visit their 65,000-square-foot store in Garland when in the Dallas area; otherwise call or write for a free catalog.

Jean's Silversmiths
16 W. 45th Street (212) 575-0723
New York, NY 10036 CK, MC, V, COD, PQ

Jean blows the others to smith-ereens with over 1,000 current and discontinued patterns in sterling-silver flatware, new and used silver, and antique jewelry. They've been tracking down discontinued patterns and hard-to-find items since 1932. We inquired about INTERNATIONAL's discontinued "Silver Rhythm" pattern and were quoted a price of $34 each for place spoons and salad forks. (Elsewhere we were quoted prices of $52 and $48, respectively, for the same items.) Probably Jean's most popular item is sterling-silver liquor labels in five different styles. Their price? $16 each. To order, send an outline of the items you want to match, noting the type of knife blade, whether it has a bright or dull finish, and whether it's stainless or silver-plated. Most orders are received in two weeks; shipping charges are only $3.50.

The Jompole Company, Inc.
330 Seventh Avenue (212) 594-0442
New York, NY 10001 CK, MO, PQ

Vault into Jompole and pay less for just about everything. Pull up a dish from LIMOGES, LENOX, MINTON, MIKASA, ROYAL COPENHAGEN, WEDGWOOD, FRANCISCAN, and lots of others for up to 50 percent off. Crystal and flatware by KOSTA BODA, ORREFORS, FOSTORIA, WATERFORD, BACCARAT, REED & BARTON, ONEIDA, LUNT, TOWLE, TUTTLE, GORHAM, and

KIRK-STEIFF, to name a few, are getting polished off at great discounts. We couldn't write off fine pens and pencils by MONT BLANC, CROSS, and PARKER, either, plus CARTIER, ROLEX, and SEIKO watches, LLADRO, HUMMEL, and SWAROVSKI figurines, and a host of other merchandise. Call for a price quote and find out how much they can save you before you jump into retail prices.

Kaiser Crow Inc.
3545 G South Platte River Drive (800) 468-2769
Englewood, CO 80110 (303) 781-6888
CK, MC, V, D, MO, B, PQ

Kaiser Crow has been in business since 1985, and their bargains are something to squawk about. All kinds of flatware flies in the face of retail: LUNT, ONEIDA, REED & BARTON, INTERNATIONAL, GORHAM, TOWLE, and other brands, up to 55 percent off. You can be sure their brochures will keep you abreast of any new discounting developments. Satisfaction is guaranteed; they ship worldwide. Price quotes are available by letter or telephone.

Kitchen Etc.
31 Lafayette Road
P.O. Box 1560 (800) 232-4070
North Hampton, NH 03862 CK, MC, V, MO, C, PQ

Kitchen Etc. whips up deals on kitchenware, china, flatware, and . . . everything *but* the kitchen sink. Save about 40 percent on casual everyday dishes to puttin'-on-the-ritz-ware in their two catalogs. The "Cook 'n' Dine" catalog is for appliances with brand names like KRUPS and BRAUN, plus REVERE WARE, WILTON baking pans and tins, CORNING WARE, CALPHALON pans, FARBERWARE, T-FAL pots, WAGNER skillets, just to whet your appetite. The "Dinnerware" catalog ran about 90 pages and was filled with the stuff bridal dreams are made of. Sugar and spice jars and everything nice. China by NORITAKE, WEDGWOOD, and ROYAL ALBERT, ONEIDA silverware, and many other delicate delights presented at great prices. Altogether a selection of quality names and products with an absolutely flawless customer satisfaction policy.

Lanac Sales
73 Canal Street
Dept. 10002
New York, NY 10002
(800) 522-0047
CK, MC, V, AE, D, DC, PQ (SASE)

Paddle the aisleways of this New York institution when you're fishing for fine china, crystal, and tableware. Save 30 to 60 percent off the retail price of china, silverware, gifts, and figurines by GORHAM, LENOX, MIKASA, ROYAL DOULTON, ROYAL WORCESTER, AYNSLEY, VILLEROY & BOCH, BACCARAT, LLADRO, and still more big names that will set the table in the lap of luxury-for-less. Normal delivery takes seven to ten days. Returns on stock items are accepted within 30 days. Write (with SASE) or call for a price quote.

Lillian Vernon
(see **Housewares**, p. **329**.)

Locator's, Incorporated
908 Rock Street
Little Rock, AK 72202
(800) 367-9690; (501) 371-0858
CK, MC, V, PQ (SASE)

Once lost, now found . . . Locator's Incorporated sells, buys, and brokers discontinued patterns of china, crystal, and sterling-silver flatware. What a scope! Their shop boasts 50,000 pieces of china and crystal in discontinued patterns, and eight times that is in their matching registry. This registry holds over 40,000 cards linking buyer to seller and vice versa. They handle all major china manufacturers in the United States, England, France, Germany, and Japan. If they don't have a particular piece available, they will keep your name on file until they locate a match and contact you. If you have a pattern to match, simply write or call, giving manufacturer, pattern, and, if necessary, a description or photo of distinguishing marks.

Marel Company
6 Bond Street
Great Neck, NY 11021
(516) 466-3118
CK, MO, PQ

Set yourself up for bargains; up to 50 percent off on tableware, including flatware, china, crystal, and giftware from Marel. You're in good company with KIRK-STIEFF, LUNT, REED & BARTON, TOWLE, LIMOGES, NORITAKE, MINTON, WEDGWOOD, WALLACE, SPODE, INTERNATIONAL, GORHAM, and other dinnerware dandies. New stuff, old stuff; flatware including sterling, stainless, and holloware; and collectible gift items are good reasons to pal around with Marel. No credit cards accepted; price quotes available by phone or letter with SASE.

Messina Glass & China Co. Inc.
P.O. Box 307 (609) 561-1474
Elwood, NJ 08217 CK, MC, V, AE, D, MO, PQ

The tables will turn and so will heads when you serve your guests from famous-name china, crystal, giftware, and barware bought for 25 to 40 percent less than retail. Entertaining brands we found: ROYAL DOULTON, MINTON, WEDGWOOD, NORITAKE, ATLANTIC, JOHNSON BROTHERS, GORHAM, AYNSLEY, and many others. The selection of patterns ranged from formal to casual. Just write Messina with the manufacturer and style you desire and they will send you a price quote. No returns are accepted on special-order items. Delivery time averages one to four weeks. Customers can request a catalog from the individual brands Messina carries, although Messina does not have its own catalog.

Michael C. Fina Co.
580 Fifth Avenue (800) 289-3462; (718) 937-8484
New York, NY 10036 CK, MC, V, AE, D, DC, O, MO, C

Fina-lize your wedding plans at this bridal registry and jewelry emporium. You'll find all kinds of glittering goodies in this distributor's catalog: sterling-silver tea services, crystal stemware, bone china, even a set of pewter goblets. Low prices and a large selection (hundreds of brands are available) put them high on our list. Prices on their sterling-silver flatware fluctuate with the silver market. Call for a catalog.

Michele's Silver Matching Service
805 Crystal Mountain Drive (800) 332-4693
Austin, TX 78733 CK, MC, V, AE, D, PQ

Michele's sterling silver simply sparkles. Seeking a solitary spoon? Over 700 patterns in stock should shake your flatware fears. Active and inactive patterns are available. They also have a silver-polishing service, will remove monograms, and are "actively buying silver." The prices are described as "affordable"; see for yourself. A bridal registry is a la carte, Blanche. Whether you need a place to shine, search for, or simply set you up with silver, Michele's sells silver by the score! Call or write for a price list of an individual pattern.

Midas China & Silver
4315 Walney Road (800) 368-3153
Chantilly, VA 22021 CK, MC, V, AE, D, MO, C, PQ

The Midas touch turns everything to discounts of up to 70 percent. Lay your hands on fine china, silver (new and used), crystal, and giftware. China comes from AYNSLEY, GORHAM, LENOX, MINTON, NORITAKE, ROYAL DOULTON, SPODE, FITZ & FLOYD, and WEDGWOOD; figurines from HUMMEL and LLADRO; ORREFORS, WATERFORD, and BACCARAT crystal; and flatware from GORHAM, KIRK-STIEFF, ALVIN, NATIONAL, ONEIDA, REED & BARTON, and many more. We've also got to hand it to their bridal registry. They'll hand over a catalog (free) or a price quote; we'd also like to point out that there's a minimum order of $25. Returns are accepted on all but special orders.

Mikasa Factory Store
6100 Avenue K (214) 881-0019
Plano, TX 75074 CK, MC, V, PQ

Set your table where East meets West by MIKASA and save up to 30 percent and more. This manufacturer's outlets express the Orient's attention to detail and beauty. Choose from dinnerware, stemware, flatware, giftware, housewares, crystal serving pieces, and frames. Now, who has room for JELL-O? Check directory assistance for the outlet nearest you; call for a price quote.

Music Box World
P.O. Box 7577 (718) 626-8153
Rego Park, NY 11374 CK, MC, V, AE, O, MO, C

Listen; they're playing our song. This delightful collection of music boxes is bound to melt any heart. Porcelain, lucite, and wooden boxes are available, and you call the tune from their list of more than 800 songs. You can even create a box with a personal drawing or photograph (a great gift for newlyweds), or engrave a velvet-lined box with a personal message. An Italian creche from FONTANINI that plays your choice of seasonal songs was $79.95; a lucite piano with goldtone trim was $29.95. Tunes range from "We've Only Just Begun" to "Swan Lake." There's something for everyone and every occasion. Picture-personalized orders can take up to two months to fill, so plan ahead. Gift items may be sent to an address other than your own; items lost or damaged in transit are replaced free of charge.

Nat Schwartz & Co., Inc.
549 Broadway (800) 526-1440
Bayonne, NJ 07002 (201) 437-4443 (NJ residents)
CK, MC, V, D, MO, C, PQ

Champagne, anyone? Or will you only accept a sip from a glass by WATERFORD? Make a toast in WEDGWOOD, GORHAM, LENOX, or many other brand names to savings of up to 45 percent. You won't be LAUFFER-ing at these low prices. You'll find all your ONEIDA and much, much more. In their 48-page, full-color catalog, you will ogle at gifts ranging from $10 to $500. We found adorable sterling rattles, and an exquisite LLADRO figurine. They all figure in as perfet gifts at passable prices. Let Nat go to bat with GORHAM, WALLACE, TUTTLE, and several others, enough to fill a GEORGIAN HOUSE. Eat like a king on ROYAL CROWN DERBY, ROYAL WORCESTER, or WEDGWOOD QUEENSWARE. Take your PICKARD if you can. If ever in the metropolitan New York area, stop by and see Nat. The showroom is filled with thousands of magnificent pieces, but Nat would never dream of making you feel like a bull in a china shop. The company offers full refunds and exchanges on your unused purchases, if returned within a reasonable time; special orders require a nonrefundable deposit of 20 percent. "High Ho Silver," don't delay!

Noritake China Replacements
2635 Clearbrook Drive (800) 562-1991
Arlington Heights, IL 60005 CK, MC, V, PQ

My kingdom for those missing NORITAKE pieces! In a frenzy over china that's been chipped or chiseled? Never fear; NORITAKE's service center is here. They'll help you find the missing pieces. Simply write with the following information: pattern name, number, and the items you're after. They will take care of the rest, so even if your china's resting in pieces, you can get ready for the eastern parade.

Oneida Factory Store
Southwest Outlet Center I-35S (817) 582-7449
Hillsboro, TX 76645 CK, MC, V, MO, PQ

ONEIDA is one up on the competition. Their factory stores can save you anywhere from 25 percent to 75 percent on stainless flatware; they sell individual pieces, three-piece serving sets, and 20-piece sets. They also feature seconds and discontinued crystal, silver, and flatware, plus coffee and tea sets. You can order by mail from them, or from any one of the other Oneida Factory Stores around the country (check your phone book for the one nearest you).

Patterns Unlimited
P.O. Box 15238, Dept. GBBM (206) 523-9710
Seattle, WA 98115 CK, PQ

Tired of plastic Mickey Mouse forks or Michael Jackson cups completing your incomplete china and silverware patterns? Use a pattern-matching service to replace those lost or broken items and restore symmetry to your table setting. With Patterns Unlimited *you* don't have to hunt for the lost in October china, crystal, silver, and earthenware from all makes and manufacturers. They do the legwork. Just write Patterns Unlimited and tell them exactly what you want (color photos or make and model numbers are good). If readily available, you will receive a reply within 30 days. If not, all requests go on file until they're filled. There's a 20-percent restocking charge if you return an item because of your mistake. Packing and shipping charges are included in the price. A service like this can keep you from being at odds over replacing odd china patterns.

Identify yourself as a *Great Buys By Mail* reader and get a 10-percent discount when you buy all of a given pattern in stock.

Pueblo to People
(See **Apparel: Family**, p. **18**.)

Red Rose Collection
42 Adrian Court (800) 451-5683
Burlingame, CA 94010 CK, MC, V, D, MO, C

Have a heart. Have a gemstone heart, to be specific. A rose by any other name wouldn't be found in this catalog. These rose quartz, hematite, and other New Age stones help calm you down, rev you up, or just make you look beautiful, and are available for around $14. Add a suede pouch (about $4) for gift-giving, and make it your last rose of summer. Weekly specials are also available.

Reject China Shop
33-34-35 Beauchamp Place
London SW3 1NU 01-581-0733
England MC, V, AE, DC, CB, IMO, C/$3

If you think it's no fun being Reject-ed, you haven't shopped here. (When it comes to classic china patterns, in most places you don't stand a chance, pricewise.) In this shop, you'll find some of the best deals around on imports. Get on their mailing list and become pen pals internationally with renowned favorites like SPODE, AYNSLEY, COALPORT, ROYAL WORCESTER, LIMOGES, WEDGWOOD, and DENBY. Discounts are 15 percent to 50 percent. Prices vary depending on shipping, but according to our British correspondent, they're "jolly good." China settings and porcelain are their specialty. If the goods you get are not-so-good (chipped, cracked, etc.), you'll get a full refund.

Replacements, Ltd.
P.O. Box 26029
1089 Knox Road (919) 668-2064
Greensboro, NC 27420-6029 CK, MC, V, AE, COD, PQ (SASE)

This company may be serving just what you need if you've got a cupboard full of mismatched crystal or china. A million pieces of crystal and china provide the promise of restoring complete place settings, even if the pattern has long since been discontinued.

Among the crystal selections carried are TEFFIN, LENOX, CAMBRIDGE, and GORHAM. China patterns include NORITAKE, WEDGWOOD, ROYAL WORCESTER, and MIKASA. Bone, fine, and earthenware discontinued china are all available from Replacements, Ltd., as are numerous non-major manufacturers. Savings here are crystal-clear, as patterns still in stock are sold one-third off retail prices, and prices on discontinued patterns are dependent on the age of the pattern. Customers are offered a full refund if dissatisfied for any reason. Send a SASE for a price quote; orders are shipped via UPS within two weeks, and charged UPS shipping charges.

Robin Importers

510 Madison Avenue (800) 223-3373; (212) 753-6475
New York, NY 10022 CK, MC, V, AE, DC, B, PQ

Robin Importers Sher-wood save both rich and poor from poverty; not by robbin' hoods but by offering 20-percent to 60-percent discounts on a large selection of stainless steel, china, cutlery, crystal, giftware and bakeware, and even tablecloths. They carry 50 brands of china and 25 different brands of flatware. Brands in this forest of imports include WALLACE, GORHAM, MIKASA, WEDGWOOD (Midwinter and Stonehenge), and ARABIA, in patterns that have made marryin' so wonderful. Hard-to-find discounted ROSENTHAL, and FRENCH LIMOGE dinnerware, VAL ST. LAMBERT stemware, and giftware set us all a-quiver. Merchandise not in stock is usually delivered within about three to four weeks. Write (including a stamped, self-addressed envelope) or call Robin with a description of what you want, and before you know it, his band of merry men (and women!) will help you.

Rogers & Rosenthal

22 W. 48th Street, Room 1102 (212) 827-0115
New York, NY 10036 CK, F, PQ (SASE)

It took us a while to get oriented, but after paddling through the paddies, we took a slow boat down the canal on our quest for china and silver discounted up to 50 percent. The bargains we found let us set an exquisite table even though there were so many hungry Maos to feed. The shop features every major advertised brand (GORHAM, WALLACE, LENOX, and WEDGWOOD). Send for their price list, but be specific about what you want. Orders are shipped UPS; allow from one to eight weeks for delivery. Rogers & Rosenthal has been a pillar in the china business for years and has served generations of satisfied customers.

Ross-Simons Jewelers
9 Ross-Simons Drive (800) 556-7376
Cranston, RI 02920-9848 CK, MC, V, AE, D, CH, CB, MO, C

At Ross-Simons "the money-back policy is guaranteed even if the wedding isn't." Discounts on top-quality merchandise were about 25 to 40 percent below retail. Brands in fine china include WEDGWOOD, NORITAKE, LENOX, and ROYAL DOULTON; in crystal, brands include LENOX and GORHAM. They also carry CONCORDE gold watches and CORUM watches, necklaces, brooches, bracelets, and more. Most orders are received in two to four weeks. A knowledgeable clerk told us about the selection. Check out their full-color catalog.

Rudi's Pottery, Silver & China
176 Route 17 (800) 631-2526
Paramus, NJ 07652 CK, MC, V, AE, O, MO, PQ

Pattern yourself after the great bargain hunters and find your pattern at Rudi's. They're shooting down the price of china, crystal, and flatware by as much as 50 percent. Tableware includes china from FITZ & FLOYD, LENOX, MIKASA, NORITAKE, ROYAL WORCESTER, and ROYAL DOULTON; crystal from BACCARAT, GORHAM, and ORREFORS; and silver from TOWLE, KIRK-STIEFF, REED & BARTON, and other big-game names. Hunt down the prices by sending a SASE or calling for a price quote. The store's open Monday through Saturday 10 a.m. to 5:30 p.m.; Tuesday and Thursday 10 a.m. to 9 p.m.; stop by when in Paramus and bag a bargain (or three).

Saxkjaers
53 Kobmagergade 001-45-331-10777
1150 Copenhagen K Denmark CK, MC, V, AE, C, B

Have a Danish. Trying to cut down? Try Saxkjaers for ROYAL COPENHAGEN and BING & GRONDAHL porcelain collector's plates for at least 30 percent below their U.S. retail price. Their limited edition and discontinued HUMMEL collectibles are their most popular items. The creation of new designs every year and destruction of the mold after each issue (i.e., planned obsolescence) makes these plates and figurines very valuable. WATERFORD crystal and GOEBEL porcelain figurines, plus silver and holiday ornaments, were also pictured and described in the brochures we received. Prices include shipping, insurance, and door-to-door delivery.

Shannon Duty Free Mail Order

Shannon Free Airport, Dept. GBBM — 011-353-61-363182
Shannon, Ireland — CK, MC, V, AE, IMO, C/$2

The luck o' the Irish will have you Dublin your pleasure and saving nearly 50 percent on handmade Irish lace, WATERFORD crystal, French perfumes, pure Irish linen, mohair wool blankets, GOEBEL and HUMMEL figurines, German music boxes, jewelry, apparel, and other gifts and collectibles. China by ROYAL WORCESTER, SPODE, AYNSLEY, ROYAL DOULTON, and WEDGWOOD at a discount will make your friends green with envy. Orders are shipped to the continental U.S. duty-free; duty paid on orders shipped to Puerto Rico, Alaska, and Hawaii will be refunded or credited to the receiver's account. The minimum credit-card order is $25; satisfaction is guaranteed.

The Silver Queen

730 N. Indian Rock Road — (800) 262-3134
Bellair Bluffs, FL 34640 — CK, MC, V, D, MO, C

The Silver Queen, wearing the crown for 20 years now, features new and pre-owned sterling-silver flatware fit for a king. Save 60 percent off the retail price of all major brands, including GORHAM, ALVIN, and ONEIDA, and 20 percent off the price of HAGERTY polishing products. Ah, a kingdom for a course in table setting is worth its weight in gold. They offer a 10-day, no-questions-asked return policy, with no restocking charge. Get in the receiving line to curtsy to this Queen of savings.

Skandinavisk Glas
4 NY Ostergade 011-45-3313-8095
1101 Copenhagen K Denmark CK, MC, V, AE, DC, MO, C/$3 (refundable), PQ

Schou, fly, Schou! A.B. Schou is Skandinavisk Glas now. The prices here definitely didn't bug us or bore into our savings. Savings were 25 to 40 percent off U.S. retail on porcelain by ROYAL COPENHAGEN, LLADRO, and HEREND, and crystal by BACCARAT and ORREFORS. This company shines with ROYAL DOULTON china, as well as miscellaneous serving pieces, too. Seconds of figurines by makers like ROYAL COPENHAGEN that have minimal flaws are reduced an additional 20 percent. Their policies include full satisfaction or your money back; no restocking charges on returns; and no minimum order. The price for the main catalog or the stemware catalog is refundable with your order. All prices include surface postage and insurance costs.

Stecher's Limited
27 Frederick Street (809) 623-5912; (809) 623-2586
Port-of-Spain, Trinidad, West Indies CK, IMO, B, PQ

Some of the best buys in the world can be found at the many duty-free shops located in the West Indies. Stecher's is a good example, with branches at the Hilton Hotel, Trinidad, W.I., and at 27 Frederick Street. They carry watches and clocks by PATEK-PHILIPPE, AUDEMARS PIGUET, SEIKO, GIRARD PERREGAUX, MOVADO, and others; china and porcelain by WEDGWOOD, ROYAL DOULTON, ROYAL CROWN DERBY, MINTON, ROYAL WORCESTER, SPODE, COALPORT, AYNSLEY, IRISH BELLEEK, ROYAL COPENHAGEN, BING & GRONDAHL, ROSENTHAL, HUTSCHENREUTHER, HUMMEL figurines, LLADRO from Spain, etc.; crystal by WATERFORD; fine jewelry from the best design centers in the world; and pens and lighters by CARTIER, DUPONT, DUNHILL, PIERRE CARDIN, PARKER, WATERMAN, CROSS, SCHAEFFER, LAMY, etc. Their cargo usually unloads for 33 percent to 40 percent off stateside prices. To get a price quote, write them with specific information about what you want. They offer folders, too, with selection and price information, free for the asking.

Sterling & China, Ltd.

P.O. Box 1665
Mansfield, OH 44901

(800) 537-5783
(800) 472-5667 (OH residents)
CK, MC, V, D, B

If your name isn't Hunt, the next best way to buy silver is to go the refinished route. Heirloom silver, silver purchased at estate sales, or just tarnished silver from a wedding long ago can be restored or replated. This company had the best prices and the most efficient service we found. Refinished versions of silver are from one-third to one-fourth the price of new silver. They also carry new silver: sterling flatware, silverplate, holloware, and stainless. Brands of new silver carried (at 25-percent to 50-percent savings!) include: INTERNATIONAL, KIRK-STIEFF, ONEIDA, REED & BARTON, GORHAM, TOWLE, WALLACE, and others (any American manufacturer). They also carry discounted off-brands like WHITING and ROYAL CREST that were previously sold door-to-door. We ordered a teaspoon, $120, which was located minutes after we called and put on reserve. It arrived promptly and in perfect condition. Orders for new silver usually arrive in two to eight weeks; previously owned silver that looks like new usually arrives in about three weeks. You'll pay postage, handling, and insurance. There's no restocking charge on items returned within 30 days.

Thurber's

2158 Plainfield Pike
Cranston, RI 02921

(800) 848-7237
CK, MC, V, AE, D, MO, C

Thurber's is practically giving away deals on gifts, plus everything your table needs to look its best. Let us present you with the facts: up to 50 percent off on GORHAM, KIRK-STIEFF, LENOX, MIKASA, YAMAZAKI, REED & BARTON, WEDGWOOD, ONEIDA, NORITAKE, and other brands of fine china and silver. Ask for their catalog, or call or write with your request for a price quote. 'Tis better to hand over less cash when receiving tableware and gift items, so check out Thurber's and save.

Tuesday Morning, Inc.

14621 Inwood
Dallas, TX 75224

(800) 999-7061; (214) 387-3562
MC, V, D, C

It's a new day at Tuesday Morning, and they've got the deals to prove it. Their closeout gift catalog was a real eye-opener, with savings of half price and more on a host of gifts to keep your place snug and chic 365 days a year. A pretty floral twin comforter set was just $99.99; needlepoint pillows that retail for $60 were $29.99. A charming lace table-topper was $29.95. Tablecloths, picture frames, clocks, desk accessories, lamps, jewelry boxes, designer throws, handbags, crystal, dinnerware, kids' benches and rugs, and more were offered at great savings. But don't put off 'til tomorrow what you can order today; quantities are limited and moving fast. Sorry; no checks, money orders, or CODs. The catalog also advertises sales dates in summer, fall, and the holiday season at their over 150 closeout retail stores in 22 states (call for the one nearest you), selling name-brand and designer gifts, crystal, china, linens, stemware, silver, porcelain, picture frames, towels, jewelry . . . at 50 percent to 80 percent off retail. Now you can shop from home through the pages of this wish book and turn a gold leaf on ever paying retail again. A new chapter in shopping history. Isn't it time you looked a gift horse in the eye and took the vow of "Never Paying Retail Again!"?

Vimari Studios
130-31st Street N.W. (800) 457-6862; (216) 825-2753
Norton, OH 44203 CK, MC, V, MO, C/$3 (refundable)

In the 224-page Vimari catalog, you'll discover a panoramic assortment of gifts and collectibles at 25 percent off. One of the only catalogs to specialize in things to collect—from thimbles to dolls, pewter to porcelain figurines. Musical carousel horses, jewelry boxes, a glittering assortment of silver and gold jewelry set with marcasites, precious, or semi-precious stones; brass, wood, and ceramic home accents; dollhouse furniture, holiday ornaments, silk plants, kitchenware, luggage, and more at great below-retail prices. The cost of the indexed catalog is refundable with an order.

Walter Drake Silver Exchange
Drake Building (800) 525-9291
Colorado Springs, CO 80940 (800) 332-3661 (CO residents)
CK, MC, V, C, PQ

So what if you weren't born with a silver spoon in your mouth? Few of us were. Somehow, over the years you have acquired a set of silver, but your set's no longer a set—you're missing a fork, spoon, knife, or other utensil. Let Walter Drake come to your rescue! Walter Drake specializes in pattern replacement and will help you identify, locate, and purchase the pattern you need. The Exchange also buys sterling flatware. When you tell them the pieces, pattern, and the manufacturer you're interested in, they'll feed the information into their computer and print out a complete itemized price list for your pattern. Prices fluctuate with the silver market, but savings on certain patterns can be substantially below suggested retail. All sterling purchased carries a 30-day money-back guarantee.

Worldwide Collectibles & Gifts

P.O. Box 158 (800) 222-1613 (orders)
2 Lakeside Avenue (215) 644-2442 (inquiries)
Berwyn, PA 19312-0158 CK, MC, V, AE, D, MO, C

Collect yourself and check out the great prices from Worldwide. They've got it together with LLADRO figurines, including current and discontinued pieces. Or a SWAROVSKI swan, even more affordable on sale, is bound to brighten your day. ROYAL DOULTON plates, WATERFORD crystal, DAVID WINTER cottages, HUMMELS, and more make this catalog hard to keep to yourself. From sports figurines to porcelain music boxes, join up with Worldwide. There is no minimum order; most orders are shipped within five days.

Computers

When it comes to computers, you may know a modem from a mouse, but there's one thing everybody *should know: in this ever-changing world of computers, technology updates itself almost daily. Month after month, year after year, prices on many items continue to drop. What is state-of-the-art today fades from sight faster than campaign promises after an election. That means if you can last a few more months without the item you want, doing so could save you some bucks. If you've just got to have some nickel cadmium batteries or the latest IBM computer, shop around and be sure to get some price quotes from mail-order companies. The savings will be worth it.*

> Here's a new twist on an old, trustworthy name—Tandy is now offering mail-order computers through its Build-To-Order plan. The twist? Customers walk into a Radio Shack store and order whatever components, programs, and accessories they want, without being influenced by what the store has in stock. The order is sent directly to the factory in Fort Worth, where the computer is assembled, programs installed, and the entire system tested before shipping. **And** it arrives at office or home within 48 hours!

800-Software, Inc.
1003 Canal Boulevard (800) 888-4880
Richmond, CA 94804 CK, MC, V, AE, MO, C, PQ

Full-price software, computers, and computer products do not compute! Plug into 800-Software and take a break of up to 50 percent on the price of computers by MACINTOSH, the computer of choice in many offices, plus PCs. Mice (or is it mouses?), monitors, keyboards, printers, modems, and other computer goodies and necessities are also available from their catalog. Never fear; software's also here, including programs to help you manage your finances, create spreadsheets, get into desktop publishing, and much more. This company's programmed for service and is user-friendly after you buy. They offer technical support and assistance if you run into any computer conundrums. If you don't see what you want in their more-than-70-page catalog, call or write (with SASE) for a price quote. Ask about their quantity discounts.

All Electronics Corporation
P.O. Box 567 (800) 826-5432; (818) 904-0524
Van Nuys, CA 91408 CK, MC, V, D, MO, C, PQ

All in all, this could be one of the largest collections of surplus and new electronics parts anywhere. They have quality merchandise at low prices (10 percent to 60 percent off depending on quantity) and fast service (except during holidays and busy seasons, all orders processed and shipped in 48 hours). Their merchandise comes from a variety of sources: OEMs (original equipment manufacturers), surplus dealers, importers, and distributors all over the world. Sometimes sales are limited but run the full spectrum from battery chargers, bell/buzzers, chassis boxes, circuit breakers, connectors, semi-conductors, fasteners, fusers, switches, relays, speakers, transformers, lights, video accessories, and wire. Minimum order, $10 with usual manufacturer warranties as indicated in their black-and-white illustrated 60-page (mostly foreign in origin) merchandise catalog.

Ben Torres Ribbon Company
590 E. Industrial Road, Unit 15 (714) 796-5559
San Bernardino, CA 92408 CK, MO, B

Tie a reconditioned ribbon 'round your old laser or dot matrix printer and save a bundle. Ben Torres, in business for ten years, refills and reconditions laser-printer cartridges and dot-matrix printer ribbons at savings of as much as 50 percent. HP laser cartridge refills were $44.95; PANASONIC 1180 ribbons, retailing at $4.95 new, were $2.50 (to recondition your old ones). Call or write for a free brochure.

California Digital, Inc.
17700 Figueroa Street (800) 421-5041
Gardena, CA 90248 CK, MC, V, AE (add 5 percent for AE)

California Digital's getting along swimmingly with those who don't want to pay full retail for computer equipment and software. The catalog reads like a computer Who's Who; names like MITSUBISHI, PANASONIC, ECLIPSE, XEROX, TOSHIBA, SAMSUNG, SHARP, HONEYWELL, CASIO, HEWLETT-PACKARD, HITACHI, IBM, and MAGNAVOX keep popping up. Terminals, video projectors, monitors, printers, accelerator boards, and laptop computers are only a few of the many items available. There's a selection of electronic musical equipment as well, like CASIO and YAMAHA synthesizers, MIDIs and MIDI software, and more. Mice, disk cases, copiers, cables, and software galore round out the serviceable 95-page catalog. They claim to have "the most comprehensive catalog of computer products" in the world. Some of the catalog items are manufacturers' closeouts and supplies are limited. No returns on special orders. Restocking charges may apply.

CMO
2400 Reach Road (800) 233-8950
Williamsport, PA 17701 CK, MC, V, AE, D, MO, C, PQ

Boot up retail computer prices with CMO and create more opportunities to save up to 40 percent. They sell complete systems, as well as components like monitors, boards, printers, modems, and software, with their own label and other luminaries in the computer industry, like EPSON, PANASONIC, OKIDATA, HEWLETT-PACKARD, CURTIS, MAGNAVOX, and NEC. A phone call or a SASE will get you a price quote; restocking fees are sometimes applicable. Returns are accepted when authorized.

CompuAdd
12303 Technology Boulevard (800) 477-4717 ext. 4450
Austin, TX 78727 CK, MC, V, AE, D, MO, COD, C

Visit the store nearest you or stay at home and shop by catalog; either way, you'll come out ahead on computer equipment and accessories. CompuAdd carries their own line of computers, adapters, head-cleaning kits, diskettes, joysticks, and more, plus OKIDATA, EPSON, PANASONIC, CANON, and TEXAS INSTRUMENTS printers. You *can* take it with you on a laptop for $1995; $2399 with a modem and CANON printer. Or look into software for everything from games to art to improving your test-taking skills. It's all in their 63-page color catalog, which offers a no-risk, 30-day guarantee, a one-year limited warranty, and toll-free technical support on any product you buy. They'll ship necessary replacements for defective parts, too. CODs, however, have a $50 minimum.

CompUSA
15182 Marsh Lane (214) 484-8500
Dallas, TX 75234 CK, MC, V, MO, COD, PQ

You'll have to stop by one of their stores to pick up a catalog (they offer several), or call for a price quote, but it may be well worth it. Saving 30 percent to 80 percent off on more than 5,000 computer-related products is certainly worth going out of your way for. Desktop, laptop; whatever you're topping off, the prices bottom out here. And their technical assistance can be invaluable when you hit a glitch you just can't seem to escape. Save your budget and retrieve your sanity with discounts galore. Call for store nearest you.

Computer Direct
22292 N. Pepper Road (708) 382-5332
Barrington, IL 60010 CK, MC, V, D, MO, C/$2.95

Since 1979, the computer-literate (and not-so-literate) have been going directly to this source for great discounts. Save up to 80 percent on computers, all kinds of software, and extras in their holiday sales catalogs. For example, 5¼" double-sided, double-density disks were going for a mere 19 cents a piece; a computer cart with shelves for printer and keyboard, extra room for storage, and a paper-feed compartment was crated and delivered for $79.95. Give them a try and test their motto: "We won't be undersold!" But beware their busy sales reps, who may keep you on the phone longer than you'd planned. Shipping by Federal Express is also available if a deadline presses you into overdrive.

Dayton Computer Supply
1220 Wayne Avenue (800) 331-6841
Dayton, OH 45410 CK, MC, V, D, MO, COD, PQ

Extra, extra; read all about paying less for computer extras at Dayton Computer Supply. Fire up the printer with new ribbons and you may be surprised by what a difference a Dayton makes. Paper, too, for the printer or fax, labels, and diskettes. They're not made by just anybody, either; VERBATIM is one starring name. Discounts run more than 50 percent in some cases, and there are hundreds of items to choose from. There's no catalog, but price quotes are obtainable by phone when you call with your computer (or printer or fax machine) model number. Customer satisfaction is guaranteed.

Disk World, Inc.
(See **Hardware, Tools, and Home Improvement**, p. **288**.)

Eastcoast Software
422 Walton (800) 877-1327 (PA residents only)
Hummelstown, PA 17036 (717) 533-8125
CK, MC, V, MO, C

Got a computer, but beached by the high cost of software? Coast into this catalog for a profusion of programs from creating spreadsheets to learning math to playing games. Dive into a slew of software, compatible with IBM (and IBM clones), MACINTOSH, AMIGA, and COMMODORE computers. Their prices on blank disks make a splash, too, not to mention cables, keyboard covers, printer paper, and other extras for around 35 percent off. Schools and businesses note: Special discounts are available for institutions. They accept returns within 30 days. Visit the Eastcoast without leaving home.

Educalc Corporation

27953 Cabot Road (800) 677-7001
Laguna Niguel, CA 92677 CK, MC, V, AE, D, MO, C, PQ

On the road again? Whether you're out for business or pleasure, Educalc can come in pretty handy. Their calculators are calculated to do more than add and subtract; they're made by HEWLETT-PACKARD and act as computers when hooked up to your PC, at home or at the office. Then they can be used, like a desktop, to save and edit information and more. Printers are available, too, as well as adapters, couplers, and other electronic necessities. If it's a regular calculator you need (sounds a little vanilla now, huh?), they carry TEXAS INSTRUMENTS, CASIO, SHARP, and other models, both new and used, for up to 40 percent less than you'd find them elsewhere. Computer paper, software, books, portable dialers, plotting pens, covers for keyboards, monitors and mice, printer ribbons, and more are available in the free Educalc catalog. Call or write (with SASE) for a price quote. They will ship worldwide; you can return items within 15 days.

Egghead Discount Software

P.O. Box 185 (800) EGG-HEAD
Issaquah, WA 98027-7004 CK, MC, V, AE, D, MO, C

Hey, Egghead, give me a break! Don't scramble around trying to find lower prices on software. The deals here are not always Benedict, as they run $5 to $10 less on average, but that still beats retail. They do have good deals on computer printing and mouse packages for children, and more than 50 products in their "Dollar Days" catalog priced at less than $30 each. Their regular return policy allows for a 30-day exchange or refund, period, though this period is sometimes extended. Special sale prices appear in their holiday catalogs.

Elek-Tek

6557 N. Lincoln Avenue, Dept. 4444 (312) 541-9000
Chicago, IL 60645 CK, MC, V, MO, C

As you might expect, Elek-Tek elects to offer high-tech consumer electronics direct to the customer. About 75 major manufacturers are carried, among them HEWLETT-PACKARD, SHARP, TEXAS

INSTRUMENTS, CANON, and CASIO in calculators, and AT&T, TELEVIDEO, EPSON, HEWLETT-PACKARD, and SHARP in computers. Percentage discounts vary, but are often substantial, particularly on more expensive items. Discounts on their accessory lines are a minimum of 20 percent off. The HP-42S scientific calculator with more than 600 built-in functions was just $85 ($120 retail), the HP-12C was $67 ($94.95 retail), and the HP-10B was $27.99 ($39.99 retail). Elek-Tek also carries a complete line of HP products. Printers, genuine IBM supplies, ribbons, paper for copiers, printers and fax machines, cartridges, modems, and much more are discounted. Merchandise is covered by the manufacturer's warranty; Elek-Tek will replace defective merchandise within the first 30 days, but won't accept returns otherwise. Their minimum order's $15; most orders are delivered within 24 hours. Write for their 98-page, black-and-white catalog.

Exsel, Inc.
2200 Brighton Henrietta
Town Line Road
Rochester, NY 14623
(800) 624-2001
(716) 272-8770 (New York State)
Certified Check, MC, V, COD, PQ

To excel in the subject of computers, tech a look at this concept. Take the best names in the business (IBM, COMPAQ, APPLE MAC), completely overhaul them, refurbish them to like-new condition, and save the end user up to 75 percent. PCs, laptaps, even telecommunications equipment is available from this 50,000-square-foot refurbishing facility. For example, an IBM AT Model 099, which originally listed at $3,995 was slashed to 10 percent of its retail price, $399. An APPLE MAC II, originally listed for $6,774 was out the door at $2,199. Since 1983, this company has specialized in the purchase (yes, they'll take trade-ins even if they've bitten the dust), refurbished and renewed preowned computer equipment, and who cares if it's not the latest model? They also remarket new computers that are manufacturers' excess inventory. There's a minimum 90-day warranty. Also other low-cost brand-name computers, printers, accessories, business phones, faxes, and electronics all tested, cleaned, inspected, and repacked. This is as close to office-tech perfect as you can get.

Global Software & Hardware
1050 Northbrook Parkway (800) 845-6225 (orders)
Suwanee, GA 30174 (800) 227-1246 (customer service)
CK, MC, V, AE, C

There's a world of software—and disks, and cartridges, and keyboards, mice, modems, etc.—in this Global catalog. Do-it-yourself tool kits started at $12.95. A LOTUS Works package with word processing, spell check, a free Global Info mouse, form-designer program, and more that lists for $487 was just $79.99! If you don't see the software you want in the catalog, call; they couldn't possibly list their entire selection in the catalog. Only one small complaint: good luck finding the order form; easier said than done! Once you've opened your order, it's yours unless the software is defective, and warranties do not apply.

Laptop Brokers
305 N. Ft. Harrison Avenue, Dept. 3902 (800) 749-6373
Clearwater, FL 34615 (813) 442-0550
CK, MC, V, AE, C

Lap up the great deals on laptop and notebook computers and printers! Laptop Brokers, one of the first (if not *the* first) laptop mail-order specialists, offers 25 percent to 50 percent off ALTIMA, LIBREX, SHARP, TOSHIBA, and other big brands in small portable computers. Bestsellers include the ALTIMA-486SX, TI Travelmate WinSX3000, and TI Travelmate 4000. Orders are shipped by UPS air; shipping prices vary. They offer a 15-day exchange policy, and 30 days for returns with a 15-percent restocking fee.

Be sure to identify yourself as a *Great Buys* reader and get a *free* mouse when you order a computer.

Lyben Computer Systems, Inc.
P.O. Box 1237 (313) 649-4500
Troy, MI 48099-1237 CK, MC, V, COD, C

When it says Lyben, Lyben, Lyben, on the label, label, label, you will like it, like it, like it on your . . . budget! We discovered a cannery of computer supplies: diskettes, ribbons, storage products, paper, calculators, phone copiers, and accessories. Lyben Computer Systems offered hot brand-name products at savings that will take a byte out of the cost of operating your computer. Their bulk package deals would keep your computer pantry stocked for years. Some of the brands carried were MAXELL, CANON, TEXAS INSTRUMENTS, and MEMOREX. The minimum order is $15 and should arrive within 10 days. You won't get stuck with a floppy deal; Lyben guarantees all products and offers full refunds.

MacConnection
14 Mill Street — (800) 622-5472
Marlow, NH 03456 — CK, MC, V, MO, COD, PQ

Get tight with MacConnection and save up to 40 percent on all kinds of MACINTOSH-related products. Hook up with loads of software, printers, modems, disks, keyboards, and more from names like VERBATIM and SONY. There's a selection of computer networking services as well. They won't leave you all by yourself, either; once you've made the connection, they keep sending you up-to-date information on the technical aspects of the products they offer. They will ship worldwide. Write for a price quote or free price list.

Marymac Industries, Inc.
22511 Katy Freeway — (800) 231-3680 (orders only)
Katy, TX 77450 — (713) 392-0747
CK, MC, V, AE, PQ

Next time someone asks "where's the beef?" send them a "shack in the box." That's what Marymac Industries just may be, the fast-food equivalent of computer sales. If you're dead set on owning a computer by RADIO SHACK, simply call or write this Houston outlet (conveniently located only hours from Fort Worth, home of Radio Shack) for a price quote, or pick up a catalog at any Radio Shack store. Discounts are usually 15 percent and they usually fill orders for computers the same day. They pay freight and insurance. So if you want TANDY or RADIO SHACK products, you better get shackin'.

MicroWarehouse
1720 Oak Street — (800) 367-7080
Lakewood, NJ 08701 — CK, MC, V, D, AE, C

Join the computer age with this educational software for novices and you'll find that full price doesn't compute. Look it up with the

Random House Encyclopedia Electronic Edition for $69; try *Learn to Speak Spanish* for $65; read like the wind with *Evelyn Wood Dynamic Speed Reader* for Windows for $29; or limber up your fingers with *Teaches Typing* by Mavis Beacon for $49, to name a few. Call for the maxi-catalog from MicroWarehouse.

Pan American Electronics, Inc.
1605 East Expressway 83 (512) 581-2765
Mission, TX 78572 CK, MC, V, C

Former Dallas Cowboys Coach Tom Landry was born in (and with) a Mission, and Pan American has its goals, too. Pan handles 10 to 15 different brands of electronics, including RADIO SHACK. Discounts are about 10 percent, with bigger discounts on quantity orders. RADIO SHACK products were marked down 10 percent to 20 percent. Your prospecting will pan out and you'll also find TVs, radios, security systems, and calculators. There's no minimum order; orders are usually delivered in eight to ten days. Shipping's free on orders of over $100. There's a three-month guarantee on purchases and a $10 restocking charge on returns.

PC Connection
6 Mill Street (800) 243-8088
Marlow, NH 03456 CK, MC, V, MO, COD, B (SASE), PQ

PC Connection has been in business since 1982 and is a great source of IBM-compatible equipment, software, and peripherals, as well as repairs on EPSON and OMEGA products. Names like LOTUS, WORDPERFECT, SUBLOGIC, CURTIS, TOSHIBA, VERBATIM, and MAGNAVOX make this connection the place to find great quality, selection, and discounts. Both price lists and specific price quotes are available. They honor warranties on all of their products; a SASE with your request will get you a price quote, or ask for a free price list.

Telemart
8804 N. 23rd Avenue (800) 634-0402
Phoenix, AZ 85021 (602) 224-9345
CK, MC, V, AE, D, COD, C, F, PQ

"Low prices are born here and raised elsewhere" screams their bold price list. Save from 30 percent to 55 percent on computer hardware, software, and peripherals; IBM compatibles, hardware, software, boards, printers, and peripherals. Input these brands: EPSON, TOSHIBA, BROTHER, HAYES, LOTUS, MICROSOFT, and others. Add $7 under 10 pounds; $10 over 10 pounds for shipping and handling. All manufacturers' warranties apply and all orders shipped within 72 hours of request.

Under-Ware Electronics
(See **Electronics: Audio/Video/Stereo/TVs**, p. **189**.)

Visible Computer Supply Corporation
(See **Office Supplies and Equipment**, p. **392**.)

Electronics: Audio/Video/ Stereo/TVs

Audiophiles and video-nuts should pick up the relevant issue of Consumer Reports *at their local library for the lowdown on high fidelity. With so many self-proclaimed electronics advisers offering their opinions, you'd be smart to start with the* facts *about turntables, readouts, and the rest of what you need.* Consumer Reports' *specialty is unbiased reporting on the advantages, disadvantages, quality, and prices of all major models of electronic equipment. You can save yourself a lot of trouble if you do your research before you buy, and then focus on the sights and sounds of great buys.*

Audio Advisor, Inc.
225 Oakes S.W. (800) 669-4434; (616)451-3868
Grand Rapids, MI 49503 CK, MC, V, AE, D, PQ

Dear Audy: My husband is tweeting me badly. Last month, he hit me and I slipped a disc. He still wants me to cook his tuner casserole before he gets home from work. More than that, if he woofs at me one more time, I'm going to unleash my fury. I can't take his constant needling. It's like a broken record. My head is spinning. What should I do to turn the tables? Signed, Played Out in Yonkers.

Dear Miss Out: Take my advice: Get rid of the bozo who's bonkers in Yonkers and check out this company. Prices average 15 percent to 50 percent less than retail, and they carry over 200 brands in mid- to high-priced, high-quality stereo and video products. Most orders are delivered in seven to ten days. There's a restocking charge of 15 percent on returns.

Bondy Export Corp.
(See **Buying Clubs and One-Stop Shopping**, p. **112**.)

Cambridge Sound Works
154 California Street, Suite 216 (800) AKA-HIFI (252-4434)
Newton, MA 02158 (800) FOR-HIFI (367-4434)
CK, MC, V, AE, D, Cambridge Card, MO, C

When an audio expert answers the phone, you must have called Cambridge Sound Works between 8 a.m. and midnight, EST. They have an audio expert on-line during those hours, 365 days of the year, but they do more than help you decide what you want. Their 68-page color catalog shows speaker systems at factory-direct prices—40 percent to 50 percent less than you'd pay for comparable equipment elsewhere. Cambridge sells its own line, designed by Henry Kloss. In addition, they offer deals on names like SONY, PIONEER, PHILIPS, and DENON. There's a 30-day satisfaction guarantee; Cambridge accepts returns for refunds on its own line, and returns for credit on other brands. They ship your order the same day if you order by 4 p.m. EST. No minimum order; orders are taken 24 hours.

Cellular Phone & Accessory Warehouse
934 Hermosa Avenue, Suite 11 (800) 342-2336
Hermosa Beach, CA 90254 CK, MC, V, C

Hold all calls until you talk to this cellular phone supplier. They can ring up long-life batteries, mobile phones by MOTOROLA, NEC, MITSUBISHI, GE, and OKI, antennas, replacement batteries, adaptors, leather phone cases, and desktop battery chargers for less than you'd pay elsewhere. Other companies told us their batteries were going for $100; Cellular Phone's started at just $49.95, and most were $59.95. They say they offer the best prices on hand-held and portable cellular telephones, too. Calling all those who wish to pay less than full price! Cellular's got your number so isn't it time you dialed-a-deal®.

Cellular World
2717 E. Beltline Road, Suite 104 (800) 723-5339
Carrollton, TX 75006 (214) 418-2233; (214) 418-1894 (FAX)
CK, MC, V, AE, D, MO, C

One ringy, dingy and you're on your way to the 21st century. Nobody in his right mind these days would be caught (dead) without a cellular phone. In fact, you should *only* leave home *with* one. In your car. In the board room. In your bedroom, or better yet, underneath the bed. If you want access to a phone, anytime, anywhere, then call home . . . to Cellular World. This company is the world's first communications superstore to offer to anyone in the country the largest selection of top name brand cellular phones (over 40 models available from manufacturers such as MOTOROLA, NOKIA, OKI, PANASONIC, SONY, NEC, NOVATEL, AUDIOVOX, UNIDEN, PIONEER, MITSUBISHI, FUJITSU, and others. And that's just the tip of the mouthpiece. Add thousands of cellular accessories such as antennas, batteries, hands-free kits, and chargers, but still, you want more? Well, how does immediate activation of your cellular phone in your area (wherever you are) with no programming charges sound? Everything is priced up to 80% off suggested retail everyday. They also carry pagers, radar detectors, and auto security systems. In addition, there are volume discounts, same-day shipping, a toll-free hotline, and a 24-hour fax-order line. Now, wait for the dial tone!

Readers special: An additioal 10 percent off first order.

Cole's Appliance & Furniture Co.
(See **Appliances (Large and Small)**, p. **40**.)

Crutchfield Corporation
(See **Cars and Auto Supplies**, p. **141**.)

DAK Industries Incorporated
8200 Remmet Avenue (800) DAK-0800
Canoga Park, CA 91304 CK, MC, V, AE, MO, C

If electronic gadgetry turns you on, turn to DAK for the latest for less. Computers, speakers, remote controls, televisions, printers, copiers, mouses (did we say that right, or is it mice?), earphones, even ice cream makers. Melt-in-your-mouth brands like: SANSUI, EMERSON, TOSHIBA, and more. Every product is backed by a manufacturer's warranty, and you have 30 days to return it if it doesn't meet your expectations. Checks take about ten days to clear, so money orders or credit-card orders are faster.

Focus Electronics
4523 13th Avenue
Brooklyn, NY 11219
(800) 223-3411 (electronic orders only)
(800) 221-0828 (camera orders only)
(718) 871-7600 (NY residents, electronic inquiries)
(718) 436-6262 (NY residents, camera inquiries)
CK, MC, V, AE, C/$3 (refundable)

Focus is no hocus-pocus place even though they juggle cameras, TVs, copiers, computers, audio, video and stereo equipment, large and small appliances, telephones, answering machines, typewriters, even film. Focus carries a full line of 22-volt appliances and electronic gadgets. They've been in business for 28 years, so they won't do a disappearing act, either. They can pull most cameras, camcorders, and VCRs out of their hat at prices "lower" than full-price retail stores. It's still a mystery as to how they do it, but then again, maybe we just weren't focusing. They have prompt shipment anywhere in the USA and abroad. Returns accepted within ten days if in original mint condition as shipped.

Harry's Discounts & Appliances Corp.
(See **Appliances (Large and Small)**, p. **41**.)

Illinois Audio, Inc.
12 E. Delaware Place
Chicago, IL 60611
(800) 621-8042
(312) 664-0020 (local residents)
CK, MC, V, F

What's that I hear? Must be the sound of prices falling. At Illinois Audio, "The best equipment" is offered at "the best prices": JVC and TECHNICS CD players, TEAC, AIWA, and SONY cassette decks, KENWOOD receivers, and more, including loudspeakers, blank tapes, video equipment, equalizers, headphones, and more.

A flier is available that lists the brands and equipment they carry; some prices are included, while you must call Illinois for others. Discounts are loud and clear—about 30 percent below list; sometimes they scream out at 60 percent with closeouts. There is no minimum order. Orders paid for by check are held three weeks, until the check has cleared. COD orders are accepted on some merchandise.

J & R Music World

59-50 Queens-Midtown Expressway (800) 221-8180 (orders)
Maspeth, NY 11378 (718) 417-8600 (information)
CK, MC, V, AE, D, C/$1.95

High fidelity is a sound virtue, 'cause nobody likes a speaker that squawks around. This maestro of music mail-order houses blends discounts of up to 50 percent with a great selection of products. Most major brands are available. Their catalog of audio, video, and electronics stuff is about 128 pages and conducts a symphony of famous-name audio and videotapes, video electronics, computers, communications items, car stereos, cameras, and binoculars. Their tape and CD selection included popular titles, vintage '80s' rock, and CD sets like *The Clash on Broadway*. The standard shipping charge is five percent of the total order.

Lyle Cartridges

115 South Corona Avenue (800) 221-0906; (516) 599-1112
Valley Stream, NY 11582 CK, MC, V, AE, D, MO, C, PQ (SASE)

Lyle be seeing you in all the familiar places . . . wherever there's a phonograph. Cartridges, replacement needles, and record care items from manufacturers including SHURE, PICKERING, STANTON, AUDIO-TECHNICA, GRADO, ORTOFON, DYNAVECTOR, and MONSTER CABLE are all discounted up to 60 percent. They also carry old 78 RPM diamond styli to play 78 RPM recordings. The minimum order is $25 by credit card; $15 by check or money order. Most orders are received in seven to ten days; shipping is by UPS. Send a SASE for a free catalog or price quote.

McAlisters, Inc.

926 E. Fremont (408) 739-2605
Sunnyvale, CA 94087 CK, MC, V, AE, COD, PQ

We had a Big Mac attack when we saw the prices at McAlisters. They previously offered discount prices and various repair services only to insurance companies, which purchased merchandise to replace fire and burglary claims. But for several years now, their incredible selection of big screen televisions, stereos, microwave ovens, computers, burglar alarms, and more has been available to the public. They sell all at $10 to $30 over cost! (SONYs, for example, were around $15 over cost, including VCRs, stereos, and more.) We compared another discounter in this book with McAlisters and found you simply have to compare each item, as discounts fluctuated. Solid savings were found on PIONEER, TECHNICS, SONY, and PANASONIC products. Savings of 30 to 40 percent were found on JENSEN, KENWOOD, SANYO, ACOUSTIC, and DATRON. If you know your stereos and electronic equipment, McAlisters offers the best savings on off-brands. There is no minimum order; no returns are accepted. Add 5 percent to credit-card orders.

Mission Service Supply, Inc.

P.O. Box 2957 (800) 352-7222
West Monroe, LA 71294 CK, MC, V, AE, D, MO, C

This company is on a Mission to save you money on audio and video equipment. And the mission is complete, sir. Microphones, cassettes, camcorders, video and audio editing equipment, mixers, PA systems, cassette decks, speakers, CD players, televisions, overhead projectors, slide projectors, and more are available from AUDIO-TECHNICA, SHURE, HITACHI, JVC, SONY, PANASONIC, and others. Most of the equipment is designated professional quality. Additional savings with bonus coupons available through the catalog. No merchandise may be returned unless authorized by customer service.

Pan American Electronics, Inc.

(See **Computers**, p. **181**.)

Percy's, Inc.

(See **Appliances (Large and Small)**, p. **42**.)

S & S Sound City

58 W. 45th Street, Dept. US93 (212) 575-0210
New York, NY 10036 (212) 944-7663
CK, MC, V, D, MO, B

Morris coded an SOS to S & S and they dashed to our rescue with the information we requested. They carry TVs, video equipment, electronics, appliances, air conditioners, and microwaves for 10 percent to 40 percent less. Almost every brand imaginable is in stock: SONY, PANASONIC, JVC, YAMAHA, SHARP, AT&T, MITSUBISHI, and others. S&S has shipped merchandise to customers around the world. There's a seven-day return policy as long as the purchased item is in the factory carton with all packing material intact; no restocking charge. Orders are usually received in seven to ten days. Standard manufacturers' warranties apply. All things considered, we'd say S&S is a City built on a "sound" foundation.

Under-Ware Electronics
601 N.W. Street #100
Wichita, KS 67203
(800) 442-1408
(316) 942-3574 (tech support)
CK, MC, V, AE, D

It's not the part that shows that's important; it's what's underneath that counts. At Under-Ware, their goal is to get the price down and your computer system up and running. The prices are generally sure things in the savings department—like a BROTHER fax machine for just $499 (list was $1895). SHARP laptops, MITSUBISHI four-head VCRs, JVC CD players, KENWOOD receivers, SONY camcorders, and more were nearly half, or less than half of list prices. They carry a lot more than just computers, and their telephone "counselors" will help you determine what you need. Under-Ware can even create computer systems to meet your individual needs. Shipping within 48 hours; overnight shipping also available if time is of the essence. And, as with all Under-Ware, support is important . . . and they've got it!

Fabrics and Upholstery

Shopping for designer fabrics like Oriental silk, camel's-hair wool, natural cottons, or linens? How about drapery and wall fabrics? Whatever your pleasure, shop these pages first. Fabric clubs offer excellent bargains for seamstresses who have special interests, such as "haute couture" fabrics. When ordering specific fabrics, be sure to include a recent sample so that colors and fabric details like width can be matched precisely. It's always a good idea to order a little more than you'll actually need, especially when buying exotic fabrics from international sources. Mistakes can be costly if you don't. And remember, with your elegant leftovers, you can always make a quilt or a pillow. Or call on one of the upholsterers listed here who can stitch 'n save for you if you prefer a ready-made family of furniture.

All American Fabrics
636 S. Lafayette Street — (704) 482-3271
Shelby, NC 28150 — CK, MC, V, samples (SASE), PQ

We bet Betsy Ross came away from this store with flying colors. They sent us a handful of tapestries, early American prints, and in-stock velvets in response to a brief letter we wrote in which we described the shape of the room we were working on, the color of the walls, carpet, and draperies, and the style of furniture we had. They had ab-salutely the best discounts we've seen (up to 75 percent on closeouts, overruns, seconds, and mill ends. In fact, they had some jacquards that retailed for $39.95 per yard for $7.98 per yard. (Velvets, jacquards, and tapestries are their hottest items.) There are no refunds or exchanges. To get samples of upholstery material, send them a SASE and specify the color and type of fabric you want.

Arctic Sheepskin Outlet
565 Co. Road T
Dept. 4249
Hammond, WI 54105
(800) 428-9276
(715) 796-2292
CK, MC, V, D, MO, B, PQ

Don't be sheepish because you paid retail. Just be aware that you could have saved up to 30 to 50 percent buying sheepskin goods like slippers, moccasins, rugs, hats, covers for bicycle and car seats, and more from the Arctic Sheepskin Outlet, where they won't get your goat. They're sheep-er than many of their competitors when it comes to sheepskin products; theirs are made at one of the world's largest sheepskin tanneries (not baaad, eh?). The store in Hammond is about 30 minutes outside of St. Paul; there's another one in Chippewa Falls, WI. Or, if you're not planning on visiting those particular pastures, send for a brochure. You can also call or write for a price quote.

Tell them you're a *Great Buys by Mail* reader and request a free gift when you place your order.

Britex-By-Mail
146 Geary Street
San Francisco, CA 94108
(415) 392-2910
CK, MC, V, AE, samples, PQ

This unique shop features top-quality domestic and imported fabrics, including many from American and European designer collections. Britex-by-Mail will bring the best of them to you, several times a year, with swatch samplers of 32 fabrics, chosen for their beauty, quality, and value to the consumer. Fabrics are seasonal and may include wools, silks, cottons, linens, knits, and synthetics, priced at a fraction of their ready-to-wear cost. Write today to receive an introductory packet of swatches and be placed on their mailing list.

Buffalo Batt & Felt Corporation
3307 Walden Avenue (716) 683-4100
Depew, NY 14043 CK, MC, V, MO, B/$1 (refundable), PQ

These big leaguers have been in the batters' box since 1919 (when mighty Casey was at batt?). While we struck out on craft felt (which they don't sell), the batting averages about 30 percent to 40 percent off—definitely a hit with us. We dugout this source for home sewers and groups who need team-ing quantities of pillow inserts, quilt batts, and fiberfill. BB&F has a minimum order of two cases. They also include a sample brochure of their own 100-percent polyester "Superfluff" products that, along with their other items, are in the same ballpark as other top-of-the-line retail batting and fill. There's a 48-hour order-processing time. Make your pitch for a $1 brochure and samples, and then make out your batting order. Orders must be prepaid with a check or money order. Phone orders are accepted using Visa or MasterCard.

Cambridge Wools, Ltd.
(See **Arts and Crafts**, p. **54**.)

Carolina Mills Factory Outlet
P.O. Box V
Highway 76 West (417) 334-2291
Branson, MO 65616 CK, B, swatches $2 or $5

What's a factory outlet in the Ozarks doing selling first-quality designer fabrics made in North and South Carolina? Who cares? All we know is that their reputation is flawless and people come from hundreds of miles to shop at the Branson store. You can take advantage of tremendous savings (30 percent to 50 percent) on fabrics used to make the clothing of ACT III, JANTZEN, JONATHAN LOGAN, LESLIE FAY, LONDON FOG, KORET OF CALIFORNIA, and JACK WINTER, among many others. Swatches are sent in coodinated colors and patterns with the designer's name shown. Now you can copy the clothing seen in your favorite boutique or department store. Specify whether you're interested in woven or knits. Then you'll automatically receive two additional mailings. They send out four sets of swatches per year, so get one set for $2 or all four sets for $5.

Clearbrook Woolen Shop

P.O. Box 8 (703) 662-3442
Clearbrook, VA 22624 MC, V, AE, C, PQ

Is the big bad wool-f of high fabric prices keeping you wide awake? Instead of counting sheep, dream of saving up to 50 percent on attractive solid, tweed, and plaid patterns in 100-percent wool. (Wool is the big item here, shorn 'nuf!) We received some stunning swatches in maroon, navy blue, charcoal, and cerulean blue, but with over 1,500 different fabrics, and all of them beautiful, we have to admit there's a lot we didn't see, too. They also offer cozy woolen blankets and throws. Prices are excellent—they range from 15 to 50 percent off, and exchanges and refunds will be made gladly, without any restocking charge. They try to ship your order the same day. Paul revered his savings when he ordered, "One if by lamb, two if by sheep."

Custom Upholstery Mart

2512 Ferris (800) 231-3368; (214) 821-4444
Dallas, TX 75226 CK, MC, V, PQ

In the heart of the upholstery district, the Childress family has been covering the Southwest from top to bottom in the finest upholstery fabrics in the country. They can start from scratch with a furniture frame (all you need to do is send them a picture of a famous upholstered piece), and they will copy it for a fraction of the original cost. Save hundreds of $$$, even thousands, and not sacrifice the quality or integrity of the furniture that designers insist you pay thousands of dollars for. If all you want is the fabric, let them roll off the famous names at 50 percent off and more. From tapestries to chantungs, chenilles to leather, if it's upholstery fabric, this is your source for custom looks-for-less.

Dazian, Inc.

2014 Commerce Street (214) 748-3450
Dallas, TX 75201 CK, COD, C

Once upon a time, there was a fairy princess, one king, two butterflies, and a white rabbit . . . sound like a story you know? You can bring it to life with Dazian. Their catalog offers theatrical fabrics, trimmings, leotards, and much, much more. Whether you are going to a costume ball or putting on your own play, you'll dazzle your audience on opening night with sequins and spangles, or you could be the king with a jewel-encrusted crown and a real scepter. Being in business more than 100 years is nothing to drop a hat at, and hats they have, in several different styles. Overall, their prices deserved a standing ovation. For a good ending to the story . . . live happily ever after with "the world's largest and oldest theatrical fabric organization." There's no minimum order, but returns and exchanges must be made within ten days, or it's curtains. The End.

The Fabric Center, Inc.
485 Electric Avenue
P.O. Box 8212 (508) 343-4402
Fitchburg, MA 01420-8212 CK, MC, V, MO, C/$2

Sometimes home is where the art is, especially when you find your decorator fabrics at The Fabric Center. Put together your own look with fabric for drapes, valances, upholstery, pillows—virtually anything you can think of. Best of all, this family business, which has been operating successfully for three generations, will save you 25 to 50 percent on most major name-brand fabrics, including WAVERLY, PAYNE, and ANDREW DUTTON. Everything from silk to chintz; even fabrics to brighten up kids' rooms. To help ensure you get the color and fabric you want, their sampling service offers 3″ by 4″ samples for 15 cents a piece; 8″ by 10″ samples for 50 cents each; or 24″ by 27″ samples for $3.95 each. For every 24″ by 27″ sample you receive, you get $3.95 in credit toward each $50 worth of fabric you order. The beautifully idea-provoking decorative 130-page catalog is worth the $2 charge. Dare to be different and save at the same time!

The Fabric Outlet
P.O. Box 2417 (800) 635-9715; (508) 468-1917
S. Hamilton, MA 01982 MC, V, MO, PQ

The name gets right to the point at The Fabric Outlet, where you can save on drapery and upholstery fabric from 36 different manufacturers. This company was in the retail business for 30 years before weaving over into the outlet lane in 1988. They have nothing to hide in the price department, but *you* can cover up a chair or couch for less—30 percent to 60 percent less, to be exact. Make a material issue of names like WAVERLY, DURALEE, SCHUMACHER, PEACHTREE, KRAVET, and ROBERT ALLEN. All fabrics are first quality, with no flaws or defects. In-stock orders are usually delivered within seven to ten days; items they must order take three weeks. Call or write with fabric name, number, and yardage for a price quote.

Fabrics by Design
325 N.E. Fifth Avenue (407) 278-9700
Delray Beach, FL 33483 CK, MC, V, MO, B/$7.50 (w/samples), PQ

Designing women (and men) set their sights on Fabrics by Design to help with their decorating needs for less. The savings aren't sketchy: save 30 percent and more on their own line, as well as those of famous manufacturers like CYRUS CLARK, STROHEIM & ROMANN, and ROBERT ALLEN. Put together scotchguarded® cotton prints, muslin, and more. There's a one-yard minimum order; returns are accepted within 14 days on uncut, unused fabric unless the order was five yards or less. Customer satisfaction is guaranteed. Price quotes are available by phone, or by mail with SASE. Samples and a price list are $7.50.

Fabrics by Phone
P.O. Box 309 (800) 233-7012
Walnut Bottom, PA 17266 CK, MC, V, MO, B/$3 (w/samples), PQ

Calling all redecorating buffs! Dial the Fabrics by Phone toll-free number for a fabric find that'll have you seeing double—because you can buy twice as much. ROBERT ALLEN, WAVERLY, FABRICUT, SCHUMACHER, WESTGATE, and most other manufacturers are represented here at up to 50 percent off. Price quotes are free by phone, and available by mail with SASE. There is a one-yard minimum order on goods they don't have in stock. Send $3 for their price list and other literature plus swatches.

Fashion Fabrics Club
10490 Baur Boulevard, Dept. 3001 (314) 993-4919
St. Louis, MO 63132 CK, MC, V, B

Some benefits are for members only, like the great savings here. You won't find any snobbish attitude, but you can get the big-bucks look with quality fabric from KORET, COUNTRY MISS, BTS FABRIC, and others, including the workrooms of J.G. HOOK. Started in 1956 by former Macy's fabric buyer David Samson, Fashion Fabrics Club (which was taken over by Samson's son, Tom, in 1986) gangs up to save you from 25 percent to 60 percent on designer fabrics. Gorgeous silk jacquards were $8.99/yard, and cool cotton prints were a hot seller at $4.99/yard. Poly-rayon blends were $6.99/yard. Satisfaction's guaranteed or your money back. Orders are usually delivered within a week.

Readers of *Great Buys by Mail* will receive one sample *free*. For a limited time, Fashion Fabrics Club will also offer a *free* one-year membership ($4.95 value) with purchase.

Global Village Imports
1101 SW Washington, #140 (503) 236-9245
Portland, OR 97205-2313 (503) 233-0827 (FAX)
CK, MO, COD, B/$5 or $7.50

Clothes that reflect your global consciousness are a hot fashion ticket, and you can make them yourself with some help from Global Village Imports. Pete Heimlich and Karen Shulman not only offer a product, they educate you on the handwoven Guatemalan and Thai single and double ikat fabrics available in a variety of vivid colors. Woven by craftsmen in Guatemala and Thailand, each design is different. It's very difficult to find fabrics like these anywhere, and even when you do, they are generally twice as expensive. Global Village offers brochures and swatch packs with a variety of colors and patterns. The Guatemalan cotton swatch pack containing over 40 fabrics was $5; swatches of Thai silks and cottons were $7.50. Cottons started at $9 to $12 per yard; silk/cotton blends were $32 per yard. Even scraps suitable for quilting for $25, included shipping. Make sure you order enough fabric to complete a project, because fabrics are so unique, a later order of an identical pattern may not match exactly. Discounts for quantity orders are as follows: $50–$99 order (5 percent discount); $100–$199 order (10 percent); $200–$299 (15 percent); over $300 (20 percent.) Personal checks are held for seven days; otherwise orders are usually shipped within 48 hours.

Harry Zarin Co.
292 Grand Street (212) 925-6134 or 925-6112
New York, NY 10002 CK, MC, V, AE, PQ

The Harry Zarin Co. has been a direct importer for 53 years and is famous for a huge, diverse selection of drapery and upholstery fabrics. This includes both imported and domestic goods at prices usually 25 percent to 33⅓ percent off department store *sale* prices. In addition to a long list of famous brands like SCHUMACHER, ROBERT ALLEN, RIVERDAY, and COVINGTON, they're one of the largest distributors of French embroidered tergal sheers. Heard enough? There's more: They're the largest mail-order business in the U.S.A. for LEVOLOR and KIRSCH blinds (including ready-mades), which they sell for at least 50 percent off. No mail orders to Hawaii, Alaska, or Canada (condolences to those far-flung folk!). Since Harry Zarin has such a large inventory of different fabrics, no samples can be sent without specific information. Write for price quote.

Home Fabric Mills, Inc.
882 S. Main Street (Route 10)
P.O. Box 888 (203) 272-6686
Cheshire, CT 06410 MC, V, MO, B, PQ

Where there's a mill there's a way to save up to 40 percent on velvets, antique satins, sheers, and textured patterns, and all sorts of "newly designed" fabrics. Accessories like drapery rods, trim, foam, upholstery supplies, thread, and pillows are also available. Though they offer a color brochure, they have literally thousands of bolts of fabric to choose from, so if you want samples, be sure to be specific. Send color samples or a swatch of fabric similar to what you want, plus a description of its intended use—bedroom, bathroom, etc. The more information you provide (style, type of furniture, other colors), the greater the likelihood they'll be able to oblige. Most orders are processed in about ten days; all sales are final. Visit their other stores in Belchertown, MA, and Scotia, NY, if you are in the area. Credit cards are only accepted on out-of-state orders; there's a minimum order of ½ yard.

Intercoastal Textile Corp.
480 Broadway (212) 925-9235
New York, NY 10013 CK, COD (cash only), PQ

Roll, roll, roll your bolts, gently down the seam! This company's products struck us like a bolt from the blue! Their 10,000-square-foot wholesale jobbers' warehouse and walk-in store has just about everything you could possibly "tweed." There is first-quality slip-cover, upholstery, drapery, and curtain fabrics (everything for home decorating), and prices are around 50 percent to 75 percent less than retail. Polyester sheers were just $1.50 to $2 per yard, and slipcover fabrics were just $2.50 to $3.50 per yard. With over 10,000 different sample fabrics, it's not surprising that they don't answer letters requesting they send samples of upholstery fabric. To get them, you must send in a sample similar to the fabric you want, or else provide a color swatch and a description of the type of fabric you need. Exchanges only if fabric was not cut.

J & J Products Ltd.
117 W. 9th Street, Suite 111 (213) 624-1840
Los Angeles, CA 90015 CK, MC, V, MO
Samples $3 (refundable)

When it comes to sewing it yourself, quality is a concern. J & J sells quality fabrics for up to 40 percent less than the competition, in all kinds of colors and materials. From flannel to cashmere, stylish to sumptuous, they've got a good selection and a $3 sample packet for each kind of fabric ("crepe," for example), including little swatches to show you the assortment of colors in which it's available. When you buy a fabric from your group of samples, they refund the sample's charge. Got it? If not, call or write J & J for more information or a price quote and leave a message on their machine. Satisfaction guaranteed.

Mary Jo's Cloth Store, Inc.
401 Cox Road (800) 342-1229
Gastonia, NC 28054 (704) 861-9100 (NC residents)
CK, MC, V, AE, D, PQ

By Jo, Mary's fabric-ating all kinds of cloth in first-quality dress goods, including calico, gingham, bridal, lace, eyelet, drapery, and upholstery fabric. (Their motto is, "If you sew it with a needle, we have it.") Most name brands are available, and now costume materials have been added to their repertoire. They also carry notions and accessories at shear savings—everything's marked up as little as possible (but enough to stay in business!). All brands of patterns are 20 percent off. Once fabric has been cut, it's yours; there are no exchanges or refunds unless the fabric was defective. Inquire about their inventory since there is no catalog. There's a small charge for samples.

Marlene's Decorator Fabrics
301 Beech Street, Dept. 2J (800) 992-7325
Hackensack, NJ 07601 CK, MC, V, MO, PQ

Marlene makes masses of material monetarily manageable. Hang up retail prices on drapes; sweep full-price upholstery fabrics under the rug, and give Marlene's a try. You'll clean up with up to half off on the price of fabrics by KRAVET, DURALEE, MICHAELS, STROHEIM & ROMANN, ARTMARK, BERGER, and others. Know the pattern and its maker. Their fabric experts can give you a price quote by phone. Or, if you're not so sure, send a SASE with a sample piece and they'll figure it out for you. There is a minimum order, which varies from one yard to three with different fabrics. Get to know Marlene's and make the most of this mail-order marvel.

Monterey Mills Outlet Store
1725 E. Delavan Drive, Dept. GBBM (800) 438-6387
Janesville, WI 53545 (608) 754-8309
CK, MC, V, MO, COD (over $100), B/$4

Fur Pete's sake, this should be fun. Fun fur, that is; synthetic style. Fake fur fabric, coats and jackets, and polyester stuffing make up the menagerie at Montery Mills, and they'll save you 50 percent off the going rate. Nothing to shake a stick at, unless you enjoy being doused with ketchup by a local animal-rights activist. These animals are aggressive discounters. Try on some cruelty-free "Dalmatian" or "seal" fabric (kitschy, kitschy coo); "shearling" (75-percent polyester, 25-percent acrylic) comes in white, light yellow, beige, and black. Faux fur is tres chic (not to mention *cheap*!), so get it while it's hot. A sample package is available for $4.

Sanz International Inc.
P.O. Box 1794 (919) 886-7630
High Point, NC 27261 (919) 882-6212
(24-hour recorded message)
MC, V, C

Take off for Sanz International for almost every major brand of wallpaper, borders, drapery, and upholstery fabric. You can afford to get draped with SCALAMANDRE, SEABROOK, ASHFORD HOUSE, CRUTCHFIELD, QUALITY HOUSE, RALPH LAUREN, and GAGNE at 30 percent to 90 percent off. In 1976, Sanz started out as a small design shop, and has since become "one of the largest in-stock dealers on the East Coast." They guarantee satisfaction and, best of all, *lowest prices*. Quantity discounts save you even more. There's a 30-day return policy. Visit their store at 1183 East Lexington in High Point or one of their four other locations, for a combination of quality and value that can't be beat.

Identify yourself as a *Great Buys* reader and Sanz will give you free regular shipping inside the continental U.S.

Shama Imports, Inc.
P.O. Box 2900, Dept. GBBM (313) 478-7740
Farmington Hills, MI 48333 CK, MC, V, COD, B

Hey Christopher, we really discovered India when we hit upon Shama Imports. They offer such variety of Kashimir Indian craftsmanship that you're sure you've gone Gandhi. Columbus couldn't have been more thrilled discovering America. You might jump the boat when you catch sight of savings up to 50 percent. We discovered a bold new land of colorful crewel embroidery in their brochure, which comes with a price list, swatches, and helpful hints. You can explore wonderful savings on multicolored hand-embroidered fabrics to cover your favorite chair, walls, or couch. You can also buy ready-made bedspreads, tablecloths, cushion covers, and other items. Queen-pleasing prices can be conquered: a full-size bedspread cost $130, cushion covers cost only $11 to $12 a piece, and unique tote bags were $13. You can return uncut, undamaged merchandise within 30 days. Normal delivery time is seven days.

Silk Surplus
235 East 58th Street
New York, NY 10022
(212) 753-6511
CK, MC, V, MO, PQ (SASE)

Re-cover your sense of fair price with fabric to die for from Silk Surplus. Savings as much as 75 percent will smooth out your budget and let you get your hands on silk closeouts from SCALAMANDRE, plus fabrics from other lines, including velvets, brocades, woolens, cottons, and more. Price quotes are available on SCALAMANDRE fabrics if you already know precisely what you want (you can also send a fabric swatch and a request by mail). Additional discounts available to the trade (decorators, for example). No returns are accepted, so be sure before they sheer.

Testfabrics, Inc.
P.O. 420
200 Blackford Avenue
Middlesex, NJ 08846
(908) 469-6446
CK, MC, V, C, B, PQ (SASE)

The luxury of a pure silk blouse or dress can be yours if you know how to sew. Silk crepe de chine was just $18.23 a yard (retail $22); silk chantung was $9.75 a yard (retail $20). Save up to 50 percent on 44-inch widths; with large orders, save even more. Wools, linens, and poly/cottons available also. All fabric is in its natural state (not printed or dyed), making Testfabrics a lifesaver for folks allergic to fabric dyes. The samples we ordered were not only lower in price, but higher in quality than most seen at full retail price. This 52-year-old company requires a $25 minimum order, accepts exchanges or refunds with proper approval, and has a 15-percent restocking charge if your dissatisfaction is not their fault. Occasionally, they will have seconds on cottons available at your own risk.

Thai Silks
252 State Street
Los Altos, CA 94022
(800) 722-SILK
(800) 221-SILK (CA residents)
(415) 948-8611
CK, MC, V, AE, COD, B

Marco didn't trek to the Far East looking for Polo shirts—rather, he wanted silk. Likewise, we were lured westward by *Vogue Patterns'* ads for 60 kinds of silks. These "pillars" of the community "catered" to our expedition and wormed their way into our hearts with shantung silk in 15 colors, natural and bleached raw silk, scarves, cotton poplin, and batik. Ready-made silk blouses, linen tablecloths, and lambswool sweaters were also available. Savings average 25 percent off on their non-sale items, and discounts are even bigger when they sell to store owners or dressmakers. Raw silk voile is probably their biggest-selling item. Preauthorized returns are accepted; they don't guarantee colors, but they'll exchange if there's not a match. Send for a brochure and see what they've been "cocoon" up for you.

Tioga Mill Outlet Stores, Inc.
P.O. 3171 (717) 843-5139
York, PA 17402 CK, MC, V, D, MO, B, PQ

Tioga houses home-decorating fabrics by ROBERT ALLEN, FABRICUT, COVINGTON, and more. They also offer help doing it yourself (with supplies for upholstering) and expert advice on decorating (details are on their order form), complete with swatches. They give price quotes by letter with SASE or by phone; returns are accepted only on defective goods. There's a ¼-yard minimum order.

Utex Trading Enterprises
710 Ninth Street (716) 282-8211
Niagara Falls, NY 14301 CK, C

Getting tired of the "what to wear" syndrome? Be a little enterprising and trade your everyday blues for an exciting new look with accessories and fabrics from Utex. With a company that caters to designers, high couture, and even royalty, you'll find yourself looking like a princess without becoming a pauper. Utex offers the largest selections of silk fabrics in North America, including Chinese as well as European silks, at discounts of 30 percent to 50 percent. Utex also carries scarves, lace, and other accessories at discounted prices. Further discounts of 5 percent to 25 percent are available with volume purchases. No minimum order required, though there is a shipping and handling fee, plus sales tax. Authorized returns are accepted; delivery takes seven days on average.

Way Station Fabric Shop
Oak Springs Road (704) 287-3637
Rutherfordton, NC 28139 CK, MC, V, PQ

This outlet sells fabric for ladies' clothing only, so don't expect to get hung up with drapery or upholstery fabric. It *is* the place to intercept good deals, though. Fabrics are sold at near wholesale prices, or about 30 percent to 50 percent less than most other places. Specify the type of fabric you want and they'll send you small samples, including information on width, price, and fiber content. From there, it's just a matter of returning the sample you like along with your method of payment (plus a minimum of $3.50 to cover postage). Fabrics are leftovers from the DONCASTER-TANNER manufacturer/retailer, so don't expect to find the same fabrics twice in this place. They ship promptly, but won't exchange or offer refunds.

The Woolrich Store
P.O. Box 130 (717) 769-7401
Woolrich, PA 17779 CK, MC, V, COD, B

Sheep chic! From "the store for outdoor people" come the richest wools, perfect for mountain life. Do what you wool—purists know to go for the golden fleece in outdoor clothing! The fabric of Woolrich's life is over 150 years old. Their woolens are sold at mill prices and remnants are sold by the pound. Chamois cloth and poplins are their biggest sellers. Less than a yard of wool was $1.85 per pound; more than a yard was $2.50 per pound. Get a pound of tartan, plaid, or solid wool by sending a SASE for samples and information. And if you're in the neighborhood (three miles off Route 220 between Lock Haven and Williamsport), you're invited to drop in for a nickel cup of coffee, a stroll through the park and their outdoor hall of fame, and a look at one of their two films about the manufacturing of woolens.

Food

Who says there's no such thing as a free lunch? Happy hours at local bars feature tacos, cheeses, chicken wings, maybe even shrimp or oysters for the patrons. (Who's going to notice a few missing egg rolls?) Gallery and store openings are a dandy way to fill up on pâté, salmon, and imported cheeses washed down with a glass of wine. (Whoops, you left the invitation at home!) Show up for any demonstration of food processors, blenders, etc. (Always something cooking here.) Watch for those nice ladies giving out samples of the latest pizza flavors in the supermarket. (Get extras—for mother.) There's a bowl of caviar dip over in the deli. GO for it. If you're a teacher, confiscate all the gum and candy before class. (Ummmm, a Cadbury bar!) Finally, if you find you must pay for your food, check the pages that follow for some delicious deals.

American Spoon Foods, Inc.

P.O. Box 566 (800) 222-5886; (616) 347-9030
Petoskey, MI 49770 CK, MC, V, D, MO, C

Ladle it on thick, or toss up a salad seasoned with oil-free dressing. It's easy, healthy, and fun with the American Spoon Foods catalog. Moon over Spoon Fruits (their own preserves), which have no sugar added. (The dried cherries packed in birch-bark baskets took care of one year's entire Christmas gift list.) Add other dried berries and fruits, nutmeats, gift assortments, salad utensils made of cherry wood, and natural pasta for something out of the ordinary. Dip into luscious honey, just $4 for 11 ounces; or try a pound of their Harvest Fruit Mix with apricots, figs, pears, blueberries, cherries, apples, and seedless raisins for $8.95. Delectable gift baskets are available, and you can create your own assortment. The colorful catalog even includes healthy recipes. What are you waiting for? Get cooking. There is a $10 minimum on all orders; CODs are not accepted.

The Amishman
P.O. Box 128
Mount Holly Springs, PA 17065 CK, MC, V, MO, B

Anyone who's ever lived in Pennsylvania has probably had scrapple. It's a nostalgic food like White Castle hamburgers. So, if you're living in Texas or Tuscalosa, you'll be glad to know that The Amishman sells scrapple-by-mail. Other Pennsylvania Dutch treats include toasted coconut, marshmallow, buttermints, a coal scuttle (a licorice novelty), Brother George apple butter, and chow chow. If you come from the city of brotherly love, you'll feel right at home with The Amishman. Minimum order, $15.

Arizona Champagne Sauces
℅ Sugar's Kitchen (800) 342-9336
P.O. Box 41886 (602) 624-3360
Tucson, AZ 85717 CK, C

The craze for NO SALT in your diet wins praises in my kitchen, so stock up on these NO SALT sauces. Three cheers for the Arizona Champagne Sauces from Sugar's Kitchen, a 16-year-old gourmet resource. There are three famous mustard sauces: hot, cajun style, and regular. Great addition to your deli platters, spreads for chicken or ham, or as a marinade. Also delicious are their vegetable dip, salsa preparation, and dry herbal spice dip. For a distinctly different taste sensation, try their mild or hot jalapeño jellies; three eight-ounce jars for $14.75. All prices include shipping. Usually one-day turnaround, depending on UPS zone.

Badger Mountain
110 Jurupa, Dept. GBBM (800) 643-WINE
Kennewick, WA 99337 CK, MC, V, B

Cheers to Badger Mountain for offering wines that fly straight to your door (with a little help from UPS). Among their intoxicating offerings sip white organic wines, Chardonnay, Seve, Mountain Blush (a blended cocktail wine), and Riesling. If that leaves you dry, try sending a tasteful gift of two bottles in a special pine gift box, or stock your cellar with six bottles that come in a stryofoam shipper. *L'chaim!*

Reader special: 10 percent off first order.

The Baker's Find
135 Woodworth Avenue (800) 966-2253
Yonkers, NY 10701 MC, V, D, DC, C

If you can bake in it or with it, chances are you'll find it in The Baker's Find illustrated catalog. Once selling exclusively to restaurants and bakeries, the company has gone public-by-mail. Items include institutional-sized rolls of plastic wrap, throwaway (or recyclable) plastic aprons, chocolate chips (in bulk), brownie and muffin mixes that boast a homemade taste, cake-decorating supplies, spices, herbs, baking ware, and more. Over 300 different items to bake and shake the retail prices down to mouth-watering discounts.

Baldwin Hill Bakery
Baldwin Hill Road (506) 249-4691
Phillipston, MA 01331 CK, COD, PQ

Sourdough bread in the European tradition comes straight to you from the Baldwin Hill Bakery. This 100-percent wholewheat bread is made from organic stoneground flour and pure well water, leavened with natural sourdough and baked over a wood fire in a brick oven. Minimum order is twelve large breads, or the equivalent in large and small breads (about $19). Orders will be shipped UPS; there's a charge for collect shipments. Orders must be received by noon on Friday before the week you would like your bread shipped.

Bates Bros. Nut Farm, Inc.
15954 Woods Valley Road (619) 749-3333; (619) 749-3334
Valley Center, CA 92082 CK, MC, V, MO, B

When we found out about their prices, we almost bought the farm. These "nuts and gourmet delights from all over the world" include candies and dried fruits as well. Exotic Turkish apricots, sesame candy, wheat germ snacks and trail mixes, almonds, pecans, cashews, peanuts . . . time for a food break. Twelve ounces of sunflower seeds, roasted in the shell, were $1; sixteen ounces of macadamia nuts were $8.75. Crunch up these raw, roasted, sliced, or mixed goodies by mail, or visit the Valley Center address. Special events like art fairs, weddings, and more take place in their eight-acre park.

Bayou to Go Seafood, Inc.
P.O. Box 20104 (800) 541-6610; (504) 468-8040
New Orleans, LA 70141 MC, V, AE, D, CB, MO, C

Put some (Cajun) spice in your life with a little help from Bayou to Go. For six years, they've been swamped with business, offering authentic Cajun food, spices, gumbo, red snapper, sauces, mixes, shrimp, crabs, oysters, sausages . . . even alligator steaks, all at 10 percent off retail. They get it there fresh with same-day pickup at your local airport. Perishables are sent in frozen gel packs. Check out their 22-page catalog for foods that are fresh and delicious.

Bickford Flavors
19007 St. Clair Avenue (800) 283-8322; (216) 531-6006
Cleveland, OH 44117-1001 CK, MC, V, MO, B, F

Bickford was born with a silver spoon in its bottles in 1917. Then in 1980, they went nationwide with their ½ ounce to 64 ounces of flavorings discounted by 25 percent when compared with prices of like products elsewhere. Almond, anise, lemon, orange, vanilla, peppermint and cinnamon oils, and more are bound to give you sweet dreams. No sugar and no salt make these old-time formulas temptingly timely. Call or write for a free price list and flier.

Boudin Bakery
132 Hawthorne Street (800) 992-1849
San Francisco, CA 94107 CK, MC, V, AE, D, C

Take a cable car—or just send a cable—to San Francisco, for a load of loaves. San Francisco sourdough at Boudin Bakery is where you exit for bread and Italian coffee cakes (panettone). Their one-pound loaves are sold in packs of two, four, or six rounds or longs; panettone comes in four-pound rounds. Knead we say more?

Cavanaugh Lakeview Farms
P.O. Box 580 (800) 243-4438 (313) 475-1384
Chelsea, MI 48118 CK, MC, V, AE, D, MO, C

Ham it up with Cavanaugh Lakeview Farms and you'll have the last laugh. Their tempting sliced hams, coated with a brown-sugar-and-honey glaze, were $64.95; half a ham (a pork cut-up?) was $36.95. Discover the other white meat with a business that's been letting you pig out by mail for over 10 years. Their 24-page catalog is free. Shipping is included in the price; however, there is a $2.75 order-processing charge.

Caviarteria
22-14 40th Avenue (800) 4-CAVIAR; (800) 422-8427
Long Island City, NY 11101 (212) 759-7410 (NY residents)
(310) 285-9773 (Beverly Hills residents)
CK, MC, V, AE, B

If you're fishing for compliments at your next cocktail party, send for this luscious catalog and serve caviar, Scotch salmon, and other delicacies, to your guests. Founded by New York City ad-man Louis Sobol, this family-operated business has been discounting fine gourmet foods for over 40 years at the same location. Russian, Iranian, or new American caviar is shipped to your door within days of being received at the Caviarteria warehouses. This means you could have fresher caviar than if you bought it at your local gourmet shop. And the savings—well, how about 30 percent! Besides caviar, this company features a wide assortment of unique gourmet specialty items such as truffles, pâtés, caviar servers, caviar spoons, and 25 varieties of "freezer pac" snacks.

Great Buys readers will receive 10 percent off on their first order.

Cheesecake Royale
9016 Garland Road (800) 328-9102; (214) 328-9102
Dallas, TX 75218 CK, MC, V, PQ

Smile when you say cheese-cake! But don't expect to eat just one slice from this bakery. These cakes are sold in the finest specialty stores in the country, but are available at half price to individuals who order direct. All natural ingredients—real cream cheese, whipping cream, hand-squeezed lemon juice, dairy butter, sour cream, and fresh fruits—are used, and no preservatives, artificial flavors, flour, or gelatin are added. Scrumptious choices include Chocolate, Key Lime, White Chocolate, Amaretto, Black Forest, Strawberry, Raspberry, and yes, New York Plain Cheesecake. Shipped overnight by Federal Express, each cake is individually pre-cut and tissue separated into 16 large slices, weighs approximately four to five pounds and is an over-generous 10 inches in diameter.

Readers special: Take an additional 10 percent off any order.

Colonel Bill Newsom's

Main Street (502) 365-2482
Princeton, KY 42445 CK, MC, V, B (includes recipes)

If you're a ham and in a class by yourself, you'll feel right at home here. Over 100 food writers have saluted this 75-year-old colonel in their articles or columns, and this one is no exception. Bill's genuine green hickory-smoked Kentucky hams are carefully selected, dry cured, slow-smoked, and aged many months by methods used for nearly 200 years. The weather in this particular area of Kentucky seems to aid in the natural enzymes that produce this melt-in-your-mouth delicacy. No chemicals and no quick-cure methods are utilized. Each ham is gift-wrapped, packed, and shipped in individual boxes. Gift cards can be included. Price at time of research was $2.89/pound with each ham weighing 15 to 18 pounds.

Cook in the Kitchen

P.O. Box 3 (802) 333-4141
Post Mills, VT 05058 CK, MC, V, MO

Peek into this Pantry for gourmet cooking mixes that won't make you raise a high-brow; they're discounted by 20 percent to 50 percent. They sell a variety of ready-made mixes such as soup mixes, pancake mixes, muffin mixes, and more to whip up like the pro's. Chef's Pantry (which was once a supplier to three- and four-star restaurants in northern New England) takes care of your budget simultaneously with your taste buds.

Deer Valley Farm

R.D. 1 Box 173 (607) 764-8556
Guilford, NY 13780 CK, MO, B/50 cents, PQ

Don't be timid about saving on organic foods, including spices, herbs, meats free of hormones, pasta, preserves, cereals, and even cookies. We got wide-eyed just reading about their meats and cheeses at up to 40 percent less than at our nearby health food store. The minimum order is $10, but alas, you've got to buy at least $150 worth to qualify for truly wholesale prices. You'll fawn all over their stores, located in Cortland, Guilford, and Oneonta, New York, when you're hunting for healthy bargains. Write (with SASE) or call for a price quote, or check out the en-deer-ing brochure for a mere 50 cents. Happy hunting, dear!

Dundee Orchards
P.O. Box 327 — (503) 538-8105
Dundee, OR 97115 — CK, B, PQ

Write for their free brochure/price list for "Yummy in your Tummy" Oregon Hazelnut butters (creamy or crunchy). Try these 100-percent dry-roasted Oregon hazelnuts (no salt, sugar, or stabilizers) in a pancake batter or a pasta salad for a taste sensation. You'll go nuts over their walnut peanut chocolate or mocha hazelnut butter.

And then, *Great Buys* readers, take 20 percent off mail-order brochure prices with your first order.

Durey-Libby Edible Nuts, Inc.
100 Industrial Road — (201) 939-2775
Carlstadt, NJ 07072 — CK, MO, F

How low can you go? Hyphenate your budget; these nuts are crazy about saving you as much as 50 percent. Pass the pistachios, pack in the pecans, and can the cashews; they're bagged and we're not shellfish (with three pounds or more, who would be?). They guarantee satisfaction and ship practically anywhere. If you just want a taste, don't call or send a SASE for a price quote; they only give 'em on bulk orders.

E.C. Kraus
(See **Kits and Kaboodle**, p. **354**.)

El Paso Chile Co.
909 Texas — (800) 27-IS-HOT
El Paso, TX 79901 — CK, MC, V, AE, C

This is the hottest tamale we've seen since Madonna. *Madre de Dios*, it's hot in here, what with all the salsas, green chiles, and other authentic Southwestern delights. Their "Adobe Hacienda," made up of a pint of chile con queso (that's a spicy cheese dip, for those "furriners" among us), a pack of chili spices, and two pints of salsa—the works—got a warm reception. Spice up your life and get a taste of the wild side.

Elbridge C. Thomas & Sons

Route 4, Box 336 (802) 263-5680
Chester, VT 05143 CK, MO, B/$1

Some companies just want to stick it to you, but not this one. They sweeten the deal on their syrups with up to half off the competition's prices. Only a sap couldn't recognize this grade A syrup as a good deal. Buy it by the half pint for $4.40 or the gallon for $39.50, or send it as a gift. Don't be sappy; this is the good stuff from Vermont. Buy in quantity to get even better discounts.

Frank Lewis' Alamo Fruit

100 North Tower Road (800) 477-4773
Alamo, TX 78516 CK, MC, V, AE, D, B

Remember the Alamo Fruit when you can't elope to your field of dreams. The cantaloupe season is limited to three weeks beginning in mid-July, when ROYAL STAR cantaloupes (of two pounds or more each) are ripe to perfection. Satisfaction with these vine-ripened fruits is unconditionally guaranteed.

Fredericksburg Herb Farm

P.O. Drawer 927 (512) 997-8615
Fredericksburg, TX 78624 CK, MC, V, AE, C/$2

Down on the farm, they keep their vim and vinegar longer than elsewhere. Why not gift a friend with the delightfully unexpected (not to mention divinely *inexpensive*!)? An etched-glass bottle of Fredericksburg Herb Farm's "Edible Flowers" vinegar was $22 for 25.4 ounces and their Edible Flower jelly was $8.50 for eight ounces. Or cuddle up with herbal teas, $3.25 for two ounces. Charmingly presented and demurely priced, they're the daintiest game in town.

Goodies from Goodman
11390 Grissom Lane (800) 535-3136
Dallas, TX 75229 (214) 484-3236 (in Dallas)
MC, V, AE, C

Since 1916, the Goodman family has been delivering delicious deals fit for meals. Feast on fruit baskets for under $30 (and up) bursting with fruit 'n' cashews, or fulfill those snack attacks with a cheese, sausage, jelly, and fruit combo; then it's on to the pages of glacé apricots, Texas pralines, neapolitan cheesecake, truffles, chocolate champagne cake, popcorn tins, or a peanut brittle pail. Then smell the roses. They are also a full-line florist, delivering "all occasion" arrangements throughout the country. But don't expect your plain Janes. Rather, they send quality with flair. Add $2.50 per shipment and your gift-giving days have only just begun. Fruits cannot be shipped to Arizona, California, or Florida. Any non-fruit gift is available to all 50 states. Complete satisfaction or replacement or refund in full.

Gourmet Expressions
6065 Forest Lane, Dept. GBBM (214) 788-5155
Dallas, TX 75230 CK, MC, V, AE, DC, PQ

Open wide and say, ah-h-h-h! This little piggy went to market and saw ambrosia for the gourmand's palate. Buying directly from the manufacturer eliminates (pardon the expression) the middle layer, thereby allowing you to savor the 20-percent to 50-percent savings. Like other off-price "category killers," this one is to die for. The price is right on their gift baskets, which they'll deliver anywhere in the country. Even your mother-in-law won't know you saved on the WATER ST. CAFE coffee or the BELGIAN chocolates. Former Neiman-Marcus epicurean-shop executives saw the writing on the wall and opened their own off-price gourmet food emporium featuring hundreds of gourmet food baskets to ship nationwide.

Great Buys By Mail readers will receive 10 percent off their first order.

Grace Tea Company, Ltd.
50 W. 17th Street, Dept. GBBM (212) 255-2935
New York, NY 10011 CK, B

What price luxury tea? Though the cost of Grace Rare Teas on a per-pound basis is among the highest of all teas in the U.S., the cost, in comparison to gourmet coffees, bottled water, or soft drinks, for example, can be low—less than 20 cents a cup. So sip the savings, Grace, and order from their selection of black loose teas: superb DARJEELING; WINEY KEEMUN ENGLISH BREAKFAST; LAPSANG SOUCHONG; and EARL GREY SUPERIOR MIXTURE and CONNOISSEUR BLEND in teabags. Instant refund if not completely satisfied. One eight-ounce canister and shipping and handling would run about $9.90 to $12.25. Their brochure gives information on the quality of Grace Teas, as well as some helpful tips on making tea, serving, storage, and gift ideas. We recommend writing rather than calling; their single black rotary phone may not be up to many calls.

Reader special: Shipping and handling is FREE on your first order.

Grandma's Spice Shop

P.O. Box 472-1111 (410) 672-0933
Odenton, MD 21113 CK, MC, V, MO, C

Catherine R. James was one Grandma who knew where it was at when she founded Grandma's Spice Shop in 1978. Coffees, teas, over 500 herbs and spices, essential and body-massage oils, preserves, butters, honey, vinegars, and kitchen gadgets discounted by 25 percent to 75 percent fill the 17-page, black-and-white catalog. Their double nut fudge coffee made us think differently about decaf, and black current tea was another plum. From salt-free pizza seasonings (85 cents per ounce) to Garden of Eden potpourri ($1.50 an ounce), we found page after page of delightful notions. Give them a call between 9 a.m. and 5 p.m., Monday through Friday, or write for a catalog. Orders are usually shipped within 48 hours; shipping and handling is $3 per order.

Great Buys By Mail readers get an additional 10 percent off on orders.

Green Mountain Coffee

33 Coffee Lane (800) 223-6768
Waterbury, VT 05676 CK, MC, V, AE, B

If a regular cup of mud isn't your cup of tea, consider a cup of Green Mountain gourmet coffee. A java jubilee is brewing, with 50 different kinds to make any coffee lover content to the last drop.

The company's signature blend, Green Mountain Roasters Coffee, is roasted fresh mere hours before it's shipped.

Readers of *Great Buys By Mail*: When you call for your free brochure, Green Mountain will throw in a gift certificate good for $5 off on your first order. I'll drink to that!

H & H Bagels
2239 Broadway @ 80th Street (800) NY BAGEL
New York, NY 10024 (212) 595-8000
MC, V, AE, C

Now is the time for all good people to take a bite out of a world-class bagel. Low in fat and high in fiber, this is the roll with a hole for the '90s. Delivered overnight right to your door, fresh from their ovens in New York City, it's no wonder *H & H* has been voted the best bagel in the world. Name your favorite: plain, cinnamon-raisin, sesame, poppy, onion, salt, garlic, pumpernickel, whole wheat, or sourdough. Choose all the same, or mix and match in 4 packs. Minimum order is 2 dozen. When they arrive, what you don't eat right away should be sliced and stored in the freezer for year-round brunching, lunching, or munching. "Like no other bagel in the world!"

Great Buys by Mail Readers receive a 10 percent discount on their first order.

The Herb & Spice Collection
P.O. Box 299 (800) 365-4372
Norway, IA 52318 CK, MC, V, C

In the '80s we got physical; now it's time to get natural. Herbs and spices make great replacements for the salt and cholesterol-clogging butter most of us have used all our lives. The Herb & Spice Collection is right on with the health program for the '90s with their selection of traditional and culinary herbs and spices, oils, teas, and more. You can even post your botanical knowledge with a poster to remind those around you that you're hip to herbs.

High Meadow Farm
20 Davis Hill Road (603) 763-2535
New London, NH 03257 CK, MC, V, C/$3

You don't have to go to the farm to get wholesome, natural food; the farm will come to you. If you can imagine whole-food *diet* meals delivered to your front door, you'll love High Meadow Farm. Precooked natural meals emphasize whole grains and include three main meals per day along with two snacks. Each day's package averages around 1,000 to 1,200 calories and includes wholesome broths, soups, brown rice, pilafs, soy milk, and other nonperishable yet nature's-own foods. Mom couldn't keep you better fed.

IGT Services, Inc.
111 Lincoln Road
Miami Beach, FL 33139
(305) 531-6300
Membership/PQ

This a la carte card provides 25 percent off thousands of restaurants in the U.S. and it certainly sounds appetizing. The idea behind the Executive/IGT charge card is to provide for your annual $50 membership, easy access to over 3,000 participating restaurants (and constant updates). You may use the card as many times per day as you like, for any meal. You sign for the full price of the meal, as if you were paying with an ordinary credit card, but IGT subtracts 25 percent from the total cost (excluding tax and tip) before they bill you. No more bulky coupon books, only a contemporary credit card way to save "mucho dinero" on dinners.

Ideal Cheese Shop
1205 Second Avenue
New York, NY 10021
(212) 688-7579
MC, V, AE, C

You can smile when you say "Cheeses" at this Second-Avenue emporium. Celebrating its 33rd anniversary, this is the haven for some of the finest cheeses in the country. This trend-setting shop was reviewed by famed Craig Claiborne in 1962 in an article in *The New York Times*, and since that time owner Edward Edelman has continued to tempt the fanciers with some of the finest and freshest cheeses from all over the world. Find exotic double and triple creams, the perfect brie, the quintessential Boursault, Danish Saga, Creama Donia, or Italian Taleggio. Experts are on hand to guide you through their extensive and mouth-watering catalog.

It's From Oregon
8065 S.W. Cirrus Drive
Beaverton, OR 97005
(800) 247-0727
(503) 641-0727
CK, MC, V, AE, D, MO, C

When you want fresh-baked bread fast, mix it up with It's From Oregon. Their DASSANT Gourmet Mixes may be just what you're craving. Eight types of beer bread (hiccup!) are available, plus Oatmeal Raisin Spice Cookie and Old English Scone mixes. Average beer bread price is $3.50. It's much easier to rise to the occasion with a little help from this catalog without putting your foot in your mouth. (Though Beaverton is also home to Nike.)

Jaffe Bros., Inc.
P.O. Box 636 (619) 749-1133
Valley Center, CA 92082-0636 CK, MC, V, D, B, PQ

Jaffe's ranch puts a healthy squeeze on high-priced organic dried fruits, nuts, grains, and vegetarian food supplements. Picky palates will go nuts over organic unsalted peanut butter priced at $9.75 for three one-pound jars; unrefined olive oil made us Pop-eyes at $23.50 a gallon. Bee pollen, honey, brown rice, rolled oats, soy and mung beans were also available, although their dried fruits (unsweetened pineapple, mango, papaya, and 15 others) in five-pound bags are a real specialty. Prices are much lower than health food stores; there's a real incentive for bulk buying (minimum on most orders is five pounds). Down-to-earth prices in their 17-page price list made us real bargain-catchers in the rye!

Jessica's Biscuit/The Cookbook People
(See **Books and Magazines**, p. **104**.)

Katie's Candies
26 S.E. Spring Street (206) 748-8967
Chehalis, WA 98532 CK, MC, V, C

Katie's a sweetie, and has the goods to prove it: truffles, caramels, coffee drops, and other handmade Northwest yummies to ruin your diet big time. We went koo-koo for their chocolates and tried not to be greedy with gift baskets. It's a sin to catalog these sweets anything but heavenly.

Kolb-Lena Cheese Company
P.O. Box 486
3990 N. Sunnyside Road (815) 369-4577
Lena, IL 61048 CK, MC, V, AE, B

Craving cheese—go directly to the Big Cheese and smile. Since 1900, Kolb-Lena has been the place to save your curds and whey.

Offering the finest in cheese gift packs stuffed with more than a dozen cheeses that are produced on the premises. Swiskers, the mouse who used to stand guard at the plant has moved to a park, so you will have to fend for yourself when it comes time to pick a gift pack. Choose Brie, Camembert, feta, and their own baby Swiss if you want to send the very best. No minimum orders and shipped UPS, usually in 72 hours. Gift packs start as low as $8. If you're ever in Illinois, visit their factory to see how the cheese is made. And then you'll have it made . . . they give free taste samples.

Le Gourmand
P.O. Box 597 (518) 643-2499
Peru, NY 12972 CK, MC, V, B

Close your eyes and picture a fancy gourmet feast, featuring products from Le Gourmand at 30 to 200 percent below other gourmet mail-order companies. We found a 17-ounce bottle of walnut oil by GUENARD, balsamic vinegars aged over 25 years (makes a great salad dressing with a dash of lemon), herbs, spices, oils, vinegars, teas, coffees, LENOTRE chocolate coatings, pastry products, and more under the names of: PAUL CORCELLET, TABLE LYONNAISE, DEAN & DELUCA, PAGES, GASTON LENOTRE, BARRAL, LA PERRUCHE, BARRY, LA BALEINE . . . They stock a wide assortment of miscellaneous foods ranging from brown cane sugar in irregularly cut cubes to hazelnut praline. Write or call for their newsletter and stay on the cutting edge of their delicacies.

Maid of Scandinavia
3244 Raleigh Avenue (612) 927-7996
Minneapolis, MN 55416 CK, MC, V, D, MO, C/$2

Cake-decorating and candy-making supplies have been less expensive at Maid of Scandinavia since 1946. Bake the cake yourself even if you've never qualified for the Pillsbury Bake-off. A baker's bargain for do-it-yourself weddings, confirmations, anniversaries, or any other special occasion will save you plenty of dough. Items like cake tops, fountains, tier sets, candy molds, sucker sticks, chocolate candy coating, and other party supplies are available in their catalog, along with instructional books on the "how-to's" of baking and creating gorgeous candies and cakes. Stick with the experts here, and you've got it maid.

Manganaro Foods

488 Ninth Avenue
New York, NY 10018
(800) 4-SALAMI (472-5264)
(212) 563-5331
CK, MC, V, AE, D, DC, CB, COD, C

Mama mia! Now that's Italian. Founded in 1893, in its present location, Manganaro continues in the same fine family tradition. Their rafters are hung with imported hams, cheeses, and provoletti. Now the taste of old Italy can be yours with their wide variety of cheeses (parmigiano, Romano pecorino, pepato, provolone, and smoked mozzarella); vinegars and olive oils; pasta; espresso and desserts (yum-m, hazlenut chocolates!) and, of course, their famous Italian-style meats. Their gift boxes and baskets are gifts no one would return. Or learn to make it yourself with their Italian cookbook, $18.95. There's a minimum order of one pound on meats and cheeses. Orders are normally shipped within two days of their arrival at Manganaro; delivery in five to ten days. Remember, Rome wasn't built in a day, either.

The Maples Fruit Farm, Inc.

P.O. Box 167
Chewsville, MD 21721
(301) 733-0777
CK, MC, V, MO, C

Maples Fruit Farm has been around almost as long as the U.S. of A., and with good reason. We'd be nutty not to appreciate prices as much as half what they are elsewhere on nuts, dried fruits, trail mixes, teas, coffees, syrups, and other goodies we're stuck on. Got a date? If not, you can find some here, along with peaches, peanuts, pears, almonds, cashews (Gesundheit!), walnuts, pecans, pineapples, and much more. Their catalog is 16 pages of good eats (and drinks) to keep you healthy, wealthy, and wise.

Matthews 1812 House

P.O. Box 15
250 Kent Road
Cornwall Bridge, CT 06754-0015
(800) 662-1812
(203) 672-6449
CK, MC, V, AE, MO, C

The war of the roses could have been won, hands down, had we known about these scrumptious cakes and candy mixes. If you're ever needing to make peace, think about mixing up a batch of "sure tastes like homemade" cakes and candies from the House that Matthew built. Why waste a lot of time whipping and sifting when you can serve up desserts like these in no time? Impress even the most discerning diners. Or how about a spot of tea by EASTERN SHORE TEA COMPANY, flavored with fruit, spices, and flowers for a fragrant change of taste? Satisfaction guaranteed.

Moon Shine Trading Company

P.O. Box 896 (916) 753-0601
Winters, CA 95694 CK, MC, V, MO, B

Love ya, love ya, honey . . . and so did Ishai Zeldner when starting Moon Shine in 1979. Ten percent on case orders may not sound like much of a discount, but not only are their products less expensive; some of them would be hard to find anywhere else! Gourmet nut butters in seven varieties, a gourmet honey collection, honey fruit spreads, special sampler collections, and a "Vermont Hardwood Honey Dipper" made our mouths water. All their products are certified kosher (they've got certificates to prove it), and recipes and serving suggestions come with every order. Buy by the case to save more. For example, California Honey Apricot spread was $2 for two ounces, $5.75 for 15 ounces, or $42.50 for 10 pounds. (At the dollar-per-ounce rate, that would've come out to $160.) The brochure had a recipe for "Honey Apricot Barbecue Baste" that is simply scrumptious. Gifts included three- and six-jar samplers, a "Tropical Rainforest Gift Collection," and holiday boxes. Altogether, a unique and luscious collection that we'll bee keeping our eye on.

Morisi's Pasta

647 Fifth Avenue (718) 499-0146
Brooklyn, NY 11215 CK, MC, V, AE, C/$2.50 (refundable)

If you think "plain" when you think "pasta," think again. It's almost "prepastarous" how many flavors and shapes of pasta Morisi's offers. Green and red pasta for the holiday season? Fruit-, fish-, cheese-, nut-, and herb-flavored pasta? No kidding, they're cranking out more than 200 varieties. Lobster linguine sounded tempting, and we lingered over red wine linguine. To give or receive, you won't find anything pasta its prime here.

Pendery's
1221 Manufacturing (800) 533-1870
Dallas, TX 75207 (214) 741-1870
CK, MC, V, AE, D, MO, B, PQ

Rumor has it that this is the place that supplied J.R. Ewing with his peppers, and you know what a hothead he was. These folks have been in cahoots since 1891 (when cowboys were really tough). Custom-blended chile powders and many other spices are sold in bulk packages, saving consumers 50 percent to 75 percent or more off those high-priced bottles in retail stores. All seasonings and spices are sold under the brand PENDERY'S. No returns on food products; no problem with refunds if the request is reasonable. No matter if it's chile today or hot tamale, you'll get a taste for the flavor of the Southwest—the hottest part of the country! Their price list is free.

Mr. Spiceman Inc.
169-06 Crocheron Avenue, Dept. G-1 (718) 358-5020
Auburndale, NY 11358 CK, MC, V, C/$1 (refundable)

One might define the changing of the seasons as spices that lose flavor as thyme goes by. Mr. Spiceman, as he's called, offers more than 130 spices and seasonings to specialty stores, ethnic restaurants, and *now* to the public at wholesale prices. Everything is carefully sealed in airtight pouches to ensure freshness. Sesame, saffron, charcoal salt, cinnamon, juniper berries, anise star, pignolia nuts, crab boil, kelp, shallots, instant herbal flash tea—it's all here, and prices are up to 90 percent off those found in supermarkets. There's no minimum order, but there's a $1.50 charge on orders under $10. Shipping is free on orders over $100; if you're unhappy, they'll exchange or refund (your option) within ten days. Do yourself a flavor, seasoned shoppers, curry up—order one of their catalogs today!

Mrs. Travis Hanes' Moravian Cookies
431 Friedberg Church Road-1107 (919) 764-1402
Clemmons, NC 27012 (919) 764-2883
CK, MC, V, MO, B

Cookies and milk will never be the same. Mrs. Travis F. Hanes bakes the finest cookies in the world from an old family recipe.

Each cookie is rolled, cut, and packed by hand. "The flavor is literally rolled into the cookie." There were six delicious flavors to choose from: "Chocolate Crisps," "Lemon Crisps," "Butterscotch," "Ginger Crisps," their original "Sugar Crisps," and new "Black Walnut." Wrapped in individual stacks in a tin container, the cookies are guaranteed to arrive fresh and in good condition. One-pound tins were priced at $13 or $13.50; two-pound tins were $23 or $23.50. Gift packs were also available. Shipping and handling was $1.50; add $4 more for cookie monsters to Puerto Rico, Alaska, and Hawaii.

Nancy's Specialty Market
P.O. Box 1302-GBBM — (800) 4-NANCY (462-6291)
Stamford, CT 06904 — MC, V, C/$2

Shop the international marketplace for specialty goods and exotic dining treats without leaving the kitchen. Hard-to-find and specialty items often leave a chef in a tither just because he can't find the necessary ingredients. Well, meet Nancy and forget running all over town looking for those hard-to-find culinary condiments. From pasta to peppers, Cajun to kosher, Nancy does the shopping in over 13 ethnic regions. Where else could you find Caribbean spices, Blue Corn Meal, dried chile peppers, shittake mushrooms, plus unique cookware and tableware . . . all from one 24-page catalog.

New Canaan Farms
Highway 290 W
P.O. Box 386 — (800) 727-JAMS
Dripping Springs, TX 78620 — CK, MC, V, MO, B

New Canaan turned us to jelly with their jams, butters, and spreads. Pumpkin Butter, Texas Pride Jalapeño Mustard, Brazos River Blackberry Jam, and Whiskey Sour Jelly ("great bourbon topping") are among the named pureed prizes. (We must admit, though, that Garlic Onion Jelly gave us a breath of relief.) From the more pedestrian Country Apple Butter and Strawberry Jam to exotic Cactus Sangria Jelly, their brochure contains a plethora of scintillating spreads, including a couple that were sugar-free. Prices were $12.95 for a three-jar gift box, or your choice of 12 jars for $36.95 (jars are 10 ounces each). Write or call for a brochure; orders taken before noon are shipped the same or next day. Shipping is included in their prices.

New York Texas Cheesecake

Dunsavage Farms
Route 2, Box 220 (800) 225-6982; (903) 675-2281
Larue, TX 75770 CK, MC, V

Former newspaper publisher Lyn Dunsavage hit the pay dirt and changed careers in mid-sentence. Now she sweet-talks her customers with her 100-year-old family recipe for homemade cheesecake baked in home-style ovens right in her farmhouse, 85 miles outside Dallas. The fruits of her labor have appeared in the Neiman-Marcus catalog, as well as reaching the finals of the International Fancy Food Competition. Available (frozen) and packed in special styrofoam boxes (add $2), the cakes can travel up to two days without refrigeration. Scrumptious cakes at *wholesale* prices include the petite, $2.50; one-pound, $9.95; two-pound, $16.95; three-pound, $22.95; four-pound, $29.95. Those prices are for the original recipe. Add 50 cents for flavors in one-pound sizes and $1 for larger sizes. Other flavors include apricot brandy, chocolate, Jamaican rum, Amaretto, Black Forest, Bababerry (similar to raspberry), and praline. Now don't we all scream for praline?

Northwest Select

14724 184th Street N.E. (800) 622-2693; (206) 435-8577
Arlington, WA 98223 B

Living well is the best revenge. And eating without pesticides helps. Eat to your heart's content with fresh-from-the-garden produce. This company lives on a 320-acre farm and produces all its own organic, spring-fed produce. And if you want to veg-out, they also offer every conceivable vegetable, fruit, or berry, picked fresh daily and shipped overnight. Imagine the pleasure of giving a gift with the real greening of life. Choose a healthy-holiday centerpiece basket or decorated garlic braids and grapevine wreaths. Call for free brochure and samples.

Northwestern Coffee Mills
217 N. Broadway (800) 243-5283; (414) 276-1031
Milwaukee, WI 53202 (715) 747-5825
CK, MC, V, AE, MO, C

The smell of coffee is said to open the pleasure centers of the brain. We find, however, that our pleasure centers respond to discounts, too. That's why we savored the savings from the Northwestern Coffee Mills Company. They are "importers, roasters, blenders and grinders of fine coffee, teas and spices." They've been in business since 1875, so they must be doing something right. Coffees included New Orleans chicory; straights (unblended) from Brazil, Costa Rica, India, and Peru; French and Vienna dark roasts; and Sumatra and Kenya decaffeinated. Buying in bulk, you can save 30 percent to 40 percent. Guatemala Huehuetenango, for example, was $6.55 for one pound, but the per-pound rate dropped to $4.50 with 25-pound orders. Northwestern uses no Robusta beans, which dilute the flavor. Suggestions on preparing their coffees are included in the brochure. Spices are offered, too, as well as extracts and dried vegetables and other seasonings. Delivery usually takes one to two weeks. Wake up to an exotic line-up of steamy gourmet coffees.

Palmer's Maple Syrup
P.O. Box 246 (802) 496-3696
Waitsfield, VT 05673-9711 CK, AE, MO, B

Some may pull up the price, but Palmer's Maple Syrup brings it back down to earth. Sample the sap and sugar from Vermont and taste the reason they've been around since 1967. Not only do they know what they're doing (the brochure told us all about it), they discount the price by about 30 percent, which is easy to swallow. Syrups fit for cooking or drizzling over your pancakes are going like hotcakes. A call or letter will get you a price quote and the brochure is free, so don't be a sap—check it out.

Paprikas Weiss Importer
1572 Second Avenue, Dept. GBBM (212) 288-6117
New York, NY 10028 (212) 288-6903
CK, MC, V, AE, C

From the wooden shelves of this 100-year-old gourmet food shop come some of the world's finest delectables. Owner Ed Weiss "has to be the greatest and fastest and most complete and thorough source of food information in the world," wrote Maida Heatter, the famous creator of *The New York Times* recipe series. The imported foods and cookware (hard to find on many local fronts) included many Hungarian specialties like PICK imported Hungarian salami, (regularly $7.98 per pound, discounted to $5 per pound), paprika paste, fresh-baked Dobosh torte (seven-layer cake) . . . even a dumpling machine. Plus cheese, pâtés, coffees, teas, and candies. Corporate gifts available with one phone call.

Pinnacle Orchards
P.O. Box 1068 (800) 547-0227
Medford, OR 97501 CK, MC, V, D, AE, MO, C

These orchards are a peach, but pears are their specialty. Then sink your teeth into other mouth-watering and healthy gourmet gift and fruit baskets, and hold the mayo. A Harvest-of-the-Month Club gift certificate is a yummy and fruitful way to remember someone (or yourself). Candies, bakery items, smoked meats, and preserves round out their delicious menu of offerings.

Rocky Top Farms
Route 1, Essex Road (800) 862-9303
Ellsworth, MI 49729 (616) 599-2352 (FAX)
CK, V, MC, MO, B

Love the old-time flavor and taste of homemade jams and jellies? Then Rocky Top Farms is the place to churn. Good ol' Rocky Top! They specialize in Michigan grown and produced products made in small batches to control the ultimate quality, utilizing only pure ingredients with no preservatives. They boast old-time recipes and a lower level of sweeteners. It's hard to choose a favorite from their Berry Preserves and Toppings, Fruit Preserves, Fruit Butters and Toppings. You'll drool over the Apricot Butter and Gram's Rhubarb Chutney. Michigan white cedar bark is crafted into gift containers for the jars, but still the recipients pine for more. You are invited on a personal tour of Rocky Top, if ever in northern Michigan. All orders shipped UPS. Prices range from $11 for a three-jar redwood gift crate to $34 for the 12-jar family pack.

Reader special: 10 percent off on your first order.

SalsaExpress
P.O. Box 3985-GBBM (800) 43-SALSA
Albuquerque, NM 87190 MC, V, C (free sample)

So what do they do "After the Stork"? Well, the founders of this successful children's catalog retired and spent a few days thinking of what else they could deliver that was a hot deal in the ole town tonight? Holy jalapeño! Stuff yourself on the finest red and green stuff in America. They carry O.G.'s all-natural green chili salsa (a three-time winner of the New Mexico Fiery Foods Award), as well as other fine salsas and spicy delights. Best yet, dip with an all-natural blue-corn tostada chip that's still warm when it arrives at your doorstep. Gourmet quality at economically epicurean prices. Just add crushed tomatoes to the packet of dry sample salsa when it arrives. Try it. You'll like it!

San Francisco Herb Co.
250 14th Street (800) 227-4530
Dept. GRT (800) 622-0768 (CA residents)
San Francisco, CA 94103 (415) 861-7174
CK, MC, V, MO, C

For the spice of life, slice off at least one-half the price for the same or similar products from the supermarket. Since they buy in bulk quantities and repackage in their own one-pound units, you can reap the benefits of wholesale prices on spices, teas, and natural foods. If you'd rather leave your heart in San Francisco but bring home botanicals (like Mexican chamomile), pine nuts, tapioca pearls, or tropicana orange pekoe blend teas, then we can't sing praises loud enough for this mail-order resource.

Great Buys By Mail readers: Additional discounts are 10 percent on $200; 15 percent on $500 orders. Minimum order, $30. Shop where the chefs shop and chop 'til you drop your food bill in half.

Schapira Coffee Company
117 W. 10th Street (212) 675-3733
New York, NY 10011 CK, MC, V, MO, B

Coffee, tea, and you can always find me—a sucker for a cup of lapsang souchong (tea) or Kenyan AA water-processed decaffeinated coffee. Any way in which I can make my life easier is high on my shopping list. Favorite blends were available by the pound within their mail-order price lists. BROWN ROAST ($5.65), COSTA RICAN ($5.90), JAMAICA BLUE MOUNTAIN ($14.75)—shipped the day it's roasted to your specifications. Beans are ground to order for the percolator, drip, vacuum, or Melitta. Naturally flavored teas like black currant or raspberry were packed 50 teabags for $3.40 and loose teas by the pound like EARL GREY or DARJEELING were $5 to $6.

Schoonmaker/Lynn Enterprises
4619 NW Barnes Road (503) 222-5435
Portland, OR 97210 CK, B

Hey, honey, here's the perfect barbecue combination. Imported French lavender honey as a glaze for indoor grilling sounds succulent to us! Savor 50-percent savings when you buy their Orangier, Printemps, Montagne, Acacias, or Tournesol honeys, as well. No returns, honey, are accepted; most orders are delivered in one week.

Schwan's Retail Customer Service Group
600 Michigan Road (800) 544-8708
Marshall, MN 56258 CK, MO, C

No, it's not your swan song. It's the Schwan man bringing you the convenience of never standing in a grocery line again. Schwan trucks bring frozen foods, like chicken patties, ice cream, and corn dogs, right to your door. Fill your freezer with cool edibles without going any farther than the driveway. There's no cost for the delivery, either. Check with Schwan to find out if they're available in your area and for more information.

Simpson & Vail, Inc.
P.O. Box 309 (914) 747-1336
Pleasantville, NY 10570 CK, MC, V, MO, C

Tea and symphony since 1929 for 10 percent to 30 percent less, *plus* coffee, accessories, and the accompaniments to both (like chocolates and preserves) are available through this fine retailer. Over 80 varieties of teas to taste, more than 50 high-grown, hard-bean coffees from Kenya AA to Mocha Java to water-processed decaffeinates. Lovely gift-giving canisters filled with teas, teaballs galore, teapots, sugar and creamer sets, maple syrups, pancake and muffin mixes, Scottish soups, pure seafood soups, Louisiana spices . . . all too mouth-watering to enumerate further. This company, more than 50 years old, is owned by Joan and Jim Harron and sells to such famous restaurants as The Russian Tea Room in New York City.

Great Buys By Mail readers can take 10 percent off their first order.

The Spice House
P.O. Box 1633
Milwaukee, WI 53201
(414) 768-8799
CK, MC, V, MO, C/$1, PQ

Sprinkle on the fresh spice and get out of the salt-and-pepper set. For 24 pages of spice information and tremendous selection, The Spice House catalog could be your home away from home. Soup bases, seasonings for tacos, salads, chicken, sausage, meats and more, herbs, spice racks, and a host of other cooking companions are hosted here. They'll put you up for up to 40 percent less than the next guy, and all their spices are ground weekly to ensure freshness. They guarantee customer satisfaction and will give price quotes by phone, or by mail with SASE.

Steel's Old-Fashioned Fudge Sauce
425 East Hector Street, Dept. GBBM
Conshohocken, PA 19428
(800) 678-3357
(215) 828-9430
CK, MC, V, COD, B

Steel yourself for the temptation that will ensue. Only the most fervent despiser of desserts and pancake syrups could say no to Steel's amaretto, praline, champagne peach, wild Maine blueberry coffee liqueur, creme de menthe, or rum fudge sauces. It would take a supreme feat of will to resist the attentions of their fresh apricot sauce, or the elegance of white fudge sauce with toasted almond. But if you're not among the strong-willed, how about sugar-free fudge, strawberry or raspberry sauce? (Only 16 calories per tablespoon.) Feel free to send one of their gift baskets, such as those featuring fudge, butterscotch, and raspberry flavors ($2 per 5.25-ounce unit a piece), or indulge yourself guiltlessly with a 9.5-ounce jar of sugar-free strawberry sauce for $3.25. If you're worried about preserving your investment, don't be; the average shelf life is one year. Wait and salivate about a week for the arrival of your order.

Reader special: 10 percent off your first order.

Sugarbush Farm
RR 1, Box 568 U — (802) 457-1757
Woodstock, VT 05091 — CK, MC, V, AE, DC, B

If you want to tap into something delicious, order this family's (made on the farm) maple syrup. What sap could resist any of their seven kinds of Vermont cheeses meticulously packaged in foil and wax? Imagine, two-year-old sharp cheddar (until you've tried it, you'll never know what two years of aging can do to fresh whole milk cheese); hard-to find sage cheese (rarely made today and delicious); or naturally smoked cheese (smoked golden for five days over a slow-burning maple/hickory log fire). Since 1945, the Ayres family has been delivering naturally good cheese, not processed or colored, at reasonable prices. Gift packs, too. Satisfaction guaranteed.

Sultan's Delight, Inc.
P.O. Box 140253-0014 — (718) 720-1557
Staten Island, NY 10314-0014 — CK, MC, V, C

Delicacies from the Middle East will melt in your mouth and not in your pocketbook. Their 16-page catalog sumptuously lists their specialties—from tahini (sesame butter), semolina, couscous, bulgur, chick peas, cashews, pistachios, packaged gift items, candied and dried fruits, filo dough, baklava, Turkish coffee to cookbooks. Savings soar to 50 percent. There's a $15 minimum order, excluding shipping. Normal delivery time is within one week.

Get an additional 10 percent off on your first order when you identify yourself as a reader of *Great Buys By Mail*.

Texas Rose Coffee & Tea
P.O. Box 536 — (817) 983-3111
Heidenheimer, TX 76533 — CK, F

If you've got a nose for Rose, your taste buds will be blooming before you know it. This quaint country store carries a selection of freshly roasted coffees, Texas Rose tea (an orange pekoe black tea they blend and pack), and several varieties of honey, spices, extracts, and other items, although only teas and coffees are sold by mail. Their coffee originates as the finest quality Central American green coffee available, which is then roasted using an old European method of dry roasting. By roasting the coffee beans slowly, the beans retain a richer flavor and stay fresh longer. Besides selling to individuals, they sell their coffee and tea wholesale to gourmet and specialty food stores. A sample pack containing one pound of their special-blend coffee and four ounces of tea was $6.25 (they pay shipping). You can also buy larger weight orders of whole bean, filter ground, or percolator ground coffee and loose teas.

Timber Crest Farms
4791 Dry Creek Road (707) 433-8251
Healdsburg, CA 95448 CK, C

You're nuts if you pay for those high-price spreads . . . at high prices. Timber Crest is knocking down the high cost of healthy eating by offering their own brands of organically grown and dried fruits, nuts, and dried tomato products in consumer-size packs and in bulk. They've been growing, drying, and packaging their own fruits since 1957; the tomatoes were added a few years ago. Dried tomatoes are great for cooking, or try tomato paste, sauce, or salsa. Then take a bite out of the big apples, apricots, pears, peaches, pineapples, star fruit, papayas, mangos, cherries, figs, dates . . . yum-m-m! Or taste some pear butter, with no sugar added. You won't believe you ate the whole thing! Trail mix is perfect for snacking on the road or for holiday gift-giving boxed or on a redwood tray. Most orders are received in one to seven days. Write for the free 13-page color catalog.

Walnut Acres Organic Farms
Walnut Acres Road (800) 433-3998
Penns Creek, PA 17862 CK, MC, V, MO, C

Naturally it's organic if it comes from Walnut Acres. Since 1946, they've been purveyors of pounds of dried fruits and veggies, nuts, seeds, herbs and spices, preserves, juices, grains and cereals, honey, salad dressing, nut butters, and more. Running anywhere from 10 percent to 40 percent below competitors, Walnut Acres sells vitamins, too. Save the planet, save yourself, and save some money for a triple win.

Wilbur Chocolate Candy Outlet
48 N. Broad Street (717) 626-1131
Lititz, PA 17543 CK, MC, V, B, PQ

While my conscience, and Richard Simmons "talk a lot," I find that I am swayed by an occasional piece of "chocolate." This company can save "consumers" 20 percent on their own brand of chocolate and confectionery items. (Any dedicated chocoholic immediately will realize this doesn't necessarily mean 20-percent savings—it means you can binge on 20 percent *more* chocolate for the same price!) Wilbur, though, also has dietetic candies, plus a selection of chocolate and confectioner's coatings in white, pink, green, yellow, and orange sunlight. Delivery takes about a week.

Wood's Cider Mill
RFD #2, Box 477 (802) 263-5547
Springfield, VT 05156 CK, MC, V, MO, B (SASE)

Woodn't it be loverly if everybody discounted everything? Until that time, we'll have to carve out our own niches, like Wood's Cider Mill, where you can save up to 40 percent on their apple cider jelly and maple syrup. Apple-y yourself to their jelly without spreading yourself thin, or sigh for their cider; whatever you buy, it's from a family company that's been in operation since 1882. Send for a brochure (with SASE) and try this New England nectar.

The Working Moms of Sweet Energy
4 Acorn Lane (802) 655-4440
Colchester, VT 05446 CK, MC, V, MO, C

Home, sweet, home. What kid wouldn't want to listen to his mother? Well, do as I say and have your fruit, but love it, too! Everyone who works at Sweet Energy is a working mother, and, naturally, what they sell is good for you: all natural, preservative-free dried fruits and nuts. Taste peanuts, raisins, pistachios, apricots, cherries, and other taste treats that nurture nutrition, too. Or try the sugar-free carob products if you're counting calories. Their catalog is free, so sit up straight, and call before it's too late.

Zabar's

2245 Broadway (212) 787-2000 (NY residents)
New York, NY 10024 CK, MC, V, AE, DC, C

Concerning Zabar's, the famous New York gourmet food store, there's good news and bad news. First, the good news—they have a fascinating little catalog that's crammed with gourmet goodies like Russian coffee cake, milk-fed white veal, and more. Just reading the names of all the scrumptious foods will make your mouth water. Now the bad news—we can't possibly list all the discounted housewares they carry. (As a company's spokesman told us, "That'll take all year!") Nonetheless, they do carry brands like OSTERIZER, WARING, GE, SUNBEAM, KITCHENAID, HAMILTON BEACH, KRUPS, and SANYO at savings of 20 to 40 percent. Choose from a large inventory of French copperware. You'll save a buck or two on gourmet and hard-to-find coffees such as Jamaican Blue Mountain Style, Kenya, Hawaiian Kona, Mocha Style, Costa Rican, and Colombian. Brew, too, through their selection of decaffeinated blends including espresso and water-processed. All coffees are roasted on Zabar's premises twice a week. If your palate exceeds your pocketbook, call for this catalog immediately.

Freebies

Did you know you could hold your place in your favorite Danielle Steel book with a free animal protection bookmark? How about arranging for your grandparents or friends who are celebrating a milestone birthday or anniversary to receive a card from President Clinton? Or a mention on "The Today Show" from lovable Willard Scott? You can do that, too, and it's free. Cooking from old New England recipes, a guide to 100 best restaurants in New York City, or giving a Braille cookbook to a blind friend are just some of the options that won't cost you a cent. Here are some tips on asking for "freebies." Ask for just one item at a time—don't be greedy. Specify what you enclose with your request: for example, "I am enclosing a stamped self-addressed envelope." SASE means a 9½-inch-long, stamped business envelope addressed to yourself. If you need to send coins, mail as few as possible and tape them inside. Write your name (LEGIBLY!), address, and zip code on both your letter and the envelope. And finally, be patient. Expect to wait a month or two before your request is answered.

AARP (American Association of Retired Persons)
Health Advocacy Services
AARP
1909 K Street N.W.
Washington, DC 20049

For a free booklet about the skyrocketing costs of health care and what you can do about them, write AARP. They offer practical tips on how to save money on medical bills, how to stay healthy, and how to get involved in the fight to hold down health-care costs. There's also a brief discussion outlining the scope of the health-care crisis.

American Baby Magazine

American Baby, Inc.
575 Lexington Avenue (212) 752-0775
New York, NY 10022

Who says a baby is no bargain? Get a free issue of *American Baby Magazine* for expectant new parents. What kind of articles will you get? The issue that was delivered to us (no, the stork didn't bring it!) contained features such as "Dear Doctor," a parent's personal story, "Medical Update," nutrition advice, job-sharing information, and a photo essay of a baby's birth. A yearly subscription is $9.97, with the first six months free. Now, if only the baby would sleep and we weren't so tired, we could read. . . .

American Foundation for the Blind

15 W. 16th Street (212) 620-2000
New York, NY 10011 C

This helpful packet will increase understanding of the problems of visually impaired students and friends. A card with raised Braille alphabet and numerals, the life of Louis Braille, and suggestions for teachers who deal with visually handicapped children in the classroom are included. Publications, aids, and appliances for the visually impaired are AFB's specialty, and their catalog of publications for and about the blind can be quite useful. They also offer a free "application kit" for creating a photo-ID card for blind persons.

American Heart Association

National Center
7350 Greenville Avenue (214) 373-6300
Dallas, TX 75231

Do you know that almost one million Americans die of heart disease every year? Do you know how to control high blood pressure? Do you know what major factors contribute to early heart attacks and strokes? You'd know these facts and many others if you read the Heart Association's sheet on heart attacks, strokes, and risk factors associated with diseases of the heart and blood vessels. In fact, these warning signs result in more premature deaths and disabilities than any other health problem. A few examples: "Strokes: A Guide for the Family"; "Living With Your Pacemaker"; "Exercise and Your Heart"; Cholesterol and Your Heart." Please note that we've given you the National Center's address, but the free or nominally charged literature is distributed by the Heart Associations's state affiliates and local chapters. To avoid delay, contact the nearest local office, which should be listed in your phone book.

American Paint Horse Association
General Store
P.O. Box 18519
Ft. Worth, TX 76118

This is the mane source for information on the American Paint Horse. Free information includes a full-color brochure detailing history, breed characteristics, and Association activities. Information is also available on Association services. Videos for loan include the A.P.H.A. National Championship Show and the World Championship Show. This comes from a city "where the West begins" and there's a high interest in horses. (Did you know a paint is not the same as a pinto, even though the colors may be the same?)

Animal Protection Institute
Free Animal Bookmark Offer
P.O. Box 22505
Sacramento, CA 95822

Want to find out everything "humane-ly" possible about cats, dogs, or birds? Send for these *free* bookmarks from the Animal Protection Institute and read about the eating, sleeping, and bathing habits of these three species of the animal kingdom. Enclose SASE along with your letter asking for "Free Animal Bookmark."

Announcements by Willard Scott
"Today" Show Office, Room 304
30 Rockefeller Plaza
New York, NY 10012

Be a star for a day. Willard Scott, the loveable weatherman of NBC's "Today" show, will announce birthdays, anniversaries, and charitable events on the air. Couples celebrating their 75th (or beyond) anniversary or individuals who have reached their 100th (or beyond) birthday can have their special day announced on national television. For those whose names are not announced, Willard will still send a birthday or anniversary greeting card. Willard will also announce charitable events on the air. Just send in the name, address, date, and the type of celebration or event at least three to four weeks in advance. Send in complete details and press releases with visual aids (if available).

Auto Safety Hotline
Consumer Information Center
Department of Transportation (800) 424-9393
Washington, DC 20590

If you're hot to get the facts on auto safety, then call the Hotline Monday through Friday, 8 a.m. to 4 p.m. This user-friendly government service provides some 20 booklets on such topics as "Child Restraint Systems"; "How to Fight Drunk Driving"; "Reports on Crash Tests"; "Fuel Economy"; "Motorcycle Safety"; and "Travel Campers' Trailer Safety."

Bel's Guide
RLH Marketing Communication
355 Lexington Avenue
New York, NY 10017

Dining out in New York City? Send a postcard to this address and ask for a (free!) guide to 100 of New York's finest retaurants. The guide was compiled by noted New York food critic Bob Lape and contains restaurants in nine categories. You can sample both moderately expensive to very expensive meals from restaurants serving American, Chinese, continental, French, Italian, Japanese, Mexican, Spanish, and seafood. *Bon appetit!*

Consumer Information Catalog
Consumer Information Center (303) 948-3334
Pueblo, CO 81009 C

What's been on your mind lately? Savings, suntans, sensible child raising? Get the scoop by requesting free information booklets from about 30 federal agencies. Such best-selling titles as: "The Confusing World of Health Foods"; "Herbs—Magic or Toxic"; "Thrifty Meals for Two"; "Your Key to Energy Efficiency"; "Cholesterol, Fat, and Your Health"; "Antidepressant Drugs"; "Generic Drugs"; "Antihistamines and Aspirin." Confirmed booklet junkies in our office have also broken down and ordered: "Nutrition and Your Health," "Consumers' Resource Handbook," and "Mortgage Money Guide."

Deak International, Inc.
Marketing Department
29 Broadway
New York, NY 10006 CK, MC, V

The firm that brings you commission-free foreign and U.S. traveler's checks will also send you a currency-by-mail form, rate guide, and brochure on foreign currency needs and investment in precious metals. They sell a currency calculator and send out a quarterly currency guide that is updated for 120 countries. Credit cards for calculator only.

Hollywood Bread
1747 Van Buren Street (305) 920-7666
Hollywood, FL 33020

Want a handy purse-size calorie and carbohydrate guide to take along to cafés and restaurants? Here's where to get one for no bread. The introductory pages give good advice: "Forget the fad diets, keep this book handy and get to know the foods you eat." About 630 foods are listed. Best of all, the guide won't cost you any dough.

L'Oreal Guideline (800) 631-7358

Why be hair-ried by the hassles of a permanently depressing perm? If you're frazzled by the frizzies or tainted by the tone of your tints, call the experts for free advice. They have a complete team of friendly professional technical consultants who are trained to help consumers. Line open from 10 a.m. to 7 p.m. E.S.T. Monday through Friday.

March of Dimes Birth Defects Foundation
Public Information Office
1275 Mamaroneck Avenue (914) 428-7100
White Plains, NY 10605

The March of Dimes Birth Defects Foundation provides the public with important information regarding birth defects and genetic disorders. "The Family Health Tree" is a colorful foldout genealogical chart useful for recording family health history. There's also a helpful list of sources for additional research on the back cover. Best of all, the booklet costs . . . $0.00!

Modern Products, Inc.
Gayelord Hauser Offer
P.O. Box 09398 (414) 352-3333
Milwaukee, WI 53209

Enclose a SASE and receive one sample each of SPIKE, VEGESAL, and low-salt VEGIT. Enough comes in each packet to flavor several soup pots. Ingredients are natural salt-of-the-earth seasonings.

Morton Salt Co.
Salt Dough Brochure
Department of Consumer Affairs
110 N. Wacker Drive (312) 621-5200
Chicago, IL 60606

"Dough-It-Yourself Christmas Decorations" is a small foldout with directions for salt sculptures. You'll find everything you knead to know to sculpt with dough: basic recipes, tool selection, hardening methods, finishing, and ideas for Christmas ornaments. "The Sodium Content of Popular Prepared Food Items" charts everything from deviled crab to barbecue sauce. Their "Measure Helper" provides data on calories in popular foods. An enticing folder, "Tickle Your Taste Buds," gives eight recipes using Morton's seasoning blend (in soups, pies, and casseroles). Fine info and free!

New Bedford Seafood Council
Promotion Department CDAU
17 Hamilton Street (617) 994-3457
New Bedford, MA 02740

For those who fancy fish, these folks offer free items that'll make your fins flap. Included are an iron-on transfer for you or your mate's T-shirt, a four-inch round blue and gold sticker (both show the council's logo, a sailor boy with a background of rope and nets), plastic litter bag, and a recipe folder of scrumptious seafood dishes that'll hook you in a New Bedford minute. (Limit your request to three items and include SASE.)

Office of Metric Programs
Washington, DC 20230 (202) 377-0944

Give us an inch and we'll take a kilometer. Like it or not, it's coming: the metric system. This office will send you an information sheet and conversion cards ASAP. While we could probably cope with the change, imagine the turmoil faced by the lowly inchworm. Talk about an identity crisis!

Penzoil Company
Gumout Division
3675 South Noland Road (816) 461-7078
Independence, MO 64055

These automotive experts offer three free informative folders: "How to Find Your Way Under the Hood and Around the Car" is appropriately described as "a quick and easy guide to preventive maintenance for the self-service customer (and anyone else who drives)." You'll discover good tips on keeping the old tank in service. "Why Use Fuel Mix Gas Treatment" and "Why Use Gumout" provide facts and figures concerning the solutions and problems of carburetion systems in modern automobiles.

Presidential Greetings Office
The White House (202) 456-7639
Washington, DC 20500

Want someone to get the recognition he deserves? Couples celebrating their golden anniversary (or beyond) and individuals who are 80 years old (and older) can get a congratulatory letter from the president of the United States. To arrange for the greeting to be sent, you need to write six weeks in advance, giving the occasion and the name(s) and address of the recipient-to-be.

Radio Shack (any retail store)
Battery-A-Month Card
Your Town, USA

Is this what's meant by a charge card? Not really, but it's a good idea. Once a month, you can get one free battery of your choice (AA, C, D, or 9-volt) from Radio Shack brand bins. No purchse is required to get a card. You may bring your card in for validation anytime during the month and pick out your battery.

Rice Council of America
P.O. Box 740123 (713) 270-6699
Houston, TX 77274

Offerings from this group will tell you everything you need to know about cooking rice. About 30 leaflets are available, but limit your selection to three, please, and send them an SASE. Subjects include: recipes for people with diabetes and allergies; microwave and conventional cooking; desserts, salads, seafood, and international favorites. "Rush-Hour-recipes" comes in large type and Braille versions (no SASE needed). Write for a complete list of their brochures or request leaflets by title.

Roman Meal Company
P.O. Box 11126
Tacoma, WA 98411

Friends, Romans, brown-baggers: lend us your ears! This company furnishes a variety of fine publications for your use. "Sandwiches Under 200 Calories With Roman Light Bread" is a booklet dieters will appreciate. Equally delicious are the menus and calorie counts for a 1,200-calorie, balanced, 14-day diet plan in "Diet and Nutrition." "Bread on the Table" offers 22 pages that will guide you to better nutrition and tell you everything you wanted to know about bread . . . from field to table. *Get Fit and Fiddle in the Kitchen* is a new creatively written and beautifully illustrated book for children that gives information on nutrition, exercises that are fun to do, and simple recipes for the beginning cook. Send for their complete list of brochures and publications (regular size SASE).

The O.M. Scott & Sons Company
Marysville, OH 43041 (800) 543-TURF
(800) 762-4010 (OH residents)

Mow the line and call these lawn-care experts for advice. Save green. Scott's lawn consultants can tell you the best products and agronomic practices to use for your type of lawn and your region of the country. They can also give you the location of the nearest Lawn Pro™ retailer. Free for the asking is *Lawn Care* magazine, a compilation of helpful lawn information published in the spring of every year.

U.S. Department of Education
Federal Student Aid Program
Dept. J-8 (303) 984-4070
Pueblo, CO 81009-0015

To receive a free copy of "Student Guide; Five Federal Financial Aid Programs, '92–'93," you may call a local office or write to them at the above address. The new version reflects changes made in 1984 for the Guaranteed Student Loan (GSL) program. Other programs described include: National Direct Student Loans; College Work-Study; Supplemental Educational Opportunity Grants; and Basic Educatioal Opportunity Grants. Restrictions have been tightened so you can't take financial assistance for grant-ed as easily. It pays to keep current.

W. J. Hagerty & Sons
P.O. Box 1496 (800) 348-5162;
South Bend, IN 45524 (219) 288-4991 (IN residents)
CK, MC, V, B

We took a shine to this company's product brochure and free half-ounce sample of silversmith's polish. It's a European formula with a tarnish preventative that is sold in jewelry stores throughout the world. Hagerty manufactures their own brand of polish (they know that nothing can tarnish your image faster than a reputation for dullness). Whether you're bringing a shine to old heirlooms or the family tea service, their products can take care of silver, brass, copper, pewter, pearls, wood, and crystal.

Women's Sports Foundation
342 Madison Avenue, Suite 728 (800) 227-3988
New York, NY 10017 (212) 972-9170
CK, MC, V, D, B

This nonprofit organization encourages women to be involved in sports. They publish guides, posters, and pamphlets. Their Women in Sports films are available to schools and community groups and the foundation publishes a guide listing scholarships to American colleges and universities. Athletic scholarships range from under $100 to "full ride." The WSF maintains a library for additional resources concerning women and sports. Brochures available.

Free TV Tickets

Many TV shows have live audiences. If you plan to be in New York or Los Angeles, write to the network's guest relations department for free tickets.

ABC
7 West 66th Street
New York, NY 10023

or

4151 Prospect Avenue
Hollywood, CA 90027

CBS
524 W. 57th Street
New York, NY 10019

or

7800 Beverly Boulevard
Los Angeles, CA 90036-2188

NBC
30 Rockefeller Plaza
New York, NY 10020

or

3000 W. Alameda Avenue
Burbank, CA 91523

Other TV Show Addresses

Jenny Jones Show
NBC Tower
454 N. Columbus Drive, 4th floor
Chicago, IL 60611
(312) 836-9400

Oprah
P.O. Box 909715
Chicago, IL 60690
(312) 591-9222

Maury Povich Show
221 W. 26th
New York, NY 10001
(212) 989-8800

Montel Williams
(800) 747-8181

Joan Rivers
℅ Don Golden
CBS Broadcast Center
524 W. 57th Street
New York, NY 10019

Sally Jesse Raphael
510 W. 57th Street
New York, NY 10019

Jerry Springer
℅ WLWT-TV
140 W. Ninth Street
Cincinnati, OH 45200

Geraldo
CBS Broadcast Center
524 W. 57th Street
New York, NY 10019

Toll-Free Directories
(800) 426-8686

Toll-free shopping means you do not have to pay for the phone call. If there's an 800 number for a company, AT &T will list it in these two directories: one for consumers ($9.95) and another for businesses ($14.95). Other specialty directories are the one for *Gifts, Catalogs and Celebrations* ($4.99) and *Travel* ($4.99).

Furniture and Accessories

Decorate your home with fine furniture in styles ranging from high-tech to traditional from such manufacturers as BROYHILL, HERITAGE, HENREDON, THOMASVILLE, STANLEY, THAYER COGGIN, and others. If you buy by mail, savings are substantial, often as much as 60 percent. On large purchases, even after paying shipping, you could still save hundreds, *even* thousands *of dollars! Look around locally and when you see something you like, send for manufacturer's catalogs or brochures for the companies we list. You'll have to provide the manufacturer's name, a description of the item, the model number, and maybe even a fabric swatch to order. There's a definite trade-off: what you save in dollars you may lose in time. Although shipping times vary widely between companies (a point you should definitely check), don't expect instant delivery. Occasionally the wait can be as long as four to six months. Remember, your local retail store pays freight, too (which you pay ultimately), and you may have to wait months for delivery, there as well, only you still end up paying full price. A definite trend is away from name brands where upholstery resources can build a piece of furniture from the basic frames and copy the most expensive lines at a fraction of the original's price.*

Annex Furniture Galleries
P.O. Box 958
616 Greensboro Road (919) 884-8088
High Point, NC 27260 CK, MC, V, B, PQ

Annex-cellent choice for all styles of furniture including contemporary, 18th century, Oriental, French Provincial . . . and some excellent manufacturers: BAKER, DREXEL, HERITAGE, THOMASVILLE, CENTURY, HICKORY, to name but a few. Savings abound from their 45,000-square-foot showroom and usually are 45 percent off from this 42-year-old firm. To find out if what you want is available, supply the manufacturer's name and style number. They will quote prices and arrange delivery (which includes set-up in your home). All orders are shipped COD.

Arts by Alexander's
701 Greensboro Road (919) 884-8062
High Point, NC 27260 CK, B, PQ

It's the same old story—one thing leads to another. Begun in 1925 as a printing company, Arts by Alexander's soon branched off into picture framing, then into accessories, and finally into furniture. That's quite an evolution. Arts by Alexander's has no ragtime brands—they carry mid-to-upper-echelon lines in accessories, bedroom furniture, chairs, mattresses and sleep products, office furniture, patio and outdoor furniture, rattan, sleepers and sofas, tables, upholstered furniture, and wall systems. Their aproximately 200 brands include such names as AMERICAN DREW, DANSEN, LA BARGE, CHAPMAN, THAYER COGGIN, CRAFTIQUE, and PULASKI. Custom framing is a specialty, and they have an extensive gallery of pictures to decorate the home or office. Discounts are 40 percent to 50 percent on most lines.

Bachmaier & Klemer
Postfach 2220
D-8240 Berchestesgaden-2
BRD, Germany 8652-5079 CK, C/$1

Birds of a feather clock together! This German clock factory sells a variety of plain or painted cuckoo clocks. Prices are 45 percent to 50 percent lower than comparable American clocks. There's a guarantee on material and workmanship for one year and they'll exchange during this period as well. If the clock has been damaged in transit, they'll replace it (but an official transport claim by a local post office must be filed). There's no minimum order and no restocking charge. So beak now or forever hold your timepiece! Cuckoo, cuckoo, cuckoo!

Barnes & Barnes
190 Commerce Avenue (800) 334-8174
P.O. Box 1177 (919) 692-3381 (NC residents)
Southern Pines, NC 28387 CK, MC, V, MO, B, PQ

Cliff Barnes is the marketing director, but you won't find him feuding with J. R. at Southfork. He's more interested in forklifts and shipping merchandise direct from the manufacturer's warehouse to you including an in-home set-up. Choose from over 200 of America's leading furniture manufacturers at 40 percent to 50 percent off. Their connections net you AMERICAN OF MARTINSVILLE, FAIRINGTON, HIGHLAND HOUSE, TEMPLE, and others of equal worth. Fill up your hearth with a dearth of name-brand living room, dining room, bedroom, and patio furniture and expect birth in eight to 12 weeks or longer. Next time you're feuding with J. R. (Jerky Retail), call Cliff for a peek at his savings.

Mention you read about them in *Great Buys By Mail* and receive a special 2-percent discount off your order.

Bedazzled/Pat Petersen and Western Decor
418 Lincoln Square (817) 261-6911
Arlington, TX 76011 CK, MC, V, D, AE, PQ

Bewitched. Bedazzled. But never be-better. This designer showroom is a class act. Enter the world of high-fashion furnishings and forget ever paying retail again. This is **the** designer that can achieve a million dollar look on a working gal's budget. All major furniture and furnishings' manufacturers represented at prices up to 40 percent off (including shipping). Their newest addition is their Western Gallery and Accessories Collection. Send a picture or photo of a unique accessory and let them do the stalking. They can find it at a discount, or duplicate it without the fancy price tag. Add gorgeous gifts, a private collection of carpeting under the PAT PETERSEN label, wallcoverings, tapestry pillows, and floral arrangements that will all stand the test of time. Go West, and discover the best.

Ben's Babyland
81 Avenue A (212) 674-1353
New York, NY 10009 CK, MC, V, MO, B/50 cents

Land at Ben's and let them baby you with 30-percent discounts. They've been a soft touch in the baby furnishings biz for more than 75 years, with strollers from APRICA, GRACO car seats, SIMMONS cribs, NIKKYS diaper covers, and more. Crib bumpers, bathing equipment (for the first plunge!), cloth diapers, high chairs, and more for nearly a third less than at other baby furniture dealers. If you don't see what you're looking for in their brochure, call or write with SASE for a price quote, with as much information about the piece you want as possible, and say good buys to nightmarish retail!

Blackwelder's
Route 18 (800) 438-0201
P.O. Box 8 (704) 872-8921 (NC residents)
Statesville, NC 28677 CK, MC, V, COD (with 50-percent deposit)
C/$10 (refundable w/gift certificate for $20), B/$2

According to the *Wall Street Journal* (which once gave this company a front-page write-up), Blackwelder's is a savings hot spot for wood-be weekend decorators. Since 1938, this family has sold furniture for less. Today, they also carry their own walnut, mahogany, cherrywood, rosewood, ash, maple, wicker, and rattan furniture. They're also known by the companies they keep: their portfolio offers over 300 different MARTINSVILLE COLLECTION English and American 17th- and 18th-century reproductions in solid cherry, oak, or pine with four different finishes. Handmade and appearing much more expensive, this look spells class. Prices in Statesville are usually 30 to 45 percent below retail! Shipping is handled by Blackwelder's own trucking line or by special contract rate with North American Van Lines (that can be lower than a common carrier rate). Blackwelder's does a booming business, so if you can't get through on one of their four incoming phone lines, keep trying.

Attention Readers: Not only will you receive the $2 portfolio

FREE upon request, but you'll receive 10 percent off any MARTINSVILLE COLLECTION purchase. You must identify yourself, though, as a *Great Buys* reader.

Bonita Furniture Galleries

P.O. Box 9143 (704) 324-1992
Hickory, NC 28603 CK, PQ

Ahhh! *Qué bonita!* Bonita has been in the furniture business for 25 years. They carry most major brands, including CENTURY, LEXINGTON, and BARCALOUNGER. But we really relaxed when we found out their prices are about 50 percent below retail. Call for a price quote with information on the manufacturer, style number, and color you want, or mail all the information with a picture and/or fabric swatch (if possible).

Boyles Furniture Sales

P.O. Box 2084 (800) 334-3185
High Point, NC 27261 (800) 334-5135 (DC, SC, VA, WV, MD, GA residents)
(919) 889-4147 (NC residents)
CK, COD (with one-third deposit), B

Boyles carries over 150 lines of furniture including HENREDON, HERITAGE, DREXEL, CENTURY, HENKEL, and 18th-century reproductions. Prices are 40 percent off the manufacturer's list price if you live in North Carolina or the surrounding states; it's 30 percent off list if you live elsewhere. From April through October, High Point has their annual furniture convention for retailers. That's a good time for customers to save with last year's market prices. Shipping charges are set by weight and assistance—they'll gladly quote the price over the phone, so call and check. They ship via their own carriers and by common carriers. Expect at least an eight- to twelve-week wait, and possibly as long as five to six months at the outside. Like many of the North Carolina furniture firms, Boyles doesn't have a single comprehensive catalog, but they'll send you manufacturers' brochures about the particular line you're interested in.

A Brass Bed Shoppe

12421 Cedar Road, Dept. GBBM (216) 371-0400
Cleveland Heights, OH 44106 CK, MC, V, MO, C/$1

Brass and more comes to you from this store! Brass beds, white iron beds, and daybeds can all be mail-ordered at 50 percent off retail. The heirloom-quality brass and white iron beds offer the best of bedtime beauty with a full refund or exchange guaranteed if not completely satisfied. Special layaway and payment plans make purchasing the perfect bedroom furniture even easier. The prices alone will give you a polished budget! Orders delivered within six to eight weeks.

Cedar Rock Furniture

P.O. Box 515-0321 (704) 396-2361; (704) 396-2362
Hudson, NC 28638 CK, B

Build your home on the rock of great savings and you'll never be sorry. Cedar Rock carries all major brands of furniture at prices up to 50 percent below retail. Rock the house with bestsellers, like LANE recliners, JAMESTOWN STERLING in solid oak, mahogany, and cherry, the BOB TIMBERLAKE collection or CRAFTIQUE bedroom furniture. Their mirrors, lamps, and Oriental rugs add to the ambience of a well-decorated house. If furniture is damaged or a manufacturer's defect is found, Cedar Rock will repair or replace it. Delivery takes an average of eight to twelve weeks. Numerous brochures for different lines are available.

Identify yourself as a reader of *Great Buys By Mail* and you will receive an additional 5 percent off on in-stock merchandise.

Charles P. Rogers

899 First Avenue (800) 272-7726
New York, NY 10022 CK, MC, V, AE, MO, C

When you want a deal on a bed, go to the top brass. Charles P. Rogers, established in 1855, is America's oldest manufacturer of brass beds, and offers them at factory-direct prices. Dreaming of hundreds of rare, one-of-a-kind beds? They've got 'em wholesale, too. Rest easy—sleep cheap!

Cherry Hill Furniture, Carpet & Interiors
Furnitureland Station (800) 328-0933
Dept. GBBM (800) 888-0933
P.O. Box 7405 (919) 882-0933
High Point, NC 27264 CK, B

Want to know how the no-show showroom saves you up to 50 percent on home and office furnishings? Look no further than this family business, established in 1933. You can join the catalog revolution by shopping by phone. Yes, from the hundreds of famous manufacturers, and by shopping direct, you don't have to wait for special sales, closeouts, or dated merchandise. More than 500 names, like HENREDON, DREXEL, HERITAGE, CENTURY, BAKER, KITTINGER, KARASTAN rugs and carpets, you're only a phone call away. No sales tax outside NC.

Cole's Appliance & Furniture Co.
(See **Appliances (Large and Small)**, p. **40**.)

Custom Upholstery Mart
(See **Fabrics and Upholstery**, p. **193**.)

Design Lighting and Accessories
1311 Inwood Road (214) 638-1311
Dallas, TX 75247 CK, MC, V, AE, PQ

These are the design lighting and accessory sources to track. Though not in Soho, they are your ticket to high-tech lighting that formerly only designers turned to. Now you, too, can save from 20 percent to 50 percent on the lights of Broadway: FLO's, ARTEMIDE, SHANOBECK, and old stand-good-buys like STIFFEL lamps and CASABLANCA fans. For the artsy-endowed with good taste, just name your preference and switch to here. Chandeliers, halogens, landscape lighting, neon, baby lamps, and more hang out to try.

Edgar B Furniture
P.O. Box 849 (800) 255-6589; (919) 766-7321
Clemmons, NC 27012 CK, MC, V, MO, C/$15 refundable

Let Edgar B furnish you with discounts of 45 percent to 60 percent below retail. Representing over 130 different manufacturers, the B stands for Broyhill as well as bargains. Edgar's a powerhouse in the North Carolina corridor for factory-direct name-brand and private-label furniture. Shop their 320-page catalog with even a consulting service to help you in the decorative scheme of things. Satisfaction guaranteed upon delivery. A 25-percent restocking charge is assessed for returns.

Emperor Clock Company
(See **Kits and Kaboodle**, p. **350**.)

European Furniture Importers
2145 West Grand Avenue (800) 283-1955
Chicago, IL 60612 CK, MC, V, D, C/$3

European chic ain't cheap, *mes cheries*, especially not around these parts. But it can be cheaper, thanks to European Furniture. "Buy direct and save," they say, on carved wood chairs, lacquer dining chairs, and more to give your home that international jet-set ambience without the jet-set debt.

Fran's Basket House
295 Route 10 (201) 584-2230
Succasunna, NJ 07876 CK, MC, V, AE, B

Rattan is dandy and wicker is quicker to rearrange from parlor to patio. Find all your lightweight furniture here including dressers, headboards, chaise longues, rockers, dinettes, bath accessories, porch furniture, even unusual baskets imported directly from Hong Kong, Poland, Spain, and the Philippines. Two to three weeks is the normal delivery time. The minimum order is $25. There's just no doubt about it: Fran's hefty selection and considerable savings does her peers one up.

The Furniture Barn
1190 Highway 74 Bypass (704) 287-7106
Spindale, NC 28160 CK, MC, V, MO, B

It's a bargain hoe-down! Bow to your partner and pick out furniture that will cost between 40 percent and 50 percent less than suggested list prices. More than 20 years in the business has made these retail barnstormers tops in the delivery department. Their brochures and brands lists show off some of the selection; hundreds of brand names are represented. Just call in and name that brand. Information will be sent post haste.

The Furniture Patch
10823 Beach Drive, SW
Dept. GBBM
P.O. Box 4970
Calabash, NC 28467
(800) 334-1614
(919) 579-7994
CK, MC, V, B

The folks that run Murrow Furniture decided to expand to a second location and put their more than 60 years' experience in the furniture business to further use here. Their goal is to provide a service to people unaware of North Carolina discounters. Save 40 percent to 60 percent on fine furnishings and accessories by STANLEY, LEXINGTON, AMERICAN DREW, and many other nationally known names. Free brochures are available to give you an idea of their lines and explain their delivery and ordering procedures. Furnish every room in the house with the three $s: savvy, savings and style.

Furnitureland South, Inc.
P.O. Box 790
High Point, NC 27261
(919) 841-4328
CK, B

When furniture comes from Furnitureland, does it follow that it's "soiled" and dirt cheap? No way; we liked what we saw here. Aside from furniture, they carry lamps, accessories, and room-sized rugs at savings averaging 30 percent to 50 percent off retail. They have a 40,000-square-foot interior-decorated showroom with special prices on already discounted samples and closeouts. (Not bad for a company that started out in 1970 with catalogs and not much showroom, huh?) Brands include THOMASVILLE, CENTURY, SEALY, HENKEL-HARRIS, LANE, SHERRILL, LA-Z-BOY, WHITE FURNITURE OF MEBANE, and over 400 others. Delivery time for upholstered goods is 90 days; for wood products, 30 to 60 days. Expect a 20-percent restocking charge (plus freight) if you return items without cause. If they don't travel to your area with their own trucks and crews, they'll connect with other truck lines who do in-home set-ups.

Genada Imports
P.O. Box 204
Dept. C-3 (201) 790-7522
Teaneck, NJ 07666 CK, MC, V, C/$1

The accent's on European furniture at Genada with an emphasis on lower prices. Originally importing furniture for wholesaling only, Genada began selling to the public because of the great savings they were able to pass on to consumers on living room, dining room, and bedroom furniture—up to 40 percent. A #703 oak dropleaf gate-leg table, 31″ by 10″ closed and 31″ by 55″ opened, was going for $109.95 plus the cost of shipping via UPS. They offer a money-back guarantee; delivery takes an average of three to five weeks.

Golden Valley Light
274 Eastchester Drive, Suite 117A (800) 735-3377
High Point, NC 27262 CK, MC, V, B, PQ

The light at the end of the tunnel is at Golden Valley Light, where floor and table lamps and ceiling fans are glowingly discounted. More than 200 manufacturers are represented here. You don't have to be very bright to find savings of up to 50 percent on major name brands. How illuminating! Don't be shocked to discover they aren't light-weights, with more than 40 years of experience in the business. Whether you're still shopping or know what you want, we're happy to turn you on to Golden Valley. Call for a price quote, or check out their free brochure. Why be in the dark about discount lighting?

Harvest House Furniture
P.O. Box 1440 (704) 869-5181
Denton, NC 27239 CK, MC, V, D, MO, B, PQ

Harvest House separates the wheat from the chaff and offers quality brands of home and office furniture at up to 50 percent off. After you request (and receive) their list of brands they carry, you can get information tailored to your needs by filling out a questionnaire and returning it with a check or money order for $6 (refundable). They they'll hand-pick the brochures most likely to meet your requirements. Price quotes are available by mail with SASE, or by phone. Check out their sales, too, where you can thresh out even bigger bargains.

Hendricks Furniture, Inc.
P.O. Box 828 (704) 634-5978
Mocksville, NC 27078 CK, PQ

This may sound SEALY, but we found bargains on a BARCALOUNGER and a BROWN JORDAN patio grouping to be at least 40 percent below retail. You'll find those same savory savings on over 200 lines including DREXEL-HERITAGE, AMERICAN OF MARTINSVILLE, CENTURY, PENNSYLVANIA HOUSE, THOMASVILLE, and others in their 20,000-square-foot showroom. Brochures are available from all the major manufacturers they represent. Freight charges vary. Don't forget, you'll be saving sales tax if you don't live in NC. If the dining-room suite is $5,000 retail plus sales tax of 5 percent ($250), and Hendricks' price is $3,000 and the weight is 800 pounds, you will only be paying about $315 for freight. The proof of the savings is in your pocketbook. Remember, most retailers order from NC, too, so when you buy from a store, you're also paying freight charges, whether you know it or not.

Homeway Furniture Co.
121 W. Lebanon Street (800) 334-9094; (919) 786-6151
Mount Airy, NC 27030 CK, MC, V, B, PQ

Save up to 45 percent when you buy directly from this North Carolina company. Make Homeway your home away from home where furniture shopping is concerned. Sink into BROYHILL, BASSET, LEXINGTON, and other big names. A list of all brands they carry (including some prices) is free for the asking, or call for a price quote if you already know what you want. Don't stay home without them.

House Dressing/International Furniture
2212 Battleground Avenue (919) 282-5800
Greensboro, NC 27408 CK, MC, V, MO, B

Whether you prefer ranch or Italian, there's furniture to fit your style at House Dressing. They're pouring out discounts of up to half off the retail prices of furniture and furnishings by hundreds of major manufacturers, including ROBERT ALLEN, ALLMARK, DILLON, VOGUE RATTAN, and WATERFORD, to name a few.

Outdoor chairs, wicker, rattan, lamps, accessories, brass, upholstery—even fabrics are available. Payment on orders under $500 is due in full when you place your order; otherwise, a 50-percent deposit is required. They ship anywhere, and offer customer pick-up, in-home delivery, common carrier, and UPS shipping. House Dressing's brochure details their ordering procedures. Cut out the overhead and dress up your house with bargains.

Ideal Home Industries
11661 Preston Road, #131 (214) 363-3232
Dallas, TX 75230 CK, MC, V, AE, MO

Get out of the retail fishbowl and swim with the sharks. This is an Ideal place to get your feet wet. Fine-quality Oriental and traditional accessories and gifts are directly imported and sold at a savings of 30 percent to 50 percent. Use fishbowls as accent pieces to the bath, the hot tub, the mantel. Use them as an end table. A planter. Even a dining-room table. Choose any accessory and have them make it into a lamp. Soapstone, inlaid screens, rosewood furniture, pedestals, chairs, chests, vases, candlesticks, and figurines all ideally suited to designer touches.

Interior Furnishings Ltd.
P.O. Box 1644 (704) 328-5683
Hickory, NC 28603 CK, Certified Check, MO, B, PQ (SASE)

Deliver me from full-price furniture! Interior Furnishings obliges, with up to half off and a variety of brand names in tables, mirrors, mattresses, lamps, chairs . . . you name it. They furnish you with several delivery options, as well, and offer a brochure that includes a brands list. Price quotes are available by phone or mail (don't forget the SASE if you want a reply!). When you order, be prepared to pay a deposit of one-third.

King's Chandelier Co.
Highway 14
P.O. Box 667 (919) 623-6188
Eden, NC 27288 Certified Check, MC, V, MO, C/$3.50

Let's shed some light on the subject of chandeliers. King's no jester—every crystal piece in the place is their own design. Lighting fixtures are crystal, brass, and pewter combinations. Chandeliers and sconces hold court in either brass or silver finish. Their 100-

page catalog is filled with every style chandelier you can swing from, as well as royal testimonials from big-name customers. Their prices are good compared to those of similar quality merchandise in a retail showroom and their designs are often better. Chandeliers and other items may be returned for full refund within five working days after receipt (customer pays shipping). Orders are usually received in two to four weeks. Debbie Boone may light up your life but King's lights up your k-night.

L.A. Design Concepts
8811 Alden Drive, Suite 11-A — (310) 276-2109
Los Angeles, CA 90048 — PQ

This national buying service allows shoppers access to the items found in *House Beautiful* or *Metropolitan Home* that are often not seen in mainstream furniture galleries. Frank Kesheshian will escort you through L.A.'s Pacific Design Center for $25 an hour, or will track down your requested order at 20 percent above wholesale. Call for price quote and more information. They carry only custom-made high-end designer merchandise that is usually purchased through an interior designer.

Lamp Warehouse
1073 39th Street — (718) 436-2207
Brooklyn, NY 11219 — CK, MC, V, AE, MO, PQ (SASE)

Watt's a nice girl like you doing in a place like Brooklyn? Saving up to 50 percent on STIFFEL lamps and every other major name-brand lighting fixture and shade available! If ceiling fans are what you're after, they have over 85 styles on display featuring such major brands such as CASABLANCA, EMERSON, HUNTER, and more. (All discounted.) Although they don't give cash refunds, they do give store credit. Send SASE with your price-quote request if you write.

Liberty Green
P.O. Box 5035 — (800) 255-9704; (919) 395-1440
Wilmington, NC 28403 — CK, MC, V, AE, MO, B

Since 1984, Liberty Green has been crafting tables, chairs, bureaus, chests, and more out of pine wood. Wholesome and distinctly American, they're well made and won't leave you pining for a bigger brand name. Go for country charm at more than half-off prices found elsewhere. Customer satisfaction is guaranteed on all their goods; price quotes are available by letter or phone; refunds are accepted within 90 days.

Loftin-Black Furniture Co.
111 Sedgehill Drive (800) 334-7398
Thomasville, NC 27360 (919) 472-6117 (NC residents)
CK, MC, V, COD, B

Loftin space? Less-than-lofty prices is one reason for lofting a letter to Loftin-Black. This 45-year-old firm can furnish you with furniture, lamps, and Oriental rugs from over 300 major manufacturers: HENREDON, THOMASVILLE, CENTURY, PEARSON, BERNHARDT, HICKORY, and others. Prices generally run about 40 percent below retail. They require a 50-percent deposit before they'll ship. Upholstered goods typically take ten to twelve weeks for delivery; case goods, six to eight weeks. In the event of a return, the restocking charge is 25 percent. They have their own trucks for delivery.

Luigi Crystal
7332 Frankford Avenue (215) 338-2978
Philadelphia, PA 19136 CK, MC, V, AE, MO, C/$1.50 (refundable)

Mama mia! Luigi Crystal has been speaking our language (the language of quality for less) since 1935, and they're very familiar with crystal lighting fixtures. Their catalog features lamps, chandeliers, wall sconces, candelabras, and chimney lamps. You'll light up at discounts of up to 50 percent on fixtures made of marble, stained glass, and crystal, plus extra accessories and parts for lamps and other fixtures you already have, such as drop prisms in several sizes for chandeliers, and glass chimneys. They can also create custom fixtures to meet your own decorating needs. Check out their catalog for fixtures that range from simple to spectacular and light up your life for less!

Mallory's
P.O. Box 1150 (919) 353-1828
Jacksonville, NC 28541 CK, C, B, PQ

Mallory's should watch their calories: Some of their furniture looks positively stuffed. This firm carries HENKEL, COUNCIL

CRAFTSMAN, SHERKILL, LEXINGTON, STANLEY, and over 35 lines of high-end merchandise (some from Europe and the Middle East). They have 60,000-square-foot showrooms in Jacksonville and Havelock, NC. Prices are discounted to 50 percent. Their slick 24-page catalog is beautifully photographed; get one, plop down at the kitchen table, and sample their furniture buffet.

Marion Travis
P.O. Box 292 (704) 528-4424
Statesville, NC 28677 C/$1

This 10-page catalog highlights, in black and white, country furniture at a fraction of what you'd expect to pay. Particularly noteworthy is the collection of ladder-back chairs with woven cord seat, armchair, and rocker styles. Though the prices quoted are for "nude furniture," custom staining in natural, oak, or walnut is available.

Murrow Furniture Galleries, Inc.
P.O. Box 4337 (919) 799-4010
Wilmington, NC 28406 CK, COD (with 50-percent deposit), B

To Murrow, to Murrow, I'll be there, to Murrow, it's only a stamp away! Located in the heart of this country's home-furnishing industry, Murrow's sprawling 66,000-square-foot showroom contains a 45,000-square-foot decorator gallery. All told, they represent over 500 famous-name manufacturers, including BAKER, DAVIS CABINET, THOMASVILLE, and HICKORY CHAIR. Prices were 40 percent to 60 percent off retail. Resident decorators are available to advise you on choices of furniture, carpeting, and accessories. A 50-percent deposit with each order is required; balance due upon delivery. Custom-upholstered furniture is available; any order can take from six to twelve weeks. There's a 30-percent restocking charge on orders already in transit. Their brochure gives a partial list of brands and company policies; go for it today!

National Furniture Gallery
15 E. 32nd Street (212) 679-2565
New York, NY 10016 CK, MC, V, B, PQ (SASE)

James has no version of a catalog to serve as your Bible on prices, but he will send you (SASE) a free list of over 60 name-brand furniture and carpet lines discounted 30 percent to 40 percent off (one-third discount off the manufacturer's suggested retail price is guaranteed). Members of King James's entourage include HERITAGE, HENREDON, THOMASVILLE, BAKER, STANLEY, and SEALY. Company policy requires model, style, and color codes before they'll issue a proclamation on prices. Shipping time varies with manufacturer.

Nite Furniture Co.
P.O. Box 249
611 S. Green Street (704) 437-1491
Morganton, NC 28655 CK, C/$25, B, PQ

First in discounts since 1945, these folks discount first-quality furniture by 40 percent and more, and they carry lines from over 200 manufacturers. Brands include THOMASVILLE, DIXIE, WRIGHT TABLE CO., SOUTHWOOD, DREXEL, HERITAGE, HENREDON, and FREDERICK-EDWARD. (Nite's the only hometown outlet for HENREDON and DREXEL and HERITAGE furniture.) Nite ships anywhere in the country, with prices that are competitive with the best discounters around. Nite has four elegant showrooms of lovely furniture on display. In-stock merchandise can be shipped within a week, but shipping times vary on items that are special-ordered. Twenty-five dollars will get you 10 pounds of catalogs (this amount is refundable with purchase, or the catalogs may be returned within 30 days for a refund). They have their own brochure; write to get a complete list of the lines they represent. They are a fully authorized dealer for the lines they represent. Good Nite!

North Carolina Furniture Showrooms
1805 NW 38th Avenue (800) 227-6060
Lauderhill, FL 33311 (305) 739-6945 (FL residents)
CK, B, PQ

After three generations in the business, these Tarheels are well-heeled! They have a rich inventory featuring furniture lines from over 400 leading manufacturers. Discounts range from 20 percent to 50 percent, so when you order from their wealth of inventory, you won't land in the poorhouse. Brands include the biggies: HENREDON, THOMASVILLE, BAKER, and CENTURY, among others. They require a 50-percent deposit to place an order; all sales are final. Most orders are delivered within six to eight weeks. Call for a price quote and be sure to ask about sale prices on samples and closeouts for further discounts.

Passport Furniture Classics
P.O. Box 571853
6303 Beverly Hills (713) 723-4303
Houston, TX 77057 CK, MC, V, AE, D, DC, PQ

Down and out in Beverly Hills? Well, take a ride down the classic side of heaven and try not to fall in love with these hand-made armoires. For $299, this is your passport to savings. Shopping the bazaars across the Atlantic including unusual finds from Scandinavia and Russia, this resource lands some of the best buys in country pine, Queen Anne, Victorian, Louis XV, and Country French furniture, antiques and reproductions. Choose from any one of hundreds of chips off the old Chippendale block with wood that's solid. Or sit on furniture not quite old enough to be classified an antique, but not new, either (20 to 99 years old). With over 150 locations nationwide, they'll even start you in your own Passport store. If not, call for inventory and tell 'em you want a Great Buy from Beverly Hills.

Phoenix Design
733 N. Wells Street (708) 328-3240
Chicago, IL 60610 CK, MC, V, D, MO, C, PQ

This Phoenix soars to great heights when the subject of high-quality, solid wood furniture is concerned. No fly by night, quality doesn't come cheap, but it does come cheap*er* with Phoenix Design. They sell fine LE CORBUSIER, MIES VAN DE ROHE, MISSION, and MACKINTOSH chairs, beds, nightstands, entertainment units, armoires, and more at savings of 50 percent to 70 percent. Call to order a catalog or get a price quote. Custom orders incur a restocking fee of 10 percent.

Plexi-Craft Quality Products
514 W. 24th Street (212) 924-3244
New York, NY 10011 CK, MC, V, MO, C/$2

Plexi-Craft sells a variety of Lucite® and Plexiglas® acrylic products, including furniture, cubes, tables, kitchen and bathroom accessories, and more. Prices were all below what you would pay in department and specialty hardware stores—about 50 percent less. Plexi-Craft specializes in custom orders, so send a sketch of what you want molded into plastic and they'll send you a price quote. Most orders are received in seven to fourteen days.

PSC Lamps
435-West Commercial Street (800) 772-5267
East Rochester, NY 14445-2298 CK, MC, V, C

For medicinal purposes, turn on two lights and call me in the morning. You'll see better with these illuminating sources, which are 100-percent guaranteed. There's no minimum order for these replacement stage, studio, graphic arts, medical, scientific, miniature, and other specialty lamps. Quantity discounts are available (PSC sells to colleges, clinics, and other organizations); orders are shipped free via UPS. Orders are shipped within 24 hours when merchandise is in stock.

Priba Furniture
P.O. Box 1329527415 (800) 334-2498; (919) 855-9034
Greensboro, NC 27409 CK, MC, V, (credit cards for deposit only), B, PQ

Don't be a LA-Z-BOY and pay retail for your home furnishings. Priba offers discounts up to 40 percent across the table. They carry about 350 major brands of furniture, lamps and accessories, carpets, fabrics and leather, shades and blinds, wall coverings, and bedding. Brands include HENREDON, BAKER, CENTURY, HICKORY CHAIR, and COUNCIL CRAFTSMAN. A 50-percent deposit is due when placing an order; balance is due prior to shipping. Shipping times vary according to availability from the manufacturer. Write or call for a price list or price quote. They'll provide catalogs on request, but you must specify the manufacturer.

Quality Furniture Market of Lenoir, Inc.
2034 Hickory Boulevard, S.W. (704) 728-2946
Lenoir, NC 28645 CK, MC, V, PQ

Just because you're Quality doesn't mean you have to forgo quantity. This place carries about 150 notable names in furniture, porch and patio lines, and area rugs to outfit the private quarters of your home. After some preliminary scouting around, we saw such major brands as BARCALOUNGER, CHROMCRAFT, DREXEL, HERITAGE, HENREDON, LA-Z-BOY, SEALY, SERTA, and THOMASVILLE, to trumpet only a few names. Prices on these decorated heroes are 50 percent to 55 percent less on average. All orders must be paid in full before shipment; delivery time depends on the manufacturer. Returns are accepted only in the case of company error. Their motto is "satisfied customers are our only advertising."

Queen Anne Furniture Co., Inc.
Route 2, Box 427 (919) 431-2562; (919) 434-4990
Trinity, NC 27370 CK, MC, V, MO, B/$3, PQ

Queen Anne's crowning glory is an average of 45 percent off on furniture. The black-and-white brochure (which comes with upholstery fabric swatches) lists brand names and shows some of their selection. Get the royal treatment on all kinds of home furnishings by Queen Anne and other manufacturers. Price quotes are available by letter with SASE, or by phone.

Rattan Factory Outlet
13396 Preston Road (214) 386-6484
Dallas, TX 75240 CK, MC, V, AE, D, PQ

Wayne doesn't play The Gin Game on any of the dinette or dining-room sets here. But he does manage to deal the best hand around on rattan tables and chairs. Straight from the manufacturer in Houston at 50 percent off, you can't get much better than that. Choose the finish and fabric and it's yours. Small five-piece sets start around $600. Dining-room sets start at $600 and go to $1,400. Custom-crafted rattan is hand-bent rather than frame-built. Etàgeres, cushions, desks, bar stools . . . lots of rattan options and wicker choices as well. The selection of fabrics is also mind-boggling. Visit showrooms in Houston, TX, or Tampa, FL, when in the area; if not, call for a price quote for shipping nationwide.

Rose Furniture Co.
916 Finch Avenue (919) 886-6050
High Point, NC 27263 CK, COD (with 30-percent deposit), B, PQ

You can Bette your fiddler Rose ain't owned by Midler. Owners Bill and Buck Kester are the grandsons of the founder and they carry on the fine old tradition of discounting 300 manufacturers' lines to the tune of 40 percent. If you're on a Rose bud-get, spend $800 to $1,000 on purchases and save $200 to $300 even after freight charges. They require a 20-percent to 30-percent deposit for orders to be placed. Rose has 13 trucks with two-man crews to set up furniture in your home. They deliver more furniture themselves than most other stores. Orders are delivered in about eight to twelve weeks, carry the manufacturers' guarantee, and are subject to a 25-percent restocking charge if returned. With an average of 1,000 pieces to deliver per week, it's no wonder their sales Rose last year.

Rubin & Green Interior Design Studio
290 Grand Street (212) 226-0313
New York, NY 10002 CK, MC, V, AE, COD, PQ

Rubin & Green has made a few changes over the past few years—now they're a full custom-design company. They carry an extensive line of 20 to 30 name-brand fabrics including SCHUMACHER, DAVID DASH, ROBERT ALLEN, and STROHEIM AND ROMANN. From these materials, they create custom-design draperies, fully upholstered furniture, and custom-designed window treatments. (They'll build furniture from the frame up, to your specifications.) They still make designer bedspreads (and comforters of goose down, lamb's wool, or Dacron) from your plans: they'll take your sample, picture, or diagram and quote prices and custom design according to your specifications. Prices are 50 percent off what you'd pay retail and sometimes more (depending on the fabric and design you choose). Interior designers are on staff at all times. The delivery time usually is four to six weeks for most orders; eight to ten weeks for furniture. Request specific information and a price quote.

Shaw Furniture Galleries
P.O. Box 576
131 W. Academy Street (800) 334-6799
Randleman, NC 27317 MC, V, B, PQ

By George, Bernard! I think Shaw's got it! They sell furniture discounted up to 50 percent, and represent over 300 top-name furniture companies, including: HENDERSON, HICKORY

CHAIR, THAYER COGGIN, COUNCIL CRAFTSMAN, CENTURY, and WOODMARK ORIGINALS. Then add the class of a brass bed; accessorize with clocks, lamps, mirrors, bedding, and lighting. They set the stage for savings with the proper discounts. A 30-percent deposit by personal check is required when ordering; balance paid before shipment is made. It takes about twelve weeks for orders to be delivered. Returns are subject to a 25-percent restocking charge.

Sico Room Maker
5000 Belt Line Road, Suite 250 (214) 960-1315
Addison, TX 75240 CK, MC, V, AE

Help put an end to the squeeze of tightening walls! Open up your room to more room for enjoyment with the addition of one of Sico's wallbed and cabinet systems. Just imagine the space you could create for play in your little one's room. Or what about that spare guest/sewing room? Endless possibilities are open to you from this seemingly endless collection of wallbeds and organized unions for keeping *all* things in their proper places.

Silk Plant Company
(See **Plants, Flowers, Gardens, and Farming**, p. **425**.)

Sobol House
P.O. 219 (704) 669-8031
Black Mountain, NC 28711 CK, C/
(\$\$ varies depending on the manufacturers—refundable with the first order)

Start your education on saving money here. Sobol bolsters your bottom line by selling furniture from over 200 companies at 45 percent to 50 percent off retail. Select from CENTURY, THOMASVILLE, SEALY, CLAYTON MARCUS, AMERICAN DREW, and others. Their most popular line is probably THOMASVILLE—small wonder—it is discounted 50 percent! There is a 30-percent restocking charge on returns; orders generally are delivered in eight to ten weeks. Sobol House will send a helpful "request for quote" form to those who write, along with instructions on how to shop by mail.

St. James Furniture
P.O. Box 729
Houston, TX 77001
(800) 926-9065
CK, MC, V, B

They proclaim themselves to be "Texas' largest hickory chair gallery store." Brands carried: HICKORY CHAIR, HENKEL-HARRIS, HEKMAN, HARDEN. With discounts up to 40 percent off, you'll never end up in the St. James Infirmary. Choose any style in over 800 fabrics like the Herford chair, retail $1,188, their price $699; or a Chippendale sofa, retail $2,405, their price $1,399.

Stuckey Bros. Furniture Co., Inc.
Route 1, Box 527
Stuckey, SC 29554
(803) 558-2591
CK, Certified Check, MO, PQ/SASE

Nearly 50 years old and not slowing down one bit, here you can save up to 50 percent on some of the senior settees in the furniture world: AMERICAN DREW, CRAFTIQUE, HENKEL HARRIS, HICKORY CHAIR, WHITE, CLASSIC LEATHER, and more. This showroom boasts a selection that includes 18th-century reproductions, Oriental, traditional, and contemporary classics. All orders must be placed in writing, indicating style numbers, finish, fabric, and quantity. A 25-percent deposit is required. An additional 1-percent cash discount is offered if payment is made in full at time of order. Normal delivery eight to sixteen weeks. Merchandise cannot be returned without a prior written agreement; otherwise a 20-percent handling charge is assessed.

Sturbridge Yankee Workshop
(See **Art and Collectibles**, p. **49**.)

Sutton-Council Furniture
P.O. Box 3288
Wilmington, NC 28406
(919) 799-1990
CK, MO, B

Sutton-Council, around since the roaring '20s, has been flapping away the high cost of furniture and rugs. They have a swinging selection of carpeting, too, all at discount prices. Head south and save on kitchen tables, chairs, entertainment centers, and bedroom furniture by COUNCIL CRAFTSMAN, LEXINGTON, HENRE-

DON, and HICKORY CHAIR. They have over 100 brands available. Delivery normally takes ten to twelve weeks. A deposit is required with one-half down and the balance on delivery.

Thomas Home Furnishings
401 S. Highway 321 (704) 396-2147
Granite Falls, NC 28630 CK, MO

Nationwide delivery, famous-brand names, and as much as 50 percent off; that's the recipe for making great deals on furniture. No need to be a doubting Thomas. Here the Home Furnishings are reduced without losing any of their value or taste. A mixture of all styles for all budgets, but don't expect to take this Thomas for granite.

ToddleTown
351 S. Sherman, Suite 104 (214) 437-2770
Richardson, TX 75081 CK, MC, V, PQ

When the baby cries, this crib swings into action and would you believe, rocks the baby back to sleep! No more rockin' and rollin' at 2 a.m. when you can barely see straight. These innovative cots for tots are full-line cribs, and hospitals are loving them. The manufacturer is TODDLETOWN, with owners Candy and Herman Munster (yes, these are their real names, no kidding). You can rock away full prices with these solid wood-constructed cribs: oak, natural, white, whitewash, and cherry at up to 50 percent off. Retail around $550/outlet price, $329. Imagine, a good night's sleep is just ahead. Call for shipping nationwide.

Turner Tolson, Inc.
P.O. Drawer 1507 (919) 638-2121
New Bern, NC 28560 CK, MC, V, MO, B, PQ

Home, cheap home for half the cost! This company offers everything you need to furnish a cozy cottage or a palatial estate. Furniture, rugs, and carpets are available at 40 percent to 50 percent off retail price and familiar names include HERITAGE, DREXEL, PENNSYLVANIA HOUSE, THOMASVILLE, and many others. More than 200 of the finest names in home furnishings let you select the style you want to enhance your hearth and home. A 25-

percent deposit is required with your order. Same-day response is given to phone orders; one week on written price quotes.

Tyson Furniture Company, Inc.
109 Broadway (704) 669-5000
Black Mountain, NC 28711-3422 CK, MC, V, PQ

What a knock-out this Tyson offers. Get into the ring and join the other winners who have been buying their furniture from this family since 1946. That's when Alfred and Betty Tyson founded the 70,000-square-foot store now run by the second generation of Tysons. You don't have to sing "Those Were the Days"; prices are still 35 percent to 50 percent below retail on average. More than 200 furniture lines all point to quality: THOMASVILLE, DREXEL-HERITAGE, SHERRILL, HICKORY CHAIR, and many more. Get familiar with their restocking fee: 15 percent on cancelled special orders. No need to get out the truck and trek to NC; they offer nationwide in-home delivery. Most orders arrive within eight to twelve weeks. Call or write for a price quote.

Utlility Craft, Inc.
2630 Eastchester Drive (919) 454-6153 (NC residents)
High Point, NC 27265 CK, B

This utility company sure is a gas—but the pain of high prices is eased considerably with the savings here. Though they specialize in solid wood, 18th-century, and colonial reproductions, they do carry all styles and looks in furniture and accessories. KNOB CREEK, CRESCENT, STATTON, HICKORY CHAIR, DAVIS CABINET, GILLIAM, HABERSHAM PLANTATION, THOMASVILLE, and WHITE OF MEBANE in dining-room and bedroom suites; in upholstered pieces, you can sit on the likes of BARCALOUNGER, FLAIR, FLEXSTEEL, SELIG, or PEARSON; pull up to an occasional table, accent with accessories and casual furniture, or bed down in a brass bed with bedding by SERTA and KINGS DOWN. Utility provides in-home delivery and set-up and requires one-third down to place an order.

Wood-Armfield Furniture
P.O. Box C (919) 889-6522
High Point, NC 27261 CK, MC, V, B

One of the high points in furniture showrooms, Wood-Armfield is one of the largest showrooms handling most major manufacturers in upper-ended lines. No snob would turn his nose up at the KNOB CREEK line of furniture; the discounts are nothing to sneeze at. As with other shops in the Furniture District of North Carolina, ordering is basically a hit-or-miss-out experience. Go to your local furniture store first, then shop from this catalog to find out if they can get the brand and model you want. Prices are 30 percent to 50 percent below retail, and shipping is by their trucks or common carrier. Brands we found included THOMASVILLE, CENTURY, HICKORY CHAIR, STATTON, VANGUARD, CLASSIC LEATHER, and DAVIS CABINET. They also offer interior-design assistance for customers. Since 1939, they've been a fashion-forward furniture dealer on the home front.

Young's Furniture and Rug Co.

P.O. Box 5005 (919) 883-4111
High Point, NC 27262 CK, COD (with one-third deposit), B

If you're Young at the heart of the furniture industry, the future belongs to you. This is an ageless source of indoor, outdoor, rattan, and office furniture, as well as bedding, lamps, clocks, and carpet at discounts up to 45 percent off (special orders receive similar discounts). In the heart of furnitureland, though not as Young as they look, these folks have been in business over 42 years and carry over 150 better-quality lines, among them such old-time favorites as BAKER, HENREDON, KITTINGER, DREXEL-HERITAGE, HENKEL-HARRIS, CENTURY, COUNCIL, and HICKORY. Young-at-heart folks can even call toll-free for advice from their staff of trained interior designers. Young's requires a one-third down payment on all orders and has an excellent delivery system, with shipping time generally varying from two to five weeks. There are no returns on custom merchandise. If you're vacationing in the area, a look at their 25,000-square-foot furniture showroom could be the High Point of your trip.

Zarbin and Associates, Inc.

401 N. Franklin Street (312) 527-1570
Chicago, IL 60610 CK, MC, V, PQ

Zarbin is located across the street from the world-famous Merchandise Mart. You can find one of the largest selections of home furnishings on display in the United States. They can save you 40 percent and more on famous-maker national brands such as PULASKI, STIFFEL, HOOKER, FREDERICK COOPER, and many more. By appointment only, their interior designers will guide you through the selection of furniture and carpeting exquisitely displayed in the manufacturers' showrooms. They offer home delivery nationwide. If you can't visit them in Chicago, write the manufacturer's name and style number for price quotation.

Handbags and Luggage

Looking for a set of traveling companions? Get a handle on these suggestions. If you want to bag a lasting bargain, buy the sturdiest, most durable luggage you can find. When it comes to the airlines, remember, no bag has a pass to first-class treatment. Airlines give baggage a beating, and you'll need bags tough enough to take it. Another suggestion: If you're a woman in business, consider buying a handbag that doubles as a briefcase. When it comes to buying a bag, know that some listings insist on a description and model number, so be specific. If you don't, you'll be more likely to get the olive snakeskin bag by DIOR rather than the straw satchel a store clerk is trying to get rid of.

A to Z Luggage

4627 New Utrecht Avenue — (800) DIAL-011 (342-5011)
Brooklyn, NY 11219 — (718) 435-2880 (NY residents)
CK, MC, V, AE, DC, CB, MO, C, PQ (SASE)

How do you spell relief? S-a-v-i-n-g-s! We found everything from A to Z . . . attachés to zippered manicure sets. Christmas comes just once a year, and when it comes, it brings A to Z's only catalog. (But don't miss their periodic sales' fliers.) The brimming book of bargains contains all kinds of luggage and travel accessories from famous makers such as HARTMANN, ZERO, HALIBURTON, ROLF, ADOLFO, LACOSTE, and SAMSONITE. Discounts were up to 50 percent. Their imported attaché items represent a particularly good buy. If you're looking for something special, send a detailed description (including style and/or manufacturer's number) of the item you want, along with a SASE, and they will give you a price quote. Their catalog represents only a portion of the A to Z inventory. By calling the company before placing an order, we found out which catalog items were on sale for further reductions. Most orders arrive in about ten days.

Ace Leather Products
2211 Avenue U (800) DIAL ACE; (718) 891-9713
Brooklyn, NY 11229 CK, MC, V, AE, MO, C/$1

With over 30 years in the business, Ira and Andy are no jokers when it comes to selling handbags, luggage, and briefcases. In fact, they hold a wild card in the bargain game. Selling all types of top-grade luggage, briefcases, attachés, small leather goods, handbags, and gift items makes them an ace in brands such as ANDIAMO, LE SPORTSAC, LARK, HARTMANN, and TUMI. Discounts run 20 percent to 40 percent off. An added attraction: clocks by SEIKO, paperweights and other desk accessories, and lots of useful travel and gift items. Ira and Andy believe that discounts should be calculated by comparison to "real retail" prices. Orders are shipped the same day they're received. Returns on unused merchandise are accepted for a full refund made within 14 days.

Al's Luggage
2134 Larimer Street (303) 295-9009; (303) 294-9045
Denver, CO 80205 CK, MC, V, AE, D, MO, C

We shouldn't have to quote scriptures to you about the strength of SAMSONITE—if you've watched the TV commercials, you've probably seen a testament to its durability. Al's offers some commanding discounts of 30 percent to 50 percent off retail on the entire SAMSONITE line. This place is a source for luggage, soft-side and hard-side casual bags, and attachés. All luggage carries a two-year guarantee. Orders are received in three to five working days. If you're planning a trip to visit the Phil O'Steens of the Middle East, you can profit with honor from the savings in this country first.

American Tourister
91 Main Street (800) 879-2686
Warren, RI 92885-4301 CK, MC, V, AE, D, PQ

American Tourister's outlets are all over the country, and more are in the works. But if they haven't opened in your neck of the woods, never fear; mail order is here. For 30 percent to 70 percent less, this is first-quality luggage that has stood the test of time. AMERICAN TOURISTER, FRENCH WEST INDIES, BUXTON, and other brands in business cases, travel accessories, and other leather goods aren't just passing through. You can call the outlet nearest you for ordering and delivery information, after you know the model number, color, and any other pertinent information. Then, expect your luggage to arrive in one piece and at least before you depart.

Ber Sel Handbags
79 Orchard Street (212) 966-5517
New York, NY 10002 CK, MC, V, AE, MO, PQ

Ber Sel Handbags offers (you guessed it) handbags. Big deal, you say? Well, in fact, it is a big deal: You can get up to 35 percent off on a wide variety of leather, exotic skin and fabric handbags, wallets, belts, and gloves. Over 20 top manufacturers (ANNE KLEIN, DIOR, PIERRE CARDIN, LISETTE, STONE MOUNTAIN, ISOTONER, and TOTES) are represented. Inquiries must include the manufacturer's style number. Exchanges are made within 30 days; most orders are received in two weeks. There's a $2 shipping charge.

Bettingers Luggage
80 Rivington Street (212) 475-1690; (212) 674-9411
New York, NY 10002 CK, MC, V, AE, MO, PQ (SASE)

Pack up all your cares and woes and go to Bettingers Luggage for all your leather needs. Whether it be attachés or briefcases, garment bags, luggage, small leather goods or trunks, pack 'em at a walloping 30 percent to 40 percent off. Names to travel by include HARTMANN, SAMSONITE, SKYWAY, AMERICAN TOURISTER, and LARK. A $5 shipping-and-handling fee will be added to your minimum purchase of $25. Expect orders to arrive in about 15 days from this company that's been fulfilling them for over 65 years.

Carole Block Handbags

1413 Avenue M (718) 339-1869
Brooklyn, NY 11230 CK, MC, V, AE, PQ

Carole has a mental Block about charging full price, so she psyches up her customers with 15 percent to 20 percent off list in the final analysis. What's more, during her twice-a-year sales, we saved 30 percent to 50 percent. The reputation of her merchandise is secure, even if her prices are a bit depressed. Ladies' handbags and small leather goods were available from Italy, the U.S., and South America in such brands as HALSTON, SUSAN GAIL, ALDANA, and VISONA. About 35 brands are carried. There's a $25 minimum order on credit-card purchases. Exchanges are accepted for store credit only. Carole's bag has been shrinking prices for over 35 years, but she's still feeling pretty Jung. Write or call for a price quote.

Classic Designs

P.O. Box 994 (508) 748-2425
Marion, MA 02738 CK, MC, V, MO, C/$1

Having style doesn't have to mean having big bills. We're indebted to Classic Designs, though, for offering up to 40 percent off on leather business accessories. Work on your image with elegant briefcases, appointment books, and more for much less than the prices elsewhere. Satisfaction is guaranteed. Flip through their catalog; call or write for a price quote if necessary.

Creative House

100 Business Parkway (800) 527-5940
Richardson, TX 75081 (214) 231-3461 (TX residents)
CK, MC, V, AE, MO, C, PQ

Before you pack it in and become unhinged looking for luggage and attachés, check out these discounts from 30 percent to 60 percent on the moderately crafted WORLD TRAVELER, JORDACHE, and MASTERCRAFT lines. Their free catalog features briefcases and leather attaché cases in many styles and colors at about half off retail; there's also a line of leather luggage and garment bags. Handbags, wallets, and other leather products are also available.

Fine & Klein
119 Orchard Street (212) 674-6720
New York, NY 10002 CK, MO, PQ (SASE)

Julius Fine and Murray Klein opened their tumultuous New York shop some 48 years ago, and you have to hand it to them, business is in the bag. Their Fine Klein-tele includes many international celebrities. Today their legendary leather repertoire consists of over 1,000 different styles of exclusive, first-quality ladies' designer handbags, attachés, and accessories. Such brands as ANNE KLEIN, HALSTON, and CHRISTIAN DIOR. All items are 30 percent off the usual retail price. Mr. Klein welcomes everyone to write him for price quotes on particular styles and brands of merchandise—if you see something in *Vogue*, chances are it's in the bag that Fine & Klein can get it for you at a substantially lower price. Orders are shipped the same day if in stock. Send a SASE for a prompt response.

Hicks USA
7070 W. 117th Street (303) 469-3615
Broomfield, CO 80020 CK, C (SASE)

For trips to the moon, don't leave earth without the "Face-shuttle"—a unique cosmetic organizer that doubles as a portable vanity. When you land, you'll be out only $12. It's heavily padded, comes in all the fashion colors, is nylon and washable, too. Another out-of-this world item is their washable duffel bag, popular among professional ball players. It's square, with pockets in both ends and a pocket in the middle of the bag. Double zippers are lockable in three sizes, with the smallest a mini-version that serves as a handbag as well, $12; medium, the size of a carry-on case, $18; and the jumbo, $22. All prices are direct-consumer wholesale prices. Shipping charges, $2 per item. Allow three weeks for delivery.

Innovation Luggage
487 Hackensack Avenue (800) 722-1800
River Edge, NJ 07661 CK, MC, V, AE, MO, PQ (SASE)

Forget the same old prices. Innovation has fresh deals on SAMSONITE galore. From carry-ons to wheeled wonders, the selection would be hard to match. The discounts were newsworthy, too; up to 50 percent. Start with luggage and move on to briefcases, portfolios, attaché cases, handbags, and more. There's a new beginning for those seeking AMERICAN TOURISTER, HARTMANN, TUMI, and other brands to carry on. Begin by learning their minimum order ($15); price quotes are available by mail (with SASE, of course) or phone.

Leather Unlimited Corp.
7155 County Highway B
Dept. GM0292 (414) 994-9464
Belgium, WI 53004-9990 CK, MC, V, MO, C/$2 (refundable)

Why limit yourself to the ready-made? Be an original and make it yourself with the Leather Unlimited catalog. We'll tan your hide if we catch you paying full price after you've read about their 30-percent to 60-percent discounts on leather kits, belts, dyes, punches, shawl sets, strap cutters, assorted leather scraps, and pieces and leather-working items galore. For the unhandy among us, there are finished goods as well, like slippers, mittens, handbags, wallets, belts, tote and drawstring bags, and more. That's pretty smooth for a business begun in a Milwaukee garage in 1971. Now they own 12 acres and have 12 employees (one for each acre?); their 64-page catalog is mailed nationally. Satisfaction's guaranteed, whether you're into Harleys or hardware; delivery takes about two to four weeks. Minimum order is $30.

The Luggage Center
960 Remillard Court (408) 288-5363
San Jose, CA 95122 CK, MC, V, AE, MO, PQ

Take heart and lug your luggage troubles to this center of savings for up to 50 percent off. Dial for a deal on suitcases, briefcases, carry-on luggage, and more. Get the last word in travelin' bags by LARK, MEMBERS ONLY, HALLIBURTON, SAMSONITE, and others. Price quotes are available by phone, or by letter with SASE. Or you can visit one of their fourteen stores in California. They have a 15-day return policy.

New England Leather Accessories, Inc.
11 Portland Street (603) 332-4526
Rochester, NH 03867 CK, MC, V, AE, MO, C/$5 (with samples)

The price of leather goods is revolting! Leave it to New England to do something about it. You won't have to ride at all for these traditionally low prices from a company that's been in business since (when else?) 1976. Just open the 12-page catalog and stand up for your rights. Save up to 30 percent on New England handbags, tote bags, and other bags great and small for storing, slinging, and saving. Everything is made, patriotically, in the good ol' U.S. of A. A five gets you the catalog and supple samples of their lovely leathers in various colors. They accept returns, too, if you're not satisfied.

Tag Air International
P.O. Box 166007 (800) 874-1204; (214) 401-0544
Irving, TX 75016 CK, MC, V, MO, F

Fly me to the moon and save a lot of wear and tear on your flight. Though she tags the flight crews as her targeted market, if it's SAMSONITE you're after, this is the place to land. Consider a first-class $243 bag here for $143. Luggage, attachés, data cases, and gifts available at economy prices by appointment only, or call for mail-order list.

Travel Auto Bag Co., Inc.
264 W. 40th Street (212) 840-0025; (212) 302-8267 (FAX)
New York, NY 10018-1574 CK, MC, V, AE, MO, C, PQ

Traveling salesmen have been purchasing their softside luggage for almost 60 years from this company and you can too! (Willie, low man on the totem pole, thought that lugging around those samples would be the death of him.) Prices are low! You'll pay 35 percent to 70 percent more for comparable-quality items in a department store. Greater discounts are given when you buy in quantity. They don't carry famous brands—they sell their own NU-EASE lines exclusively. Their most popular lines include soft-sided luggage on wheels, wheeled hard-fiber cases, hangers, wall systems, canvas garment bags, professional steamers, collapsible rolling racks, and their latest, collapsible and stackable luggage that can be folded and stored underneath the bed. They have a 30-day return policy and a three-month guarantee against defects. Most orders are shipped within 48 hours. Write or call for a catalog and see for yourself.

Hard-to-Find and Unique Items

Okay, we'll 'fess up: Some of the following companies (sob, sob) don't sell discounted merchandise. Diehard bargain hunters like us hate to admit it (sniff, sniff), but it's true: You can't get everything *wholesale. We've put these companies in our book because we felt the nondiscounted (boo-hoo) goods they carried were unusual enough to merit a listing. We've been preaching all along that variety is the spice of a shopper's life, so thanks to these listings, if you absolutely can't get it wholesale, well, at least you can* get *it. There are times when you just can't find what you want, no matter how hard you try. That's why this section is here. If you shop by mail, you'll have more luck finding what you want. (And that's nothing to cry about!)*

Allen's Shell-a-Rama

P.O. Box 291327, Dept. 1327 (305) 434-2818
Ft. Lauderdale, FL 33329 CK, COD, C

Allen's sells seashells by the seashore—at wholesale prices. Wanna good buy on a bivalve? They've got 'em—but that's not all! Craft shells are their biggest sellers, but they've also got decorator, collector, and specimen shells, cut and dried shells, exotic tropical air plants; coral, shark's teeth, sea horses, sand dollars, books about shells and shell-craft, original kits unavailable anywhere else, and gifts and novelties. There are over 1,000 all-natural items ranging in price from 10 cents to $200. If you're not satisfied with your shells, ship 'em back for a refund.

Ameba Catalog
1732 Haight Street (800) 292-6322
San Francisco, CA 94117 CK, MC, V, AE, D, MO, C

We'd Haight to let this one get away. Let original clothing engulf you from Ameba. They feature "Manson clothing," silkscreens, psychedelic wear, jester hats, leggings, hooded sweatshirts, and other one-of-a-kind and unusual fashion declarations. There's a 60-day return policy; no restocking fee. Most orders arrive in two to six weeks from the San Francisco beat.

Beitman Co., Inc.
(see **Sewing Machines and Notions**, p. **437**.)

Comfortably Yours
2515 East 43rd Street
P.O. Box 182216 (800) 521-0097
Chattanooga, TN 37422-7216 CK, MC, V, AE, D, DC, CB, MO, C

Now for a catalog that says you never have to grin and bear it again. Whatever it is that makes you uncomfortable—whether it's soggy crackers, cigarette smoke, cold feet, or hot steering wheels, here is a company that devotes itself to things that make life easier. For example, if you're tired of a steering wheel that's too hot to touch in summertime, try their folding sun deflectors. There's a portable chair, a wheeled travel bag, a digital blood pressure monitor, and more. Disabled persons will find a wide assortment of comforting products from contoured canes to contoured shower chairs. Spot remover, wooden beaded car-seat covers, heaters, and many more ingenious products round out the selection.

The Company of Women
(see **China, Crystal, Silver, and Gifts**, p. **152**.)

Consumer Guide to Home Repair Grants & Loans
C.E.R.C. Grants
134 Evergreen Place (800) USA-0121
East Orange, NJ 07018 CK, MC, V, MO, C/$13.95
(including postage, 184 pages)

Write for your copy of this book today if you're one of the many home-owners who are unaware that regardless of your income, there are federal, state, and local programs that will help you with the repair and remodeling of your home. There are even programs that give you money for repairs that does not have to be repaid or money loaned below market levels or with no interest at all. In many areas, utility companies will either do energy conservation work free or at low cost and in other places will lend home-owners money at no interest to pay the contractor of their choice for the necessary work. Over 4,000 sources of grants and subsidized loans to choose from. Form letters are included to help get your information to the proper agency.

The Juggling Arts
5535 N. 11th Street (602) 266-4391
Phoenix, AZ 85014 CK, MC, V, MO, COD, C/$1

This company rarely goes for the juggler vein with their range of juggling equipment like spinning plates, clubs, fire torches, balls, and such. Perfectly balanced aluminum spinning plates and bowls are their best-selling items. Most of their merchandise is slightly less expensive than other mail-order firms, but their real claim to fame is that "there are no props of equal quality in retail stores." (The business was started when the owner, a member of a family of professional jugglers, could not find quality props for her act.) A set of three cloth balls filled with rice was $10.95, while a set of three rings 11 inches in diameter was $14.95. Fire torches (designated, appropriately enough, "Not for the Beginner") were $35.95 for a set of three. A new line of books, including *Just Juggle, Want to be a Juggler?, The Juggler's Manual of Cigar Box Manipulation and Balance,* is also available. Delivery usually takes about a week. They give a 100-percent refund if requested.

Left Hand Center
210 West Grant, Unit 2
Dept. 7792 (612) 375-0319
Minneapolis, MN 55403 CK, MO, C/$2

Lois Ruby would like to give you a few left-handed compliments, like left-handed kitchen items, scissors, mugs, rulers, T-shirts, and more. The catalog featured an extensive selection of left-opening greeting cards for all the right occasions. They also have instruction books, portfolios, and notebooks for lefties. Turns out Miss Ruby has her left *and* right hands in a number of different projects, but this one is right on!

When ordering the catalog, be sure to request a free left-handed greeting card and tell them you saw it in *Great Buys*.

Mature Wisdom
(See **Buying Clubs and One-Stop Shopping**, p. **117**.)

The Non-Electric Heritage Catalog
Lehman Hardware and Appliances
P.O. Box 41 (216) 857-5441
Kidron, OH 44636 MC, V, C/$2

If your electricity has just been turned off or if you've been turned off by modern times, get back to basics and reacquaint yourself with some quaint and useful appliances. Among the many offerings we found: dough mixers, noodle makers, corn dryers, lard presses, gas and kerosene refrigerators, butter churns, hand-operated clothes washers, hog-scrapers, apple parers, and cream separators. A six-quart WHITE MOUNTAIN ice cream freezer was a bargain at $125, and wood stoves were also a good buy (some EPA exempt models were as low as $169). There's a $3 surcharge for orders under $20. Free shipping, and it usually takes between five and ten days to receive your order. The Lehman family operates two stores in Holmes and Wayne counties right in the heart of Ohio's Amish country. Why are you waiting? Send for their unique 128-page catalog today.

Objects by Design
P.O. Box 11825 (800) 872-7501
Roanoke, VA 24022 CK, MC, V, AE, MO, C

The object of our affection is this catalog. Though not for lovers of everyday low prices, it is a catalog for creative, one-of-a-kind home furnishings. Hammocks, baskets, lawn sculptures, sleek and stark furniture, and even a medicine cabinet assume artistic proportions in this colorful collection. Designer furniture like Yin-Yang tables, zig-zag candlesticks, and fantastic telephone tables; your not-for-prime-time rugs, clocks, trash cans, kitchenware, and more, are available, needing no rhyme or reason. The "Great Values for Under $30" section was more our speed, including a unique traveling briefcase barbecue, a cedar log birdhouse, and a fish griller. Most orders are shipped UPS; gift certificates are available.

Russian Dressing/The Daily Planet
P.O. Box 1313 (212) 334-0006
New York, NY 10013 CK, MC, V, MO, C/$2

Their line is "the party's over," but in this flip-flop catalog, it's just beginning. Russian Dressing pours out unique offerings such as an old Paul McCartney album of hits released only in the USSR, a leather baseball cap, hand-painted holiday folk ornaments, genuine Russian military gear, and more. The Daily Planet features environmentally conscious T-shirts, colorful Tibetan bags, Dan Quayle watches, recycled rubber shoulder bags, and more. These products are not cheap; in fact, most are downright expensive. But many of the items would be practically impossible to find elsewhere, and the witty catalog is food for thought. Ten percent of the profits from the Russian Dressing half go to groups that are forging stronger links between the former Soviet Union and the U.S. and cleaning up Eastern Europe's environment; and another 10 percent go to nonprofit environmental organizations.

The Scarlet Thistle Studio
P.O. Box 280781 (214) 328-9856
Dallas, TX 75228 CK, MO

The Scarlet Thistle Studio is the home for the Humpback Whale and African Elephant T-shirts. Masterfully silk-screened by this artist, a portion of the profits are donated to various organizations working to protect endangered species worldwide. Each design is hand silk-screened on 100% heavyweight cotton T-shirts. Sizes S, M, L, XL, and XXL (this one does double duty as a night shirt). Price is $20 each ($1 more for XXL). Texas residents add sales tax. Allow four to six weeks for delivery.

Seventh Generation (800) 456-1197
Colchester, VT 05446-1672 CK, MC, V, MO, C

Environmentally correct consumers find shopping here an ecological windfall. Turn the tide to recycling. Choose GreenCotton clothing, water conservation, and organic products, and consider yourself part of the aware generation. Seventh Generation sells recycled paper, rubber shoulder bags, composters, light bulbs that are more energy-efficient, net shopping bags, unbleached cotton clothing, towels, and sheets, and organic shampoos, soaps, and cleaning agents. Perfect as gifts or for yourself, so you can be kind to the planet to ensure an eighth generation. Returns are accepted for refund, exchange, or credit.

The Southpaw Shoppe
P.O. Box 2870 (619) 239-1731
San Diego, CA 92112 CK, MC, V, AE, C

Give this shoppe your paw and they'll send you a flea catalog. The camaraderie among lefties is evident by the number of T-shirts, bumper stickers, buttons, and other paraphernalia having to do with being left-handed. Functional items such as scissors, cooking utensils, musical instruments, how-to books for calligraphy, embroidery, guitar, golf, writing, and even ego-boosting (*The National Superiority of Left Handers*) won't leave you feeling "left out."

The Vermont Country Store
P.O. Box 3000 (800) 362-2400
Manchester Center, VT 05255-3000 CK, MC, V, MO, C

The "Voice of the Mountains" is saying, "Save!" Want a goose-feather comforter, a turtleneck sweater, a French angora hat, or a long-reach snow brush for your car windshield? Then you've come to the right place. This delightful black-and-white catalog features dusting cloths, woven tablecloths, sturdy shoes, pajamas, cookies; even men's MUNSINGWEAR briefs, all made with old-fashioned quality and at reasonable prices. These days, a quality 100-percent cotton flannel shirt at the low price of $31.50 is something to write home about. There are holiday catalogs, too. They ship immediately, unless otherwise specified. Gift certificates are available; returns are accepted for exchange.

The Warner Bros. Collection
4000 Warner Boulevard (800) 223-6524
Burbank, CA 91522 CK, MC, V, MO, C

Hey! I tawt I taw a Bugs Bunny T-shirt! I did! It was in the Warner Bros. Catalog, the perfect place to find a present for all the Looney

Tunes on your list. T-shirts, sweats, mugs, figurines, watches, jackets, and other novelties to tickle your funny bone and reminisce. Hard-core devotees also devour the many books, tapes, and CDs from other Warner TV shows, movies, and recording artists. Prices aren't low, but the merchandise is a gas: a Coyote "Acme" dynamite alarm clock that explodes instead of ringing, was $50; a Yosemite Sam apron was $22. Orders paid for by check are held for two weeks; returns are accepted for refund or credit. That's all, folks!

What On Earth Catalog
2451 Enterprise East Parkway, Dept. GBBM (216) 963-6555
Twinsburg, OH 44087 (24 hours a day/ 7 days a week)
CK, MC, V, C

This collection is dedicated to environmentally correct objet's d'art. Yes, Dorothy, there is life after Kansas, but it better be good for "What's on Earth." This catalog is a collection of fun, off-the-wall-fashion and decorative gifts, but we ooh-h-h and oz-z-zed over their 100-percent heavyweight cotton T-shirt statements such as "The Recycled Oz," and "Re-Cycle" (with a great-looking bicycle in the center). From fashion plates to wear or decorate, it's hard to beat the salt of the earth's selection here.

Reader special: $5 off your first order.

Hardware, Tools, and Home Improvement

Whether you're renovating your home or just building a classy sandbox, tools and hardware can be expensive. They are often hard to find locally at discount prices, and that means you can really get nailed. If you have to spend a fortune on tools, that do-it-yourself home repair project can end up as a do-it-to-yourself budgetary disaster. Hook up with these listings for brass and porcelain faucets, chain-saw winches, hydraulic presses, hardware, tools, underwater sweepers, or a pair of woodchopper's chaps. It's no fun getting hammered by high prices, and if you use these listings, you won't!

Aristocast Originals Inc.
6200 Highland Parkway, Suite I — (404) 333-9934
Smyrna, GA 30082 — CK, MC, V, MO, C/$5

Make your castle one-of-a-kind with Aristocast Originals. Aristocast sells moldings, medallions, cornices, and other indoor and outdoor architectural accents at prices about 50 percent lower than those available elsewhere. These are made in England and are easy to install. There is no minimum order; returns are accepted for a 20-percent restocking fee.

Artic Glass & Window Outlet
Route 1, Box 157 (800) 657-4656; (715) 796-2292
Hammond, WI 54015 CK, MC, V, D, MO, C/$4 (refundable)

What a pain in the neck to price-check for windows, doors, patio doors, insulated glass for solar homes, sun rooms, etc. Look through this looking glass first before you buy elsewhere for savings from 50 percent to 70 percent off list. A ten-year replacement guarantee is offered on glass seals. They can custom-build any size, in any shape in double or triple pane, tempered or untempered glass, and are an authorized dealer for WEATHER SHIELD windows, doors, and patio doors. Delivery time—about six days to almost every state in the USA (49, actually, to date).

Bailey's, Inc.
P.O. Box 550
Highway 101 (707) 984-6133
Laytonville, CA 95454 CK, MC, V, MO
C/$2 (full year's subscription)

Paul could have saved himself some Bunyans by using this 64-page cata-log for supplies. We saw items ranging from extra-large dogs (claws), preferred by experienced timberfallers, on down to a toy chain saw for the little cut-up. Woodsmen can lumber along in CHIPPEWA brand boots at savings ranging from 30 percent to 50 percent off list price. Significant discounts on chain saws didn't go against our grain, either. WORK SAFE, McCULLOCH, PIONEER, HOMELITE, in fact, hundreds of brands were carried and were waiting for the right jerk to make them roar to life. Their magnetic first-aid kit came just in the nick of time. Returns that aren't their fault are charged a restocking fee. Be the first chip off your block to axe for a catalog. Folks living in the South can write Bailey's at P.O. Box 9088, 1520 S. Highland, Jackson, TN 38314, or phone them at (901) 422-1300. Easterners can catch up to them at P.O. Box 14020, 3 Selina Drive, Albany, NY 12212, (518) 869-2131.

The Bevers
P.O. Box 12 (214) 272-8370 (after 4 P.M.)
Wills Point, TX 75169-0012 CK, MC, V, MO, C/$2 (refundable)

Busy as a beaver building, fixing, and repairing? Then sharpen your teeth on prices 20 percent to 50 percent below retail on nuts and bolts by the bucket, as well as a den full of general merchandise. No specific brands, just dam bustin' quality at low, low prices. Orders are shipped immediately within three days of their receipt. Money back on returned merchandise. Don't get flooded with the high cost of building, just "Leave It to The Bevers."

BRE Lumber
10741 Carter Road (616) 946-0043
Traverse City, MI 49684 CK, MC, V, MO, PQ

These prices'll floor you. BRE is putting down solid teak, cherry, maple, and other woods for paneling, flooring, and molding, at discounts of up to 30 percent and more. It costs $15 to get a group of their samples and a price list, but that may end up saving you big bucks. Send a SASE or call for a price quote; no catalog or brochure is available.

Burden's Surplus Center
1015 West O Street (800) 488-3407 (orders)
Lincoln, NE 68501-2209 (402) 474-4055 (information and inquiries)
CK, MC, V, AE, D, C

Burden's won't load you down with high prices. They've been selling industrial surplus equipment for 60 years, including pressure washers, spraying equipment, compressors, motors, pumps, valves, hydraulics, winches, and security equipment at the lowest possible prices. They obtain merchandise from business closings, design changes, and closeouts, and pass along the great deals for farms, homes, and industries in their 148-page catalog.

Camelot Enterprises
P.O. Box 65, Dept. GBBM (414) 857-2695
Bristol, WI 53104-0065 CK, MC, V, MO, C/$2 (refundable)

In a kingdom of high prices, it's nice to find a palace priced right. Camelot Enterprises offers a realm of champion tools—fasteners, electric tools, and shop equipment—knightly enough for Sir Lancelot. The empire strikes back with brand names like MILTON, TRUECRAFT, GENERAL, CHICAGO TOOL, and K-D. They have enough to fill a moat, at a very noble savings of up to 50 percent and more. Orders take one day to two weeks. Tools carry anywhere from a 90-day to a lifetime warranty, depending on the manufacturer. No minimum order, and there is a ten-day return policy for those of you who might commit treason. So, if you are tired of blue-blooded tool prices, get off your throne and get on the phone.

Cisco/Chanute Iron & Supply Company
1502 West Cherry (316) 431-9290
Chanute, KS 66720 CK, Certified Check, MO, PQ

Don't let the local hardware store sink your hopes for do-it-yourself heating and plumbing repairs. Sinks, swimming pool chemicals, tools, INSINKERATOR disposals, DELTA faucets, pumps, fixtures, and all kinds of plumbing supplies will keep you afloat for as much as 40 percent less. Names like WHIRLPOOL, MAKITA, MOEN, and OWENS-CORNING keep bobbing up, too. The minimum order is $10. They don't offer a catalog, but don't let that throw a wrench into your plans; Chanute Iron & Supply Company could help you nail down a deal. Call for a price quote, or send a SASE with your request.

Continental Lawn Mower Mfg. Co.
3205 E. Abrams (817) 640-1198
Arlington, TX 76010 CK, MC, V, B, PQ

Great grass-cutting prices on riding lawn mowers aren't a continent away; they are but a phone call away. With probably the least expensive riding mowers in the country, this manufacturer cuts corners, offering their mowers by mail, as well as to customers who save freight by driving to their 43,000-plus-square foot factory. Construction on the eight-horsepower basic is all steel; parts are under warranty for one year from the factory. The engine is a four-cycle BRIGGS & STRATTON with authorized dealer warranty. It has a three-position with reverse transmission, chain drive, safety, clutch, adjustable cutting height, can carry 500 pounds, and comes assembled. Basic price was $529. It's like buying a car. You add to the options and price. Pneumatic wheel, four-wheel rear drive, blade, padded and/or spring seat, grass catcher, and high-speed sprocket are just some of the extras. Orders paid in cash or with a money order are received in about one week. There is a 15-percent restocking charge on unused mowers that are returned.

Crawford's Old House Store
550 Elizabeth Street, Room 795 (800) 556-7878
Waukesha, WI 53286 (414) 542-0685
CK, MC, V, AE, B, PQ

Crawford's specializes in products for the restoration of old houses, like textured wall coverings from England, their own attractive wood corner protectors, ceiling medallions; plus CHICAGO FAUCET and imported plumbing items. Brochures specific to the merchandise you're interested in are available. If you already know what you want, call for a price quote; their friendly staff will be glad to help. There is a $10 minimum order on credit cards. Returns incur a restocking charge that varies with the order.

Direct Safety Company
7815 S. 46th Street (602) 968-7009
Phoenix, AZ 85044 CK, MC, V, AE, MO, PQ

Play it safe at work and at home with the right safety equipment. Direct Safety offers a secure environment for discounts of up to 30 percent on safety goggles, gloves, and other protective gear. Clean up your act with first-aid kits, or protect your home with a fire extinguisher. Equipment for detecting radiation, carbon monoxide, metal, smoke, and more was also offered. If it makes homes or businesses safer, you're likely to find it here. Price quotes with SASE or by phone; customer satisfaction is guaranteed. There may be a restocking charge on returns.

Disk World, Inc.
4215 Main Street (800) 255-5874
Skokie, IL 60076-2046 CK, MC, V, D, COD, C, PQ

Go around the World at 50 percent off—Disk World, that is. They've been selling (what else?) disks, printer ribbons and labels, disk storage cases, cartridges, paper for fax machines and printers, blank video tapes, and more in their catalog since 1983. BASF, VERBATIM, and MAXELL disks cost about half what they do elsewhere; video tapes start at under $2.50. The well-traveled computer customer won't have any trouble recognizing these deals. They'll ship worldwide, too, and satisfaction's guaranteed. They have a 30-day return policy. Call or write for a price quote.

E.T. Supply
(See **Surplus and Volume Sales**, p. **472**.)

Gilliom Manufacturing Inc.
P.O. 1018 (314) 724-1812
St. Charles, MO 63302 CK, MC, V, MO, C/$2, PQ

Keep this number handy, man. If you're into power tools, Gilliom has the plans and tools for build-it-yourself band saws, lathe drill presses, wood shapers, circular saw tables—all designed to save you $50 to $250. They also carry kits of metal parts so you can build your own power tools. We saw plenty of parts and accessories such as V-pulleys, line shafts, work lights, motors, and sanding drums. Don't expect to find name-brand items: everything's their own GIL-BILT brand. All parts are heavy duty and guaranteed for one year against mechanical failure due to defects. There is no minimum order; restocking charge on returns. This is definitely a place for things that go bump and grind in the night.

H & H Manufacturing & Supply Co.
P.O. Box 692 (205) 872-6067
Selma, AL 36701-0692 CK, MO, COD, C, PQ

Topple prices on chain-saw chains (are we repeating ourselves?) with Saw Chain, H & H Manufacturing's mail-order division. Drop the price of guide bars, too, plus sprockets, logging equipment, and more, by as much as half. CRAFTSMEN, ECHO, PIONEER, STIHL, and JOHN DEERE are trusted names in serious equipment and tools, so check with H & H before you go after a tree for the holidays or fireplace. A SASE is required with mail-in requests for price quotes; phone calls are also accepted. If the merchandise is faulty in any way, return it for replacement.

Harbor Freight Tools
3491 Mission Oaks Boulevard (800) 423-2567
Camarillo, CA 93011-6010 CK, MC, V, AE, D, MO, C/$2

For everyone from the serious mechanic to the weekend do-it-yourselfer, Harbor Freight Tools' catalog features loads of automotive tools and equipment that are bound to come in handy. Heavy-duty jacks, 20-gallon parts washers, PITTSBURGH wrench sets, MCCULLOCH chain saws, paint sprayers, PORTER CABLE sanders, scroll lathe chucks, workbenches, air compressors, ladders . . . and more with budget-wrenching savings as much as 55 percent off. Orders of $50 or more are shipped free; no mail orders are accepted for customers in AL, HI, Guam, the Virgin Islands, or Puerto Rico; call-in credit card orders only. The 30-day return policy allows for refunds or replacements. Next-day and second-day deliveries are available.

Leichtung "Handys"
4944 Commerce Parkway (800) 321-6840
Cleveland, OH 44128 (216) 831-2555 (OH residents)
CK, MC, V, AE, D, MO, C

Leichtung got *my* attention with their 86-page irresistible catalog of deals. Scattered throughout the four-color slick shopping book are tools, hardware, gardening equipment, automotive, and housewares. A full set of taper drills was 20 percent off the regular price. Other best-sellers included an equi-pressure clamp for $24.99, a 36-piece paintbrush set composed of one-, two-, and three-inch brushes for $14.99, a 15-piece router bit set for $89.99, and a multi-height gauge for $9.99. Returns within 90 days for refund. Satisfaction—rest assured.

Mail Order Plastics, Inc.
56 Lispenard Street (212) 226-7308
New York, NY 10013 CK, MO, C

What do photographers, mad scientists, and high-school girls have in common? (No, not a porno flick called "Dr. Tickle and Mistress Hide.") They all find plastic doo-dads for less from this mail-order company. Beakers and measuring cups are perfect for the home-photo buff. Funnels, trays, vials, and pitchers make the home lab more efficient. A wide assortment of compartmentalized boxes store earrings, buttons, and even love notes for the teenager. If it's plastic, chances are you can get it here at a good price. Case discounts are offered; minimum order, $50.

Manufacturer's Supply
P.O. Box 167
Dorcester, WI 54425-0167
(800) 826-8563
(800) 472-2360 (WI residents)
CK, MC, V, MO, C

Manufacturer's Supply is *the* do-it-yourself-and-save mecca for the handyman and -woman. If your nonhuman machinery breaks down (like a lawn mower), this is the 167-page sourcebook to savings of up to 50 percent. Parts to make 'em new again plus lots of tools and stuff. (You don't need to be the *Super Handyman*, Al Carrell, to know how to nail a good deal on the head.) Over 10,000 parts: small engine parts, chain-saw parts, cycle parts, lawn-mower parts, snowmobile parts to ship to parts unknown. Brands named were GRAVELY-HAHN, ARCTIC CAT, HUSQVARNA, OREGON, and HELICOIL. Orders shipped within 24 hours; the minimum order is $10.

RSP Distributing
(See **Surplus and Volume Sales**, p. **473**.)

Master Mechanic Mfg. Co.
P.O. Box 757
280 S. Pine Street
Burlington, WI 53105
(800) 877-8350; (414) 763-2824
CK, MC, V, AE, MO, C

Mastermind a plot to save about 20 percent to 35 percent on a wide range of mechanical items and tools from this 47-year-old company. We saw hydraulic presses, winches, drill presses, air compressors, electric motors, pumps, electric tools, etc. The Master Mechanic alternators can guard against disaster in case of power outages; the 1,500-watt direct-drive generators were real-l-ly big sellers. There are good prices on gas engines and winches as well. Brands include BLACK & DECKER, MILWAUKEE TOOL, GRESEN HYDRAULIC, PRINCE HYDRAULIC, BRIGGS & STRATTON, KOHLER, and ONAN generators. Orders are shipped immediately: Most are received in 10 days. No restocking charge for orders returned within 10 days. Their 60-page catalog is electrifying.

McKilligan Industrial and Supply Corp.
435 Main Street (607) 798-9335
Johnson City, NY 13790-1998 CK, MC, V, COD, C/$5 (refundable)

Selling to industries and high-school shop teachers is the main business of McKilligan, but individuals can purchase hardware, tools, electronics, graphic supplies, and craft materials at up to 35 percent off list prices, too. The encyclopedic catalog costs $5 (refundable) and lists over 70,000 items. We usually look for companies *without* vises, but at these prices, we'll make an exception. Other good buys: a STANLEY Powerlock tape measure with a half-inch blade and a two-meter metric gradation and a 15-piece home-owner's basic tool kit. Watercolor supplies by GRUMBACHER were discounted 20 percent to 30 percent. Kits for stained glass, model cars, model rockets, and miniature houses also available. Ceramics equipment and molds were also featured. The McKilligan catalog is worth buying as a reference work for quick price comparisons. When it comes to variety, we think this is one of the best.

Monarch
2744 Arkansas Drive
Dept. GBBM (201) 796-4117
Brooklyn, NY 11234 CK, MC, V, MO, B

Ingenious radiator enclosures for 30 percent off butterfly off the shelves at this specialty store. Born in 1980 as the mail-order division of Elmwood Enclosure Company, they cater mainly to those restoring or maintaining older homes. The covers are functional as well as attractive; they can even create bookcases! Monarch's brochure tells you all about getting accurate dimensions for the cover you need, and shows several different styles. Once you've found one you like and you have the necessary measurements, you can call or write for a price quote. The enclosures are not returnable; delivery is made in approximately four to six weeks.

The New England Slate Company
R.D. #1, Burr Pond Road (802) 247-8809
Sudbury, VT 05733 CK, MO, C, PQ

They're slated to offer up to 50 percent off on new and "used" slate here, plus the tools necessary to put on slate roofs. This long-lasting roofing material comes new or salvaged, and can be custom-cut or colored to suit your needs. Not sure how to do it? New England Slate offers an instructional book, as well as gloves, nails, and other supplies. They can also help you keep the home fires burning with slate for hearths, floors, and more. If historic home or building improvement is on your agenda, slate a date with New England; check out the catalog or call or write (with SASE) for a price quote.

The Non-Electric Heritage Catalog
(See **Hard-to-Find and Unique Items**, p. **280**.)

Northern Hydraulics, Inc.
P.O. Box 1499
Dept. 17646
Burnsville, MN 55337
(800) 533-5545
CK, MC, V, D, MO, C

Give your budget a lift with Northern Hydraulics and discover tools and equipment at up to 50 percent off. Come up to HOMELITE, MCCULLOCH, SKIL, BLACK & DECKER, COLEMAN POWERMATE, and other names in generators, tool kits, sanders, protective clothing, welding equipment, winch accessories, and a lot more. Once you've been exposed to Northern Hydraulics' free 135-page catalog, you will be a regular viewer. Returns are handled on an individual basis by their customer service line (above); most orders are received within ten working days.

Quad Machinery
46 Huyler Street
P.O. Box 2228
South Hackensack, NJ 07606
(800) 342-8665; (201) 288-4070
CK, MC, V, AE, MO, COD, C

We thought Boring Heads was a new punk rock band that played in boring bars until we read this 400-page catalog with the bright orange cover. Extensive product specifications, illustrations, and photographs make this a valuable tool for buying everything from small items like drill bits and screws to large-ticket items like band saws and surface grinders. Prices are nailed about 40 percent to 60 percent lower than list prices. Some entries offered additional deductions, bringing the savings to 80 percent in some cases. If you're a mechanic, small manufacturer, or weekend handyman, it is well worth your time to look through this catalog. An additional 20-percent discount is given when a check accompanies an order. The minimum order is $50.

Red Hill Corporation/Supergrit Abrasives
P.O. Box 4234
122 Baltimore Street (800) 822-4003; (717) 337-1419
Gettysburg, PA 17325 CK, MC, V, MO, C

Redhill keeps you in the black with 50 percent off on abrasives, hot metal glue guns, and glue sticks. They stock SUPERGRIT sandpaper, belts, discs, and more, plus SUPERTACK 3000 glue sticks. For example, 3″ × 21″ sanding belts were $8 for a box of ten; 9″ by 11″ brown aluminum oxide sandpaper sheets, 80 grit, were $13 for 50 sheets. When in the area, visit their retail store in Biglerville, PA, about six miles north of Gettysburg. There is a $25 minimum order; returns are accepted if merchandise is defective. Orders are generally shipped within 48 hours. Write or call for a free 20-page catalog.

Renovator's Supply
Millers Falls, MA 01349 (800) 659-2211
CK, MC, V, C/$3 (refundable)

They've got the handle on everything: brass doorknobs, drawer pulls, brass and porcelain faucets, chandelier prisms, door hinges, fancy letter boxes, weathervanes, brass bolts and hooks, copper lanterns, and the "world's largest selection of brass switch plates." They carry over 1,500 hard-to-find hardware items. Everything a renovated home needs to feel secure is featured in this 48-page catalog at savings up to 70 percent. (Knock on wood.) Most of the unique items are specially produced for owners Claude and Donna Jeanlz: the others are imported from around the world. They'll exchange items, give credit, or refund the purchase price if not satisfied. Their magazine, *Victorian Homes*, is for anyone young at heart renovating old homes.

Saco Manufacturing & Woodworking
P.O. Box 149 (207) 284-6613
Saco, ME 04072 CK, MO, F (SASE)

Posted: no high prices. Pine is fine, but poplar is popular, too, in Saco's line of posts. Posts for mailboxes, outdoor lighting fixtures and porches, to be exact, and they're straight with you on the price, which is as much as 50 percent less than elsewhere. The posts aren't finished; that's where the handy member of your household gets to show off. Lamp posts come in standard heights from eight to 12 feet, center-bored; other sizes are available. Pine canisters, in 12", 20", and 30", too. Tell them which flier you want (newel posts, canisters, lamp posts, or "Colonial Columns") when you send a SASE.

Safe Equipment Co., Inc.
Route 1 (800) 755-3862
P.O. Box 61 (919) 285-5679
Wallace, NC 28466 CK (personal and certified), MO, C

Better SAFE than sorry. Don't go down the tubes financially paying full price for pumps, suctions, and BRIGGS & STRATTON engines when you can save 35 percent. There is no minimum order. Orders paid by money order or certified check are shipped immediately. There is no restocking charge because there are very few returns. Happy motoring, folks.

South Bound Millworks
P.O. Box 349 (508) 477-2638
Sandwich, MA 02563 CK, MC, V, MO, C/$1 (refundable)

Pull the curtain on expensive curtain rods, wooden and wrought-iron shelf brackets, iron kitchen and bathroom fixtures, and other hardware. South Bound offers them for 50 percent off, which means it's curtains for full price. Woodn't it be nice to hang your towel on a stylish rack? Their catalog (about 26 pages) features drawings rather than photographs, but still gives you a good idea of the merchandise available. They have a 14-day return policy. Bolt for these functional and decorative rods and brackets, but brace yourself, you won't be paying retail.

Tools on Sale
216 W. Seventh Street (800) 328-0457; (612) 224-4859
St. Paul, MN 55102 CK, MC, V, D, C

Like the name says, tools are always "on sale" here. Power tools and related accessories from BLACK & DECKER, MAKITA, MIL-

WAUKEE, DELTA, PORTER CABLE, BOSCH, and other popular brands are available at 45 percent off regular retail. It's easy to trust a company that's been around for 60 years. Older means they're getting better, too. A catalog with prices this low is never "boring." There is a 15-percent charge, plus shipping, on returned items. Normal delivery time is between seven and ten days.

Trend-Lines, Inc./Woodworkers Warehouse Outlet

375 Beacham Street
Chelsea, MA 02150

(800) 767-9999 (order hotline)
(800) 877-7899 (customer service)
(800) 884-8951 (technical questions)
(800) 366-6966 (to order free catalog)
(617) 884-8951
CK, MC, V, AE, D, MO, C

Working on wood for a cabinet or a cradle requires the right tools for the job. Come out of the woodwork and go to the Trend-Line catalog, more than 70 pages of sanders and saw blades, plus a whole lot more. (What hidden meaning is there in those FREUD saw blades?) We came, we looked, and we saw. Saws galore, woodbits, dowel rods, glue kits, air hammers, workbenches, doll house furniture, T-squares, canister lights, and more from BLACK & DECKER, SKIL, DELTA, HITACHI, and RYOBI, among others, are bound to leave the competition in the sawdust; you'll save as much as 50 percent. Sales catalogs have even better deals. They have a 30-day return policy (except on custom-made merchandise); the minimum credit-card order is $20.

Turnkey Material Handling Co.

P.O. Box 1050
Tonawanda, NY 14151-1050

(800) 828-7540
CK, MC, V, AE, MO, C, PQ

Around since 1946, Turnkey will rev up your budget with 50 percent off on storage equipment for tools and supplies and more. This turnkey catalog offers a variety of sizes, from small to industrial, in steel and plastic, to be used commercially or in your own garage. The big 116-page catalog also offers office chairs, tarps, wheeled ladders, emergency lights, lifts, wastebaskets, work benches, and other heavy-duty merchandise. Customer satisfaction is guaranteed; authorized returns may require a 20-percent restocking fee. The minimum order is $25; price quotes by phone, or letter with SASE.

Vintage Wood Works
513 S. Adams — (512) 997-9513
Fredericksburg, TX 78624 — CK, MC, V, D, MO, C/$2

If it's always been your fairy-tale dream to live in a gingerbread house, here's your chance! Vintage offers a selection of gingerbread trims to make your home your castle. Ah, a kingdom for some stairways, gables, newel posts, porch supports; everything to charm your way through the Victorian era with accents 30 percent less. The catalog is specific about sizes, so you can find a princely fit for your needs. Discounts are available on quantity orders; satisfaction's guaranteed.

Whole Earth Access
822 Anthony Street — (800) 829-6300
Berkeley, CA 94710 — CK, MC, V, MO, C

Get access to some of the best prices on woodworking tools from a company established in 1969 and you'll unearth savings of up to 40 percent. Whole Earth Access's catalog features saws, drills, sanders, and other equipment by BLACK & DECKER, MAKITA, SKIL, MILWAUKEE, DELTA, and others, plus compressors and safety items. Get the big picture and altogether great discounts on all kinds of woodworking needs. Put the whole earth in your hands, for free, through their 48-page catalog.

The Woodworkers' Store
21801 Industrial Boulevard — (612) 428-2199 (credit-card orders)
Dept. GBBM — (612) 428-2899 (customer service)
Rogers, MN 55374 — CK, MC, V, AE, D, MO,
C/$2 ($1 refunded with first order)

Planning on a project with plywood? Dabbling in drilling and driving? Whether it's a rocking horse or an entertainment center, you can make it yourself for a lot less, and save even more with what's in store at The Woodworkers' Store. Since 1955, they've been offering a variety of woodworking supplies like inlay bands, specialty and face grade veneers, hardwood lumber and trim, carvings, kits, models, buttons, caning supplies, braces, computer desk hardware, shelving, locks and bolts, and much more. You'll want to run out to the garage and start building when you see the 98-page catalog, in which the merchandise is clearly displayed and each page is marked by category. They offer a good selection of woodworking books, as well. Returns should be accompanied by a packing slip; satisfaction is guaranteed. Orders are processed in 24 to 48 hours.

Woodworker's Supply, Inc.
5604 Alameda Place, N.E. (800) 645-9292; (505) 821-0500
Albuquerque, NM 87113 CK, MC, V, D, MO

Wrench yourself away from regular list price; Woodworker's Supply features a big catalog with more than reasonable prices on more than just a screw or two. Saws of all kinds (circular, table, etc.), glue scrapers, veneers, finishes, sanders; in short, just about anything you might need for woodworking. The right tools at the right price can make a big difference, and at 30 percent off, you can buy three times as many! (How's that for black-belt shopper logic?) A minimum order of $5 would work, unless you're in Canada (then it's $25). They accept returns and guarantee satisfaction, so branch out and try discount for a change.

World Abrasive Company
1866 "U" Eastern Parkway (718) 495-4301
Brooklyn, NY 11233 CK, C, F

The people here thankfully aren't noted for their abrasive personalities, even when they're worn out. (They certainly didn't rub us the wrong way!) World Abrasive has sanding belts, discs, sheets, rolls, and other sanding accessories at nitty-gritty dirt band bargain prices. Their world also includes wire wheels, goggles, oil stones, and grinding wheels for those who like the grind of everyday life. Top-name brands like NORTON are available, and prices are about 30 percent to 50 percent off retail. Most orders are received in one to two weeks. No restocking charge or minimum order; refund or exchange on returns.

Zipp-Penn Inc.

P.O. Box 10308 (800) 824-8521
Erie, PA 16514 CK, MC, V, D, MO, COD, C, PQ

When Charlene the Chain Saw needs a new wardrobe, Zip-Penn zips in with accessories to outfit her in style. We saw discounts up to about 45 percent on replacement parts for lawn mowers, chain saws, small tools, and accessories. (Bargains like that made our chain saw break into a snaggle-toothed smile.) Chain saws are probably the best buys; safety equipment for chain-saw users is also reasonably priced. They have a 32-page catalog with eight small versions that come out every six months. Orders are shipped from their warehouse within 24 hours. All merchandise carries an unconditional 90-day warranty. Write for their famous "Zip-O-Gram" listing many bargains if you want to put an end to further chain-saw massacres.

Health, Fitness, and Vitamins

Now, more than ever, it pays to stay both physically and fiscally healthy! Throw out those baggy, gray sweats and jump into some super-fit deals! Save on items from home gyms and great-looking fitness wear to natural vitamins. Having a fabulous body and a healthy life-style is not only fashionable but smart these days! Need a boost to your life-style? Visit your local natural foods store or contact a good nutritionist to learn how to combine vitamins for best absorption. My mother taught me, it pays to shop around. Oftentimes, the same product will be priced quite differently by various companies. So save money and look and feel better with style and grace—without paying a well-conditioned arm and a leg.

Barth's
865 Merrick Avenue
Westbury, NY 11590
(800) 645-2328
(800) 553-0353 (NY residents)
CK, MC, V, C

Barth is both a manufacturer and distributor of vitamins and health products. Although they "stress quality rather than low price," their mailers announce frequent sales during which savings can range up to 70 percent. (Who says you can't have both quality and low price? Production costs affect quality, but marketing costs—which often account for most of the price—can be cut by savvy management without affecting quality.) Barth's stresses new ideas in nutrition with the use of unique formulas of natural ingredients in their line of cosmetics, as well. One hundred of Barth's extra-strength HI-C-PLEX 500 milligram tablets of vitamin C with wild rose hips, 100 milligrams of bioflavinoids, 50 milligrams of rutin, and 25 milligrams of hesperidin were reduced from $6.95 to just $3.13. Natural selenium was reduced from $11.75 to $9.95 (for 100 tablets), and their timed-release All Day B-100 Complex tablets were reduced from $17.50 to $7.88 for 100. Expect a $15 minimum on credit-card orders.

Better Health and Fitness
5201 New Utrecht Avenue, Dept. GBBM (718) 436-4801
Brooklyn, NY 11219 CK, MC, V, AE, PQ

Most places pump up the already-high cost of exercise equipment and sporting goods, but Better Health muscles in with discounts of 20 percent to 70 percent. Hop aboard a TUNTURI, TROTTER, BODYGUARD, VECTRA, and PARABODY—just some of the names in fitness, health club, leisure, and rehabilitation equipment that are lookin' good here. Since 1977, Better Health and Fitness has been exercising their ability to sell for less. Take advantage of heart-stopping deals from a company whose clients include many corporations, hotels, and other institutions. Call or write for a price quote.

And lucky you: As a *Great Buys By Mail* reader, you're eligible for a special offer—an additional 5 percent off on any order.

Creative Health Products
7621 East Joy Road (800) 742-4478
Ann Arbor, MI 48105 (313) 996-5900
CK, MC, V, AE, MO, C

Creative Health Products has one of the best selections of high-tech ways to bring your performance into the 21st century. They offer heavily discounted medical scales and other health-related paraphernalia, such as a wide range of pulse monitors to monitor your heart rate accurately. Then there's a "spirometer" for testing your lung capacity. And if you're ready to invest in a body fat measuring device, look no further. They offer simple-to-use body fat measurers for $7.25, to digital, computerized ones for $349. Read all about it in a 22-page guide called "How to Measure Your

Percentage of Body Fat" for $2. Maximize your healthy regime with strength and flexibility testing tools, blood pressure kits from $25.50 to $134, a heartminder for exercise equipment to tell you if you're under or over your target heart rate (discounted from $179 to $129), sports watches, exercise bikes, and 200 different models of weight scales, all sold at discounts of 10 percent to 40 percent. They also sell a wide range of wrist, ankle, and specialty weights (like the kangaroo weights) at substantial discounts, along with stretch ropes. For high-tech fitness options, you can't beat the low prices here.

Tell them you're a *Great Buys* reader and receive an additional $5 off on your first order over $20 or an additional $10 off on your first order over $75.

Eden Ranch
P.O. Box 370 (310) 455-2065
Topanga, CA 90290 CK, MC, V, MO, B

You can lasso Eden Ranch's own 100-percent natural line of vitamins and health-care products in this brochure. One of their dietary supplements is protagen, a digestive enzyme that supplements the body's hydrochloric acid supply and is said to aid digestion in people who suffer from a lack of HCL in the stomach. One hundred tablets were $6.50, 250 were $13.50, and 1,000 were $45. Pancroenzyme, a supplement to pancreatic enzymes in the digestive tract, was $9 for 100 tablets, 250 tablets for $19.25, or 1,000 for $67. No upset stomachs here as satisfaction is guaranteed.

Effective Learning Systems, Inc.
5221 Industrial Boulevard, Dept. GBBM1 (800) 966-5683
Edina, MN 55439 (612) 893-1680
CK, MC, V, AE, D, C

Effective Learning Systems offers tapes in both subliminal (messages only your subconscious can hear under soothing sounds of sea or music) and standard versions. One interesting program is Slim Image II, which offers motivation, affirmations, and visualizations for those on a diet. As a daily support partner, audiotapes can be an effective adjunct to your diet and fitness routine (and who doesn't need that extra help to stay away from chocolate chip cookies?). This catalog offers discounts on multiple purchases and accessories such as a SONY portable cassette player with dual alarm and radio

($69.95), pillow speaker for listening to tapes in bed without forcing your mate to listen, too ($11.95), and a combination sleep mask and earphone ($17.95).

The Fitness Store
6000 West Campus Circle Drive, Ste. 101 (214) 644-7610
Irving, TX 75063 PQ

Working up a sweat over the price of exercise equipment? Equip yourself with a battery of discount fitness gear from here. The Fitness Store sells new and used equipment at a discount. Sometimes working at cross-purposes is just the ticket to get you in shape; work out a budget and call or write the fitness store for a price quote.

Freeda Vitamins
36 E. 41st Street (800) 777-3737; (212) 685-4980
New York, NY 10017 CK, MC, V, MO, COD, C, PQ

Feel Freeda gulp these power-packed dietary wonders. Vitamins aren't hard to swallow when they're priced up to 30 percent to 50 percent below usual market prices. Mega-vitamins, minerals, amino acids, nutrients . . . starch-free, vegetarian, and kosher-approved. (They're on the Feingold Association of the U.S.A. approved food list!) We felt peppier just scanning the selection in their 36-page catalog. There is no minimum order, and unopened merchandise can be exchanged for something of equal value. Remittance required with first order to establish credit. Just about every food supplement on the market today was offered under the Freeda label by this friendly, family-owned pharmacy who has offered fast, quality, and efficient service since 1928.

Special: Get 25 percent off their already discounted prices just by identifying yourself as a *Great Buys* reader.

Harvest of Values/Hillestad International Inc.
1545 Berger Drive (800) 535-7742
San Jose, CA 95112 (800) 356-4190 (CA residents)
CK, MC, V, MO, C

Thresh out the savings on vitamins, minerals, supplements, hair and skin care products, detergents free of phosphates, and other body bounties for both children and adults at this Harvest of Values.

Their 32-page catalog features prices about 40 percent below what you'd pay elsewhere and provides a complete breakdown of ingredients. Customer satisfaction is guaranteed, and returns are accepted within 30 days. Orders over $35 include shipping.

High Meadow Farm
(See **Food**, p. **214**.)

L & H Vitamins
37-10 Crescent Street (800) 221-1152
Long Island City, NY 11101 (718) 937-7400 (NY residents)
CK, MC, V, D, C

At L&H, you'll find the ABCs in vitamins with such names as SCHIFF, PLUS, THOMPSON, STANDARD PROCESS LABS, NUTRI-DYN, as well as over 100 other national brands. Discounts are a standard 20 percent, plus there are several 40-percent-off sales during the year. Their 64-page catalog features every conceivable nutritional supplement, including the (kitchen) zinc. There's no minimum order; returns are accepted within 30 days; orders are shipped out the same day they're received. The SCHIFF Acidophilus with Goat's Milk caught our eye with alluring copy that said: "Natural aid for introducing friendly organisms to the lower intestines—20 million living lactobacilli in every capsule." Yum-m! Hope none of those little creatures has claustrophobia. A new catalog is published quarterly.

L.L.Bean
Fitness Catalog (207) 865-3111
Freeport, ME 04033-0001 CK, MC, V, AE, C

L.L. Bean publishes a beautiful fitness specialty catalog; one came with a really valuable little *Guide to Fitness* that included information on starting a fitness program. GORE-TEX® running suits (the miracle material that is waterproof, windproof, and breathable), that fold into a briefcase for running on business trips or lunch hours ($86 postage paid), a pedometer for measuring your walking distance ($16), as well as other products with brand names like NEW BALANCE, AVIA, and HEAVYHANDS®. These catalogs sell out quickly, so you must be on their list to be sure to receive yours.

Lotus Light
P.O. Box 1008 (414) 889-8501
Silver Lake, WI 53170 CK, MO, C

Lotus Light the way to find just about everything in body care products as well as bulk herbs and spices that you might hope to find in the best-stocked whole foods store. Scrub with natural body care products that do not contain any animal by-products. Soak up the savings with a wide variety of mineral bath products and bath soaps. While you're making your skin feel h-m-m-good, make the inside of your body feel better, too, with their different herbal formulas and dietary supplements. Herbs and spices can be bought in bulk, by the ounce or by the pound. They also carry Chinese ginseng products and remedies, along with other traditional folk remedies. Shipping will cost 15 percent up to $25; and 10 percent of the total after $25.

Mega Food
P.O. Box 325 (603) 434-6254
Derry, NH 03038 CK, MC, V, C

Mega Food exclusively offers one of the only brands of vitamins that are made out of food (making them nonsynthetic). Whether you want a once-daily multi-vitamin or the full spectrum of 100 different vitamins, minerals, and food nutrient factors, Mega Food has it all. B-complex, vitamin C, stress formulas, and mineral formulas are just a few of the 21 multivitamin products available. Their ONE-DAILY brand was available at $12.75 for 45 tablets. So a little tab should do ya!

Nutrition Headquarters
1 Nutrition Plaza (618) 457-8103
Carbondale, IL 62901 CK, MC, V, C, F

Put your money where your mouth is and feel good about it. Nutrition Headquarters offers a healthy dose of vitamins, high potency formulas, minerals, and amino acids, as well as health and beauty aids, and weight-loss products at substantial savings. We obtained 50 tablets of L-Glutamine 500 milligrams for $4 ($5.95 elsewhere). They also carry a wide selection of pure natural herbs in capsule or tablet form. Reading the catalog is enlightening for the uninitiated. Minimum order of $15 on credit-card orders.

Quantum Fitness
1341 West Main Road (800) 521-9996; (401) 849-2400
Middletown, RI 02840 CK, MC, V, B, PQ

If you're trying to stay on track, exercise-wise, we found no better source for home fitness equipment than Quantum Fitness (formerly Healthtrax International). Perhaps because these friendly folks manage health clubs themselves, they really know the ins and outs of the exercise regime. Want to know which multistation gym really holds up under family use? Or which exercise bike won't leave you limping? Ask the experts here. They offer top-of-the-line, first-quality equipment at near wholesale prices, and pride themselves in follow-through and customer service. And when your fit new body requires an even more challenging workout, check into their trade-up equipment option. Prices are too low to quote here, but discounts are substantial on over 100 manufacturers' products. Bimonthly newsletters feature updates on new equipment.

Rainbow Hot Tubs and Spa, Inc.
4796-A Schuster Road (614) 459-0909
Columbus, OH 43214-1951 CK, MC, V, D, COD, C/$5

When in Rome, do as the Romans. You might think you're in Rome when you see the selection of hot tubs and spas offered by Rainbow. We certainly found a pot of gold at the end of Rainbow Hot Tubs and Spas. They offer a bath house of spas, saunas, steamers, solariums, and tanning beds. You'll take a dip when you see their plunging prices of up to 60 percent off. They carry LANDIA, SKYTECH, LA SPAS, CURTIS FRP, FOUNTAIN VALLEY, GALAXY, and enough others to satisfy any Roman bather—Caesar. For all of the sun worshippers, KLAUS and others offer a selection of tanners. So, after riding in your chariot all day, come home to a hot tub or spa and relax somewhere under a rainbow.

Star Professional Pharmaceuticals, Inc.
1500 New Horizons Boulevard (800) 274-6400
Amityville, NY 11701 (800) 645-7171 (NY residents)
CK, MC, V, MO, C/$1

Twinkle, twinkle, little Star,
Through the mail you're not so far.

If I gulp your vitamin weaponry,
Will my bod, too, become then, heavenly?

We checked out their 48-page catalog and liked what we saw. Specials change as the catalogs change. Prices on their house-brand (STAR) vitamins deserve a gold star for being up to 85 percent lower than comparable retail products, but their brand-name goods were priced remarkedly close to retail. They also carry natural health and beauty aids and gifts. Premium gifts are offered with orders. Star guarantees satisfaction: if after 30 days of use you aren't completely satisfied, you can return the unused portion for a total refund. Shipping is $2.50 on all orders; there's a $15 minimum on credit-card orders.

Stur-Dee Health Products
105 Orville Drive (800) 645-2638 (orders only)
Bohemia, NY 11716 (516) 889-6400
CK, MC, V, COD, C

Stur-Dee's carries their own brand of drugstore products like vitamins, minerals, cosmetics, etc., formulated to their specifications. Many of their products are natural and contain no sugar, artificial color, or starch. Prices on house vitamins, minerals, cosmetics, healing agents, and aloe vera products averaged a sturdy 15 percent to 30 percent lower than most national brands; they also offer gifts with orders. Orders are delivered ASAP. Folks on their mailing list periodically receive advance catalogs announcing sales.

Sunburst Biogranics
838 Merrick Road (800) 645-8448
Baldwin, NY 11510 CK, MC, V, COD, C/$1

"Combat dietary deficiencies with all-natural (no preservatives, no artificial flavorings or color) supplements!" says Millie Ross. Her family sells the preferred form of vitamin C, calcium polyascorbate, 625 milligrams, 100 tablets for $4.99. Spirulina—a protein food praised by dieters and joggers—was $4.99 for (100) 500-milligram tablets (a special offer). You can also pep up pets by getting them to pop pet vitamins. Discounts are 20 percent off and more; brands include SUNBURST, FUTURE BIOTICS, RACHEL PERRY, NATURE'S WAY, and SCHIFF. (We don't want to B-complex; check out their 48-page catalog and C for yourself.) All orders are processed within 24 hours and require a $2 handling charge. Full refunds are given within 30 days.

Taffy's by Mail
701 Beta Drive (216) 461-3360
Cleveland, OH 44143 CK, MC, V, AE, C/$3

Dancers get to wear the best clothes. Dancewear makes great, stylish streetwear as well as great fitness wear. Taffy's offers the best selection of fashion for dancers, aerobic athletes, gymnasts, and even cheerleaders. Just about everything comes in regular sizes and hard-to-find extra-large sizes (have you ever tried to find extra-large warm-up pants? Taffy's had them for $9.50). There are "gotta dance" shoelaces, the full line of CAPEZIO dance shoes, from ballet to tap (the classic character pump with the two-inch heel is one of the most comfortable dress shoes you can wear; at $70 in flesh or black, it's a foot-saving bargain), and great leg warmers (over 30 colors including electrics in lime, orange, pink, rose, and yellow for $8.95). Every possible style of leotard, unitard, and tights is available in a rainbow of colors, with kids' sizes, too. Resources for dancers and teachers: records, videos, magazines, and teaching tools.

Vienna Health Products
54 Phillips Way (412) 342-2525
Sharon, PA 16146 CK, MC, V, C/$1

Want to work out in the convenience and privacy of your own home? It's actually possible to build your own weight-training benches and stations, at great savings. Vienna Health Products provides kits with pre-cut heavy wall two-inch-square steel tubing, hardware, upholstery, detailed prints, and instructions. Welding and painting is required, however. There are more than 40 kits available, either assembled or unassembled pre-fab. The savings by doing-it-yourself can be substantial—up to 75 percent! An unassembled T-bar rowing kit sells for $155, while the same machine already put together rows for $235.

Vitamin Specialties Company
8200 Ogontz Avenue (800) 365-VITA
Wyncote, PA 19095 (215) 885-3800
CK, MC, V, C

Here's a well-established (around for more than 50 years) company you'll want to specialize in if you're prone to vitamin deficiencies.

This source will have you back on your feet in no time, nourishing your bank account as well, with prices at 40 percent to 60 percent off retail on brands of vitamins, dietary supplements, over-the-counter drugs, and cosmetics. Compare actual prices by ordering their 96-page catalog. All products are manufactured under the Vitamin Specialties brands. We checked and found that approximately half of the products offered were 100-percent natural. Merchandise is guaranteed to meet all F.D.A. requirements. Unopened merchandise may be returned within 30 days for a full refund or credit.

Great Buys readers are entitled to an extra 10 percent off on orders over $20, as well as free shipping.

WSA Community Pharmacy

341 State Street (608) 251-3242
Madison, WI 53703 CK, MC, V, MO, C

From State Street, that great street, comes this mail-order catalog with an old-fashioned apothecary feel. Step into modern times without feeling the sting of modern prices when buying vitamins, health and beauty aids and homeopathic remedies for common afflictions. WSA has natural remedies for everything from acne to allergies, along with a host of herbs and herbal extracts, natural skin and hair care products, and more. Their prices are low and selection is wide. Call for a catalog or a price quote on your favorite botanical products before you hit the health store at organically produced prices.

Western Vitamins

P.O. Box 694040 (800) 777-9847
Miami, FL 33269 CK, MC, V, MO, C

Get along to Western Vitamins, pardners, for savings on products designed to care for your physical and mental well-being. Vitamins, herbs (along with a section describing their purposes), natural nail hardeners and moisturizers, capsules to do everything from rid your body of cellulite to suppress your appetite, and more are available for less here than at many health-food stores. Round up products for both men and women, including aloe vera- and crystal-deodorant, jojoba shampoos, collagen hand and body lotion, and soaps. Lose weight, get fit, or just maintain your health with this stampede of runaway good deals. They have a 100-percent money-back guarantee; shipping and handling is free on orders over $30.

Years to Your Health
503 East Second Street (214) 579-7042
Irving, TX 75060 CK, MC, V, AE, C

Add years to your health and dollars to your wealth by shopping here. If you know goto kola from Coca-Cola®, you'll find over 500 botanicals to choose from at prices 30 percent to 50 percent lower than most health-food stores. This husband-and-wife team offers one of the largest selections in the country of bulk herbs, potpourris, spices, teas, and vegetarian vitamins. They carry their own line of products through their catalog, so isn't it time you discover the exciting and wonderful world of herbs and healthy living?

Health and Medical

The next time your doctor writes you a long-term prescription, don't rush to the corner drugstore to have it filled. Send it to a prescription service! You can save as much as an additional 60 percent over their discounted prices, for example, by substituting generic compounds for brand-name drugs. Whether you're buying a juice extractor, contact lens, or a hearing aid, compare prices before you buy. Be specific about your requirements and shop-buy-phone!

Action Mail Order Drug
P.O. Box 787
Waterville, ME 04903-0787

(800) 452-1976 (customer service, Monday–Friday, 8:30 A.M.–5 P.M. EST); (207) 873-6226
CK, MC, V, AE, D, C, PQ

Put Action to work and forget about waiting at the corner drug store. When you send a prescription from your doctor, Action's registered pharmacists fill it and usually send it out same day. Customers should send for refills seven days before their medication will run out, in case of unforeseen delays. Started in 1976 to provide an important service to residents of rural New England, Action has built momentum nationwide. They even offer competitively low prices on generic and over-the-counter drugs. Call for a catalog, which includes an order form and prices on their generic vitamins, minerals, diet aids, allergy and cold medications, and more. (Prices aren't printed on prescription drugs due to price fluctuations, but a phone call will get you a price quote guaranteed for 30 days.) Add 75 cents for handling on up to three pounds. The brochure we saw came with a $5-off coupon.

America's Pharmacy Service, Inc.
P.O. Box 10490 (800) 247-1003; (515) 287-6872
Des Moines, IA 50306-0490 CK, MC, V, B, PQ

One of the largest mail-order pharmacies in the country (they stock over 10,000 prescription and nonprescription items), America's Pharmacy expresses the sentiment that "you can save more money by buying generic vitamins and prescriptions instead of higher priced national brands." America's prices on generic alternatives represent savings of 25 percent to 60 percent off the cost of advertised brands. Generic equivalents are chemically identical to brand-name products and are approved by the F.D.A. They also carry vitamins and minerals, A through zinc; aspirin, cold capsules, sleep aids, creams and ointments; even hearing-aid batteries and blood-pressure kits. All orders are guaranteed to be correct in quantity and strength. Refunds or exchanges are made within 30 days. There is no charge for shipping via UPS or parcel post, although there is a 75-cent handling fee.

Anatomical Chart Co.
8221 Kimball (800) 621-7500
Skokie, IL 60076 CK, MC, V, AE, MO, C/$6

This medically correct and colorful, fun-filled 71-page catalog has something for anyone interested in the human body, space, physics, genetics—even exercising. A large selection of books for children offers an explanation on everything—from the history of the dinosaur to more contemporary issues such as puberty; while the adult section delves into dentistry, medicine, weight control, getting rid of unhealthy bad habits, and more. Read on. There are books on drawing the anatomy for artists, and books for healthy eating for cooks. Or how about a *Merck Manual*? They're all available at stripped-down prices. Then, let the videos begin: videos on yoga, exercising with arthritis, preventing heart attacks, prenatal care, and many more. High selection and low prices make them a thumbs-up. They offer gift wrapping, too, for that pre-med student on your list. Orders are usually shipped within five to ten days; there's a 30-day return policy.

B & B Company, Inc.

P.O. Box 5731 (208) 343-9696
Boise, ID 83705 CK, MO, MC, V, COD, B

B & B is doing a booming business with their Bosom Buddy. This is a breast form made of nylon and cotton that contains small pillows filled with one-and-a-half ounces of very small glass beads, an alternative to more expensive silicone-filled forms (that can cost twice as much). Costs per form run from $60 to $65, and forms fit sizes 32AAA to 46DDD. They are designed to be comfortable and fit either right or left sides. Satisfaction is guaranteed.

Bruce Medical Supply

P.O. Box 9166 (800) 225-8446
411 Waverly Oaks Road (617) 894-6262
Waltham, MA 02254 CK, MC, V, MO, COD, C

A professional no-pin-stop sphygmomanometer (doesn't exactly roll off the tongue, does it?) may not be your idea of an im-pulse purchase, but at least you can get a blood-pressure reading without getting the squeeze put on your wallet, too. This company's 56-page catalog offers a complete line of medical supplies (in such brand names as SQUIBB, HOLLISTER, SUNBEAM, 3M, DANSAC, NU HOPE, COLOPLAST, FOSTER GRANT, MENTOR, DEPENDS, and BARD) at savings of 20 percent to 60 percent. Coupons are offered on select items. Heating pads, walking aids, bathroom aids, and a wide range of ostomy products bring medical and monetary relief to those with colostomies, ileostomies, and urostomies. (Ostomy products are what they're best known for.) Bruce gives full refunds or exchanges within 60 days, and there's no restocking charge. Credit-card orders are shipped out the same day as they're received; orders paid by check are held until the check clears.

Clover Nursing Shoe Company

1948 East Whipp Road (513) 435-0025
Kettering, OH 45440-2921 CK, MC, V, F

If you're an R.N., let Clover nurse your budget back to health. Their NURSEMATES nursing shoes are up to 35 percent off retail.

Normally retailing at $60, they can be had from Clover for just $35. Choose from 14 styles, in sizes 5 to 12, in widths from slim to double wide.

Conney Safety Products
3202 Latham Drive (800) 356-9100
P.O. Box 44190 (800) 362-9150 (WI residents)
Madison, WI 53744-4190 CK, MC, V, AE, D, MO, C

Solving safety problems built this company into a major source for saving money in the workplace or on the home front. Accidents can occur anywhere, and after nearly 50 years in the business, Conney's catalog offers discounts on safety equipment as well as fast service. You can buy first-aid supplies at a quantity discount based on your annual first-aid-dollar purchases, as well as take advantage of the Big Buck Savings throughout this four-color catalog. You can save up to 50 percent on Conney brands. Products include safety glasses, dust masks, disposable earplugs (great to block out your teenager's rock music), fire extinguishers, rubber gloves, Band-Aids®, Ace bandages, antiseptics, burn remedies, feminine hygiene products, and more.

Contact Lens Replacement Center
P.O. Box 1489 (516) 491-7763
Melville, NY 11747 CK, MO, B (SASE), PQ

You'll soon see clearly why you wouldn't want to pay full price for contacts. Contact Lens Replacement Center can save you as much as 70 percent. See what I mean? Name-brand gas-permeable, disposable, extend-wear, hard, and soft lenses are available to replace the ones that got away, dribbled down the drain, or got scratched or ripped. You'll be able to envision the best for less with great prices on BAUSCH & LOMB, WESLEY-JESSEN, and HYDROCURVE lenses, among others. Check out the sunglasses, too, even if you're not a shady character.

Continental Assn. of Funeral & Memorial Societies
2001 S Street N.W.
Suite 530 (202) 745-0634
Washington, DC 20009 PQ

You don't have to be a dead-icated *Shopper* to avoid a grave mistake on a funeral. There are almost 200 nonprofit Memorial Societies in the U.S., more in Canada. Most are staffed by volunteers. These folks are committed to "simplicity, dignity, and economy in funeral arrangements." While most members emphasize services with closed caskets and immediate burial (or a memorial service following cremation), you can nail down a traditional American funeral at lower costs with pre-need counseling. Call or write: They'll send a packet that includes a donor's card, list of societies in your area, plus *all* members listed with them. It could help you avoid coffin up your estate in your move from here to the hereafter.

Elite Eyewear
10992 NW 7th Avenue — (800) 321-1819 (orders)
Dept. GBBM12 — (305) 754-5894 (customer service)
North Miami, FL 33168 — CK, MC, V, AE, D, MO, B, PQ

The Elite meet here to beat the high cost of eyeglass frames and sunglasses. Get upscale names like POLO, GUCCI, ARMANI, CARRERRA, DIOR, and many more for much less. Up to 56 percent less than retail optical stores, as a matter of fact. Look down your nose at a pair of POLO Classic Deluxe frames for $75 ($129 retail), or GUCCI 2105s for $92 (retail $199.95). You can call for a price quote once you get the manufacturer's name, color, size, and style of the frames you want; just be sure to say you're an Elite Eyewear customer. Checks are held seven days; otherwise, frames are shipped the same day they receive the order.

The Eye Solution, Inc.
P.O. Box 262 — (419) 683-1608
Galion, OH 44833 — CK, MC, V, MO, C

Clean your contacts without cleaning out your wallet. Well-known names in contact-lens-care products like ALLERGAN, ALCON, and BAUSCH & LOMB for as much as 70 percent off will clean, rinse, and disinfect your lenses with solutions, or even with cleaning machines. The catalog is free, so see (better) for yourself. There's a $30 minimum order.

A Guide to Health and Consumer Toll-Free Hotlines
Essential Information
P.O. Box 19405
Washington, DC 20036 — B/$1

Jam-packed with essential toll-free resources that'll answer your most quintessential questions, this handy guide has got your number! Published by a Washington, DC, nonprofit group, it covers two basic categories—health and consumer concerns. For example, medically speaking, one good number is for the source to call to donate your organs for research (The Living Bank). Just send $1 for booklet to address above.

Health-Hotlines
NLM Information Office
8600 Rockville Pike
Bethesda, MD 20894

FREE booklets on the many sources for medical help. Over 250 organizations that can help answer your health-related questions with their addresses and toll-free numbers such as:

- 800-4-CANCER (Cancer Information Service)
- 800-662-HELP (National Drug Information Referral Line) and
- 800-336-4797 (National Health Information Center)

Hidalgo
45 La Buena Vista, Dept. GBBM
Wimberley, TX 78676
(800) 786-2021 (orders)
(512) 847-5571 (information)
CK, MC, V, AE, D, CB, DC, C

Sunglasses and prescription eyewear are Hidalgo specialties, so look to them before paying full price again. Save 30 percent to 60 percent off on their own brand, plus RAY-BAN frames, are available in a variety of styles. Scratch-resistant lenses, cases, and a special anti-reflective coating can also be ordered. When in the area, visit the store in Wimberley and get a hands-on look at their eyewear. There's a 30-day money-back guarantee; normal delivery time is from one to seven days.

Lens Express, Inc.
2780 Gateway Drive
Pompano Beach, FL 33069
(800) 666-LENS (666-5367)
(305) 772-3698 (international)
MC, V, AE, D, C, PQ

Race over to the Lens Express and save up to 70 percent on brand-name contact lenses. This club ($25 for a three-year membership) offers price quotes on lenses that could save you a bundle. So make it snappy; look into their free catalog and let your eyes roll, with new lenses usually shipped within 24 hours. More information is available upon request.

LenSmart
One Elm Street (800) 231-LENS
Tuckahoe, NY 10707 CK, MC, V, AE, PQ

You don't need a PhD to get smart with LenSmart. BAUSCH & LOMB, ACUVUE, ALLERGAN, DURASOFT, NEWVUES, and SOFTCON are a few of the brand names in contact lenses that LenSmart offers at 40 percent to 70 percent off. Get Smart. All it takes is a phone call, a credit card, and your prescription. They offer additional savings through their membership plan. Orders are shipped in vials that have been factory-sealed. LenSmart offers a 100-percent guarantee on their products. Call to make contact(s) with savings.

Majestic Drug Co., Inc.
711 E. 134th Street (212) 292-1310
Bronx, NY 10454 CK, MO, B

When you're out on a camping trip and your filling plunks into your cup of coffee, DENTEMP can fill in for a dentist. This filling mix, developed by a dentist, temporarily replaces lost fillings, loose caps, crowns, or inlays so you can keep on talking while the stuff is caulking. They also carry health- and skin-care products (which they manufacture) at prices roughly comparable to retail, but you get 10 percent off on a $25 order. There's a 10-percent restocking charge on returns and no minimum order. Orders are shipped out within 24 hours; most are received in five to ten days.

Masuen First Aid & Safety
P.O. Box 901 (800) 831-0894
Tonawanda, NY 14151 CK, MC, V, AE, MO, C, PQ

Masuen to the rescue! Call 800-831-0894 instead of 911 for emergency treatment for first-aid and safety kits for the car or home. The catalog's 48 pages help stop the hemorrhaging of runaway costs by supplying aids and antiseptics from the mundane to the more sophisticated, from bandages to sphygmomanometers. They also sell preventive safety equipment like goggles and gloves. Put safety first and save as much as another 30 percent with their quantity discounts. There's a minimum order of $25; price quotes are offered by letter or phone.

Mature Wisdom

(See **Buying Clubs and One-Stop Shopping**, p. **117**.)

Medi-Mail, Inc.

P.O. Box 98520 (800) 331-1458
Las Vegas, NV 89193-8520 CK, MC, V, MO, B, PQ

Getting sick over the high cost of getting well? Well, we recommend a membership dose in a pharmacy that mails prescriptions right to you, at a discount, no less. Medi-Mail can save you as much as 80 percent on the cost of generic vitamins and medicine, and no contraindications on their prices on prescriptions, either. Members of organizations like the AARP, Hadassah, Pace, American Federation of Police, and others can realize even bigger savings. There's a minimum order of $2.50, or $10 when you order with a credit card. Call or write for a price quote and/or their brochure for membership details. Shipping is included in the price of your order.

My Choice Plan (MCP)

P.O. Box 418 (800) 336-7310 (membership
Teaneck, NJ 07666 and application)
(800) 637-9792 (Rx refills and
doctors' call-in line)
MC, V, MO, PC, B, PQ

There is nothing more important than good health, and this is of prime importance to this company. At last someone has finally gotten a grip on out-of-control drug prices. This is *the* source for physical as well as fiscal recovery. Make My Choice Plan your choice when it comes to low prices on name-brand and generic prescription drugs, over-the-counter items, and medical supplies delivered right to your door. Membership is *free*, and prices quoted included delivery. It is truly one-stop drug store shopping at its best. Now hear this! MCP also accepts insurance assignments, files your claims, and will bill your insurance company for its portion. Seniors get special discounts. All FDA-approved drugs are available. MCP staff is very knowledgeable in the field of AIDS drug therapy. Generics are also available and afford even greater savings. Prescriptions are filled and delivered within two days. Overnight delivery upon special request. Write or talk to one of their counselors by phone for more information.

National Contact Lens Center
3527 Bonita Vista Drive (800) 326-6352
Santa Rosa, CA 95404-1506 CK, MC, V, MO, B

Save 40 percent to 75 percent on all nationally available brands of soft contact lenses. Paying to see clearly at a little over cost is just what the doctor ordered. Great for replacement lenses, but not for an original prescription. You will receive their brochure describing and listing company policies, price list, order blank, and guarantee in just a few days. Order time—approximately one to two weeks.

Pharmail Corporation
P.O. Box 1466 (800) 237-8927
Champlain, NY 12919-1466 (518) 298-4922
CK, MC, V, MO, B, PQ (SASE)

Pharmail's prices on prescription drugs and vitamins are as much as half what you'll find in the local drugstore. If your medicine's not included on their price list, call or write (with SASE) for more information. Quantity discounts are offered to save you even more if you can buy several months in advance. Shipping is included in the price of your prescription; the minimum order's $10 ($4.99 per prescription).

Prescription Benefit Services, Inc.
P.O. Box 1540-GBUY (800) 222-4727) (membership/$15)
2646 Highway Avenue (800) 228-6149 (prescriptions)
Highland, IN 46322 CK, MC, V, AE, D, $15/annual membership

Prescription Benefit Services wants to save you money on prescriptions, and deliver them right to your doorstep. They offer all name-brand and generic drugs, except Class 2 narcotics. All medications are discounted to the level of the best possible price for your area of the country. For a $15 yearly membership, you'll get the assurance that your prescription(s) will be filled and shipped to you within one day of its receipt, and UPS delivery takes only a few days. Maintenance drugs, like blood-pressure and birth-control medications, can be received on a regular basis; just send in your doctor's prescription the first time, then call in and request refills. Stay well.

Prism Optical, Inc.
10992 N.W. 7th Avenue, Dept. GB12 (800) 637-4104 (orders)
North Miami, FL 33168 (305) 754-5894 (customer service)
CK, MC, V, AE, D, MO, C

Take a closer look at the Prism catalog before you get framed for higher prices on eyeglasses and save 30 percent to 40 percent off retail optical-store prices. With a written prescription from your eye doctor or a pair of the glasses you wear now, Prism can grind impact-resistant lenses to fit into a pair of frames from their catalog or your old frames. Some plastic frames were as low as $35; metal bifocal frames were $24. Men's, women's, and unisex frames were available, as well as eyeglass cords, sports and safety goggles, and lens tinting and repair. They can even put your prescription on file, so all you have to do is order frames next time. Express service is available for fast delivery; single-vision lenses are usually shipped four working days from the time you send in your order.

Retired Persons Services, Inc.
500 Montgomery Street (703) 684-0244
Alexandria, VA 22314-1563 CK, MO, C, PQ

Some things only improve with age, like your eligibility for special discounts. Retired Persons Services, a division of the AARP (American Association of Retired Persons), offers AARP members the chance to join for $5 and save as much as 80 percent on the cost of prescription and nonprescription medicines, vitamins, skin- and hair-care products, reading glasses, and other practical items that make for life's little pleasures. Check out the catalog's price listings, coupons, and general information if you're an AARP member. Customer satisfaction's guaranteed.

Ric Clark Company
36658 Apache Plume Drive (805) 947-8598
Palmdale, CA 93550 CK, C

You'll grin ear-to-ear to hear 50 percent and more savings on nationally advertised brand name hearing aids. They'll create prescription aids from your audiogram, but they don't make custom ear molds, so you must buy yours locally. Although we found no savings on batteries, repair costs did average about half what we found elsewhere. A $10 deposit is required—they'll refund it if you're dissatisfied or apply it to the price of your order. There's a one-year guarantee and 30-day trial period. Orders are air-mailed first class the same day they're received. Sounds good—particularly when you consider this business was begun more than 20 years ago as an adjunct to Ric's retirement. Though no credit cards are accepted, they will finance at a 10 percent rate of interest.

Rite-Way Hearing Aid Co.
P.O. Box 597635 (312) 539-6620
Chicago, IL 60659 CK (terms available), B, PQ

Hear ye! Hear ye! Are you oppressed by excessive hearing-aid prices? Have manufacturers got you by the eustachian tubes? Rise up, one and all, for the days of lib-ear-ation are at hand. Make a price pilgrimage to a land of economic freedom, to a new land of discounts! Rite-Way sells hearing aids the right way—at 50 percent off! Batteries are 25 percent off and repairs are about 25 percent lower than you'll find in the retail Homeland. Brand names include ROYALTONE, DANAVOX, and others occasionally. All aids are available for a 30-day trial period and carry a one-year unconditional guarantee (and a six-month warranty on repairs). They'll send you an impression kit for custom ear molds. Select from behind-the-ear, all-in-the-ear, eyeglass, and body aids.

SelectQuote Insurance Service
140 Second Street (800) 343-1985, ext. 293
San Francisco, CA 94105-9807 CK, MO, PQ

As a broker for 18 companies, SelectQuote helps you find a policy to meet your needs. They deal only in term life insurance, and their service is free. They will send quotes by mail. Now who says there's nothing free in this life? All of the companies are considered top-rated by insurance guidelines.

Signature Dental Plan
Dept. 2096
200 N. Martingale (800) 346–0310
Schaumberg, IL 60173 CK, MC, V, AE, D, DC, Montgomery Ward, B

This dental plan, currently available in 36 states, is a great way to save 30 percent on the cost of 170 dental services. The plan includes free oral exams and bite-wing-X-rays. SDP's network includes some 3,000 dentists who have been screened for excellence in health care, facilities, and cleanliness. Peridontal (gums), endodontics (root canals), prosthodontics (dentures), and oral surgery are available, besides fillings, crowns, and other general restorative dentistry. You may cancel at any time for a pro-rated refund of unused dues. Coverage usually begins two weeks from the receipt of your application.

Great Buys readers get a 13-month membership for the price of 12 months. The $72 annual fee covers all dependents of the member.

Surgical Products, Inc.
99 West Street (800) 229-2910
P.O. Box 500 (508) 359-2910
Medfield, MA 02052 CK, MC, V, AE, MO, C

If you're in need of financial support when it comes to support hosiery and underwear, look no further. The Support Plus catalog's pages contain items that are behind you every step of the way. Panty hose, stockings, lumbrosacral and abdominal supports, disposable pants, guard rails, and other personal equipment and apparel are available at discounts from 15 percent to 30 percent less than retail prices. There's a $20 minimum with credit cards; there's no charge for the catalog. And thank you for your support!

Housewares

Why go to Belgium for waffles when you can iron out a not-so-syrupy bargain right here? Need some SABATIER knives for slicing that elegant pâté en route? You'll find some sharp bargains here. Celebrate St. Patrick's Day with a set of genuine Irish ale tankards. Raise your cooking to haute cuisine with CALPHALON cookware. Americans are entertaining more and more in-house and with the right housewares and cookware, you'll set the culinary standards for good taste at your next progressive dinner party. And what dinner party would be complete without a clean plate? Measure up with a KRUPS coffee machine and have your guests begging for MOULI, MOULI!

Bernie's Discount Center, Inc.
821 Sixth Avenue — (212) 564-8758
New York, NY 10001-6305 — CK, MC, V, AE, MO, B, PQ

Plug into the discounts and save about 30 percent on electronics, office equipment, appliances, and more. Bernie's been dealing in bargains since 1948 and sells everything from hairdryers to fax machines. Names that are discounted: TOSHIBA, MITSUBISHI, HAMILTON BEACH, WEAREVER, WHIRLPOOL, BLACK & DECKER, BRAUN, SONY, RCA, BROTHER, PANASONIC, JVC, and many others. Small appliances are shipped all across the country, but larger items are shipped only in the New York area. Call or write for a price quote; bear in mind that the brochure only shows you the tip of the inventory iceberg where selection's concerned. Visa and MasterCard are accepted only for in-store purchases, and American Express charges are shipped to billing addresses only. Orders are shipped to Canada via UPS only.

Betty Crocker Enterprises
P.O. Box 5000 (612) 540-2464
Minneapois, MN 55440-5000 CK, MC, V, C

Betty's sweet-talking us again, this time with kitchenware and silver. When you buy GENERAL MILLS products you get "points" (on boxtops), which can then be used toward purchases from the catalog. You can pay cash, too, but using points, called the THRIFT option, saves you the most money if you usually purchase GENERAL MILLS products. In addition to cake pans, measuring spoons, mixers, cookie-making tools, wooden spice racks, pans, and the like, you'll find ONEIDA silverware (on which you can save as much as 77 percent), porcelain china, and crystal. Cookbooks for microwaving, making appetizers, cooking healthy, and more are also offered. Even kids can get in on the act with toys and games.

Bondy Export Corp.
(See **Buying Clubs and One-Stop Shopping**, p. **112**.)

The Chef's Catalog
3215 Commercial Avenue (800) 338-3232 (credit-card orders)
Northbrook, IL 60062-1900 (708) 480-8312 (customer service)
CK, MC, V, AE, D, MO C/$3

Ooh-la-la! Cuisine is an art, and this company's 40- to 60-page full-color catalog displays 1,001 gourmet cookware items, fine foods, and imaginative gifts from around the world to help you create those epicurean delights. From HENCKELS gourmet kitchen tools to KITCHENAID mixers to plastic Swedish spatulas that won't melt in your mouth, let alone on the stove, The Chef's Catalog serves up top brands like CUISINART, CALPHALON, KRUPS coffee makers, SIMAC electric ice cream makers, MOULI salad makers, and more at money-saving, mouth-watering reductions. Discounts range to 40 percent. Cactus-shaped muffin tins, foolproof skewers for kabobs, and a wok for the grill were just a few of the "can't live without" items we saw. There's no restocking charge, and exchanges and refunds are made if you're dissatisfied. Most orders are received within eight working days. Wok, don't run, to this ingenious collection for the "cooking enthusiast."

Clothcrafters, Inc.
P.O. Box 176, Dept. GBBM
90 Rhine Street
Elkhart Lake, WI 53020
(414) 876-2112
CK, MC, V, MO, C

Smile and say "cheesecloth"—it's just $3.50 for two yards. Cheesecloth can be used for straining, keeping salad and parsley fresh for weeks, or for a variety of other purposes, like converting cottage cheese into yogurt. Other favorites include hickory-stripe denim aprons, 100-percent cotton, for $10; and a denim market tote (big enough to hold a paper grocery bag) with front pocket for $10. There's no minimum order, no restocking charge, and refunds are given on request. Orders paid for by check will be shipped in two weeks; credit-card orders go out immediately.

Colonial Garden Kitchens
P.O. Box 66
Hanover, PA 17333-0066
(800) 752-5552 (orders)
(717) 633-3330 (customer service)
CK, MC, V, AE, D, CB, DC, MO, C/$2

There's nothing behind the times about this Colonial's kitchen, but fortunately, the prices are a little old-fashioned. A 12" pan that serves as a wok, skillet, or roasting pan; a microwave potato ring; a banana slicer; a bread baker; it's all here waiting to be taste-tested for less. In addition, they offer pillows, storage racks, drawer and closet organizers, and other items that help keep the cook within arm's reach of the ingredients. There's a $15 minimum on credit-card orders; refunds are available for dissatisfied customers. Cook with new-fangled equipment at less-than-current prices.

A Cook's Wares
211 37th Street
Beaver Falls, PA 15010-2103
(412) 846-9490
CK, MC, V, AE, C/$2

Gourmet goodies galore! Confirmed cooks and budding bakers alike will enjoy every page of this delicious, 46-page catalog. Pots and pans, bakeware, gadgets, food processors, and more are available, all at 20 percent to 50 percent off the retail price. Too many cooks never spoil the bargains here. Experienced owners personally handle each order and test all equipment before placing it in the catalog. From spice racks to sweet sauces, chocolate to crystal, this business meets all your taste requirements. Detailed descriptions of the merchandise make your selection simpler. Superior products include ROSTI utensils, CUISINART food processors, LE CREUSET copper pans, KRUPS appliances, TAYLOR WOODCRAFT butcher-block tables, PILLVUYT porcelains, and much more. With more than 1,300 items and cookbooks packed into these pages, you're sure to find plenty that pleases your palate. They offer a 30-day return policy. All items carry a manufacturer's guarantee.

Factory Direct Table Pad Company
1036 North Capitol — (800) 428-4567
Suite C-210 — (317) 631-2577 (in IN)
Indianapolis, IN 46204-1007 — CK, MC, V, AE, D, F

Did you know that up to 60 percent of the price of a custom-fit table pad goes to the measurer? Factory Direct Table Pad Company lets you do the measuring (in five minutes or less!). Cut out the middleman and realize a drastic price reduction. They even guarantee a proper fit—every time. Factory Direct makes pads like they were made 50 years ago, maintaining a tradition of excellence. All pads are hand-tailored, have washable leatherette tops, cotton or velour backing, are spill-resistant, and fold easily for convenient storage. Mat and color selection mailed to assist you in choosing just the right style for your table. Flyer with material and color-selection card sent upon request. Satisfaction guaranteed.

Fivenson Food Equipment, Inc.
324 S. Union Street — (800) 632-7342
Traverse City, MI 49684 — (616) 946-7760 (MI residents)
CK, Certified Check, MC, V, AE, D,
C/$3 (refundable)

You can pay cash, you can lease with Fivenson's own exclusive leasing plan, or you can charge it—anyway you cook it, if you're in the kitchen for professional food service equipment and furniture, this is it. Save from 40 percent to 60 percent across the counter for under-counter dishwashers, fryers, mixers to handle from five to 140 quarts, folding tables and chairs, and more. The advantages of buying from their huge inventory are immediate service and great prices. Now don't tell me you don't have room for dessert!

Fuller Brush
P.O. Box 1020 (800) 522-0499; (919) 744-8047
Rural Hall, NC 27098-1020 CK, MC, V, C

Been brushed off lately? Not if you've used the Fuller Brush line for all your household chores. Knock, knock. Who's there? Now, you only have to answer to the postman. The Fuller Brush Home Catalog makes it easier. Products like the Magic Cart, a broom closet on wheels; ten-year light bulbs; back-saving, long-handled brooms and dustpans; precision physicians' scales; Spray 'N Sparkle eyeglass cleaners; a deluxe safety grab bar for the tub; you'll never know what you're missing until you've tried it and it saved your life. All backed by a 100-percent satisfaction guarantee, with Federal Express service for those who can't wait. You'll receive a $25 gift certificate with orders of $250 or more.

Handart Embroideries
Hing Wai Building, Room 106
36 Queen's Road Central 011-852-5-235744
Hong Kong CK, MC, V, AE, C

We're not above taking a Handart with items like these. This company stocks embroidered tablecloths, kimonos, shirts, blouses, and other Oriental items at about 20 percent below retail. As we flipped through Handart's Xeroxed price sheets, we saw hand-crocheted lace tablecloths, children's Kung Fu–style pajamas in sizes 2 through 14, hand-crocheted doilies and place mats, as well as ladies' pure-silk flower-print scarves. Satin sheets for a queen-size bed were easy to slip on. Jade ornaments and ivory hand-carved ornaments were priced to please everyone's pocketbook. Handart goes out on a limb to offer a full refund if the customer is dissatisfied for any reason.

Home Decorators Collection
2025 Concourse Drive (800) 245-2217
St. Louis, MO 63146-4178 CK, MC, V, AE, D, DC, CB, MO, C

We found a houseful of values between the sheets of this catalog, including the (bathroom) sink. Grandfather clocks, bathroom fixtures, chairs, tables, mailboxes, sinks, toilets, medallions, mirrors, Tiffany-style lamps, and more to accent your own house beautiful on a budget. In-stock orders are shipped within 24 hours; there is no charge for shipping on exchanges. Watch for holiday-sales catalogs for the best buys.

Kaplan Bros. Blue Flame Corp.
(See **Appliances (Large and Small)**, p. **41**.)

Kitchen Bazaar
4401 Connecticut Avenue N.W. (202) 244-1550
Washington, DC 20008 CK, MC, V, D, AE, MO, B

The name of this company not only describes our kitchen, but some of our cooking, too! Bizarre! This full-color kitchenware catalog includes gourmet cookware and serving dishes with some items during their periodic sales simmering at up to 75 percent off. (The mere thought sets our blood to boiling!) January is traditionally their clearance month; that's when they gather their slow sellers and slash prices to the bone. Brands included CALPHALON, LE CREUSET, CUISINART, BRAUN, and COPCO. There is no minimum order; orders usually arrive in 14 to 21 days. If you're in the Washington, DC, area, drop into one of their stores. They've been cookin' for 22 years and the staff is exceptionally knowledgeable.

Kitchen Etc.
(See **China, Crystal, Silver, and Gifts**, p. **158**.)

Land O' Lakes Catalog
P.O. Box 1692 (612) 481-2781 (customer service)
Center City, MN 55012-0992 CK, MO, C

Keep the proof of purchase when you buy a pound of Land O' Lakes butter, and shop for some lower-price spreads. Those seals can be used toward items in their catalog, and could save you more than 50 percent off average retail prices on cookware, housewares, and appliances. Butter up to CORNING WARE cookware sets, REED & BARTON flatware, ROYAL DOULTON crystal and china, and more. A child's silverplated bunny bank from REED & BARTON, at $32 suggested retail, was $16.50 with six Land O'

Lakes "points"; a BRAUN Citromatic juicer, retailing for $39.95, was $26.75 with six points. Even irons and hand vacs were included. One of the nicest presentations we've seen in a proof-of-purchase catalog, with 48 colorful pages of buttery bargains for those who use Land O' Lakes products. Make sure you read the information about their point system carefully; some are margarine-al. Orders take up to six weeks to arrive; no credit cards are accepted.

Lillian Vernon

510 S. Fulton Avenue
Mt. Vernon, NY 10550

(804) 430-5555 (customer service)
(914) 633-6300 (orders)
CK, MC, V, AE, D, DC, C

Mail-order magic at fun-filled prices. Often 40-percent to 70-percent discounts are packed into the pages of this can't-resist catalog! No person is left out. There's something for everyone, on anyone's gift list. You'll flip . . . through the pages and see puzzles, games, clothing, accessories, baby items, party items, gift wrap, stationery, housewares, bed and bath doodads, a one-stop shopping book with low prices at every turn. What kid wouldn't lay down and die for a "super kid" beach towel, nature stickers, or a leaf and flower press? What hostess wouldn't swoon over an elegant gift such as a hand-painted porcelain lotus flower, a Victorian-style fireplace fan, or a pearl-shaped porcelain jar? Gifts in Lucite®, crystal, rattan, and linen let you find something for even fussy friends or forgotten relatives. Gifts for the home, office, and automobile give a unique and personal touch to gift-giving. Take two aspirins and call for this catalog in the morning if you are experiencing the buyer's blues. Orders are shipped UPS and come with a 100-percent customer satisfaction guarantee.

Markline

1 Komer Center
Elmira, NY 14903

(800) 992-6754 (orders)
(215) 244-9447 (customer service)
CK, MC, V, AE, MO, C

Mark my word. Markline is full of neat gift ideas and personal treasures backed by their 60-day guarantee. Special perks like $5 worth of "Markline Dollars" redeemable toward a future purchase hold much promise for the future. Call today for their catalog and check out products like their remote light-control system that turns on the lights in your house before you enter, a folding toboggan, a clothes shaver to bring new life to worn sweaters, a bathroom telephone with AM/FM radio and toilet tissue holder, a Vegas slot machine, a SILENT NIGHT pillow that supposedly prevents snoring and migraine headaches, and a JUMP START that gives your car a boost without leaving the driver's seat!

Open House
200 Bala Avenue (215) 664-1488
Bala-Cynwyd, PA 19004 CK, MC, V, PQ

Cookware, tableware, table linens, and more are at prices that close down the competition at this Open House. CHANTAL, LIBBEY, FITZ & FLOYD, LE CREUSET, NIKKO, GUZZINI, MIKASA and CALAPHON are only a smattering of the names close to our hearts. Open your eyes to cutlery and tablecloths, too; it's all about 40 percent less than list prices. This House has been Open since 1960; give them a call or send a letter for a price quote.

Paris Bread Pans
500 Independence Avenue S.E. (202) 544-6858
Washington, DC 20003 CK, MO, B, PQ

Founder Clyde Brooks writes that after living in Paris many years, he didn't want to give up French cuisine—especially the light, crusty bread that the French are famous for. He developed his own bread recipe, but when he was unable to find pans like those used in France, he designed his own pans. A set of double pans making four loaves costs $12, and a four-pan set was $18, or about 40 percent less than in retail gourmet shops. Other items offered include a San Francisco sourdough pan and recipe, and oversize cookie sheets to utilize the whole oven. Shipping charges are included in the price. Our Mr. Brooks says you can save plenty of dough by baking your own.

Peerless Restaurant Supplies
1124 S. Grand Boulevard, Dept. 7223 (800) 255-3663
St. Louis, MO 63104 (314) 664-0400
CK, MC, V, MO, C

Founded in 1947, Peerless Supplies the savings; you supply the cook. Get cookin' with 40 percent off the retail price of kitchen and dining supplies like LIBBEY glassware by the case, WEAREVER and VOLLRATH pots and pans, white and colored chef's aprons, VULCAN ranges, and TRAULSEN refrigerators (to name some of their best sellers). Over 2,000 manufacturers in the food-service industry are represented. Returns are accepted within 30 days; 90-percent credit is given on stocked items, 80-percent on special orders. Expect in-stock items delivered within two weeks.

Pfaltzgraff Pfactory Outlet
2900 Whiteford Road
York, PA 17402
(800) 999-2811 (customer service)
(717) 757-2200
CK, MC, V, AE, DC, C/$1 (refundable)

They say it's "pfabuloous, pforever, pfantastic!" It's PFALTZGRAFF stoneware, glassware, and copperware. Every piece is made from natural materials, hand-finished and hand-decorated. They offer a world of wares for your kitchen counter or dinner table—platters, soup tureens, casserole dishes, wine goblets, gravy boats, mugs, copper chambersticks, and cookie cutters. Stoneware is safe in microwave ovens, freezers, and dishwashers and is chip-resistant.

The Pine Cone
P.O. Box 1378
Blake Building
Gilroy, CA 95021
(408) 842-7597
(408) 842-4797
CK, MO

You might have to suck in you stomach for this one, but it'll be worth it. This miracle Mini-Vac is a revolutionary new tool for cleaning minute particles of dust and debris from hidden and hard-to-reach places. Unlike compressed air, which simply disperses the pollutants, Mini-Vac vacuums them away FOREVER! Mini-Vac is the tool for all reasons and seasons. Perfect for computers, camera equipment, typewriters, stereo equipment, automobiles, and a myriad of household uses. The Mini-Vac goes for $26.95. Your satisfaction is guaranteed.

Plastic BagMart
904 Old Country Road
Westbury, NY 11590
(800) 343-BAGS
(516) 997-3355
CK, MC, V, MO, B (SASE)

It's in the bag! This factory outlet for plastic bags has a bag full of bargains for you. We found over 300 sizes and strengths of bags.

They also have cinched compactor bags, too. Their prices are something to brag about. One hundred extra-heavy industrial-type bags with a 56-gallon capacity cost $34.95. Or maybe you're not trying to bag an elephant, in which case, the light kitchen and office bags cost only $24.95 per 1,000. Whether you are baggin' big or storin' small, the Plastic BagMart has them all . . . fat, skinny, short, or tall. You won't get caught holding the bag, though, because there is a money-back guarantee. So get on your Mart, get set, go!

Potpourri
120 North Meadows Road
Medfield, MA 02052
(800) 388-7798
(800) 688-8051 (customer service)
CK, MC, V, AE, D, MO, C/$2

Add a little potpourri in your life and smell the rewards of your labor. A little price tag and a lot of thought goes a long way. Circling the globe for inexpensive gifts is this company's forte. Jewelry, home accents like mugs, wall hangings, copper wind chimes, plaques and pictures, handbags, knickknacks, rugs, and watches appear at every turn of the page. Potpourri offers a delightful assortment of decorating, entertaining, and gift ideas for the whole family at prices perfectly suited to the budget-correct. Gift wrap and gift cards also available.

Protecto-Pak
P.O. Box 5096
Longview, TX 75608
(903) 757-6092
(903) 297-3985
CK, MO, F/$2 (w/samples), PQ (SASE)

Winding up a bag lady is worth your while here. Zip it up in a Protecto-Pak plastic bag and store the savings, as much as 50 percent below retail. Store food, silver jewelry, pills, or just about anything else in these bags, which come in sizes from 2" by 2" to 13" by 15". Or have Protecto-Pak print your company name on them and use them at work (the minimum order for printing is 10,000) if your storage needs are great. The minimum order is $10.

Richardson Specialty Company
1905 Swarthmore Avenue
Lakewood, NJ 08701
(908) 367-2900
CK, MC, V, AE, MO, C

Clean up your act! This mail-order specialty company comes up smelling like a rose. Its cleaning products are dirt's worst nightmare, like "White Wizard," "Wood to Wood," "Avenge," and "Housekeepers Secret." "Lano Wash" and "Lano Rinse" are especially effective in the washing machine for clothes that have seen more grime than time. No stains/all gains by not making a clean sweep of your budget.

RSP Distributing
(See **Surplus and Volume Sales**, p. **473**.)

Signatures and Starcrest of California
19465 Brennan Avenue (800) 777-0327
Perris, CA 92379 (714) 943-2021
CK, MC, V, AE, MO, B

Sign up for Signatures and Starcrest if the handwriting's on the wall. These two collections of very reasonably priced housewares, gift items, clothing, jewelry, silk plants, bed and bath linens, and accessories are easy on the eye and easy on the pocketbook. Sent in a package of loose pages, each individual item is photographed in color and priced to sell from a $10 manual can opener to a bracelet watch for $26. Sunglasses, crystal sun catchers, tote bags, a series of VHS nature videos, amethyst earrings, a brass doll cradle, and a calligraphy set were some of the offerings available in their monthly mailings. Special gifts and incentives add to the savings and their ultimate appeal.

Weston Bowl Mill
P.O. Box 218 (802) 824-6219
Weston, VT 05161 CK, MC, V, MO, C

We were never much for the GE College Bowl, but the Super Bowl's another story. (Yea! Cowboys!) When it comes to fielding a team of quality products, Weston Bowl just about bowls us over. (Their housewares aren't your everyday run of the mill, either.) Maple, birch, elm, and beech trees sacrifice their roots to become salad bowls, cheese boards, knife holders, pine sugar buckets, stools, coffee tables, shelves and racks, canisters, and jewelry boxes. Everything is beautiful (as Ray Stevens used to sing), and comes in your choice of natural, dark lacquer, or sans finish. About 70 percent of their inventory is their own; they distribute the remaining 30 percent from other manufacturers. Prices are reasonable since they are factory direct. Restocking charges vary depending on the item; orders are shipped in about two or three days. There's a $5 minimum order ($20 with credit cards). Request their retail catalog: There's also a wholesale catalog for businesses buying in bulk (over $50).

The Wine Enthusiast
404 Irvington Street
P.O. Box 39 (800) 356-8466
Pleasantville, NY 10570-0039 CK, MC, V, AE, D, MO, C

Time to sip and save! This aromatic catalog is 48 color pages of wine accessories and more. More than 12 years in the business has aged this company to perfection. Cheers to decanters, wine glasses, ice buckets, corkscrews, wine cellars, and other elegant accoutrements at discounts of 30 percent. We toasted books, too, on fine vino appreciation. Satisfaction is guaranteed; there is a 30-day return policy.

Zabar's
(See **Food**, p. **231**.)

Jewelry

Who can resist the pristine glitter and glamour of exquisite jewelry, the sparkle and fire and inner radiance of a fine gem? Many a stone has unlocked the romance and passion of a woman's heart. The mystery and quiet beckoning of beauty, the silent impact of all that glitters indeed is gold. And whatever your heart desires, you'll find in the following pages. Whether sifted, mined, or plucked from the ocean's floor, it's all here—everything from low-cost gems and cultured pearls from the Orient to high-grade diamonds from New York's famed jewelers on Forty-Seventh Street. The more specific you can be about what you want, the more satisfied you'll be with your selection. Remember, the bigger the carat, the heavier the stone; and the higher the karat, the purer the gold.

Adco Company
P.O. Box 10949 — (312) 337-7804 (order)
Chicago, IL 60610-0949 — (312) 327-1637 (customer service)
CK, MC, V, MO, C

We're talking costume jewelry here, the kind in drugstores, not the stuff that Tiffany charge accounts are made for. But any teenager would find these pages exciting. Earrings represent the largest selection of "fun" jewelry we've seen in one place—ranging in style from "cultura" pearls to a pair of tropical fishes to dangling globes and lobsters! For all the fashion trends and fads, the gal on a budget will be well prepared with earrings, bracelets, rings, and necklaces priced from about $2 to $13. With orders over $50, you will receive a special gift.

Bennett Brothers, Inc.
(See **Buying Clubs and One-Stop Shopping**, p. **112**.)

Brilliant Ideas
332 W. Sunset (800) 678-3033
San Antonio, TX 78209 CK, MC, V, AE, D, MO, C

Call them copycats, but they'd rather save you money than be original. This company got the bright idea of offering copies of fine designer jewelry for a lot less than the real thing. Rings, necklaces, earrings, bracelets, and brooches sparkle with faux pearls, diamonds, rubies, sapphires, emeralds, and more in gold electroplate and sterling silver. B.I. copies designs by CHANEL, BULGARI, DAVID WEBB, and others, and puts out a catalog every fall. There's a minimum charge order of $20; no CODs are accepted. San Antonio, Austin, and Houston are home to Brilliant Ideas boutiques.

Diamond Essence Co.
6 Saddle Road (800) 642-4367
Cedar Knolls, NJ 07927 CK, MC, V, AE, D, MO, C/$2

Forget about the glass-scratching test; these *simulated* diamonds do scratch glass, but they only scratch the surface of your bank account. Set in 14K gold, Diamond Essence's "Ruby Essence,"® "Emerald Essence,"® and other dazzling deceptions cost a fraction of the price of genuine diamonds. They're not putting you on, but putting these on won't cost you an arm and a leg. Jewelry is shipped in velvet gift boxes; delivery takes approximately three to four weeks. There's a 100-percent guarantee.

Fantasy Collection
5952 Royal Lane, Suite 103 (800) 527-6983
Dallas, TX 75230 (800) 492-9209 (TX residents)
(214) 361-1411
CK, MC, V, AE, C

Just half the printed price is your price from this 44-page color catalog of faux gems extraordinaire. All stones are the trademarked

Diamagems® grade AAA cubic zirconia, machine cut, and hand polished in Europe. Rings are set in 14K yellow or white gold in sizes 6 for ladies, 9 for men. There is a sizing charge for larger or smaller ring sizes. This beautiful selection includes the Emergems® (emeraldlike gems that would make your friends green with envy). All fancy shapes: pears, marquises, ovals, emeralds, heart shapes, tri-angles, and radiants that radiate from the pages. Cultured pearl classics, gold chains (herringbone, rope, and cobra), as well as genuine ruby, sapphire, and emerald creations are all available. No more fantasy; they are 50 percent off the retail price.

Fortunoff Fine Jewelry & Silverware, Inc.
(See **China, Crystal, Silver, and Gifts**, p. **154**.)

Helena Windsor Collection
37 Eleventh Avenue (800) 346-9666
Huntington Station, NY 11746-2252 CK, MC, V, AE, MO, C

Look the fashion plate without dishing out your entire food budget on these bijoux. Add some oomph to your wardrobe with inexpensive, knockout jewelry and accessories from the Helena Windsor Collection. Even the Duke of Windsor would fall in love with these crowning jewels without bankrupting the Lloyds of London. The Helena Windsor Collection features copies of classic as well as original designs at piercing and nonpiercing prices. How about circling the globe with an art deco–style watch for around $30, or a classic Roman numeral model for less than $20? These timepieces, bracelets, necklaces, earrings, and pins are right on time. There is a $20 minimum credit-card order; satisfaction is guaranteed or your money back.

House of Onyx
#1 North Main (800) 844-3100
The Aaron Building (800) 992-3260 (KY residents)
Greenville, KY 42345 (502) 338-2363 (AL, HI residents)
CK, MC, V, MO, C

This house is built on the premise that onyx-ty is the best policy, so if rocks are your quarry, you'll find agates, loose diamonds, opals, sapphires, emeralds, tigereye, malachite, and blue topaz here at 50 percent and more off retail. (With these prices, we could afford twin purchases of these Gem-in-eyes and we could still bask in the lapis of luxury.) Onyx is the specialty of the house; they're the largest dealer in carved onyx in the U.S. All merchandise carries a 100-percent satisfaction guarantee; the minimum order is $25; and their 56-page catalog is free.

International Gem Corporation
3601 Hempstead Turnpike (516) 796-0200
Levittown, NY 11756 CK, C/$2

If Scarabs are scarce at your local jewelry store, check out the International Gem catalog for watches, bracelets, and earrings. There's also cloisonne bracelets, rings, earrings, and pins; necklaces of semi-precious stones like garnets, onyx, agate, lapis, amethyst, and adventurine; coral twistable necklaces; rose quartz gemstone hearts; and other unique additions to complement the perfect look and all discounted by about 40 percent. Their rhinestone pins and fresh-water pearl jewelry were among their most popular items, at $5 to $25. Returns are accepted with authorization, and deliveries are normally made within 10 days. Travel to International Gem Corporation, where the faraway gets affordable.

Jewelry Depot
6222 Richmond Avenue, 7th Floor (800) 231-3368
Houston, TX 77057 CK, MC, V, C, F

For starters, Jewelry Depot is the place to go for the gold! A winner in every race when the line-up is jewelry. Bridal sets and semi-mountings from here to eternity. If you have a fatal attraction to stones, this is where they are to die for. Cuts such as the baguette, round, princess, marquise, emerald, or trillion in loose precious gems and diamonds, Diamonds from $1,000/kt and up begin your wholesale shopping buying frenzy. Then it's off to the rope chains (there are zillions of them), or bracelets, or charms, or earrings. No stone is left unturned. Eliminate the middle man, and go directly to the source that had previously been supplying many of the national jewelry chains in the country. Greet the manufacturer at the Jewelry Depot. At last you'll have a friend in the business.

Readers receive a special discount with order.

Kenya Gem Company
801 N. Harvard Avenue (800) 523-0158
Ventnor, NJ 08406 CK, MC, V, AE, DC, B

This one's a gem for those who want a rock with a price that won't rock the boat. KENYA Gem made us ask, "Friend or faux?" Their simulated diamonds allow the gem set to go out and about without naked wrists, ears, or fingers, and still protect their investments: the real McCoy is under lock and key while these pseudo stones come out to play. Cleverly faceted and crafted, KENYA gems started at about $75 a carat, a far cry from their diamond cousins. And KENYA's booklet urged us not to confuse them with cubic zirconia. The order form contains a clever cut-out ring sizing strip, so they'll ring up the perfect size. Orders are delivered via UPS or registered mail. There's a 10-day return-for-refund policy.

Michael C. Fina Co.
(See **China, Crystal, Silver, and Gifts**, p. **160**.)

Nature's Jewelry
27 Industrial Avenue (800) 333-3235
Chelmsford, MA 01824-3692 CK, MC, V, AE, D, MO, C

Naturally, the environment's on everybody's mind, and Nature's Jewelry reflects that consciousness with a catalog of earthly delights. We saw gold-plated earrings and bracelets featuring reminders of endangered species, lovely sterling-silver pieces, jewelry with an Egyptian-inspired motif, and crystal pendants in one of their color catalogs. Holiday and seasonal pieces are also offered. All jewelry is unconditionally guaranteed. An additional $10 gets your order shipped overnight.

One at a Time
3313 Grandview (915) 949-6788; (817) 692-0895
San Angelo, TX 76904 CK, MO, B

Bet you can't buy just one at a time! This jewelry designer, Leslie Reeves, creates intricate, one-of-a-kind jewelry just for kids. The brochure only gives a sampling of the possibilities, and custom requests are welcome. Guatemalan "worry dolls," ceramic fruit and vegetables, ribbons, baskets, and chains woven into necklaces, so not to worry. She also designs hair clips, earrings, pins, and hatbands, as well as hand-painted T-shirts in southwestern motifs. Save 30 percent to 35 percent by ordering direct. When care instructions are followed, all items are guaranteed. Allow two weeks for UPS delivery; $4 shipping and handling.

Palm Beach International
6400 E. Rogers Circle
Boca Raton, FL 33499
(800) 448-5619
(407) 994-2211 (customer service)
CK, MC, V, AE, D, MO, C

Another scandal is brewing in Palm Beach. Is it . . . or is it not the real thing? There is Hope in them thar diamonds, especially if you can save as much as 80 percent on cubic zirconia versions. Bask in the sun and bask in the bargains. In the mail-order business for over 35 years, Palm Beach is the place to sift through the sand and separate the good, the great, and the fake. But, not to be forgotten, who said diamonds are not a girl's best friend? Not I. Here there are savings on genuine diamonds, sapphires, rubies, cultured pearls, onyx, and coral, as well as the faux stones. Lifetime "no-questions-asked" guarantee with full refund is your assurance of reliability. The prices given in the catalog are full-retail prices; you use a table to calculate the savings on the iceman cometh-for-less.

R/E Kane Enterprises
15 W. 47th Street
New York, NY 10036
(212) 869-5525
Certified Check, MO, C/$2, PQ (SASE)

More than a good citizen, Kane is a good entrepreneur as well. While you likely won't find her muttering "rosebud" on her deathbed, you may, if you listen closely, hear the words "Cubic Zirconia" pass from her lips. This company delivers Cubic Zirconia for $10 per diamond carat. Now that deserves an Oscar.

Rennie Ellen
15 W. 47th Street
New York, NY 10036
(212) 869-5525
Certified Check, MO, C/$2, PQ (SASE)

If, as Frank Sinatra sings, New York's a city that doesn't sleep, does it follow that this jeweler rocks around the clock? (To quote Bill

Haley.) You'll have to find out for yourself—we forgot to ask. But enough of our glittering comedic gems! We left no stone unturned in a fruitful search for bargain diamonds in the Big Apple. Happily, we found Rennie Ellen in the perfect setting. As a consumer advocate and one of the few women in the industry, Rennie's wholesale diamond-cutting business will polish up to 75 percent off the price of all jewelry items. Her catalog offers pendants, necklaces, bracelets, and chains sparkling with sapphires, rubies, and amethyst stones. There is a money-back guarantee; most orders are delivered in 10 to 15 days.

Ross-Simons Jewelers

(See **China, Crystal, Silver, and Gifts**, p. **166**.)

Samarth Gem Stones

P.O. Box 6057
61-63
Colaba, Bombay 400 005
India

0091-22-2183512
IMO, Bank Draft, Postal Order
B/$1 (refundable)

Since 1962, Samarth has been exporting and manufacturing gemstones at wholesale prices. Cut and polished precious and semiprecious stones, earrings, pendants, bracelets, and straight-drilled bead necklaces are available through their thick brochure, in which the prices are clearly displayed. This company has made a name for itself with a record that's free of complaints. They promise that your orders will be exported directly; their minimum order is $200.

Great Buys readers get 20 percent off on their first order; be sure to identify yourself and request the discount specifically.

Script Craft Jewelry

P.O. Box 2279
Santa Cruz, CA 95063

(800) 777-1169
CK, MC, V, AE, MO, B

If you're a plain Jane, step aside for curly Shirley. This inventive jewelry is made of gold wire, fashioned into the shape of your personal monicker. The wire, of 12K rolled gold, is guaranteed not to tarnish, fade, or discolor as it proudly spells out your name in curving script. Pins, necklaces, bracelets—even tie chains—tell the world your name and that you're proud of it. (Initials only are available for the shy.) Write or call for a free color brochure showcasing this reasonably priced and unusual, peculiarly American, art form, practiced by the Script Craft family for three generations.

Stecher's Limited
(See **China, Crystal, Silver, and Gifts**, p. **168**.)

The Swiss Konnection
5520 LBJ, Suite 332 (214) 233-0627
Dallas, TX 75240 CK, MC, V, AE, COD, C

A cut above any other furrier, it may seem ludicrous to stuff a 40-percent to 50-percent-off sable coat in your mailbox, but trust me, no matter what size you are, it'll fit. Primarily a source for mink, dahhling, but connections can also be made on blue, white, red, or silver fox, Canadian lynx, beaver, coyote, and sable. Although this retailer is also a full-service discount jeweler, we couldn't resist highlighting their fur collection, too. All brand-name and fine jewelry offered, including watches and accessories, lighters, pens, clocks, and crystal, custom-made creations (just send them a picture), and loose stones, their specialty. Save one-third to one-half on items made to retail from $300 to $50,000. Merchandise returned for exchange or credit (except special orders), and no refunds unless returned within 72 hours. Minimum order, $100.

T. M. Chan & Co.
P.O. Box 33881 Bank or Certified Check, Postal Order, C
Sheung Wan Post Office
Hong Kong

Ever wonder what happened to Charlie Chan's heirs? The great sleuth's namesakes have cracked the case of the overpriced piece of electronic equipment. We grew suspicious when we priced the Asahi PENTAX ME camera with a 50mm f/1.7 lens and case at $277 (about what the catalog distributors offer on a regular basis without across-the-ocean anxiety). However, the watch selection clued us into a SEIKO Sports 100 watch for only $99 (retail $215) and ROLEX watches in the sub-$1,000 category. We detected similar bargains (savings of 30 percent to 50 percent) on their high-quality clothing tailored from the finest British and Italian fabrics.

Bank check, money order, certified check, or cashier check (no credit cards) must accompany every order before shipping. All goods come with a one-year warranty; insurance is extra.

Vanity Fair (also S.A. Peck & Co.)
55 E. Washington Street 539
Chicago, IL 60602
(800) 235-3000
(312) 977-0300
(IL residents call collect)
CK, MC, V, AE, MO, DC, C

Since 1921, S.A. Peck has been specializing in jewelry design and diamonds. Because they import and manufacture fine jewelry and eliminate the middleman's profit, they offer savings from 35 percent to 50 percent. Their merchandise is top quality and priced perfectly. We saw, for example, a well-priced modern octagon-shaped GRUEN 18K goldtone Swiss quartz, ultra-thin calendar watch at 40 percent off retail. Their 30-day money-back guarantee is underwritten by Lloyds of London. They also offer the free service of inspecting and ultrasonically cleaning your jewelry for you. An appraisal is included with all diamond purchases.

Van Moppes Diamonds
Albert Cuypstraat 2-6
1072 CT
Amsterdam, Holland
(3120) 761254
MC, V, AE, DC,
C/$5 (refundable with purchase)

In today's world of inflated diamond prices, you don't have to stick your finger in a dike to get lower prices. Just let your fingers do the walking and give Van Moppes a call. They will be happy to send you their catalog containing selections of 400 designs from the collection of over 2,000 models of jewelry. They have been in business since 1828—longer than Holland has had dikes. This is Amsterdam's most famous diamond factory. Mr. Arnold J. Van Moppes represents the eighth generation in this family business. All of their items are made with 18 carat gold. Their stones are cut with the world-famous Amsterdam cut—a cut above the rest. This family has eliminated the costly middleman to give you the lowest possible prices. These precious diamonds took thousands of years to be created and cannot possibly be described with words. They must be seen to be appreciated. Before you buy a gem for your hand, check prices with this man from tulip land.

Vintage Timepieces
12900 Preston Road, Suite 500 (800) 833-3159
Dallas, TX 75230 (214) 392-4281
CK, MC, V, PQ

Time is on your side when you buy from these buyers of vintage PATEK and ROLEX watches made before 1955. A blast from the past could help you keep up with the times—of your appointments. The latest, says Don Meyer, is not necessarily the greatest, especially when it comes to wrist and pocket watches, coins, and fountain pens. Strap on one of his deals and help your budget stay in tick-tock shape. He buys high, sells low.

Wild Rose Studios
P.O. Box 387 (701) 245-6356
Westhope, ND 58793 CK, MO, C/$1

Finding this gem in North Dakota was no easy matter. Nonetheless, we found it . . . and since 1972, they've generated a loyal following. You'll go Wild over their selection of Jade and Hematite, as well as the latest craze—New Zealand Sea Opal (deep blue) jewelry. A less expensive line, called Gold 'n' Stones, is also available for the less endowed. Choose from a large variety of Alaskan, North Dakotan, and other hat and lapel pins, worry stones, natural stones, bangles, and charms. We became attached to their line of magnets and ornaments, too. High-quality, reasonable prices (save 10 to 40 percent), and service all rolled into one. All items are real gems and stones, nothing is glass or fake. Most settings in 23K Hamilton gold plate. Two-week delivery, a five-year warranty. Orders less than $10, add $1 postage and handling.

Kits and Kaboodle

Remember that first do-it-yourself project? You were five, and you used half a paper plate and some crayons to make a gift for your mother, and she thought that it was the most beautiful paper plate-half in the world. You're probably more skillful when it comes to working with paper, crayons, and paint—not to mention wood, cloth, and metal—by now. At least we hope so! (Come to think of it, maybe it's time you made another gift for Mom.) Do-it-yourself projects have come a long way from primitive designs made on paper plates with broken crayons. Today you can build a grandfather clock or a baby's cradle; assemble a greenhouse; ferment some wine; repair an antique trunk; construct a computer; wire a stereo; or even build a three-bedroom house, or a houseboat. All it takes is time, determination, and knowing where to buy your supplies. Get yarn, woodworking tools, optical accessories, beekeeping supplies, jewelry-making instruments, doll-house furniture, leathercrafting materials—almost anything to indulge your creative spirit. Be crafty; order by mail or phone and make bargain-hunting part of your diversion. When it comes to saving money, "where you get it" is as important as "what you get."

The Bartley Collection
29060 Airpark Drive, Dept. 8225 — (800) 227-8539
Easton, MD 21601 — CK, MC, V, D, C

You take the lowboy and I'll take the highboy from this elegantly photographed catalog of 18th-century antique-furniture-reproduction kits. These gleaming wood furniture pieces will hold candles, brandy, the White House china (in reproduction, of course), or even your collection of murder mysteries. All kits are complete and include solid brass hardware, all finishing materials, stains and varnish, and complete instructions. There's even a form included for replacement of any pieces that might turn up missing. All kits can be ordered finished or unfinished. Bartley's catalogs come out eight times per year, and each catalog contains a selection of new kits. Refund and exchange privileges extend for 30 days for items returned in their original condition; missing, defective, and freight-damaged parts will be replaced at no charge during the same period. Orders are shipped immediately.

Brew City Supplies
P.O. Box 27729 (414) 425-8595
Milwaukee, WI 53227 CK, MC, V, MO, C

Brew City's brewing up great deals on everything you need to make your own beer. Chug-a-lug. They guarantee the lowest prices, or up to 50-percent savings on supplies from JOHN BULL, COOPERS, GLENBREW, MUNTON & FISON, and others. Oak chips, thermometers, brushes, cappers, yeast, siphons, spigots, filters, funnels, glasses, and more are included in the black-and-white catalog. Their JOHN BULL Home Beer Making Kit retails for $45, but is available at Brew City for $29.95, and contains "everything you need" to brew five gallons at home. Brew City offers prompt refunds on all merchandise returned within 15 days (but no refunds on food items). Most orders are shipped within 24 hours of their receipt.

Brewmaster
162 Steam Mill Road (607) 594-3743
Odessa, NY 14869 CK, AE, B

Ale, ale, the gang's all here! Is this for you? Of Coors it is! Serious and recreational beer guzzlers nip beer prices in the Bud with their very own Brewmaster beer-making kit. We've known men who became Hamm's after just one taste. (There's many a sip 'twixt cup and lip!) Besides beer-making supplies, we heard through the grapevine that they carry all of the better winemaking supplies, too. Known nationwide and in Europe, Asia, Africa, and Australia, a random sampling of items for sale included: Canadian Ale Kit (12 gallons); light beer kit (95 gallons); Old English Stout Kit (6.5 gallons); along with malts, hops, and yeast. The savings are from 40 percent to 50 percent below standard prices on these unique, delicious home brews. These Premium brews from imported hops create an alcohol content of over 5 percent. Glassware, barrels, equipment, and books are available. Their latest line of kits, "Froth for the Gentry," makes an improved-quality beer for the discerning. Orders are shipped via UPS every two days.

Customers who order and mention *Great Buys* will receive a 5-percent discount.

BYX (Bill Your Ex)
3960 Laurel Canyon Boulevard, #437 (213) 850-5522
Studio City, CA 91604 $14.95 (plus tax and shipping)

Got a deadbeat dad (or mom, for that matter) who needs constant nudging when it comes time for the support checks to be forked over? Well, here's a do-it-yourself kit that will make the job of billing and record keeping of the court-ordered support payments easy (good for alimony payments, too). Take control of the situation and treat what's owed you impassionately with triplicate NCR invoices, mailing envelopes, return envelopes, first and second past due notices and a simple record keeping ledger. And don't relax when you hear that ole refrain, "The check is in the mail." Seeing is believing.

Cane & Basket Supply Co.
1283 S. Cochran Avenue (213) 939-9644
Los Angeles, CA 90019 CK, MC, V, AE, DC, CB, C/$2

In a Testament to the Genesis of evil, Cane was Able to weave himself a tale of woe. Fortunately, you won't become a basket case if you make the right sacrifices and stay out of trouble. Boasting "the largest selection of caning and basket supplies in the world," these folks can give advice in hand-weaving chair seats, choosing the appropriate tools and materials, or selecting oils and varnishes for the right finishing touches. (And that's the unvarnished truth!) Prices are 20 percent to 40 percent lower than you'll find in craft stores carrying similar products. C&B also sells complete kits of woods and weavings for footstools and chairs, for those who want to keep their idle hands busy in their own and not the Devil's workshop. Returns are accepted with no questions asked. Shipping's the same day. Check out their 20-page catalog.

Cherry Tree Toys, Inc.

P.O. Box 369 (800) 848-4363 (orders)
408 S. Jefferson (614) 484-4363
Belmont, OH 43718 CK, MC, V, D, MO, COD ($2.95 fee), C/$1

Whirligigs—clever variations of weather vanes and wind toys—the ones you used to see atop old barns or fence posts most often in the Northeast or Midwest—are available here in do-it-yourself kits, Cherry Tree Toys liked them so much, they designed more than 30 whirligig plans so that you, too, could "forecast" the weather. Know the wind's direction by watching an entire array of whirligigs ranging from mallard ducks, cardinals, and loons to woodchoppers, milking farmers, baseball players, and airplanes—and many more—spin in the wind. Cherry Tree Toys' full-color catalog not only has whirligigs and toys, but plans for dollhouses, clocks and music boxes, parts, and a variety of kits for all skill levels. The easiest kits to make are precut and pre-drilled and require only sandpaper and glue for assembly—while the more challenging kits contain only the plans and the special turned wood or metal parts. Also available are toy, craft, game, and furniture parts in maple, oak, walnut, and cherry, in addition to nontoxic finishes and general toymaking and woodworking supplies.

Clothkits

24 High Street, LEWES (0273) 477111
E. Sussex BN72LB MC, V, Sterling Cheques, Sterling Postal/
England Money Orders, EuroCheques made out in
Sterling, Access, Eurocard, C

Talk about a success story. For 18 years, this luscious 58-page color catalog has covered many satisfied shoppers from top to bottom with designer outfits that you make from a CLOTHKIT. This original screen-printed kit allows you to save your creative input. Those unwilling to do it "their way" can choose from pages of ready-made clothes for adults and kids. Their kits are especially designed for nimble-fingered folks who have found dressmaking tough. Paper patterns are eliminated either by printing the cutting lines directly on the fabric or are offered already cut out and ready to sew. Instruction sheets are a snap. To coordinate with each kit, you can choose ready-made knitwear, hosiery, and accessories, along with original toys and household items. Perfect gifts for your entire family. Full refunds or exchanges if not completely satisfied.

Constantine's
2050 Eastchester Road
Bronx, NY 10461
(800) 223-8087
(800) 822-1202 (NY residents)
CK, MC, V, AE, MO, COD, C

Constantine's claim is "everything for better woodworking," and who would disagree? This 177-plus-year-old company offers kits, materials, tools, and books for everything from backgammon table tops to dollhouse miniatures. With Constantine's supplies you can build a ship model or guitar, or make a cabinet or clock. Inlays, overlays, cane and rush supplies, whatever your pleasure, their catalog of many colors has probably got something to assemble. Prices aren't discounted, but they are competitive: Constantine's merchandise qualifies as hard-to-find items. Their library is as extensive as their selection of specialty tools. There's a $15 minimum order with charge card; a $10 minimum with cash. They stand behind everything they sell, and will give full refunds or exchanges if you're not satisfied. Orders are usually delivered in seven to ten days.

CR's Bear and Doll Supply Catalog
P.O. Box 8
Leland, IA 50453
(515) 567-3652
CK, MC, V, MO, C/$2; $4 in Canada;
$7 in foreign countries

The cost of cuddlies can be un-bear-able, but CR's will save you about 33 percent and more on the cost of making teddy bears and dolls. Kits, supplies, and patterns, including their own original designs, are available here. Supplies featured in their 16-page catalog include everything the well-made bear is wearing this season: glass eyes, fur fabrics, mohair, stuffing, and joints. Dolls were decked out in shoes, wigs, hats, porcelain parts, glasses, and more. Music boxes and stands were extra touches. CR's also had books on doll and bear making, and finished vinyl dolls. It's a great way to make a friend!

EFS
Everything you Need to Know To Save the Earth Kit
1407 Foothill Boulevard, Suite 38107
La Verne, CA 91750 CK

Raise your planetary consciousness and be part of the solution. This kit includes information on recycling and conserving water and energy, along with a cotton shopping bag, water-saving shower heads, toilet dams, and rescue aids. The cost of the entire kit is $44.95, plus $4 shipping. Help save the day for future generations.

Emperor Clock Company
Emperor Industrial Park (205) 928-2316
Fairhope, AL 36532 CK, MC, V, AE, D, MO, C/$1, PQ

Look at the Emperor's new clocks from the world's largest manufacturer of grandfather clocks. It's no wonder—they sell grandfather clock kits at factory-direct prices. Clock movements are included. (What's a grandfather clock without its pacemaker?) They also have wall clocks in cherry, walnut, and other fine woods. If you're still not a handyperson, you can buy the clocks assembled. You'll still save a bundle over retail prices, and you'll save time. Emperor also carries butler tables, chests, desks, and entertainment-center kits. Complete instructions, screws, and hardware are included. Expect your order to arrive in three to six weeks. Movements are warranted for three years.

Four Seasons Greenhouses
(See **Plants, Flowers, Gardens, and Farming**, p. **416**.)

Frank's Cane and Rush Supply
7252 Heil Avenue (714) 847-0707
Huntington Beach, CA 92647 CK, MC, V, MO, C

Rush to Frank's and take a seat—or at least the makings of one. Their selection included cane webbing, wire-fiber rush, wicker, rattan, and binding cane for weaving replacement seats after somebody decides to stand up on one. Frank's also offers chair-making kits, basket-making materials, books, and upholstering tools and supplies. All this is put together at about 40 percent less than prices elsewhere.

Frostline Kits
2525 River Road (800) 548-7872; (303) 241-0155
Grand Junction, CO 81505 CK, MC, V, D, AE, C

Baby bunting and clothes for hunting; saddlebags for models; backpacks for dogs; robes and booties for humans; comforters and tents; even a do-it-yourself (imitation) bear rug are among Frostline's wide variety of sew-it-yourself outdoor clothing and equipment. Expect a mountain parka to arrive in about three to four weeks. There's a six-month refund period, and they'll exchange in the case of faulty materials. That should take the chill off.

Go Gart
(See **Cars and Auto Supplies**, p. **143**.)

The Green Pepper
941 Olive Street (503) 345-6665
Eugene, OR 97401 CK, MC, V, COD, C/$1

I'm a pepper, you're a pepper, but these folks are Green Peppers (and when you're hot, you're hot!). Buy the patterns alone or the complete kits to make colorful, fashionable clothes for camping, galloping, pedaling, crossing the country, or schussing down the slopes. This company specializes in active sportswear patterns, fabrics and notions in brands like GREEN PEPPER, GORE-TEX®, KLIMATE, THINSULATE, and DACRON II HOLOFILL. Hard-to-find fabric for rainproof/waterproof clothing is their best-selling item. Price reflects 50 percent or more savings over comparable ready-mades. We saw patterns for vests, jackets, parkas, ski suits, running suits, as well as book bags, saddle bags, and cargo bags all designated by asterisks to denote the degree of sewing difficulty. Fabrics and notions needed for each pattern are also included in their catalog. They also provide "pre-cut kits" as an educational service to junior and senior high-school home-economics teachers. Novice to experienced sewers can find something in this slick, black-and-white-photographed catalog. There is no minimum order or restocking charge, and refunds or exchanges are made on merchandise returned in its original condition. Wouldn't you like to be a Pepper, too?

Green River Trading Co.
Boston Corners Road
R.D. 2
P.O. Box 130 (518) 789-3311
Millerton, NY 12546 CK, COD, C/$6

Have a barn-building party (or put up a garage for a noble steel steed) with kits from Green River. Their specialty is rustic-looking log cabin kits, and they'll sell you blueprints or help you design your own. Prices are 20 percent to 40 percent less than conventional prices. There's no minimum order, no restocking charge on returns, and exchanges or refunds are honored up to 60 days after delivery. All materials are warranted for one year. For those who want to avoid slivers from timbers, Green River sells novelty log siding—for the log look without the log. Green River also publishes and sells Western art, originals and limited editions, and—get this!—they raise and breed Texas Longhorn Cattle.

Herrschners, Inc.
2800 Hoover Road (800) 441-0838; (715) 341-0560
Stevens Point, WI 54481 CK, MC, V, D, AE, MO, C

Herrsch-a-buy, herrsch-a-buy, little baby. And rest assured that the selection of handcraft kits for little ones is tremendous. Baby afghans, bibs, mobiles, towels, buntings, sweater sets, and quilts can be made from easy-to-use kits. That's not all—lacy Victorian blouses, pillows, sachets, even garters and hankies can be fashioned. Afghans are the biggest seller at Herrschners if one considers the number of pages devoted to them. Embroidered tablecloths were well represented. Quilts were, too. Christmas ornaments, dolls, latch rugs, and needlepoint kits make this catalog worth ordering.

Hobby Shack
18480 Bandilier Circle (800) 854-8471
Fountain Valley, CA 92728-8610 (800) 472-8456 (CA residents)
(714) 963-9881
CK, MC, V, MO, COD
($4.95 charge), C

Hobby Shack's color catalog displays hundreds of souped-up, radio-controlled models of boats, planes, and cars bound to stretch the imagination of kids and adults alike. They carry SUTABA, AIRTRONIX radios, and MAGNUM engines; elaborate designs, bright colors, and assorted scale sizes are available. Many accessories, tools, and supplies are available at up to 50 percent off. Regular customers gain special status and receive the *Sport Flyer* (which touts special sales during the year). There is no minimum order ($25 minimum on COD), no restocking charges, and if you place an order, the catalog is free.

Hobby Surplus Sales

P.O. Box 2170, Dept. GBBM
287 Main Street
New Britain, CT 06050
(800) 233-0872 (orders only);
(203) 223-0600
CK, MC, V, D, C/$3

You're bound to go loco when you see the great prices and selection of LIONEL and AMERICAN FLYER trains and train repair parts. While they have one of the best selections of trains we've seen (from giant size LGB to tiny N gauge), their huge illustrated catalog features thousands of items and specializes in offering a full selection of hobby kits and supplies for everyone in your family. You will find a wide variety of new, as well as hard-to-find, out-of-production model cars, trucks, ships, planes, radio tools, and more. Most are on sale for discounts of 20 percent to 70 percent. Closeouts and discontinued merchandise went off the road at wheely low prices. Want to explore space? Why not build a model rocket that really flies thousands of feet and then parachutes safely back to earth? Feeling steamed up? Their selection of real operating steam engines from Europe will fascinate and educate. For a comprehensive guide to family-centered activities that will open the door to hours of creative fun, get the Hobby Surplus catalog! Hobby Surplus guarantees your satisfaction; returns are accepted within 30 days.

Mention *Great Buys By Mail* and get the *$3* catalog for *$2*.

Hudson Glass Co. Inc.

(See **Arts and Crafts**, p. **66**.)

Huston Dolls

(See **Toys**, p. **482**.)

The Iron Shop
P.O. Box 547 (800) 523-7427
400 Reed Road CK, Certified or Bank Check, MO
Broomall, PA 19008 MC, V, AE, D, C

Climbing the stairway to paradise is made easier when you want to climb in the appropriate circles. For a spiral-staircase kit, step up to The Iron Shop. This manufacturer offers kits that include all necessary fasteners and instructions, and also provides accessories like extra spindles (for child safety) or special handrails, and spindle and center-pole cap designs. These stairs vary in diameter from 3′ 6″ to 7′ 0″, and were priced from $425 to $1,575. Visit their showrooms/warehouses in California, Florida, Texas, Illinois, and Connecticut; maps of their locations are included in the catalog.

E. C. Kraus
Wine & Beermaking Supplies
9001 E. 24 Highway (Winner Road)
P.O. Box 7850 (816) 254-7448
Independence, MO 64053 CK, MC, V, MO, C

Distill, my art! A loaf of bread, a jug of watermelon wine, and thou art on the way to enjoying the fermented fruits, flowers, and vegetables of thy labors. Kraus's 16-page illustrated catalog features a library of information, plus a large supply of yeasts, extracts, equipment, and accessories for beer and wine private production. Fruit juices and additives for making wine are their biggest-selling items. There is no charge for shipping, satisfaction guaranteed, and delivery is usually in about a week. No restocking charge on returns, either. All you need to supply is the women (or men) and song.

Kuempel Chime Clock Works
21195 Minnetonka Boulevard (800) 328-6445; (612) 474-6177
Excelsior, MN 55331 CK, MC, V, C

These grandfather clock kits are made by real grandfathers! Their full-color catalog **a**) introduces you to the little old clockmakers who create the clocks; **b**) tells you how the business began; and **c**) offers accolades and testimonials from satisfied customers. You can buy just the clock plans, just the molding packages, or an entire kit containing all case pieces. A selection of melodic clockworks is sold separately. If time flies when you're having fun, a project from Kuempel should speed you on our fun-filled way.

Leather Unlimited Corp.
(See **Handbags and Luggage**, p. **275**.)

McKilligan Industrial and Supply Corp.
(See **Hardware, Tools, and Home Improvement**, p. **292**.)

Milan Laboratory
57 Spring Street (212) 226-4780
New York, NY 10012 CK, MC, V, MO, COD, C, (SASE)

Discover the secrets of Forbidden Fruit, Roman Punch, and other magical nectars of the gods by concocting them in the confines of your own kitchen. Milan is a complete headquarters for beer-bellied brewers and bibulous imbibers of wines and spirits. They have chemicals, extracts, preservatives, barrels, corks, and a host of other supplies to make your alcoholic elixir-making easier. Their catalog devotes a whole page to extracts to mix with alcohol, sugar, and water to make instant (and discounted) liqueurs and cordials. Discounts fermented at 50 percent: the brands were Milan's own. There's even a wine doctor in the house who can diagnose errant brews, mismixed batches, and lifeless spirits.

Miles Homes
P.O. Box 9495 (800) 328-3380
4700 Nathan Lane (800) 642-3200 (MN residents)
Minneapolis, MN 55440 CK, MO, C/$10

Miles to go before you sleep in one of these ranch-style, split-level, one-and-one-half, and two-story houses. The Miles people specialize in making your impossible dream of home ownership a four-walled reality. Their designs are modern and simple, but solid and homey-looking. Homes are available with decks and vaulted ceilings—some have separate dining rooms. Of course, the homes are precut and then you're on your own. One of their biggest selling points is that there's no money down and the homes are financed at below-market rates. You need good credit and a lot of homing devices. Miles has 16 national sales offices and five distribution points, plus design centers and model homes on display.

Music Maker Kits
423 Main Street (612) 439-9120
Stillwater, MN 55082 CK, MC, V, AE, COD, C/$1

Has the high cost of beautiful musical instruments been a cross to bear? Then Music Maker should bring heavenly music to your ears. They offer a cathedral of 25 different acoustical instruments for you to construct from kits. You can bring the hills alive with the sound of music by constructing a guitar, a Mountain Banjo, or a mandolin. At these prices, you should be picking and grinning. With a little patience and time, you could build a beautiful gothic harp. That's something to harp about. The company carries a variety of useful kits that could provide you with porch swings, hanging chairs, wooden trains, airplanes, kitchen knives, and more. If you decide you can't quite get it together, just return your unfinished kit for a full refund.

New England Cheesemaking Supply Co.
85 Main Street
Dept. 85 GBBM (413) 628-3808
Ashfield, MA 01330 CK, MC, V, COD, C/$1

Get a slice of these cheesemaking kits and you may never settle for store-bought again. You'll melt at the sight of a basic kit, including everything you need to get started, for just $22.95. Champagne yeast, a home milk pasteurizer, an electric cream separator, a cheese press, mold powders, and more will set you on the road to a cheesier way of life.

Great Buys readers will receive their $1 catalog free.

Rollerwall, Inc.
(See **Windows and Walls**, p. **523**.)

Squadron Mail Order
1115 Crowley Drive (214) 242-8663
Carrollton, TX 75011-5010 CK, MC, V, AE, D, MO, C/$3.50

Tanks to this defender of discounts, model airplanes, motorcycles, bombers, battleships, tanks, and other "militaria" are available at savings of 30 percent to 70 percent off retail. This is one of the country's foremost dealers of airplane kits, with a selection that ranges from a simulated World War I biplane to an exact replica of a Navy fighter detailed down to the cockpit and decals. A fascinating selection of books for the model builder is available, many concerning a particular branch of the armed services. Squadron owns their own publishing company and markets publications though this mail-order business. Minimum order is $10.

Taylor's Cutaways and Stuff
(See **Arts and Crafts**, p. **74**.)

Texas Greenhouse Co.
(See **Plants, Flowers, Gardens, and Farming**, p. **426**.)

Tower Hobbies
(See **Toys**, p. **484**.)

Vienna Health Products
(See **Health, Fitness, and Vitamins**, p. **308**.)

Wilderness Log Homes
P.O. Box 902
Rural Route 2, U.S. 85
Plymouth, WI 53073
(800) 237-8564 (800-BEST LOG)
(800) 852-5647 (WI residents)
CK, MC, V, AE, MO, COD (with 50 percent down), C/$9

Want your kids to grow up to be president? Raise them right—in a log cabin! Wilderness Log Homes provide just what their name says, but their dwellings are not the rough-hewn, thatch-as-thatch-can variety. The logs are handcrafted and (would you believe?) custom-designed. Homes have a woodsy charm and blend in well with the environment provided you don't erect one in midtown Manhattan! They're available with up to five bedrooms, cathedral ceilings, studies, dining rooms, and almost as much elbow room as the great outdoors. Their most popular model is the "Cumberland," a 1,700-square-foot cabin with two porches and cathedral ceiling. Those favoring modern comforts and energy efficiency will be interested in their "Insulog Kits," in which the logs have been split and filled with insulation and the interior is finished with sheetrock. These units have ceilings with an R-value of 40 and side walls are R-30. Prices are good when compared with others in the same business; not surprising as they own their own mill. Kits are shipped on flatbed trucks, and usually go out about four weeks after you place your order.

Lingerie and Underwear

Whether you wear your underwear as outerwear, it's all in the name of fashion. From cuddly robes to curl up in around the fire, to a sexy peignoir to light someone's fire, these sources won't put a damper on your budget. Brand' names from top to toe for both men and women will keep the '90s shopper spic 'n' spandex for the next decade or two. JOCKEY into position and say BALI-hoo to full-price lingerie and underwear.

Chock Catalog Corp.

74 Orchard Street — (800) 222-0020; (212) 473-1929
New York, NY 10002 — CK, MC, V, MO, C/$1, PQ

This business is chock full of nuts who love these heavenly bargains on undergarments. We found savings of 25 percent off hosiery and underwear for the whole family—a fitting discount for well-fitting unmentionables fit for newborns to grandparents. They've got CARTER'S pj's, undies, and blankets; HANES and BVD briefs and boxer shorts; BURLINGTON socks; HANES pantyhose and much more. We're told their most popular brand name items are their men's briefs from MUNSINGWEAR, at three for $10.50 (retail three for $14); women's LOLLIPOP bikinis and panties were three for $7.50 (retail three for $10). Orders are usually delivered within two weeks, and returns and exchanges are accepted within thirty days.

D & A Merchandise Co.
22 Orchard Street
New York, NY 10002
(212) 925-4766
MC, V, C/$2 (one-time fee), PQ

Elliot Kivell calls himself The Underwear King, and with a business in business since 1946, he's had more than a brief reign. D & A treats their customers royally with 25-percent savings on men's and women's robes, underwear, and lingerie. Ninety percent of their merchandise is branded, and famous names aren't exactly feudal and far between. You'll see HANES and BERKSHIRE panty hose; panties and bras by LILY OF FRANCE, OLGA, WARNER, MAIDENFORM, CARNIVAL CREATIONS, LILYETTE, BALI, VASSARETTE, and FORMFIT RODGERS; DANSKIN tights; LORRAINE camisoles; MUNSINGWEAR, JOCKEY, and BVD T-shirts and briefs; and BURLINGTON, INTERWOVEN, CHRISTIAN DIOR, and WIGWAM socks. Bra sizes run to 48 and panties to size 12. Most orders are received within two weeks. (An exception was a $2,000 underwear order mailed to an Arab sheik in Europe; not surprisingly, that took a little longer!) No time limit on returns; cash refunds are given. Be specific when requesting a price quote as to line and style number, size, and color. Shipping costs $2.50, except to Alaska and Hawaii. As Elliot so demurely put it, "Why pay more?"

Damart
3 Front Street
Rollinsford, NH 03805
(800) 258-7300
(603) 742-7420 (NH residents)
CK, MC, V, AE, D,
($15 minimum for cards), C

We're talking underwear, folks! Who's going to know . . . Thermolactyl underwear, exclusive to Damart, will keep the north winds out. The 48-page catalog makes no mention of their factory seconds, but call the toll-free number and ask if any items from the catalog are available in seconds. The only possible drawback from this tasty underwear is that thermolactyl material cannot be thrown in a dryer. Even so, it is touted as fast drying, and there is no retail equivalent available anywhere. Besides offering an assortment of colors and styles (button-downs, long-sleeves, vests, etc.), Damart also stocks an assortment of heavy-duty socks.

Eisner Bros.
(See **Apparel: Family**, p. **13**.)

Goldman & Cohen, Inc.
55 Orchard Street (212) 966-0737
New York, NY 10002 CK, MC, V, AE, PQ

This dynamic duo carries over 50 of the finest names in lingerie and loungewear, at savings ranging from 20 percent to 70 percent. (The usual discount is probably more like 40 percent to 50 percent.) Their inventory is mostly first quality, with an occasional select irregular. You'll also find bras and lingerie by EVE STILLMAN, VASSARETTE, KAYSER, BALI, LILY OF FRANCE, and others; WARNER bras and daywear were also available from 20 percent to 70 percent off. Sizes in bras ranged from 32A to 44D; in lingerie from petite to extra-large. Exchanges are made, but the item must be clean, the tickets must still be attached, and you must have the receipt. There's a $15 minimum on credit cards. Shipping's $2.50 on orders under $50; $3 on orders up to $100. In-stock merchandise usually arrives in about a week; three to four weeks for things not on hand.

Howron Sportswear
(See **Apparel: Family**, p. **15**.)

Isaac Sultan & Sons, Ltd.
332 Grand Street (800) 999-1645
New York, NY 10002 CK, MC, V, AE, COD, PQ

Bravo! Bravo! We played the understudy of undergarments here and decided this was a class act for brassy brassieres in broad(way) sizes (32A to 50DD). Current and discounted styles and hard-to-find large sizes in bras get very favorable reviews. Sultan's the sheik of cheap chic, and if you know your lines, you'll score 20-percent savings on lingerie by BALI, POREET, MAIDENFORM, and a crowd of others. Give them the style number of the item you want and they'll find it. Shipping's a flat $2.50 charge; there's no minimum order; and your tickets to comfort should arrive in a week or two. No wonder folks keep coming back for an encore! Send them a postcard giving the manufacturer, style number, size, and color to get a price quote; they prefer to have only serious buyers use their phone number.

Just My Size
P.O. Box 748 (800) 522-0889
Rural Hall, NC 27098 CK, MC, V, D, MO, C

Just My Size is the catalog of choice for full-figured women who want style as well as substance in their lingerie. Panty hose and stockings from HANES, slips, camisoles, girdles, underwear, even socks, sweatpants, fleecy cardigans, and tank dresses in a variety of colors. Bras that are reasonably priced at around $18 a piece are even less when you buy two or more—some as low as $13.50 each. Slightly imperfect panty hose go for 50 percent off. Designed to fit you *and* your budget.

L'eggs Showcase of Savings
P.O. Box 843 (919) 744-1170
Rural Hall, NC 27098-0843 CK, MC, V, D, MO, C

In addition to irregular hosiery and slightly imperfect and first-quality lingerie, first-quality activewear such as T-shirts, leotards, tights, boxers, and turtlenecks are available at discounted prices. Their colorful catalog featured men's and women's style and size charts for easy ordering; pages were tagged to indicate first-quality or imperfect merchandise. Postage varies depending on the amount you purchase: for under $10, you'll pay $1.60; for under $20, you'll pay $2.40, etc. Get a L'EGGS up on the competition's prices with names you trust.

Maidenform
New Braunfels Mills Street Plaza
651 Highway 81 East (512) 620-7366
New Braunfels, TX 78130 CK, MC, V, MO (with credit card)

Maidens in waiting can get into form for less here. 'Twas both boom and bust in all discounted styles of MAIDENFORM bras, including OSCAR DE LA RENTA. Underwire models were $9-$10 and up; slightly imperfect (one once opened wide during a speech, oops!) began as low as $7; $16-$20 and up for OSCARs. Save up to 60 percent on first-quality, discontinued, and closeout merchandise in bras, panties, camisoles, half and full slips, and garter belts.

Mayfield Co. Inc.
303 Grand Street (212) 226-6627
New York, NY 10002 CK, MC, D, V, PQ

Mayfield knows hose, and theirs go for 20 percent to 25 percent off retail. They carry a full line of lingerie, hoisery, and underwear in brands such as BERKSHIRE, BONNIE DOON, BALI, BARBIZON, CHRISTIAN DIOR, VASSARETTE, OLGA, WARNER, MAIDENFORM, FORMFIT, and HANES. Bras range in size from teen to size 48DD, and hoisery comes in all sizes. Merchandise is guaranteed to be first quality; exchanges and refunds are made as long as the item is still intact. It's usually about a week before you receive your order. There's a $25 minimum order, so you may have to do some stocking up.

Mendel Weiss
91 Orchard Street (212) 925-6815
New York, NY 10002 CK, MC, V, COD (when over $50), C, PQ

Weiss up and become bosom buddies with Mendel Weiss. His 30-percent to 70-percent discounts will keep you abreast of inflation. A treasure chest of lingerie lines included PLAYTEX, OLGA, MAIDENFORM, BALI, WARNER, and others in bras, girdles, panties, garter belts, slips, camisoles, caftans, robes, bodysuits, swimsuits, cruise wear, car coats, and raincoats, hostess gowns, and peignoirs. Bras are their claim to fame (like the PLAYTEX Cross Your Heart tricot for $11.55/ retail $16.50) and, if needed, they also carry mastectomy forms. But don't forget the sportswear: cotton Ts by FRUIT OF THE LOOM, sweats from LEE, and more. Special orders take about two weeks; you should receive standard orders in about a week. No minimum order; refunds and exchanges are made within 30 days.

Great Buys readers get a free 50/50 T-shirt with any order exceeding $100.

National Wholesale Co., Inc.
Hosiery Division
400 National Boulevard (704) 249-0211
Lexington, NC 27292 CK, MC, V, AE, C

Does thigh-priced lingerie leave you feeling crotchety? Now all your dollars don't have to go to waist! Brief-ly summarizing, National

Wholesale carries ladies' bras, panties, girdles, gowns, robes, hosiery, and socks, ranging from tummy tamers, body slimmers, and surgical hose, to ankle, thigh-, and knee-high hose. (Their thigh-thinner panty hose for slimming thighs, squeezing bulges, and diminishing saddlebags are particularly popular, but don't let the camisoles and slips slip by, either.) We found sheer savings from heel to toe (and on up!) with queen-sized control top panty hose. Regular panty hose are available at good prices, too: order a half-dozen at a time. Even pugnacious men won't fight their prices on boxers, T-shirts, and socks. Most orders are received in five days; everything has a money-back guarantee.

Petticoat Express

318 W. 39th Street — (212) 594-1276
New York, NY 10018-1407 — CK, MO, B

If you've got it, flounce it. You'll save 40 percent when you buy direct from this petticoat manufacturer. In sizes 4 through 20, Petticoat Express offers four of their most popular styles: a double-ruffle floor-length bouffant for just $26, retail $48; floor-length flounce bouffant for $21, retail $36; tea-length bouffant for $18, retail $32; and floor-length A-line flare for $19, retail $32. Refunds and exchanges are accepted, and orders are usually received in two weeks.

Red Flannel Factory

73 South Main
P.O. Box 370 — (616) 696-9240
Cedar Springs, MI 49319 — CK, MC, V, D, C

Turn back the clocks to 1949 and remember the founding fathers of the Red Flannel Factory. It was then that they first produced their now-famous pajamas, undergarments, robes, and shirts white and red for the entire family (even the dog). Now, past forty and still going strong, their outlets offer their entire line at 20 percent to 30 percent less than retail. Write for a free catalog and curl up for a good night's sleep, cheap.

Roby's Intimates
121 S. 18th Street, 2nd Floor
Philadelphia, PA 19103
800 878-8BRA
(215) 751-1730 (PA residents)
CK, MC, V, D, C/$1, B, PQ (SASE)

Whether it's your basic undercover bare necessities or fit-for-life leotards, tights, or sports bras, Roby's Intimates offers some of the best bargains in the business. Name brands like MAIDENFORM, VASSARETTE, FORMFIT, PLAYTEX, and KAYSER are available at a discount of 20 percent to 50 percent, and DANSKINS can be ordered for 25 percent off their retail price. Dressing great while getting your body in shape doesn't have to be expensive. Send the name of the manufacturer and style number for a price quote.

Mention *Great Buys By Mail* and get 30 percent off *only* on your first order over $50.

Sock Shop
Sweetwater Hosiery Mills
P.O. Box 390
Sweetwater, TN 37874
(615) 337-9203
CK, MC, V, MO, COD, B

This place should help knock your socks off—at least as much as 30 percent. Made in the U.S.A., women's and girl's panty hose from as low as $1.39, including support irregulars at that price; queen sizes at $1.59; control-top sandalfoot at $1.85; and sport panty hose, first quality, at $3.39. Knee-highs for 69 cents; bobby socks, 49 cents; cuff sport socks, 70 cents; irregular pom poms for 59 cents. Other items include panties, men's socks, FRUIT OF THE LOOM underwear (briefs, boxers, T-shirts, etc.), boys' and girls' socks and anklets, and boys' FRUIT OF THE LOOM underwear ($4.59 for the three-pair package). For orders under $10, please add $2.50 postage. With orders over $10, postage is free.

The Smart Saver
P.O. Box 209
Wasco, IL 60183
CK, MO, C

Save up to 30 percent when you put your faith in this firm believer in discounted bras, girdles, and other foundations. Their girdle size guide makes it easy to find the perfect fit. Get it together and shop smart with their free illustrated catalog.

Musical Instruments

You may have a musical gift, but like a St. Bernard puppy, it may turn out to be an expensive gift to feed. The cost of music lessons, a good quality instrument, and sheet music can really sound a sour note. By careful shopping, you can usually play out the scenario at less than retail without sacrificing quality. Consult a professional to get advice on what to buy for your skill level, then shop by mail. Most major manufacturers are carried by the companies listed in this section. Some offer group discounts, trade-in policies, and free trial periods. That leaves us with a song in our heart.

A.L.A.S. Accordion-O-Rama
16 W. 19th Street — (212) 675-9089
New York, NY 10011 — CK, MC, V, B

No wonder their competition keeps saying "Alas!" A.L.A.S. squeezes out almost unbeatable savings of 15 percent to 45 percent on accordions, concertinas, electronic accordions, and amps. They're known in the industry as "the electronic accordions specialists." While that might not sound impressive to some, it's gotten them on "Late Night With David Letterman," and you can't knock success. They carry all top brands, including EXCELSIOR, PAOLO SOPRANI, HOHNER, CORDOVOX, ELKA, POLYTONE, FARFISA, SCANDALLI, ARPEGGIO, and AVANTI; that's not so surprising since they've been direct importers of musical instruments and in sales and service for over 35 years. There's a 10-percent restocking charge on returns; orders can take up to two weeks to be delivered.

Altenburg Piano House, Inc.
1150 East Jersey Street (800) 526-6979
Elizabeth, NJ 07201 CK, MC, V, AE, MO, B, PQ (SASE)

Tired of playing the full-price game? Try listening to a different tune, like the one Altenburg Piano House is playing: at least 35 percent off on the keyboard of your dreams. Pianos and organs by Altenburg's own hands, and most other major brands, were right in tune with our budget. Their brochure gives you the lowdown on a full range of organs and pianos, so you can decide if they're playing your song.

Carvin
1155 Industrial Avenue (800) 854-2235
Escondido, CA 92025 CK, MC, V, C

Trivia pursuit: What on earth do Frank Zappa and Roy Clark have in common? (No, not generic quiche or the sound of one wave slapping.) Here's a clue: Jefferson Starship, Rush, and Heart are also strung-in on this deal. Give up? The answer is Carvin, a manufacturer who has drummed up quite a reputation among professional musicians. No one's got the blues over their "X" amps (a hot number in their line of amplifiers), and their electric guitars are good pickin'. Not only are these goodies available at a 40-percent savings when rated against comparable name brands, but they offer a 10-day free trial period, and if not satisfied, you can return the product with "no strings attached." Expect delivery in about two weeks. Their color catalog is far-out and free.

CMC Music, Inc.
1385 Deerfield Road (708) 831-3252
Highland Park, IL 60035 CK, MC, V, D, MO, PQ

Don't let anybody Conn you into buying an organ, piano, or synthesizer elsewhere before you check out the low prices at CMC—up to 50 percent off on KIMBALL, TECHNICS, KAWAI, and others. Those who play the 88 know the sound of a good deal when they hear one; so get a price quote on one of these beauties and pedal off with a bargain. Manufacturers' brochures are available for specific items.

Discount Music Supply
41 Vreeland Avenue, Dept. GBBM (201) 942-9411
Totowa, NJ 07512-1120 CK, MC, V, C

Band together and play nice; there's no time for fussing and feuding with sounds that are exuding 30-percent to 70-percent savings. Rock around the clock with equipment from here. Roll out a JIM DUNLOP Crybaby that lists for $129.50; DMC customers pay only $62.50. MAXIMA strings, listing for $21.95, were only $10.95. We heard the deals on SHURE microphones loud and clear, too; just $98.95, as compared to $141.25. Orders already in stock shipped within 24 hours; full refunds are available within 14 days.

Discount Reed Company
P.O. Box 6010, Suite 496 (818) 990-7962
Sherman Oaks, CA 91403 CK, MC, V, MO, B, PQ

Blow off the rest and stick with the best. The best price, that is, like up to 45 percent off on the cost of reeds for clarinets, oboes, saxophones, and other woodwinds. Soft or hard by JAVA or JONES. Even if your style is twice the reed (doubles), you'll find what you need at a discount from Reed. (And if you don't, call and blow the whistle.) They also sell supplies to care for your instrument. Satisfaction guaranteed.

Elderly Instruments
P.O. Box 14210 (517) 372-7890
Lansing, MI 48901 (517) 372-1212 (Dial-a-Ditty-a-Day)
CK, MC, V, D, MO, C/$5

Old instruments never die; they just retire to Elderly Instruments until they find another good home. ROLAND, GIBSON, FENDER, YAMAHA, CRATE, and other names in guitars, keyboards, amps, and other equipment are going for a third less than the prices at other dealers, new or used. A catalog subscription is $5, or free to regular customers. Their used stock is constantly changing, and they keep you informed of new offerings monthly. Plug into Elderly for rare recordings, too, and books on all kinds of musical history and esoterica. One researcher grooved with their "Dial-a-Ditty-a-Day," Elderly's picks-of-the-day service (free except for long-distance charges). Satisfaction is guaranteed; there's a five-day return policy for refunds, exchanges, or credit.

Fred's String Warehouse
212 W. Lancaster Avenue — (800) 677-2882
P.O. Box 328 — (215) 775-9472
Shillington, PA 19607 — CK, MC, V, D, MO, C/$1

Don't fret over the high prices of strings today. If you're a guitar, bass, banjo, violin, or any other stringed instrument player, you'll save up to 50 percent at this warehouse. All items are either shipped directly in the factory carton or inspected thoroughly at the warehouse before packing. Experienced musicians man the phones and can answer most musical questions. MARTIN, MARQUIS, VEGA, GIBSON, D'ADARIO, LABELLA, and ROTO SOUND are just a few names you're likely to hear. Orders shipped via UPS in three days in most cases.

Giardinelli Band Instrument Co., Inc.
7845 Maltlage Drive — (800) 288-2334
Liverpool, NY 13090 — CK, MC, V, AE, D, MO, C

This company is instrumental in helping you save as much as half on—you guessed it—band instruments. From brass to woodwind, Giardinelli has instruments and accessories by the score. Their catalog, 123 pages, sets forth their offerings from first chair to last. Customer satisfaction is guaranteed; returns are accepted. They even offer institutional discounts for the leaders of the band.

Interstate Music Supply
P.O. Box 315
13819 W. National Avenue — (800) 837-BAND
New Berlin, WI 53151 — CK, MC, V, MO, C

If you get your kicks by saving a bundle, you're on the right road. Cruise into Interstate for *all* major brands of band instruments, guitars, amps, drums, and more. What began as a small music store/teaching studio in 1974 has grown to employ over 50 people and seven repair technicians who all want you to find a good instrument at a good price. Crossing interstate's lines will save you 20 percent to 50 percent. Most orders are shipped within 24 hours of their receipt. A full refund, less the cost of shipping, will be given on merchandise returned within ten days. Cut your engine and your cost at Interstate.

Jazz Aids

P.O. Box 1244 (812) 945-3142
New Albany, IN 47150 CK, MC, V, MO, C

Established as a leader in the jazz education field for nearly 30 years, this company carries about 1,000 instructional jazz and jazz improvisation items. They are well known for selling the PLAY-A-LONG book and record sets, but their wide range of music and books should keep you jamming long into the night. For the beginning student or established pro, a romp through this catalog will stir up feelings of desire, so have your checkbook handy.

Kennelly Keys Music, Inc.

5030 208th Street S.W. (800) 426-6409; (206) 771-7020
Lynnwood, WA 98036 CK, MC, V, AE, D, MO, C, PQ (SASE)

Kennelly Keys strikes a familiar chord with the budget-conscious. Their musical instruments suit the needs of everyone from jazz enthusiasts to marching band members to would-be rock stars, and all starring at 50 percent less than list. ARMSTRONG, CONN, GIBSON, BOSE, EMERSON, and PEARL are just a few of the stellar performers here. There is a $25 minimum order. Would this Washington tell a lie?

Keyboard Outlet

14235 Inwood (214) 490-5397
Dallas, TX 75244 CK, MC, V, AE, D, MO (90 days same as cash), PQ

Roll over, Beethoven, to the Keyboard Outlet. Tickle the ivories for less here, including professional-quality used equipment, all in excellent condition. Some on consignment (used), some repossessed (new) from stores and banks, and all priced BELOW WHOLE-

SALE. Find such renowned names as ROLAND, YAMAHA, MIDI, KORG, and others. Inventory changes daily, and software is available, too. Sounds good to me.

Lone Star Percussion
10611 Control Place (214) 340-0835
Dallas, TX 75238 CK, MC, V, B

Lone Star beats down on the price of all kinds of drums, brushes, books, mallets, sticks, effects, and books. Their "Discount Price List" is a concise brochure with a convenient table of contents to direct you to the drumming accessories of choice. You can't beat 'em. All merchandise in their extensive 47-page price list is in stock; shipping and insurance charges are $4. Only credit cards are accepted on telephone orders. So, try to control yourself.

Mandolin Brothers, Ltd.
629 Forest Avenue (718) 981-3226
Staten Island, NY 10310-2576 CK, MC, V, AE, D, COD, C

If strings are your thing, put the finger on these guys and strum up some savings. Their 64-page catalog displays electric and acoustic guitars, banjos, autoharps, and, of course, mandolins at prices that won't make you fret. They specialize in "vintage" instruments (1833 to 1969), but they also carry the finest brands of new instruments. A few of their more notable customers have been Bob Dylan, Joni Mitchell, Bob Seger, Stephen Stills, Judy Collins, and Elliot Easton of The Cars. Discounts are 30 percent to 40 percent on brands like GUILD, C.F. MARTIN, OVATION, SIGMA, GIBSON, YAMAHA, and DOBRO guitars; GIBSON, STELLING, GOLD STAR, WILDWOOD, and WASHBURN banjos; and GIBSON, STELLING, GOLD STAR, WILDWOOD, and WASHBURN mandolins. Mandolin Bros. is the largest dealer in the world for C.F. MARTIN guitars, and they sell many vintage MARTIN guitars and GIBSON mandolins, as well. There's a full guarantee on all items shipped, with a 72-hour trial privilege. (Customers should phone them during the trial period if they are dissatisfied and return the instrument by UPS or mail for a full refund of their purchase price, less shipping charges.)

Manny's Musical Instruments & Accessories, Inc.
156 W. 48th Street (212) 819-0577
New York, NY 10036 CK, MC, V, AE, D, MO, PQ (SASE)

Manny's is musically inclined to save you half what you'd normally pay. Stars in their selection include BOSE, LUDWIG, KORG, ROLAND, PEAVEY, OVATION, MARTIN, and WASHBURN. Around since 1935, Manny's is handy with a discount, and they can help you find it if they don't have it in stock. Send a SASE with your price-quote request if you want it by mail; otherwise, a phone call will do.

Metropolitan Music Co.
P.O. Box 1415 (802) 253-4814
Stowe, VT 05672 CK, MO, C/$1.25, PQ

This Met is also alive with the sound of music, selling basses, cellos, violins, and other stringed instruments. They also carry strings, pegs, bows, shoulder and chin rests, fingerboards, tools, bags, books, and other helpful accoutrements for flawless fiddling. And they won't string you out on the prices; they're about 40 percent to 50 percent off in many cases. There is a minimum order of $15, we noted.

Music Maker Kits
(See **Kits and Kaboodle**, p. **356**.)

The Music Stand
1 Rockdale Plaza (603) 448-3832
Lebanon, NH 03766 CK, MC, V, AE, D, MO, C

Novelties and knickknacks kick up their heels from Broadway musicals, films, and other performing arts to fill the 80 pages of The Music Stand's catalog for a lot less than you'd pay at a theater gift shop. Whimsical personalized watches, towels with a classical art motif, jewelry inspired by musical instruments, tragedy- and comedy-mask clocks, plus sweatshirts, T-shirts, and mugs galore to advertise your musical preferences. Dance to ballet-inspired items, personalized rubber stamps, the perfect plaque for a beloved band director, and more, all at entertainingly low prices. It's nobody's fault with their 100-percent, no-fault guarantee, even on personalized items.

National Music Supply of Florida

P.O. Box 14421
St. Petersburg, FL 33733

(813) 823-6666
CK, MC, V, COD, C

When it comes to musical accessories, this company has them coming out the kazoo! National Music Supply is a national supply house for schools of music, as well as a main supply source for professional and student musicians. They offer special boutique items, as well as VCR equipment, clock, and repair tools. The catalog featured over 1,300 items discounted 30 percent to 60 percent off retail. While the majority of products are accessories, such as microphones and music stands, NMS does carry some instruments, like SELMA BUNDY 1400 clarinets and BACH STRAD trumpets. Every conceivable accessory from mouthpieces and ligatures to drumsticks and cymbals is represented at substantial savings. Even xylophones can be called from home. An additional 15-percent savings on all music orders from major publishers. Their 250-page catalog is free.

NEMC

P.O. Box 1130
Mountainside, NJ 07092

(800) 526-4593
(201) 232-6700 (NJ residents)
CK, MC, V, AE, MO, C

AT NEMC (National Educational Music Company), you can picc-o-lo-priced instrument from a clarinet to a violin. They carry over 900 instruments, and prices are up to 50 percent off the list price; 60 percent in some cases. Inflation-fighter offers deserve an additional round of applause. All major manufacturers are represented (ARMSTRONG, SIGNET, and others), and what they don't have in stock, they'll special order. Your order should come in ten days to two weeks; there are no restocking charges levied on returned merchandise. If your child is taking music lessons, this is a good place to pick up a horn without blowing a lot of cash. Minimum order on accessories is $100.

Patti Music Corp.
414 State Street (800) 777-2884 (orders)
Dept. 4226 (608) 257-8829 (customer service)
Madison, WI 53705 CK, MC, V, D, C

Strike the idea of paying full price for piano or organ music and teaching aids; the key issue here is saving money. Patti plays our song with discounts of up to 25 percent. Metronomes, manuscript paper, statuettes, and hundreds of titles to choose from make them a paying proposition. Patti was established in 1936 as a retail store and opened its phone lines in 1982. All major publishers are represented in its catalog, 69 pages of keyboarding bliss. Get in tune with its return policy: It applies to merchandise that is defective or sent in error. Most orders ship within 24 working hours of their receipt.

P.M.I.
P.O. Box 827 (201) 863-2200
Union City, NJ 07087 CK, MC, V, AE, D, MO, C, B, PQ

"When you're looking for that big break, P.M.I. can be instrumental" was their line, not ours. We'll toot their horn, too, for lines of first-quality, professional musical instruments and accessories in over 100 major brands, including GIBSON, ROLAND, FOSTEX, and PRO AUDIO PRODUCTS. Discounts ranged from 30 percent to 40 percent. We learned from their catalog that they are the only mail-order company that deals in custom-made and modified guitars. They've done a number of instruments for rock groups. Besides guitars, they have keyboards, brass and woodwind instruments, and multirecorders. Orders are drop-shipped when possible directly from the manufacturer when P.M.I. gets your order and full payment. Additional freight charges run about 3 percent. There's a $10 minimum order, 30-day exchange or refund policy, and 10-percent restocking charge on returns. Checks are held for 15 working days.

Rhythm Band, Inc.
P.O. Box 126
1212 E. Lancaster (800) 424-4724
Ft. Worth, TX 76101-0126 CK, MC, V, D, C

What's a band without Rhythm? This company principally sells to elementary schools, although they do sell to individuals at the same reduced rates. (There's no minimum order.) Prices are about 20 percent lower than you'll find in retail music stores. Their full-color catalog displays rhythm instruments like bells, bongos, castanets, cymbals, drums, glockenspiels, kazoos, maracas, rhythm sticks, ukuleles, and xylophones. Popular items include the RB1545 Chromaharp, which is $250 retail, sold by Rhythm Band for $135; and AULOS A103N recorders, retail $7.50, discounted to $4.45. There is no return policy; orders arrive in about a week. Now, isn't it about time to get on the Rhythm Band method of saving money?

Sam Ash Music Corp.
401 Old Country Road — (800) 4-SAM ASH
Carle Place, NY 11514 — CK, MC, V, AE, B, PQ

There's so-nata bagpipe, marimba, or accordion Sam can't lay his hands on! Sam Ash, with its seven stores and multimillion-dollar inventory, is trying its darnedest to be the lowest-priced, best-quality music store in the country. They've got "one of the world's largest inventories of musical instruments, amplification, sound reinforcement, professional audio equipment, sheet music, and accessories." They're not kidding around—they've even got stage lighting and industrial video equipment. Founded in 1924 by prominent New York violinist and bandleader Sam Ash, the business offers every major name brand in instruments, synthesizers, and sheet music. Synthesizers are their hottest-selling item. Prices are excellent, usually 30 percent to 70 percent off retail. Triple guarantees are offered on all instruments, including original factory guarantee, Sam Ash's guarantee, and a guaranteed trade-in policy. There's a $25 minimum order; orders usually are received in about two weeks. Get on their mailing list for their newspaperlike periodicals.

Shar Products Company
2465 S. Industrial Highway
P.O. Box 1411 — (313) 665-7711
Ann Arbor, MI 48106 — CK, MC, V, D, COD, C

The family that plays together, stays together. (At least that's the impression the family photo in their catalog gives.) For over 30 years, the Avsharians have stood for selection, service, and low prices (up to 50 percent lower on instruments and accessories) for folks strung out on stringed instruments. They've got strings, accessories, cases, instruments, and repair supplies at respectable discounts, while SUZUKI materials, books, and reams of sheet music are available at full price. (They don't restrict themselves when it comes to brands; their policy is to "straddle various" manufacturers.) Strings, cases, and accessories are their biggest-selling items. Orders arrive in about a week; satisfaction is guaranteed. Shar's regular discount catalog and their catalog of 600 most-requested sheet-music pieces for strings are free.

Weinkrantz Musical Supply Co., Inc.
870 Market Street, Suite 1265 — (415) 399-1201
San Francisco, CA 94102-2907 — CK, MC, V, MO, C

Weining about the cost of stringed instruments? Violins, cellos, basses, and violas by KARL HAUSER, ROTH, ENESCO, HELMUT MAYER, SUZUKI, and other luminaries are represented in the Weinkrantz catalog for as much as 50 percent off. Accessories tie in, too, like strings, bows, music stands, timely metronomes, and cases. Satisfaction is guaranteed; there's a $10 minimum order with credit cards.

West Manor Music
831 East Gunhill Road — (800) 228-8790 (orders only)
Bronx, NY 10467 — (212) 655-5400 (information)
CK, MC, V, B, PQ (SASE)

Mind your Manors! This is one house where you'll feel right at home. West Manor "has been selling musical instruments and accessories to school boards and individuals across the country since 1952." They offer up to 45 percent off, and a one-year warranty against manufacturing defects. Gifts are given with purchases of $200 or more, such as a set of 20-point diamond earrings in 14K gold with orders of $200 or more or a piccolo case with purchases of $400 or more. Most orders are received within seven days.

The Woodwind/The Brasswind
19880 State Line Road — (800) 348-5003
South Bend, IN 46637 — (219) 272-8266 (IN residents)
CK, MC, V, AE, D, C

We don't remember the question, but the answers, my friend, are blowing in The Woodwind and The Brasswind catalogs. Despite sounding like twin condo developments, The Brasswind and The Woodwind are stores specializing in instruments for serious musicians. If you specify your catalog preference, you can rustle through their price sheets and select from a very extensive list of quality instruments discounted about 40 percent. Instruments included piccolos, flutes, bassoons, oboes, saxes (and accessories) in the Woodwind catalog; fluegelhorns, trombones, trumpets, French horns, euphoniums in Brasswind. They make repairs, too. There's a two-week return privilege, and even an installment plan on some instruments where no interest is charged. All instruments are completely tested before being shipped. Check out their Woodwind 80-page catalog, Brasswing 80-page catalog, 60-page drum catalog, 50-page string catalog, and the Rock and Rhythm catalog, 80 pages of electronic instruments.

Office Supplies and Equipment

"You've got to spend money to make money." How often have you heard that? It's a business cliché, but it's true—most of the time. It shouldn't be true, though, when it comes to shelling out for office supplies and equipment. They're not investments, they're expenses, and if you don't watch your costs, before you know it, your company will be expended rather than expanded. Kaput! So what can you do? Cut corners! Cut out the middlemen! Cut out the overhead! Buying office supplies and equipment from a discounter is a good way to begin. Forms, ribbons, pencils, pens, calendars, etc., are all available at a discount through the mail. Larger purchases such as typewriters, computers, word processors, dictaphones, and faxes are also a way to cut through the red tape and put your company's finances in the black. Shop around and try different products, but when it comes to ordering, place your order buy phone. It may take a little longer to get, but remember, "Haste often makes waste."

Alfax Wholesale Furniture
370 Seventh Avenue, Suite 1101 (800) 221-5710
New York, NY 10001-3900 (212) 947-9560
CK, MC, V, MO, C

If you get all your facts straight, you can save up to 50 percent on lockers, hat racks, park benches, and computer work stations. Alfax Wholesale Furniture's free 64-page color catalog offers institutional and office furnishings that can be used at home and are built to last at least as long as your business. Quantity discounts are available (they sell mainly to companies), and they guarantee you'll find "everything is satisfaxual".

Bernie's Discount Center, Inc.
(See **Housewares**, p. **323**.)

Brown Print & Co.
P.O. Box 935 (818) 286-2106
Temple City, CA 91780 CK, B/$2 (with samples)

Brown Print is anything but neutral when it comes to making an impression. They leave their mark making "exotic" business cards and letterhead stationery. Customers and colleagues are bound to remember these distinctive designs that say you care enough to present the very best. Over 100 types of cards are available, plus unique and unusual artwork for letterheads. There's no catalog, but this exclusively mail-order company does offer a price list along with a generous group of samples for $2. All their work is guaranteed even if they don't make a sale. The custom goods are delivered in 10 to 17 working days from the receipt of order.

Business Envelope Manufacturers, Inc.
900 Grand Boulevard (800) 275-4400; (516) 667-8500
Deer Park, NY 11729 CK, MC, V, AE, MO, C

Don't feel sorry for these envelopes—they're made to take a lickin'! BEM will "envelope" you in business statements, invoices, stationery, ledgers, labels, ribbons, jumbo markers, and more at factory-direct prices. Imprinted business envelopes were priced as much as 40 percent below retail (a discount that definitely didn't leave a bad taste in our mouth). With savings like that, it's not surprising that envelopes are their most popular item. If you don't believe us, just take a look at their 48-page catalog! There is a $20 minimum order with credit cards, everything's fully guaranteed, and you can expect to receive your order in about ten days.

Business & Institutional Furniture Company
611 N. Broadway (800) 558-8662; (414) 272-0248
Milwaukee, WI 53202 CK, MC, V, D, MO, C

If you need a desk, workstation, chair, or other vital tools of your trade and are discouraged by the meager selection and high prices found locally, a catalog like Business & Institutional could save you money and time. They've been in *their* business since 1960, helping *other* businesses and offices meet their furniture needs. Due to their background, they're best at quantity discounts, but they're not bad at one-on-one deals, either. An institutional-size inventory of name brands and a 15-year guarantee make them qualified "officionados."

Business Technologies
426 W. Fifth Street (800) 397-5633
Dubuque, IA 52001 CK, MC, V, MO, C, PQ

Get down to Business Technologies and the difference will register immediately. The difference is about 33 percent off list price on the price of cash registers by SHARP and others, plus supplies and accessories. Since 1985, this company's been helping businesses find the right register for the job, with the latest state-of-the-art extras like computerized help with tips and taxes. Call or write for a price quote, or request a catalog; minimum order is $10 (not a hard bill to fill). Ring up the profit side of the coins, not the debits.

Chiswick Trading, Inc.
33 Union Avenue (800) 225-8708
Sudbury, MA 01776-0907 (800) 638-9899 (FAX)
(508) 443-9592
CK, MC, V, AE, MO, C

Bag a bargain at Chiswick Trading. In the mail-order business for 18 years, they know how to sack it to you. They sell shipping and packaging supplies, zip-lock bags, tape, and mailing labels through their 64-page catalog. Or choose from their selection of 7.5 million poly-bags. The savings are about 50 percent off retail. Most orders go out by UPS ground, and are processed and shipped within 24 hours. Expect to wait three to four days for delivery.

Colwell Business Products
P.O. Box 9024 (800) 637-1140 (orders)
201 Kenyon Road (800) 225-1448 (customer service)
Champaign, IL 61826-9024 (800) 222-4890 (IL residents)
CK, MC, V, AE, C

Make it your business to send for this catalog. Their motto is "stationery and forms for price-conscious businesses." They have a catalog devoted exclusively to computer and word processing forms and supplies. Over 300 software packages are included with forms for accounts payable, payroll, statements, labels, and invoices. Colwell had the best prices we found on printed business cards in the country.

DAK Industries Incorporated
(See **Electronics: Audio/Video/Stereo/TVs**, p. **185**.)

Damark
(See **Buying Clubs and One-Stop Shopping**, p. **114**.)

Dinner + Klein
P.O. Box 3814 (800) 2-DINNER; (206) 682-2494
Seattle, WA 98124 CK, MO, C/$5

The bargains here are signed, sealed, and delivered. "Printing and mailing for less" are Dinner + Klein's forte. They say they'll print up catalogs, brochures, and fliers on time and on budget. Their own catalog includes details on preparing camera-ready art, price lists, information on tabloids (enquiring shoppers want to know), and charts of standard ink colors. They've been in business since 1948, and even offer consultants to help with your printing questions.

Disk World, Inc.
(See **Hardware, Tools, and Home Improvement**, p. **288**.)

Educalc Corporation
(See **Computers**, p. **177**.)

Elek-Tek
(See **Computers**, p. **177**.)

Executive Photo and Supply Corp.
(See **Cameras, Opticals, and Photographic Equipment**, p. **123**.)

Exsel, Inc.
(See **Computers**, p. **178**.)

Factory Direct Furniture
225 E. Michigan Street, Suite 11 (800) 972-6570
Milwaukee, WI 53202-4911 (414) 289-9770
CK, MC, V, C

Direct your attention to Factory Direct and pay up to 70 percent less for office and home furnishings. Organize your workday around a computer workstation, add chairs and other more direct furnishings for the job by MILL, STYLEX, and BPI, and you're off to a good start. LA-Z-BOY chairs listing for $488 were sitting pretty for $279.75. They'll get it to you directly (in about two to five weeks); returns are subject to round-trip shipping charges. Take a look at their free catalog or call for a price quote to point you in the direction of the discounts.

Fax City, Inc.
P.O. Box 38182
2711 B Pinedale Road (800) 426-6499; (919) 288-1735
Dept. 1111 CK, MC, V, AE, C
Greensboro, NC 27438-8182

Just the Fax, ma'am. Well, not entirely; fax machines, yes sir, plus copiers, and supplies are this business's forte, and the fact is, they can save you as much as 50 percent off retail prices. SHARP, RICOH, MAGNAVOX, CANON, MURATA, QUASAR, and SANYO are among the names you've seen before. (And, one might say, they've been copied, but never duplicated.) They'll run off even more famous brands when asked. Begun in 1985 by Patricia Adams, this company ships worldwide. There is a 15-percent charge on returns; deliveries are usually made the same week the order is received.

Identify yourself as a *Great Buys* reader and get 10 percent off the already discounted price for your first order of fax paper only.

Fidelity Products Co.
5601 International Parkway (800) 328-3034
P.O. Box 155 (612) 536-6500 (MN residents)
Minneapolis, MN 55440 CK, MC, V, AE, DC, D, C

Fidelity's own brand of opaque correction fluid was truly discounted, but the buys on corrugated modular storage systems ranked even higher in our files. We didn't see soon enough the writing on the wall with their anti-graffiti urethane, which protects against aerosol spray paint, felt pen, and most other staples of visual vandalism. They carry over 1,800 products for the office, factory, or warehouse, including temporary files, packaging tapes, and containers, and first-aid kits (OSHA-approved). Prices are about 15 percent to 20 percent less than retail, and up to 40-percent savings on quantity purchases. Thirty-day free trial with a full refund during that time. Delivery of orders is usually within seven to ten days. There are three catalogs to choose: one for business products (100 pages), one for office products (63 pages), and one for graphic arts (67 pages).

Frank Eastern Co.
599 Broadway (800) 221-4914; (212) 219-0007
New York, NY 10012-3258 CK, MC, V, MO, C

Message from the boss: Keep this company on file—under "M" for memo-rable. Savings are up to 50 percent off retail on business and institutional equipment. They've got chairs, files, bookcases, storage units, panel wall systems, desks, tables, and a wide selection of computer workstations. Over 300 prominent office brands are carried, including LA-Z-BOY with ERGONOMIC chairs, one of their specialties. There's a $75 minimum order with credit cards; standard manufacturers' warranties apply. You'll get your order in about three weeks. They've been in business since 1946, so it's about time you checked out their catalog with its complete selection of office and institutional seatings in wood, chrome, plastic, or combinations.

Grayarc
Greenwoods Industrial Park
P.O. Box 2944 (800) 562-5468
Hartford, CT 06104-2944 CK, MC, V, MO, C

Prices are falling gracefully at Grayarc, where you can pay half as much for a bevy of business and office products. Their general business catalog, for example, features business forms, envelopes, memos, mailers, BROTHER typewriters, SEIKO and ROYAL calculators, cash registers, clocks, copy machines, office furniture, and more. They even print-to-suit with their custom-printing service for letterheads and other corporate statements. Never fear, they offer a 30-day return policy.

Hunter Audio-Photo Ltd.
(see **Buying Clubs and One-Stop Shopping**, p. **115**.)

Jilor Discount
1020 Broadway (516) 374-5806
Woodmere, NY 11598-1202 CK, AE, PQ

The daily grind is much easier with the right office machines. Jilor brews bargains on calculators reduced 20 percent and more by makers like CANON, SHARP, and TEXAS INSTRUMENTS. Or get keyed up on typewriters by SMITH-CORONA, OLYMPIA, and BROTHER. Get the message? They've got answering machines by CODE-A-PHONE (commercial model), GE, and PANASONIC all recording record savings. Also available is ORANGE MAGIC, the wonder all-purpose cleaner that whisks away stains and dirt, grease, ink, and gum from cars, motors, boats, driveways, pet stains—just about anything. It's the stuff New York is using to remove the graffiti from its subways—so here's proof that at least our recommendation need not be erased. Call if you require service on calculators, answering machines, or dictaphone equipment. There's a $75 minimum order with credit-card orders; orders are shipped immediately or as soon as the merchandise is available. Their newest additions are the SELECTRONIC electronic reference products such as the "Random House Electronic Encyclopedia," the "Electronic Bible," the Berlitz WC 20 Spell Checker for 100,000 words, the "Berlitz Interpreter"—even a "26 Language Translator."

Great Buys readers get a free pint of Orange Magic (an $8 value) with their first order.

L & D Press
P.O. Box 641
78 Randall Street (516) 593-5058
Rockville Centre, NY 11570 CK, MO, F

Congratulations! You're starting your own business. You'll probably be needing the following items from L & D Press: business cards, envelopes, letterhead, announcements, stock forms, reply messages, invoices . . . the list is endless, but there is a light at the end of the tunnel. When pressed, you can save up to 50 percent on printing and office supplies with L & D Press. We found incredible deals on business cards available in 18 popular type styles. A very convenient order form is provided for guaranteed accuracy. Maybe you're tying the knot instead, and want to announce it to the world. You can shout it from the rooftops or order announcements from L & D and save. Correspond in style with luxurious stationery at notably lower prices. Select from two styles: Princess or Monarch, with matching envelopes. More than 30 years in the business is very impress-ive, too. If you don't want to save money, it's none of our business!

Lincoln Typewriters and Micro Machines
111 W. 68th Street (212) 769-0606
New York, NY 10023 CK, MC, V, AE, O, MO, PQ

Typewriters, calculators, and more are available from this honestly less-than-retail business. Log up to 40 percent off on these and other items, including cartridges and ribbons. If OLIVETTI, BROTHER, MINOLTA, and IBM are your type, why pay more? Other key supplies are available, too, but there's no catalog, so call for a price quote. The minimum order is peculiarly $14.50.

Mail Center USA
One De Zavala Center
12734 Cimarron Path, Suite 104 (512) 699-0311
San Antonio, TX 78249 CK, MC, V, D, MO, C/$5

Deep in the heart of Texas, something big is coming off; it's the prices on office supplies. The selection in their Texas-sized catalog (more than 300 pages) features discounts from 30 percent to 40 percent on supplies by ROLODEX, VERBATIM, MONT BLANC, CANON, CURTIS, and others. Getting the max for the minimum charge is just $15. (Discounts climb with the amount of your purchase, starting at 30 percent for $15 and going to 40 percent for $100 and over.) Sales catalogs (which are free), offering as much as 70 percent off, make us Texans even prouder. Authorized returns are accepted; satisfaction is guaranteed.

Misco
One Misco Plaza (800) 876-4726
Holmdel, NJ 07733 (908) 264-1000 (NJ residents)
CK, MC, V, AE, COD, C

Misers love company. And since 1977, Misco has sold computer supplies and accessories to thousands of them. Misco's own ribbons, storage cases, and furniture, plus VERBATIM and 3M disks and more, are available through their color catalogs. Greater discounts are available when you buy in quantity. Misco offers a one-year 100-percent-satisfaction guarantee; you must contact the company before returning any merchandise. Orders are shipped within 24 hours. End of sentence.

National Business Furniture, Inc.
222 E. Michigan Street (800) 558-1010 (national)
Milwaukee, WI 53202 (800) 558-9803 (customer service)
(800) 242-0030 (WI residents)
CK, MC, V, MO, C, PQ

Far-out! This company outfitted a wing of the American Embassy in Senegal. Apparently word reached those diplomats in Africa about the diplomatic prices charged here. Nothing is as revolutionary as even-handed pricing! What's that to you? Well, you don't have to be a continent away to take advantage of the in-continent bargains here. In fact, you can shop for over 40 top-drawer brands without ever leaving your desk, just by flipping through any one of NBF's catalogs. Names like COLE, GLOBE/COSCO, LA-Z-BOY, HIGHPOINT, INDIANA DESK, O'SULLIVAN, and SAMSONITE are all available direct from the manufacturer, not to mention great prices on computer furniture. Discounts run about 30 percent; volume orders get you even bigger savings.

NEBS, Inc.
500 Main Street (800) 225-6380; (508) 448-6111
Groton, MA 01471 CK, MC, V, AE, MO, C

Make your office feel all-write by taking care of business with discounts on carbonless business forms, sales slips, envelopes, invoices, labels, files, and check-writing systems. Prices won't put you out of business, either. Most of their over 300 items carry the NEBS brand. Small businesses are their biggest customers. No shipping charges on orders prepaid by check; orders come in about six working days. Check out their catalog for the full story.

Office Furniture Center
1400 E. Devon Avenue (800) 343-4222
Elk Grove, IL 60007 CK, MC, V, MO, C

Officially, this is the place for those who work at home . . . or just want an efficient space in which to write out the bills. You can work out a deal with these folks for 30 percent to 50 percent off on chairs, bookcases, workstations (those computer colleagues), and more. Make your day's work reflect in your bottom line and never pay full price on names like INDEPENDENT DESK and STACOR. Their in-stock selection is commendable; price quotes are available by letter or phone. There's no charge for their 32-page catalog.

Percy's, Inc.
(see **Appliances (Large and Small)**, p. **42**.)

Quill® Corporation
100 S. Schelter Road (714) 988-3200 (AK, AZ, CA,
Lincolnshire, IL 60069-3621 HI, ID, MT, NV, OR, UT, WA, WY)
(404) 479-6100 (AL, FL, GA, LA, MS, NC, SC, TN)
(708) 634-4800 (all remaining states)
CK, MC, V, MO, C

Quill may sound like a name inspired by a porcupine, but the prices here are anything but prickly. This company serves only businesses, institutions, and professional offices. (If you are unprofessional, don't bother!) With over 600,000 accounts, their business-to-business business needles their competition. As one of the largest mail-order office products firms in the nation, Quill has outstanding values down the line. Their 61-page catalog is well worth a look; you'll find everything from 3M diskettes (at 31 percent to 45 percent off), typewriters, lamps, attachés, and office furniture, to those important office incidentals like tape, staplers, assorted pads and paper, pens, ROLODEX files, and printer ribbons, to name a few. All things considered (and they do have all things!), we'll save our barbed comments for a company less fortified with merchandise than Quill.

Rapidforms, Inc.
301 Grove Road (800) 257-8354
Thorofare, NJ 08086 CK, MC, V, COD, C

Rapidforms fills the bill and fits the mold to a T. Save up to 40 percent in one of their six catalogs, including Manufacturing and Wholesale, Holiday and Everyday Cards, Auto Repair, Contractors, Retail, and Repair Service. Each catalog offers a full selection of forms, as well as other items necessary to get the job done, such as price labels and plastic bags in the *Retail* catalog, and stationery, work orders, and memos in the *Manufacturing* catalog. Since 1939, Rapidforms has been providing thousands of forms rapidly; they seem to be getting even speedier with age. Take the fast track to savings and ensure the competitive edge with a little help from your friends.

The Reliable Corporation
1001 W. Van Buren (800) 735-4000
Chicago, IL 60607 CK, MC, V, AE, C

We all need somebody to lean on when the economic crunch pinches our bottom line. Thanks to Reliable, you can stay in the black and you won't see red when it comes to buying office supplies. This deep discounter of brand-name products features their own line of computer paper, WEYERHAEUSER copy paper, desk chairs, binders, MURATA office fax machines, CASIO adding machines . . . they'll even give you a coffee break on coffee by SANKA, HILLS BROTHERS, MAXWELL HOUSE, and FOLGERS, starting at just $17.75 per case. Diskettes, cartridges, tape, mailers, and more are all discounted; buying in quantity saves you even more.

There's free delivery on in-stock items, and a "hassle-free" return policy. Orders taken by 4 p.m. your time are shipped the same day.

Robert James Co., Inc.
P.O. Box 530 (800) 633-8296; (205) 640-7081
Moody, AL 35004 CK, MC, V, AE, O, MO, C, PQ (SASE)

Robert James, in business since 1939, makes it their business to supply office supplies at a savings of up to 60 percent. Knock off early and take a look at one of their catalogs (one is called simply the *Office Supply* catalog; the other is *Hospitality Supply*). Included in their office supplies: paper for copiers, filing cabinets, desks, typewriter ribbons, envelopes, mailers, forms, and more. The *Hospitality Supply* catalog featured travel-sized toothpaste and shampoo, cleaning carts, industrial-sized trash cans, lamps, and other hotel/motel and restaurant-oriented supplies. Robert James offers a 30-day return policy, and price quotes by phone or letter with SASE. Call for the catalog of your choice.

Rochester 100, Inc.
P.O. Box 1261
851 Joseph Avenue (716) 544-3414 (call collect)
Rochester, NY 14603 CK, MO, B, PQ

Buy direct from this manufacturer of vinyl plastic envelopes and holders. They are "clearly" invaluable to organize, transport, store, or protect important documents, manuscripts, proposals, floppy disks, mag tape, data cards and sheets, word processing records, and related data. Whew! Their modern factory produces hundreds of different dies and has the capacity to manufacture holders up to size 26 × 38. Fast service and low prices are their buywords since they sell by mail and phone only. No follow-up salesman will call you if you request information. Call collect for further information and free samples upon request.

Safe Specialties, Inc.
215 Center Park Drive, #650 (800) 695-2815; (615) 675-2815
Knoxville, TN 37922 CK, MC, V, D, MO, C/$1 w/SASE, PQ (SASE)

Interested in putting something under lock and key? From valuable business documents to your child's first tooth, there's a safe to keep it safe, and Safe Specialties has it. Unlock savings of 30 percent off list on their own lines, as well as safes by most well-known manufacturers. In the wall or underfoot, a cleverly disguised safe can safeguard your investments and your budget at the same time. Call or write for a specific safe, or check out their catalog. Shipping is included on some orders.

Simon's Data Services
215 W. Loockerman Street (800) 274-6667
Dover, DE 19901 CK, MC, V, F, PQ

Fax machines are the wave of the future, and Simon's is one of the best places to ride the wave for less. When you have to face the fax, look to TOSHIBA, CANON, MINOLTA, SHARP, PANASONIC, RICOH, EPSON, and PANAFAX, starting as low as $499 (as opposed to $899 list). Simon sez his prices and inventory are subject to change on a daily basis; call to order or get a price quote. All their machines come with $100 worth of free MCI long-distance service, and they don't charge freight or sales tax. No catalog is available, but they do have a price list that offers fairly detailed information, including list prices and ordering details.

Staples, Inc.
100 Pennsylvania Avenue
P.O. Box 9328 (508) 370-8525
Framingham, MA 01701-9328 CK, MC, V, AE, D, MO, C

Add to your cupboard plenty of staples so you'll never run out of office supplies. Staples packs a punch in the discount department, where they clip your spending on office supplies by big names like AT&T, 3M, CANON, MURATA, CROSS, FABER CASTELL, CASIO, VERBATIM, and others. They even have office furniture! Whatever the "form" of supplies you need, get the fax and copy down this information. There's no minimum, and a 30-day return policy on goods in their original packages. There is, however, a $25 flat delivery rate on furniture; $30 for New York residents. Look into their membership cards and visit one of their approximately 150 stores in 15 states (listed in their catalog).

The Stationery House, Inc.
(See **Party and Paper**, p. **399**.)

Turnbaugh Printers Supply Co.
104 S. Sporting Hills Road (717) 737-5637; (717) 737-5734
Mechanicsburg, PA 17055 CK, C/$1 (with price list)

If full-price printer parts and supplies do not compute at your home or place of business, check out Turnbaugh and turn into a discount believer. Everything from paper to printer machinery is available in their catalog, which comes with price lists. Under the same ownership since 1931, Turnbaugh's special sales offer savings of 20 percent to 30 percent. Most orders are delivered within ten days. Get turned on to Turnbaugh and add up the difference.

20th Century Plastics, Inc.
3628 Crenshaw Boulevard (800) 767-0777
Los Angeles, CA 90016 CK, MC, V, AE, D, MO, C

Mold yourself into a savvy saver with 20th Century's plastic office supplies. The office of the future uses binders, plastic storage sheets for transparencies, file folders, and more, without paying tomorrow's prices. See-through discounts as much as 35 percent on these and other products; they can also be imprinted with the name or logo of your office, department, etc. Quantity discounts are available. Enter the 20th Century with contemporary services such as a 30-day return policy, exchanges, refunds, or credit when requested.

U.S. Box Corp.
1296 McCarter Highway (718) 387-1510
Newark, NJ 07104 CK, Certified Check, MO, C

Don't box me in! Just land me land, lots of lands with great discounts on boxes, wrapping paper, tape, mailing envelopes, tissue paper, excelsior, bows . . . everything I need to send a gift or mail an important document. U.S. Box Corp. delivers the all-American way . . . at more than half off. Even stone figures for decorating, velvet boxes for jewelry, baskets, and display cases are available. There are a couple of catches, though: The minimum order is $150, and they don't accept returns. However, buying in quantity does save you more, and samples are available for $2. Unwrap great discounts; when you buy big, you save big!

Value-Tique, Inc.
P.O. Box 67, Dept. GBBM (201) 461-6500
Leonia, NJ 07605 MC, V, AE, D, DC, CB, C/$1

Get a lock on a good, safe deal with Value-Tique safes. Manufacturers include secure names like AMERICAN SECURITY, PROSTEEL, SENTRY, FICHET, and GARDALL. A SENTRY Professional Quality "PQ" safe that can be bolted to the floor, two cubic feet, was $289.95, delivered (list $395 plus freight) in the continental U.S. This safe is fire-resistant (UL listed), with a large locking bolt, two deadbolts, and a combination lock. Check with Value-Tique before you turn the key to the competition; you could save as much as 35 percent, but be sure of what you want. It's a safe bet they won't accept returns. Orders are normally delivered in four to twelve days.

Viking Office Products
P.O. Box 6114
13809 S. Figueroa Street (800) 421-1222
Los Angeles, CA 90061 CK, MC, V, C

This Viking won't pillage or plunder; he's out to rescue you from regular retail. His office supplies are very reasonably priced. This Viking also publishes sales catalogs offering you savings of as much as 78 percent! Charge in for Viking's own copier paper and office chairs, CARTER'S Hi-Liters and Marks-A-Lots, BOSTON electric sharpeners, brand-name printer ribbons, binders, folders, OVERALL correction fluid—even a desktop vacuum! Savings come on like gangbusters, and on orders of $25 or more, delivery is both free and overnight. It's hard to argue with deals like that, or with Irwin Helford's (president of this Viking) smiling face on the catalog's cover.

Visible Computer Supply Corp.
1750 Wallace Avenue (800) 323-0628
St. Charles, IL 60174 CK, MC, V, AE, DC, MO, C, PQ

The spotlight is on computer and office supplies, and the savings here are Visible. Paper, disks, cables, waste cans, notebooks and notebook paper, highlighter pens, paper shredders, and much more—even telephones—are featured in over 250 pages in their free catalog. Price quotes are available by mail or telephone. They guarantee customer satisfaction, offer discounts when you buy in quantity, and have a 30-day refund/credit/exchange policy.

Vulcan Binder & Cover
P.O. Box 29 (800) 633-4526
Vincent, AL 35178 CK, MC, V, AE, COD, C

It's no myth that Vulcan can run circles around the competition when the subject of ring binders is concerned. Shop direct at this manufacturer of folders, easels, displays, and holders; (custom requests or stock orders available). Advertise your company name, or just add that professional touch to office manuals, records, and presentations. The selection of colors are virtually limitless. In addition, there are leather portfolios, I.D. card–making machines, overhead projectors, briefcases, and other goods to make the climb to the top as easy as looking down at the pages of this catalog. Vulcan soars when it comes to stock ring binders by direct mail. The minimum order to use a credit card is $25.

Party and Paper

Party, party, every day, but novel ones weren't created in a day. First, start with some nouveau invitations. Voila! *Then, call on these creative colleagues to help make a new person out of you (or close to the gorilla your dreams). You can twist balloons into dachshunds, star-spangle the night sky with a breathtaking fireworks display, or dig into a tin of delicious popcorn or fortune cookies. Hundreds of fun-loving and specialty trinkets are available from the companies found on the following pages. Seek and ye shall find that there's nothing new under the sun (or underwater), except—watch out for motorized shark fins!*

Acme Premium Supply Corp.
4100 Forest Park Boulevard
St. Louis, MO 63108-2899
(800) 325-7888 ext. 23
(314) 531-8880 ext. 23
CK, MC, V, MO, COD, C, B

Throwing a party, or just decorating to celebrate a holiday season? Festivities are more festive with favors and other premium novelties especially when the novelty is they're half off. Acme Premium's general catalog and seasonal update brochures are home to all kinds of toys, games, and novelties. Stuffed animals galore, plastic bugs, tinsel wigs, promotional baseball caps, bingo cages, silly keychains, toys that "talk" to you, and more have been included in past catalogs.

The toys are intended for ages five and up, and there is a $100 minimum order. Twenty-five percent is required in advance on COD orders.

The American Stationery Co., Inc.
100 Park Avenue (800) 822-2577; (317) 473-4438
Peru, IN 46970 CK, MC, V, D, C

Since 1919, this company has been providing the Write Stuff and saving you 40 percent to 50 percent in the process. Personalized stationery, wedding stationery, and accessories (reception needs) is the American way. Embossed stationery and notes were $16 here; $28 retail. Deckle-edge stationery was $10.50; retail, $22. Wedding invitations, thank-you notes, hand-drawn calligraphy stationery, Crane papers, with exclusive designs on some; well, what are you waiting for, start writing for their free catalog now. Normal delivery time is within three to four weeks.

Great Buys readers will get 250 address labels *free* with any order. Just identify yourself as a reader, write "Free Address Labels," and include the personalization you'd like.

Current
The Current Building (719) 593-5990
Colorado Springs, CO 80941 CK, MC, V, C

In the high country of Colorado, Current carries stationery and gift items, and if you go with the flow, it's hard to go wrong. The current Current catalog is over 88 pages and displays calendars, all-occasion cards, gifts, date books, stationery, wrapping paper, recipe cards, and birthday party kits in many attractive designs. They carry 500 to 600 different items. Gift wrap and greeting cards are their big sellers. Discounts depend on the number of items ordered: price breaks come with the eighth and sixteenth items ordered, and savings can climb to 45 percent. (It's another way to save some Current-cy.) Their guarantee's a good one: You must be totally satisfied or they'll replace your order or refund the money. It's comforting to know you won't have to fight against the Current here.

Idea Art
(See **Arts and Crafts**, p. **66**.)

Island House Rubberstamps
8924 Cartagena Place (214) 328-9856
Dallas, TX 75228 CK, C

Stamp out all creative urges and make sure that they are all environmentally correct. Cindy Lewin has translated her artistry and concern for endangered species to a unique and comprehensive rubber stamp collection that is perfect for creating your own stationary, envelopes, invitations, wrapping paper, or greeting cards. You might even use it to make wallpaper, personalized toilet paper, business or enclosure cards, post cards . . . wish you were here. The stamps include archeological treasures, 1930s sea planes, and a variety of other fun images not found in your everyday stationary store.

Readers receive a 10 percent discount off their first order.

L & D Press
(See **Office Supplies and Equipment**, p. **385**.)

La Piñata
Number 2 Patio Market
Old Town (505) 242-2400
Albuquerque, NM 87104 CK, MC, V, COD, C/$1 or SASE, PQ

These amigos are piñata perfectionists! Vent your frustrations on traditional motifs (bulls, donkeys, pedros, stars) or seasonal characters (reindeers, Santas, pumpkins, witches, Easter rabbits). They come in three sizes ranging from $3.50 to $20. This family-run business has a life-size bull that's been no small provocation to the shop cat for many years. If you want a custom job done (they've created a sexy lady, a four-foot Idaho Potato, and a Dallas Cowboy . . . no relation), just provide a picture and the size and they'll give you a price quote. Send SASE for current price list. Most orders can be delivered within a week (via UPS); a special two-day service is available. They will refund or replace your order if not satisfied.

Tell them you're a *Great Buys By Mail* reader and get even better discounts on large purchases.

Love Letters, Inc.
Dept. LL60
1752 Westwood
Los Angeles, CA 90024
(800) 448-9673
CK, MC, V, AE, MO, C/$1

If you don't know how to say it, maybe you should take a lesson from *Cyrano* and let someone else say it for you. Letters for birthdays, anniversaries, weddings, Mother's Day, and other holidays and special events are done in calligraphy and personalized for each client by Love Letters. Each letter is then rolled and tied with a ribbon for the final touch of class. The catalog allows you to read each letter in its entirety and pick the one that says it perfectly for you. Custom letters and papers upon request. The average price of letters was $16.95; one two-page letter was $20.95. Allow four to seven days for delivery; overnight or second-day delivery is available.

Love Letters' Catalog is usually $1, but it's free to readers of *Great Buys*.

Palmer Sales
3510 E. Highway 80
Mesquite, TX 75149
(214) 288-1026
CK, MC, V, MO, COD, C

Smart party planners know a good thing when they see it. Celebrate the discovery of this one without running all over town doing the paper chase. For discounted party supplies, fund-raising products, decorations, carnival supplies, religious items, balloons, toys, and holiday decorations, this must be the place. Palmer Sales supplies the goods to celebrate any occasion: birthdays, weddings, anniversaries, and holidays. They offer a 30-day return policy with a restocking charge of 10 percent, and a free catalog.

The Paper Wholesaler
Greco Paper
795 N.W. 72nd Street
Miami, FL 33150
(305) 836-1400
CK, MC, V, MO, C/$3

Party on with Paper Wholesaler. Their catalog'll put you in the spirit with up to 30 percent off on party paraphernalia like plates, cups, paper tablecloths, napkins, hats, invitations, and party favors. You're also invited to save on supplies for party *goers*, like gift bags and bows. Or you can get down to business with industrial-sized containers of party munchies, including popcorn and peanuts, cake-decorating supplies, brooms and cleaning equipment (to ease the aftermath), and more. Unopened, unused items may be returned within 30 days. Cheers!

Paradise Products, Inc.
P.O. Box 568 (800) 227-1092; (415) 524-8300
El Cerrito, CA 94530-0568 CK, MC, V, MO, C/$2

We thought Paradise Products consisted of apples, fig leaves, and serpents until we looked through their catalog and discovered nothing was lost. They've got party goods for 23 international and nine seasonal themes with tempting discounts of up to 50 percent on an assortment of favors, posters, crepe paper, hats, banners, flags, and masks (in their Party Host line). Say "Aloha!" to Hawaiian orchids and packets of beach sand or "How!" to an Indian peace pipe. You can even save a fortune, cookie, on fortune cookies for your next Chinese party. Finding the proper decorations to set the mood for a fifties or sixties party is no problem when you flip through this company's 88-page catalog. There's a $30 minimum order—if you order less than this amount, you must pay a service charge. All items are guaranteed to be as represented in the catalog, with shipments guaranteed to arrive on time (not fashionably late) for the party and in perfect condition, or they'll cheerfully refund your money.

Rocky Mountain Stationery
11725 County Road 27.3 (303) 565-8230
Dolores, CO 81323 CK, MO, F w/samples/$1
and double-stamped SASE

If you're hard pressed to find charming correspondence note cards, well, press on. Address these botanical beauties and pay half as much as you might in a ritzy boutique. Designed by artist Rose Ruland, these cards feature designs created with pressed flowers and leaves, and oil paints. Collections are available in assorted colors, in sets of 12 cards with envelopes, and sell for under $10. For a sample and a list of prices, send $1 with a double-stamped SASE.

The Stationery House, Inc.
1000 Florida Avenue (800) 638-3033
Hagerstown, MD 21741 CK, MC, V, AE, DC, CB, C

Foiled again, but this time it's gold foil stamping at the Stationery House. These folks help stamp out high prices with their gold-stamped, thermograved raised print designs suitable for personal or professional stationery. Selection runs the full spectrum, including stock logos and design ideas for a new business in need of a professional upgrade. Let's face it—you're saving up to 40 percent by ordering thermograved stationery direct rather than through a printer; therefore, you won't incur any extra typesetting or paste-up charges. The Stationery House claims they can match your current design or artwork, regardless of your choice of paper, ink, color, or type style, whether it be thermograved raised print, flat offset lithography, genuine engraving, hot foil stamping, or blind embossing, for less than the competition.

U.S. Box Corp.
(See **Office Supplies and Equipment**, p. **391**.)

Pets and Vets

Four-footed family members need love just like everyone else, but they also need their own supplies. You may not know it, but there are mail-order companies specializing in pet supplies. You don't have to roam all over town to find Rover a leash. Collar a bargain on a dog or cat collar, or buy toys, grooming supplies, vitamins and medical supplies, and hair clippers or hoof trimmers for your racehorse, ocelot, or Great Dane. Some mail-order firms even keep a veterinarian on staff to give you free advice. That's a deal that should set everyone's tail to wagging!

Advanced Consumer Products
P.O. Box 87766
Dept. GBBM — (800) 677-9090
Canton, MI 48187 — CK, MC, V, MO

Here's the picky cat's preference—the disposable cat-litter box. These cardboard wonders eliminate dust and odor problems, scattered litter, messy disposal, and box washing. They can be set up in just 30 seconds, and, one week later, thrown away. This product is made in America from recycled products and is assembled by physically challenged workers. Cat tested and approved, $2.95 each.

AVP (Animal Veterinary Products, Inc.)

P.O. Box 1326 (800) 962-1211
Galesburg, IL 61401 CK, MC, V, AE, PQ

Our pet peeve has always been paying too much for pet-care products. No more, my pet. AVP is *the* catalog to consult whenever purchasing your pet's health and hope chest. Get HAUGEN Pet Products at great prices. From simple ("cosmic catnip") to specialized (poodle hair dryer), the items fulfill every need a pet owner or pet-shop keeper might have. Feeders, furniture, scoopers, skin care, chokes and chewies, clippers, collars, piddle pads, vitamins, odor eaters, and litter pans . . . are you panting? Instead of saying "Out, damn Spot," treat your pet with some TLC from AVP. After all, it's a dog-eat-dog world out there. No catalog, but they will give price quotes by phone, and ship without a hitch.

Beef Rawhide

161 Riverdale Avenue (914) 969-1537
Yonkers, NY 10701 MC, V, B, PQ

Have Fido chew on this for a change—curls, rib rolls, chew sticks, pretzels, donuts, and of course, 100-percent all-beef rawhide, basted with a freeze-dried liver coating for enhanced flavor and added nutritional value. Or what about compressed rawhide chips in red and white—all at factory-direct prices. Bark if your dog brakes for bargains. Write for free brochure/price list. No handling charge for orders over $20. Arf!

Daleco Master Breeder Products

3340 Land Drive (219) 747-7376
Ft. Wayne, IN 46809 CK, MC, V, MO, COD, C/$4 (refundable), PQ

If you're fishing for complimentary aquarium supplies, here's the next best thing. Fish swim in bliss with "The Aquarists Supply Manual" from Daleco. Everything from filters to foods are included; some items are discounted as much as 40 percent. You'll get along swimmingly with buys from MARDEL, HAWAIIAN MARINE, AQUARIUM SYSTEMS, VORTEX, and others; they even have charts to help pinpoint your finned friends' infirmities. Order more than $30 and get shipping free; more than $50 and they'll refund the price of the catalog (which doubles as a handy reference guide if you're into these bubbling buddies). They will accept authorized returns only.

The Dog's Outfitter

P.O. Box 2010 (717) 384-5555
Hazleton, PA 18201 CK, MC, V, MO, COD, C

If Fifi's not looking first class lately, or Sampson is not quite sartorially correct, how about putting on the dog from The Dog's Outfitter. They've got everything a dog could want, doggone it, like flea shampoos, bones, gates, toys, collars and leashes, feeding bowls, supplies for abandoned newborns, carriers, cages, grooming brushes, and more. And let's get candidly catty for a moment; that includes goods for cats, too. RING 5, ZODIAC, OSTER, and BIO-GROOM were some of the names we answer to here, along with the great discounts; up to 50 percent off! They guarantee customer satisfaction (people and pets); the minimum order's $50. Most items include shipping.

Echo Products, Inc.

44635 Westminster (313) 453-3131
Canton, MI 48187 CK, MC, V, MO, COD, C/$1

Echo's a place for resounding bargains in small animal supplies, especially for the tropical marine varieties, like fish. Branded items are available, including SUPREME filters; VORTEX filters; GEISLER foods for dogs, cats, and birds; and TETRA fish food. A complete line of books on pets and pet care is great late-night reading at discounts of 25 percent. Check out their catalog—you won't want to miss the amusing "Tropical Fish Problem Solver Chart" that's included. Dive in while the discount's cool.

The Herb Garden

P.O. Box 949 (803) 237-9300
Pawleys Island, SC 29585 CK, MC, V, MO, B

If you flee at the site of parasites on your pet, but shudder to think of spraying them with toxic sprays, The Herb Garden may become your pet's ecologically correct mail-order company. Their all-natural pet products, made with ground herbs and other natural ingredients, include flea collars, dips, oils, and powders, as well as vitamin supplements, odor controllers, medicines to relieve scratching and allergies, and catnip mice. "Designer mice" for cats, filled with catnip or valerian root, were $4.50; Dermasol therapeutic lotion to relieve skin irritations without alcohol or steroids was $7 for four ounces. They offer a "holistic pet consultation," as well, which involves analyzing your animal's fur to determine health and nutritional problems. These environmentally safe products won't give you cause to pause over pet care. Orders over $50 are shipped free; there is a minimum of $15 on credit-card orders.

J-B Wholesale Pet Supplies, Inc.
289 Wagaraw Road, Dept. GBBM (800) 526-0388
Hawthorne, NJ 07506 CK, MC, V, AE, D, C

You supply the love, and let J-B fill in with the more pragmatic supplies. This catalog is slanted toward professionals, but you'll also find plenty of items your garden-variety animal lover can enjoy. Stainless and plastic feeding bowls, fly traps, wall-mounted feeding dispensers, scoopers, grooming brushes and mat combs, shampoos, flea collars, beds, and more, plus a large selection of books on health, showing techniques, pet psychology, and breeding. This 75-paged, indexed catalog showcases pet products at 50 percent to 60 percent off. Hoof 'em over to their outlet store when in Hawthorne, New Jersey, and show your appreciation.

Jeffers Vet Supply
P.O. Box 100 (800) JEFFERS
Dothan, AL 36302-0100 CK, MC, V, MO, C

Surely you'll be able to care for your cat or cattle with something from Jeffers' 131-page catalog. In a jiffy, you can bet on Jeffers for vet supplies for most four-legged animals. Livestock goods for horses, pigs, goats, cattle, sheep, and poultry include milking equipment for your divine bovine, incubators, grooming tools, antibiotics, and more. Owners of more citified pets will feel at home with the abundance of necessary cat and dog supplies. Save as much as half off regular retail and keep your pet pals groomed for the '90s. Jeffers accepts returns; quantity discounts are available.

Kennel Vet Corporation
P.O. Box 835
1811 Newbridge Road (516) 783-5400
Bellmore, NY 11710 CK, MC, V, AE, D, COD, C/$1
(free to readers)

This company is the purr-fect place to fill your small pet supply needs! Take a nip at a full range of health, grooming, and playtime products for dogs, cats, and other small animals. A complete line of vaccines, sprays, ointments, and grooming aids keeps your pet looking and feeling stylish and secure. Take a paws at prices that promise a savings on tools for professional care: grooming tables, stand dryers, clippers, trimmers, and nail groomers. Latex and hard rubber toys for pets offer plenty to keep you both entertained for hours. Brand-name supplies such as LAMBERT KAY, VET-KEM, ST. AUBREY, RING 5, OSTER, MID-WEST, and GENERAL are all available below retail. Learn more about caring for your pet with an extensive selection of pet-care books. Orders of $60 or more include shipping, and customers outside of New York don't pay sales tax. Orders shipped via UPS.

Offer to *Great Buys* readers: free catalog, brochures, and samples.

Mail Order Pet Shop
1338 N. Market Boulevard (800) 366-7387
Sacramento, CA 95834 CK, MC, V, AE, D, MO, COD, C

Maybe "Mail-Order Pet *Supply* Shop" would be more accurate; they don't sell live animals here, just the goods to keep 'em once you've got 'em. Aquarium supplies for neophyte and advanced hobbyists (but no tanks), filters, bird, cat, and dog supplies, toys, collars, shampoos, everything to help you stamp out high prices for pet care. Swim with the sharks at 50 percent off normal pet-shop prices and help keep your head above water.

Master Animal Care
P.O. Box 3333
Lake Road (717) 384-3600
Mountaintop, PA 18707-0330 CK, MC, V, D, MO, C, PQ

Master Care has the Midas touch when it comes to the golden rule for Great Buys. Their four-color 72-page catalog features pet products galore, like cages and carriers, automatic feeders, bones, herbal shampoos, leashes, and grooming tools at up to 40 percent off. Masterfully, they take charge of customer satisfaction by accepting returns, as well as providing price quotes without a bark.

The Natural Pet Care Company
2713 East Madison
Seattle, WA 98112
(800) 962-8266
(206) 329-1417 (in WA)
(206) 329-9211
CK, MC, V, C

Pamper your pet the *au natural* way. Now the environmentally correct pet owner can enter the New Age with products that are both safe and effective but do not contain dangerous chemicals. For example, you can eliminate fleas on your pets, and at the same time treat your indoor environment without serious toxic after-effects. This catalog offers not only flea products such as herbal pet powders, pyrethrum powders, citrus oil coat enhancers, and the miracle cure of diatomaceous earth but a line of Dr. Goodpet's natural medicines, a line of vitamins called "treatamins," yeast and garlic bits for snacks, and a home dental kit for dogs and cats. No kiss and tell after-smells with these smackers. All orders shipped UPS with charges based on dollar amount ordered (from $3.75 and up). Two-day air in continental U.S., double shipping charges; outside continental U.S., triple shipping.

Northern Wholesale Veterinary Supply
P.O. Box 2256
Brockford, IL 61131
(800) 356-5852
CK, MC, V, D, MO, COD, C

Ro-meow, Ro-meow, wherefore art thou with my chow? The Montagues and Cat-ulets may have been battling tooth and claw in Shakespeare's day, but today when it comes to problems like worms and fleas, the battle's over. Northern Wholesale carries a complete line of 6,000 animal health products (including PFIZER and ELANCO brands) discounted as much as 50 percent. Check 'em out: their 110-page catalog is free. A veterinarian is available to answer questions. How ducky can you get!

Omaha Vaccine Company, Inc.
3030 L Street
Omaha, NE 68107
(800) 367-4444; (402) 731-9600
CK, MC, V, D, MO, COD, C

My doggie door cost $79.95; in the catalog, a comparable one was $10.25. So—even the best of shoppers can be led astray from the path of good sense and admits she's been had. Whether it's for your dog, cat, or horse (or for your akita dog who's like a horse), you're sure to find something and save 20 percent to 50 percent while you're at it. After over 25 years of customer and vet satisfaction, you can expect their jam-packed, illustrated 290-page master catalog in about ten days and another week for your order. The minimum order's $50. In addition to the master catalog, which includes dogs, cats, horses, swine, sheep, and cattle supplies, there are two others. One just for horses, dogs and cats; the other, sheep, swine, and cattle. Moo-ve over. All catalogs are free.

Pet A Vision, Inc.
P.O. Box 222 (800) TABBY TV
Lyndon Center, VT 05850 CK, MC, V, AE, MO, F

And the winner is. . . . in the pet category, a runaway hit for indoor couch cats. *Video Catnip* is 25 minutes of VHS videotape–viewing pleasure no housecat should be denied. Opening with a few bars of human music, then it's on to the meat and potatoes. Twenty-two minutes of a "cats only" sequence sure to turn heads and wax nostalgic. Guaranteed to be 90-percent effective at driving indoor cats wild (not so successful, however, with outdoor ones, who are continually catting around). The tape consists of squirrels on film, along with chipmunks and birds; a tantalizing smorgasbord of edible critters in 21″ of viewing pleasure. The video is available for $19.95, which includes shipping. Write for a free flier to preview this coming attraction and treat your furry friend to a mesmerizing menagerie of entertainment tonight.

Pet Warehouse
P.O. Box 20250, Dept. GBBM
3189 Plainfield Road (800) 443-1160
Dayton, OH 45420 CK, MC, V, D, C

Our pet-agrees we should never pay full price for pet supplies from major animal houses. But at Pet Warehouse, their bark is as good as their bite (out of our budget). Expect bargains at every turn of the page, bursting at the seams with deals on fresh- and saltwater aquariums, as well as supplies for birds, dogs, cats, small animals, and reptiles. No creepy crawlers need apply for the 50-percent to

70-percent savings; they're available to everyone just for the asking. Most orders are shipped within 24 to 48 hours; there's a 15-day money-back guarantee.

Petdoors USA
4523 30th Street West, Dept. GBBM (800) 749-9609
Bradenton, FL 34207 (813) 753-7492
CK, MC, V, C

Don't let the screen door hit them in the face at full price. These doors let them come and go safely at whim, without whinning. PLEXIDOR, PET-EZE, HALE, CLEARTHRU, BORWICK, PET-WAY, and PET MATE were a few of the names we saw, all priced well below what you'd find in a pet store. "For cats to Great Danes," they have something to fit every size, color, and pace. They also carry unusual or hard-to-find supplies, like a Flea Vac, an outdoor pet toilet (with a mini septic tank), games, and self-grooming implements to teach your kid a thing or two. The full purchase price will be refunded on items returned within 30 days; most orders are shipped via UPS within 24 hours, although second-day and next-day shipping is available.

R.C. Steele Co.
P.O. Box 910
1989 Transit Way (800) 872-3773
Brockport, NY 14420-0910 CK, MC, V, MO, C

Get a Steele of a deal from this company, founded in 1959 and bent on saving you up to half the regular retail price on pet care supplies and books. Mostly dog supplies, though, are featured in the catalog (about 70 pages), with a passing nod to cats and fish. From bones to beds, the prices are pared to the bare bones. There is a $50 minimum order, and returns are accepted. Whether you're a vet, run a grooming shop, or just have a pet in the family, R.C. Steele drives quite a wheely.

That Fish Place
237 Centerville Road (717) 299-5691
Lancaster, PA 17603 CK, MC, V, MO, C/$2

Something's fishy here. Before you flap a flipper over the price of aquarium upkeep, try this catalog from a company that's been bubbling for almost 20 years. Keep it warm; keep it clean; keep 'em fed; keep 'em healthy with heaters, filters, and feeders; plus lights, air pumps, plants, and more, for as much as 50 percent off. Schools of books are also available, too, along with some cat, dog, and bird supplies. There is a minimum order of $25 for live plants and $15 for dry goods. Returns are accepted, but there may be a restocking charge of 15 percent.

Tomahawk Live Trap Co.

P.O. Box 323 (800) 27A-TRAP (orders only)
1416 E. Mohawk Drive (715) 453-3550
Tomahawk, WI 54487 CK, MC, V, COD, B

Honest Injun, palefaced animal lovers can snare savings without putting the bite on their four-footed friends. Tomahawk Live Trap makes humane traps and box-type cages for catching, holding, and/or transporting wild and not-so-wild beasts like mice, chipmunks, beavers, raccoons, and skunks. This is the only company that makes traps approved by the U.S. government for humane societies. All traps are built to last. (One long-term customer wrote: "Your traps and Zippo lighters are the only products that have kept their quality throughout the years.") Since they're factory direct, prices are excellent. Orders are shipped out the same day. Get set to spring into action!

United Pharmacal Company, Inc.

P.O. Box 969, Dept 95
GBBM93 (816) 233-8800
St. Joseph, MO 64502 CK, MC, V, AE, D, C

We wanted to throw rice when we saw all the bridle and grooming supplies in United Pharmacal Company's 176-page catalog. Say "I do" to prices of 30 percent to 70 percent off antibiotics, vitamins, insecticides, and horse tack—in fact, on everything needed to care for a dog, cat, or horse. Take your vows of "Never Paying Retail Again!" and start with do-it-yourself vaccines. You'll save about 80 percent off vet's fees with no prescription needed for catalog items. PET TABS vitamins, 60 per jar, were just $3.95 (retail, $6.50). Newfangled clumping-style cat litter was $11.95 for a 16-pound jug, as opposed to $19.95 retail. There's a $10 minimum order.

Delivery in three of four working days, a 30-day return policy, and manufacturers' warranties make this more than a one-night stand.

Wholesale Veterinary Supply, Inc.
P.O. Box 2256 (800) 435-6940
Rockford, IL 61131-0256 CK, MC, V, D, MO, COD, C

Get it wholesale at Wholesale! From hair-clippers to hoof-trimmers, they've got everything you need in vitamins, supplements, prescriptions, medical supplies, shampoos, and insecticides for your Flicka, Benji, or Morris. Everything is discounted up to 50 percent, including popular brands like LAMBERT KAY, FARNAM, and PET-TABS (pet vitamins). You'll also find items like wonder wormers, anti-mating spray (only on four-legged animals—shucks!), spray cologne and deodorant, flea bombs, JIM DANDY horse treats, and carrying cages. For something even more exotic, buy a cow-chip penholder. There's a full-time, in-house veterinarian who answers your questions at no charge. All their catalogs are free, including the master (all animals; about 250 pages), one for small animals (cats, dogs, horses; 150 pages), and one for farm animals (cattle, sheep, swine; 100 pages). About 80 percent of their items are shipped free—the others are marked FOB in the catalog. There's no restocking charge on orders returned within 30 days, but you must call first. Minimum order is $30.

Wow-Bow Distributors, Ltd.
13-B Lucon Drive (800) 326-0230
Deer Park, NY 11729 CK, MC, V, AE, MO, COD, C

This is the catalog of choice for anyone concerned about his pet's health. Health foods for pets, including cats, dogs, and horses, are cruelty-free and designed to nourish and maintain your beloved companion. Vegetarian dog foods, "Cat Croutons," biscuits, meat-based foods free of chemicals, toxin-free flea-control products, and books on natural health care and nutrition for pets are available in this four-legged collection. They'll even bake canine cakes and cookies for your pet's birthday. Wow-Bow offers a 100-percent satisfaction guarantee, with no restocking charge on returns. Orders are shipped within 24 hours.

Plants, Flowers, Gardens, and Farming

Grow your own fruits and vegetables, raise chickens, repair your tractor, landscape your yard—you'll reap the benefits of a healthier life-style and a heartier bank account. Start with high-quality seeds, add good soil and weather, fertilize with tender loving care, and—watch your garden grow. From apples to zinnias all ripe for the picking. When ordering live plants or seeds, be sure to consider your native soil conditions and local weather. If you're not sure a white flowering dogwood will make it through the night in the dead of winter, consult a local nursery or the mail-order supplier before you order.

Bluestone Perennials Inc.
7211 Middle Ridge Road
Madison, OH 44057
(216) 428-7535
CK, MC, V, AE, D, MO, C

The Bluestone catalog kind of grows on you. The 500 or so varieties of perennial plants remind us of birthdays; they crop up every year with practically no coaxing. If you admire the beauty of flowers found bordering lawns or being grown in gardens for display, here's a chance to try your green thumb at saving some green cash. Not only does Bluestone offer an outstanding array of flowers, but their prices are very reasonable. Care is taken to package the plants and a full money-back guarantee is given. The four-color catalog features a description of all plants, shade and lighting requirements, price, and, in some cases, photographs. Colorful reading.

Breck's Dutch Bulbs
6523 N. Galena Road (309) 691-4610
Peoria, IL 61632 CK, MC, V, AE, D, MO, C

These light bulbs—and dark bulbs, too—are imported from Holland. Before you start shaking in your wooden shoes at the thought of the price, relax; they're as much as 50 percent less here than elsewhere, so reach for their anemones, cuddle their crocuses, and enjoy the irises, worry-free. Tulips are center stage, in a variety of gorgeous shades, plus hyacinths, snowdrops, jonquils, and daffodils. Breck's maintains a staff in Holland to oversee the bulbs' production. If you're not happy with your bulbs, even after they've grown, Breck's will give you a replacement, exchange, or refund. That's a bloomin' bargain! Want to go Dutch?

Brookfield Christmas Tree
P.O. Box 2490
1970 Palmer Street (703) 382-9099
Christiansburg, VA 24068 CK, MC, V, B

Bah! Humbug! It's Christmas time again. Time for the annual, hectic hunt for a tree in a forest of high prices. Here is a version of *A Christmas Carol* that will lift even Scrooge's spirits: The Spirit of Christmas *Past*—Humbug! Bruised, crushed, dried-out trees that were shipped thousands of miles and show every mile. Your living-room floor is blanketed with needles, and your wallet is a lot thinner. The tree is dead, and the special day hasn't even arrived yet. Besides that, you had to fight the crowds for a not-so-jolly tree. The Spirit of Christmas *Present*—Ho! Ho! Ho! Capture the elegance and tradition of a Christmas spent in the Blue Ridge Mountains of Virginia. Brookfield Plantation offers a very unique service that will make your Christmas merry. They deliver beautiful, carefully nurtured, hand-selected, fresh trees directly to your door. Each tree is guaranteed to bring joy to your heart, or you will get a full refund. Mike and David have one of the largest evergreen farms on the east coast with over one-half million of the very best white pines. They are the first growers to ship a tree direct to your door. Every tree arrives fresh and crisp in its own package since it's shipped the same day it's cut. The prices will make you Dancer and Prancer on the rooftops. Santa himself couldn't deliver a better deal. The Spirit of Christmas *Future*—Noel! Noel! No more tree hassles, ever! You can relax, Ebenezer; throw out that plastic tree and bring the wonderful fragrance of fresh pine indoors. Get beautiful, handcrafted, fresh pine wreaths and lifetime tree stands uniquely designed to eliminate the need to trim those beautiful lower branches. Fraser firs and blue spruces are offered for the pickier, their price a little stickier. Now, that's a Christmas carol even Dickens would appreciate. Here's a little stocking stuffer we almost forgot: All orders must be placed each year by December 17.

Butterbrooke Farm

78 Barry Road (203) 888-2000
Oxford, CT 06478 B/$1 or SASE

It's back to nature for mail-order shoppers. Whether gardening for pleasure, profit, recreation, or appetite, Butterbrooke Farm has the seeds to sow. For 30 percent to 70 percent less than prices elsewhere, this company will provide a wide variety of seeds to choose from. Butterbrooke Farm caters to the veggie gardener by offering 75 varieties of seeds in their brochure. These seeds are pure, open-pollinated strains, which means any seeds you save from your own produce will grow to be just as beautiful as their parents. Because these seeds require a short growing season, they are ideal in areas like New England. Furthermore, these seeds are chemical-free, which should please the organic purists among us. Butterbrook owners Tom and Judy Butterworth have formed a seed co-op. Associate membership is $12.50; supporting membership is $25; and lifetime membership is $250.

Calyx & Corolla

1550 Bryant Street, Suite 900 (800) 877-7836; (800) 800-7788
San Francisco, CA 94103 (415) 626-3781 (FAX)
(415) 626-5511
CK, MC, V, AE, MO, C

Why be ordinary? Go for the exotic in tropical flowers, plants, and herbs direct from their greenhouses to you. A few fresh-cut items include pink-fringed carnations, mini-carnations, long-stem roses, and birds of paradise. Dried items include rose topiary trees, wreaths, even a pepperberry heart wreath. They also offer potted plants and seasonal items. Calyx & Corolla eschew the everyday for the unusual and manage to save you money, too. Don't be a shrinking violet; explore these lush and lovely alternatives to another bedraggled begonia. All fresh-cut items arrive within 24 to 48 hours.

Caprilands Herb Farm
534 Silver Street
Route 44 (203) 742-7244
Coventry, CT 06238 CK, Certified Check, MO, B

Travelers will be glad to know owner Adlema Simmons conducts tours through the farm from April 1 to December 27 for a small fee. The next best thing to being there is receiving a copy of their very concise brochure, which includes a healthy selection of medicinal and decorative herbs ranging from rosebuds and lavender to musk, clove, and orange blossoms. Most herbs are sold in small packages, but you can get quarter-pounder packages of lemon verbena and half-pounder packages of rosebuds and lavender blossoms. Books, postcards, incense, potpourri, coat hangers, note paper, necklaces, and spinning wheels are also available. There are three shops: a gift shop, a greenhouse, and a book store. Prices are reasonable, although they are not discounted. Unfortunately, many herbal wreaths are too fragile to ship.

Carino Nurseries, Inc.
P.O. Box 538, Dept GBBM (800) 223-7075
Route 403 North (412) 463-3350; (412) 463-7480
Indiana, PA 15701 CK, MC, V, C

Come, my dear little ones, and I'll tell you about a great little nursery called Carino, where barefoot seedlings and transplants are about 50 percent less than conventional nursery prices. Colorado blue spruce, Douglas firs, Canadian hemlock, and white pine are some of their most popular varieties. And it's no fairy tale; orders of 500 or more plants can save you another 50 percent! Spring shipping, so the story goes, is from March 20 through May 15; fall shipping is from September 15 through October 31. Christmas tree planting stock, wildlife food and cover, nut trees, and cut Christmas trees are included in their color catalog. They'll even tell you when to plant. There's an additional 10 percent added for UPS shipping.

Central Michigan Tractor & Parts
2713 North U.S. Hwy 27 (800) 248-9263
St. Johns, MI 48879 (800) 292-9233 (MI residents)
(517) 244-6802
CK, MC, V, COD, PQ

Till we till again, here's a source for 50-percent savings on "good used tractor and combine parts" for the farm. When they answer the phone, expect them to say "Tractor Salvage." They have parts for all makes and models, rebuilt starters, reground crankshafts, reconditioned cylinder heads, plus cylinder blocks. Discounted diesel and gas engines for tractors and combines are also available. There's a 30-day guarantee on all parts, refunds given. Orders are shipped within 24 to 48 hours. Check out their "23-acre facility" when in the area, with over 7,000 bins of parts and reconditioned starters, generators, and more.

Dairy Association Co., Inc.
Lyndonville, VT 05851-0145 (800) 232-3610; (802) 626-3610
CK, MO, COD, B

Hay, a horse is a horse, of course, of course, and it behooves him to have, what else, soft hooves. (If you don't believe us, just ask Mr. Ed!). Along with the GREEN MOUNTAIN HOOF SOFTENER, get a supply of BAG BALM dialators to keep Elsie from uddering sounds of distress during milking. (BAG BALM's their best-selling item.) KOW KARE and TACKMASTER products are also available at considerable savings. Credit is issued on receipt of returned merchandise, but call first; they accept on a prepaid postage basis only upon their authorization.

Daylily Discounters
Dept. 1080 (904) 462-1539
Route 2, Box 24 (800) DAYLILY (orders only)
Alachua, FL 32615 CK, MC, V, AE, D, MO, C/$3 (refundable)

These delicate flowers don't shrink from offering hard-core savings. Daylilies bred by famous hubridizers in all sizes, shapes, bloom seasons, and colors are available at savings of 50 percent and more. They offer the Stella de Oro, the world's best-selling daylily, which typically sells for $12.95 to $15.95, for $3.95; prices are even lower when you buy in quantity. A detailed description of each flower, details on growing zones, and gorgeous photographs are included in their color catalog. Daylily Discounters ship within 48 hours unless otherwise specified; 100-percent satisfaction guaranteed. Hi-lily, hilily, how-low!

Dutch Gardens
P.O. Box 200, Dept. GBBM (908) 780-2713
Adelphia, NJ 07710 CK, MC, V, AE, C

Rooted in Dutch Gardens, this company deals exclusively in narcissus, iris, daffodils, amaryllis, lilies, dahlias, tulip bulbs, and other flowers shipped direct from Holland. Prices average about 30 percent to 50 percent below retail; some prices, however, were comparable to retail. Tiptoe through their tulip bulbs for their biggest selling item. Each flower carried is pictured in full bloom in their exceptionally attractive 244-item catalog, with the growing time, bloom size, and other pertinent information. An additional 10-percent discount is given on orders over $70. They will replace bulbs that don't grow the first year. Minimum order with credit cards is $20.

Flickinger's Nursery
P.O. Box 245 (412) 783-6528
Sagamore, PA 16250 CK, MC, V, COD, C

Is the Little Woman pining for some firs? You don't have to think mink to spruce up your love life! For 44 years Flickinger's has been needling their customers and providing a hedge against inflation. Small trees are their specialty, and prices are from 50 percent to 75 percent lower than you'll find in most nurseries. We saw seedlings and transplants of bristlecone pine, Colorado blue spruce, Douglas fir, Canadian hemlock, European white birch, and white flowering dogwood. There's a $30 minimum order, so you may need to branch out and chop up your order with friends. How does 100 five- to nine-inch Japanese black pine seedlings for $24 sound? Stumped? One thousand are just $130. Don't beat around the bush (or go barking up the wrong tree)—write for their free catalog. Note: This company's stock is grown for the Northeast, Midwest, and some coastal Southern states, so westerners will have to look elsewhere.

Florist Products, Inc.
2242 North Palmer Drive (800) 828-2242
Schaumberg, IL 60173 CK, MC, V, AE, MO, C, PQ (SASE)

Good prices on gardening goods are sprouting at Florist Products. Save your green on green-thumb necessities like insecticides, plant food, fertilizers, flats, and gardening tools, or get serious with a greenhouse. Either way, you'll save up to 50 percent off list price on garden gear like JIFFY and CORONA. Returns are accepted on unused merchandise; you can call or write (SASE) for a price quote.

Four Seasons Greenhouses
5005 Veterans Memorial Highway (516) 563-4000
Holbrook, NY 11741 CK, MC, V, AE, MO, C

This company's greenhouses have been used for many special projects and solar demonstrations, including the Department of Energy's demonstration house at Brookhaven National Laboratory. Their catalog provides extensive information, accompanied by excellent photography of the many types of maintenance-free features and accessories that are available. Color charts, diagrams, and other catalog features give facts and figures that can help you make a decision, whether it be for your home or business. Delivery usually takes about three to four weeks.

Frans Roozen
Vogelenzangseweg 49
2114 BB Vogelenzang
Holland MO, C

For over 55 years, this family has been offering bulbous bargains on tulips and singing a song of savings on over 1,000 different varieties of bulbs. Prices are comparable to other discount bulb imports from Holland, with savings planted in the 10-percent range. There is a money-back guarantee if your complaint is reasonable. Flowers are always guaranteed.

Fred's Plant Farm

Route 1
P.O. Box 707
Dresden, TN 38225-0707
(800) 243-9377
(901) 364-3754
CK, MC, V, D, COD, C/$1

One potato, two potato, three potato, four; and a lot, lot more. Fred's Plant Farm grows ten varieties of sweet, sweet spuds. Centennials, Nancy Halls, Jewells, Beauregarde, Red Nuggets, White Yams, Yellow Yams, Jaspers, and Algolds were the sugar-coated varieties offered one spring. "We grow our own seeds and plants." Fred guarantees to ship strong, well-rooted plants, or your money back. No dud spuds in his garden or yours. You won't be caught holding the hot potato. Fred pays all shipping charges and sends you a free "growing guide." You won't be yammering over these wholesale prices either. There's no minimum order, so don't be a potato head, and order from Fred.

Gardener's Supply Company

128 Intervale Road
Burlington, VT 05401
(802) 863-1700
CK, MC, V, D, MO, C

From earthworms to "the Cadillac of composters," there are dozens of ways to improve the odds of your gardening success, and Gardener's Supply Company is out to help you find them. They offer PaperPots, biodegradable pots held together by water-soluble glue; "Energy Buttons" for fast fertilizing; small, reasonably priced greenhouses; chippers, dusters, pruners; even a Bat House! Don't gamble with expensive gardening goods; try Gardener's Supply and save yourself both time and money. More information is available on their greenhouses (see catalog order form); credit-card orders have a $25 minimum. Most orders are shipped within 24 to 48 hours after receipt.

Glass House Works Catalog

P.O. Box 97
10 Church Street
Stewart, OH 45778-0097
(614) 662-2142
CK, MC, V, MO, C/$1.50

The "esoterica botanica" in this catalog might tax even the most earnest taxonomist. However, for those of you who know a ficus from a fuchsia, this is an excellent reference work and source for rare and unusual varieties of home and greenhouse plants. If they don't have the plant you want listed in their copious catalog, send them the common name or scientific name, description, where you saw it growing, and a copy of any articles that mention it. The catalog describes color, shape, lighting requirements, prices, and other commentary useful to home-growers. Allow six to eight weeks for shipping; add $7.50 for postage on all orders. Add an additional 60 cents per plant for air UPS or air parcel post. Minimum order is $10 plus postage.

Gurney's Seed & Nursery Co.
110 Capital Street (605) 665-4451
Yankton, SD 57079 CK, MC, V, D, MO, C

If the grass is always greener on your neighbor's side of the fence, try Gurney's. They carry more hybrid plants, bulbs, trees, seeds, and gardening supplies than you've probably ever seen before. Over 4,000 items from African violets to zucchini are bursting out of their colorful catalog. Prices are better than you'll find in most retail plant and gardening stores. We've grown accustomed to their face during their one-cent sales. Their crop of novelty items, like grow-your-own bird seed, yard-long cucumbers, loofah sponges, tobacco, horseradish, and even praying mantises represents good buys. A nice perk, Gurney's "Complete Growing Guide," is sent with all orders.

Hickory Hill Nursery
Route 1, Box 390A (703) 942-3871
Fisherville, VA 22939 CK, Certified Check, B

These Hickory Hillbillies aren't afraid to turn over a new leaf, or an entire layer of topsoil, with their TROY-BILT ROTOTILLER POWER COMPOSTERS, manufactured by the Garden Way Manufacturing Company. Their price list showed 12 models of roto-tillers, with most discounted 10 percent to 20 percent. Prices on various attachments are also discounted. (Discounts vary with the season.) Our experience with roto-tillers has been akin to plowing behind a bucking Brahma bull while gripping a jackhammer, but at least here, the prices won't shake you up.

Hoffman Hatchery, Inc.
Main Street (717) 365-3694
Gratz, PA 17030 CK, B

They've been hatching since 1948, and the Hoffmans think that's a feather in their cap. If you think a bird in the hand is worth two in the mail, just look at their prices (cheep, cheep!). Commercial and fancy breeds of chickens, ducks, geese, quail, turkeys, hens, swans, even peafowl are available. In addition to animals, Hoffman's carries equipment for small flock raisers. Brooders, feeders, coops, picker fingers . . . everything you always wanted to know about chicks but were too chicken to ask is contained in their brochure. In case you haven't been able to put one aside, they even sell plastic nest eggs. A copy of "Basic Fundamentals on Raising Goslings, Ducklings, Guineas, Chicks, and Turkeys" is indispensable reading for some, as is the bulletin concerning the raising and feeding of ducks on a budget.

J.E. Miller Nurseries
5060 W. Lake Road (800) 836-9630; (716) 396-2647
Canadaigua, NY 14424 CK, MC, V, AE, D, MO, C

No need to be a John E. Appleseed with John E. Miller. His catalog includes pages of apple strains including "old-fashioned" favorites, along with many other quality fruit trees. Prices are competitive, with walnuts being their most popular line. Everything comes with a one-year guarantee against failure. Replacements are offered at no charge ($3.25 handling fee only) up to one year from any shipping season. There's a $10 minimum on charge orders. Their catalog is packed with facts and tips on all aspects of growing.

K. Van Bourgondien & Sons, Inc.
P.O. Box 1000 (800) 622-9997 (orders)
245 Farmingdale Road (800) 622-9959 (customer service)
Babylon, NY 11702 CK, MC, V, AE, D, MO, C

You've come a long way, from Babylon. Contemporary gardeners get on the stick and order through the catalog without pussyfooting around. You may not find Tiny Tim tiptoeing throughout this 63-page catalog bursting with color, but you will find flowers. Lots of them. They specialize in bulbs from Holland and the U.S. at up to

50 percent off. Check out the caladiums, giant dahlias, gladiolus, and lots o'lilies of all sorts, plus Japanese anemones and ferns. Returns are accepted and refunds given if there are problems with an order upon receipt; all orders are shipped at the proper planting time, unless otherwise specified.

La Vie En Rose
82 Christopher Street (212) 366-4010
New York, NY 10014-4252 MC, V, AE, MO, PQ

A rose by any other name wouldn't smell as cheap. Order a dozen long-stemmed for $35 anywhere in the continental United States, and they'll be shipped Federal Express. Many other varieties, including dry roses, are available in the store, but you'll have to negotiate the price. Orders are accepted Tuesday through Friday.

The Ladybug Company (Bio-Control Products)
Oro-Quincy Highway (916) 589-5227
Berrycreek, CA 95916 CK, MO, C, PQ

Question: What winged wonder fearlessly fights for your garden's glory, risking life and limb in a never-ending struggle against those horticultural hell-raising insects that feast on your foliage? It's a Ladybug. (No, this is not some flipped-out refugee from a religious cult, or a six-legged feminist crusader of the insect world—the Green Hornet doesn't have a wife.) Ladybugs are insects that brunch on the bugs that munch on our flowers, shrubs, and trees. They make gourmet meals of mealy bugs (mealy bug Bourguignonne), leafhoppers (hoppers au gratin, with bay leaf), and aphids (aphids a la mode). If beetles in your juice and crawlies in your clover are driving you buggy, write Bio-control for a price list of their beneficial bugs. Lacewings, Chinese praying mantises, and trichograma are also available. Biological warfare can be cheaper and safer than insecticides. And all these antennaed mercenaries ask for is a free lunch. Live delivery is guaranteed.

Long Distance Roses
P.O. Box 7790 (800) LD-ROSES; (719) 537-6737
Colorado Springs, CO 80933 CK, MC, V, AE, DC, CB, Postcard

Flowers to go! Fresh roses and orchids can be sent almost anywhere in the United States via Federal Express at a price sometimes lower than your neighborhood florist. (What price convenience?) Overnight floral delight is offered for most areas, with a few locations requiring up to two days. Roses come in your choice of colors—red, pink, or yellow, with other colors available on special occasions. Roses by any other name will cost $49.95 per dozen. All flowers are guaranteed fresh, or a complete refund or replacement is provided. Call or write for a postcard to shop from; checks must clear before orders paid for by check will be sent.

Mellinger's Inc.

W. South Range Road (800) 321-7444
North Lima, OH 44452-9731 CK, MC, V, D, MO, C

Since 1927, Mellinger's has been in the gardening business, and now they're reaping what they've sown. Their 120-page catalog is full of seedlings, seeds, shrubbery, gardening tools, herbs, vines, fertilizers, bulbs, chemical and organic pesticides, small greenhouses, books, and more, at up to 45 percent off. Some of the items found here would be hard to locate elsewhere, like seeds for exotic plants. There is a $10 minimum on credit-card orders; a 10-percent restocking fee may be charged for authorized returns.

National Arbor Day Foundation

100 Arbor Avenue (402) 474-5655
Nebraska City, NE 68410 CK, MC, V, AE, MO

For a $10 membership, you can harbor great buys on trees from the National Arbor Day Foundation. They sell bare-root trees for a third of regular retail prices, some even less. Members receive *The Tree Book*, a plant identification and cultivation reference book that doubles as a catalog; and, every two months, an *Arbor Day* newsletter. Unfortunately, they don't ship to Alaska, Arizona, California, or Hawaii; shipping periods are between October 15 and December 10 (Fall), and February 1 through May 31 (Spring). Contact the Foundation for more information.

Nor'East Miniature Roses, Inc.

P.O. Box 307 (508) 948-7964
Rowley, MA 01969 CK, MC, V, MO, C

Things are looking a little rosier since we found out we can save up to 30 percent on miniature roses. (See, good things do come in small packages!) Whether you're green with enthusiasm or an old hand, Nor'East's 16-page catalog will tickle you pink . . . or red, orange, apricot, mauve, white, or yellow. There's a beginner's kit to get your started, and a great selection to keep you growing, from tree roses to micro-minis; even a flowery book on the subject. There is a $20 minimum order with credit cards, and returns are accepted if plants don't grow up satisfactorily (too bad they don't give you that option with kids!). Large orders mean larger discounts.

Noweta Gardens
900 Whitewater Avenue (507) 932-4859
St. Charles, MN 55972 CK, C

Carl Fisher, founder of "Beautiful Gardens" (translation of the Indian word *noweta*), has been growing gladiolus for 63 years and he's glad, which is to be expected from a man surrounded by happy friendship flowers. Varieties for sale are Buttercup Dancer, Gladheart Hallmark, High Seas, and Lavender Dream. Minimum bulb order is $15, but you receive a 20-percent discount with orders of $250 or more. Usual shipping season runs from March to June; orders are sent by UPS and filled in accordance with planting seasons in customers' regional areas. They send out 10,000 catalogs a year, so get in line for a free one.

Park Seed Co.
Cokesbury Road (803) 223-7333
Greenwood, SC 29647-0001 CK, MC, V, AE, D, MO, C

Park's the place to park your trowel at your barren backyard. Plant yourself a garden with seeds, bulbs, plants, and all the gardening accoutrements to complete the fete-for-less. Delicate calla lillies, sinuey shrub roses, succulent wax beans and stringbeans, crunchy carrots and corn, perfect potatoes and tomatoes; whatever your gardening palate, you're likely to find it in Park's 131-page catalog, complete with pictures of all kinds of flowers and vegetables, plus helpful gardening hints. Fan and ladder trellises, pyramid planters to make maximum use of minimal space, electric sprayers, a children's seed collection, and much more are available. Park guarantees "to deliver quality goods that satisfy you completely," and sets forth a very reasonable replacement policy in the catalog. Park ships bulbs and plants until May 28; earlier for southern planting zones.

Pinetree Garden Seeds
Route 100 (207) 926-3400
New Gloucester, ME 04260 CK, MC, V, AE, C

Pining for some seeds to call your own? Fret no further; Pinetree's 176-page catalog is bound to ease your seedy sorrows. Seeds, spring and fall bulbs, tubers, onion sets, garden tools, perennial plants, and more are available at up to 35 percent off. Bring up a blaze of begonias, gladiolus, lillies, and irises, or plant your garden with Pinetree seed packets; they're "smaller quantities for the home gardener." Pinetree has been in business since 1979, and guarantees everything 100 percent. Most orders are delivered in one to three weeks.

Pony Creek Nursery
Nursery Lane
P.O. Box 16 (715) 787-3889
Tilleda, WI 54978 CK, MC, V, COD (with 25 percent down), C/$1 (refundable), PQ

Are visions of sugarplums and cherries break-dancing in your head? That's the pits, man. Maybe you've been aiming for an organic diet or maybe you are just a flower fancier. Whatever your plant preference, you can stock your greenhouse with seeds, fertilizers, insect repellents, and more from Pony Creek. A full assortment of ORTHO garden products, plus tree seedlings of all varieties including their best-seller, Colorado blue spruce, is available. Price breaks mean the more seedlings you buy, the better your savings. Get on your way to healthier eating, beautiful landscaping, and sizable savings. Shade trees and about 50 different varieties of flowering shrubs are also available. Pony Creek will replace (ONCE!) any shrub, tree, or evergreen that dies in its first growing season and is returned with the guarantee slip by November 1 of the year it was purchased. Price quotes are given by phone.

Prentiss Court Ground Covers
P.O. Box 8662 (803) 277-4037
Greenville, SC 29604-8662 CK, MC, V, MO, B/50 cents

They've got you covered! Give your lawn a new look with cushioning ground covers. A variety of textures add that special touch to banks, slopes, and rock gardens. More than 50 varieties of ground covers, including day lilies, fig vine, algerian ivy, honeysuckle, and phlox let you choose the creative—and inexpensive—landscape option. And, at up to 50 percent below retail cost, these ground covers are a beautiful buy for any budget. Ajuga, pachysandra, and cotoneaster are also available. These practical problem-solvers are the scenic solution to humdrum lawns. Top-grade stock lets you enjoy maximum ground coverage for a minimal price. A large selection of varieties and colors creates covers with a refreshing new look. Prices include shipping and handling, and orders are shipped within one week.

Reich Poultry Farms, Inc.

R.D. 1 (717) 426-3411
Marietta, PA 17547 COD

If your poultry has been looking paltry, you've come to the Reich place. Mr. Reich's been in the poultry biz for 48 years and ships baby chicks from February through November. All orders are shipped Air Parcel Post, Priority Mail—and usually arrive anywhere in the U.S. or Canada overnight. Savings come with volume. If you buy only 15 or so chicks, the price may be better in a local feed store. (Hens-forth, you'll have to order in large quantities to get the better price.) Besides chickens, Reich ships equipment and veterinary supplies.

R.H. Shumway's

P.O. Box 1, Dept. 6724
571 Whaley Pond Road (803) 663-9771
Graniteville, SC 29829 CK, MC, V, D, MO, C/$1 (refundable)

Established in 1870 in Rockford, Illinois, by Roland H. Shumway, the "pioneer American seedman," Shumway's offers "good seeds cheap." They're sowing seeds of contentment by offering seeds, plants, trees, and gardening supplies for about 40 percent off. The 55-page indexed catalog, illustrated with Victorian-style wood engravings, even contains a dictionary of herb uses. Returns are accepted for full refund or credit; most orders are delivered within 48 to 72 hours.

Rosehill Farm
P.O. Box 188 (800) 285-5538; (410) 648-5538
Galena, MD 21635-0188 CK, MC, V, MO, C

Everything's coming up miniature roses at Rosehill, for about a third less than elsewhere. The roses are available in a variety of colors and sizes, including red, apricot, blush, orange, yellow, gold, pink, lavender, and white, and micro-minis, climbing roses, and sweethearts. The bigger your order, the more you save; orders of ten or more warrant an additional 10 percent off; more with larger orders. There is a $20 minimum on credit-card orders. Visit Rosehill's store on Gregg Neck Road when in or near Galena.

Silk Plant Company
14885 North 83rd Place, Dept. GBBM (602) 483-0100
Scottsdale, AZ 85260 CK, MC, V, AE, MO,
C/$3 or $10

Why get real? These bloomin' beauties are impossible to kill, and they're as much as 60 percent less than retail. Silk Plant Company offers a complete line of imported plants, trees, cacti, flowers, and the baskets and containers to pull them all together. Their 20-page black-and-white catalog costs $3; or you can examine their 200-page color catalog for $10. Plant it here for drop-dead savings! They charge a 15-percent restocking fee on returns, which are accepted in seven to fourteen days.

Smallholding Supplies
Pikes Farmhouse
East Pennard, Shepton Mallet 074-986-688
Somerset, BA4 6RR, England CK, MC, V, Access, Eurocard, C

Are you starting your own small farm? Maybe you operate a larger corporate farm. If so, you may find Smallholding Supplies can save you moo-cho dollars. They are the cream of the crop when it comes to supplying the farmer with any imaginable farm item. Items long forgotten can be found here at the prices of long ago. We found their 49-page catalog filled with hundreds of items such as an Italian milking machine that should make your cow jump over the moon in delight. Listen to these cheesy deals: cheesecloth, molds, butter churns, yogurt machines, and other milky items were offered at prices way below retail. Tether your cow in the heather with a tethering stake, or shear your sheep cheap with electric shears. Not a baa-d deal. Prices will be quoted and discounts negotiated for larger orders. Remember it's coming from England, so it might not make it for tea.

Smith & Hawken
25 Corte Madera (415) 383-4050
Mill Valley, CA 94941 CK, MC, V, AE, D, MO, C

Gardeners on the grow will love every page of this catalog! Indoor and outdoor gardening is made simple with the items offered by Smith and Hawken. Year-round gardeners everywhere will appreciate the English-cottage greenhouse with coordinating shelving, staging, and benches to make the most of your plants. Garden furniture in a water-resistant teak finish lets you enjoy your self-made Eden, or if redwood is more to your liking, enjoy the hand-carved redwood seating group. Aluminum garden furniture in a Victorian style was available, too. To help your garden grow, look into the large selection of tools, pruners, and garden accessories. Everything for the gardener was available in this full-color catalog. All you add is sunshine and enthusiasm! An unconditional guarantee was offered on all items. Orders shipped within one week of their receipt; more to customers on the east coast.

Sunshine Miniature Trees
7118 Greenville (214) 691-0127
Dallas, TX 75231 CK, MC, V, MO, PQ

Let a smile be your umbrella by letting a bonsai into your life. A little touch of the Orient, for indoors or outdoors, with a bonsai miniature tree. Add mystery to history while this delicate and intricate tree (that's as small as a houseplant) graces an entry table. They have beautiful bonsai trees, ranging in price from $7.98 to $1,000. Over 38 varieties of bonsai trees to mediate. They will deliver or ship anywhere and the staff is knowledgable.

Texas Greenhouse Co.
2524 White Settlement Road (817) 335-5447
Ft. Worth, TX 76107 CK, MC, V, COD, C/$4

Red-faced over greenhouse prices? There is no reason to be hot-headed over hothouses with Texas Greenhouse kits. (When you build your own greenhouse, only your plants will get steamed.) Since 1948, this company has manufactured their own greenhouses and accessories so their prices are factory-direct. About 15 to 20 brands are carried, including MODINE heaters and CHAMPION coolers. Prices are competitive. Most orders come in six to eight weeks; there is a one-year guarantee; a 15-percent restocking charge on returns. You'll have to put down a 50-percent deposit with your order, balance due on delivery.

Records, Tapes, and CDs

Hear ye, hear ye! Are your ears itching for some music? Scratch the itch, but avoid a pain in your pocketbook. Mail-order companies offer sound bargains on records and tapes. Loop-the-loop with cassette tapes of your favorite crooner, or get in the groove with CDs at irresistible prices. Whether you lull yourself to sleep with a lullaby, or set your eardrums to throbbing with the pounding and roaring of Heavy Metal as it crashes onto the sandy beach of your brain, you'll find what you want at a price you can afford. And that's a deal worth listening to.

Adventures in Cassettes
Metacom, Inc.
Dept. P200
5353 Nathan Lane — (800) 328-0108
Plymouth, MN 55442 — CK, MC, V, AE, D, C

Travel to a faraway land, solve a mystery, or take a trip into the past, all in the privacy of your own home. Adventures in Cassettes offers a selection of vintage radio shows, featuring Jack Benny, Gangbusters, Sherlock Holmes, Amos and Andy, and others; foreign-language tapes; children's audio tapes (so they can use modern media yet still use their imaginations); health and wellness programs; and, of course, music. Adventures' prices are competitive.

They accept returns within 30 days for refund, credit, or exchange, and most orders are delivered within two weeks.

Identify yourself as a *Great Buys By Mail* reader and get 25 percent off the price of the goods on your first order only. Offer expires February 1, 1994.

Barnes & Noble Bookstores, Inc.
(See **Books and Magazines**, p. **102**.)

Berkshire Record Outlet, Inc.
Route 102 Pleasant Street, RR1 (413) 243-4080
Lee, MA 01238 CK, MC, V, C/$2

Forget ephemeral popular music stores; this one's a classic. Berkshire's been around since 1974, selling classical records at classic prices. Closeouts and overruns on classical compact discs, LPs (dust off that old Victrola!), and cassettes are bound to perk up your ears, at prices lower than you'd pay elsewhere. There is a $2 charge for Berkshire's catalog, to pay for first-class postage (nothing tacky about these guys). Minimum order with credit cards is $15. Take a look at the catalog and you'll soon discover they ain't just whistling Dixie!

Bill's Records
8136 Spring Valley (214) 234-1496
Dallas, TX 75240 CK, MC, V, AE, PQ

Good golly, Miss Molly, do you like to dance? And rock 'n' roll? Catering to the young "in" crowd with what to wear and what to play and what to pin up. Standing still in this place is impossible. Jump and start. Even the staff was animated and knew their stuff, musically speaking. Love to rap? Talk and shout 'til the wee hours on the weekends. Never miss a beat. The inventory of records, cassettes, CDs, T-shirts, and posters makes your head spin. Some of the best prices on new and used tapes, CDs, collectible records, and rock memorabilia in the country. Incredible selection! And along came Bill's, no ordinary record store. Tune in to the star search here.

Bose Express Music
The Mountain, Dept. GBBM01
Framingham, MA 01701
(800) 451-2673 (orders); (508) 879-7330
CK, MC, V, AE, MO, C/$6 (refundable), PQ

Whatever your musical taste, you're sure to find a taste of it at Bose. They offer thousands of CDs and albums to workout, and movie videos at 10 percent to 30 percent less than prices found elsewhere. The catalog, nearly 250 pages, lives up to its promise of price, selection, and service with coupons and additional catalogs as they become available. Plus, its cost is refunded with your first order. Choose from a selection that includes everything from speed metal to opera—every album in print—from "the largest and most complete CD catalog in the world." Shipping and handling is $3.95 per order; price quotes are available. All products are guaranteed; defective merchandise will be replaced.

Coronet Books & CDs/Cassettes
311 Bainbridge Street
Philadelphia, PA 19147
(215) 925-2762
CK, MC, V, MO, C, PQ

Sound the fanfare! Coronet plays it straight with up to 30 percent off on a jazzy collection including 15,000+ recordings. Classical, rock, rhythm and blues, big band, soundtracks, Broadway musicals and shows, pop, and country selections are offered, and with orders of ten or more recordings, shipping is free. Blow it on music here; at Coronet, you can buy three times as much and rock 'til you drop.

Critics' Choice Video
800 Morse Avenue
Elk Grove Village, IL 60007
(800) 367-7765
CK, MC, V, AE, D, MO, C

Family videos, classic oldies, animated films, arts, science, sports, and fitness videos are some entertaining features in this color catalog. Everyone from Marilyn Monroe to Dirty Harry to Richard Simmons to keep your VCR smokin' and the price of movie-watching down—from $9.95 to about $20. New releases, alas, don't come so cheap; they're $94.95, and their price goes down in 30 to 60 days. Get fit, see the latest flicks, or even learn another language with the help of a video tape or two (or three, or four . . .). Books on films and filmmakers are also available and make great gifts for the movie buff in your life. Orders are delivered from five to seven days after Critics' Choice receives them; orders are accepted 24 hours a day, seven days a week.

Discount Books & Video, Inc.
P.O. Box 928
Vineland, NJ 08360-0928
(609) 691-7726
CK, MC, V, MO, C

If you're having trouble finding great prices on great books, the search stops here. Discount Books & Video has a name that pretty much says it all. They sell publishers' overstocks and other books, plus discount videotapes and audiotapes. Everything from fiction to politics (wait a minute; isn't that the same thing?), medicine to metaphysics, at savings of up to 90 percent! They offer CDs and tapes, too, including rock, classical, jazz, and opera, plus self-help tapes. Videos feature educational programs, oldies, and sports. They have a 30-day return policy; the minimum order is $15 with credit cards.

Double Time Jazz Records
1211 Aebersold Drive
New Albany, IN 47150
(812) 945-3142
CK, MC, V, MO, C

Double-Time is working overtime to bring you hard-to-find jazz records in half the time at half the price. Whew! Jamie Aebersold has made a name for himself (and apparently a street, too) in the jazz business. Collectors know who to call for cutouts, out-of-print, and esoteric jazz selections from the '30s to the present. Mainstream, bebop, modern, and swing are well represented in this huge inventory. Their 88-page catalog lists over 5,000 selections, with over 1,000 LPs alone.

Forty-Fives
P.O. Box 358
Lemoyne, PA 17043-0358
CK, MO, C/$2 w/SASE

These stars in the record business are twice as cool at half the price. Both new and collectible oldie 45s have made the charts at Forty-Fives—the price chart, that is. Forty-Fives offers a price list of singles from the '50s to the present, and even tells you if the record's in good shape. Most of them cost about $1, and, as any modern music lover will tell you, that's historical in itself. (CD and cassette singles go for quite a bit more!) Here's how it works: You send in your order, and Forty-Fives lets you know whether they have your requests in stock (the price list titles are subject to change). If you're the C & W type, send them $1 and ask for their country list. Get your hands on some divine vinyl before there's no more to be had!

Harmonia Mundi-USA

3364 S. Robertson Boulevard — (310) 559-0802
Los Angeles, CA 90034 — MC, V, C/$3, PQ

Send your money to Harmonia Mundi—not for Blondie but for imported recordings on the HARMONIA MUNDI, RCA, HYPERION, UNICORN-KANCHANA, CHANDOS, PERFORMANCE RECORDINGS, HONG KONG, and ORFEO labels among others. This company, a division of Harmonia Mundi-France, is a wholesaler to record stores, although they will help individuals get unusual items. If you know records, this may be a valuable source for hard-to-find titles.

Hunter Audio-Photo Ltd.

(See **Buying Clubs and One-Stop Shopping**, p. **115**.)

J & R Music World

(See **Electronics: Audio/Video/Stereo/TVs**, p. **187**.)

Kicking Mule Records, Inc.

P.O. Box 158 — (707) 926-5312
Alderpoint, CA 95511-0158 — CK, MC, V, D, MO, C, PQ

If you've got the blues for some great recordings, Kicking Mule may have just the kick your music collection needs. Folks who've got it real bad for folk, blues, and acoustical sounds of music can find tapes and records by their favorite artists in this catalog, and the prices are great. Most are *well* below list prices; during sales, prices can plunge even farther! CDs, for example, were selling routinely for $12.95; LPs, for around $1.50 each. Kicking Mule's own label is represented, of course, along with ROUNDER, SUGAR HILL, and others. There are also video recordings to help you learn to play the guitar, dulcimer, or banjo. Kicking Mule offers price quotes by phone or letter.

Music in the Mail
P.O. Box 1
Brightwaters, NY 11718 CK, C/$1

We've received plenty of notes in the mail, but never one with such sound advice. Music in the Mail, in business since 1969 and selling classical CDs only since 1984, operates as a cooperative classical buyers' service for serious record collectors. They offer factory-sealed classical CDs, and, as of 1991, used classical LPs, for $1 or less above the dealers' cost. That adds up to savings of about 33 percent. CHANDOS, TELARC, HARMONIA MUNDI, HUNGAROTON, and 250 other classical CD labels are available. Defective CDs are exchanged only for the same title; orders are sent out in 30-day cycles. They request that all correspondence be accompanied by a SASE.

Musiquarium Used CD Club
P.O. Box 7151
Rochester, MN 55903 CK, MO, B/$2 (refundable)

Swim in this groovy ocean and school yourself in saving on the green stuff on CDs. They may be even cheaper here than in your local used-CD store. A six-month Musiquarium membership is $7.50 (or $12 a year), which gets you a bimonthly newsletter listing CDs other members are offering for sale. Rock, pop, country, jazz, soundtracks, and other categories are listed, and you can add titles of your own that you're looking to sell. For $2, you will get the latest newsletter and more membership information; if you join, the $2 will be deducted from your orders.

Publishers Central Bureau
(See **Books and Magazines**, p. **104**.)

The Record Hunter
507 Fifth Avenue (212) 697-8970
New York, NY 10017 CK, MC, V, AE, D, C

Got a minuet? If you've got a bad case of Saturday Night Fever and have been itching for some entertainment, step out in style to the classical big symphony sound of Mozart, Haydn, Beethoven, Schubert, Strauss, or Mendelssohn at good discounts. Names like Dvorak, Smetana, Borodin, and Khachaturian compose a Slavonic festival of sound. The Record Hunter has more than just classical music, though—a lot more! They stock records of all types of music and have one of the biggest selections of compact discs in the U.S. CDs range in price from $7.97 to $14.97. Another feature sets them apart: they operate a search service and will ferret out any record or title that is still in print. Most orders are received in seven to ten days.

Rose Records
214 S. Wabash Avenue (312) 987-9044
Chicago, IL 60604 CK, MC, V, C

Everything's coming up Rose's. Record prices can present a thorny problem, but this place can soft-petal a solution. While we never promised you a Rose bargain, albums at below-list prices smelled like a pretty sweet deal. Budding classical music lovers will find scores of selections, although folk, pop, blues, soul, and jazz albums also sprout in their catalog and are available for the picking. If you're like most folks, you'll receive your order in about a week. A nice arrangement for those who like to face the music without paying the piper.

Script City
(See **Books and Magazines**, p. **105**.)

Wholesale Tape and Supply Company
P.O. Box 8277 (800) 251-7228
Chattanooga, TN 37411 CK, MC, V, AE, D, COD, C, PQ

If you draw a blank when asked where blank tapes can be found for less, let us fill you in on Wholesale Tape and Supply. Their 30-page, black-and-white catalog features blank audio and video tapes, sold by length (10 minutes to 120 minutes are standard). They sell their own brand of audio tape, as well as tapes by other major brands, such as MEMOREX and MAXELL. They also offer videotape duplicating services. There is a minimum order of ten tapes for video; price quotes are available by phone.

Zip Video

14375 Myer Lake Circle
Clearwater, FL 34620
(800) 552-0211 (US)
(800) 551-0211 (Canada)
CK, MC, V, AE, B

Why leave town to see a new house, building site, or any other potential investment? Zip Video, in business since 1989, zips to the location for you, films the object or site in detail according to your specifications, and returns with a videotape, saving you from ever having to leave the house. Boats, cars, property, homes, and more can be assessed from your living room, saving you hundreds or thousands of dollars, not to mention time. Video costs start at $100 and vary with each assignment, your choice of Hi-8, VHS, Beta, or Super VHS tapes. Videos are delivered in 24 hours.

Sewing Machines and Notions

Sew? Sew buttons. And bows. Bangles. And bright shiny beads. Baste, hem, and haw no more for these needles can set the fabric straight. For a wide assortment of sewing needs and notions, as well as the machines, themselves, thread your bobbin to the stars in this section. Tie a yellow ribbon around your finger so you don't forget to shop-by-phone.

A. Feibusch Corporation
30 Allen Street — (212) 226-3964
New York, NY 10002 — CK, MO, PQ (SASE)

Zip to Feinbusch for zippers of all kinds! For over 50 years, they've been selling big zippers, little zippers, red zippers, blue zippers—you name the size or color, they've got their teeth in it. At 50 percent below retail, you can zip up YKK and other brand-name zippers, and if they don't have what you want (hard to imagine), they'll make you a custom zipper to fill the bill. They carry a colorful assortment of threads, too, as well as other sewing notions. Sorry, no catalog, but you can mail a request with a SASE (and fabric swatch, if possible or necessary), to help them match colors. They ship worldwide.

Bee Lee Co.
P.O. Box 36108
2714 Bomar Avenue (214) 351-2091
Dallas, TX 75235 CK, MC, V, COD, C

Bee Lee-ve us when we say this is *the* source for "sewing supplies with a Western accent." With 191 different colors and styles of Western snap fasteners and trims, you'll have the C & W crowd sewn up in no time. You'll snap to attention, too, when you see their tremendous selection of snaps and their excellent prices! Trims, threads, buttons, interfacings, and zippers from the finest manufacturers are also displayed in their free 24-page color catalog. Brands include WISS scissors, DRITZ notions, and WHITE sewing-machine needles priced well below retail. Most merchandise is discounted between 20 percent and 50 percent. Shipping charges are standard: on orders up to $5, it's $1.25; the maximum charge is $2.50 for orders over $20. Most orders are shipped in two to three working days maximum.

Beitman Co., Inc.
170 Elm Street (203) 333-7738
Bridgeport, CT 06604 CK, MO, C

Tired of buttoning your head against the wall? Let Beitman and the Boy Wonder blast out of the Beit-cave in the Beit-mobile and race to your aid. This company custom-covers belts and buttons from fabric, leather, suede, or even plastic that you supply. It's a way of getting the buttons and accessories to match the materials in your own home-sewn garments. Everything is made-to-order, except leather tabs and some buckles. Prices are often lower than those found in custom-sewing shops, usually about 10 percent less. There is a $5 minimum order, and all merchandise is guaranteed machine-washable. Shipping is paid by the company; your order will probably arrive in about a week. Pick up the Beit-phone or write to put these not-so-comic superheroes in stitches.

The Button Shop
P.O. Box 1065, Dept. GBBM (708) 795-1234
Oak Park, IL 60304 CK, MC, V, C

Full-price buttons and other "basic sewing supplies" will have you in stitches once you've seen them for 30 percent to 50 percent off at The Button Shop. They began in 1900 with tailor supplies, and 40 years later went into the mail-order business. Today, with its fourth-generation button masters, The Button Shop is as reliable as it is economical, offering zippers for trousers, skirts, necklines, jackets, and coat linings, plus thread, cuffs, scissors, tailors' chalk, sewing-machine oil, and a whole lot more. The brands aren't sew-sew, either: TALON, DRITZ, PRYM, and YKK were some of the names we button-holed. Their best-selling items are zippers cut to any length up to 120", black and white elastic, and bulk items. Send them a fabric swatch and they'll find matching thread and buttons. Returns are accepted within 30 days; they ship the same day you order via UPS.

Clotilde, Inc.
1909 S.W. 1st Avenue (800) 545-4002 (customer service)
Ft. Lauderdale, FL 33315-2100 (800) 772-2891 (order line)
CK, MC, V, MO, C

If waiting for your department-store credit bill every month keeps you on pins and needles, maybe you should take up sewing. Clotilde got the notion to compile a catalog of hard-to-find notions such as glass-head silk pins, deerskin "pioneer" thimbles, a "third hand" to speed up hemming and embroidery work, and many more. We found patterns and books for smocking, quilting, and even French hand sewing. The discounts run about 20 percent on all items listed in the attractive (and fun!) 76-page color catalog.

Derry's Sewing Center
430 Street Ferdinand (314) 837-6103
Florissant, MO 63031 MC, V, MO, B/$1 (SASE)

Derry's needles the retail competition with up to 40 percent off on sewing machines and parts. Follow the thread of discounts to SINGER, SIMPLICITY, and NECCHI machines and PANASONIC vacuum cleaners. They also offer a service department if your sewing machine warranty's still intact. Call or write for a quote on the machine of your dreams; otherwise, $1 and a long SASE will get you a brochure.

Discount Appliance Centers
(See Appliances (Large and Small), p. **40**.)

Ident-ify Label Corp.
P.O. Box 204
Brooklyn, NY 11214-0204 CK, B

Crafters will find personalized labels to sew into their gifts available from this mail-order company. Printed in red and black on durable white cotton, the labels are 2½- by 1¹⁄₁₆-inch with pinked edges. Several label styles are available. Campers will find a less expensive tape that can be sewn onto everything. Allow two to three weeks for delivery.

MidAmerica Vacuum Cleaner Supply Co.
(See **Vacuums**, p. **514**.)

Newark Dressmaker Supply, Inc.
6473 Ruch Road
P.O. Box 20730, Dept. 0909 (215) 837-7500
Lehigh Valley, PA 18002-0730 CK, MC, V, D, C

Sew you're looking for oceans of notions, materials, and supplies? Find needles, hand and sewing thread in bulk, displayed in this company's 59-page catalog. They carry basic fabrics like muslin, crinoline, and buckram. The LILY line of crochet cottons and weaving supplies, elastic, zippers, ribbons, bindings, bobbins, doll-making supplies, craft felt, and much more are also available. Discounts range from 10 percent to 50 percent off, with bigger discounts with bigger orders. (They'll give a $2 gift on orders of $25 and more.) The best buys are probably on appliqués; they're 50 percent off. More savings are built-in; you'll automatically save 10 percent on orders over $50. Shipping is $2.50 for orders under $10; $2.75 for orders more than $10. Delivery is within seven working days.

Sewin' in Vermont
84 Concord Avenue (800) 451-5124
St. Johnsbury, VT 05819 (802) 748-3803 (VT residents)
CK, MC, V, COD plus $2.50, B, PQ

"Why pay through the nose when you can save throuth the mail?" Sewin' in Vermont has sewn up the market on mail-order sewing machines with low, low prices that will keep you in stitches. We found a common thread of excellent values running between domestic as well as foreign-brand sewing machines. Their most popular brand is SINGER, as you'd expect, but PFAFF, a European model, is also in demand. Prices of about 30 percent below retail on most models won't leave you hemming and hawing. Inventory is maintained on the premises: credit-card orders are shipped the same day; orders paid by check are delayed until the check clears. (A stitch in time saves—period.) Merchandise is returnable for 30 days; refunds or exchanges are made depending on the problem. Write for manufacturers' brochures and price lists; soon you'll be bob, bob, bobbin' along.

Singer Sewing Center of College Station
1667 Texas Avenue South — (800) 338-5672
College Station, TX 77840 — CK, MC, V, D, PQ

You'll burst into song when you catch sight of the savings at SINGER. Their sewing machines and vacuums are humming for 20 percent to 40 percent less. Brands they carry include their own, as well as PANASONIC, JUKI, PRINCESS, HOOVER, EUREKA, and RICCAR. The SINGER 9113 model, which lists for $579, can be mail-ordered for just $295. (They're playing our song.) Or get in tune with a PANASONIC 6347 vacuum for $245, retail $299.95. They guarantee all merchandise, but offer no refunds, and their exchanges are limited. Check out their store locations in Houston and Waco, TX, and Pittsburg, KS, when in the area.

Solo Slide Fasteners, Inc.
166 Tosca Drive
P.O. Box 528 — (800) 343-9670
Stoughton, MA 02072 — CK, MC, V, AE, MO, COD, C, PQ

Got a notion to sew? Sew does Solo Slide, and they'll help with tailoring supplies like TALON zippers, pins and needles, elastic, scissors, buttons, zipper parts (that's where the "Slide" part comes from), sewing machines by SINGER, and more. We couldn't keep our lips zipped about saving up to 50 percent on sewing needs of all kinds; even acolytes were raring to make it themselves. Fasten your eyes on their free catalog (about 30 pages), or call for a price quote. They have a 30-day return policy and a $25 minimum order.

Suburban Sew 'N Sweep, Inc./The Sewing Machine Outlet
8814 Ogden Avenue (800) 642-4056; (708) 485-2834
Brookfield, IL 60513 CK, MC, V, AE, D, B

Relax at Suburban, your store-next-door for up to half off on sewing machines and vacuums. The names are familiar: WHITE and SINGER sewing machines and ORECK vacuum cleaners. Four-thread sergers were a popular item at $279. SINGER electronic machines started at $479. Suburban became a family operation in 1975, but was a family-owned franchise for 21 years before *that*. Brochures are free for the asking, and price quotes are available by phone. Returns are accepted three days after receipt of order.

Shoes, Boots, and Hats

You'll take a shine to the fancy footwork listed in this section. In fact, it's a "shoe-in"! How about buying a pair of old-fashioned cowboy boots, just for kicks? Substantial savings could spur you on. And if Chief Big Foot's been on the warpath lately, don't criticize until you've walked a mile in his moccasins. Maybe he doesn't know about all the size AAAAA to EEEE shoes available by mail. For loafers, tassels, topsiders, saddles, espadrilles, or sneakers, look here first for special buys. You'd be a heel not to.

Boot Town
10838 N. Central Expressway (800) 222-6687
Dallas, TX 75231 CK, MC, V, AE, D, DC, CB, C, PQ

One of Texas's finest boot merchants mails his boots out of town for the same great discounts. Over 30 top-quality brands are available: LUCCHESE, TONY LAMA, RIOS, JUSTIN, DAN POST, NOCONA, ACME, LARRY MAHAN . . . in the most exotic skins of lizard, snake, ostrich, antelope, cowhide, and more. Sizes 6½ to 13 for men, 4 to 10 for women, and children's sizes. Call for customer assistance with the brand and size and Boot Town will ship within a few days. They also carry the most popular "name blank" belts, hats by RESISTOL and other major brands, and a variety of buckles including CRUMRINE initials. Western shirts and jeans by LEVI, WRANGLER, LEE, and PANHANDLE SLIM, to boot. Expect your order to arrive in about two weeks. They'll give refunds or exchanges on unworn boots; there's no restocking charge on returns.

Cahall's Department Store/Cahall's Brown Duck Catalog
(See **Apparel: Family**, p. **10**.)

Capezio Factory Store
Southwest Outlet Center
I-35 NE, Suite 107 (817) 582-7396
Hillsboro, TX 76645 CK, MC, V, AE, D, MO, PQ (Phone)

If the shoe's price fits, buy it. Capezio's factory stores sell shoes by big names at small prices: ROCKPORT, DEXTER, PAPAGALLO, LIZ CLAIBORNE, BANDOLINO, ARPEGIO, and others leave their footprints on the sands of time. Don't be poorly shod when you can step in style and still save. Call for a price quote with precise information about the brand, style, color, and size shoe you want.

Chernin's Shoes
1001 S. Clinton (312) 922-5900
Chicago, IL 60607 CK, MC, V, C

Our hearts churned after discovering Chernin's. We didn't even have to butter up our husbands to step aside so we could order our shoes. Thousands of famous brands are sold at reasonable prices, like EASY SPIRITS, usually $72, for $54. Extra-narrow, extra-wide, extra-long, extra-short . . . size 'em up. Their selection of wingtips, oxfords, demi-boots, boat mocs, hiking boots, penny flats, pumps, boots, and athletic shoes for men, women, and children is an amazing "feet." They have several locations in the Chicago area, but you don't have to walk a miracle mile to save on soles. Put your foot down, and shop by phone.

Clover Nursing Shoe Company
(See **Health and Medical**, p. **313**.)

Dazian, Inc.
(See **Fabrics and Upholstery**, p. **193**.)

Deerskin Place
(See **Apparel: Family**, p. **11**.)

Hanover Shoe Company
440 North Madison (800) 426-3708; (717) 633-8400
Hanover, PA 17331 CK, AE, D, CB, MO, C

Hand over the shoes, and make sure the price is right! At Hanover, medium-to-better-quality shoes by ROCKPORT, TIMBERLAND, NIKE, NEW BALANCE, CLARKS OF ENGLAND, and (who else?) HANOVER were a shoo-in for a great deal. How does 40 percent to 60 percent off the retail price of men's and women's shoes grab you? Step up for PALM BEACH brand suits, too, as well as shirts and ties. This nationwide chain has its headquarters in Hanover, but their catalogs will bring them right to your door.

Just Justin
1505 Wycliff Avenue (800) 292-BY-A-BOOT
Dallas, TX 75207 (214) 630-2858 (Dallas residents)
CK, MC, V, AE, D, C

Are high-priced cowboy boots about to put you on Boot Hill? Get some relief! Discounts run 40 percent to 70 percent off normal retail here—that should spur you on to action! The selection's great (they have over 20,000 pairs of boots in stock), but just as you'd expect with a name like Just Justin, you won't find any labels besides JUSTIN. To order, send your size in regular shoes (men's or women's) and Justin will send you the size you need. Shipping's preset at $10 for a pair of boots; you'll probably receive your order in about a week to ten days. They'll exchange or give refunds if there's a problem.

Justin Discount Boots & Cowboy Outfitters
P.O. Box 67 (800) 677-BOOT; (817) 648-2797
Justin, TX 76247 CK, MC, V, C

Check out this color catalog for a real discount hoe-down. Over 50 pages of how the West was won wearing westernwear, including shirts, coats, WRANGLER jeans, and, of course, JUSTIN boots. Slip into a pair in a variety of styles, or rope a belt up to 40 percent off retail. Justin gives price quotes by phone or letter. Unworn returns are accepted.

Manny's Millinery Supply Co.
26 W. 38th (212) 840-2235
New York, NY 10018 CK, MC, AE, V, MO, C/$2, PQ

This company is no longer veiled in secrecy. Hats off to Manny's for an average savings of 33 percent on hats, bridal accessories, and "millinery supplies": bugle-bead appliqués, trims, fringes, buttons, feathers, fabric flowers, braid, hat stretchers, hat boxes, display racks, and more. Hundreds of hats fill the catalog, in straw, felt, and fabric. Fabric-covered hat forms are available, too, as well as bridal headpieces, lace parasols, gloves in velvet and satin, beaded and jeweled hatpins, boas, fans, ring pillows . . . the list goes on. Bear in mind that the minimum order for hats is three (buy fewer and you must buy at least $15 in other merchandise); for other items, the minimum order is $25. Orders may be shipped all over the world, and they'll give you a price quote over the phone.

Masseys Direct Footwear Merchants
601 Twelfth Street (800) 462-7739
Lynchburg, VA 24504 CK, MC, V, AE, D, MO, C

Masseys says they have your size, and with widths from AAAAA to EEEE, sizes 3 to 14, we don't doubt it. Masseys sells women's pumps, dress shoes, flats, slings, espadrilles, sandals, loafers, shoes for walking, cross-training, and tennis, and much more. Names include REEBOK, EVAN-PICONE, EASY SPIRIT, COBBIE, BIRKENSTOCK, BASS, and many more for working, playing, or a night on the town. Massey's prices are reasonable, and they offer a free 31-day "trial," details of which are included with each order. Add $4.95 to cover shipping and handling "for as many pairs as you like."

Minnetonka-By-Mail
P.O. Box 444, Dept. GBBM (212) 364-6266; (212) 365-7033
Bronx, NY 10458 CK, MO, C/$1

Get the real thing—Minnetonka accessories and casual footwear for the whole family—at prices comparable to and sometimes lower than the knock-offs seen in local stores each summer—up to 30 percent off. Minnetonka produces several interpretations of the fringed and tied moccasins with beaded "Thunderbird" design, with choice of sole type (crepe, boat, soft, and polyurethane, etc.) A 16-page catalog shows off a variety of boots, booties, and more at prices from about $15 to $60. They offer a 60-day refund or exchange policy; most orders are delivered in a week to ten days.

Okun Brothers Shoes
356 East South Street, Dept. GBBM93 (800) 433-6344
Kalamazoo, MI 49007 (616) 342-1536
CK, MC, V, D, MO, C

Oh Brother! Okun Brothers offers the easy way out when shopping for shoes. EASY SPIRIT pumps, DEXTER loafters, NEW BALANCE tennis shoes, ROCKPORT casuals, ADIDAS and REEBOK tennis shoes, and more for men and women at about 20 percent less than retail; often tapping out at 25 percent. (Now, that's what we call brotherly love!) Is your size hard to find? No problem. Women's sizes 4 to 13 in AAA–EEE widths, and men's sizes 6 through 16 in widths AA–EEEE, are available. Most orders are delivered within five to ten days, and satisfaction is guaranteed. The catalog we saw included a special offer of $5 off on orders of two pairs of shoes; $10 off for three pairs.

Reader special: $5 off when you mention *Great Buys By Mail*.

One Shoe Crew
86 Clavela Avenue
Sacramento, CA 95828

Join this crew if your feet are two different sizes, or you're an amputee, have a clubfoot, wear a brace, or have some other problem affecting one foot. One Shoe Crew will set you up with a partner to share the half of the pair you don't use. There's no charge to register for the service, but there's a small fee when a partner is found. Just write to them with the following information: name, address, telephone number, shoe size, width, and an idea of what you're looking for.

Orchard Street Bootery
75 Orchard Street (212) 966-0688
New York, NY 10002 CK, MC, V, AE, DC, PQ

We almost couldn't see the tree-mendous discounts through the forest of inventory at Orchard. There's nothing seedy about this establishment—when it comes to footwear, they're the apple of our eye. You can't help but pick something from Orchard's crop of shoes for the well-heeled woman. MARTINEZ VERLO, PETER KAISER, and others are available in leather loafers sandals, slippers, and evening wear. Prices are unseasonably reasonable at 25 to 30 percent below retail, but the usual harvest is 20-percent savings on shoes to cover sizes 5 to 10, in B and C widths. There are no refunds; they exchange or give store credit only. Orders go out the same day as received. Write or call for more information; be sure to have the style and model number of the pair you want.

Road Runner Sports
(See **Sporting Goods and Apparel**, p. **462**.)

Sara Glove Company, Inc.
(See **Apparel: Family**, p. **20**.)

The Sole Source
8400 A Hilltop Road (800) 827-3765
Fairfax, VA 22031 CK, MC, V, MO, B, PQ

They're all heart when they saved your soles. And being as they're the only authorized ROCKPORT and CLARKS OF ENGLAND repair center in the country, they qualify as the "Sole Source." In business since 1983, they'll repair *any* shoes, with your satisfaction guaranteed. Resoling, cleaning and polishing uppers, new laces, and minor repairs of eyelets are optional. Expect shoes to spend four to five days laid up in the shop, plus transport time.

Wide World of Sporting Goods
(See **Sporting Goods and Apparel**, p. **469**.)

Zoo Shoes
9848 Harwin Drive (713) 780-8858
Houston, TX 77036 CK, MC, V, MO, PQ

If your little animals are restless, take 'em to the Zoo! Zoo Shoes will keep your kids and your wallet happy, with kids' jogging shoes with animal motifs. Velcro closures are easy for little hands, and sturdy elastic under the animal faces makes for easy on and off. There's a corresponding animal footprint on the tread, too! Sizes are infants 1 to 4, child 5 to 12, and youth 12½ to 3, with monkeys, raccoons, dinosaurs, frogs, penguins, koalas, and killer whales making up the menagerie. Adult's shoes are available, too, by REEBOK, NIKE, LA GEAR, FILA, and CHAMPION (Zoo's own brand). Call for a price quote on the shoes of your choice.

Sporting Goods and Apparel

Whether you're a middle-aged athlete fighting off flabby thighs and a growing paunch, or a superbly conditioned young adult with the body of a Greek god, getting into the swim of things is what counts. Here you will find everything you'll need for sports, indoors or out. From basketballs to bass lures by mail, you'll sink or swim with the savings here. When ordering hiking boots or running shoes, always send along an outline of your foot since sizes can vary, even within the same brand. If you telephone for information, ask if there's a floor model of what you're looking for that's on sale. Buying a floor model is a great way to save even more on keeping with your fiscal regime.

Allyn Air Seat Co.
18 Millstream Road — (914) 679-2051
Woodstock, NY 12498 — CK, MO, COD, B (SASE)

Who cares about "fanny fatigue"? Lots of people, that's who. If you are a peddle pusher, truck driver, taxi driver, cycle rider, or just going down the highway, you care about your derriere. Is your rump in the dumps? Never fear, Allyn Air Seat Co. is here. We found the perfect solution for tired tooshies. Allyn's offers air cushions for just about everyone and you won't be paying out the bazooka for them. An air-filled seat cover for a motorcycle was only $35, including shipping. The model attaches in minutes and stores easily when not in use. The seats bring up the rear only one-fourth inch and never need refilling. No ifs, ands, or butts about it—these seats are the "kiss of comfort." They also offer covers for small tractors and snowmobiles. Here's a treat for your seats: the prices. They are up to 50 percent below retail, and deliveries are mailed immediately upon order. So move your tail and get your order in the mail.

Alpine Range Supply Co.
5482 Shelby (817) 572-1242
Ft. Worth, TX 76140 CK, MC, V, D, MO, PQ

Shoot straight from the hip and save a few shells. This company supplies hunting-related reloading equipment, primers, casings, presses for pistols, books, and more that will save you about 10 percent (more during sales). Rifle through their inventory by phone for a quote; or when you're in the Dallas/Ft. Worth area, practice on any one of their four pistol ranges, a rifle range, three skeet fields, and a trap field.

Austad's
P.O. Box 5428 (800) 759-4653
Sioux Falls, SD 57196-0001 CK, MC, V, AE, DC, C

Comó está, Austad? If you've been engolfed with the urge to hit a little white ball, bogie on down and putt in an order here. Since 1963, Austad's has stocked a complete line of quality golf gear (RAM, WILSON, MACGREGOR, and other leading manufacturers) at prices up to 40 percent less than retail. With an outstanding selection at fair prices, Austad's won't put a divot in your green. Their full-color catalog features clubs, bags, carts, shoes, training aids, sportswear, accessories, gifts, and even exotic golf vacations. Many items are made exclusively for Austad's by leading golf manufacturers. Orders are shipped within 48 hours, usually by UPS, so most orders are received within one week, two weeks maximum. If golf is your handicap, this store and mail-order company should treat you in a fairway.

Bart's Water Ski Center, Inc.
P.O. Box 294 (800) 348-5016; (219) 834-7666
North Webster, IN 46555 CK, MC, V, AE, D, COD, C

Are you having trouble keeping your head above waterskiing costs? We didn't find that sink-or-swim attitude at Bart's. He carries slaloms, ski vests, swimsuits, T-shirts, and many other waterskiing accessories. Save up to 40 percent on toys for fun in the sun. You'll be jumping over the wakes when you see his lake of brand names: JOBE and AMERICAN, to mention a couple. Would we KIDDER you? Just look at the bargains from O'BRIEN and CONNELLY. What a hotdog of a deal! Bart's 48-page, full-color catalog is especial-ski nice. You won't get splashed in the face if you don't like your order; Bart accepts returns up to 30 days for any reason.

Bass Pro Shops
(See **Boating Supplies**, p. **97**.)

Berry Scuba Co.
6674 N. Northwest Highway (800) 621-6019
Chicago, IL 60631 CK, MC, V, AE, D, C, PQ

Full retail is all wet. Don't get soaked when you go for good prices on scuba gear. The 40-page Berry Scuba catalog will get you out of that shark pool and into their own line of scuba gear: fins, masks, tanks, diving watches, spears, and more at wholesale prices. You can save as much as 40 percent on NIKON, DEEP SEA, U.S. TECH, SEATEC, and other big names in the scuba biz. Call for a price quote or a copy of their free catalog.

Bike Nashbar
4111 Simon Road (800) NASHBAR
Youngstown, OH 44512-1343 CK, MC, V, D, C

Sports enthusiasts will move right along to catch the bargains in this biker's shopping bible. For both the serious and semi-sedentary biker, Bike Nashbar carries the finest equipment at the finest prices we've seen in a long time. Racing and recreational bikes, touring bikes, and street bikes are all available from this company. Major brands, such as SHIMANO, SUNTOUR, and the Bike Nashbar brand were carried at up to 40 percent off retail price. Accessories such as bike pumps, water bottles, shoulder holders, helmets, shoes, and mirrors were included in the tour de bargains. Already own a bike you just can't part with? Chances are, you can order its repair and replacement parts through this catalog, such as chains, brake levers, cranksets, and flywheels. Deluxe seats, tires, fenders, and tool kits are also available at discount prices. Indoor enthusiasts will also appreciate the stationary trainers to keep in shape year-round. Sporty racing jerseys, caps, and sunglasses round out the racing gear. Orders receive fast shipping and a 100-percent guarantee of satisfaction.

Bowhunters Warehouse, Inc.

P.O. Box 158
1045 Ziegler Road
Wellsville, PA 17365

(717) 432-8611 (orders)
(717) 432-8651 (customer service)
Certified Check, MC, V, COD, C

We wanted to talk to an expert, so we asked William to Tell us where to target in on discount hunting bows. (We figured he must know something—he was wearing an Arrow shirt.) Since he aimed to please, we got the point instead of the shaft. It's no surprise he referred us here—this company is the world's largest archery distributor with over 7,500 bows in stock. BROWNING, BEAR, JENNINGS, TSE, DARTON, and MARTIN hunting bows can all be sighted in their 136-page catalog at a discount! Tree stands, targets, broadheads, camouflage clothing, and accessories were also available. Less discriminating single girls a-quiver with the notion of doing a little beau-hunting can even find a selection of turkey calls to help them bag a Tom (or Dick or Harry). Bowhunters Warehouse carries over 100 different brands with discounts running 40 percent off retail. The best bets for bargain-hunting come during the Christmas season. There's a $15 minimum order; most orders are shipped within 24 hours.

Cabela's

812 13th Avenue
Sidney, NE 69160

(800) 237-4444 (orders)
(800) 237-8888 (customer service)
CK, MC, V, C

Anyone for singing praises in a Cabela's choir? While we're big believers in being in harmony with nature and in tune with the outdoors, our voices may be a bit too corn-husky for this Nebraska firm. Prices are good—from 10 percent to 75 percent off on their own brand of high-quality outdoor gear. They handle all kinds of equipment and clothes for fishing, hunting, and camping (but no guns), with their own brand of down jackets being particularly popular. There is no restocking charge and no minimum order. Five catalogs are issued annually.

Campmor
P.O. Box 997 (800) 526-4784; (201) 445-5000
Paramus, NJ 07653-0997 CK, MC, V, AE, D, MO, C

Get on a camping campaign with Campmor! Prices are as much as 50 percent off on brand-name camping and outdoor supplies. Tents, goose-down sleeping bags, bicycle touring accessories, backpacks, COLEMAN stoves, and lots more—everything you'll need to survive in the outdoors is displayed in their 120-page catalog. Other brands you'll discover include WOOLRICH, NORTH FACE, and COLUMBIA. We compared the price of VICTORINOX, the original Swiss-Army knife, with the price charged by a local retailer and found a 30-percent savings. Refunds are given within six months of your purchase. The minimum phone order is $20.

Central Skindivers
160-09 Jamaica Avenue (718) 739-5772
Jamaica, NY 11432-6111 MC, V, AE, D, PQ (SASE)

Get in the swim with scuba gear from Central Skindivers. You won't feel the sting of retail; here's a ray of discount sunshine with up to 40 percent off on suits, masks, fins, and other gear. Flip for DACOR, SHERWOOD, SEATEC, and other names in the diving game. They aren't flops in the shipping department, either; that's included in the price. There is a $75 minimum on credit-card orders.

Cheap Shot Inc.
294 Route 980 (412) 745-2658
Canonsburg, PA 15317 CK, MO, C

If you're not gun shy, fire away at full price and limited selections! Cheap Shot has been covering your gun and ammunition needs from A to Z (not just the popular brands) since 1976, and is even listed with the Better Business Bureau. Their 16-page black-and-white catalog will give you an idea of their inventory. They ship the day they receive your order. You can save as much as 30 percent on some items. Some restrictions and regulations apply; see the catalog for details.

Cycle Goods Corp.
2801 Hennepin Avenue South (800) 328-5213
Minneapolis, MN 55408 CK, MC, V, AE, DC, O, C, PQ

Are you failing your cycle class? Are you finding the high prices above your level? Maybe you need *The Handbook of CYCL-OLOGY*, published by Cycle Goods Corp. It will offer financial aid with savings of 10 percent to 40 percent and have you aceing the course. This handbook offers more than 100 brands of bicycles and related clothing, accessories, and parts. You'll pass your finals with flying colors with brands like KIRTLAND, CINELLI, OAKLEY, and others. We found scholarly deals on triwheel carriers, ATMOS pumps, and kickstands. We scheduled our classes in style, wearing NIKE shoes and AVOCET skin shorts. Cycle Goods has a liberal refund policy and a 30-day guarantee, so you won't have to cram for a refund. Pass Cycl-ology and graduate from high prices.

Dinn Bros.
68 Winter Street
P.O. Box 111 (413) 536-3816
Holyoke, MA 01041 CK, MC, V, C

There's a soccer (player) born every minute. Why else would the brothers Dinn sell so many trophies and plaques? (Just for kicks?) We saw every conceivable type of trophy, ribbon, medal, wall plaque, desk accessory, etc., in their 48-page catalog, with factory-direct wholesale prices up to 70 percent off retail. Swimmers, golfers, runners, bowlers, skiers, skaters, weight-lifters, tennis-baseball-basketball-football players, as well as speakers, champion dogs, horses, bulls, and big fish are all represented in walnut- and marble-based trophies. Up to 40 letters of engraving are free. Orders over $200 are shipped free (if prepaid or paid for by credit card).

Down Generation/Sylvia & Sons
(See **Apparel: Family**, p. **13**.)

Eisner Bros.
(See **Apparel: Family**, p. **13**.)

The Finals
21 Minisink Avenue, Dept. GBBM
Port Jervis, NY 12771
(800) 431-9111
(800) 452-0452 (NY residents)
CK, MC, V, AE, D, C

Just for the halibut, when you're serious about swimming, don't forget to take The Finals. Make a splash for less cash in their own brand of factory-direct swimsuits priced at $32 for women and $18 for men. Lycra suits for men and women are their most popular. Discounts are given on quantity purchases—they'll knock up to $9 off the price for 12 or more swimsuits in the same style number. We tracked down running gear such as brightly colored nylon lined shorts for $12 and matching tank top for $10. Warm-up pants in eight attractive colors were $32. Goggles, bags, swim caps, and other accessories, so it's no longer sink or swim. Count on a 10-percent team discount; $25 credit-card minimum; seven- to ten-day delivery time on most items.

Fish 'n' Shack
(See **Boating Supplies**, p. **98**.)

The Fitness Store
(See **Health, Fitness, and Vitamins**, p. **303**.)

Foxbat Golf Equipment
15105 Surveyor
Addison, TX 75244
(800) 933-2775; (214) 239-5200
CK, MC, V, AE, PQ

Get discontinued and closeout high-quality professional FOXBAT equipment at moderate prices from this golfing outlet. For those seeking a great deal on a pro line set of clubs that can even be custom-crafted to compensate for your handicap, these are the folks to call. Get into the swing of things with their golf bags, hats, and shirts, too. A PGA is on staff to answer any of your questions. The equipment, though, speaks for itself. One aspiring Arnold Palmer in Florida swears FOXBAT'S clubs improved his game by ten strokes. Their overall prices are affordable and up to par.

Golf Haus
700 N. Pennsylvania (517) 482-8842
Lansing, MI 48906 CK, MC, V, C, PQ

'Fore you swing into action and get teed off, tally up the savings at the Haus named #1 Discounter in America by *Family Circle*! With prices slicing 40 percent to 70 percent off retail, you can make your pitch to Golf Haus and save yourself a long drive, as well as some green. Golf Haus carries DUNLOP, WILSON, TITLEIST, HOGAN, PING, and MACGREGOR in putters, woods, irons, balls, accessories, and more. Best-sellers include LYNX V-Tech Drivers, at a list price of $310, sold here for $140 plus free headcover; and TOMMY ARMOUR 845 Irons 3-9PW, listed at $640, for $375. There's a $50 minimum order; exchanges or full refunds are given on returns. Most folks get their order in ten days. They ship freight free within the continental United States, and have a free catalog upon request.

Identify yourself as a *Great Buys* reader when you buy a complete set of clubs, woods, and irons for a *free* set of four headcovers, a $20 retail value.

Golfsmith International
10206 North I-H 35 (800) 456-3344 (in U.S. & Canada)
Austin, TX 78753 (512) 837-4810
CK, MC, V, D, COD, C

From a most humble beginning in the basement of Carl's Plainfield, NJ, house in 1969 and a few hundred dollars, Carl and his brother Frank Paul began a business that's going strong to this day. In fact, they might be the world's largest supplier of custom clubs, repair components, and accessories even though the majority of those sales outside of their Austin retail locations is by mail order. If you want to tighten your grip on prices, too, plan on saving 10 percent to 30 percent or more off suggested retail prices. Check out one of their catalogs, including one for clubmaking components and supplies, and one for accessory merchandise, including golf apparel, clubs, and more. The best discounts are available on their components, for those talented enough to build their own clubs. Orders are shipped via UPS ground; there is no minimum order.

Holabird Sports Discounters
9008 Yellow Brick Road
Baltimore, MD 21237
(410) 687-6400
CK, MC, V, B

A little birdie told us where you can save from 20 percent to 50 percent on major brand-name sporting goods. Holabird Sports Discounters will have you strutting proud as a peacock in REEBOK, PRINCE, SPALDING, WILSON, AVIA, and an entire flock of others. Whether you are into squash, racquetball, tennis, golf, or running, you can find all the accessories and equipment you need cheep, cheep at Holabird, "the most complete racquet/footwear company nationwide." We were happy as a lark about the bargains we found in their brochure. Holabird is a songbird of savings. Here is something to make you sing: They will ship your order within two days. Be a bird in paradise with Holabird. Returns are accepted with no restocking fee.

HTC, Inc.
(See **Apparel: Family**, p. **14**.)

Kirkham's Outdoor Products
3125 S. State Street
Salt Lake City, UT 84115
(800) 453-7756
(800) 486-4161 (UT residents)
CK, MC, V, AE, D, MO, COD, B, PQ

After a hard day of camping and hiking, at night we like to sleep intents-ly. Kirkham's carries the exclusive line of SPRINGBAT® tents, manufactured in their factory. Kirkham's tents are sold only factory direct, without dealers or distributors, resulting in a direct price to the consumer, so it's difficult to compare prices, although prices are certainly competitive. Price comparisons are difficult also because Kirkham's tents often have more features and use better quality materials in their construction than their competitors. Choose from many styles and sizes; from one-person pup tents (for dogged outdoor buffs), to family tents sleeping six (for those into group sacks). Kirkham's refund policy is hardly tent-ative: SPRING-

BAR® tents are warranted to be free from defects in material or workmanship for ten years. There's no restocking charge; most orders are shipped within 24 hours.

L.L. Bean
(See **Health, Fitness, and Vitamins**, p. **304**.)

Ladylike Ski Shop
203 N. Ballard
Wylie, TX 75098
(214) 442-5842
CK, MC, V, AE, MO, PQ

There is NO better source for skiwear in the country. We're talking 30 percent to 70 percent off on RAICHLE "VIVA" boots, COLUMBIA BUGABOO parkas, PACIFIC TRAIL jackets, COLUMBIA WHIRLIBIRDS, SUBELLO two-piece suits, and more for the entire family. From toddlers to XXXL men, you'll find all the gear to slush and slide. Now carrying equipment, too. Call for a price quote.

Las Vegas Discount Golf and Tennis
4405 Paradise Road
Las Vegas, NV 89109
(800) 933-7777; (702) 892-9999
CK, MC, V, AE, D, DC, CB, C, PQ

You have to know when to hold 'em and know when to sell 'em at a discount. Since 1974, Las Vegas has gambled on selling the very latest in golf and tennis equipment, at prices far below retail, and the gamble's paid off. Over 50 major brands in pro-line golf clubs, shoes, bags, racquets, balls, gloves, as well as a complete line of accessories are slotted in their company, and when we pulled the right lever, brands like WILSON, BEN HOGAN, PING, SPALDING, ST. ANDREWS, PRICE, and ELLESE came up. Tennis department expanding as we lobbed over to net some additional bargains. Love it! Discounts range from 20 percent to 40 percent. Most orders are delivered in seven to ten days. Returns are subject to a 10-percent restocking fee (if used or worn). Ninety percent of their merchandise is in stock; about 10 percent must be drop-shipped. They put all their cards in their free 48-page catalog (put out every six months) and continue to come up a winner.

Mega Tennis Products (Rayco)
1434 University Avenue (800) 228-2373
San Diego, CA 92103 CK, MC, V, COD, F, PQ

The string's the thing! Tighten those purse strings with savings on strings, tennis rackets, and racket-stringing machines at Rayco. Most of their customers are folks who've set up their own racket-stringing business, but that could be you. Stringing your own racket would save you the double markup on strings plus the labor charge. Delivery times vary: strings are stocked, and you can get them the next day if requested; rackets and stringing machines are drop-shipped from the manufacturer. (Some stringing-machine manufacturers are in Europe.) There's a $3 service charge on orders under $50.

Overton's Marine/Overton's Water Sports
(See **Boating Supplies,** p. **100**.)

Performance Bicycle Shop
P.O. Box 2741, Dept. 22609 (800) 727-2453
One Performance Way (919) 933-9113
Chapel Hill, NC 27515-2741 CK, MC, V, D, C

Go for it and perform like a champion (with a little help from Performance Bicycle). Their cycling apparel and equipment will have you rolling right along. They sell their own brand, as well as NIKE, BOLLE, SHIMANO, and others. Popular buys included PERFORMANCE rims starting as low as $25; their road and mountain tires, $12 and up; PBS helmets, $29 and up; and PBS gloves, $10 and up. Race into their full-color, 79-page catalog and ride out a winner. There is a 100-percent guarantee on all merchandise; orders are shipped via UPS and received in seven to ten business days.

Great Buys readers can get a *free* guide to bicycle maintenance and repair with their first order; be sure to ask.

Performance Diver
P.O. Box 2741, Dept. 60299 (800) 727-2453
One Performance Way (919) 933-9113
Chapel Hill, NC 27515-2741 CK, MC, V, D, C

How's this for making a big splash? You can save yourself around 25 percent when you buy the Performance brand. They make their own line of apparel and scuba-diving equipment, and stock merchandise by NIKE, BEUCHAT, BOLLE, CITIZEN, SEIKO, and others. Full quarter-inch NEOPRENE wetsuits were just $159.95 here (retailing at $300). One-hundred-percent Lycra skins were $39.95 ($100 retail); VITESSE regulators were $169.95 (retail $200); and Power Fins were just $29.95 ($60 retail). Come on in—the prices are fine!

Identify yourself as a *Great Buys* reader and be sure to request a free pair of sunglasses with your first order.

Performance Golf
One Performance Way, Dept. 800009 (800) 727-2453
Chapel Hill, NC 27515-2741 (919) 933-9113
CK, MC, V, D, C

Drive in a great deal on golf apparel and equipment. Prices on Performance goods are up to 50 percent less than other nationally advertised brands. In addition to their own line, they carry POWER-BILT, ADIDAS, SLOTLINE, ETONIC, H & B, and SPALDING. Clubs ranged in price from $189 to $799 for a full set. GORETEX rainsuits were $139 to $367, and golf shoes were priced from $40 to $135. Get in the swing and forget about trapping yourself in regular retail prices. There's a 100-percent customer satisfaction guarantee.

Pro Shop World of Golf
8130 N. Lincoln Avenue (800) 323-4047 (order line)
Skokie, IL 60077 (708) 675-5286
CK, MC, V, D, B

High prices are enough to knock the dimples off any Titleist, so why fall into the (sand) trap of paying retail? Stay away from the rough—you can stop driving and start to putter around at home if you trust a Pro. This place claims to have "the largest golf inventory in the world," with 24,000 square feet of selection. Hazards are few with names like WILSON, LYNX, MACGREGOR, BEN HOGAN, PING, RAM, SPALDING, and other brands in clubs, golf carts, golf balls, drivers, wedges, utility irons, shoes, and gloves—especially when prices are 20 percent to 50 percent off! PRO LINE golf equipment is their most famous line. They don't give refunds but do make exchanges. Credit-card orders are shipped the next day; orders paid by personal check are delayed until the check clears the bank. Most orders are received within seven days (inside the U.S.). The shipping charge is $6: there's a 10-percent restocking charge on nondefective, unused merchandise returns. Since everything is first quality, you can rest assured that when it comes to ordering a bag, shirt, etc., you won't find a hole-in-one. Their price list is free.

Professional Golf & Tennis Suppliers, Inc.
7825 Hollywood Boulevard (305) 981-7283
Pembroke Pines, FL 33024 CK, MC, V, AE, DC, CB, MO, B (SASE)

Hit it! If you can smash it with a racquet or slice it with a club, chances are you'll find it here. Tennis, squash, racquetball, and golf make for a mix of garb and gear in this catalog that'll leave you breathless. (We got worn out at the mere *thought* of playing all these sports.) We hate to drop names but . . . Professional offers TITLEIST, WILSON, MACGREGOR, and LYNX golf clubs and accessories, including bags, balls, gloves; tennis racquets, balls, and more from DUNLOP, WILSON, SPALDING, HEAD, and others; and squash equipment from VOIT and LEACH just to get your game plan in order. Step into their brochure and come home a swinger. Add additional three percent charge on Visa and MasterCard orders.

REI Co-op
1700 45th Street East (800) 426-4840 (orders)
Sumner, WA 98352-0001 (800) 828-5533 (customer service)
CK, MC, V, MO, C

Aside from their walk-in stores, REI has one of the best catalogs displaying outdoor clothing and equipment. Their niche is state-of-the-art climbing and camping gear, cross-country skiing, bicycling items, and fashion sportswear. Mountain-climbing gear is their claim to fame. (Jim Whittaker, one of the first Americans to climb Mt. Everest, was a former company president.) Mail-order prices are somewhat downhill from full retail. REI carries many top-quality products by famous-name manufacturers like JANSPORT, SIERRA DESIGNS, WOOLRICH, KELTY, and MOUNTAIN HOUSE foods, to name a few. Their own PEAK VALUE brand offers comparable quality to big-name brands but at reduced prices, a good way to save on the cost of outdoor recreational gear. REI's more than three million members save even more. For a $10 membership fee, you can share in the company's profits at year's end and receive a rebate of what usually amounts to about 10 percent of the cost of your year's purchases.

Road Runner Sports
6310 Nancy Ridge Road
Dept. BUYS
San Diego, CA 92121
(800) 662-8896 (customer service)
(800) 551-5558 (orders)
CK, MC, V, AE, D, MO, C

This company will run circles around its nearest competitors. Leave full-price retailers in the dust in fitness and running shoes, clothing and accessories for 20 percent less. ASICS, NEW BALANCE, REEBOK, and SAUCONY for shoes, and DOLFIN and HIND running apparel won't make you an also-ran. This family business, started in a garage in 1983, has grown to be "the nation's largest distributor of running shoes." Road Runner guarantees customer satisfaction; most orders are received in five to seven working days. Don't get caught paying full price. They also offer a Walking Catalog. Whether you walk, or run, you should never experience the agony of de-feet and pay through the nose.

Ruvel & Co., Inc.
(See **Surplus and Volume Sales**, p. **473**.)

Sailboard Warehouse, Inc.
300 S. Owasso Boulevard, Dept. GBBM
St. Paul, MN 55117
(800) 992-SAIL
(612) 482-9995
CK, MC, V, AE, D, C/$3.95

Shove off for adventure, and don't let the price of your sailing equipment sink your spirits. All major brands of sailboards, car racks, wetsuits, booms, and masts can be had at Sailboard Warehouse, at prices 15 percent to 50 percent less. Let the "largest retailer of sailboards in the U.S." set you on a course for everything from books and videos to sailing hardware. Safe delivery and satisfaction are guaranteed.

Great Buys readers receive the $3.95 catalog *free*.

Sampson & Deliah
7324 Reseda Boulevard, Suite 208
Reseda, CA 91335
CK, MO, C/$5 (refundable with order), PQ

Only an Olympian could have created the sexy, body-revealing leotards, swimsuits, and playwear featured in Corinna's Fitness Fashions. This catalog is inspiring enough to tape to your refrigerator, for "Corinna" is none other that Cory Everson, two-time Ms. Olympia body-building champ and owner of the ultimate '90s physique. Once you see how she looks in these great fitness outfits, you'll want to head straight for the gym. Her free $10 gift with orders over $100 is just added motivation. Shipping and handling costs ranged from $1 to $4, depending upon the cost of your order. Send the name of the manufacturer and the style number for a price quote.

Samuels Tennisport
7796 Montgomery Road
Cincinnati, OH 45236
(800) 543-1153
MC, V, AE, D, MO, C

This company's a smash at selling tennis, squash, racquetball, and badminton equipment at savings up to 35 percent. They're serving up HEAD, SPALDING, YONEX, PRINCE, SLAZENGER, WILSON, and EKTELON racquets, court shoes, running shoes, eyeguards, gloves, stringing machines, water bottles, grips, tapes, shuttles, and more. Popular buys included an EKTELON Strobe racquetball racquet, at a list price of $250, selling here for $175; NEW BALANCE 997 running shoes were $70 ($110 list); and a HEAD Discovery tennis racquet, at a list price of $325, was $279. Exchanges may be made with no fee, but a 15-percent restocking fee is charged on returns. Most orders are delivered within one week.

The Shotgun News
P.O. Box 669
Hastings, NE 68902
(800) 345-6923 (subscriptions only)
(402) 463-4589
CK, MC, V

We got a kick out of the reaction they triggered. This high-caliber publication aims to offer "the finest gun buys and trades in the U.S." Shoot, for only $20. You'll be hit with 36 issues; that's one issue three times per month (or 72 issues for $39). You can really get loaded on 108 issues for $58. If you want a sample copy to rifle through before you subscribe lock, stock, and barrel, send $3. After you subscribe, expect to wait four to six weeks before you receive your first issue.

Soccer International, Inc.
P.O. Box 7222 (703) 524-4333
Arlington, VA 22207-0222 (6:30 A.M. to 10:30 P.M. EST)
CK, MO, C/$2

Is your goal saving money? Well, soccer to you. With Soccer International, you can kick high prices away. Without much coaching, you can buy uniforms, equipment, books, games, novelties, bumper stickers, patches, and more—all with soccer motifs at savings up to 30 percent and more. Quantity discounts for quantity purchases possible. Nowhere else could we find soccer items in team quantities. That's the team spirit! Names like UMBRO, BRINE, and MITRE will have you scoring points in pre-season. For starlight soccer players, kick up a lighted soccer ball; for crib kickers, try a soccer-ball crib toy with a foot that kicks to music. If soccer has gone to your head, then you'll love their soccer caps that look like a soccer ball. There is a $15 minimum order.

Spike Nashbar
4111 Simon Road, Dept. GBM2 (800) 937-7453
Youngstown, OH 44512 CK, MC, V, D, MO, C

Have a ball at Spike Nashbar, or just walk a mile (or a million) in a volleyball player's shoes. Volleyball shoes for men and women by MIZUNO and AVIA, women's apparel by DANSKIN, and SPALDING balls were only a few of the offerings in a recent Spike Nashbar catalog, the headquarters for serious volleyball enthusiasts. From kneepads to nets to instructional videos, they'll Spike it to you for less. They offer a 100-percent-satisfaction guarantee, same-day shipping, and overnight delivery for an additional $2.85.

Sport Europa
7871 NW 15th Street
Miami, FL 33126
(800) 695-7000 (orders)
(800) 333-2188 (customer service)
(305) 477-9341 (Dade County residents)
CK, MC, V, AE, D, MO, C

Give your body a workout, but let your wallet rest for a change. Here you can save as much as 40 percent when you buy direct from the factory at Sport Europa. They offer their own brand of diving suits, running and cross-training wear, and apparel for aerobics and bodybuilding. Their 56-page color catalog features recreational clothing, too, for those who'd prefer to play less seriously. Warm up in their warm-ups, or resort to casual wear like stretch-fit pants. Either way, your budget gets a break.

Sport Shop
P.O. Box 340
Highway 11 North
Grifton, NC 28530
(800) 334-5778
CK, MC, V, D, MO, C

Hit the bulls-eye and aim for the Sport Shop catalog when tracking down 30-percent to 50-percent savings on archery and hunting equipment. Their 63-page catalog contained sport boots, cresting lacquers, arrow-making supplies, instructional videos, silencers and carrying slings, plus a host of other pointed items. Returns are accepted when accompanied by a note explaining the problem (a lover's quarrel is unacceptable). Orders are shipped within one to two days of their receipt.

Sportswear Clearinghouse
P.O. Box 317746Y3
Cincinnati, OH 45231-7746
(513) 522-3511
CK, MC, V, COD (only via UPS), B

Clear the way for up to 70 percent on overruns of printed sportswear with corporate logos, sports teams, or other written matter. T-shirts, sweatshirts, golf shirts, athletic socks, nightshirts, and more are available from a variety of different brands, which can't be determined beforehand, in youth sizes through adult extra large. T-shirts were five for $14.25, or ten for $27.90 plus shipping and handling. Five youth size Ts were $7.90. Unused returns are accepted within 30 days of their receipt. Money orders and charge orders are delivered in approximately five days; personal check orders take 18 to 20 days. Check out their gift offers on orders over $30.

Strand Surplus Senter
2202 Strand — (800) 231-6005 (charge orders only)
Galveston, TX 77550 — (409) 762-7397 (TX residents)
CK, MC, V, AE, B/$1 (refundable)

"The world's only surviving general government surplus store" is what the owners call it and they're right. We've been there: just blocks away from the beach, surrounded by the beautifully restored buildings downtown, and always full of enthusiastic shopping tourists. They've got everything from pith helmets (and appropriate machetes) to camouflage cotton pants and Italian army pullover sweaters (both $39.95). Mess kits, tools, medals, hiking accessories, and just plain campy things that occupy the stuffed racks and packed bins while shoppers maneuver their way through the crowded aisles. Everybody buys something. Don't miss it if you're in Galveston. Minimum order $10.

Sunglasses USA
469 Sunrise Highway — (800) USA-RAYS
Lynbrook, NY 11563 — CK, MC, V, AE, D, DC, CB, MO, C

You've got it made in the shades from Sunglasses USA. Cool-hand Lukes and Lucy's sport RAY-BANs in assorted styles at prices that are hot—about 33 percent less than elsewhere. Styles for driving, rugged, or chic looks are available from this 10-page color catalog. Popular styles included "Wayfarers," retailing $74, for $46.10; and large metal "Aviators," retailing $76, for $49.30. Returns are accepted within 30 days for an exchange or refund. Most orders are delivered within 10 days.

Reader special: 10 percent off the already wholesale prices when mentioning *Great Buys*.

Survival Supply Co.
P.O. Box 1745, Dept. GBBM — (916) 621-3836
Shingle Springs, CA 95682 — CK, MC, V, C

Survive the economic crunch (or Armageddon) with "emergency preparedness supplies," outdoor and camping equipment, and foods that can be stored for long periods, all at 10-percent to 30-percent savings. Military foods and books on survival are two of the big sellers at Survival Supply. Check out their catalog and you may live to tell about it. Returns are accepted within 30 days with approval; orders paid for by credit card or money order are usually delivered within one week.

Telepro Golf Shop

17622 Armstrong Avenue (800) 333-9903
Irvine, CA 92714-5791 CK, MC, V, D, MO, B

When a professional golfer answers the phone, that's par for the course. This company goes a little further to make mail-order shopping easy. Their brochure features a large selection of famous-name golf clubs in a variety of precise specifications. You'll match these clubs to your shaft flex, shaft length, and swing weight to get the right one. If you don't know all of these things, there is a questionnaire to help Telepro help you. A little birdie told us we'd find discounts of up to 40 percent.

The Tennis Co.

30860 Southfield Road (313) 258-9366
Southfield, MI 48076 CK, MC, V, PQ

Tennis Pro is your ace on the court of saving money on tennis equipment. And in fact, this is no backhanded compliment. They themselves boast they are the "best tennis store in the Midwest," with 8,300 square feet to prove it. Tennis shoes and racquets, plus golf equipment and more from REEBOK, AVIA, DUNLOP, PRINCE, HEAD, and others are discounted by an average of 20 percent. Call for a price quote with all the necessary information and let them save you money. Advantage, shopper.

Todd Uniform, Inc.

3668 South Geyer (800) 458-3402
St. Louis, MO 63127 CK, MC, V, AE, D, MO, C, PQ

Suit up for 30 percent less than you'd pay elsewhere and leave your budget lookin' good. Todd Uniform has work shirts for men and women in a variety of colors, plus jackets, coveralls, T-shirts, aprons . . . even baseball hats that you can personalize with your name or logo. Quantity discounts will save you even more. (They must be doing something right; they've been around since 1881!) They offer price quotes by phone or letter, and satisfaction is guaranteed.

Trophyland USA, Inc.
7001 W. 20th Avenue (800) 327-5820
P.O. Box 4606 (800) 432-3528 (FL residents)
Hialeah, FL 33014 CK, MC, V, AE, D, C, PQ

By now you must be an accomplished reader of catalogs. This one is full-color and 96 pages. Why not reward yourself for your expertise and give yourself a medal, plaque, award, or trophy from this family-owned store and mail-order company? After all, you've earned it. Trophyland carries a complete line of trophies, medals, plaques, desk sets, charms, and show ribbons at factory-direct savings, up to 70 percent! All wood is walnut and the marble is imported from Italy. Engraving is free. Most orders are shipped within four days. They'll replace orders in the case of their error; otherwise there are no refunds or returns. There is no minimum order, although they prefer orders over $25. Shipping is prepaid on orders over $200.

UT Golf
2346 West 1500 South (800) 666-6033
Salt Lake City, UT 84104 CK, MC, V, D, C

Bogie on over to UT Golf by way of their 60-page color catalog. Get out of the trap of paying full price (that really tees us off!) and shop direct. UT manufactures their own line of golf clubs, and also sells BROWNING equipment. You won't get shafted, either. All types of shafts, grips, etc., are available, and all products with the UT GOLF label come with a one-year warranty. If an order was incorrectly filled and must be returned, they'll even pay for return shipping. There is no minimum order.

Wearguard Corp.
P.O. Box 400 (800) 888-2900; (617) 871-4100
Hingham, MA 02043 CK, MC, V, AE, COD, C/$1

If you're worn out wearing boring casual work clothes or uniforms, why not spruce up your wardrobe here with personalized uniforms, work clothing, and rugged casual apparel, along with silk-screened and embroidered hats, Ts, and jackets. Weekend Editions (56 pages) are specialized mini-versions of their big catalog (96 pages) and would fit into anyone's outdoor wardrobe needs. New England–type separates and footwear, flannel shirts, and chinos for the football games—all factory-direct priced at 10 percent to 30 percent off. Brands include HERMAN'S, TIMBERLAND, HANES, WRANGLER, and ADIDAS. Customer satisfaction is guaranteed 100 percent of the time—or your money back. Expect a response in one or two days. In addition to their mail-order division, WEARGUARD has 50 retail locations throughout the Northeast. Call their toll-free number above for the location nearest you.

Wide World of Sporting Goods
220 S. University — (305) 475-9800
Plantation, FL 33324 — CK, MO, C, PQ

Been looking for some sporting shoes to complement your sporting life? Well, the Wide World of Sporting Goods (formerly The Athlete's Corner) is a great place to tie one on. This place has NIKE basketball shoes, ranging from canvas shoes to leather ones. Good sports will find sporting goods for tennis, racquetball, running, and basketball—shoes, rackets, and clothing. Leading brands in sporting goods like NIKE, ADIDAS, NEW BALANCE, and EKTELON huddle here before making tracks to go a-courtin'. Clothing brands include OCEAN PACIFIC, DOLPHIN, RAISINS, HOBIE, and HEAD. Savings were around 30 percent to 40 percent on most items; team orders are welcome. Unused merchandise can be exchanged or money refunded; there's a 15-percent restocking charge on returns. Most orders are shipped within 48 hours and are received within seven days.

Wiley Outdoor Sports, Inc.
Dept. 0024
P.O. Box 5365
1808 Sportsman Lane
P.O. Box 5307 — (205) 837-3931
Huntsville, AL 35816 — CK, MC, V, MO, C

Here's your chance to get a shot at hunting, camping, and archery equipment, plus outdoor apparel, footwear, and cutlery. For about

30 percent to 50 percent less than elsewhere, Wiley offers riflescopes, binoculars, spotting scopes, camping gear, and reloading equipment in their annual 160-page catalog. This small, family-owned business offers great service and a knowledgeable staff. Returns are accepted within ten days on unused merchandise; orders are shipped the day they're received.

Surplus and Volume Sales

Ever wondered where to find uniforms for medical technicians, seafood restaurant waiters, or French maids? (You haven't?) Do you know where to get Portuguese camouflage berets, utility paint tanks, and deluxe naked leather and down vests? (You don't?) Well, maybe you were just thinking about where to get Korean War–vintage genuine U.S. Army–issue hand-powered generators, and grenade belts from World War I? (You weren't! Amazing!) If you answered "yes" to any of the above questions, you've come to the right place. Buying overstocks or buying in multiples usually means savings, as you'll see from the following dealers. (Incidentally, if you didn't do very well on our test, don't feel bad. Many people don't. We're easy—you can still look through this section anyway. And better luck next time.)

American Science & Surplus
601 Linden Place
Evanston, IL 60202
(708) 475-8440
CK, MC, V, MO, C/$1

It's alive! The thrill of creation can be yours with odds and ends from American Science & Surplus. American's rag-tag selection of surplus includes lab wear, motors, tools, electronics, books, and other "weird stuff" for the junior mad scientist or anyone else who enjoys a technical challenge. Savings can be gargantuan (up to 95 percent), especially compared to the cost of the same merchandise new. Formerly known as Jerryco, American has been in business since 1937, and selling by mail since 1978. They accept returns in 15 days, except on special-order merchandise; the minimum order is $10.

Blair
1000 Robins Road
Lynchburg, VA 24506
(804) 845-7073
CK, MC, V, COD, C

Mary, this one's O-Kay. Without being caddy, we were in the pink with all these BLAIR beauty products at wholesale prices. This plant operates as a dealership, but you determine your own quota. Buy for yourself or for friends at wholesale prices. Cosmetics, fragrances, health aids, costume jewelry, home products, and small gifts, plus food products such as spices, are available. Blair guarantees products and has been in business since 1920. For more information, check out their free catalog.

E.T. Supply
P.O. Box 78190
Los Angeles, CA 90016-8190
(213) 734-2430
CK, MC, V, MO, C, PQ

E.T., call home. This company is offering very down-to-earth prices on military and industrial surplus. Savings of up to 90 percent are enough to grind down even a hardened spendthrift. E.T.'s catalog features heavy-duty equipment like pumps and generators, plus hardware, tools, and bits and pieces for electronics repair. Some brand-name items are found like diamonds in the rough, like MOTOROLA and WESTINGHOUSE, but sometimes, parts is parts, right? They'll give price quotes by letter or phone, and returns are accepted (a 15-percent restocking fee is charged with some items).

Mass. Army & Navy Store
15 Fordham Road
Boston, MA 02134
(800) 343-7749
CK, MC, V, AE, MO, C

You can a-Mass a marvelous eclectic wardrobe here complete with genuine U.S. and European military garb, like Foreign Legion caps and Vietnam jungle boots. Names like LEE, LEVI'S, SCHOTT, WOOLRICH, TIMEX, and CONVERSE are campy collections for your camping or survival gear, as well as outdoor clothing. Their catalog is jam-packed with a multitude of interesting and unique military surplus items—some even useful and practical. They have two stores in the Boston area: one at 1433 Massachusetts Avenue, known as Central War Surplus; and one on Boylston Street. Satisfaction guaranteed or your money back. There's a 10-day return policy.

RSP Distributing
P.O. Box 2345 (213) 542-0431
Redondo Beach, CA 90278 CK, MO, C/$6 (refundable)
B, and Sales Kit/$2

Talk about closeout heaven. This 200 page catalog sure offers enough items: jewelry, gifts, novelties, housewares, cutlery, survival products, auto accessories, tools, toys, office supplies and accessories, clothing, electronics . . . whew, exhaustive enough to tire even the consummate shopper. Save up to 90 percent on closeout merchandise and save up to 60 percent off suggested retail items in this catalog. You can choose to be the ultimate consumer of these goods, or resell them for a profit. Many products are covered by a factory warranty; others can be returned postpaid to RSP within 30 days for credit.

Ruvel & Co., Inc.
4128–30 W. Belmont Avenue (312) 286-9494
Chicago, IL 60641 CK, MC, V, C/$2, PQ

Boy, did the military serve us when we enlisted the help of Ruvel's catalog. This store has all types of army-navy surplus goods. Clothing (flier's jackets, pith helmets), camping goods (sleeping bags, snowshoes), dummy grenades, gas masks, knives, British hurricane lamps, poison-resistant full-body aprons, and blood pressure kits are just a few of the items from their extensive inventory. Most items are about 20 percent less than retail. No license or permit is necessary to buy any of their merchandise. There's a 30 day policy on items returned in the same condition as when shipped; items ordered in error or returned for a refund are subject to a 20 percent restocking charge. The catalog is $2; free with an order of $10 or s-more.

Telephone

Low-Cost Long-Distance Service

Though Southern Belles have changed a lot since the days of Alexander Graham Bell, so has the telephone. They now come in all shapes, sizes, and colors. You can get video displays, speakers, cordless models, hook-ups to your computer, mobile cellular, and pocket-size versions that fit in your briefcase. Automatic redial, mute buttons, call-waiting, call-forwarding, the list is endless. But, who gets the No-Bel prize for long-distance service is ever-changing. The war of the words is celebrated between the Bells, Sprint, and MCI, so monitoring the lowest of the low rates is always recommended. However, as of publication date, we have found that the following company is the lowest to date.

Leading Edge Communications, Inc.
Attn: D. J. Goodwin
10724 Garland Road, Suite 300
Dallas, TX 75218
(214) 324-1484; (214) 896-4747

This newcomer to the long-distance rates arena is a boon to residential and small-business-users. Talkers, save on long-distance usage anywhere from 5 percent to 35 percent off your current billing (if you're using the Big Three).

As an individual or small-business-user, the rates are as low as most major corporations receive. But have no fear, LEC uses all the major carriers. If you are paying more than 18 cents per minute during the day/12 cents for nights and weekends, or the commercial flat rate of 16 cents per minute, you've paid too much!

There's also discount 800 service and the lowest calling-card rates available (varies with state). So, don't delay. Sign up today and start dialing with saving dollars.

Tobacco

Modern literature has elevated smoking to an art form. Who can imagine Ashenden without an Indian cheroot, Lady Brett without a Gauloise, or Hercule Poirot or Sherlock Holmes without their pensive pipely puffings? It's almost inconceivable that a deep-thinking detective would not, at some point during his ruminations, light up his pipe and surround himself with slowly curling and snaking wisps of smoke. Maybe you haven't been immortalized (yet on the big screen or in a steamy best-seller)—no matter, you can still find the pleasure and relaxation of a pipe or after-dinner cigar one of life's small satisfactions. From the mundane to the exotic, from corncob pipes to handmade cigars—order your supplies by mail. The merchants in our book offer a great selection and the savings are even greater.

Famous Smoke Shop, Inc.
55 West 39th Street, Dept. QBBM 93 (800) 672-5544
New York, NY 10018-3803 CK, MC, V, House Accounts
COD ($3 extra), C

Handmade, all-tobacco cigars are shipped anywhere in the world the same day they're ordered via Airborne Express. You can use your Visa for a TE-AMO PRESIDENTE, or you may open up an account with Famous Smoke Shop and charge all you like. Send PARTAGAS to your papa or MACANUDOS to your mama. They have a huge selection of name-brand cigars and tobaccos, plus pens by MONT BLANC and CROSS, at 30 percent to 50 percent off. Their catalog is free and informative, so why don't you pick one up and . . . read it sometime.

Fred Stoker & Sons

P.O. Box 707 (800) 243-9377
Route 1 (901) 364-3754; (901) 364-5419
Dresden, TN 38225-0707 CK, MC, V, D, COD, C

One dip or two? Aromatic cherry, mild Cavendish, Stoker's chocolate mint, coffee, pineapple, or apple. Ice cream anyone? No, not ice cream, but sweet cigars and pipe and chewing tobaccos for the choosy chewer or picky puffer. Stoke on this: Fred has been around since 1940. Now that's something to chew on. Peter Piper picked a peck of BRIAR pipes and then he smoked them. You're not a smoker or a chewer? How about popping your top over genuine, yellow hybrid popcorn? Or you can slurp on their sweet deals on sorghum-flavored table syrup. You'll want to put Fred Stoker & Sons tobacco in your pipe and smoke it at bulk-rate savings.

Iwan Ries & Co.

19 S. Wabash (800) 621-1457; (312) 372-1306
Chicago, IL 60603 CK, MC, V, AE, D, DC, CB, F, PQ

Don't have money to burn? Then don't waste it on expensive cigars, pipes, tobaccos, ashtrays, lighters, pouches, or humidors for cigars or cigarettes. They're all less costly at Iwan Ries—as much as 60 percent less. They have a selection as good as their prices, and fliers to show you the goods; just call. There is a service charge of $1.50 on orders under $10.

J-R Tobacco of American

I-95 at Route 70 (800) JR-CIGARS
Selma, North Carolina 27576 CK, MC, V, D, AE, COD, C

When in Dallas, J.R. likes ch-Ewing his tobacco, but in New York, he joins the fogeys in puffing stogies at 30 percent to 60 percent off. This company sells 40 percent of the premium cigars bought in the U.S.! J-R carries handmade cigars (every quality brand offered) from such exotic lands as the Dominican Republic, the Philipines, Honduras, Brazil, Costa Rica, Nicaragua, and Mexico. They also have the J-R alternative cigars, which are discounted reproductions (40-percent to 60-percent savings) of such renowned smokes as EL CAUDILLO, FLAMENCO, DON TOMAS, DON DIEGO, MONTECRUZ, HOYO EXCALIBUR, HOYO DE MONTERRERY, MACANUDO, PARTAGAS, RAMON ALLONES, REY DEL MUNDO, ROMEO Y JULIETA, ROYAL JAMAICA, JOYA DE NICARAGUA, FLOR DEL CARIBE, and CUESTA REY. To go with their alternative cigars, you'll enjoy their offbeat catalog. If you're huffin' and puffin' to smoke your house up, the mail's your trail to this Southfork of New York cigars. To mask any telltale signs of cigar smoke, they also sell designer fragrances for men and women at profoundly aromatic prices as well as designer writing implements like MONT BLANC. When on the road to savings, stop by their outlet in North Carolina.

Marks Cigars
8th and Central — (800) 257-8645
Ocean City, NJ 08226 — CK, MC, V, AE, MO, C, PQ (SASE)

Smoke out the savings and find "the world's greatest cigars at below wholesale prices" from Jody Kish at Marks Cigars. Since 1947, this firm has been smokin' with ROYAL JAMAICA, HOYO DE MONTEREY, TE-AMO, ARTURO FUENTE, and other famous cigar brands at about 33 percent off. The catalog even tells you the cigar's ring size, length, wrapper color, and country of origin. You can call or write (with SASE) for a price quote if you don't see what you want in the catalog. Visit their store in Ocean City at 8th and Central from 7 a.m. to 9 p.m., seven days a week, when in the area.

Nurhan Cevahir
Istiklal Caddesi
Bekar sokak No. 12/4 — (907717) 1444123
Beyoglu, Istanbul — IMO, Bank Draft (through Osmanli Bankasi, Karakoy, Istanbul), F

Comparable hand-carved genuine-block meerschaum pipes are at least twice as expensive elsewhere as they are at Nurhan Cevahir. Put that in your pipe and smoke it. Each pipe is guaranteed first quality and comes loose inside the bowl with a label ensuring the quality of meerschaum used. Each pipe is wrapped in a plastic envelope and individually packed in a cardboard box with the picture and style of the pipe.

Thompson Cigar Company
5401 Hangar Court (813) 884-6344; 800-237-2559
Tampa, FL 33634 CK, MC, V, AE, D, DC, MO, C

Thompson's color catalog, which runs about 50 pages, features Thompson's own brand of cigars, along with brands like HOYO DE MONTERREY, ROYAL JAMAICA, H. UPMANN, PARTAGAS, and CUESTA REY, plus lighters, tobaccos, pipes, ashtrays, and other accessories. Thompson has more than a cigar or two up its sleeve; in addition to their catalog of smoking items, they offer linens and items for "casual living," including gifts. There is no minimum order, and there is a 30-day return policy.

Toys

Toys aren't just for kids! From the smallest to the tallest, from the youngest to the oldest, you can find something special for the perennially young at heart. Let your fingers do the walking through a wonderland of toys from dinosaurs to dolls, bears to balloons. You don't have to wait for Santa's sleigh; these catalogs are available year-round. So plan ahead for that special "child," big or small; sit back and watch 'em have a ball.

Ace Fireworks
P.O. Box 221 — (800) 334-4ACE
Conneaut, OH 44030 — Cashier's Check, MC, V, C

You light up my night! Connoisseurs of the finer things of light can shatter the stillness and split the night skies with any one of 1,000 different types of fireworks available here. They've got bottle rockets (their biggest seller), Roman candles, ladyfingers, and countless firecrackers, and everything is priced 20 percent to 30 percent below retail. You can get "Class C common fireworks," including "happy lamps" and "baby magic blooms" in two to three days by mail. There's a $50 minimum order, but there's no charge for shipping. You must be 18 or older to order. Satisfaction guaranteed, and apparently a lot of folks are: Ace has been in business for over 30 years.

Acme Premium Supply Corp.
(See **Party and Paper**, p. **394**.)

Archie McPhee & Company
P.O. Box 30852
Dept. GB01
Seattle, WA 98103
(206) 782-2344
CK, MC, V, C/$1

Everything from the avant-garde to the extremely bizarre is yours for the buying from Archie McPhee & Company. Named for a relative of the owner who, we're told, was responsible for taking the first dance band to China in 1924, Archie McPhee was founded in 1980. Those hard-to-find items you'd forgotten you wanted as a child are available at nearly the same prices they were back then. If you're in the market for rubber insects, rodents, or fish, this is the place to shop. Whining cicada keyrings, Dr. Science mugs, Mona Lisa brooches, potato guns that shoot real potato pellets, and Frankie and Annette dolls make gift-buying from this catalog outright outrageous. The 63-page catalog, which contains a coupon good for $5 off your first order over $25, also stocks rubber eyeballs, rubber chickens, disguises, and glow-in-the-dark goods. Prices are all 10 percent to 30 percent below retail, and there's a 100-percent-satisfaction guarantee. Requests and orders are shipped within two working days of receipt. When in the neighborhood, check out the wacky Archie McPhee Outlet Store at 3510 Stone Way, North Seattle.

The $1 Archie McPhee catalog is free to *Great Buys* readers.

CR's Bear and Doll Supply Catalog
(See **Kits and Kaboodle**, p. **349**.)

Dollsville Dolls and Bearsville Bears
461 N. Palm Canyon Drive
Palm Springs, CA 92262
(800) CAL-BEAR (orders only)
(619) 325-2241 (customer service and inquiries)
CK, MC, V, AE, D, C/$1

The store with an English accent would love to save you from 10 percent to 30 percent on their collector teddy bears and dolls, from ALEXANDER to ZOOK, English, European, and "artist" bears.

These cuddlies are definitely works of art. They charge a flat $3 for shipping per item in the continental U.S., and ship orders the day they're received whenever possible. Their liberal return policy is to replace, exchange, or give credit for up to one year. If you just can't bear to sleep alone, or want to display your good taste, put your arms around one of these and give 'em a big bear hug.

Hoover Bros/The Teachers Store
2050 Postal Way
P.O. Box 660420 (214) 634-8474
Dallas, TX 75266-0420 CK, MC, V, D, C

This arsensal for teachers (or parents who'd like to help) eases the war on boredom and the Blackboard Jungle. Materials for grades K–6 make the grade with paints, art accessories, teaching aids, pens, pencils, puzzles, posters, software, games, award ribbons, and thousands of stickers. You won't get stuck with high prices! The catalog is a store-plus-more. Getting decorating ideas for kids' rooms is a real side attraction. You won't believe the selection in this HUGE catalog!

Huston Dolls
7960 U.S. Route 23 (614) 663-2881
Chillicothe, OH 45601 CK, MC, V, D, C/$2

Hey, doll, goin' my way? You are if you're looking for handmade porcelain dolls and doll kits. Collectible replicas of antique American, French, and German dolls are available from Huston, from delicate newborn dolls to kits of Elvis, Shirley Temple, and the Presidents and their First Ladies. Huston's, in business for over 60 years, also offers a doll house and miniature doll catalog ($10). Prices range from a $15.95 imported doll from RUSS to a $390 "First Moments" doll made of porcelain. Over 250 dolls available, from clowns to cherubs to babies, all crafted and selected with a fine-tooth comb.

Into the Wind
1408 Pearl Street (800) 541-0314 (orders)
Boulder, CO 80302 (303) 449-5356
CK, MC, V, AE, D, MO, C

Don't let your plans for starting a new hobby be up in the air. Send for this catalog but beware, there *are* strings attached. Into the Wind offers one of the largest selections of kites and wind socks available by mail. Kites range from traditional silk Chinese birds and butterflies to space-age nylon airfoil. Each kite's description in the colorful catalog offers information on flying characteristics and features as well as the level of proficiency required to operate it. There are kites just for children, kites for fighting other kites, and kites for decorating your pad. Prices range from a modest model for $7.99 to a four-pound stunt kite for $495. Boomerangs and wind chimes were also found in this catalog.

Johnson Smith Co.
4514 19th Street, Court East ((813) 747-6645
Bradenton, FL 34203 CK, MC, V, AE, D, MO, C

After getting a whiff of the Johnson Smith catalog, I was ready to place my order for a herculean wristband, rotating spaghetti forks, a leather bullwhip, a ventriloquist's dummy, live "sea monkey" character masks (for those with minor personality disorders?), phony blood, alien ears, monster teeth, motorized shark fins, an electric talking toilet, liquor lollipops, and The Last Supper purse wallets. Over 1,600 unusual offerings from around the world are available. This company, more than 75 years old, has two good-sized catalogs: *World of Fun* and *The Lighter Side*. They contain almost everything you could ever want in the way of jokes, novelties, costume jewelry, hobby items, electronics and radio stuff, magic, and Halloween items. Prices are generally below retail. Delivery time is about three to four weeks, but they'll give refunds or make exchanges immediately if there's a problem.

La Piñata
(See **Party and Paper**, p. **396**.)

Lilly's Kids
Lillian Vernon Corporation (804) 430-5555
Virginia Beach, VA 23479-0002 CK, MC, V, AE, D, DC, MO, C

Stop kidding yourself. When it rains, it pours. And this catalog is the salt of the earth with affordable and money-saving, imaginative, and educational kids' stuff. First-class travelers can travel the backroads without the usual boredom with many fun-filled hours of driving pleasures. Turn your wheel to "Games on the Go" or the "Busy Box Steering Wheel" for small-fry backseat drivers. Pick a pumpkin jack-o'-lantern costume or end those harried hair-dos with a set of three playtime wigs. Take a bow in a glamorous one-shoulder tulle netting gown if a pageant is up and coming. Explore scientific endeavors, back-to-school bargains by the pagefuls, dolls, dollhouses, tap dance videos, bathtime splash specials, rainy-day activities, all at prices that are scaled down to size. You'll flip . . . through the pages and see puzzles, games, clothing, accessories, baby items, party items, gift wrap, stationery, housewares, bed and bath doodads, a one-stop shopping book to toy with at every turn. What kid wouldn't lay down and die for a "super kid" beach towel, nature stickers, or a leaf and flower press? Take two aspirins and call for this catalog (part of the Lillian Vernon empire that strikes back against the buyer's blues). Orders are shipped promptly and come with a 100-percent customer-satisfaction guarantee.

Museum of Fine Arts, Boston
(See **Art and Collectibles**, p. **47**.)

Natural Baby Co., Inc.
(See **Apparel: Baby's and Children's**, p. **4**.)

Palmer Sales
(See **Party and Paper**, p. **397**.)

Pueblo to People
(See **Apparel: Family**. p. **18**.)

RSP Distributing
(See **Surplus and Volume Sales**, p. **473**).

Squadron Mail Order
(See **Kits and Kaboodle**, p. **356**.)

Tower Hobbies
P.O. Box 778 — (800) 637-4989
Champaign, IL 61824 — CK, MC, V, D, MO, COD, C/$3 (refundable), PQ

Model yourself after Tower Hobbies customers and forget paying outrageous prices on remote-controlled cars, trucks, planes, and more. Tower's are the latest thing, not rejects from five years ago, and they're as much as 60 percent less than those in most hobby stores. One 14-year-old research assistant was delighted with the mere *thought* of this 290-page catalog full of planes, trains, and automobiles (not to mention ships), which includes model kits, tools, batteries, fuel (they're not just for little kids anymore!), radios, and anything else you'll need to get your choice of models up and running. Serious enthusiasts will recognize names like COX, DUMAS, TOP FLITE, LANIER, and KYOSHO. Start your engines and go for the gold!

Toy Balloon Corporation
204 E. 38th Street (212) 682-3803
New York, NY 10016 CK, MO, C

You could go around the world with their balloons and still not run out of ideas for your next party. There's plenty of hot air around this place—helium balloons, latex balloons (all sizes), mylar balloons with custom imprinting—blow 'em up and let the good times roll. Since 1985, this has been a complete center for balloon accessories and party supplies. Three dozen minimum on custom printing. The more you buy, the more you'll save—as much as 70 percent over your neighborhood party store. Exchanges are accepted on unprinted materials, less 20 percent handling charge, provided goods are returned unused in good condition. There is a $3 minimum charge for shipping and handling.

Travel

Get out of the house! If the world is your oyster, get up out of your oyster bed and listen to these pearls of wisdom. You don't have to be rich to travel first class. Try an airline broker or contact one of the travel clubs who offer a country-club atmosphere, group travel rates, and the camaraderie and fellowship of fellow sightseers to the world's ports-of-call. Pack your bags at a discount (see Handbags and Luggage), and have your frequent-flyer ticket in hand. For reservations, without mental reservations, book a room through a Bed & Breakfast program, or stay in a dorm—even with confirmed reservations in advance. See the countryside on your bicycle or trade your Pacific condo for a picturesque bungalow in Kennebunkport. The sky's the limit—not your pocketbook! And though it still seems preposterous that folks pay a membership fee to access the warehouse clubs, travel clubs are in like Flynn.

Air Fare Busters
5100 Westheimer #555 — (800) 232-8783
Houston, TX 77056 — CK, MC, V, AE, D

For international travel, this is the way to straighten up and fly right. With the air-fare wars ebbing and waning as the crow flies, you might as well learn the ropes and give this air-fare company a try, Buster. A flight to Milan was $202 *less* than the discounted price at Air Value. Head off into the sunset: Moscow, $990; Hong Kong,

$980; Frankfurt, $722; Geneva, $748, and no membership fees to get these low prices. Other than watching the classifieds, hidden fares, having a frequent-flyer ticket, or being married to a pilot, there's probably no better way to save on the long hauls.

Airhitch
2790 Broadway, Suite 100 (800) 326-2009; (212) 864-2000
New York, NY 10025 B

Airhitch is for the flexible traveler who wants a great low fare to western Europe. Contact Airhitch first, with a five-day range in which you can fly. Airhitch guarantees to get you there within this range. They don't guarantee that they'll get you to the city of your choice, but if they can't, they'll get you as close as possible. Then, once Airhitch has sent you information, return it with full payment for your flight, giving three preferences to destinations in Western Europe. At the time of this writing, prices (all one-way) were $169 from the east coast; $269 from the west coast; and $229 from other possible destinations in the U.S. and Montreal. In the case of a sold-out flight, Airhitch will book you on the next available flight. Homebound vouchers may be purchased in the U.S. or in one of four European locations. Airhitch stresses the fact that they provide service primarily in spring, summer, and fall. Sunhitch operates similarly, but primarily in winter: December through April. Get away to someplace warm and sunny (e.g., the Carribean) for just $189 round-trip. Send for a Sunhitch informational brochure. Checks are not accepted for payment later than two weeks before your range of flight dates. New Yorkers may go to the office in person. If you're up for an adventure, hook up with Airhitch.

America at 50% Discount
Taste Publications (800) 248-2783
1031 Cromwell Bridge Road (410) 825-3463
Baltimore, MD 21204 MC, V, $49.95/annual membership

Get a taste of the better price of America and save 50 percent. Enroll in this program for hotel discounts and sleep your way cross-country for less. Select the hotel from the participating hotels in this directory, and call direct for reservations. When you arrive, show your membership card at check-in. Rooms are available to members when hotels are not booked solid, but when you check out, at least the sting of full price won't bite you.

American Youth Hostels, Inc.
P.O. Box 37613 (202) 783-6161
Washington, DC 20013-7613 MC, V, B

Students who want to see the U.S.A. or foreign countries have resorted to this inexpensive housing alternative for years. With over 6,000 hostels located in 70 countries, AYH appeals to travelers of all ages who think spending from $7 to $15 a night for a "delightful surprise" is the best deal in the land. Dorm rooms are the norm. Fees are reasonable: a Junior Pass (17 years and under) is $10; a Senior pass (18–54 years) is $25; and a pass for those 55 and over is $15. Family Passes cost $35; Organizational Passes are free to nonprofit organizations, such as schools, scouting groups, etc. Life Passes are $250. Members receive a friendly copy of *Hosteling North America*, a guidebook to hostels in Canada and the U.S.A. The cost of this book, which runs about 350 pages, is $7 to nonmembers, which includes postage and handling. A free brochure titled "Explore the World" is available free. Hostel la vista!

Bent Tree Travel
16000 Preston Road, Suite 306 (214) 490-1122
Dallas, TX 75248 (9 A.M.–6 P.M. weekdays;
10 A.M.–2 P.M. Sat CST)
CK, MC, V, AE, DC, D, MO, PQ

Tired of faring poorly in the confusing travel market? Try calling Nancy DeWitt or any of her highly trained staff at Bent Tree Travel for personalized service. They'll guarantee the lowest fares or refund the difference. You won't get bent out of shape when you learn they don't exclude reservations with low-fare airlines. Bent Tree handles corporate accounts as well as leisure clients, and offers free ticket delivery. How's that for a fare deal?

Best Fares Discount Travel Magazine
P.O. Box 170129 (800) 880-1234; (817) 261-6114
Arlington, TX 76003 MC, V, AE

Here's the magazine for travelin' fools who aren't spendin' fools. *Best Fares* keeps track of travel promotions that the public doesn't hear about. Promotions, they say, that "sound too good to be true . . . but *are* true." All offers are investigated and must be legitimate to be included in the magazine. These great discounts include up to 50 percent off at over 10,000 hotels, up to 30 percent off the lowest fares to Europe and the South Pacific, and more. How would you like to save $100 on air fare by buying a romance novel? Or travel to Australia for $1,000, getting a few hundred dollars knocked off the price of your next flight, to boot? Samples of the magazine aren't available, but they do offer a pro-rated refund if you decide your subscription wasn't worth it. Subscriptions are $58 per year for 12 issues and, believe me, well worth it!

Bike Vermont

P.O. Box 207-LF (802) 257-2226
Woodstock, VT 05091 CK, MC, V, C

Roll over rolling hills and tour the verdant countryside, quaint towns, and historic inns of Vermont, one of America's most scenic states. Bike from inn to inn at your own pace, with singles, couples, and families. Tours are leisurely and are suitable for beginning to advanced cyclists. Friendly leaders conduct the tours; thank goodness, they're able mechanics, too. A support van carries luggage for the (comfortably small) group. Reservations require a deposit of $125 per person for weekend tours and $300 for midweek tours. (The fee is fully refundable up to three weeks before the tour is scheduled, and 100-percent credit is given for cancellations later than that.) BYOB, or rent a bicycle from them. The beautiful photos in their catalog made us want to sign on the dotted line and pedal into a Vermont sunset.

Campus Holidays USA

242 Bellevue Avenue (800) 345-2775; (201) 744-8724
Upper Montclair, NJ 07043 MC, V, AE, D, Agency Checks, B, PQ

Campus holidays offers discounts primarily to students, but adults can also save big here. Tours to Europe, South America, and Asia for ages 28 to 35 are a specialty, as well as discount airfare and backroads touring, and travel to England, Scotland, and Wales. They can even save you money on car rentals in combination with other travel tours. Call for information and a brochure specific to your needs.

Campus Travel Service
P.O. Box 8355
Newport Beach, CA 92660 CK/$14.50

What a way to go! Just write for a copy of *U.S. and Worldwide Travel Accommodations Guide* and get in on college and university guest lodgings for just $12 to $24 dollars a day. Just send a check for $13, plus $1.50 for first-class mail, to the above address and receive the latest edition of this invaluable guide to more than 725 colleges in the U.S. and abroad, including London, Australia, and New Zealand (among *many* others), where dormitory lodgings are available by the day, week, or month. They vary from single and double rooms to bedroom apartments and suites with kitchens. Most are open to the public during the summer—some year-round. Over 35 universities in England alone offer bed and breakfast for one-third the cost of regular lodgings. The guide provides daily room rates, available dates, types of accommodations, activities, food services, addresses, phone numbers, and housing officials to contact for reservations.

Capitol Reservations
1730 Rhode Island Avenue NW, (800) VISIT-DC (847-4832)
Suite 302 (202) 452-1270
Washington, DC 20036 (local residents)
B, F

A free hotel reservation service? What a capitol idea! Capitol Reservations provides *free* hotel reservations (but not free hotel rooms) in downtown Washington, DC, and nearby suburbs. Reserving through this service can save you 30 percent to 50 percent on the nightly cost of a hotel. They say their rates, available year-round, are always the best, and all hotels have been screened for cleanliness and safety. Call for a free brochure and rate list, updated each season.

Carla's Cruise Corner
15770 Dallas Parkway, Suite 130 (800) 338-6259
Dallas, TX 75248 (214) 239-9103
CK, MC, V

Carla's been setting sail for over ten years and promising every cruise "sold at a discount." How could you ever say no to a 3-, 4-,

7-, 10-, 20-, or yes, even a 30-day cruise? In fact, you may even want to wave good-bye forever. But think about cruises with spa meals. If not, expect to eat ten meals a day and drink like a fish. Cruises are wonderful and self-contained, budgetwise and funwise. On board, all types of activities like trapshooting, exercising, bridge, and dance lessons. Beginners usually like The Carnival Cruise, which is a 7-day cruise costing around $1,100 per person for an inside cabin, plus port taxes. This includes round-trip air fare and transfer to and from the ship. You would be responsible for land excursions, cocktails, and any gratuities. Not bad for a week off shore, though.

Carlson Travel/Cruises Only!
28592 Orchard Hills Road
Farmington Hills, MI 48018
(800) 445-1666
Credit is determined by each tour company, B

Travel plans up in the air? Carlson Travel and Cruises Only! can bring the expenses down to earth. Now you can trip the flights fantastic, have a wingding, and not create a flap! From North American Elk hunts in the Canadian Rockies to African safaris in the shadow of Kilimanjaro, these folks will arrange the details of your trip so you're left with the fun-in-the-sun fundamentals of having a good time. Travel without travail! CT/CO's owner, Annette Langwald, has great contacts with all the cruise companies, and Cruises Only! has developed the most thorough list of cruise vacations in the country. Shake your marimbas on the Royal Caribbean or Norwegian Caribbean cruises, or find yourself a Czech mate on an international cruise.

Colonial Vacations
1945 Hoover Court
Birmingham, AL 35226
(800) 548-2812
MC, V, $21.95/year

Return to the days of yesteryear, when vacations were affordable. Get out your copy of GREAT AMERICAN TRAVELER and find out how to travel the countryside in the U.S., Canada, Mexico, Puerto Rico, and Hawaii . . . at half the price. This directory also offers discount coupons to Alamo, National, and Budget rent-a-cars. Allow two to three days to get your card.

Commercial Travelers Association
P.O. Box 76400 (800) 392-2856
Atlanta, GA 30358 Annual Newsletter/$5 USA; $7.50 Canada

If you consider yourself a regular business traveler, then you might consider joining this association. You know how tough it is to negotiate a good deal on airfare when you are a business traveler and need to change flight plans practically in mid-flight. Well, with numbers comes clout and "volume is the name of the plane." Benefits other than discount flights include a Visa card; discounts on car rentals, tires, even gasoline; a health insurance and retirement plan; and an in-house travel agency. Sounds like a winner in the business of putting a cap on uncontrollable travel expenses.

Concierge
P.O. Box 2320 (800) 346-1022; (303) 444-2724
Boulder, CO 80306-2320 CK only, $70.00

Meet your own personal concierge for service and savings at luxury (and some not so luxurious) hotels and resorts around the world. Make your own reservations from the property list with your membership packet, and discounts will be up to 50 percent off. These are confirmed reservations subject to availability. Show your card and take advantage of discounts on air fare, cruises, condo and car rentals, too. There were over 90 four- and five-star properties, from Norway to Arizona. For example, Camelback Inn and Mountain Shadows in Scottsdale, Arizona, to the Steingengerger Hotels and Resorts in Europe. Expect some budget properties, too, like select Comfort Inns and Howard Johnsons. Not all properties are created equal.

Consumer Reports Travel Letter
P.O. Box 53629
Boulder, CO 80322-3629
Subscriptions $37 one year; $57 two years
Single Copies/ $5

Other people know something you don't about traveling for less, and they probably learned it from *Consumer Reports Travel Letter*. Get the lowdown on special programs offered by airlines and hotels that could save you plenty of moola, travel tips, and more. CityScope gives you the lowdown in a specific city, from the best rates on taxis to hotels, from Atlanta to Prague. Find out where to go for lower prices and better bargains from a publication that's not likely to be biased (they don't accept advertising).

Council Charter
205 E. 42nd Street (800) 800-8222; (212) 661-0311
New York, NY 10017 MC, V, MO, F

This division of CIEE (see below) offers budget charters to Western Europe for all ages. Add-on flights also available from most major U.S. cities to connect with these flights leaving New York. Travel from New York to Paris, London, Brussels, Madrid, Málaga, Amsterdam, Rome, and Milan, for example, with no advance booking required. There are no minimum or maximum stays; fares are booked each way, and mix 'n' match fares are available to save you even more. Council books with major carriers and offers frequent departures. Spring bookings are available through October; winter bookings begin in late August or early September for trips through the following March. Council Charter fares have no hidden charges and no required Saturday overnight. They also stand firmly behind their advertised prices. A unique low-cost cancellation waiver is available for all flights. Call for a general flier and specific information.

Council on International Educational Exchange (CIEE)
205 E. 42nd Street (212) 661-1414
New York, NY 10017 CK

A book on student work/study/travel abroad opportunities, called *The Whole World Handbook*, is available for $12.95 (payable by check) plus postage from CIEE, or you can check out their free magazine, *Student Travels*. Their International Student I.D. Card can save you up to 50 percent on airfare, plus international and domestic rail, bus, ship, and ferry tickets, tours, and accommodations. In addition, the Council offers work programs in Great Britain, Ireland, France, New Zealand, and other countries. Academic programs, such as language-study programs, are offered for anyone over 17. CIEE has over 38 offices, located near college campuses, throughout the U.S., and offices in Europe and Japan. Call for more information and see the world the old-fashioned way.

Cruise Advisors, Inc.
2442 Northwest Market Street (800) 544-9361; (206) 784-9852
Seattle, WA 98107 CK, MC, V, AE, B

Write or call for your free **Alaska Discount Cruise Guide**, which lists the discounts available (some as much as 20 percent to 25 percent) on cruises to Alaska. Alaskan cruises from May through September. But don't discount cruises to Mexico and the Caribbean, either. They're discounted, too . . . up to 25 percent. Personal services provided, such as trying to match you with a cruise line that specializes in your age group and budget. Free brochures on destinations and cruise lines.

The Cruise Line
260 N.E. 17th Terrace (800) 327-3021
Miami, FL 33132

Where else but the ports of embarkation would you expect your ship to sail? And with this free membership program offering both advance bookings as well as last-minute travel, you will be able to save up to 50 percent. A toll-free hotline and newsletter for additional information is available and a list of cruise offerings.

Cruise Marketplace
939 Laurel Street (800) 826-4333 (U.S.)
San Carlos, CA 94070 (800) 247-4003 (Canada)
(800) 826-4343 (CA residents)
(415) 595-7750 (Bay area residents)
CK, MC, V, AE, D, C

Set a course for adventure with Cruise Marketplace, where you can reserve your spot on a cruise for as little as $5 during specials. They have over 100 years of experience in the travel industry, and their rates "reflect the maximum discount possible." Sail away on the CARNIVAL, PRINCESS, ROYAL, or any of the major cruise lines and save enough to not jump ship. Deposits range from $5 to $500, and Cruise Marketplace sends written confirmation upon receipt. Call or write for a cruise catalog with rates and ports-of-call information.

Cruises Worldwide

16585 Von Karman, Suite A (800) 6-CRUISE
Irvine, CA 92714 (714) 975-1211
CK, MC, V, AE, D, B (SASE)

This port is calling you to savings. Cruise on any line in the world with Cruises Worldwide. A major agent for PRINCESS, CARNIVAL, and NORWEGIAN cruise lines, they offer discounts on many cruises, as well as last-minute specials. Cruises Worldwide is a full-service travel agency that has been in business for ten years and is listed with the Better Business Bureau. Call before your next get-away and get away from the high cost of cruises. Send a SASE for a FREE listing of their cruises. And don't forget to mention when you book a cruise if you will be celebrating your birthday on board. Something special's sure to happen.

Tell them you're a *Great Buys* reader when you book a cruise. If the cost is $1,000 or more, request on-board credit of $25 per person, or $50 per cabin. If the cost is under $1,000, request a free photo album to fill with memories of your cruise.

Discount Cruises

(800) 882-9000

All aboard, starboard, and set your sails to the wind. Sail away on a discount cruise that washes high prices to the tide. Choose the Caribbean or the Pacific as your destination, and pack the sunscreen and swimsuits but make your reservations early. Ships fill up fast (with people, not water). Sit down, sit down, you're rockin' and rollin' the boat. "If it floats, they have a discount on it!" For example, a ROYAL CARIBBEAN, seven-night cruise to Ocho Rios, Grand Cayman, and their own private island including air fare from Dallas/Ft. Worth was under $1,000 per person (not including port taxes), as was the NORWEGIAN CRUISE LINE to the Caribbean and Mexican Yucatan peninsula; the SEABREEZE, which is not as luxurious, could be had for under $900.

Discount Travel Passbook/Great American Travel Spree

2252 Dixie Highway (313) 333-1300
Waterford, MI 48328 CK, MC, V, D, $25 (reader price $7.95)

Don't take off without it! This coupon book is your ticket to great travel discounts all across the country. Save up to 50 percent off the rack rate on hotels, and 10 percent to 50 percent on restaurants, tourist attractions, and car rentals. Go in style, not into debt, with a book that pays for itself over and over again.

Identify yourself as a *Great Buys* reader and you'll get the book, a $25 retail value, for just $7.95.

Entertainment Publications
2125 Butterfield Road (800) 477-3234; (313) 637-8400
Troy, MI 48084 CK, MC, V, B

Remember *A Tale of Two Cities*? Well, here's a tale about cities and two-fers. *Travel America at Half Price* ($32.95, including shipping and handling), includes 2,500 half-price hotel coupons around the U.S., Canada, and Mexico, plus discounts on dining and tourist attractions like the San Diego Zoo. There are also discount books for travel in Eastern and Western Canada, cities in Europe and Israel, and specific cities throughout the U.S. (such as Orlando and Las Vegas). Their bed-and-breakfast club ($22.95 for membership) offers 25 percent off at bed and breakfasts throughout the U.S., Canada, Great Britain, and the Caribbean, along with a list of reservation services. Deals like that beat the Dickens out of paying full price. Call for more information or a brochure on any one of the books.

Express Hotel Reservations
3800 Arapahoe Avenue (800) 356-1123
Boulder, CO 80303 Credit (varies with hotels)

Working exclusively in Los Angeles and New York, Express secures discount reservations in 40 hotels. They give priority to savings and a high level of customer service, and their goal is to offer the best possible deal at the best possible hotel. They visit the hotels they deal with, and know the staffs and neighborhoods firsthand. There is no minimum number of reservations, and the credit cards they accept vary with hotels. Then, please do not disturb! Do not confuse this company with Hotel Express International, which is a multilevel sales company selling hotel rooms at a discount.

Ford's Freighter Guide (818) 701-7414
19448 Londelius Street (818) 701-7415 (FAX)
Northridge, CA 91324 CK

Some people have to get away come hull or high water. Freight travel can cut costs way down and from what some salty dog adventurers say, "It isn't bad!" You'll even have access to the passenger lounges, dining rooms, studies, and outdoor decks. The food is excellent, the ride is generally smooth, and the boat's not as crowded, as they claim. To find out more about the 46 cargo/passenger lines, send $7.95. CA residents, please add 6½-percent sales tax. Send $14.95 for a single subscription; $20 for a subscription plus periodic updates throughout the year.

Frequent Flyer/Official Airline Guides

(800) 323-3537
MC, V, AE, D

Take advantage of your frequent-flyer status with this magazine. You'll learn about ways to use your frequent-flyer mileage to save on hotels, rental cars, and more. When we called we heard about "Gaining Control of Corporate Travel Expenses," a free booklet being offered to readers. Publication subscription prices vary. Call for detailed information.

Great Expectations

P.O. Box 8000-411
Sumas, WA 98295-8000

Even if you didn't graduate *summa cum laude*, you can still sign up to find a classmate of equal proportions with a classified ad in *Great Expectations*. Every Tom, Dickens, and Harriet can place a free ad to find that soulmate to join on a backpacking trek through the Andes, or anywhere else for that matter. This is **the** source for matching travel companions and off-the-beaten-track destinations, cultural conclaves, and budget-minded consumers. Subscription is $18 for six issues; $32 for twelve.

Hideways International

P.O. Box 1270
Littleton, MA 01460

(800) 822-9798
(800) 486-8955 (in MA)
(508) 486-8252 (FAX)
CK, MC, V

Hideways International, as its name implies, represents little-known, out-of-the-ordinary secret escape spots where memories are etched for a lifetime. This full-service travel resource specializes in premier villa and condo rentals (great money-saver for traveling with families), yacht charters, special cruises, intimate inns and resorts . . . even castles and ranches. Your membership ($79 per year) entitles you to their quarterly newsletters giving the "inside scoop" on new places, a personal travel service for air fares, and money-saving discounts. From Antigua to Wyoming, Grenada to Quebec, this is the way to go in style. The guide details handicap access, whether your pets are welcome, plus a myriad of details on every property.

FREE four-month trial membership for readers of *Great Buys*.

Home Exchange International
30 East 33rd Street — (212) 689-6608
New York, NY 10016 — General information (SASE)

If you're planning a stay in another country, or even away from home in the U.S., consider contacting Home Exchange International. For a one-time fee (about $50), they'll set up a "home swap" between you and another party. You let them know the details of your trip, and, once a trading partner is found, pay a variable closing fee. For exchange information, send your phone or fax number, approximate travel dates, and SASE to the address above.

Inside Flyer Publications
4715-C Town Center Drive — (800) 333-5937
Colorado Springs, CO 80916 — CK, MC, V, AE, DC, MO

This monthly magazine helps you make the most of your frequent flyer mileage. You can always make time in your busy schedule to catch up on articles telling you how to save money on car rentals and hotels. Information on current frequent-flyer programs is also given. A subscription is $33 per year, or $55 for two years.

Interhome, Inc.
Swiss Chalets — (201) 882-6864
124 Little Falls Road — MC, V, C/$5
Fairfield, NJ 07004

This New Jersey–based company is linked by computer to Switzerland and can book reservations to more than 3,000 Swiss chalets and condos in major resort areas. From budget-priced studios to posh villas, they can also handle your reservation at over 100 Swiss hotels. Edelweiss, Edelweiss.

International Home Exchange Service

INTERVAC U.S. (415) 435-3497
P.O. Box 190070 (415) 956-3447 (FAX)
San Francisco, CA 94119 CK, MC, V, B

Choose a home exchange from a list of thirty countries, including Japan, Brazil, Australia, Morocco, Poland, Zimbabwe, and New Zealand. And your home can be a rewarding experience for someone from another country or some other part of the U.S. in return. Membership is $35 per year, plus postage and handling. The current brochure gave information about home exchange, subscription form, and listing deadlines. To expedite membership, exchange information can be sent by fax. When a fax is used payment must be with Visa or MasterCard, but photos may not be sent by fax. Home exchange is possible anytime during the year, including summer, Christmas, and Easter vacations.

International Travel Card/ITC-50

6001 N. Clark Street (800) 342-0558
Chicago, IL 60660 $36/annual membership
CK, MC, V, AE, D, B

Join the ITC-50 club and hitch your wagon to the stars. This investment will pay back in great dividends on savings from 30 percent to 50 percent on hotels across the world. Bed down for the night at a participating Hilton, Marriott, Days Inn, Radisson, plus 2,500 others. Hotels sign up individually, not by chains, even in Hawaii. With your membership, you also get a personal, embossed membership card, an up-to-date directory listing of all participating motels, hotels, and resorts, a TravelAlert guide containing information about money-saving tips and cruises, and a $10,000 Mutual of Omaha travel insurance certificate. Application and brochures sent upon request. Thirty-day money-back guarantee.

Last Minute Cruise Club

Village Travel Service
870 Ninth Street (213) 519-1717
San Pedro, CA 90731

Just what the doctor ordered at the last minute. If you can leave with short notice, you might be able to save up to 50 percent on cruises worldwide.

Marv Golden Discount Sales, Inc.
8690 Aeor Drive, Suite 102 (619) 569-5220
San Diego, CA 92123 CK, MC, V, AE, D, C

Up, up, and away with the flyaway-for-less plans for pilots only offered at Marv Golden. Private pilots soar to the savings here. Take off with aviation supplies, including headsets, intercoms, transceivers, computers, GPS systems, and books by DAVID CLARK, TELEX, SIGTRONICS, SOFTCOM, PILOT AVIONICS, PALTOR, GARMIN, TRIMBLE, and ICOM. You'll be flying high at 20 percent to 40 percent off retail. Safe landings are ensured and returns are accepted within 30 days, provided items are returned in perfect condition. There is no restocking charge.

Now Voyager
(212) 431-1616 (Monday-Friday 11 A.M.–5 P.M.; Sat 12:30–4 P.M.)
(212) 431-1616 (6 P.M.-11 A.M. for current destinations, prices, lengths of stay, and last-minute super reduced fares)
CK, MC, V, AE (additional fee for credit-card use)

Register for a year for $50 and unlimited travel (round-trip if needed) to various destinations for up to 75 percent off on all major airlines as a courier. Europe, South America, Caribbean, Los Angeles, the Far East, Mexico, and more are on courier routes. Freight companies exchange your baggage space for a package they need to transport, and limit you to only one carry-on bag. Cancellations on international flights not refundable; but you can cancel with two weeks' notice for domestic flights with certain restrictions. You can book up to two months in advance, but there's only one person per flight. For more recorded information, call the number above.

Odyssey Network
c/o Charles River Travel (617) 237-2400
118 Cedar Street $20 membership
Wellesley, MA 02181 CK, MC, V, AE, MO

Seek and ye shall find a traveling companion, thus avoiding the costly "single" surcharges often assessed if you are going solo. This full-service travel agency plays matchmaker as well as money-saver to this members-only network.

The Phone Booklet
P.O. Box 88, Dept. 1234
West Redding, CT 06896 B/$2

If you're on the road again, check out this collection of toll-free numbers for travelers. "The Phone Booklet" contains hundreds of 800 numbers to use in contacting credit-card offices, airport limousines and buses, car-rental services, tours, casinos, hotels, motels, airlines, resorts, auto and travel clubs, and vacation rentals. Write for your copy, and don't leave home without it.

The booklets are normally $2 apiece, but *Great Buys* readers get *two* for $2.

Players Club International
26541 Agoura Road, Suite 100
Casabasas, CA 91372
(800) 275-7600
(800) 525-6600 (brochure)
Membership for two: $144/year,
CK, MC, V, AE

If you're ready to throw in the towel, why not throw the dice instead and get twice the fun at half the price. This club offers discount rates at casino-hotels and negotiates special air fares to the gaming parts of town. Deal the deck in the Caribbean, Las Vegas, Atlantic City, and Hawaii. In Atlantic City, stay at the Resorts Hotels for $70 (regular $85) and receive 25 percent off show tickets. In Vegas, stay at the Hilton for $29.50 to $34.50 and receive an additional 25 percent off your restaurant bill and show tickets. If you still have money left after the slots, why not shoot your wad at any one of their discount cruises—some are even half off.

TravelAlert
100 Executive Way, Suite 110
Ponte Vedra Beach, FL 32082
(800) 822-2300
CK, MC, V,
$49.95/with access code to
give to travel agencies and airlines

Join the over 2.5 million happy campers who've hopped aboard this membership club to achieve 50-percent savings on participating Marriotts, Hyatts, Hiltons, Sheratons, Holiday Inns, Ramada Inns, Days Inn throughout the U.S. and in over 70 foreign countries. Membership in TravelAlert allows you to book direct to the airlines using your special code as well as to over 40,000 participating travel agencies. Lots of last-minute cruises, tours, and condo rentals, too. In fact, there are over 750 club-recommended travel offers updated daily, car-rental discounts, and more. For example, a one-day tour in Hawaii, 5-hour morning cruise, snorkeling and lessons and a barbecue lunch was $56/ club price $49.95. Or a trip to Great Britain (excluding air) for seven days' and six nights' lodging, car rental, and continental breakfast daily was $105 (regular price $405), and a Bahamas four-night cruise departing from Ft. Lauderdale was $434 (regular $870). Some specials even include airfare. No risk trial 90-day membership with a money-back guarantee. TravelAlert lists its last-minute deals in the airlines' computer reservations system; therefore, you can check availability, reserve it yourself, or book through your travel agency once you know your code.

Travel Avenue
180 North Desplains (800) 333-3335
Chicago, IL 60661 (312) 876-1116 (in IL)

A money-saving alternative to the traditional commissioned-based travel agency (with the exception of planning an in-depth vacation package or around-the-world tour), this company charges an $8 service fee for domestic flights and rebates an 8-percent check off airfare price with ticket. International flights: $20 service fee and you'll get an 8- to 15-percent rebate. Receive an additional check (even after posted discounts) of 5 percent with proof of hotel stay or car rental. Tours and cruises, save 8 percent and a fee of $20 (for cruises less than $1,000) and $40 (for cruises over $1,000). Guaranteed lowest published fares and rates. Ask about specials called "The Ultimate Deal."

Travel Companions Exchange, Inc.
P.O. Box 833, Dept. US (516) 454-0880
Amityville, NY 11701 CK, MC, V, AE, B

This is no Amityville horror! The Travel Companions Exchange has served thousands of single, divorced, and widowed people all over North America since 1982. It is the largest, most successful nationwide "match-up" service for singles aged 20 to 80 who don't want to go alone. This company has been featured on "PM Magazine" and in articles in major newspapers such as the *Los Angeles*

Times, *The New York Times*, and *The Boston Globe*. Travel Companions Exchange is run by Jens Jurgen, a veteran consumer-oriented travel writer. "It's a great way to make new and interesting friends and save money at the same time," says Jens. The cost of membership varies, depending on the length and other factors explained in their brochure. The newsletter prints a number-coded list of its members, as well as the destinations for which members are seeking companions. A half-price Quest Card entitles its bearers to hotel discounts, and is also available to members. If you're looking for a same-sex companion, membership is $36; for an opposite-sex companion, the price rises to $66 (based on a six-month membership). The newsletter subscription alone is $24; sample copies, $4.

Tell them you read about them in *Great Buys*, and be sure to mention that it's a publication of the Underground Shopper. You'll get a two-year subscription and membership for the price of a single year.

Travel Consortium Group

(800) 228-8345;
(214) 717-0777
CK, MC, V, AE, D

With their Dallas location and two in California, this consortium can save you money when the subject of traveling is discussed. For business or pleasure, call their hot line (800-228-8345) that operates 24 hours to get the current monthly specials and information. Enroll in their travel club to get bonus dollars and savings. Members can enjoy air-fare savings up to 30 percent and up to 50 percent on cruises and U.S. hotels. For example, a few of their monthly May specials included a seven-day cruise on the Carnival line (without Kathie Lee) with savings up to $600 per cabin; or how about a two-for-one, 15-day trans-Atlantic cruise to Europe; or a seven-day cruise to Mexico for $495 aboard the COMMODORE. On the air-fare line, in spite of the price wars, international flights to London, round-trips were $510; Paris, $690; Frankfurt, $699, and to the South Pacific, $819. Happy Sales.

Travel Smart
40 Beechdale Road
Dobbs Ferry, NY 10522-9989
(800) 327-3633
MC, V

This newsletter, published monthly at $5 an issue or $37 annually, is full of helpful hints and shrewd suggestions to help you cut the cost of travel. "Pay less, enjoy more" is their slogan, and with this informative publication, you may do just that. The issue we saw included the inside skinny on traveling domestic business class, traveling to Russia as a Peace Corps volunteer, suggested travel books, unusual trips (like baseball road trips), reasonably priced dining, "unusual travel goodies," and much more. They also added a section on free brochures and inexpensive books to send away for. Call for subscription information.

Travel Smarter (800) 992-8972
88 Bleecker Street (212) 982-3771
New York, NY 10012 CK, MC, V, AE

Sneak into the Ritz with the Loyal Order of Poobahs and enjoy great low rates on hotel rooms given to convention- and group-goers. This monthly newsletter provides you with a listing of convention dates and corresponding discounts on hotel rates and air fares. A sample (current) issue is $10; 12 months for $95.

Travelers Access c/o CUC International
707 Summer Street (800) 458-1028
Stamford, CT 06901 MC, V

Join Travelers Access for a $39 membership fee and get access to the lowest available rates on cruises, air travel, car rentals, resorts, and more. A three-month trial membership is available for $1. If you buy a full membership and are dissatisfied, Travelers Access offers a complete money-back guarantee for up to a full year. Call for more information and access the deals worldwide.

Travel World Leisure Club
225 W. 34th Street (800) 444-8952
New York, NY 10122 CK, MC, V, AE

Tired of traveling with the riff-raft? Well, honker up to the finer things in life and live the life-style of the rich and famous. Even they love a bargain! This club caters to the high-flying, high-fallutin' travelers who only stay at luxury properties and eat in five-star restaurants in New York. Of course, the only difference is the price.

Travltips
Cruise and Freighter Travel Association
P.O. Box 188 (800) 872-8584
Flushing, NY 11358 B

Where can I go on a freighter? What are the accommodations and what is the food really like? How much time will we have in port? What about visas, immunizations, age and health restrictions? These are some of the questions answered in a free pamphlet available from Travltips. Freighter travel is not for everyone, and shipping is always a freighter's main concern, with passengers "along for the ride." Nevertheless, freighter travel is becoming increasingly popular, as shown in the bi-monthly newsletter published by the association that features first-hand accounts of voyages worldwide, written by the members themselves. Leisurely and unregimented days, spacious accommodations, good food, and the companionship of no more than a dozen passengers make freighter travel a delightful way to cross the Atlantic, and the low cost makes it an excellent, economical value for travelers with more time than money on their hands.

Trendsetter Travel Inc.
777 S. Central Expressway #4C (214) 480-0727
Richardson, TX 75080 (17-B) CK, MC, V

Setting the trend for the future means keeping the prices low. Air fare to Honolulu, Hawaii, was taking off for $560 (Delta's price was still $802). Vacation specials were available everywhere. Sail away on a cruise for as little as $395. And the agent managed to be friendly, despite phones ringing off the hook. *Se habla español* and Yiddish. *Oy vey!*

Unitravel Corporation
1177 N. Warson Road (800) 325-2222
St. Louis, MO 63132 CK, Cashier's Check, MC, V, AE, MO

Call for information from this money-saver. They don't offer brochures, but will gladly tell you about their flights to Europe and throughout the U.S. for less. Contact them at least one full month before the date you want to depart, and, if you're able to be flexible, you might fly away with a heavenly deal.

Urban Ventures, Inc.
P.O. Box 426 (212) 594-5650
New York, NY 10024 (212) 947-9320 (FAX)
CK, MC, V, AE, D, CB, MO, B

We'll venture a guess that urbane urbanites (or others) venturing to the Big Apple aren't after some seedy, slice-of-life slum as an abode to abide in. Most folks aren't. If that describes you, you'll find Urban Ventures to be very accommodating. This service offers single rooms, private suites, and elegant apartments in good neighborhoods right in the core of the Apple. Prices range from $40 to $65 for single rooms; $65 to $90 for a double. Apartment prices started at $85 for a one-bedroom studio or about $190 a night for a two-bedroom. (They are the only place in New York where short stays in apartments can be booked.) We're told that their prices are less than those charged by other similar booking services. Urban Ventures also offers additional services such as securing theater tickets, steering you to moderately priced restaurants, and guiding you to top tourist attractions. If you opt out, there's a $20 cancellation fee that is applied to any future booking; no-shows and same-day cancellations must pay for that night.

Vacation Outlet/Last Minute Travel Reservation Center
1249 Boylston Street (617) 267-8100
Boston, MA 02215

Doing what they do best, this is *the* source if you need to make a fast getaway. If you want the best vacations around with personal attention from a travel expert, too, go underground, to a Filene's Basement location in Boston and check out The Vacation Outlet. Giddy-up and go for less . . . 20 percent to 50 percent less. If your plans can tolerate quality leisure vacations at the lowest possible prices, have they got a deal for you! They buy seats that have not sold in volume at a discount and pass those savings on air/hotel packages, cruises and club vacations to the most popular destinations including Mexico, the Caribbean, Florida, Las Vegas, Hawaii, and Europe on to you. So what's the hitch? Waiting until the last minute to hop aboard helps, but not always necessary. If you're a shopper in the '90s and understand the nature of "living the good life . . . at half the price," then you can trip out on a Carnival Cruise to the Bahamas, a week at a Club Med hideaway, an American Airlines Flyaway Vacation to . . . get the picture? If you're flexible with your departure date, you can fly with the best of them. The only difference is that you can sit at the captain's table without experiencing indigestion at having paid full price. *Bon voyage*!

Visiting Friends, Inc.
A Round Robin of Hospitality (409) 297-7367
P.O. Box 231
Lake Jackson, TX 77566

Visiting Friends is a private group of people from all across the country that offers singles and couples the opportunity to use the guest room in participating homes on a time-exchange basis as a means of staying with compatible folks in other parts of the country. This network is an excellent supplement to hotel accommodations, with the visits individually arranged, and the privacy of each member protected. A newsletter is sent at no charge to members two to four times per year. Registration for lifetime membership is $25 and first-time Host Home per trip (one to six nights) is only $20, with each additional Host Home on the same trip (one to six nights in each home) $15. These low charges are *per visit*, not *per night*!

Readers of *Great Buys* get a 40-percent discount on registration for lifetime membership, PLUS 25-percent discount on first exchange fee.

White Travel Service, Inc.
127 Park Road (800) 547-4790 (US and Canada)
West Hartford, CT 06119 (800) 547-4790 (in CT)
(203) 233-2648
(203) 236-6176 (Cruise Hotline, 24 hours, 7 days)
CK, MC, V, AE, D, B, PQ

White is right on the money when it comes to savings on your next cruise. In fact, they are considered one of the best cruise specialists in North America. Check the Cruise Hotline, if you don't believe me (see number above). Their brochures lit a fire under our cabins. Enjoy the Royal Caribbean "Sovereign of the Seas" for a seven-night Caribbean cruise sailing from Miami to RCL's private island, San Juan, and St. Thomas for only $799 including air fare. This was no misprint. Save up to $2,000 per room! And the sales are set from there. To Bermuda, to Brazil, to Alaska, to Mexico, to

Scandinavia, to Russia. From the "QE II" to the Holland American lines, it's neither sink nor swim. Just sit back and relax.

Worldwide Discount Travel Club
1674 Meridian Avenue, Suite 206 (305) 534-2082
Miami Beach, FL 33139 CK, MO, B

Take off on your dream vacation and save up to 65 percent off usual and customary charges. Cruises, air tours, and international air fares are all included in club packages. Worldwide Discount Travel Club specializes in filling slots on cruise ships, charter trips, and tours that remain empty close to departure dates. Every 25 days, their Travelog newsletter informs members of upcoming travel opportunities. Members pay a $50 annual family membership fee to keep abreast of vacation savings. This club caters to retired people, teachers with long vacations, and busy professionals who can't plan several months in advance for their vacations. By dealing direct with tour operators, cruise lines, airlines, and charter wholesalers to find out space availability, discounts are secured. Air transportation packages also available one to six weeks before departure, and cruises are offered from one week to several months before departure. Travelers get the same treatment as those who pay full fare. Trips are generally noncancelable and nonrefundable upon purchase.

Identify yourself as a *Great Buys* reader and save $10 off the $50 membership.

The Y's Way
224 E. 47th Street (212) 308-2899; (212) 308-2899
New York, NY 10017 B/SASE plus 65 cents postage

Y spend? The network of YMCA lodging centers spans North America from coast to coast in 38 cities in the U.S., Canada, and five overseas countries. Their City Package Programs feature New York, New Orleans, Seattle, Washington, DC, and Hollywood, with meals, sightseeing tours, and tourist information. Perfect for those who don't care for fancy hotels and just want to travel the Y's Way. Information is available at most local YMCAs, but trip arrangements must be made through the New York office. Payments must be made in advance and in full. Free 23-page brochure with SASE, No. 10 size with $.65 postage.

Air Fare Brokers/ Discounters

You can fly the friendly skies without a membership fee through select travel clearing houses. You can order your discount tickets by phone. You can often depart many major U.S. cities; even the Eurailpass is available at a discount. Unsold airline seats for last-minute departures (one to seven days) can really save the day for budget travelers. One call is all it takes.

Access International
250 West 57th Street — (800) 825-3633; (212)465-0707
New York, NY 10019 — MC, V

Council Charters
205 E. 42nd Street, 16th Floor — (800) 800-8222
New York, NY 10017 — (212) 661-0311
MC, V

Destinations Unlimited
400 Madison Avenue — (212) 980-8220
New York, NY 10017 — MC, V, AE

Intravco Travel Centers
211 E. 43rd Street, Suite 1303 — (800) 482-8785
New York, NY 10017 — (212) 972-1155
MC, V, AE

Travac
989 Sixth Avenue — (800) 872-8800; (212) 563-3303
New York, NY 10018 — MC, V

UniTravel
11177 N. Warson Road — (800) 325-2222; (314) 569-0900
St. Louis, MO 63132 — MC, V

Car Rentals

Consider some of these "cheapo" but "they still run" cars with a toll-free call. And call around to see who'll give you the best deal—even the biggies. Even though you may belong to a club that offers discounts on rental cars, or there may be a special promotion being offered, it pays to price-check by phone. Remember to check your own car-insurance policy before you get suckered into being sold a rider for additional protection at the car-rental agency.

Agency Car Rental	(800) 321-1972
Alamo	(800) 327-9633
American International	(800) 527-0202
Auto Europe	(800) 223-5555
Budget	(800) 527-0700
in Canada	(800) 268-8900
Dollar	(800) 800-4000
EuroRent USA	(800) 521-2235
Hertz	(800) 654-3131
National	(800) 227-7368
Rent-a-Wreck	(800) 535-1391
Sears Rent-a-Car	(800) 527-0770
Thrifty	(800) 367-2277
Ugly Duckling	(800) 843-3825
Value Rent-a-Car	(800) 327-2501

Travel: Budget Motels with Toll-Free Numbers

"Budget motels" are an alternative to luxury hotels or motel chains with cocktail lounges and conference rooms. All of these no-frills lodging chains offer a clean room with the basic comforts, but without the high price spreads. Different parts of the country have different chains, but here are some with toll-free numbers so you can check 'em out. (Hint: Have paper, pencil, and major credit card available when calling 800 lines for reservations.) For a national directory of budget bunks where Tom will leave the light on for ya, write: Motel 6, 51 Hitchcock Way, Santa Barbara, CA 93105; or phone (805) 682-6666.

NAME	NUMBER	HOME OFFICE
Budgetel	(800) 4-Budget	212 W. Wisconsin Milwaukee, WI 53203
Best Western	(800) 528-1234	P.O. Box 10203 Phoenix, AZ 85064
Budget Host Inns	(800) 283-4678	P.O. Box 10656 Ft. Worth, TX 76114
Chalet Suisse	(800) 258-1980 (800) 572-1880 NH residents	Chalet Drive Wilton, NH 03086

NAME	NUMBER	HOME OFFICE
Days Inns	(800) 344-3636 "Incredible Clubs"	LCS 120 Brighton Road Clifton, NJ 07012
Econo Lodges (Friendship Inns)	(800) 553-2666	10750 Columbia Pike Silver Spring, MD 20901
Econo Lodges	(800) 453-4511	10750 Columbia Pike Silver Springs, MD 20901-4494
Econo Travel	(800) 446-6900	6135 Park, Suite 200 Charlotte, NC 28210
Economy Inns	(800) 826-0778	755 Raintree Drive, Suite 200 Carlsbad, CA 92009
Excel Inns	(800) 356-8013	4706 E. Washington Madison, WI 53704
Family Inns of America	(800) 251-9752	P.O. Box 10 Pigeon Forge, TN 37868-0010
Hampton Inns, Inc.	(800) HAMPTON	6800 Popular Avenue Suite 200 Memphis, TN 38138
Motel 6	(505) 891-6161	14651 Dallas Parkway Dallas, TX 75240
Red Carpet Inns/ Scottish Inns	(800) 251-1962	1152 Spring Street Suite A Atlanta, GA 30309
Red Roof Inns	(800) THE-ROOF	4355 Davison Road Hillard, OH 43026
Super 8 Motels	(800) 848-8888	1910 Eighth Avenue NE Aberdeen, SD 57401
Susse Chalet	(800) 258-1980	Chalet Drive Wilton, NH 03086
Travelodge	(800) 255-3050	1973 Friendship Drive El Cajon, CA 92920

Vacuums

Here's something to consider the next time you have to defrost your refrigerator. Reverse the airflow on a canister vacuum and direct the stream of warm air to eliminate the frost in your freezer? Want to know a way to add a fragrant scent to any room? Add a cotton ball of your favorite fragrance to the bottom of your vacuum cleaner bag, and smell sweet all over. Check out a BISSELL of these resources the next time you want to make a clean sweep of your carpets and rugs. From canisters, uprights, shampooers, to heavy-duty machines, the following will keep you in the green.

AAA All Factory Vacuums, Floor Care & Ceiling Fans
241 Cedar
Abilene, TX 79601
(915) 677-1311
CK, MC, V, COD, DC, Layaway,
B/$2 (refundable with first order to *Great Buys* readers)

Vaccinate yourself against high-pressure salespersons selling high-price vacuums—the prices here are innocuous enough! First-quality brand-name dirtbusters like KIRBY, RAINBOW, FILTER QUEEN, HOOVER, EUREKA, PANASONIC, COMPACT, as well as MASTER CRAFT (a line of commercial vacs and floor-care products), are discounted up to 50 percent and 75 percent on some makes! AAA is one of the oldest and largest mail-order vacuum and floor-care discount stores in the country. Your satisfaction is

100-percent guaranteed or your money back. AAA issues their own product-protection guarantee for up to three years on "door-to-door" makes, and provides factory-authorized warranties in your own locality for most other makes. Quality ceiling fans are another money-saving opportunity and a proven means of lowering energy bills during both summer and winter.

Don't forget to mention you read about AAA in *Great Buys* so you can get your $2 back with order.

ABC Vacuum Warehouse
6720 Burnet Road (512) 459-7643
Austin, TX 78757 CK, MC, V, AE, COD, B, PQ

There's a sucker born every minute. That's why ABC doesn't want you to be taken in or get left holding the bag. Although science tells us there is no such thing as a perfect vacuum, we found some of the best brands (RAINBOW, KIRBY, FILTER QUEEN, PANASONIC, ROYAL, and ORECK) discounted up to 50 percent. That's probably why business has been picking up since 1977 for owner Ralph Baccus. KIRBY cleaners are warranted for parts and service for two years. All others have a one-year warranty for parts and service. Merchandise is shipped within 24 hours; most of their customers receive their orders within five to seven working days. They give full refunds within 15 days (excluding shipping charges). Before you buy a vacuum from a door-to-door salesman, check out the prices here. Readers get free shipping.

Derry's Sewing Center
(See **Sewing Machines and Notions**, p. **438**.)

Discount Appliance Centers
(See **Appliances (Large and Small)**, p. **40**.)

MidAmerica Vacuum Cleaner Supply Co.
666 University Avenue (612) 222-0763
St. Paul, MN 55104-4896 CK, MC, V, AE, D, O, MO, PQ

Sure, they've got vacuums by EUREKA, HOOVER, BISSELL, and more, brand new and up to half off. So what else is new? They also carry bags, attachments and parts, plus parts for blenders, toasters, pressure cookers, coffee makers, and other kitchen appliances. There's no catalog, but if you know which vacuum you want or what you need to fix it yourself, they'll quote you a price over the phone or by mail. You must order at least $15, and quantity discounts are available. Now that you know the dirt, you can sweep anything under the rug at savings of 50 percent.

Oreck Corporation
100 Plantation Road (504) 733-8761
New Orleans, LA 70123-9989 CK, MC, V, AE, DC, MO, C

Since 1963, Oreck has been making a clean sweep in housewares and appliances, especially vacuum cleaners and floor polishers. Don't brush off these same high-power vacs used by institutions because here you can save up to 25 percent or more. The catalog features mini-vacs, a hypoallergenic tank vacuum, rug shampooers, buffers, polishers, and bags by the case to keep your place spic-and-span on the cheap, plus emergency spotlights, kitchen islands, multi-band radios, and more. Send it back within 30 days if you're not satisfied and they'll refund your money.

Singer Sewing Center of College Station
(See **Sewing Machines and Notions**, p. **440**.)

Suburban Sew 'N Sweep, Inc./The Sewing Machine Outlet
(See **Sewing Machines and Notions**, p. **441**.)

Windows and Walls

Here's a tip on how to measure your windows when buying blinds. To avoid any confusion when giving the sizes for your blinds inside a window, remember the width *is the measurement taken from left to right, the* length *is taken from top to bottom, and the* sill *height is the measurement taken from the floor (or counter top) to the window sill. Ask for free installation instructions when ordering your blinds. Installing them yourself isn't difficult and will save you labor charges.*

Alexander Wallpaper
2964 Gallows Road (703) 560-5524
Falls Church, VA 22042 CK, MC, V, PQ

This Alexander is Great. The mystery's solved. Once we discovered where the cover-up began, it was easily said and done. First-quality WAVERLY and SUNWORTHY wallpapers, and coordinating wallpaper borders, all for at least 30 percent off. The minimum order is a unit package—that's one double roll. Orders are filled and shipped within 24 hours; their refund policy is 30 days from the date of invoice shipment, providing the package is unopened.

American Blind Factory
28237 Orchard Lake Road #105 (800) 351-1150
Farmington Hills, MI 48334 (313) 553-7773
CK, MC, V, AE, D, DC
MO, B, PQ, Samples

Save 70 percent to 85 percent off manufacturers' retail prices at American Blind. They're pulling the shades on full price, with their own in-house brand, plus majors like LEVOLOR, DELMAR, and LOUVER DRAPE. With 40 years in the business and two million satisfied customers, they're your window to the discount world. Mini- or micro-aluminum custom blinds, verticals, pleated shades, and wood blinds in 1" and 2" widths also an open-and-shut case. All products are guaranteed to be first quality; if not, they're returnable. Orders of three double rolls or more can be returned if you change your mind. For a price quote, send them the name of the wallpaper book the paper came from and the pattern number. For quotes on blinds, send the manufacturer, measurements, and manufacturer's color number. If your blinds are not shipped in five days, they are FREE.

American Discount Wallcoverings
1411 5th Avenue (800) 77-PAPER (777-2737)
Pittsburgh, PA 15219 CK, MC, V, D, MO, PQ (by mail with SASE)

We didn't give this discounter their walking papers with brands like IMPERIAL, GREEFF, RALPH LAUREN, and WESTGATE, and pleated shades and mini-blinds from LEVOLOR, BALI, and FLEX-ALUM at 40 percent to 70 percent off. Give them the length and width of window, pattern name, color, and trim specs, and you'll get a price quote quicker than you can say DELMAR, DELMAR, DELMAR. There's no minimum order; wall-covering orders are usually received in about seven to ten days; window treatments in four to five weeks. There's a 20-day exchange or refund period on full bolts of wall covering (less 25-percent restocking charge); no returns on custom window treatments or wall coverings, or cut rolls.

Benington's
1271 Manheim Pike (800) 252-5060
Lancaster, PA 17601 PQ

No need for a PhD to understand how the savings of 35 percent to 70 percent on any make of wallpaper, fabric, and border computes to money in your pocket and decorative covering on your walls. Same-day processing of your order. All it takes is knowing which manufacturer and pattern number you want and a toll-free call. That's all, y'all.

Best Discount Wallcoverings
P.O. Box 1286
417 Jackson (800) 328-5550
St. Charles, MO 63302 Cashier's Check, MC, V, MO, PQ

They say they're "not the biggest—just the best." Take them up on their offer of 35 percent to 75 percent off most major brands of wall coverings. You'll pay no tax outside of Missouri, and price quotes will be given when you give them the book and pattern number. No returns or exhanges are accepted unless the merchandise is defective, in which case they'll replace it. There's no minimum order, but orders under $25 do incur a $2.50 service charge.

The Blind Spot
2067 N. Central Expressway
Suite 102 (800) 527-4585; (214) 669-1383
Richardson, TX 75080 CK, MC, V, AE, DC, B, PQ

If you want elegant window treatments at affordable prices, you've got it made in the shade with The Blind Spot. They've got LEVOLOR and GRABER mini-blinds, LOUVERDRAPE and GRABER vertical blinds, and woven woods and window shades at up to 70 percent off suggested list. Everything is first quality and custom made. Other brands include ROBERT ALLEN, SCHUMACHER, and JOANNA SHADES. Supply style, color, size, and model number and the store will send you an informative product brochure that tells you how to measure your window for blinds and shades. The Blind Spot also carries a great selection of fabrics, bedspreads, baskets, and feather dusters at discounted prices. They'll also send you a price list to determine the cost. Call and talk to Muriel Porter or any other member of their very helpful and knowledgeable staff.

Custom Windows & Walls
32525 Stephenson Highway (800) 772-1947; (313) 585-3026
Madison Heights, MI 48071 CK, MC, V, D, B

Make the most of your windows and walls without making a dent in your budget. This mail-order company carries micro- and mini-blinds at maximum savings, with discounts up to 60 percent. Choose from LEVOLOR, DELMAR, BALI, and LOUVERDRAPE to add the newest fashion trends to your windows. Roman shades by KIRSH let you cover your windows with woven woods that save energy and add beauty at the same time. Pleated shades and wood-slat blinds offer additional style—and savings! Your walls could be covered by names including WALLTEX, BIRGE, and IMPERIAL at 25 percent to 50 percent below retail prices. A complete selection of colors and patterns are available in a variety of textures. No refunds available on custom-made products and limited refunds offered on wallpapers. Lifetime warranties from manufacturers offered on most window treatments. Michigan residents pay 4-percent sales tax and all orders are shipped promptly.

Decorette/Blinds Direct

1901 W. Parker Road
Plano, TX 75023

(214) 964-3580 (call collect)
CK, MC, V, D, B, PQ

Decorate with the Decorette from top to bottom. Up to 80 percent off name brands (manufacturers' list prices): mini-blinds and micro-blinds, PVC and fabric verticals, one- and two-inch wood blinds, pleated shades, and HUNTER-DOUGLAS duettes. Decorative fabrics with all the famous-name brands. Dress up windows with custom draperies, or dress down with custom bedspreads. Call for up-to-the-minute decorating-on-a budget prices.

Direct Wallpaper Express

370 Hall Street
Phoenixville, PA 19460

(800) 336-WALL
(215) 935-6876 (customer service)
(215) 935-2146 (local residents)
CK, MC, V, AE, D, MO, B, PQ

Take the fast lane to discount wallpaper. Let Bob Hepp and his staff save you money on all brands of decorator wall coverings, from 40 percent all the way to 78 percent with quantity discounts. If you send in a sample, their fantastic color-imaging computer system can identify a wallpaper pattern even when another dealer has altered it! Orders of $50 or more come with a free how-to-hang-it kit. Coordinating fabrics are available, too, as well as window treatments, including Silhouettes by HUNTER-DOUGLAS, a combination horizontal blind and pleated shade. Returns are accepted according to manufacturers' policy, usually within 30 days. There's a 25-percent manufacturer restocking fee. By the time you get to Phoenixville, you won't be sorry you shopped by phone.

East Carolina Wallpaper Market
1106 Pink Hill Road — (800) 848-7283
Kingston, NC 28501 — (919) 522-3226 (local)
MC, V, PQ, samples

This little shopper went to market. And this little discount shopper went to East Carolina to stock up on most major brands of wall coverings. In business for about 20 years, they can save you 40 percent or more when you price-check by phone, or they can send samples when you call with a detailed description of the paper you're looking for. Returns are accepted within 25 days, for a 25-percent restocking charge. Nothing could be finer than this wall-paper marketer in east Carolina.

Elite Blinds Manufacturing
701 E. Plano Parkway — (800) 783-3548; (214) 881-0233
Plano, TX 75074 — CK, MC, V, D, F, PQ

Even bargain shoppers like to hang out with the Elite. Why not, who would know the difference from a name brand and a private label anyway? They all look the same through our rose-colored glasses, and perform the same shady functions. But here, their brand of custom-made blinds are 70 percent to 80 percent less than the brand name. Verticals, pleated shades, mini- or wood blinds; you name it, they're available here. Select wallpapers and drapery fabrics can also be had for about 40 percent off. Since most orders are custom-made, Elite does not accept returns. Most orders are sent out in a week to ten days.

Floorcrafters Wholesale
(See **Carpets and Rugs**, p. **132**.)

Hang-It Now Wallpaper Stores
10517 F N. Main Street — (800) 325-9494; (919) 431-6341
Archdale, NC 27263 — CK, MC, V, AE, PQ

Hang-It-Now, in business for 11 years, told us they have no catalog because there's too much available on the market today, and besides they carry most of it. Major names like LINDEN STREET, YORK, SUNWORTHY, and SEABROOK were available at 30 percent off and more. There is no minimum order here, and shipping is free. Returns are accepted according to distributors' specifications, usually in 30 to 60 days, but a 25-percent restocking fee is charged.

Harmony Supply
P.O. Box 313
18 High Street
Medford, MA 02155
(617) 395-2600
CK, MC, V, PQ (phone)

Does your wallpaper hang limp as a wilted wallflower? Well, then write Harmony and give your roomful of blues something to sing about! In business for more than 43 years, Harmony has received great press from magazines like *Women's Day*. Smart women would rather use Harmony and tune into savings of up to 60 percent. This company carries over 2,500 patterns in wall coverings, as well as FLEXALUM and LEVOLOR blinds. They've got whatever wallpaper you could want. Discounts are good on special orders but even better on in-stock merchandise. In-stock merchandise can be returned for a full refund; 25-percent restocking charge on special orders. No brochures or price lists; send them a pattern number and Harmony will send you the pitch.

Harry Zarin Co.
(See **Fabrics and Upholstery**, p. **197**.)

Headquarters Window & Walls
82 Speedwell Avenue
Morristown, NJ 07960
(800) 338-4882
CK, MC, V, AE, D, MO, PQ

This is your Headquarters for virtually all major brands of wall coverings and window treatments. The prices are good, and get better when you buy in quantity. The minimum order is one double roll; smaller orders are charged a $3.99 fee. Why cover your walls or windows with anything less? Returns are not accepted unless rolls are damaged or defective; most orders are received in ten to fifteen working days.

Peerless Wallpaper
700 Connor Road (800) 999-0898
Pittsburgh, PA 15228 Cashier's Checks, MC, V, AE, D, MO, PQ

Peerless stands alone with wall coverings and borders at up to 75 percent off, and coordinating drapery fabrics for 10 percent to 25 percent off. IMPERIAL, UNITED, and most other major brands are available, and quantity discounts will save you even more. They'll send you samples if you call with details of what you're looking for, or offer price quotes if you already know what you want. Fabrics are nonreturnable, but returns are accepted within 45 days on unopened paper. There is no minimum order.

Pintchik Homeworks
2106 Bath Avenue (800) 847-4199; (718) 996-5580
Brooklyn, NY 11214 CK, MC, V, MO, C

A penny pincher's paradise. This Pintchik could save you 40 percent to 75 percent off manufacturers' list price on most name-brand, custom-made window treatments. In business since 1912, they finally got into the mail-order act in 1980 and started posting record sales on window and wall treatments from the major hitters: LEVOLOR, BALI, and GRABER, to name a few. No returns are accepted, but if your order is defective, they will remake it. Take a look at their free, 20-page color catalog, or visit one of their six retail locations in New York City.

Priba Furniture
(See **Furniture and Accessories**, p. **261**.)

Rafael
(See **Bed and Bath**, p. **95**.)

Robinson's Interiors
225 W. Spring Street, Dept. 2LB (800) 458-2426
Titusville, PA 16354-0427 (814) 827-1893
CK, MC, V, AE, D, C/$2

Hello Mrs. Robinson. Instead of falling for her and being half her age, you'll fall in love with her selection at half the price. A complete selection of wall coverings and coordinated accessories at discounts up to 50 percent off are available. Borders and coordinating fabrics, along with a complete selection of bedspreads, curtains, and matching accessories for a "total decorator look" without the decorator expense are waiting to be assembled. Most orders shipped within 24 hours via UPS. Satisfaction guaranteed; refunds given within 30 days. Their 43-page catalog with actual wall-covering samples is available for only $2.

Rollerwall, Inc.
P.O. Box 757 (301) 680-2510
Silver Springs, MD 20918 CK, MC, V, MO, C

What do you get when you cross a wallpaper pattern with a paint roller? ROLLERWALL, of course! This company claims you don't need any talent (hey, that's us!), and they guarantee "delightful results." Lots of different designs enable users to apply paint on plain walls in intricate designs. Their introductory offer was a "four rollers for the price of three" deal. Four to six weeks is the usual delivery time; there's a 30-day refund or exchange policy. Some of their letters from satisfied customers are from set designers and hotel owners.

Ronnie Draperies
145 Broad Avenue (201) 945-1900
Fairview, NJ 07022 (212) 964-1480 (NY residents)
CK, MC, V, AE, C

Since 1925, Ronnie has sold its own original designs in draperies, bedspreads, and curtains at 20-percent to 50-percent savings. Hang up with a wide selection and many styles that are comparable to those found in the best retail stores. Bedspreads and draperies come lined or unlined, and Ronnie also offers thermal insulated draperies for the warming trend. LEVOLOR verticals and mini-blinds are also available. There's a $50 minimum order, a 10-percent restocking charge, and most orders are delivered in two to three weeks. Check the section in their full-color catalog (published twice yearly) on how to measure for draperies before ordering.

Rubin & Green Interior Design Studio
290 Grand Street (212) 226-0313
New York, NY 10002 CK, MC, V, AE, COD, PQ

Rubin & Green has made a few changes over the past few years—now they're a full custom-design company. They carry an extensive line of 20 to 30 name-brand fabrics including SCHUMACHER, DAVID DASH, ROBERT ALLEN, STROHEIM AND ROMANN. From these materials, they create custom-design draperies, fully upholstered furniture, and custom-designed window treatments. (They'll build furniture from the frame up, to your specifications.) They still make designer bedspreads (and comforters of goose down, lamb's wool, or Dacron) from your plans: They'll take your sample, picture, or diagram and quote prices and custom design according to your specifications. Prices are 50 percent off what you'd pay retail and sometimes more (depending on the fabric and design you choose). Interior designers are on staff at all times. The delivery time usually is four to six weeks for most orders; eight to ten weeks for furniture. Request specific information and a price quote.

Sanz International Inc.
(See **Fabrics and Upholstery**, p. **200**.)

Shibui Wallcoverings
P.O. Box 1268 (800) 824-3030
Santa Rosa, CA 95402 (707) 526-6170 (CA residents)
CK, MC, V, COD, C/$4

Shibui knows the paper chase can leave you climbing the walls. This company carries handcrafted textiles, grasscloths, and string wall coverings (all imported from the Orient) at approximately 50-percent to 60-percent savings. Wall coverings are natural in texture, color, and material. Their kit of 80 samples of wall coverings (which comes with the catalog) costs $4. Do-it-yourself instructions and tools are available. There's no minimum order; the restocking charge is 10 percent on returns; orders are shipped within two days; shipping charges are $10 for orders under $100, no charge on bigger orders.

Shuttercraft
282 Stepstone Hill Road, Dept. 1226 (203) 453-1973
Guilford, CT 06437 CK, MC, V, MO, B

These exterior and interior wood shutters and fastening hardware are used for restoring older homes and adding charm to modern ones. The shutters are custom-sized; one popular model is the 2½″ wide-blade plantation shutter, available for inside or out. Shutters are not returnable except with approval. Orders are usually delivered in six to eight weeks. Shuttercraft doesn't have a minimum order, saying they've handled everything from a single pair to a theme park in Japan. Call for one of their five brochures on the shutters you want.

Silver Wallcovering, Inc.
3001-15 Kensington Avenue (800) 426-6600; (215) 426-7600
Philadelphia, PA 19134 CK, MC, V, AE, D, COD, C

Wonderful walls can be yours at a price that's pure gold from Silver Wallcovering, Inc. Home decorating at a discount isn't just a dream, it's a way of doing business with this company. Many of the things needed to complete or create the atmosphere to make your house a home can be found here, all at 30 percent to 50 percent below what you'd pay in other stores. Wallcoverings, window treatments, and wall decor were all included in the selection of savings. We found most national brands with no minimum purchase required, so check here first, no matter how large or small your decorating needs may be. A 30-day return or refund was offered on damaged materials. Prices included shipping and handling and response time was only three to seven days.

SmartLooks
101 South Greenville (800) 229-Look (5665); (214) 699-7160
Richardson, TX 75081 CK, MC, V, D, PQ

Ok, smarty pants. It's time you use your head and get smart. Today, nobody pays retail. And today, nobody doesn't like a decorator look. Why sacrifice quality, name brands, service, and style when SmartLooks rolls out the red-carpet treatment. Name-brand window treatments from the finest manufacturers: LEVOLOR,

HUNTER-DOUGLAS, BALI, LOUVERDRAPE, the Silhouettes by HUNTER-DOUGLAS, woven woods, plantation shutters, odd-size windows, shades that pull from the top . . . or the bottom, custom wall treatments from windows to headboards, table drapes to pillow shams, and their famous Exterior Rolling Shutters, which they manufacture. These outside shutters provide maximum energy efficiency, privacy as well as security, and are operated electronically inside your home. Now, here's the smartest part: everything's 35 percent to 70 percent off.

Wallpaper Now

3511 S. Main Street — (919) 431-6341; (919) 434-1598
Archdale, NC 27263 — CK, MC, V, PQ

Also known as Your-Hang-It-Now® Discount Wallpaper store, this five-year-old company wasn't born yesterday when it comes to discounts. They lop a whopping 30 percent to 90 percent off the price of each roll, so don't put off until tomorrow what you can Wallpaper Now! This company offers 25,000 papers and coverings, so if you can't find something you like, it's not their fault. Brands like SUNWORTHY, YORK, MILLBROOK, UNITED, and IMPERIAL are worth looking into, and SCHUMACHER is sure to make you order. Grasscloths are particularly popular. Wallpaper Now will match the cuttings you send and will mail out samples. They pay shipping—so get your wallpaper now.

Wells Interiors Inc.

7171 Amador Plaza Drive — (800) 547-8982
Dublin, CA 94568 — CK, MC, V, PQ

This company is a leading supplier of window- and floor-covering products at blinding discounts of 50 percent to 60 percent off conventional retail and 80 percent off department-store prices. They carry a diverse inventory of window blinds, carpeting, blind cleaners, mini-blinds, verticals, and pleated shades: all types of window coverings. Nationally known brands make up about 95 percent of the inventory and include LEVOLOR, LOUVERDRAPE, KIRSCH, and DELMAR. No minimum order; shipping is usually free; most orders come in about four weeks. Orders are accepted by phone, but putting them in writing reduces the possibility of error. Remember to measure your windows correctly; there are no returns on custom-cut orders. All's well that ends well at Wells.

Wholesale Verticals, Inc.
713 Brooklyn Avenue, Dept. 3333 (800) 762-2748
Baldwin, NY 11510 CERTIFIED CHECK, MC, V, D, C

We stood up and took notice of window treatments for 70 percent to 80 percent less. Verticals, minis, duettes, and pleated shades are among the blinding deals here. Names include KIRSCH, LOUVERDRAPE, HUNTER-DOUGLAS, GRABER, LEVOLOR, and BALI. Samples, brochures, and catalogs are available, including one from BALI and a selection of Wholesale Verticals' custom fabrics and woods for blinds. Measuring instructions come with samples and brochures. Since all work is custom, returns are not accepted; most orders are delivered in two to three weeks.

Yorktowne Wallpaper Outlet
2445 S. Queen Street (800) 847-6142; (717) 741-3873
York, PA 17402 CK (in advance), MC, V, AE, D, PQ

Yorktowne told us they carried so many brands, it would be best to tell us what they *didn't* have: VILLAGE, GRAMERCY, SCHUMACHER, or WAVERLY. On the brands they *do* have, however (which are included in their more than 2,000 books), you'll save at least 35 percent. They do have a minimum order of one double roll. Returns on uncut double rolls are accepted within 30 days for a 25-percent restocking fee. Borders are not returnable.

Category Index

Company Index

FOR THE BEST IN PAPERBACKS, LOOK FOR THE [illegible]

In every corner of the world, on every subject under the sun, Penguin represents quality and variety – the very best in publishing today.

For complete information about books available from Penguin [illegible] and how to order them, write to us at the appropriate address below. Please note that for copyright reasons the selection of books varies from country to country.

In the United Kingdom: For a complete list of books available from Penguin [illegible]

In the United States: For a complete list of books available from Penguin [illegible]

In Canada: For a complete list of books available from Penguin in Canada [illegible]

In Australia: For a complete list of books available from Penguin [illegible]

In New Zealand: For a complete list of books available from Penguin [illegible]

In India: For a complete list of books available from Penguin [illegible]

In Holland: For a complete list of books available from Penguin [illegible]

In Germany: For a complete list of books available from Penguin [illegible]

In Spain: For a complete list of books available from Penguin [illegible]

In Japan: For a complete list of books available from Penguin [illegible]